THE HISTORY *of* PITTSFIELD

BERKSHIRE COUNTY

MASSACHUSETTS

From the Year 1800 to the Year 1876

Compiled and Written, Under the General Direction of a Committee

BY

J. E. A. Smith

By Authority of the Town

HERITAGE BOOKS
2018

HERITAGE BOOKS
AN IMPRINT OF HERITAGE BOOKS, INC.

Books, CDs, and more—Worldwide

For our listing of thousands of titles see our website
at
www.HeritageBooks.com

A Facsimile Reprint
Published 2018 by
HERITAGE BOOKS, INC.
Publishing Division
5810 Ruatan Street
Berwyn Heights, Md. 20740

Entered, according to Act of Congress, in the year 1876, by
The Town of Pittsfield,
In the Office of the Librarian of Congress at Washington, D.C.

Originally published 1876: Springfield, Massachusetts
Clark W. Bryan & Co., Publishers, Printers and Binders

— Publisher's Notice —

This facsimile reprint was produced by using a rare original book which was very fragile and somewhat damaged. Parts of some of the pages were so brittle that they had broken off, taking with them a word here and there. This is apparent on pages 381, 382, 722 and 726. Pages 323 and 324 were so damaged that they had to be re-typeset. Missing words or parts of words are indicated by dashes. We feel the contents of this book warrant its reissue despite these blemishes and hope you will agree and read it with pleasure.

This edition, previously published in two volumes, has been combined into a single volume.

International Standard Book Numbers
Paperbound: 978-0-7884-1305-6
Clothbound: 978-0-7884-8556-5

PREFACE.

In presenting the second volume of the History of the Town to the citizens of Pittsfield, we have to apologize for some vexatious delay, which, however, finds its compensation in the fact that some important portions of the work have been made correct, where it would have been impossible to do so had the story been finished at a much earlier date.

Our intention has been to give prominence to those events, enterprises, and institutions which have had an essential bearing upon the town's prosperity. We have also desired to do some justice to the men who have given it character, and labored for its good. In some instances, lack of material has rendered it impossible to accomplish this as fully as we could wish; and possibly we may have sometimes erred in judgment; but we have sincerely aimed to be impartial, and believe that substantial justice has been done.

The original plan of the work was to make the earlier portions more full than the later: indeed, to give but a brief skeleton of recent affairs; it being exceedingly difficult to make contemporary history satisfactory to those wh have taken part in it. We have in a few instances departec from this course, for reasons which will suggest themselv(to the reader. And now, in order that the size of the bc may not exceed reasonable limits, we have been obliged omit accounts of several gentlemen, and of enterprises recent date which had already been prepared.

PREFACE.

For the same reason we make this presentation of our work very brief, trusting that the charity of our fellow-citizens will suggest to them an excuse for such faults as they may discover, and for what may appear to them unfortunate omissions. We may, however, claim that the Record here contained is one of which any town may be proud; and one which will show that few towns have contributed so much to the general history of the country, in all its departments.

Pittsfield, July, 1876.

CONTENTS.

HISTORY.

CHAPTER I.

PITTSFIELD, A. D. 1800.

Preliminary—The village mapped and described—Old houses still standing—Excellence of the joiner-work—Buildings which have been destroyed—The village witling—Anecdote of the Berkshire hotel—Shade-trees, flower-gardens and shrubbery—Popular appreciation of the beautiful in nature—Stores—Major Israel Stoddard—Influence of method of first settlement on distribution of population—Streets, roads, traveling and transportation. 3

CHAPTER II.

POPULATION—EMIGRATION—NEWSPAPERS—POST-OFFICES—[1787-1800.]

Census of 1800—Increase and decrease of Berkshire towns—Causes of emigration—Anecdote of Phillips Merrill—Early newspapers—American Centinel—Berkshire Chronicle—Local items—Advertisements—Influence upon agriculture, manufactures and morals—Publishers' troubles—Post-riders—Scarcity of paper—Berkshire Gazette—More post-riders and the first post-office 20

CHAPTER III.

AGRICULTURE—MANUFACTURES—MERCANTILE AFFAIRS—[1787-1805.]

Farming universal—Deterioration of soils—Agricultural teachings—Products—Price of land—Prices of stock and farm-products—Fulling-mills—Iron forges—Tanneries—Potasheries—Oil-mills—Nail-factory—Early mercantile business—Trade by barter—Patriotic merchants—What goods were sent to market—Joshua Denforth—Simon Larned—John B. Root—Trade in 1798-1805 . . . 30

CHAPTER IV.

DOMESTIC AND SOCIAL LIFE—MANNERS AND MORALS—[1790-1810.]

The interior of houses—Dress—Household labor—Tea-parties—Social gaieties—Spinning-bees for the minister's wife—Hunting-match and club-suppers—Dancing-parties; their pleasures and their dangers—Freedom of manners—Influence of the wars and foreign intercourse on morals and manners—Customs in connection with dancing-parties—Bundling—Use and abuse of ardent spirits—Habits of Col. Oliver Root—Liquor-selling—Varieties of wines and liquors in vogue—Early efforts for temperance-reform—Doctor Rush's essay upon the effect of alcohol—He favors wine, beer and punch—Gambling—Lotteries—Imprisonment for debt—Unequal laws—Reforms of the nineteenth century . . 49

CHAPTER V.
SOME LEADING CITIZENS—[1800-1810.]

Charles Goodrich—Woodbridge Little—Rev. Thomas Allen—Dr. Timothy Childs—David Campbell—Henry Van Schaack—Oliver Wendell—Henry H. Childs—Thomas Allen, Jr.—Jonathan Allen—Rev. William Allen—James D. Colt—Samuel D. Colt—John B. Root—Oliver Root—Lemuel Pomeroy—Phinehas Allen—Jason Clapp—John W. Hulbert—Ezekiel Bacon—The generation as a whole—The town epitomized. 68

CHAPTER VI.
POLITICAL FEUDS, AND DIVISION OF THE FIRST PARISH.

Political rancor of the age—Exaggerations of tradition—Illustrative anecdote—State of American politics—Sources of political bitterness peculiar to Berkshire—Berkshire federalists and democrats characterized—Elder Leland, Theodore Sedgwick and Rev. Thomas Allen—Obnoxious sermons preached by Mr. Allen—Woodbridge Little's letter of complaint—Mr. Allen's reply—Action of the dissatisfied—Advice of the Berkshire association of Congregational ministers—Mr. Allen annoyed by newspaper-scandals—The Berkshire *Reporter*—Letter from Mr. Allen to Mr. Little—Union parish incorporated—Difficulties in organizing a new church solved by an *ex parte* council—Church of Union parish instituted—Names of members—Proposals for the resignation of Mr. Allen—Ordination of Rev. Mr. Punderson over Union church—Health of Mr. Allen; he preaches an election-sermon at Boston; writes a historical sketch of the town and county; his death; monuments to his memory. 90

CHAPTER VII.
THE METHODIST AND BAPTIST CHURCHES—CONGREGATIONAL ZEAL FOR THE RELIGIOUS INSTRUCTION OF THE YOUNG—[1800-1812.]

Inequality of the Massachusetts laws—Reorganization of the Baptist church—Rev. John Francis—Charter of the Methodist parish of Pittsfield and other towns—Secession of reformed Methodists—Dissenters from all churches—Philosophical religionists—Obstacles to the new churches—Rev. Mr. Hibbard—Congregational plan for the instruction of youth in religion 135

CHAPTER VIII.
EARLY WOOLEN MANUFACTURES—[1800-1812.]

State of American manufactures in 1800—First woolen-mills in America—Arthur Scholfield—Birth, parentage and education—Emigrates to America—Commences business at Byfield—Removes to Pittsfield—Makes broadcloths, carding-machines, spinning-jennies and looms—The first Pittsfield factory—James Strandring's manufacture of comb-plates—Elkanah Watson's efforts for Berkshire woolen-manufactures—Statement of his manufacture of broadcloth from his own merino wool—A woolen manufacturing company formed—It fails—Scholfield establishes a woolen manufactory—His difficulties—The Pittsfield *Sun's* statement of manufactures in 1809—Close of Arthur Scholfield's life. . 158

CHAPTER IX.
BEFORE THE WAR—[1800-1812.]

Business-activity—Establishment and failure of the Berkshire bank—Other business-losses—Building of a democratic hotel—Names of prominent democrats—Park square and its business-surroundings—Drum-factory—Jonathan Allen, 2d—Pomeroy's gun-factory—Ordination of Rev. William Allen. . . 181

CONTENTS. vii

CHAPTER X.

WAR OF 1812—CANTONMENT AND DEPOT FOR PRISONERS OF WAR—[1811-1815.]

Politics and political influences in Pittsfield—Names of prominent politicians—News of declaration of war received, and its effect—The Cantonment established—Barracks erected—Troops arrive—Dinners for the soldiers—Social intercourse and officers' balls—Recruiting and drilling—Major Melville as organizer and manager of the post—Slanders against him met and refuted—The 9th and other regiments called to the front—The Cantonment a depot for prisoners of war—Major Melville as agent for prisoners and deputy marshal—Escape of prisoners attributed to federalists—Stables converted into prisons—Incidents—Unruly prisoners—Prisoners released at close of the war and unwilling to return to Canada—Berkshire regiments in the war—Pittsfield officers—Dinner to General Ripley. 192

CHAPTER XI.

THE WAR OF 1812—POLITICAL EVENTS CONCERNING IT—THE MILITIA—PEACE—[1812-1815.]

Opening of the war, and position of parties concerning it—Resolutions of Pittsfield in support of the national government—Washington Benevolent Society—Celebration of Washington's birthday—Election of John W. Hulbert to congress—Spies arrested and prisoners of war escape—Critical position of the country—Massachusetts militia called out—The question of their command-in-chief—Patriotic action of Pittsfield—The militia-system and Pittsfield militia—Berkshire militia marched to Boston—Chaplain Billy Hibbard's account—News of peace received with joyful demonstrations 226

CHAPTER XII.

THE DIVIDED PARISH—PASTORATES OF REV. WILLIAM ALLEN AND REV. THOMAS PUNDERSON—REUNION—[1810-1817.]

Divorce of town and parish affairs—Temporary change in the mode of supporting public worship—Ordination of Rev. William Allen—The town appropriates moneys for a school-fund—Misapplication of the same to the purposes of the First parish, and controversy concerning the same—The First church continues the discipline of its seceding members—Measures looking towards reunion, and obstacles to them—Death and benevolent will of Woodbridge Little—The fathers of the church characterized by Rev. Dr. Humphrey—Rev. Messrs. Allen and Punderson propose reunion, and resign to facilitate it—Their dismission—The churches agree upon a basis of reunion—It is consummated under the auspices of an ecclesiastical council 262

CHAPTER XIII.

PASTORATE OF REV. DR. HUMPHREY—[1817-1823.]

Changes in the mode of transacting parish-business—Rev. Heman Humphrey chosen pastor—Sketch of Dr. Humphrey—His installation at Pittsfield—State of the Pittsfield parish—Doctor Humphrey's fitness to harmonize its conflicts—Pastoral work—Catalogue of Bible-class—Sunday-school—His release of dissenting members of the parish from the payment of taxes—Condition of the dissenting parishes—A remarkable revival—Its effects on morals and feuds—Fourth of July, and St. John's day—Mr. Humphrey is invited to the presidency of Amherst collegiate institute—Opposition to his acceptance—His own doubts—Accepts under the advice of a council—Farewell to Pittsfield—His return—Residence and death there—Interesting incidents 281

CONTENTS.

CHAPTER XIV.

CONSTITUTIONAL CONVENTION OF 1820—AMENDMENT TO THE THIRD ARTICLE OF THE BILL OF RIGHTS—ABOLITION OF SEATING THE MEETING-HOUSE—[1820-1836.]

Opinions and votes of Pittsfield regarding the convention—Equality of religious sects before the law—Amendment of the bill of rights offered and advocated by Hon. H. H. Childs—Rejected by the convention—Senatorial apportionment upon a property-basis—Changes in the political-year—Vote of Pittsfield on the several amendments—Reforms in the constitution finally obtained—Curious advertisement of Sylvester Rathbun as Methodist committee-man—Legislative action upon the amendment of the bill of rights—Proposition to change the pews in the meeting-house into slips and to abolish the seating-system—Doctor Humphrey's description of the old system—Names of seating-committees from 1790 to 1830—Evils of the seating-system—Plans for change—Change effected 305

CHAPTER XV.

THE BERKSHIRE AGRICULTURAL SOCIETY FOR THE PROMOTION OF AGRICULTURE AND MANUFACTURES—[1807-1830.]

Agricultural societies in Europe and America prior to the Berkshire—The just claims of the Berkshire society to precedence—Evidence and acknowledgment of its beneficial influence throughout the country—Biographical sketch of Elkanah Watson—His removal to Pittsfield and exhibition of merino sheep under the Elm—He advocates the establishment of an agricultural society and the introduction of merino sheep—Independent cattle-show in 1810—Its influence upon Berkshire sheep-culture—The society incorporated—Its first cattle-show—Premiums, and prophetic address by Elkanah Watson—Berkshire system of agricultural fairs gradually developed—Ingenious device to interest women in them—Organization of the society's work—Plowing-match and viewing-committees introduced—Marked effect of the society's effort upon Berkshire agriculture—Pecuniary difficulties—Contributions of Pittsfield—Aid granted by the Commonwealth—Efforts to make the shows migratory successfully resisted—Death of Mr. Watson—Ode by William Cullen Bryant. 316

CHAPTER XVI.

MEDICAL COLLEGE AND MEDICAL SOCIETIES—[1784-1875.]

Preliminary action—Dr. O. S. Root—Application for charter—Nature of the opposition to it—Charter granted—Lecture-course before the charter—First faculty and trustees—Purchase of Pittsfield hotel-building—Subscriptions and endowment—Town action and grant—Popular dread of resurrectionists—Exciting cases of "body-snatching"—Anecdote of Timothy Hall—Provisions for anatomical study at the medical college—Doctor Goodhue elected president—Sketch of his life—Lyceum of natural history—Sketch of Prof. Chester Dewey—Death of Doctor Goodhue—Dr. Zadock Howe elected president—Dr. H. H. Childs made president—Connection with Williams College dissolved—Equality of the two medical colleges of Massachusetts recognized by the State Medical Society—Death of Professor Palmer—College-building burned—Relief by grant from the legislature and citizens' subscriptions—New college erected on South street—Dr. H. H. Childs resigns his professorship—Decline of the college—Clinique established—Doctor Timothy Childs—Efforts to restore the prosperity of the college—*Berkshire Medical Journal*—The institution dissolved and the building sold—Lyceums and alumni—History of Berkshire medical societies—Pittsfield Medical Society established—Vaccination introduced into Berkshire. 352

CONTENTS. ix

CHAPTER XVII.
DETACHED SUBJECTS—[1820-1840.]

Population—Business-changes—Agricultural bank—Fires and first fire-engine—First mutual insurance-company—Stock-insurance company—Berkshire Mutual Fire-Insurance Company—First grading and planting the park—Abel West—Visit of General Lafayette—The temperance-reformation—Explosion of a powder-magazine. 377

CHAPTER XVIII.
PROMINENT CITIZENS—[1812-1860.]

Thomas Melville—Henry Clinton Brown—William C. Jarvis—Samuel M. McKay—Thomas Barnard Strong—Henry Hubbard—Edward A. Newton—Ezekiel R. Colt—Nathan Willis—Dr. Robert Campbell—Dr. John Milton Brewster—Solomon L. Russell—Berkshire hotel and incidents. 398

CHAPTER XIX.
CONGREGATIONAL CHURCHES—[1824-1875.]

First Church and Parish—Rev. Mr. Bailey—Rev. Dr. Tappan—Rev. Mr. Yeomans—Revivalist preaching, and division of the church—Six ex-pastors of the Congregational churches become college-presidents—Rev. Dr. Brinsmade—Rev. Dr. Todd—Church-statistics—Rev. Mr. Bartlett—Encouragement of sacred music—The first organ and other instrumental music—Trustees of the ministerial fund—Parsonage bought, burned and rebuilt—The church hires the Union Parish meeting-house for a lecture-room—Building struck by lightning—Objections to its use—A new lecture-room built—The church of 1794 damaged by fire, sold and removed—A stone-church built—A stone-chapel built—South Congregational Church and Parish—Measures preliminary to colonization—Organization of parish, and first members—New church begun and burned—Rebuilding—Organization of church—Pastorate of Rev. Dr. Harris—Succeeding pastors—New organ—Second Congregational Church. 416

CHAPTER XX.
CHURCHES AND TOWN-HALL—[1812-1875.]

First Baptist Church—Methodist Episcopal Church—Wesleyan Methodist Church—St. Stephen's Church—Town-hall—St. Joseph's Church—Church of St. Jean Le Baptiste—German Lutheran Church—Synagogue Ansha Amonium—Shaker Society. 435

CHAPTER XXI.
WOOLEN, DUCK, COTTON, PAPER AND FLOURING MILLS—[1808-1875.]

State of manufactures in 1812—Effect of Scholfield's machinery—Seth Moore's rope-walk—Root, Maynard & Co.'s duck-factory—Housatonic woolen and cotton mill—Pittsfield woolen and cotton company—Their mills built; leased to L. Pomeroy and Josiah Pomeroy—Sold to Josiah Pomeroy & Co.—Bought by L. Pomeroy & Sons—Berkshire agitation for protection to American manufactures—Henry Shaw—Pontoosuc woolen-factory built—Hindrances to success—Saxony sheep introduced—Henry Clay's visit to Pittsfield—The Stearns family and their factories—The Barker brothers and their factories—The Russell factories—The Peck factories—Taconic factory—Pittsfield woolen-factory—Bel Air factory—Tillotson & Collins's factory—Pittsfield cotton-factory—Coltsville paper-mill—Wahconah flouring-mills—Shaker flouring-mill—Osceola River flouring-mill. 465

CONTENTS.

CHAPTER XXII.
TURNPIKES AND RAILROADS—[1797-1875.]

The turnpike-system—Third Massachusetts, or Worthington, turnpike—Pontoosuc turnpike—Favorable pass through the mountains—Obstacles to the plans of the company—Final success, and opening excursion to Springfield—Proposed canals—Railroad from Boston to the Hudson river—Explorations for a route made—Theodore Sedgwick — Discussion of the railway-system in the newspapers—Public meetings—Patent railroad from New York to Pittsfield proposed—Further prosecution of the project for a railroad from Boston to Albany—Hudson and Berkshire railroad constructed — Peculiar charter of the Western railroad—Books of subscription opened — Contest and decision concerning the route through Berkshire—The road completed and opened—Depots in Pittsfield—North Adams railroad—Stockbridge and Pittsfield railroad. 5

CHAPTER XXIII.
FIRE-DISTRICT AND WATER-WORKS—[1795-1875.]

Old fire-department — Organization of fire-district — Purchase of fire-engines—Housatonic and Pontoosuc engine-companies—Greylock hook-and-ladder company — List of engineers—Steam fire-engines — Fires — Early water-works—Ashley water-works—Sidewalks, sewers, and main drains. 5

CHAPTER XXIV.
BERKSHIRE JUBILEE—[1844.]

Origin of the jubilee—Preparatory measures—Reception and public exercises—Farewell-addresses—Biographical sketches of George N. Briggs, Julius Rockwell and James D. Colt. 5

CHAPTER XXV.
BURIAL-PLACES AND CEMETERIES—[1754-1875.]

Earliest burial-places—Condition of the first central ground—Movements for a new ground—Purchase of the First-street ground—The town-lot—Grants and sales of portions of the first burial-ground—Friends object to the removal of the dead—A rural cemetery proposed—Town grants a site to a cemetery-corporation—Preparation of the grounds — Their dedication — Subsequent history — St. Joseph's cemetery. 5

CHAPTER XXVI.
THE CIVIL WAR—THE SOLDIERS' MONUMENT AND IMPROVEMENT OF THE PARK—[1861-1872.]

Pittsfield soldiers of 1775, and 1861, compared—Pittsfield Guard—Allen Guard—First soldiers for the war—Henry S. Briggs—Pollock Guard and Tenth regiment—William Pollock—Twentieth and Twenty-first regiments—Lieutenant-Colonel Richardson—Western Bay State or Thirty-first regiment—Thirty-fourth regiment— Camp Briggs—Thirty-seventh regiment—Forty-ninth regiment—General W. F. Bartlett—Eighth regiment—Other regiments—Bounties—Recruiting and patriotic speeches—S. W. Bowerman—Labors of the selectmen—Ladies aid-societies—Death of a patriotic young lady—Mrs. C. T. Fenn—Mrs. J. R. Morewood—Soldiers' monument—Improvement of the park—Dedication of the monument—Speeches of General Bartlett and Hon. Thomas Colt—Oration of George William Curtis. 6

CHAPTER XXVII.

LIBRARIES AND ATHENÆUM.

Early private libraries—Pittsfield social libraries—Pittsfield Young Men's Associations—Berkshire Athenæum—Thomas Allen—Calvin Martin—Phinehas Allen—Thomas F. Plunkett—Rev. Dr. Todd—Henry L. Dawes. 640

CHAPTER XXVIII.

[MISCELLANEOUS—[1800-1876.]

Agricultural society—Schools—Newspapers—Removal of county-buildings—Banks and insurance-company—Academy of Music—Abraham Burbank—Edward Learned—John C. Hoadley—New manufactures—Valuation and census. . . 662

HISTORY.

HISTORY OF PITTSFIELD.

CHAPTER I.

PITTSFIELD, A. D. 1800.

Preliminary — The village mapped and described — Old houses still standing — Excellence of the joiner-work — Buildings which have been destroyed—The village witling—Anecdote of the Berkshire hotel—Shade trees, flower-gardens and shrubbery — Popular appreciation of the beautiful in nature—Stores—Major Israel Stoddard — Influence of method of first settlement on distribution of population — Streets, roads, traveling and transportation.

IN the first volume of this work, we related the history of the township of Pittsfield from the time when it was the hunting-ground of the Mohegans, until about the year 1800, reserving, however, a few points, chiefly concerning manufactures, agriculture, and political affairs, subsequent to the Shays rebellion, in order to treat of them more consecutively in connection with their fuller development.

In resuming our task, our first endeavor will be to paint, or at least to map, the town as it stood at the close of the eighteenth century; to portray some of its leading citizens; to depict its social and domestic life; to describe its physical condition in regard to agriculture, commerce, manufactures, and the means of intercommunication with the world beyond the mountains which surround it; in fine, to render the reader as familiar as we may with the Pittsfield of seventy-five years ago.

We select this period in which to gather up the scattered threads of our narrative, and to arrange them for continuation, because the year 1800 was a grand landmark in the history of the town, as well as of the country; when, with the change in political domination, there began a more gradual, but quite as decided, change in social views and habits, a new departure in the direction of milder laws, and a lessened reverence for prescriptive absurdity and wrong entrenched behind antiquated forms. In

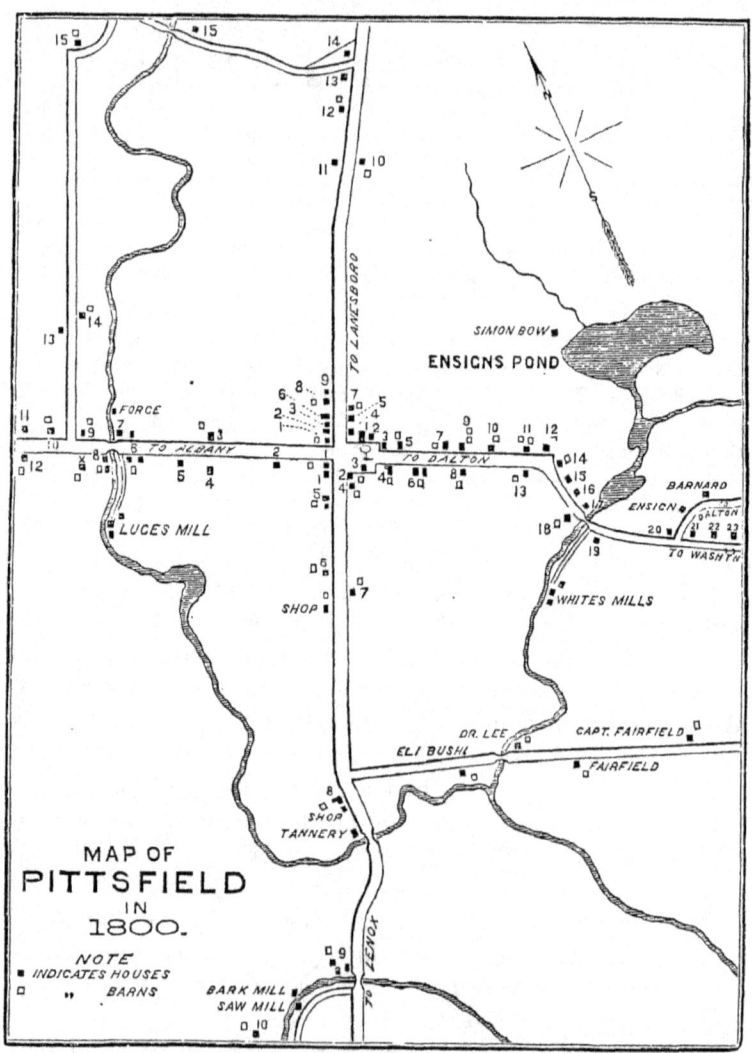

town-affairs a more than usual number of new men began, about that time, to become prominent; new industries were introduced, and new interests began to develop themselves.

We shall attempt to build our description of the central village

HISTORY OF PITTSFIELD. 5

by the aid of a map compiled from the best authorities which we have been able to consult; the description of travelers who visited the town at that time; the vivid memories of venerable citizens; the faithful delineations in the local and advertising columns of contemporary newspapers, and the guidance of nearly contemporary maps and plans.

MAP OF PITTSFIELD, A. D. 1800.

REFERENCES.

Road to Lanesboro (North street).
1. Darius Larned.
2. ———, goldsmith.
3. Wilcox, shoemaker.
4. Blacksmith shop.
5. Jonathan Allen, store.
6. Hickcock, sexton.
7. Thomas Allen, Jr.
8. Jared Ingersoll, tavern.
9. Shed.
10. Joseph Allen.
11. Fothergill.
12. Colonel Easton.
13. Joseph Hale.
14. Stephen Mead.
15. Thomas Brown (negro).

Road to Albany (West street).
1. James D. Colt.
2. Slaughter-house.
3. Dr. Timothy Childs.
4. Widow Cook.
5. Azariah Root.
6. John Snow.
7. George Randow.
8. Joel Dickinson, house and shop.
9. Zebediah Stiles Langworthy.
10. Siah Stiles.
11. Dr. Kitteridge.
12. Rufus Allen.
13. William Miller.
14. Dr. Timothy Childs, farm-house.
15. John U. Seymour.

Road to Lenox (South street).
1. J. & S. D. Colt's store.
2. John Stoddard's (store and post-office).
3. Hay-scales.
4. Stalham Williams.
5. Ashbel Strong.
6. William Hollister.
7. Ezekiel Root.
8. Captain Daniel Weller.
9. Major Dan. Weller, house and tannery.
10. Enoch Weller.

Road to Dalton (East street).
1. Meeting-house.
2. Town-house.
3. P. Allen's printing-office.
4. John Chandler Williams.
5. Rev. Thomas Allen.
6. John Strong (Lemuel Pomeroy).
7. William Mellen.
8. Thomas Gold.
9. Joshua Danforth (store and post-office).
10. Simon Larned.
11. Perez Graves.
12. Captain Jacob Ensign.
13. Oramel Fanning.
14. ——— Wadsworth.
15. Septimus Bingham.
16. Eli Maynard.
17. Tannery.
18. Ebenezer White.
19. Z. Burt.

The road upon which the residences of Dr. Lee, Eli Bush, and Captain Fairfield are laid down is Honasada street. A forge is laid down upon the map, north of the crossing of the river by West street, but it had been removed previous to the year 1800.

The village thus mapped is described by the Duke de la Rochefoucault Liancourt, a French exile who traveled through the United States in 1795-7, as "A small but neat town, containing several large and handsome houses of joiner's work." President Dwight, in his travels, speaks of it in similar terms, and we have evidence of the excellent joiner work in a considerable number of houses which were erected previous to 1800, and are still among the better class of dwellings; some of them among the most luxurious mansions of the town. We will enumerate most of them, specifying the principal changes which have been made in their exteriors, so that the reader familiar with the town as it is in 1875, may gain some idea of what it was in 1800.

The building designated as No. 6 East street, was erected by Captain John Strong, of revolutionary fame, and was kept for many years by him, and by his son of the same name, as a tavern. In the year 1800, when it was purchased by Lemuel Pomeroy, it was a two-story, gambrel-roof house, very similar in appearance to the homestead of John Chandler Williams which stood next west of it. Mr. Pomeroy substituted a third story for the gambrel-roof attic; and his son, Mr. Robert Pomeroy, who succeeded him, has since built a large wing on the south-east corner.

The John Chandler Williams' homestead, known to the present generation as the Edward A. Newton house, then stood on the corner of Park square and East street. It was erected by Colonel James Easton, who intended it as a residence for his son; but, owing to his pecuniary difficulties, it was sold about the close of the revolution, and before its completion, to Mr. Williams, by whom it was finished. In order to make room for the court-house, it has been removed a little east, to the corner of Wendell avenue; but its external appearance has been little changed.

The square mansion, No. 5 South street, was built in 1792, by Hon. Ashbel Strong, by whose heirs it was owned until 1862, when it was purchased by George and David Campbell. It has been subjected to a few alterations, but its appearance is not essentially altered.

The Dr. John M. Brewster homestead, No. 10 East street, built by Colonel Simon Larned, previous to 1790, remains quite unchanged. The large, square house erected by Thomas Gold,[1] and designated No. 8 East street, is now the residence of T. F. Plunkett; a mansard-roof has been added to it, and a more elaborate portico takes the place of that across which "Tall poplar trees their shadows threw;" it has otherwise been carefully protected.

[1] After the death of Mr. Gold, this mansion became the summer residence of his son-in-law, Hon. Nathan Appleton. Mr. Appleton's daughter became the wife of Henry W. Longfellow, and the poet gave a new charm to her home in the ballad of "The Old Clock on the Stairs;" the subject of which stood on the broad landing of the staircase which ascends from the spacious entrance hall. The description of the house in the poem is literally accurate, and its story is equally truthful. We may add that "the old-fashioned hospitality," which "used to be," still is.

The meeting-house, which faced the park, is now the gymnasium of Maplewood Institute, where it retains, externally, all its architectural features except the belfry, for which an observatory has been substituted.

Outside the district covered by our map, the large, square flat-roofed mansion, now the residence of J. R. Morewood, was built by Henry Van Schaack, in 1781, with extraordinary care and liberal expenditure; and was for many years much the best-built edifice in the town. The wooden walls were lined with brick, and the carpentry exhibits a perfection of skill which excites the admiration of modern workmen who are called upon to make alterations in it. Repairs are rarely needed. It is little changed except by the removal of the broad chimney and the old-fashioned balustrade which surrounded the roof.

Mr. Van Schaack removing to his native place, Kinderhook, in 1807, sold his house in Pittsfield to Elkanah Watson, a gentleman of very similar tastes, and the founder of the Berkshire Agricultural Society, who occupied it until his removal to Albany in 1816. It was then purchased by Major Thomas Melville, who resided in it until 1837, and was succeeded by his son, Robert Melville. For some years previous to its purchase by Mr. Morewood, in 1851, it was kept as a boarding-house, and numbered among its guests Henry W. Longfellow, Nathaniel Hawthorne, Herman Melville, and President John Tyler.

The Van Schaack mansion stands upon the east side of South street, a mile below the park. On the adjoining estate, upon the south-east, and about a quarter of a mile distant, stands the broad-chimneyed, hospitable-looking old dwelling, built some years previous to 1800, by Captain David Bush, under whose rule, and that of his son, it was a famous inn. It faces upon Wendell street; and now, but slightly changed in its general outline, it is the summer home of the family of the late Allan Melville. The old place had the good fortune, in 1852, to be purchased by Herman Melville, then in the freshness of his early fame. Mr. Melville named it Arrow-Head, from the Indian relics found on the estate, and made it a house of many stories; writing in it, besides Moby Dick, and other romances of the sea, the Piazza tales, which took their name from a piazza built by the author upon the north end of the house, which commands a bold and striking view of Greylock and the intervening valley. "My Chimney and I," a quaintly humorous essay, of which the cumbersome old chimney—overbearing tyrant of the home—is the hero, was also written here, as well as "October Mountain," a sketch of mingled philosophy and word-painted landscape, which found its inspiration in the massy and brilliant autumnal tints presented by a prominent and thickly-wooded spur of the Hoosac mountains, as seen from the south-eastern windows, at Arrow-Head, on a fine day after the early frosts.[1]

Of a still earlier date than Arrow-Head or Broad Hall, was the cottage erected about the year 1767, by Woodbridge Little, Esq. and occupied by him until his death in 1813. It still stands near the crossing of the Boston and Albany railroad by Beaver street and is little changed. It is owned by Mr. Frederic C. Peck.

In the west part still remain, almost precisely as they stood nearly a hundred years ago—save time's mellow coloring—four houses. That built by Captain William Francis, and in which that influential citizen and ardent patriot lived and died, is still owned and occupied by his descendants. That built by Robert Francis, is now owned by Edmund French, and that of Rev. John Francis, in which the Baptist church was re-organized, and where many of its earlier services were held. That erected by Mather Wright was long occupied by the late Linus Parker.

In the same vicinity is still another interesting and well-preserved specimen of the dwellings of the fathers; a square, flat-roofed house, the second story slightly projecting over the first. It stands on West street, south of Lake Onota, and is still known to the older residents of the town as the Jesse Goodrich tavern, although the builder, who gave it his name, has long since passed away, and the sign that used to swing before it long ago ceased to creak. Mr. Goodrich was a worthy man and a thorough builder. and his tavern is one of the best-preserved relics, being unchanged externally, and showing within the solid old-fashioned wainscoting and balusters. Even the boards which, at a much later date, divided the once-popular ball-room into smaller apartments, are of a breadth marvelous at this day.

Among the houses which have disappeared, there was, of course, a larger proportion of inferior dwellings than among those which remain; for the more nearly perfect the material and

[1] Herman Melville, and his brother, who succeeded him in the ownership of Arrow-Head, were nephews of Major Thomas Melville.

workmanship, the greater was the probability of preservation. In 1800, however, very shabby and uncomfortable abodes were, on the main streets, extremely rare.

There was no mansion fully equal, in all respects, to Major Van Schaack's; but some were nearly so, and many would still be called handsome and commodious, except by those who deem all the modern improvements absolutely essential to comfort.

By far the greater number of the more modest dwellings have perished, and we have neither space nor data to reconstruct them; but we will try to recall a few of the more conspicuous.

On what is known as the "Berkshire corner" of North and West streets, was a building of considerable size, with a gambrel roof; but it had undergone, in parts, some alterations, precisely of what character there are different reports. It was occupied as an inn by Captain John Dickinson, Darius Larned, Captain Joseph Merrick, and by Solomon L. Russell and brother. In 1798, the landlord was Captain Dickinson, and his daughter, Parthenia, afterwards Mrs. Curtis T. Fenn, was born in it at that late. In 1800, it was kept by Darius Larned. In 1810, Captain Joseph Merrick, an earnest federalist, was the host and proprietor, and having, as the democrats alleged, refused to provide them a Fourth of July dinner, they determined to erect, and did erect, on the opposite side of the park, a handsome hotel of three stories, one of whose glories was a spacious hall for the accommodation of political meetings, public dinners, and dancing parties. Now, Captain Merrick's inn had also a hall, in its gambrel-roof, which had long been occupied by Mystic Lodge of Free Masons, and for various other purposes of such a room. Captain Merrick was determined not to be eclipsed in so important a point by his new rival; but he kept his own counsel, and no one suspected his purpose until, one fine morning, Major Butler Goodrich, with whom he had made arrangements, appeared upon the ground with a large force of men and prepared material, and so rapidly was the work done, that before rumor could gather a curious crowd to speculate and criticise, a spacious third story had taken the place of the gambrel-roof. Captain Merrick, his brother Masons, and the federal public generally, had a hall of which they were proud, and which came in excellent good play when the Washington Benevolent Society was shortly after organized.

The Messrs. Russell having succeeded Captain Merrick in the

proprietorship of the inn, it was accidentally burned in 1826, and gave place to the still more favorite Berkshire House, which they erected the next year.

On the opposite corner, formed by South and West streets, was the two-story, gambrel-roof building—a mate, when it was built, to the inn—which was occupied, in 1800, as a dwelling-house by James D. Colt, Jr. One or two years afterwards, Mr. Colt erected the residence south of his store, now owned and occupied by George W. Campbell, and was succeeded in his previous home by Hon. John W. Hulbert.

No. 3 East street, assigned on the map to Allen's printing-office, was a gambrel-roof cottage, which had been built by Rev. Thomas Allen, as a store for his son Jonathan, who commenced his business life in it. It had been the printing-office of three newspapers previous to the *Sun*. In 1809, it was removed to North street. It will often re-appear in our story. Next south of it, the parsonage of which a description and view were given in our first volume, was still the home of the village pastor.

On Honasada street, the Long House, built by Colonel William Williams, and which has been previously described,[1] continued in good preservation, and it was owned and occupied by Joseph Shearer, a thrifty citizen, who had thriftily married the colonel's widow.

Of the same model was the Ingersoll tavern, famous as a barrack and a depot for prisoners in the Shays rebellion. This noted hostelry stood in the rear of the present south corner of North and Depot streets, facing east, with an ample court-yard in front. In much later years, when it had been abandoned by the Ingersoll family, it was known popularly as "Fort Necessity," partly from the tradition of its warlike uses, and partly because families removing to Pittsfield, in days when there were no superfluous dwellings, were compelled to pass their novitiate in this crazy edifice until a better home could be built or provided for them. The well, whose water is sadly deteriorated by impure surroundings, is still known as the "Fort Well."

Dr. Timothy Childs, in 1800, lived in the square flat-roof dwelling, which still stands, on the hill opposite the present Boston and Albany railroad depot, a part of the ministry-lot bought

---

[1] This description erroneously gave it a gambrel-roof. It was angular.

by him of the town in 1774. Attached to it as an L, is the gambrel-roof cottage which he built soon after the purchase.

In the year 1800, the dwelling-houses of Pittsfield were divided in about equal proportions between the gambrel, angular, and flat-roofed. Of those which first succeeded to the log huts of the earliest settlers, the greater number had the gambrel-roof, and were of one story, although the meeting-house, the school-house, the parsonage, the "Long House" of Colonel Williams, the residence of Colonel Oliver Root on West street, and some others were angular.

The flat-roofs began to come in fashion about the close of the revolution, and in 1800 were still the modern style. They were often surrounded by a railing of ornamental balusters, the posts of which were surmounted by urns or globes. Fences of a similar style enclosed the ample court-yards of the square mansions which generally sustained this class of roof. About the date of the incoming of this style of domestic architecture, Henry Van Schaack brought from Hartford, in his saddle-bags, the slips from which grew the Lombardy poplars introduced into Berkshire county; and this soon became a favorite shade-tree,—if a bundle of twigs, so stiff, so straight, so tall and slender, and so little umbrageous, could properly be styled a shade-tree. The Lombardy poplar is inseparably associated with our ideal of the statelier homesteads in the era we are endeavoring to depict. Before the year 1800, they had found a place in many of the court-yards of Pittsfield, and we may safely introduce them, in all their youthful freshness, keeping guard, like so many grenadiers, over the residences of Henry Van Schaack, Rev. Mr. Allen, John Chandler Williams, Dr. Timothy Childs, Ezekiel Root, and the first James D. Colt, as well as, doubtless, over many other homes which have kept no memory of their faithful service.

They had, however,—especially around the tasteful homes of Thomas Gold and Henry Van Schaack — their newly-planted rivals, in the more broad-leaved and generous button-woods, destined, not like the poplar to outlive the popular favor, but to perish of premature blight when their venerable and ample shade was most dearly prized.

A taste for the cultivation of flowers and ornamental shrubs had already manifested itself, although far from universally or even commonly. In the very first interval of rest after the

French and Indian wars, we found the garden of Colonel William Williams adorned with, at least, the pink, the carnation and the gilly-flower. In 1800, the flower-beds of Pittsfield, which were generally placed conspicuously in the front court-yards, exhibited, in addition to the noble old favorites of Colonel Williams's garden, the hollyhock, the sun-flower, the morning-glory, the sweet pea, the marigold, and others upon whose petals there still linger, in many memories, the roseate glow, the balmy aroma, and the dewy freshness of life's morning; and which are, therefore, held in the heart's esteem above all the wealth of the conservatory.

Of the flowering shrubs, the principal were the rose and purple lilac; of flowering climbers, now and then, a honeysuckle; of non-flowering climbers, the woodbine and the native grape.

As yet, native shade-trees received little attention from the gardener, and wild flowers none at all; but, as nature planted them, they served well the place of all others with the mass of the people. Few, if any of the hundred-acre home-lots, which stretched across the center of the township, from east to west, were, as yet, entirely denuded of their groves. On many, considerable relics of the original forests still flourished. Within a few rods of the park, on West and South streets, were thickly-wooded hemlock-swamps.[1]

Beyond the settling-lots, a large, perhaps the greater, portion of the "squares" into which the "commons" were divided in 1759-60, were still uncleared. With the elms, oak, pine, maples, chestnut, and other trees of these woods, were thickly intermingled the sweet-brier, the azalea, the mountain-ash, the sumach, the wild cherry, the moose-wood, and the white thorn, so close to every house that although their beauty must have often held the rapt gazer in charmed admiration, none thought of transplanting them.

It would be most unjust, indeed, to censure, as without appreciation of the beautiful in nature, or even as without a keen sense

---

[1] Mrs. C. T. Fenn remembers, when a young girl, parting often with a favorite companion—the latter being compelled to pass through the "swamp-road," on South street, on her way home—that she waited, calling to her by way of encouragement, until she reached the opening on the other side, now the head of Church street. Report located wolves in the wooded recesses, afterwards the garden of Rev. Dr. Todd, from which fearful cries were heard at night. A tangled swamp extended from near the west side of South street to the present line of the Housatonic railroad, and from West street nearly to the present West Housatonic street.

of her charms, all those who thought it but a vain labor to bring together exotics from the ends of the earth, when not only the fair, wild, flowering shrubs, which we have named, were scattered in profusion close around their homes, but the gorgeous laurel, with its glossy foliage, the trailing arbutus, luxuriously delicate of hue and fragrance, the fairy-tinted and quaintly-shaped lady's slipper, the columbine in her harlequin garb of red and yellow, the gentian with her fringed ruff of deepest blue, the asters, white, blue, purple and orange, the violets and houstonia cerulea clouding the earth, the clustering anemone, the adder's-tongue, the wake-robin, the wild pink, and other forms of floral loveliness, peeped from every thicket and spangled every field; when the myriad plumes of the purple orchis, and the pickerel-weed, invaded the waters of every stream; and, higher up their banks, the scarlet splendor of the cardinal-flower dazzled the eye; and, most beautiful of all, on the bosom of every lake floated the pure white lily of the waters.

In painting the homes of the fathers, we must surround them with a thousand forms of native grace and beauty which have withdrawn from our own; and it would be a libel upon the blood we inherit, to declare that they in whose veins it ran seventy-five years ago, because they did not seek to augment the charms with which untutored nature sought to delight them, were therefore insensible to their influence. No less would it be a libel upon history, when we remember how the early discoverers exhausted hyperbole in their description of the new world's glories, to say that the children of these same men, when they came to dwell among these same glories, were struck with an inane blindness which prevented their enjoyment of them. Not even the privations, unintermitted toil, and frequent suffering of pioneer life could have effected that transformation.

No, we may depend upon it, that the descendants of the generation to which belonged Drake and Raleigh, Hudson, the Cabots and the other voyagers of glowing story; and the ancestors of the race who claim Bryant and Longfellow and Lowell, did, with tender and true appreciation, enjoy the splendors of field and forest which the voyagers who went before them, and the poets who came after, celebrated with like fervor. And that appreciation was none the less genuine because it was casual, unstudied, and not often eloquently expressed; the golden thread interwoven by nature with a life otherwise of somewhat rude and somber texture, not that inwrought by culture with warp and woof of silken leisure.

In making these natural flower-gardens and their sheltering grove thus prominent in our picture, we do not, then, unduly magnify what the men and women of 1800 regarded lightly; but give its just place to a feature which went far to satisfy their craving for the beautiful, and contributed much to relieve the barren aspect of a town of generally-unshaded streets, and courtyards for the most part unadorned by shrub, or vine, or flower; even if, as was most likely to happen, they were not deformed by unsightly objects.

Nor must we forget another source which brought its aid to the same end; the apple orchards, which, planted near almost every house, afforded, all summer, a fair and cheerful sight; but in the season of blossoming, thick flecked the scene with clouds of splendor rivaling the most fleecy that float in the skies of June. Such, and with such surroundings of trees, shrubbery and flowers, were the abodes of the people of Pittsfield, about the beginning of the nineteenth century. Their places of mercantile business were few and unpretending, but respectable, and such as were usually found in flourishing market-villages.

On East street, at the corner of Second, was the two-story gambrel-roof store of Colonel Joshua Danforth; its gable-end facing East street. A little below was a similar store but of only one story, occupied by Graves & Root.

On the corner of North street and Park place with the gable-end and entrance facing on the latter was the store built by Jonathan Allen, in 1798; a plain, neat building with an angular roof. Next north, on the site of the Allen block was the small one-story steep-roofed "medicine-shop," built in 1796, by Dr. Timothy Childs. On South street, facing the west end of Bank row, was built about this time by J. D. & S. D. Colt a handsome wooden store, large for its time, of two stories with an angular roof. It still stands, having been removed to West Housatonic street. Opposite the Colt store on the corner of Bank row and South street, was a similar store which was built by Hon. Ashbel Strong, and occupied by his brother-in-law, John Stoddard.[1]

[1] Major Israel Stoddard, the noted loyalist of Pittsfield revolutionary story, and son of Colonel John Stoddard, the Northampton "great New Englander,"

From the Stoddard store to the house of John Chandler Williams, was a vacant space.

From the foregoing hints and outlines the reader, with a little aid from imagination, will perhaps be able to gain a tolerably correct idea of the village of Pittsfield, in the year 1800.

In examining the map, it will be noticed that dwellings are much more thickly scattered along the streets running east and west than upon those intersecting them at right angles; and the same difference would be observed if it had been extended to embrace the whole of the original settling-lots. There were two causes for this. First, the great highway between Boston and Albany ran through East and West streets. But secondly, and chiefly, it arose from the mode in which the lots were originally laid out. There were, it will be recollected, three tiers of hundred-acre farms, lying side by side and extending from the east to the west through the center of the township. One of these tiers reached the whole length of the town, while that north of it fell a mile and a half short of the Dalton border, and that upon the south something more than two miles short of the Hancock line; the three ranges being separated from each other by roads seven rods wide. They were also intersected by a road, seven rods wide, running nearly through the center of the township from north to south, and now known as North and South streets, and in the east and west parts by other roads. The extreme width of these

---

joint proprietor with Colonel Wendell, and Edward Livingstone, of Poontoosuc, died in 1872, of consumption, aged forty-one. He lies buried with his widow and several of his children on the eastern slope of Pontoosuc Hill in the Pittsfield cemetery; where his grave is marked by a large old-fashioned tombstone, bearing this exceedingly-apposite epitaph :

> "In life, uninfluenced by the breath of fame,
> The great, the true, the just, thy constant aim;
> Praised or not praised, in death affects thee not,
> By whom remembered or by whom forgot.
> A heap of dust is all remains of thee;
> 'Tis all thou art, and all that we shall be."

His daughter Mary, the grand-daughter and namesake of the "Honored Madam May," of provincial polite society, and a lady equally worthy of honor, was married in 1792, to Hon. Ashbel Strong. And in this connection there comes to us a traditional anecdote, which, at once, illustrates the decline in the reverence which the people had bestowed upon the wealthy and magisterial classes, and introduces a character now rarely met, but which, seventy years ago, made merriment in the streets of almost every New Entiers of settling-lots at the point where they were intersected by North and South streets, and where the tiers were complete, was only about six hundred rods. The length of the central tier which lay south of East and West streets, was something over six miles; that of the others about four miles. Now, the lots had a frontage from east to west of eighty rods, while their depth was two hundred rods. It will be seen that only three of these lots could lie upon each side of North and South streets, while one occupied each eighty rods of each side of the six miles of East and West streets, and the four miles of Honasada street.

The terms of the grant required a house to be built upon each of these sixty-three lots within a brief period after the first settlement; and, although the terms were not strictly complied with, and sometimes two lots were consolidated, yet it was not many years before there was an average of one house to every eighty rods on the last named streets; making an unusually-compact agricultural settlement. On the other hand, the "commons," or the territory outside the settling-lots, retained by the original proprietors, embraced a strip one and a half miles wide on the south side of the town, and another two and a half miles wide on the north; and were with a trifling exception not open to occupation until 1760, and, even then, instead of being offered in oblong parcels of moderate size, suited to the means of the young farmers and leading by their form and arrangement, as well as by positive

gland town, the village rhymesters, who, with coarse and often caustic, wit, played the part of court-jesters to the "Sovereign people." Generally they were somewhat weak or disordered in intellect; but, whether so or not, they were always licensed.

Mr. Strong was fourteen years older than his wife, and in his days of courtship, one day meeting one of this witless-witty class, he challenged a display of his powers. The response was the following doggerel:

> "Old Ashbel Strong,
> He stubs along
> Up to his farm and fodder;
> The people say,
> Who live that way,
> He's courtin' Molly Stoddar."

Plain, and rather irreverential, "Molly," observe, and no longer "Honored Madam." But the Honorable suitor is said to have "stubbed along" without further parley. The curt record of the marriage styles the bride Mrs. Polly Stoddard. John Stoddard, who kept a store on Bank row, was a brother of Mrs. Strong, and was born in 1773.

agreement, to the erection of farm-houses somewhat after the order of a village street—the "commons-lands" were divided into squares of from two hundred and thirty to three hundred acres each; some of which long remained the property of those to whom they fell by the partition of 1760.

Some of the original owners, such as Colonel Wendell, Major Israel Stoddard, Captain Charles Goodrich, Israel Dickinson and the Partridges, reserved large farms for their own use. But, with these exceptions, the owners of the squares were generally well inclined to sell their lands in lots convenient for the purchaser, with no more restrictions than prudence dictated for the prevention of awkward and unsalable remainders. And probably the majority of the farms sold were of very moderate dimensions. Some contained no more than fifty acres. But the new-comers—not restricted, like the sixty pioneers to a confined section, not like them compelled to take the poor lands with the good, and no longer attracted to a defensible vicinage by the fear of lurking savages—selected their homes wherever the fertility of the soil, convenient water-power, neighborly associations, the course of the highways, the state of their purse, and an infinitude of other considerations, led them.

But to return to the system of roads, in Pittsfield, which was distinguished for its regularity. The road from Lenox to Lanesboro, of which North and South streets were a part, extended through Pittsfield nearly in a straight line, passing through the present site of the high-school house, and over the hill north of Maplewood Institute, and that west of Pontoosuc Lake. East and West streets, as now, extended from a point half a mile east of the park, in a straight line to the Hancock borders. Owing to the swamp east of that point, the highway diverged thence south-east, through Water and Elm streets. These intersecting roads, practically only two, may be considered the trunk, or base, of the whole system. From North street, about half a mile north of Maplewood, a street turned a little to the north-west and passing near the present entrance of the cemetery, joined and continued through Otaneaque street; forming the avenue by which the people of the North woods, and several of the forge neighborhoods, reached the central village. Wahconah street was not yet opened. Farther north a road, crossing the outlet of Pontoosuc lake, wound along its west side. From South street, Honasada street—one of the originally-reserved roads—was actually opened eastward to the Dalton line. Westward, there continued to be an unmade portion until the line reached a point near Oceola village, whence it was completed to the foot of the mountain. Beyond the river, South Mountain street wound along the base of the hill from which it takes its name. From Otaneaque street, to the western extension of Honasada street, three roads ran north and south crossing West street. From West street, also ran Onota street, north to Seymour's iron forge. On West street again, east of the river, Mill street led south to Luce's mill. From Honasada street, Shearer's lane ran south along the east side of the farm which had been owned by Colonel Williams; and from the same street a road ran south and south-west, to "Rock mountain;" now known as the Sikes district, famous for its very hard and peculiarly-stratified granular quartz.

Northward from Elm street, extended Dickinson street, or the east road to Lanesboro. There were some other roads in various parts of the town; but the lack of recognizable landmarks would render an attempt to describe them unintelligible to most readers.

The roads by which the people of Pittsfield reach the great market-towns which they were accustomed to visit, have undergone material alterations. Travel towards Boston was through East and Elm streets, and thence by a street now partly discontinued, past the Woodbridge Little place, to the Dalton line, where it met the Worthington turnpike to Northampton. The road to Albany ran as at present through New Lebanon. The road to Hudson wound through South street, and South Mountain street, and thence by Barkersville, Richmond, and West Stockbridge. It is many years since the Pittsfield portion of this route has been used commonly as a thoroughfare. In 1800, however— Kinderhook and Hudson being the market-towns most convenient for Pittsfield trade and the landings where Berkshire merchandise, coming up or going down the Hudson, was generally transhipped, and where Berkshire travelers took sloop to New York city—a greater amount of mercantile travel passed over the Richmond road than over any other in Pittsfield. This road could also be reached from the west part, by any of the streets leading from West to West Honasada street. But how slowly pre-eminence was gained by, or accorded to, the present business center of the town is shown by the fact that the great convenience and reduction of distance afforded to it by the opening of West Housatonic street was not obtained until 1825, nor in its best form until 1827; long struggles in town-meetings being required to accomplish it.

The earliest communication with the towns in southern Berkshire, and in Hampshire county, and with Hartford and other Connecticut towns, was through Wendell street. The majority of the first settlers probably entered Pittsfield by this road; those from Hampshire county, coming by the road from Blandford to New Marlboro. But in 1800 the most direct road was through South street, and the travel upon it was probably greater than upon any other except the Richmond road.

These avenues of communication were imperfectly constructed and often out of repair. Frequently, for considerable distances, they passed through dreary patches of wood. Corduroy roads were not yet dispensed with in crossing swamps. The vigorous traveler, therefore, preferred to make even long journeys in the saddle; and it needed that wagons should be stoutly built in order to encounter the rudeness of the highway. The trials of the teamster's patience and muscle were severe; but luckily, at brief distances, substantial taverns offered refreshment for man and beast. Nevertheless, the best relief was offered by the season of winter with its gliding roads; and it was enjoyed to the full.

CHAPTER II.

POPULATION—EMIGRATION—NEWSPAPERS—POST-OFFICES.

[1787–1800.]

Census of 1800—Increase and decrease of Berkshire towns—Causes of emigration—Anecdote of Phillips Merrill—Early newspapers—American Centinel—Local items—Advertisements—Influence upon agriculture, manufactures and morals—Publishers' troubles—Post-riders—Scarcity of paper—Berkshire Gazette—More post-riders and the first post-office.

BY the census of 1800, the population of Pittsfield was 2,261, distributed more uniformly than in more recent periods through what had been the original settling-lots, but much more sparsely in what had been the "commons." During the preceding nine years the town had become the most populous in Berkshire; the others having a population of over one thousand, being Williamstown, 2086; Sheffield, 2050; Sandisfield, 1857; New Marlboro, 1848; Great Barrington, 1754; Tyringham, 1712; Adams, 1688; Lanesboro, 1443; Cheshire, 1325; Lee, 1267; Stockbridge, 1261; Hancock, 1187; Otis, 1102; Richmond, 1044; West Stockbridge, 1002.

By the census of 1791, the population of these towns was: Pittsfield, 1992; Williamstown, 1769; Sheffield, 1899; Sandisfield, 1581; New Marlboro, Great Barrington, 1373; Tyringham, 1397; Adams, 2040; Lanesboro, 2142; Lee, 1170; Stockbridge, 1336; Hancock, 1211; Richmond, 1255; West Stockbridge, 1113.

The increase of population in Williamstown was very much due to the incorporation of Williams College in 1793. The decrease of Lanesboro, Adams and some other towns arose, in part at least, from the setting off of a part of the territory which for the purposes of the census, had been included with them.

But from the year 1791, far onward into the present century there was a constant and exhaustive drain upon the population of the entire county, by emigration to enticing farming regions then newly opened in western New York and in Ohio. Previous, indeed, to the year named, we find in the Pittsfield newspapers, advertisements of lands, not only in Ohio and New York, but in Vermont and Canada. In the *Chronicle* of April, 1789, Silas Goodrich advertised lands in several Vermont towns to be sold on liberal terms by auction "at the gaol-house at Great Barrington." In July, 1789, Mr. Leonard Chester published a long and glowing advertisement of lands in Canada, "to be confirmed" as to title "by himself and Lord Lanaudiere"—probably one of the provincial manor-lords.

Possibly, Mr. Chester may have allured to his patent, some Tory with an obstinate hankering for the shadow of royalty; but we have no information of any such case, and the status of the Berkshire loyalists was not at that time such as to render them impatient of the republican regime. The virgin territory of Vermont was more attractive, and there was a large emigration to that state. Indeed in Rutland county, a new Pittsfield, modeled after the old Berkshire home even to its park and elm, arose under the auspices of the grand old pioneer, Captain Charles Goodrich.

But, although by no means trifling in numbers, the emigration to Vermont was small compared with that which set towards western New York. As early as 1788, companies were formed for emigration to the Genesee valley. In 1790, the glowing advertisements of the Ohio company began to appear; and, from that time on, speculators and land-agents used all the allurements which they so well know how to apply, to entice the Berkshire farmers from their decried acres to the extolled fertility of the West. These enticements were met by those who loved the old home, or were interested in preventing its depopulation, and who presented counter arguments and statistics as forcibly as they could. For many years this wordy warfare went on, the friends of migration portraying the newly-opened regions as a very paradise; the woods full of all manner of game, the soil prolific beyond precedent, and the climate delightful and healthful; while those desirous of retaining population denied all the attractive qualities of western New York and Ohio, with still greater exaggeration. The reports from those who had emigrated were equally conflicting. Now a letter would overflow with the account of marvelous crops, sparkle with stories of adventure, and revel in reminiscences of achievements in hunting; and now another would be filled with stories of disease and death. Many returned with doleful confessions of homesickness. Among the latter was Mr. Phillips Merrill, who, in 1813, when a youth of perhaps twenty years, was sent by his father, Captain Hosea Merrill, to build a saw-mill upon a tract of land which he owned in the Genesee valley. He spent the summer in executing his task; and on his return, his father told him that a Mr. Clark who owned the farm at the south end of Pontoosuc lake, wished to exchange it for the Genesee lands and saw-mill; but that, intending to give them to himself, he had refused. "Father," said Phillips in reply, "I have lived in that country all summer, and built you the best saw-mill in York State, but I wouldn't spend my life there if you were to give me the whole country. The sun rose every morning in the west, and there was nothing at all homelike about it." The result was that Mr. Clark removed to Genesee, and Mr. Merrill grew rich by intelligent farming and shrewd business management in Pittsfield.

There were many with temperaments unsuited for pioneers, whose experience was like that of Mr. Merrill. But for all this, the Genesee valley was of marvelous fertility; the western reserve of Ohio was incontestably a country to be desired; the farms of Berkshire were fast becoming exhausted as wheat producers; the advertisements of the emigrant companies, and the —not entirely gratuitous—eulogisms of editors and correspondents, in their descriptions of the West, grew more frequent and more glowing. The tide of western migration swelled in volume. Paulding's description of the Yankee abandoning his half-finished shingle palace, to push forward with his tow-headed brood—the vanguard of empire—to a log cabin in the West, was no caricature. It found its original upon every highway which led towards the promised land.

The *Pittsfield Sun* of June 2d, 1801, attributes the decrease of population in many Berkshire towns to the emigration to " the new lands in Genesee, and other parts of New York, especially the Chenango purchase." "Settlements," said the *Sun*, "which cover whole townships in several counties in New York, are composed almost entirely of emigrants from Berkshire county."

The State of Connecticut, to which, in the settlement of the ownership of public lands, the western reserve in Ohio had fallen, presented extraordinary inducements to settlers by offering the fertile lands of that territory in exchange for farms in New England. Her agents were busy in Berkshire county, and succeeded in effecting many exchanges of this sort. It is not many years since that State owned lands thus obtained; among others that which surrounds Lake Ashley, the source of the Pittsfield water-works, and that in which lies the valuable bed of granular quartz, from which the Lenox Glass Company obtain their supply of sand.

To this migration, Pittsfield, although not depleted like some of her sister towns, contributed many of her valued citizens; valued, although not always successful in business. Those who had long struggled under that burden of debt and mortgage, which we endeavored to describe, among the causes of the Shays rebellion, abandoned their long deferred hope of retrieved fortunes in the old home, for fresher promise in new fields; and generally not in vain. We find in the brief but suggestive records of the church, touching stories of the gift to members—who had been prosperous and prominent, but who had become indigent through intemperance—of the means of removing to new homes in Genesee, where they might begin life anew. And it is pleasant to find the families, thus gently and not unkindly thrust out into the wilderness, in the next generation among the most thriving and honored in the very garden of the Empire State.

The habits of intemperance, thriftlessness and dissipation generally, which existed in the years immediately following the revolutionary war, still continued, although diminished by the healing power of time. Of some other peculiarities which at this period led to the impoverishment of the unwary, we shall speak in treating of its social and moral aspects. It is sufficient here to say that they were more numerous and more powerful than they now are, especially as affecting those classes of society which, by their decorous requirements, throw the most effectual safeguards around their members.

It will be seen that, in addition to the restless desire of bettering their condition by change of location, the allurements of distant promise, and impatience of ill-success at home, which continually push on population towards the Pacific, there were powerful stimulants to migration during the earlier years of the century, which no longer exist, or are greatly diminished.

We return to the consideration of the means which enabled Pittsfield—notwithstanding the loss of the county courts, and the drain made by the West upon her population—to show an increase of two hundred and sixty-nine souls between the census of 1791 and that of 1800. It is worthy of remark that all the towns through which ran the great highways crossing Berkshire from the east to the west gained in population. But the chief agencies which advanced Pittsfield were agriculture, commerce and manufactures—not an uncommon combination, and the same which still prevails. But the order of their precedence has become reversed; it now being manufactures, commerce and agriculture. We will consider them, for the sake of convenience, in still another order, and in connection with another influence which had an extremely beneficial effect upon the prosperity of the town.

This influence came from the early newspapers of the town; of which the first was the *American Centinel*, published by E. Russell. The first number of this sheet was dated December 1, 1787, at which time there were only two other newspapers in Massachusetts west of Worcester, the *Hampshire Herald*, commenced at Springfield in 1782, as the *Massachusetts Gazette*, and the *Hampshire Gazette*, whose long and honorable career, not yet ended, began at Northampton in 1786.

All the information we have regarding the *Centinel* is derived from a single tattered copy of the second number, which is believed to be the only relic of the paper in existence. It is printed on a sheet ten by eighteen inches in size, and the greater portion of its space is occupied by two or three prosy essays. The advertisements are very few, but still the most interesting portion of the paper. The editor, however, evidently intended to make his columns when under way more readable, as is indicated by the ambitious couplet which he placed at their head:

" Here you may range the world from pole to pole,
Increase your knowledge, and delight your soul."

But alas, the *Centinel* here vanishes from view, having no doubt very soon met the fate foreshadowed in its second number, in which Mr. Russell "returns his thanks to those gentlemen who expressed their anxiety to have the printing-office in Pittsfield, by engaging him to print a certain number of papers; and begs leave to inform them that he has a large number of papers on hand for which he has yet received nothing, and which he wishes those gentlemen to call for, according to agreement. If agreements are not fulfilled, the *Centinel* must stop."

Mr. Russell had found the same experience of printers' patrons which Benjamin Franklin had met before, and many another since.

The *Centinel* was succeeded by the *Berkshire Chronicle*, which occupied the same office, and probably used the same type and press. Its birth seems to have followed hard upon the death of its predecessor, the first number being published May 8, 1788, "by Roger Storrs, near the meeting-house,"—the little, old first meeting-house, it should be remembered, which stood upon East street, in line with the printing-office; there being, as yet, no "park."

The first issue of the *Chronicle* is missing, but most of the numbers, from May 15, 1788, to June 17, 1790, are preserved.

For the first thirty numbers the new paper was only twelve inches by eight in size; but with the thirty-first number, December 19, 1788, it was enlarged to the respectable dimensions of eighteen inches by ten.

Throughout its course the *Chronicle* exhibited marked editorial skill, tact and spirit. The motto,—

"Free as the savage roams his native wood,
Or finny nations cleave the briny flood,"

gave promise of something not quite so ponderous as the essays of the *Centinel;* and the expectation excited was satisfied by able moral, political and economical articles, relieved by lighter sketches, anecdotes and verses, and by the foreign and domestic news of that exciting period, all prepared in compact and readable form. The local columns, although not so full as we could wish them for our present purpose, were more so than those of later Pittsfield journals. The advertisements came from all parts of the county, although few were from the extreme southern towns. Many of them were of a character which shows that the cost of advertising must have been small; but no tariff of prices was given, and it is probable that special bargains were made in each case; legal, mercantile and other classes of advertisements paying different rates,—a practice of which some relics remained, until very recently, in the newspaper business of the county.

The editor manifested a lively interest in that great advance of the industrial arts which was then beginning under the ardent, laborious and intelligent efforts of the best and most patriotic minds in the country. In the first number of his paper, he gave emphatic notice that "the printer would be happy to receive and publish any communications of improvements in the arts, especially those of agriculture and manufactures;" and the essays which he did publish, although not original, were not far behind those of later days.

In the number for September 14, 1789, were published eleven excellent rules, by the celebrated Dr. Rush, of Philadelphia, for the conduct of a newspaper, and, however it may have been in regard to some of the others, the editor faithfully followed the ninth: "Let the advancement of agriculture, manufactures and commerce be the principal objects of your paper. A receipt to destroy the insects which feed upon the turnip, or to prevent the rot in sheep, will be more useful to America than all the inventions for destroying the human species which so often fill the columns of European newspapers." Mr. Storrs, however, seems, as a practical editor, to have very well known that, whatever may be the principal aim of a newspaper, that aim will be best attained by devoting a considerable, perhaps the greater, portion of its space to other subjects. A paper devoted entirely to the discussion of the gravest objects, as recommended by Dr. Rush, would have soon met the fate of Mr. Russell's *Centinel,* and left its aims to such help as they could get from technical essays. The *Chronicle,* on the contrary, with its racy variety, must have been a welcome visitor in every home; a pleasant companion to the apple-basket and cider-mug, in the broad and cheery blaze which illumined Berkshire firesides in those old winter evenings; while withal, its usefulness was enhanced rather than impaired by its genial traits.

But newspaper-publishing in 1789 had its troubles and its difficulties among the Berkshire hills. There was but a single post-office in all Western Massachusetts—that at Springfield, to which all mail-matter for the present counties of Hampshire, Berkshire, Hampden and Franklin was sent. Post-riders, not employed by the government but a sort of private mail-carriers, obtained the letters and newspapers of their customers from the Springfield office, and, riding their several routes on horseback, distributed them at the doors of those to whom they were directed. The same important agents took the local newspapers from the printing-offices, and delivered them to subscribers. Often they purchased the papers from the publisher, and dealt directly with their customers at their own risk. In regard to the circulation of his paper, and the collection of his dues, these agents were a great convenience; but as the rider from Berkshire only visited Springfield once a week, and the chances for his delay by storms or otherwise were great, the facilities for obtaining news from abroad might well be considered small and precarious. Even in winter the post generally rode his circuit on horseback, but so bulky was the currency of the interior at this period that an occasional trip with some vehicle was indispensable. Thus on February 13, 1789, "Alvin Wolcott, post-rider," informed his customers that he "proposed, the next week, to go his circuit in a sleigh, for the purpose of transporting the pay which shall be ready for him at that time." The printer, like the merchant and others, was obliged to take the greater part of his dues in produce; and he was very glad if it was in linen rags—as yet cotton was not in general use—for which he also offered to exchange good writing paper. There was great scarcity of printing paper, and the newspapers, whose publishers experienced great trouble from this source, constantly urged housewives carefully to save their rags; an economy which they seem to have learned with difficulty. So great was the dearth of paper that in March, 1789, Mr. Storrs gave notice that, for this reason, he "would for the present publish only half a sheet, but as soon as these obstacles were removed, would print a half-sheet extraordinary."

The scarcity of paper was not the only difficulty with which Mr. Storrs had to contend. On the 15th of May, 1789, he, at the close of his first volume, thanking his "subscribers for their past favors," informed them that the paper would be suspended for two or three weeks, during which he asked a payment of old dues, and an addition of new subscribers." "It must," he observed, "be apparent to every person of discernment that the establishment of a new and precarious business, in an infant country, must be attended with many difficulties and expenses unexperienced in those more populated and matured;" for which reason he hoped his customers would more readily comply with his request. He had engaged a supply of paper, and the difficulty of obtaining it being removed, he expected in future to serve his customers without interruption. The publication was resumed and continued, at least until June 17, 1790. The number printed on that day was the fifty-first of the second volume. Whether it was continued longer is uncertain, but the last issue showed no signs of flagging. In politics the *Chronicle* was federal, but moderate, although earnest. In morals it opposed intemperance, and the still more fashionable vice of gambling; including lotteries, although their advertisements were found in its columns, and they were patronized and conducted then, and for many years afterwards, by the gravest personages in church and state.

The influence of this excellent journal upon the town must have been large, and its citizens should enroll the name of Roger Storrs among those entitled to their grateful remembrance.

The *Chronicle* was succeeded by a paper whose very name is forgotten, but of which we have a vague tradition as published for a time by a Mr. Spooner, who removed to Windsor, Vermont.

On the 18th of January, Nathaniel Holly, Orsemus C. Merrill and Chester Smith issued the first number of the *Berkshire Gazette*, a sheet of nineteen inches by twelve, bearing the mysterious motto, "Man is man, and who is more." Sixteen numbers of the *Gazette* are preserved, and represent a respectable newspaper. But we miss the pleasant and varied miscellany of the *Chronicle*, its practical essays upon arts, agriculture and morals, and especially its lively interest in home affairs. The only information we are able to gather from it concerning local matters is derived from the advertisements. But the increasing violence of party spirit is clearly shown in the political articles.

Mr. Merrill withdrew from the firm in June, 1798, and Mr. Holly, in March, 1799. Mr. Smith, in assuming the sole charge of the paper, made the subscription-price, delivered at the office, one dollar per annum, "as previously;" one dollar and fifty cents if delivered by carrier or post-rider. Advertisements not exceeding twelve lines were inserted three times for one dollar, and three weeks longer for thirty-eight cents; longer advertisements in proportion. This was the first time that the price of subscription or of advertising was mentioned in the Pittsfield newspapers.

The *Gazette* ended with the year 1799, and in the following October, J. D. & S. D. Colt called upon those indebted to its publisher, for payment, by an advertisement in the *Pittsfield Sun*, which then succeeded to the printing-office ; but by no means to the political principles or the ephemeral existence of its predecessors.

Four newspapers were thus printed in Pittsfield between the years 1787 and 1800. And small as their pecuniary success seems to have been, their influence upon the town for good was not slight. They attracted attention to it as a business and political center, extended intelligence among its people, and fostered all its best interests.

Among the incidental benefits which they bestowed were increased postal facilities. When the *Chronicle* was established, not only was there no post-office in the county, but the post-riders were very irregular in their circuits, their visits being sometimes at long intervals. But in January, 1790, Mr. Storrs, with excusable pride, announced that " the printer of the *Chronicle*, ever endeavoring to furnish his customers with the earliest intelligence, had engaged a post to ride *weekly* from his office in Pittsfield to Springfield on Mondays, and return on Wednesdays, with the papers published in the different states of the Union; when matters of importance [brought] by them will be published in the *Chronicle* on Thursday, and immediately circulated to the several towns by the different post-riders."

The local newspapers in 1790 furnished their own postal facilities, and the people could obtain their letters and other mail matter by the agencies thus provided. The first post-office in Berkshire was established at Stockbridge in 1792, probably through the influence of Hon. Theodore Sedgwick, of that town, who was the first representative in Congress from the district. The second was at Pittsfield, in 1794 ; and it is fair to infer that the publication here of the newspaper had its influence in obtaining it. A post-office was established at Great Barrington in 1797, and at Williamstown in 1798. There was no other in the county until 1800, when one was opened at Lenox, which had been made the shire town in 1786, for its " central position." Lanesboro, in 1801 obtained the same favor.

CHAPTER III.

AGRICULTURE—MANUFACTURES—MERCANTILE AFFAIRS.

[1787-1805.]

Farming universal—Deterioration of soils—Agricultural teachings—Products —Price of land—Prices of stock and farm products—Fulling-mills—Iron forges—Tanneries—Potasheries—Oil-mills—Nail-factory—Early mercantile business—Trade by barter—Patriotic merchants—What goods were sent to market—Joshua Danforth—Simon Larned—John B. Root—Trade in 1798-1805.

AGRICULTURE.

COMMERCE and manufactures were, even prior to the nineteenth century, no mean elements in the business of Pittsfield. Still agriculture was the chief employment of its people. Even those engaged in other avocations were generally also practical farmers. The clergyman was an enthusiastic, skillful, and personally-industrious farmer. The lawyer, the merchant and the physician each owned and cultivated his farm. So did the clothiers, the tanners, and most, or all, of the iron-masters.

Of the character of the cultivation bestowed on the fields, we can aver with some positiveness that it was not altogether so rude and unintelligent as is often represented.

Secretary Charles L. Flint thus epitomizes the history of the deterioration of New England soils: "The soil [originally] was rich in mould—the accumulation of ages—and did not require very careful cultivation to secure an abundant return. But years of constant cropping exhausted its productiveness when other lands were taken, to be subjected to the same process. The farmer raised wheat, year after year, upon the same land, till the soil became too poor, and then he planted corn; and when it would no longer grow corn he sowed barley or rye; and so on to beans."

Owing to the later settlement of Berkshire, this process of deterioration, on a greater portion of its soil, did not pass much beyond the first stage before it was arrested by intelligent manuring. Nevertheless the unthrifty practice of constant cropping without the application of fertilizers was general in Berkshire quite as late as 1800. We have the diaries of three Pittsfield farmers of good repute, between the years 1777 and 1798, and there is no mention in them of any artificial enrichment of the soil, although the dates of other farm operations are minutely given. Indeed, it is said to have been a question with some whether it were better to remove an old barn to a new location, or haul away the accumulations around it, which were considered merely a worthless nuisance. Any use of the valuable agents provided by nature for the nourishment and renovation of the soil was contemned by the masses as mere fancy farming,—good enough for gentlemen of leisure, but a waste of labor for hard-worked men.

Of course, the cultivation of wheat upon soils thus drained of all wheat-producing elements, grew unprofitable, and was abandoned. But before the second step had been taken in the downward path, more intelligent views began to prevail. And the germs of this reform were sown, not only long before the institution of the Berkshire Agricultural Society, but more than ten years before the opening of the nineteenth century. The *Chronicle*, on the fifteenth of May, 1788, began the publication of a series of essays upon agriculture, copied from a work then just issued in New York; and they extended through ten numbers of the paper, filling from one and a half to three columns in each issue. "The success of farming," said the writer, in introducing his subject, "depends principally upon the collecting of manure; on a proper change of crops; on good tillage, or ploughing the ground properly, and keeping it clean; on the choice and management of stock; and on the management of the orchard and its produce." "Upon these articles" he "made some notes, chiefly collected from Mr. Young's Farmer's Tour through Europe, published in 1771." These notes contained axioms and instructions, not essentially differing from those given in the most recent agricultural text-books. Great economy and thoroughness in the saving of manures was emphatically urged; directions were given for composting; the value of liquid manures was explained, and some modes of saving that of the stable were pointed out—among which the simple expedient of absorbents was, however, not mentioned. Of the rotation of crops it was said: "A succession of the same sort of crops will speedily exhaust the best land. For this reason the skillful farmer changes his crops every year." The order of succession most approved was that practiced in Norfolk, England: "1, turnips; 2, barley, with clover feed; 3, clover; 4, wheat." Some preferred in the third and fourth years clover, and in the fifth wheat. Others found the following formula extremely beneficial: "1, turnips; 2, barley; 3, clover two years; 4, buckwheat."

Carrots, cabbages, beans, peas, etc., were recommended to vary the ordinary hay-diet of stock. Carrots were specially commended. "No milk, cream or butter," it is said, "can be richer than what is got from carrots, all through the winter and spring; no food will carry on a hog quicker or fat him better than raw carrots; cows and oxen may be fattened on them completely; horses do very well on them; and sheep eat them very greedily." "When the soil is rich and deep, the culture of carrots is very profitable."

The following are the author's instructions as to manuring with lime: "I have in the course of seven years put on as many thousand bushels of lime, in a great variety of modes. With reference to farming for wheat, rye or corn, every one takes his own method. It is impossible to form any general rule to suit all soils. The method must depend on the quality of your land. If the land be much worn out, it will take the less quantity of lime. The soil best adapted for lime is a loamy ground inclining to sand. At least, I have found it to answer best; although I have heard of great things being done with lime on clay. Deep ploughing in the first instance ought to be practiced, but shallow ploughing after the lime is laid on." Other directions for the use of lime are given, and also elaborate instruction as to the proper treatment of particular crops, as well as upon other agricultural topics.

Such was the agricultural reading which the Pittsfield newspaper furnished, three years before the organization of the New York Society for the Promotion of Agriculture, Arts and Manufactures, and twenty-three years before the Berkshire County Society was incorporated. The meetings of the former society, commencing in 1791, elicited by their discussions a great fund of information, the result of experiments made by men of unusual ability, and sufficient pecuniary means. This information, printed in their "Transactions" and other publications, and in the newspapers, scattered agricultural knowledge throughout the country, awakened thought, and, although more slowly than could have been wished, brought about improved practices.

Although it cannot be pretended that the advice and instruction so lavishly bestowed on the farmers was very speedily adopted by them, to the displacement of life-long practices and hereditary prejudice, it cannot, on the other hand, be supposed that men like Charles Goodrich, Eli and Oliver Root, the Cadwells, the Fairfields, Hosea Merrill, the Wrights, the Churchills, and a host of other intelligent Pittsfield farmers, were slow to examine, to discuss, and perhaps experiment upon, the new theories. And in fact we find them gradually adopted years before the institution of the Agricultural Society, and preparing the way for the co-operation of the best farmers of the county with Mr. Watson in that undertaking. Of course then, as now—and doubtless in greater numbers—there were instances in which obstinate stupidity persisted in robbing the earth until there was nothing more left which it had the skill to abstract; but it is not true that the mass of Pittsfield farmers pursued this course. There never was a time, except in exceptionally cold seasons, like those of 1816 and a few succeeding years, when Indian corn was not a successful crop on most farms whose soil had been originally adapted to it. The "run-down" farms were a more infrequent exception in the earlier than the later portions of the century. And for this stay of the downward progress of its agriculture, the county was indebted in a great measure to the teachings of pamphlets and newspapers, which we may be sure were fully discussed in the nightly gatherings at the village stores and taverns, and in neighborly visits around the great farm-house fireplaces.

And, if the teachings of the writers had all been rejected, still the mere incitement to thought would have been of incalculable advantage; for while the new theories were considered, the old practices must have also been reviewed, and the reasons for them questioned, with the result sometimes of modification, and sometimes of entire change, whether in the manner recommended, or on some original plan.

Some of the farmers kept journals of their work, giving the

dates at which they began and ended planting, hoeing and harvesting each particular crop, some of their operations in stock-raising, observations on the weather, and the like; but little is to be gathered from them concerning the methods of cultivation or amount of product. We learn, however, that the principal crops were Indian corn, flax, barley, oats, hay, buckwheat and apples. Wheat also continued to be a staple crop on many farms. Mr. Cadwell records, that in the spring of 1794 he paid eight dollars for his seed-wheat. No mention is made in any of the diaries which we have of potatoes, pumpkins, squashes, turnips or beans, nor of peas as a farm-product, although considerable crops of most of these articles appear from other evidence to have been raised.

Of garden luxuries, green corn, green peas and cucumbers were the chief, and the first appearance of each is every year chronicled with marked glee.

Great attention was paid to the breeding of horses and mules, many of which were sent to the West India and other markets. Some of the wealthiest farmers made a specialty of this branch of their business. The newspapers were filled with glowing advertisements of the qualities and pedigrees of favorite stallions. The Narragansett stock was particularly prized for hardihood, bottom and speed; and the justice of this reputation is proved by the rather startling story that Capt. Charles Goodrich, when eighty years old, rode a horse of this breed, one summer day, from Pittsfield, Vermont, to Pittsfield, Massachusetts—one hundred and four miles—starting after sunrise in the morning, and sleeping at home the same night.

The beef-packing of the merchants, and the use of hides by the tanners greatly encouraged the raising of cattle, and also led to the profitable practice of purchasing lean or young cattle from the drovers, to be fattened for sale. And the animals raised, although by no means equal to those of our present pastures, were quite as far from being the scrawny, ill-conditioned beasts which they have sometimes been represented. The Duke de la Rochefoucault Liancourt says that the county of Hampshire fattened large numbers of cattle, yearly, for the market; and, speaking of the whole state, adds, that "the pastures were covered with a fine breed of cattle, and also a large number of horses, which latter he did not think remarkable for beauty;" excellent testimony to the character of Massachusetts cattle from one familiar with the best herds of Europe.

On the western side of Berkshire, the Dutch, before the transfer of the province to the English, had imported from Holland a small plump breed, many of whose descendants found their way to Pittsfield, where the cows were highly prized as milkers. Indeed, the "little Dutchies" were the favorites of many dairies. With the Dutch and English imported breeds, the Berkshire hills were not, in 1800, without very fair cattle.

Sheep were found on every farm sufficient to supply the domestic loom with a coarse wool, and the farmer's table with quite as coarse mutton. The Merinoes did not reach Berkshire until several years later. The swine were a "coarse, long-legged, large-boned, slab-sided, flab-eared, sharp-nosed generation, better fitted for sub-soiling than to fill a pork barrel;" so that, while beef-packing was a large and profitable business, pork afforded but an unimportant item. Mr. William Cadwell records in his diary in 1793, the slaughter of one hog weighing two hundred and forty-one pounds, and of another which weighed two hundred and five pounds. These seemed to have been considered of fair size, although they appear strangely small in comparison with the ordinary weights of the later breeds; not to speak of the monstrous masses of fat which attain the honor of cattle-show prizes and newspaper-paragraphs.[1]

The price of land is stated by the French author, whom we have before quoted, at "from six to twenty-five dollars an acre—the same as in New Lebanon;" and his statement is confirmed by such deeds of that period as we have had opportunity to examine.

The following "list of prices for 1795," was found in the town assessor's book for that year:

Middling (average?) horse,	$30.00	Middling cows,	$12.00
Three-year-old, do.	15.00	Three-year-old cattle,	12.00
Yearling, do.	10.00	Two-year-old cattle,	7.50
Middling oxen,	40.00	Yearling cattle,	4.00

[1] In May, 1795, Mr. Cadwell, who was a skillful and prosperous farmer, although not among the richest in the town, gives the following list of his cattle: "2 oxen, 5 cows, 4 three-year-olds, 9 two-year-olds, 4 yearlings, 6 calves, 1 bull." At the same time he had about thirty sheep, "a few swine, turkeys, geese, hens," and undoubtedly one or more horses.

Swine per lb.,	$0.03	Hay per ton,	$5.00
Wheat per bu.,	1.00	Pork per lb.,	.08
Rye per bu.,	.50	Beef per lb.,	.04
Corn per bu.,	.40	Cheese per lb.,	.08
Peas and beans per bu.,	.67	Butter per lb.,	.12
Oats per bu.,	.25	Flax per lb.,	.08

Pittsfield Archives, p. 56.

MANUFACTURES.

In the earliest period of the town—less than seven years after the close of the French and Indian wars had given the security essential to the development of its resources—we found, in the first fulling-mill and the first iron-forge, the germs of that manufacturing interest which has since grown to so over-shadowing importance; and, before the close of the eighteenth century, manufactures began to form a valuable portion of its business, although here, as elsewhere in Massachusetts, agriculture and commerce continued to absorb to a great degree both enterprise and capital.

The clothiers flourished, and, although several of the Berkshire towns which afforded water-power had also their fulling-mills, those of Pittsfield brought to it much trade. The farmers' wives and daughters carded their wool, spun their yarn, wove and sometimes colored their fabrics at home; but all, except those intended for the most common wear, were sent to the clothiers to be fulled, dressed (sheared), and, if that had not been already done, dyed.

The fulling was done by the aid of a small water-wheel; the other processes by hand. The dressing was performed with a huge pair of shears, made expressly for the purpose, one blade of which lay flat upon the cloth, while the other closed upon it as they went rapidly snipping over the surface. The clothiers differed greatly in their skill as dyers, and some of them obtained a reputation among the good-wives which long outlasted their trade; but, if tradition does them no injustice, in most cases the colors, especially the jaunty blue, were anything but fast. The wearing of a new suit—a bridal suit, it might be—for a single day, left the unfortunate exquisite of a sadly mouldy hue, which he who was content with the humbler butternut, escaped. Claret, also a favorite color of that day, was very skillfully imparted. Mr. Stearns, the ancestor of the later manufacturers of that name, obtained a high reputation by the brilliancy and permanency of his scarlets, a fashionable color for the cloaks of both ladies and gentlemen.

The appearance of these home-made cloths, when sent home by the clothier, neatly pressed and folded, was by no means so inferior to that of modern stuffs, as might be supposed.

There were four fulling-mills, or clothier's shops, in Pittsfield; that built by Aaron Baker, at the present Barkersville, about 1767, purchased by Valentine Rathbun, in 1770, owned in 1800, by Dan Munroe, and sold the next year to Daniel Stearns; that of Jacob Ensign at White's mills on Water street; that of Deacon Matthew Barber, erected by him, in 1776, in connection with a saw-mill, on the site of the present Wahconah flouring-mills; and that owned by Titus Parker, on the Cameron brook in the south-east corner of the town. The mills were thus scattered in different sections: Barber's being a mile and a half north, Stearns' three miles south-west, Parker's three miles south-east, of Ensign's. We have no means of ascertaining the exact amount of business done by either or all of them; but it must have been considerable, and much of it drawn from neighboring towns.

Another lucrative employment was found in the manufacture of malleable iron, and the working up of the product into various salable articles. The first allusion to this business is in the town records for the year 1767—the same in which Jacob Ensign received permission to build his fulling-mill. The town then refused to give Capt. Charles Goodrich anything for building a road from his iron-works,[1] which stood where Taconic village now does, to Keeler's mills, now Pontoosuc. So that it seems, the iron manufacture was introduced into Pittsfield by the most energetic and enterprising business man among its early settlers, and that it, a little, antedated the woolen manufacture.

Goodrich's forge passed through several hands, and continued in operation until about the year 1806. In its later years it was worked by Capt. George Whitney, and his four sons, Joshua, Asa, Noah and Porter, who performed the greater part of the

[1] It is worthy of note, that, upon the same site, Lemuel Pomeroy, a man in many respects strikingly like Captain Goodrich, afterwards had his musket factory; a business suggested by, and the natural successor of, the early forge. Captain Goodrich was the friend and political confrere of Mr. Pomeroy, when the former was very old, and the latter a young man.

labor with their own hands. In addition to the manufacture of iron, they forged it into anchors, ploughshares and other articles which, beside the home-demand, found a ready market in Hudson and elsewhere. The first iron axletree made in Pittsfield, was forged by them for their own wagon; and the excellence of their workmanship is attested by the fact that, as late at least as 1872, it was still in use on a farm wagon in the West Part, having lasted about seventy years. They also placed the first tire upon a pair of wheels; a pair used by Capt. Hosea Merrill in his lumbering business, in which they broke down under some of the rough and rapid work required in connection with the cantonment in the war of 1812. But, notwithstanding the superior skill of the Whitneys, their industry and good character, their business proved a failure, and the forge passed out of their hands.

The second forge was built by Capt. Rufus Allen in 1775, on the west branch of the Housatonic, a few rods above the West street bridge; but the dam, in spring, superficially flooded so large an amount of soil which was left exposed to the sun in the dryer months, that fever and ague, and other low fevers, resulted; rendering it necessary after a few years to demolish it, and abandon the forge.

Afterwards, about the year 1788-9, Captain Allen, in company with Caleb Merrill, Simon Larned, and Elisha Camp (Thomas Gold acting as attorney for the latter), erected a forge on Onota brook, a few rods above its junction with the Housatonic, and near where it is crossed by Otaneaque street.

A little farther up the same stream, near the present location of Peck's lower mill, was the forge of John U. Seymour; and, still nearer the lake, on the site of Peck's upper mill, was that of Aaron Hicock. At Coltsville, on the site of the present paper mill, John Snow built a forge where he made a large quantity of iron.

Thus we have knowledge of six iron-forges, which were erected in Pittsfield, between 1767 and 1800—and which, with one exception, continued in operation some years after the latter date. They finally became unprofitable from the building of furnaces in the modern style at places which, like Lenox and Richmond, furnished coal and ore abundantly, and in close proximity.

The ore used in Pittsfield, was at first chiefly obtained in boulders, of great richness and purity, which were found scattered over the fields, or buried in the drift; a large deposit in the gravelly hill between Seymour's and Allen's forges, now St. Joseph's cemetery, and probably others in different parts of the town. A rich deposit of similar boulders is now known to be buried on the east shore of Lake Onota, and many have been found in excavations for railroads and streets. Occasionally also they appear in old stone walls; and scattered lumps of similar ore are yet to be found in the neighborhood of Coltsville. But, for practical purposes, so far as was then known, this resource was exhausted years before the forges were abandoned; and ore was brought to them from Cone's and other mines, in Richmond and at the Shakers' in West Pittsfield; the latter of which was excavated before the year 1810, to the depth of sixty feet. The selectmen of Pittsfield, however, in reply to questions propounded by the General Court, reported in 1794, that they "knew of no mines or minerals in the town," and that "the ore used here came from Richmond, etc."

The early forges of Pittsfield and vicinity made malleable iron from the ore, but not by a single process. They were, however, very different structures from the blast furnaces and bloomaries by which the same object is now attained with vastly greater economy of labor and raw material. And in some respects they differed from those generally in use at that time in England and Eastern Massachusetts.

We have a detailed description of that built by John Snow, at Coltsville, from Mr. Phillips Merrill, who, in his youth, was accustomed to draw ore for it, and perfectly remembered its construction and operation. It did not differ much, except in size, from an ordinary blacksmith's forge. The hearth was about four and a half feet high, and twelve feet square. The center was slightly hollowed. In front a small aperture, across the top of which a bar or plate of iron was fixed, served to draw off the melted cinders which settled in the depression; the aperture, at the commencement of the operation being closed with clay, and tapped with a pointed iron bar when occasion required. Above the hearth the forge was open in front and on its two sides, and its back was like that of a common smith's forge. The chimney, which overhung the whole hearth, was supported by the back and by two iron pillars. The blast was supplied by two leathern bellows fourteen feet long—one on each side—driven by water-power.

Alternate layers of ore (prepared by roasting), charcoal, and lime flux, in proper proportions, were heaped in a rounded, or pyramidal, pile upon the hearth; additions being made as the fusion progressed, and the melted cinders being drawn off as before described.

The metal itself was never perfectly liquefied, but assumed a semi-fluid form in which it was occasionally lifted with levers, in order to let the cinder separate itself more freely. Finally, it was deposited on the hearth; an imperfectly-rounded mass, somewhat more crude than our pig-iron, and technically known as a *loop*.

This loop, still at a red heat, was next dragged, by means of a long hook, to the front of the hearth, and there beaten with a sledge-hammer, for the double purpose of expelling loose cinders, and bringing it into shape to be handled with the tongs, and fitted under the trip-hammer. This process was called shingling the loop.

When brought to the proper shape, the mass was re-heated, if necessary, and then, being lifted with tongs, was placed on a huge anvil under a heavy trip-hammer driven by water-power. At first the loop was so large that there was little space above it for the hammer to rise and fall. So that the blows were little more than a moderate tapping; but as it was reduced to shape, and more and more of the cinder expelled, the force of the strokes increased, until the loop became a perfect bar of malleable iron. The loop, after the shingling, and before being placed under the hammer, was generally about as heavy as a stout workman could well lift—perhaps two hundred pounds. The daily average product of a Pittsfield forge was, according to one authority, from one hundred to one hundred and fifty pounds of iron. Mr. Merrill thought it was somewhat more. There was wide diversity in the quality, as those who used chains and other articles requiring great tenacity in the metal, soon discovered; a large proportion being very inferior to that of the Messrs. Whitney.

The iron-makers sent a portion of their product directly to market, either in bar or in anchors and other manufactured articles. This was especially the case with the Whitneys; one of the sons, Porter, devoting himself almost exclusively to the mercantile part of their business. But much of the iron from the other forges was bartered with the town merchants. Persons very recently living remembered seeing Mr. Seymour trudging to the village with a bar of iron on his shoulders, to return laden with goods for his workmen. Some of the iron thus bartered was sent to market by the merchants; but a great deal was used by the neighboring blacksmiths, on whom the people depended almost entirely for many domestic utensils, farming implements and mechanics' tools, now almost as exclusively manufactured in large establishments, and by the aid of machinery; except where, as with the old-fashioned cranes, hooks and trammels, which then hung in every kitchen-fireplace, they are dispensed with altogether.

Third among the manufactures of Pittsfield, in the order of time, but second, if not first, in the value of its production, was that of leather, for which there were three tanneries of considerable note. The first was probably built by Capt. Daniel Weller, on the north bank of Wampenum brook, on the west side of South street. In 1795, Captain Weller sold twenty-three acres of the south end of "lot No. 28 South," which included this tannery, to his son, the major, of the same name. The next spring he purchased ten acres of the north end of the same lot, where he built another tannery, if one had not already been built there, on the north bank of the Housatonic and on the west side of South street. His son, Enoch, had a bark-mill[1] on the little water-power on Wampenum brook below South Mountain street, from which he supplied tan to his father and brother, and perhaps to others.

In 1798, James Brown, who had learned the art and mystery of tanning from Capt. Nathan Pierson, a noted and wealthy tanner of Richmond—whose niece he married, built a tannery next to the Elm street bridge on Water street. Some years before, but how many cannot now be ascertained, he had established similar works on the north side of Silver lake. Whether they were abandoned immediately on the completion of the new, is not known. In 1800, Mr. Brown admitted his brother, Simeon, a partner in the Water street tannery, and for a long time, under

[1] It is doubtful whether this mill was exclusively owned by Enoch, as his father, in 1806, bequeathed a fourth part of the saw-mill, which had taken its place, to another person. It would be interesting to learn when this mill was built, as it is claimed that the first of the kind ever run by water-power, was erected at Northampton, in 1794; but we have not been able to do so.

the proprietorship of the brothers, as well as subsequently in other hands, it has had a remarkably-prosperous history.

Single vats were probably scattered in different parts of the town, as shoemakers and saddlers then learned the art of tanning as part of their trade; while the process of manufacture in vogue was so simple, the materials so cheap and abundant, and the demand for the product so great, that many farmers were led to enter into the business in a sort of household-way.

These conditions also rendered the manufacture upon a larger scale very profitable, and moreover favored the manufacture of boots and shoes; so that tanneries and shoe manufactories multiplied so greatly in all parts of New England, that, although the number in Pittsfield was considerable, and afforded a valuable source of local wealth, they did not give the town any special prominence for that branch of manufactures in the State; of which a single county, Middlesex, had seventy tanneries, some of them of very large product.

The opportunity to use coal at the iron-works, and bark in the tanneries, largely reduced the cost of clearing the forests; and this expense was still further counterbalanced by the utilization of ashes in the manufacture of potash, so that every portion of the tree was made a source of profit, although the earth was robbed of valuable fertilizers. For the product of the potashery, as for iron and leather, there was a ready sale at fair prices, both for the home and foreign market; the American potash being highly esteemed in the latter.

The process of manufacture was, and under similar circumstances still is, simple even to rudeness and wastefulness. The wood was usually cut into lengths of eight or nine feet; piled in heaps containing from one to three cords; and, when half dry, burned. The ashes were placed in large tubs whose bottoms were covered, six or eight inches deep, with brush-wood, above which was a three-inch layer of straw. Water was then filtered through the mass, till all the soluble matter was carried off in the lye which passed through an aperture in the bottom of the tub, into a proper receptacle.

This lye was then placed in large iron-kettles, and boiled until the evaporation left the matter held in solution in a solid form: a dark, almost black, crust, known to the workmen as "brown salts," having a strong alkaline and acid taste. These salts consisted of a very large proportion of potash mixed with more or less carbonaceous matter, vegetable salts, and a little earth. This mass was thrown into a cast-iron kettle of considerable thickness, and subjected to a red heat for one or two hours, and most of the combustible matter was consumed. The residuum, when cold, was broken up, packed in tight casks, and sent to market—the American potash of commerce. It contained from five to twenty-five per cent. of pure potash, with impurities in various proportions, depending very much upon the care exercised in collecting the ashes after the burning of the wood.

In the ruder districts, all the processes of the manufacture were carried on by the farmers in the woods, and many potash-kettles might doubtless have been seen in the Pittsfield forests. As a general thing, however, it was more profitable to carry the ashes to the potasheries of the merchants, who paid eight pence a bushel for the best quality. Of these potasheries, that of Graves & Root, was opposite the tannery on Elm street; that of Colonel Danforth, in the rear of his store; that of Simon Larned " a little east of the meeting-house;" and that of J. D. & S. D. Colt, on West street, a little east of Center street; and each seems to have done a thriving business.

The staple manufactures of Pittsfield, at the beginning of the nineteenth century, were thus: cloth from household-looms, finished by the professional clothiers; malleable iron and its sub-products; leather; and potash.

To these may be added a quasi-manufacture, as lucrative, perhaps, as either of the others: the beef and pork packing carried on by the merchants; some of whom thought it more economical at least at times, to send the animals "on the hoof" to be slaughtered and packed at Hudson, although most of them had their own slaughter and packing houses.

There were several grist-mills; and saw-mills sprang up wherever there was water-power for them.

There were also several minor manufactories of a peculiar character. In one of Luce's mills, linseed oil was made, and the residuum pressed into cakes for fattening cattle; the lean beeves bought of drovers, and fattened by merchant-packers, furnishing a constant demand for the latter product. Another utilization, it will be observed, of otherwise waste material, as the primary object of raising flax was to supply the household-looms.

After Capt. Rufus Allen's ill-placed forge-dam was demolished, John and Jabez Colt built one of more moderate height, on which they placed a manufactory of cut nails, which was in operation in 1800, but how much later we cannot determine.

The manufacture of wrought nails was early a household employment in New England; and in Pittsfield, as elsewhere, many farmers' families had little anvils upon which the boys worked at their leisure, producing a supply for their own use, and generally a surplus to barter at the village-stores. Economy of time, as well as material, ruled the hour.

This home-manufacture continued in some families as late as 1800, although about 1777 a nail-making machine was introduced; an awkward worker, producing only a headless article, but improved, previous to 1825, by one hundred and twenty-three patents. The Pittsfield works were among the earlier, and were probably unable to meet the competition of larger capital and improved machinery.

MERCANTILE AFFAIRS.

Commerce contributed no inconsiderable item to the wealth of the town, and, as in all new countries, the dealers in merchandise were, in one particular, merchants in a stricter sense than those who merely dispense to their customers the goods purchased at wholesale in metropolitan markets. They were the medium for the interchange of the products of the Berkshire farm, loom, forge, anvil and tannery, for the luxuries and necessaries brought from the great centers of trade. They acted as middlemen in the outward, as well as the inward, course of traffic.

Of the earliest merchants of Pittsfield, and the nature of its traffic, we have scant information. Col. James Easton kept a store in connection with his tavern, and it would appear from entries in Rev. Mr. Allen's diary, that Capt. John Strong kept at least a few articles of merchandise. Probably most of the taverns kept some goods in their bar-rooms, varying in amount with the enterprise and means of their proprietors. David Noble, the patriotic and ill-fated captain of the minute-men, certainly carried on a considerable mercantile business at the West Part; but both he and his brother officer, Colonel Easton, seem to have had stores separate from their taverns.

We have no means of ascertaining the amount or method of

their trade; but what we know of them leads us to believe that they fully availed themselves of the opportunities offered by a new country for the shipment of furs collected by the Indians and Indian-like white men; of wheat which the virgin soil produced with that luxuriance which generally fringes the borders of civilization, and the other home-products which have been enumerated. Captain Noble had in store, when he was summoned to the field by the Lexington alarm, much grain and cloth, which he afterwards, with noble generosity, contributed to supply the wants of the army laying siege to General Gage, in Boston.

The business of Captain Noble and Colonel Easton was broken up by the war, in which both fought and suffered grandly; both sacrificed the greater part of their fortunes, and in which one died during the most arduous and,—as regards the daring exploits and extreme privations patiently borne by the soldiery,—one of the most glorious campaigns of the American armies, the first incursion into Canada. We refer again to these gallant men in order to remind the merchants of Pittsfield that the earliest of their number furnished splendid examples, which have not wanted worthy followers whenever their country has demanded similar self-devotion; although never since has the opportunity offered for that grandeur of patriotism which characterized Noble and Easton.

Captain Noble's goods were chiefly sent to Cambridge, by his direction, in 1775, for the use of the army; but Deacon Josiah Wright appears to have continued the store on its old site, on the north side of West street, beyond Lake Onota; and "store-keeping" occurs so naturally to the tavern-keeping mind, that probably other parts of the town were accommodated with at least a few "store-goods" in their numerous bar-rooms.[1]

But, well as we should like to know how the early citizens of Pittsfield, and its housewives, were able to purchase their daily supplies, it would be of more interest to learn what goods the town sent to market in the old times, and through what channels; but upon these points we have no precise information. During the war, it is likely that the iron, cloths and buckskins,

[1] Captain John Strong, who kept the tavern now the Pomeroy Homestead, was an educated man, a graduate of Yale, and an able politician as well as a genial landlord; but some of these qualities were not likely to aid him greatly as a trader.

which must have been among the principal articles of export, were absorbed chiefly by the demands of the army. This was certainly true of horses, cattle, and other agricultural products.

When trade was not thus interrupted, home-made goods and the productions of the farm were interchanged among neighbors, generally without the intervention of a shop-keeper. Producers sometimes carried their goods personally to such markets as Albany, Kinderhook and Hartford; but, unless their product was large, it was bartered with the leading traders of the town, who, in their turn, bartered it in large markets. Purchases were also sometimes made directly by the consumers, at the greater centers, either on the occasional visits of the customer, or through some accommodating friend. The town's representative in the Great and General Court, was often overburdened by his constituents, with commissions of this kind ; and in one instance, at least, was instructed by the town-meeting " not to purchase any goods in the town of Boston, beyond what was necessary for the use of himself and family." Whether this action was dictated by some petty hostility of the moment towards the capital, or was thought necessary in order to break up a system of brokerage which interfered with legislative duties, or for some other reason, we cannot now determine. At the close of the revolution, Pittsfield shared largely in the benefits conferred upon western Massachusetts and eastern New York, by the migration from the sea-board, of active and intelligent men who, relieved of public employment, sought new fields for their restless enterprise. Two of this class began a mercantile business in Pittsfield: Col. Joshua Danforth, whose life and character were sketched in our previous volume, and Col. Simon Larned, of Pomfret, Connecticut, who, like Colonel Danforth, had served with great credit in the army of the revolution. According to Dr. Field, these gentlemen came to Pittsfield in 1784, and commenced business as partners. If this is true, the connection probably arose from friendship formed in camp. It could not, however, have long continued, as we find by advertisements that they were soon carrying on trade separately, Colonel Danforth occupying the store built by him on the corner of East and Second streets ; Colonel Larned a similar store a little farther east.[1]

[1] Such is the tradition ; but, if Dr. Field's statement is correct, the first store must have been built by Danforth and Larned jointly.

Traffic was carried on for the most part by barter. Coin was scarce, Continental money had become entirely discredited, and there were few banks. What articles for barter were furnished by Pittsfield and its vicinity, we learn from the advertisements in the *Chronicle* and the *Gazette*. In October, 1788, Colonel Danforth wanted a hundred pounds of lamb's wool—merinoes had not yet come in for the finer products of the loom—and a number of good shipping-horses. In the same month, " having received a complete assortment of goods from New York," he offered to sell them at a low rate for cash, wheat, flax-seed, pork, beeswax, iron or ashes; at the same time announcing his revolt against the credit system, then almost universal, in the following paragraph: " And, as said Danforth is determined not to sell his goods on credit, those gentlemen who make him ready pay, may expect to have his goods very cheap." He made a special offer of salt in exchange for flax-seed. In December, he advertised payment in rum, brandy, loaf and brown sugars, coffee, chocolate, tea, tobacco, red-wood, alum, wool-cards, brimstone, German steel, salt and dry goods, for ten thousand bushels of good ashes, for which he would give the highest prices. He also made a particular call for pork and beeswax on the same terms.

Simon Larned published similar advertisements, offering European goods, West India goods " and cotton" of the best quality, in exchange for the best house-ashes at eight cents a bushel. He also offered nails for wheat.

These advertisements indicate the nature of the early barter traffic of Pittsfield; and, not to multiply quotations, we add only one, which shows Colonel Danforth in the character of a broker in public securities, for which his former position as pay-master in the army, had in some degree qualified him:

PUBLIC SECURITIES.—CASH, and the highest price given for Final Settlement Notes—Loan-office certificates of this and other States—Indents and Massachusetts State notes, at the store of Joshua Danforth in Pittsfield. Cash is also given at the above store for wheat, rye, corn and shipping-furs."

This advertisement appeared in February, 1790, when the national credit was rapidly appreciating under the influence of the lately-adopted federal constitution, while the disposition which was to be made of the different classes of public debt was by no means determined; so that, all over the country, an active speculation in state and national securities, sprung up.

Passing onward to the years 1798–9, when light is thrown upon business through the columns of the *Berkshire Gazette*, we find that great changes had taken place during that brief interval. Col. Simon Larned had been succeeded in his store on East street by Perez Graves who, after conducting business for awhile alone, admitted as a partner his salesman, John Burgoyne Root, one of the sons whom that stout old loyalist, Ezekiel Root, had burdened with the names of His Britannic Majesty's commanders in America. Mr. Root was a very accomplished gentleman, a prominent citizen, and a leading democrat. In business he was interested in manufactures and agriculture, as well as commerce.

Joshua Danforth retained his old store. With the building of the meeting-house and town hall, the center of business was passing westward to Park square, where Jonathan Allen & Co., John Stoddard and J. D. & S. D. Colt all had stores of some pretension on the sites mentioned in our description of the village in 1800. Dr. Timothy Childs had built his medicine-shop on North street.

Both coin and bank-bills were still scarce, and trade was generally carried on by barter. In order to facilitate this, a system of mutual credit arose, the parties settling accounts at brief and stated periods, if they were wise, although this rule was far too loosely followed, which proved an excellent thing for the lawyers. Moving appeals for settlement, supplemented by threats of an attorney, were among the most common advertisements in the newspapers; and frequent failures showed the effect of the credit system upon the dealer.

A more perfect classification and organization of trade, indicated an advance towards the character of a market-town. Stores, with a general assortment of goods for country-trade continued to predominate, but in some, dry goods, and in others, groceries, were advertised as specialties.

Thus much for the Center. Rev. Robert Green still continued his store on Elm street, but with reduced proportions; and Horace Allen supplied the people of the West Part from his "general assortment."

CHAPTER IV.

DOMESTIC AND SOCIAL LIFE—MANNERS AND MORALS.

[1790-1810.]

The interior of houses—Dress—Household labor—Tea-parties—Social gaieties.—Spinning-bees for the minister's wife—Hunting-match and club suppers—Dancing-parties; their pleasures and their dangers—Freedom of manners—Influence of the wars and foreign intercourse on morals and manners—Customs in connection with dancing-parties—Bundling—Use and abuse of ardent spirits—Habits of Col. Oliver Root—Liquor-selling—Varieties of wines and liquors in vogue—Early efforts for temperance reform—Dr. Rush's essay upon the effects of alcohol—He favors wine, beer and punch—Gambling—Lotteries—Imprisonment for debt—Unequal laws—Reforms of the nineteenth century.

DOMESTIC life in Pittsfield, as in all New England, except the richer commercial and maritime towns, was simple, unpretending and economical. Even the more stately residences were in most respects plainly furnished. A richly-carved mahogany side-board, perhaps, with sofa and chairs to match, a massive dining-table, and card-tables of quaint pattern; a fine, large old mirror, a tall Dutch or English clock, its works of brass and its dial showing some curious device, either for astronomical information or simply for ornament. Some pieces of plate, not of the most artistic design, but of standard silver; a set of genuine china-ware, ornamentally deformed in the true oriental fashion; and the never-forgotten punch-bowl of silver, china or glass, surrounded by a bold and glittering array of cut-glass decanters and goblets. These sufficed for parlor-furniture. Paneled wainscoting, and cornices of ornamental joiner-work, relieved the monotony of the walls, which were also hung with imported paper, usually of a brilliant, if not gaudy, design. Generally there were suspended from them the portraits of, at least, the master and mistress of the house, in some cases the work of very eminent artists, but more often of some ordinary traveling painter. The huge old fireplaces were inclosed in wooden mantels, frequently of an exceedingly handsome character, and their furniture, if not mostly of brass, was neatly decorated with that metal. There were sperm or wax candles in silver, or at least silver-plated candlesticks, for grand occasions; but tallow-candles, in brass or iron, served for ordinary use. In the chambers, the high, four-posted bedstead with its stately canopy of some showy material—a nocturnal enclosure condemned as murderous by modern sanitary science—was matched by window-curtains which hung in ample folds of a similar fabric.

Thus much of luxury, mansions of the more pretentious class had attained. But there were many modern improvements yet lacking. The only carpets were those home-made of rags; a household product which had been very recently introduced by Mrs. Van Schaack, and was not yet generally adopted. The first loom-woven carpet was brought into town by the wife of Dr. Timothy Childs, and covered a space about nine feet square, in the parlor of the house. The first carpet covering a whole floor was laid in the parlor of John Chandler Williams, and was a plain-figured brown and green ingrain. Within a few years it covered the floor of the choir of St. Stephen's church. For the most part, floors in all classes of houses were merely sprinkled with white sand. Painted floors were an innovation of somewhat later date, and were denounced by old ladies of conservative habits as dangerous, from the liability to slip upon them. The introduction of stone, instead of wooden, door-steps was resisted on the same ground.

From those in the first grade of houses, furniture and finish gradually diminished in quality, and as to some articles, in their essential character, as means or taste diminished. The sofa became "a settle," or a sort of wooden settee; the side-board became of a less costly material and construction; the mirror grew smaller; a wooden clock of Pittsfield or Lanesboro manufacture —and very excellent "makes" these were—took the place of the imported article. The chairs were of marvelous strength and comfortable shape, as many of them, remaining to this day, bear witness; but like the most of those, indeed, in the more costly houses, the material was no longer mahogany, and the carving was missing. Pewter took the place of silver; plain crockery of china, and glassware grew less in quantity and of inferior cutting.

Paper-hangings rarely concealed the plaster-walls, upon which hung, instead of the oil-portrait, or the wax-miniature, the profile "snipped out" by artists who went from house to house, and often produced a more recognizable likeness than their more ambitious brethren of the brush were able to achieve. The joiner-work became less elaborate; but the carpenter was still chiefly relied upon for ornamental effects, and he concentrated his efforts around the fireplace, whose furniture showed less and less of brass, and more and more of the work of the village blacksmith. The chambers were less stately in their adornments, and some of even the middle class slept less grandly, but it is to be hoped more healthfully, in bedsteads absolutely uncanopied. Tallow-candles were the only light, and it was well if, upon special occasions, they were molded and not dipped; and the candle-sticks were of brass rather than iron.

In dress there was somewhat more of distinction between classes, than in furniture. The gentlemen of the wealthy and professional orders, wore the ordinary costume of the same classes in the cities, at least upon dress occasions. The ladies of the like position in society, had their silk robes, although not changed with every wind of fashion, and not used for daily wear. The home-made fabrics of wool were finished in very respectable style, and were generally worn by men. The use of calico by the women had, since the revolutionary war, become almost universal; but home-made linens were also much worn, a pattern of blue check being the most common. The dress of both men and women was intended to conform, as nearly as possible, to the fashion of the day. This fashion, under the influence of the French revolution in taste, which accompanied that in government, was rapidly changing, especially in the dress of men. Small clothes, knee-breeches, cocked hats and queues, were giving way to the more simple and convenient modern styles; and, as many clung to the style of garments to which they had been accustomed, a dress assembly of the earlier years of the nineteenth century, presented a variegated appearance. About the same time, the congregation in church must have been brilliant with the scarlet cloaks which were fashionable for both sexes.

In the household, economy and industry were almost universal. There were few appliances and inventions to relieve the labor of the housewife. The work of cooking, washing, sewing, and the like, was done by main strength. The cook must lift the huge iron pot, which hung on the crane out-swung before the blazing fire; and deposit and withdraw the baking in the deep, brick oven, with the long, wrought-iron shovel. The laundress performed her task by pounding the soiled clothes in a barrel of water with a heavy pestle—even the fluted washing-board, having not yet been invented. Water was to be drawn from the cistern or well, by the most unaided process; the long well-sweep being the best mechanical assistance to be had. There were the unpainted floors to be scrubbed, and an excessively-broad surface of wainscoting and other joiner-work to be kept clean. And when all this was done, came the spinning, the weaving, the brewing, the candle and soap making, and other toils now unknown to the housewife. And, even yet further—for almost every dwelling was, to a certain extent, a farm-house—there were the duties which, as the students of health tell us, still overburthen and prematurely wear out the farmer's wife. With all this, and the large families of children, which were almost the rule, it is no wonder that the percentage of mortality among women was large, and that those who sustained themselves were accounted marvels of capability.

Many families had colored servants, mostly fugitive slaves from New York or Connecticut, or blacks who, having purchased their freedom, had emigrated from those States. Some of these attached themselves faithfully to kind employers with whom they remained for years; others were hired as their services were required. Other than these, servants there were none. Most households, however, included in their number "hired help;" American girls or men who lived with the family on terms nearly or quite of equality, and frequently intermarried with its younger members. Of course, in proportion to their faithfulness, they relieved the mistress of the house from the arduous labors which we have just enumerated; and her deftness in the manufacture of woolen cloths, bed and table linen, helped many a busy handmaiden in her conquest of the heir of the farm.

The tables of all moderately well-to-do people were plentifully, temptingly, and not inelegantly, spread. There was much hospitality, and visiting friends were always welcome to most firesides. But the entertainment whose discontinuance the ladies have most occasion to regret, was the tea-party which brought them together with no male element to check the flow of soul. Nothing could be more charming than one of these assemblies, especially if. it happened of a summer evening before sunset, the open windows rendering it practically a garden-feast among the apple-blossoms or lilac-blows; or at least amid the odors of new-mown hay.

The social life of Pittsfield, from the era when the community began to recover from the pecuniary difficulties which followed the revolution, until after the war of 1812, was more genial, merry and unconstrained, than at any period before or since. If there lingered, among a few families, who had been tories or very conservative whigs, some traces of the old provincial aristocracy, inducing them to maintain the peculiarly-painful position of the *ancien regime* of a country-village—an already quaint and not very obtrusive ornament to it—they affected very little the general aspect of society, which went on its pleasant ways, with or without them, as it might chance.

Social gatherings were frequent, and characterized by much innocent gaiety. Public balls, and not quite so public "assemblies," private dancing-parties, tea-parties, hunting-frolics, corn-huskings, ministers' "bees," followed each other in rapid succession, and not without frequent intermingling of resultant weddings. Still another class of festivities, less generally remembered, were the evening-suppers, at which the choicest of substantial country-luxuries—from the goose and turkey, down to the pumpkin-pie and the nut-cake, not forgetting apples, chestnuts and cider—were served in turn at the houses of circles of friends, who formed a kind of informal club; the most flourishing of which was the Woronokers, composed of immigrants from Westfield, and their descendants—a right hearty and jovial set of men, noted for stalwart frames, vigorous and manly intellects, integrity of character, and devotion to the democratic party.

Of the ladies "bees" for the benefit of the minister, we can give an idea in no better manner than by copying accounts of two of them, from the columns of the *Chronicle*. The first, from the issue of July 3, 1788, is as follows:

Thursday last, forty-five young ladies of this town, met at the house of Rev. Mr. Allen, and presented his consort with fifty-five runs of yarn spun in the best manner, as a sample of their industry, generosity and amity. The afternoon was spent in cheerfulness, perfect good humour and conviviality. So brilliant an appearance of youthful bloom, politeness and decency of behaviour, on such an occasion, could not fail of inspiring the mind with ardent expectations of their answering the description of Solomon's virtuous wife, Proverbs, 31st chapter: "She seeketh wool and flax, and worketh willingly with her hands. She layeth her hand to the spindle, and her hands hold the distaff. She maketh herself coverings of tapestry; her clothing is silk and purple. Her husband is known in the gates where he sitteth among the elders of the land. She looketh well to the ways of her household, and eateth not the bread of idleness."

A few months after this, the married ladies took their turn at the spinning-wheel, and the *Chronicle* thus tells the story:

Thursday the 9th inst., (Oct.) four and twenty married ladies of this town, assembled at the house of Rev. Mr. Allen, and among various other instances of respect and liberality, presented his consort with twenty-six runs of woolen yarn, the fruit of their industry. Such like repeated instances of amity and benevolence, not only entitle them to the blessings of the liberal soul that deviseth liberal things, which shall be made fat, and of him who watereth, of being watered himself by a richer abundance of the divine blessing; but cannot fail of producing the most beneficial influence on the other sex by softening the ferocity of the human mind, by promoting industry and diligence in their occupations in life, and by becoming productive of friendship and all the social virtues.

Hunting-matches, in those days of abundant game, furnished the occasion, and the most substantial viands, for many a merry evening's feast. The *Chronicle* tells of one, for instance, where a party of young men, although reduced in numbers by stormy weather, after a day's hunting, met, one October evening, in 1788, at Captain Cadwell's tavern, and "produced upwards of seventy gray squirrels and partridges, of which they made an elegant supper, and spent a festive evening in the greatest harmony, and jocund festivity." Constant allusions are made to similar feasts.

No event, from an ecclesiastical council to a military training, was suffered to pass without the accompaniment of festal entertainment, or at least very generous and convivial hospitality.

There was something very pleasant in this keen and general enjoyment of every variety of social life, and it is no wonder, that those living now, in extreme old age, look back upon it with delighted memories, and love to recount the festal scenes of their early youth. But this excess of social pleasures had its dark, as well as its bright, side. There were—not necessarily, in the kind of amusements then popular, and considered innocent, but certainly in the circumstances under which they were indulged, and in the degree to which they were carried—temptations to which the virtue, even of the best, too often yielded. More than half a century before the settlement of Pittsfield, a marked decline— perhaps a re-action—from the severity of the Puritan life, had come to be lamented by good men. The Reforming Synod, assembled at Boston in 1679, in " a solemn testimony," addressed to the general court, presented a long list of grievous sins which even then prevailed, closing with intemperance, "including the heathenish and idolatrous practice of health-drinking, and heinous breaches of the seventh commandment." "The people," said Cotton Mather, "began notoriously to forget their errand into the wilderness."[1]

Forty-eight years afterwards, things do not seem to have improved; for when, in 1727, Jonathan Edwards became pastor of the First Church in Northampton, "that great and good man," says a writer in the *Congregational Quarterly*, "found that parish fully sharing in the degeneracy of the times. Vice prevailed, especially among the young. Intemperance and tavern haunting abounded. There was utter insensibility to the claims of religion. There was indecent behavior in the sanctuary. There was licentiousness among the youth. 'It was their manner,' says the watchful pastor, 'very frequently to get together in conventions of both sexes for mirth and jollity; they would often spend the greater part of the night without any regard to order in the families they belonged to.' Saturday night being regarded as part of the Sabbath, Sunday night was the gayest of the week."[2]

In receiving this statement, we must make great allowance for the author's stern censorship of social pleasures which many equally good men deem innocent; and which few now denounce as grossly sinful. His "conventions of both sexes" may have been merely dancing-parties continued late into the night: not an unusual occurrence at any era. Some portion of every community are obnoxious to his worst censures, and it can hardly be believed that even a large minority of the people of Northampton were guilty of the more serious faults named. At the worst, we must only believe that a certain looseness of discipline and

[1] Congregational Quarterly, April, 1869.
[2] Congregational Quarterly, Vol. XI, p. 72.

freedom of manners, led to too frequent instances of vicious conduct. And, with this qualification, the description of manners and morals may be transferred to the state of things in Pittsfield in the twenty-five or thirty years following the revolution, and, with somewhat more of qualification, for several years later.

President Edwards, soon after his ordination, set himself to stem the growing tide of irreligion and consequent immorality; and, it is said, gave its first effective check by a pointed discourse against "Sabbath-evening dissipation and mirth-making." This work he perfected and established, by a series of discourses upon justification by faith, "convincing his people of their need of distinct, substantial, ascertainable change of heart;" and resulting in a very remarkable revival of religion. "Three hundred," we are told, "were notably renewed in a population of two hundred families." "A thorough reformation of morals followed." For fifty years there had not been so little disorder and vice.[1]

We can readily credit the efficiency which this religious agency is stated to have had in changing the manners and reforming the morals of Northampton; for a similar revival in 1822 effected a similar revolution in the general tone of society in Pittsfield; exercising an influence upon it which is very powerfully felt even yet.

But, although much of President Edwards' work at Northampton was doubtless enduring, even his grand abilities were insufficient to cope with the social tendencies of the age, and the more liberal theology with which his predecessor, Rev. Solomon Stoddard, had indoctrinated the Northampton church. And about the time that emigrants from that section succeeded in first making a permanent settlement at Pittsfield, the most eminent of American theologians was driven from his country-pulpit, on acount of "his opposition to the prominent doctrines of his predecessor, and certain disciplinary measures to which he had resorted," and "to which his church was unaccustomed."[2]

Something of the liberalism, both in doctrine and in discipline,

---

[1] This revival, which took place during the pastorate of Rev. Dr. Humphrey, who was aided by the distinguished revival preacher Rev. Asahel Nettleton, is described in the chapter of this work devoted to that period. One of its chief results was a stricter discipline in the church, whose membership was enlarged so as to include a large portion of those who gave tone to society.

[2] Holland's Western Massachusetts, Vol. 1, page 246.

which was so potent in the Connecticut valley, seems to have characterized many of the more influential first-settlers of Pittsfield; causing the difficulty in selecting the first minister, and perhaps preventing the union of some in the initial organization of the church. But from that organization onward, there is no hint of any heresy broached in the pulpit, or permitted in the church. The covenant and the articles of faith were as strict as the strongest Calvinist could demand. "The Scripture truth of the new birth was never lost sight of" by the preacher. "The half-way covenant" was never adopted by the church. Discipline was strictly enforced in the case of open and acknowledged sins, such as gross intemperance, breaches of the seventh commandment, unchristian quarreling and fighting, and family disturbances. But moderate daily drinking, no one considered to be an evil, dancing was not proscribed, and there were much more dangerous practices which were not even mentioned.

Throughout the province, with the amelioration of manners, the decadence of morals which had been rebuked by the early preachers, had continued, checked only at intervals and in limited localities. This decadence was greater in sea-ports and in larger towns, than in smaller interior communities; but few altogether escaped it. There were at work agencies of evil, more potent than any theological heresy. The contact of the youth of maritime towns with sea-faring and trading adventurers—generally of questionable, and often of unquestionably infamous, character: smugglers, slavers, and even now and then pirates—communicated a moral poison, which, to some extent, disseminated itself through the interior. Still more general, if not more pernicious, was the effect of the French and Indian wars, which, for a series of years, compelled a large portion of the young men of the province to spend long intervals in camp, freed from the restraints of society, tempted by the seductions of military license, and contaminated by association with the mercenaries of the army.

Life in camp, in bivouac, on the march, or even at the best in the little home-garrisons, must have tended sadly to relaxation of the stern manners and morals of the Puritans. The soldiery of the Pilgrim commonwealth were no longer, as a whole, of the Cromwellian school. It was much if the regimental commanders were able to maintain among them a wholesome physical police.

The best officers could do no more than to mourn over the moral delinquencies of their men.[1]

Perhaps the most pestilent source of this demoralization was the example and conversation of the regular troops drawn from the dregs of the population of Great Britain, but who being sent over by the home-government, and commanded by distinguished officers, were naturally regarded by many of the raw provincials as models of what a soldier should be.

The lessons thus learned, with others of the same character, if not more deleterious, were more deeply impressed, by our French allies in the revolutionary army, and were carried home to every village; not indeed with sufficient power to destroy the hereditary virtues of New England, but with an influence which, for a time, abated the old stern reprobation of vice, and in a marked degree relaxed that strictness of social decorum, and that delicate sensitiveness of womanhood, which society always finds a wholesome protection. Some examples of the customs of the era of which we write, in Pittsfield, will illustrate our meaning. The parties, balls, huskings and other "conventions of young people of both sexes," gathered their participants, not from a limited circle in thickly-peopled villages, but from widely-scattered farm-houses, and even from neighboring towns; especially Dalton and Lanesboro, where some popular belles resided. The invitations having been given, when the assembly was to be at a private house, or the time and place announced if in some public hall, the young men proceeded at night-fall on horseback, each to the house of some lady who had accepted his escort, and who promptly mounted the pillion behind him and clasped his waist. In this pleasant fashion the pair, sometimes with others but often alone, rode from one to six miles, on the lonely roads.

Arrived at the ball-room or parlor, the dance—happily, the floor was as yet innocent of waltz and polka—was kept up until long after midnight. A feast of substantial luxuries was provided,

---

[1] Letters of Col. William Williams, Col. Seth Pomeroy and others. We have a letter, in the Thomas Colt collection of manuscripts at the athenæum, written during the French and Indian war, in which a colonel, sending to an officer in his rear two degraded women who had followed his camp into the hostile New York forests, then swarming with savages, begs that they may be carefully sent beyond the army lines, as they had already demoralized two or three companies.

and we may be sure was partaken of with a hearty relish. The ladies sipped their wine, and cider, and did not disdain the more homely, but also more seductive, flip; or yet more tempting cordial; while the gentlemen indulged in even more fiery and exciting beverages.

The night's festivities over, the party separated and the guests returned, as they had come.

We do not mean to be understood, that every social gathering in the town was precisely like that here described. In some houses there was less of license on account of religious scruples; and in some a more refined breeding effected the same chastening. But in general, social assemblies were as represented; and in hardly any was it possible to avoid the more dangerous incidents described. Participation in the amusements condemned by President Edwards was not deemed inconsistent with Christian character, except by a few Methodists; and church-discipline did not meddle with any line of conduct unless it developed itself in definite and palpable violation of moral law. And such offenses very rarely occurred in comparison with what the temptations and opportunites would lead us to apprehend. In all new-settled countries, where freedom of intercourse between the sexes is, in a degree, a matter of necessity, female chastity becomes a law and a protection to itself. In most cases it was so in the early days of Pittsfield. There were, however, and it could hardly have been otherwise, sad and notable exceptions. But it is to be remembered that the customs, and the errors which arose from them in Pittsfield, were not specially prevalent or marked in that town. They were universal, and in many sections of the country more pronounced. There was a still coarser class of dancing-parties than those we have described, frequented by a lower order in society, and more debasing in their effects upon morals. These were held in the less respectable taverns, and were called, as similar assemblies now are, "shake-down" balls, and it is certain that their effect upon morals was only evil. Chastity indeed was hardly looked for or expected in the class which attended them.

Another source of evil, in all except among a few of the more refined families, was the practice by affianced lovers of what is known as "bundling." This custom prevailed over the whole country, and is thought by the most learned authority upon the subject, to have been brought home by prisoners returning from Canadian captivity. It was, however, universal long before the settlement of America in all the northern countries of Europe, and was quite as unlimited in all their colonies; so that there seems to be no reason to look for any extraordinary source for it in any one of them. It was known to the Germans of Pennsylvania, to the Dutch of New York, and to the French of Canada. If it did not appear in the earliest days of New England, it was doubtless due to the scrupulous watchfulness of the Puritans. And when that watchfulness diminished, the old custom spontaneously revived. It is a favorite theory of those who form theories without close examination of data, that practically no harm came of it: but the record shows that, while the practice continued, the co-habitation of respectable betrothed parties before marriage was exceedingly common, and it met with little or no reprobation from the community; while the church condoned the sin, or passed it over with a very perfunctory reprimand. It is to be remarked, however, that society which looked very leniently upon ordinary cases of seduction, placed its heaviest ban upon the man who took advantage of this practice. And it therefore happened that the promise of marriage was rarely broken.

The use of ardent spirits, wine and beer was almost universal: their abuse was very common. They were offered to the visitor on the most ordinary calls, and to refuse them, except for the most manifest special reasons, or by the extremely rare persons who were known never to taste them, was considered by many hosts an affront. A friendly glass was expected to accompany the most ordinary transactions between man and man. They were an essential element on all social and ceremonial occasions. Not only were they brought forward at military elections and parades, civil elections and inaugurations; but no ordination of a clergyman, no dedication of a church, was complete without them. And some of these ecclesiastical occasions in the early part of the present century are credited by tradition with a scarcely seemly exuberance of convivial mirth. At all social parties, at all gatherings of special gladness, such as weddings and births; at all meetings of special sadness, such as funerals; wines and liquors were provided, and, more than at any other time, it was considered rude, and perhaps unfriendly, to refuse the proffered glass. It is related of Col. Oliver Root, the strictest of temperance men, according to the standard of that era, that it was his invariable custom in his later years to tender his congratulations personally on the birth of each child in the somewhat prolific district of the West Part; and that, upon each call, the happy father invariably hastened to concoct for him a particularly-aromatic glass of sling, although it was observed that he never more than barely tasted the tempting beverage. He shrewdly suspected that when he left, the concocter took care that the remainder of the glass should not be lost.

It was the custom in Colonel Root's household, every Saturday to brew a sufficient quantity of a mild ale to last as a beverage for one week, that being as long as its strength would preserve it. Cider of course was with them an ordinary drink. But every year the temperance colonel purchased a half-barrel of whiskey, as indispensable to enable his laborers to endure the toils of haying, although he never partook of it himself. In the shops kept by the most respectable and scrupulously-virtuous citizens, ardent spirits and wines were, until long after this date leading articles of merchandise; almost always heading the list of goods advertised in the newspapers. To show the kinds of spirits favored by that generation, we copy from an announcement by Sanford and Robbins, whose store was on the corner of North street and Park place in 1809. Of fifty articles enumerated, the first sixteen are:

"St. Croix Rum, Jamaica Spirits, Cogniac Brandy, Spanish Brandy, Raspberry Brandy, Holland Gin, Molasses, Soap, Lump and Brown Sugar, Madeira, Vidonia, Sherry, Lisbon, Port and Malaga wines." In other parts of the list, we find "Cordials, Stoughton's Bitters, and London Porter."

But common as the use of alcoholic stimulants was, and venial as occasional indulgence in them to excess was considered, a marked improvement in that regard was perceptible between the years 1786 and 1800. That class of habitual intoxication which had sprung from a desire to drown the sense of helplessness and hopelessness, which at the first-named date overwhelmed so many, had been greatly lessened by the revival of national prosperity; although not before an invincible habit had fixed itself upon many persons.

The very excess to which the evil of intemperance had grown, helped in some degree to work its own cure. Men shrunk from indulgencies when their result became palpable and revolting; and if they did not totally abandon the cup, confined the use of it, so far as they had strength of will, within moderate bounds.

Nor had philanthropic effort been wanting in opposition to the use of ardent spirits as a beverage. In the year 1788, the newspapers of the whole country—and among them the *Pittsfield Chronicle*—in compliance with the request of a Philadelphia organization, published Doctor Rush's celebrated essay, "An enquiry into the effects of ardent spirits upon the human body." In this work the direful effects of alcoholic drinks, in the form of distilled liquors, were faithfully depicted, and scientifically explained; and its general diffusion must have had much beneficial result. Doctor Rush, however, maintaining a doctrine still held by a large number of the medical faculty, advocated as a substitute for spirits, the use of wine and beer, both of which he recommended " as very wholesome liquors in comparison." Indeed he eulogized beer as "abounding with nourishment," and wine as " both cordial and nourishing." "The effects of wine upon the temper," said he, "are in most cases directly opposite to those of spirituous liquors. It must be a bad heart indeed, that is not rendered more cheerful and more generous by a few glasses of wine." Punch also met the reformer's favor, as " calculated, like wine and beer, to lessen the effects of hard labor upon the body. The spirit of the liquor is blunted by its union with the vegetable-acid. Hence it possesses, not only the constituent parts, but most of the qualities, of cider and wines." He adds, however, that, " to render this liquor innocent and wholesome, it must be drank weak, in moderate quantities, and only in warm weather."

Such were the teachings of the leading advocate of temperance near the close of the eighteenth century; and very few of his followers advanced beyond his stand-point until the remarkable total-abstinence movement of 1828. It may be well believed that they did not very seriously check the convivial habits of the richer class, or prove very convincing either to the higher or lower orders in society.

A vice almost as universal as intemperance, and almost as deleterious, was that of gambling in its various forms. Games of chance were frequently engaged in to the ruin of individual fortunes. A passion for horse-racing which had been patriotically suppressed during the revolution, revived at its close, and a race-course was established in the vicinity of the present Pleasure park. But the most prevalent form of gambling was by lottery, which was, not only undiscouraged by the church and the state, but continued to be favored and maintained by both. One was established in the county of Berkshire for the aid of Williams college, and managed under the auspices of its pious and reverend trustees and faculty. The *Sun* newspaper, was filled with advertisements of the schemes of lotteries in other states, of which its editor was the local agent. Few denounced them as an evil, and the best men in the community did not hesitate frequently to try their fortunes by the purchase of tickets. The multitude, following this example, thronged to the shops of the ticket-venders, and the result was a dissipation of property in the thriftless pursuit of illusory hopes, and the gradual sinking into poverty of those who were dreaming of sudden wealth poured out from the cornucopia of that goddess of fortune who was so temptingly depicted on the tickets and advertisements of the various companies.

Imprisonment for debt, so far as regarded the closeness of the confinement and the unhealthfulness of prisons, was not so cruel and revolting as it was described at the epoch of the Shays rebellion. Prisoners from whom no attempt to escape across the lines into other states, which lay in inviting proximity, was feared, were allowed the "liberty of the yard;" that is, they had the privilege, unless the creditor objected, of spending the day wherever they pleased within the limits of the county-town, returning at night to the jail. Still, the old credit-system in business continued to prevail, and it was still protected by as relentless a law, as relentlessly resorted to, as ever. The majority of creditors did not scruple to avail themselves of all the power which that law gave them over the persons of unfortunate neighbors with whom they had been living on the ordinary terms of neighborly friendship; and, so much was this deemed a matter of course that, on the release of the debtor, the old relations were often, perhaps generally renewed, as if nothing had occurred to interrupt them. Instances of what would now be called barbarous rigor—disregard for the dictates of ordinary humanity—and forgetfulness of intimate friendships, are however still remembered as happening all through at least the first quarter of the present century. And family-feuds, not even yet extinguished, arose from them.

The struggle to abolish the law under which such practices were possible, was long and earnest. The democrats of Pittsfield and Berkshire, as elsewhere, warred against it with spirit. Articles attacking it in every form were frequent in the columns of the *Sun*, which never let an opportunity pass to illustrate its cruelty, or to prove its inefficiency in accomplishing the ends for which it was kept upon the statute-book.

The compulsory support of public worship, with its incidental partiality to the standing-order, and the property-qualification, which created different classes of voters and deprived the poorest of the right of suffrage altogether, still maintained their place among the laws to whose fundamental principles, and whose general character, they were so repugnant that they stood out as glaring inconsistencies.

It will be perceived, from the foregoing pages, how gigantic an advance has been made, both in morals and in law, during the past seventy-six years. It was the work of the men who lived and labored during the first forty years of that period, to fight the battles from which that advance chiefly resulted. If we shall find their achievements in this conflict less splendid and less striking than those of the revolutionary fathers, less marked in their effects upon the material prosperity of the town than those of later days, let us be sure that they were surpassed by neither in their beneficial influence upon the happiness of those who have come after them; as those who won them were inferior to none in generosity of sentiment, and pure devotion to justice and right.

The reader need not be reminded that the obnoxious laws which have been mentioned, and the odious manner in which it was the custom to make use of them, were heir-looms bequeathed from more barbarous ages, preserved by the more timorous classes as talismans essential to the maintenance of social order, and the protection of vested rights. But it was also true that the moral and social evils which have been described, were also relics of less advanced ages. The noxious vapors of too lax judgment of moral wrong, of too lenient consideration of libertine habits, of insufficient guardianship of the outworks of virtue—

vapors which had for ages been generating throughout the great world—began to spread inward through the atmosphere of New England, whose purity had at first been so sternly guarded against infection: an infection, it is to be observed, as old as the seduction of the mother of mankind. It is to be farther remarked that the purity of New England was only as yet subjected to contagion; had felt some of its evil effects, but was not fatally or radically infected. Toleration of some dangerous social practices and a general freedom of manners, which, in the revolt of the community against too stringent censorship, had become excessive, were sure, by that very excess, to cause a re-action in the opposite direction. The undisturbed foundations of correct moral sentiment were yet firm enough to render such a result certain.

It is not a novel remark that men of earlier epochs are not to be tried by the standard of morals which governs those of more advanced eras. This axiom cannot, it is true, be pleaded in defense of the toleration of, or indulgence in, those gross vices which are in terms condemned by the divine law; although we naturally view with somewhat more leniency, those who follow the multitude to do evil, than those who stand out conspicuously in opposition to a virtuous popular sentiment. But setting aside these extreme and exceptional offenses—and leaving out of consideration, also, those acts, such as the selling and the moderate drinking of alcoholic beverages, concerning which the opinion of the world is still divided—the remark quoted applies with great force to the case before us. Some of the moral evils which have been described as prevailing in Pittsfield from seventy-five to a hundred years ago, and even extending into later days, were then only condemned as such by the severest school in religion; others, like gambling by lotteries, only suspected of evil by the keenest observers, were held, by the very censors of public and private conduct, to be positive benefits, and were used by them, without scruple, to advance any costly public enterprise. It will be observed that President Edwards selected for his sternest reprobation, the custom of the social dance; an amusement which, with the restraints which modern society throws around it, is now held by the community at large, to be perfectly innocent; while other practices of his time, which "betray themselves to every modern censure" are not even mentioned. It does not follow, of course, that they were approved by President Edwards; for it was his method of effecting reforms in morals, to apply the axe at the root of the tree of evil, in the form of spiritual and religious truth, leaving special branches to perish of themselves. It may safely be inferred, however, that the offenses unmentioned by him, did not shock him as they now would shock ordinary men. It is certain that they did not at all shock good men at the time of which we write. And we are not to condemn them that they disobeyed moral laws which had not yet been discovered.

And the distinction to be observed between a practice at a period when it is regarded as innocent, and the same practice when it has been discovered to be extremely detrimental to individuals and society, extends farther than to the mede of condemnation which is due to him who indulges in it. It affects the consequences of these practices in an important particular. In both cases they are evils, and their direct evil results in both, inevitably follow, each after its kind; but when indulged in by those conscious of their nature, and of their consequences, they become also vices; and not only produce the harm inherent in them, but deprave him who follows them. And if his offense involves a violation of positive enactments by divine, or legitimate human, authority, so much the deeper will be the essential degradation of his manhood. Thus, when the trustees of Williams college established and conducted a lottery for the benefit of that institution; when Phinehas Allen was the agent in selling tickets for the benefit of equally-praiseworthy objects; and when Rev. Thomas Allen bought, as his diary informs us that he did, lottery tickets for himself and his children, the countenance which they all gave to this species of gambling, undoubtedly led to the impoverishment of the people, and tended to induce, in many, habits of idleness and a desire for unearned wealth. But, as they acted with no suspicion of these results, and would certainly have refrained if they had been warned of them, their actions did not at all remove them from the side of right and virtue in their eternal conflict with wrong and vice. Their dealings with the lottery no more tainted or depraved their moral nature than transactions in wheat, lumber, or cotton-goods would have done; while he who does the same thing to-day in defiance of knowledge and in violation of law, at once enrolls himself in the army of vice, blunts his sense of right and wrong, and depraves his whole nature.

So, in another department of morals, with regard to the practice of bundling. In an age when it was nearly universal, and was looked upon as a matter of course, and when the limits to which it was subjected were well understood, compliance with it, however dangerous it proved in many cases, afforded no presumption against virtue; while, under the greater refinement and more fastidious requirements of later days, such a presumption would be inevitable.

We make these suggestions, obvious as they must appear to most readers, as there are always those ready to plead the sins of good men of old, as a precedent and an excuse for their own; while others are willing enough to cite the apparent weaknesses of the old time, as evidences to disparage its virtue.

Believing the whole truth regarding the past essential to the best interests of the future, we have not attempted to exaggerate the excellencies, or conceal the weaknesses of the fathers; but we think that the reverence in which they should be held, will not be at all diminished by this, if they are scanned with proper regard to the place which they occupied in the march of the ages.

CHAPTER V.

SOME LEADING CITIZENS.

[1800-1810.]

Charles Goodrich—Woodbridge Little—Rev. Thomas Allen—Dr. Timothy Childs—David Campbell—Henry Van Schaack—Oliver Wendell—Henry H. Childs—Thomas Allen, Jr.—Jonathan Allen—Rev. William Allen—James D. Colt—Samuel D. Colt—John B. Root—Oliver Root—Lemuel Pomeroy — Phinehas Allen — Jason Clapp—John W. Hulbert — Ezekiel Bacon—The generation as a whole—The town epitomized.

THE year 1800 found, still prominent among the citizens of Pittsfield, many who had been active in its affairs during revolutionary and provincial times, and who generally retained the characteristics which had marked their earlier career.

Capt. Charles Goodrich, who in 1752 became the first settler of note in Poontoosuck plantation, and whose peculiar, but large and honorable part, in the earlier history of the town, we have chronicled, was in 1800, at the age of 81, as resolute, as energetic, and as combatant in his federal leadership, as he had been in 1776-81, when we knew him as the champion in doubly-rebellious Berkshire, of the government at Boston which, with the banner of revolt and independence in one hand, clung desperately with the other to that broken reed of legitimate rule, a mutilated and forfeited royal charter.

Woodbridge Little, still, at 59, in the full vigor of his intellect, with the pen and the living voice, displayed the same ability in his advocacy of federalism, and the same dread of popular power, that he exhibited when he plead the cause of the tories and the conservative whigs against the violent radicalism of the revolutionary committees of Berkshire. Mr. Little's abhorrence of change was constitutional, and extended to lesser matters as well as to politics. A curious illustration of this trait in his character occurred in his later years. The roads from north-eastern

Berkshire, including the great Boston highway through Windsor and Dalton, reached East street, then the principal business section of Pittsfield, by a road which ran directly south from a point near Mr. Little's house, to Elm street; a very circuitous route. In the year 1806 a proposition was made in town-meeting to open what is now known as Beaver street in a direct line from Mr. Little's house to the foot of East street, affording a very great convenience to himself and the public. But it broke up the old order of things, brought him a little more in contact with the world as it was—a very small corner of it, then, to be sure—and disturbed a little the old form and dimensions of his farm; and, true to his conservative instincts, he opposed the new avenue with the bitterest vehemence, and was able to postpone its construction until 1811.[1]

Mr. Little died in 1813, retaining his resentment to the last, and leaving directions that his funeral-procession should pass over the old road, and by no means over the new avenue, which he had never used in life; neither winter's storms nor summer's suns having ever once driven him to deviate from the true conservative route to church and post-office; although he had been compelled by stress of circumstances to accept the new federal-republican government, as a tolerable substitute for royal rule.

In considering those days of absorbing political strife, political classification naturally first suggests itself, and another leading federalist whose connection with public life, although in 1800 he was but forty-seven years old, dated back to revolutionary times, was John Chandler Williams. A little eccentric in manner, as it seems to have been thought good for dignitaries to be, but revered for much professional learning, for the soundest wisdom and the most incorruptible integrity in matters both great and small, Mr. Williams transacted his business as a lawyer and magistrate in the quaint and dusty office in the northwest corner of his gambrel-roofed mansion, where he began the practice of his profession in 1782, and where he continued it until his death. Taking an active, earnest and decided part in all classes of public affairs, he of course met many earnest, active, and decided opponents; but few, if any, continued their hostility to him after the passion of the conflict had subsided.

[1] The final vote to build the road passed in 1810, but it was not opened until 1811.

Prominent among the magnates of the town, was Thomas Gold. This gentleman, a son of Rev. Hezekiel Gold of Cornwall, Connecticut, was born in 1760, graduated at Yale college in 1778, and commenced the practice of the law at Pittsfield in 1782. Like most of the graduates of Yale who early became residents of Pittsfield, he was a man of elegant culture and refined tastes. As a lawyer he was able and shrewd to a marked degree. In matters of public as well as of private business, he was enterprising, discreet and clear-headed. We shall find him occupying positions of great responsibility in the town and in public institutions, with advantage to his constituents. As a politician he was active and ambitious, but the voters did not implicitly trust him, and he was more successful in acquiring property than in obtaining office. We have noticed his early escapade as a participant in the Shays rebellion; but growing years had taught him conservatism, and in 1800 he ranked with the most decided federalists.

Ashbel Strong, a lawyer of ability and a man of scholarly tastes, was a federalist of some note. He was born at New Marlboro, January 19, 1754, the son of Rev. Thomas Strong, the first minister of that town, who was a native of Northampton and a graduate of Yale. Ashbel graduated at Yale in 1776, having been admitted to the Berkshire bar two years before. In 1792 he married Mary, or as the town-record has it "Polly," daughter of Major Israel Stoddard, and granddaughter of Hon. Israel Williams of Hatfield. He represented Pittsfield in the legislature of 1799 and was appointed county-attorney in 1802. Having no children of his own, he educated in his family two nephews and a niece. He died in 1809.

Another man long of note and influence in town, was Capt. David Campbell. Captain Campbell was the grandson of Rev. John Campbell, a Scottish divine, who having received a classical and theological education at Edinburgh, emigrated to America in 1717, and in 1724 became pastor of the church in Oxford, Mass. His grandson removed to Pittsfield about the year 1790. He was a man of large and varied information, of a genial and generous temperament; active, but cool and of the shrewdest judgment, in his business-affairs. It can hardly be said of such a man that he was fickle in his pursuits; but he certainly made frequent changes in them, being by turns, farmer, trader, tavern-keeper and manufacturer. There is a tradition, of suggestive exaggeration, that there was not a desirable piece of real-estate in Pittsfield that he did not at some time own. In politics he was a federalist. In person those who knew him late in life describe him as portly, dignified and commanding.

Last, but far from the least, of the federalists of the eldest generation, was Henry Van Schaack, who still loved to descant on the virtues of Washington and Adams to his neighbors; to the lawyers who at every adjournment of the court at Lenox flocked to his hospitable mansion; the trustees of Williams college, who made it their rendezvous on their way to commencement;[1] and to the magnates of the federal party, who, including Hamilton, were from time to time his guests, and with whom it was his greatest pleasure to share his rich wines and sparkling cider.

Mr. Van Schaack had been a very thorough and intelligent student of the federal constitution, and appears to have been more perfectly satisfied with its guaranties of stability in government than were many of his fellows in politics, who, although they had never been tories, yet distrusted the new order of things as without sufficient powers of self-preservation. Mr. Van Schaack was, however, not a mere politician. He had become a scholar of fair attainments in many branches of learning, without the aid of schools; but he did not undervalue their advantages, and was the ardent friend of educational institutions of every grade. We have already described his strong interest in religious affairs, and his arduous exertions in behalf of the equality of all denominations before the law. In business, although his

---

[1] It was the custom for the Rev. Mr. Judson of Sheffield, the trustee in the county who lived farthest south, to pick up his colleagues along the route, so that they arrived at Williamstown in a body. The southern members, on reaching Pittsfield invariably partook of the good cheer of their associate, Mr. Van Schaack; and under the influence of his cider and madeira, many a solemn witticism and grave joke were perpetrated. Mr. Judson, the only democrat on the board, was subjected to much good-humored banter for his politics' sake; but the shafts of wit which were aimed at him could not have been very fatal, since it was considered a brilliant sally when, the host having asked Mr. Judson whether he would have federal or democratic cider, and he answering, as was expected, that he preferred the democratic, received a glass of a particularly hard beverage; while the rest of the party were smiling over that which "equalled the best champagne."

early life had been spent in mercantile pursuits, and although he was not dependent on the product of his farm, he was a skillful, enthusiastic and industrious practical farmer, in which connection a characteristic anecdote is told of him. One Jones, a neighbor whose passion for talking federal politics knew no bounds, nor distinction of time or place, called upon him while he was at work in his potato-field, and began upon his favorite theme. "Yes, yes," interrupted Mr. Van Schaack impatiently, "Yes, yes, neighbor Jones, I know all that well—very well. Adams and Pitt are great and good men—very great and good men; and Tom Jefferson and Napoleon are rascals, *very* great rascals; no doubt about it, neighbor Jones. And democracy is going to be the ruin of the country, and federalism is the only safe and sound doctrine; no doubt about it at all. I know all that, neighbor Jones, well, *very* well,—but potatoes must be hoed!" And, that being the duty which just then lay nearest to him, he set about it with a vigor which utterly discomfited poor Jones, and sent him away with a budding suspicion as to the faithfulness of his veteran leader.

A devoted ally and highly-prized counselor of the Pittsfield federalists, although only a summer-resident, and not a voter in the town, was Judge Oliver Wendell of Boston. Judge Wendell took a deep interest in the political conflict which raged in Pittsfield with exceptional bitterness even in that era of bitter political strife, and as his patriotism was long-tried and unquestioned, his name was of great value to the cause which he espoused.

Passing to the democrats of the earliest generation, Rev. Thomas Allen is first met; as energetic, as earnest and as uncompromising as a leader of the Jeffersonian republicans, as he had been of the radical revolutionary whigs. He loved democracy, as under some name he had always loved it, as the very perfect flowering of Christianity; and he hated federalism, as he had always hated the royalty, which he firmly believed that he detected under its mask. If he contended against this half-disguised foe with too little charity for those who differed from him, it must be said also, that it was with utter disregard of his own comfort and pecuniary interests. If he gave up to party too much of the energies and talents which, we conceive, might have been better employed in behalf of religion, education, or the merely material affairs of the town, we must remember that it was to contend for principles whose triumph, he honestly believed, was essential to any wholesome and permanent development of those great interests.

But, deep as was his concern in political affairs, and devoted as his labors were in behalf of Jeffersonian doctrines, it is to be doubted whether he, to any very censurable degree, neglected for them, any of his more immediate duties. In the heated discussions of the day he was charged with giving the time which ought to have been spent on his sermons to indite political articles for the *Sun;* but it seems clear that the style and substance of his pulpit-labors were acceptable even to those who objected to "the introduction of affairs of state" in them, and it is likely that the opportunity afforded of expressing his views in the columns of a newspaper, often counteracted the temptation to interlard a sermon with them. As to other pastoral labors, even the children of federal families retain a loving memory of his tender and sympathizing manner in performing them. His regard for common schools, which he so generously manifested when a scantily-paid young minister, continued to the last. It is evidence of his faithful parental care that in the year 1800, he was surrounded by sons, to all of whom he had given a good—and to two of them a classical—education, and all of whom by his aid entered upon active life under favorable auspices. Nor was he less regardful of his daughters. Indeed, his story is full of incidents showing the warmth of his parental love. Let these features in the character of the man and the minister, be remembered when we are called upon to relate the part which his views of right compelled him to take in the heated political conflict which divided the town and the church into two hostile parties.

Another leading man, quite as decided in his political opinions, but rather less emphatic and energetic in their defense, was Dr. Timothy Childs, who, at the age of fifty-two, was at the head of his profession in Pittsfield, although not so exclusively its physician, as when in 1775 the town-meeting requested him "to return from the army, as it was very sickly here." We have already sketched his character.

Col. Joshua Danforth still kept his store on East street, but, the federalists being in power, had lost his office of postmaster, which probably did not tend to mollify his political feeling.

Still, earnest and well-defined, as his opinions were, his knowledge of mankind, acquired in the army and by business-contact with many classes, had taught him a toleration unknown to his associates. It had also been his good fortune to meet the enemies of his country only in open conflict on the battle-field, while they had grown morbidly vindictive towards, and distrustful of, all political opponents, in the more rancorous encounters of pen and tongue; as well as by a constant, jealous watch of the machinations of the concealed adherents of Great Britain: many of whom they still found arrayed against them under a new name. The soldier was enabled to preserve a generous trust which cankered in the politician.[1]

Among the most influential and able leaders of the democrats, was Simon Larned, who was born in 1756, at Thompson, Conn. He was an officer of merit in the revolutionary war, and at the close of that contest, he removed in 1784 to Pittsfield. From 1792 to 1812 he was high sheriff of Berkshire, and in 1804 was elected to congress to fill the vacancy caused by the resignation of Hon. Thomson J. Skinner. In town-affairs he took a leading part. He is described as "a man of few words, deep judgment, and of rare wit and humor."

While so many of those whose services extended back into the past century were thus in the full vigor of life, several young men, natives of the town, began about the year 1800, to take an active part in its affairs.

Dr. Childs and Rev. Mr. Allen were especially happy in sons who inherited their political and religious opinions, and defended them with ardor and ability. We briefly sketch the early life of those afterwards most prominent in town-affairs.

Thomas Allen, Jr., was born in 1769, graduated at Harvard in 1789, and was admitted to the bar in 1792. He commenced practice at Sheffield, but soon removed to his native town. In his profession, he is represented to have been "skillful, learned and eloquent;" "and also," adds his eulogist, "just and merciful." No meaningless praise in times when mercy, at least, was far from the chief attribute of the law. His temper, by nature placid and not easily ruffled, was fiery enough when roused: placable and forgiving when the immediate cause of irritation was

---

[1] By a typographical error in the first volume of this work, Col. Danforth's birth-place was given as "Weston." It was Williamstown.

removed. Earnest, unwavering and uncompromising in his political faith and conduct, a forcible and persuasive speaker, of agreeable figure and address, it is no wonder that he was the idol of the democratic party of his vicinity, who had few representatives in the legal profession. Still he was no bigot of party, and had qualities of head and heart which won him the esteem and friendship of the best among those whom he most strenuously opposed in public affairs, as was emphatically shown at the time of his death. He was elected representative in 1805, and died at Boston, while serving a second term, March 22, 1806. His last illness, which was very painful, lasted twenty-three days, during which his bedside was watched by leading men of both political parties. His funeral services were conducted by Rev. Dr. Baldwin, an eminent Baptist divine of Boston, and the most conspicuous champion of the voluntary system of supporting public worship. His pall-bearers were his classmates, Rev. Dr. Kirkland, President of Harvard University; Rev. Wm. Emerson, D. D., pastor of the First Church in Boston, and Geo. Blake, Esq., together with Hon. Harrison Gray Otis, speaker of the House, Perez Morton, who had been the democratic candidate for speaker, and Hon. John Wells, a prominent member. Among the carriages in the funeral-procession was that of the democratic governor, Sullivan, and the remains found rest, where they still repose, in the tomb of the federal Wendells in King's Chapel burial-ground.

Jonathan Allen was born in March, 1773, and passing his boyhood amid the turmoils of the revolution and the internal troubles which followed, he received such education as could be obtained from the village-schools, and from his father, who, it will be recollected, was a scholar of more than ordinary attainments in classical and historical lore, and moreover a diligent student of political and moral economy.

With such preparation, Jonathan Allen began his business life, about the year 1795, by opening a store in the small gambrel-roofed building on the south-west corner of the Allen homestead lot. He was a man of active mind and versatile talents, which led him into various enterprises, public and private, and involved him in the varying fortunes which are the usual results of such a temperament. But he possessed in an eminent degree the family traits of energy, perseverance and elasticity of purpose, which carried him safely through, or over, every difficulty. Hon. Henry Hubbard, who knew him long and intimately, described him as "sedate, but cheerful, of great liberality, impartiality and fortitude, and as exerting always a considerable, and sometimes a leading, influence in the state-legislature, of each branch of which he was several times a member." "He was one of those," added Mr. Hubbard, "who, although too young to be an actor in the scenes of the revolution, were yet molded by it in character." The opinions and feelings thus formed were intensified, by the contest in which, from his earliest youth, he saw his father engaged, against those whom, under various names, he deemed the enemies of his country's liberties. It thus happened that, although a young and busy merchant, he was early found deeply engaged in the Jeffersonian politics of the day.

Throughout his life he continued devoted to the same principles, and many of his happiest intellectual efforts were made in political addresses, either from the voice or pen, during the many years in which he was chairman of the democratic county-committee. In these addresses, as well as in those before the agricultural society and on like occasions, he displayed singular clearness and vigor of thought and expression, and a very wide range of knowledge. The large influence which he enjoyed was legitimately acquired, and judiciously exercised.

William Allen was born in January, 1874, and graduated at Harvard in 1802. In his later years he was widely known as professor in Dartmouth, and president of Bowdoin college, and as the author of several literary works; the most valuable of which was his "Biographical Dictionary," the first of its class in America, and a volume displaying very industrious research. Earnest in his convictions and little tolerant of adverse opinions, he favored strong, if not arbitrary, measures in the repression of what he considered error. With less knowledge of human nature than his brothers, he often failed of carrying his points by pressing them, not so much too strenuously as with too obvious stress. But few men excelled him in conscientious regard for duty, in genuine benevolence, in love for right and hatred of wrong, as he saw them. As a writer, his style, although somewhat prolix, was pure and scholarly. As a preceptor, he was one of the most learned in the country, in his time; but he failed as the governing-head of a college by attempting to enforce too strictly the letter of the

Yours affect'y
Th. H. Childs

law, relying too little on the better traits of student character. As a clergyman, adhering strictly to the orthodox Congregational church, he preached its doctrines and administered its discipline faithfully. In 1800, he was only sixteen years old, but we shall find him a few years later defending his father in a very able pamphlet.

Henry Halsey Childs, son of Dr. Timothy Childs, and grandson of Col. James Easton, was born in 1783, and graduated at Williams college in 1802; manifesting at his graduation qualities which continued to distinguish him through life.

At that time all the faculty and, with one exception, all the trustees, were federalists, and very earnest ones. Young Childs was quite as strenuously of the opposite party, and the commencement oration, which he submitted to the president for approval, was filled with the rankest Jeffersonian democracy: little short of blasphemy in the judgment of the academic critics while his laudations of the new president, whom they regarded as an infidel in religion and a Jacobin in politics, were profuse. Of course this odious heresy was strictly interdicted. But on commencement day when Childs mounted the stage, instead of the harmless sentences which had been substituted and approved, out came the condemned heresies, trebled in force by the resentment of the young politician. "Childs! Childs!" exclaimed the astonished president. But those who knew the speaker in his later days will readily believe that no presiding officer could silence Henry Childs, with words, when he was bent upon talking. The orator went on to the end, amid mingled applause and hisses; for though his sympathizers were few on the platform, they were many on the floor.

We relate this incident simply as very characteristic of one who afterwards filled a marked place in the history of the town. A bold, self-reliant and impulsive man, it would have been strange had he not sometimes erred. Energetic, enthusiastic and generally practical, thoroughly devoted to whatever he undertook, he was for the most part successful.

We have already mentioned J. D. & S. D. Colt as commencing, in 1799, a prosperous mercantile business. Both were also men of strong personal qualities, interested and influential in town and other public affairs, and decided, although not violent, politicians of the federal school. James Denison Colt, Jr., the senior partner, born in 1767, had in 1800 already occupied places of trust in the town-government, and won an enviable reputation, which he retained through life, as a man of sound intellect and the most correct principles both in business and in morals. Samuel Dickinson Colt, born in 1779, was in 1800 barely twenty-one years old. He was only the half-brother of his partner, being the son of Capt. J. D. Colt by his second wife, Miriam, daughter of Col. Wm. Williams; from whom he inherited a lively and mercurial disposition with somewhat of that "magnificent spirit," which, according to his epitaph, distinguished his maternal grandfather.[1]

John Burgoyne Root, born in 1778, was the son of Ezekiel Root, and afforded the rare instance of a son of a royalist espousing warmly the democratic cause; resenting, perhaps, in this way the unpatriotic name which had been inflicted upon him. We shall find Mr. Root enterprising and active in business, quick to take part in the improvement of American wools, and the introduction of new manufactures. His manners were eminently pleasing and his temperament genial and kindly. Elected town-clerk in 1806, he was re-elected in 1811, and every year from that date until his death in 1838; a longer time than this office has been held consecutively by any other person.

Another citizen of influence, and one never willingly inconspicuous in public matters, was Joseph Shearer, who had married Hannah, widow of Col. Wm. Williams. Her first husband died in 1785, leaving, to satify the demands of his creditors, barely £175, of which £75 were absorbed in the charges of administration. His widow, however, proved to be wealthy, holding all his real estate by some previous transfer or settlement. This wealth,

---

[1] Capt. James Denison Colt, who had been a man of property and influence in Pittsfield almost from its first settlement, lived until 1809. The Colt family date back to Thomas Colt of Carlisle in the English county of Cumberland, whose son Thomas was chancellor of the Exchequer, and held other honorable places under Edward IV. This second Thomas died in 1476. The family traits of respect for law and established institutions, and a rigid faithfulness to public and private trusts, which distinguish the Berkshire branch of the family to this day, characterized its progenitors in the earliest record we have of them. One of its members lost an estate by adhering to the fallen fortunes of Charles I, and another refused to retain the favor of Charles II. at the sacrifice of his parliamentary duties, or to surrender to him, for any bribe, the charter of the city of Leominster, which had been committed to his charge.

of course, attracted many suitors, but she maintained her independent widowhood,—a state to which she seems to have been better adapted than any other,—until she was wooed by Joseph Shearer, who, if tradition does not belie him, won the widow and her lands by the venerable equivoque of asserting that "he loved the very ground she trod on." There remains, however, the fact that Mr. Shearer had a remarkably fine person, pleasing manners, and much adroitness; which may have made an impression upon Mrs. Williams, although she was twenty-six years his senior. But, be that as it may, their union was an unhappy one. The bride does not appear, under any circumstances, to have been exactly an angel in the household,[1] and had she been so, with the great disparity in age between the parties, the result would have been doubtful. As it was, Mr. Shearer's polite disclaimers of impatience to be rid of his wife, sounded like irony, and she openly accused him of plotting her death by leaving an open well into which she stepped, by mounting her upon an unbroken colt, and by other such ingenious marital devices. Once he was brought to trial before Justice John Chandler Williams, but the evidence failed to sustain the charge. She lived, however, until 1821, when she died of old age at ninety-one. Mr. Shearer died in 1838 at the age of eighty-two. He was a thrifty and shrewd business man. An earnest and decided democrat, he was highly esteemed by his party as well for his subtle counsels as for his liberal contributions. In public matters he was generous—to confess the truth, ostentatiously so—and the town to this day enjoys the benefits of some of his gifts, while that which he bequeathed to relatives, when he died childless, long since passed away from those to whom he gave it, and who had little good from it.

About the year 1800, the "old hive" in the Connecticut valley, to which Pittsfield already owed so much, sent out a new migration, in which, among other worthy citizens, were three young men, who built up, each, a prosperous business, and became prominent in the affairs of the town. They were Lemuel Pomeroy, Phinehas Allen and Jason Clapp.

Lemuel Pomeroy was born at Southampton, August 18, 1778.

---

[1] Of Col. Williams's three wives, his friend Col. Stoddard said: "He married first, Miriam Tyler, for good sense, and got it; second, Miss Wells, for love and beauty, and had it; third, Aunt Hannah Dickinson, and got cheated like the devil."

His family claim descent from Sir Ralph de Pomeroy, a favorite knight of William, the Conqueror, upon whom that monarch conferred extensive domains in the counties of Devon and Somerset, in the former of which the superb ruins of his castle of Berri-Pomeroy still attract the admiration of the tourist. Some of Sir Ralph's descendants had a less favorable experience of royal rule; and in 1636, Eltweed and Eldred Pomeroy, brothers, and represented to have been "men of liberal and independent minds," flying from the persecutions of Archbishop Laud, emigrated from Devonshire to Dorchester in Massachusetts. In 1637, following a line of migration then common, the brothers removed to Windsor in Connecticut. When Eltweed was ninety years old, he removed to Southampton with his son, Eldad, who received a grant of one thousand acres in that town, on condition that he should there establish himself as a gunsmith and blacksmith; a tract still known as "the Grant," and still in the possession of one branch of the family.

The trade of the smith, as we have before stated, embraced in colonial times many branches now transferred to special manufactories; and they were all pursued with skill and profit by successive generations of the Pomeroys, who had a knack of always being as their ancestor was represented at the first in Dorchester, "men in good circumstances and respectable standing." From Eldad in the first Massachusetts generation to Edward in the seventh, it is the boast of the family that it has never lacked a man to stand at the anvil. Eldad was called to Hampshire county for his great repute as a gunsmith. General Seth employed many men in the various branches of his art, and was as skillful in making muskets as in using them. His firearms were not only celebrated throughout the English colonies, but were held in the highest estimation by the French and Indian foe, who spared no effort to obtain them by fair means or foul.

Lemuel came to Pittsfield in 1799, bringing with him the same anvil which his ancestor had carried up the narrow Bay Path along the banks of the Connecticut, from Windsor to Southampton, and which his descendants still preserve among the most precious of their heir-looms.[1]

---

[1] Lemuel Pomeroy was sixth in descent from Eldad, viz.: *First* generation in Massachusetts, Eldad; *second*, Medad, a lawyer at Northampton; *third*, Ebenezer, who was one of the commissioners for the settlement of Sheffield,

THE HOMESTEAD. RESIDENCE OF ROBERT POMEROY, Esq.

In 1800 he married Miss Hart Lester of Griswold, Connecticut. In the same year he purchased the present Pomeroy homestead on East street.[1]

The homestead-lands extended to Pomeroy avenue, and in a shop on the south-eastern corner, Mr. Pomeroy laid the foundation of his fortune; his business being, as it seems, somewhat extensive and varied, for between 1800 and 1804 we find him advertising, in addition to general blacksmithing, pleasure-sleighs, wagons and plows all of his own manufacture and in considerable quantity; and in 1804 " a large number of wooden and iron axletree wagons, and two hundred good plows, complete for use." In 1805 his shop was burned; but, although the loss was great enough to be sensibly felt by him in that stage of his affairs it did not impede his progress, and he immediately erected in its place a larger and better building, which being soon devoted chiefly to the finishing of muskets, was known in its later days as " the old musket-shop."

In character Mr. Pomeroy was one of the most remarkable of the business-men who have flourished in Pittsfield. Clear-headed, of rare judgment, bold and far-seeing in enterprise, and of inflexible purpose, his career as a manufacturer was one of almost uniform success. In town-affairs, he was generous and public-spirited, although apt to be imperious and self-asserting; resolute to have the controlling voice in such matters as interested him; which were many.[2] In politics being a federalist, he could not be otherwise than a very decided and ardent one. What he believed firmly, he always defended warmly. A large-hearted and large-minded man, of commanding mien and dignified presence, he was for many years among the most conspicuous figures in the history of the town. There is perhaps none to which it is more deeply indebted for its material prosperity. A very well defined specimen of the class of men sent by the Connecticut valley to Pittsfield, was Lemuel Pomeroy.

and for establishing the Indian mission at Stockbridge; an influential and active man in the public affairs of western Massachusetts; *fourth*, Seth, a noted officer in the French and Indian wars, and in the revolution; *fifth*, Lemuel, who lived and died on "the Grant" at Southampton; *sixth*, Lemuel of Pittsfield.

[1] See chapter 1.

[2] It was one of the acute remarks of his friend, Hon. E. R. Colt, that "there would be no living with Mr. Pomeroy, if he were not almost always right."

In the year 1800, came also, Phinehas Allen, as firm and fiery in his adherence to Jeffersonian democracy, as Mr. Pomeroy was in his abhorrence of it. His father, Solomon Allen, was a brother of the Pittsfield minister, and had been an officer of merit in the war of the revolution and in the militia-campaigns against the Shays rebellion.[1] Late in life he became a minister of the gospel, and although lacking in theological science, succeeded in founding four churches, with an aggregate membership of two hundred, in previously waste places in Hampshire county and western New York. In 1820, having retired from the ministry, at the age of seventy, he visited Pittsfield, called at every house, and in each, after reading a portion of scripture, and exhorting all the members of the family to serve the Lord, he prayed fervently for the salvation of their souls.

Phinehas, his oldest son, was born at Northampton, August 11, 1776. Having served his apprenticeship in the Hampshire *Gazette* printing-office, and worked one year as a journeyman in Springfield, he removed to Pittsfield in the year 1800, upon the invitation of Rev. Mr. Allen, and established the *Sun* newspaper. The four papers previously printed in the gambrel-roofed cottage, owned by Mr. Allen had been of federal politics; but had probably been favored by him for their beneficial influence in other directions. But the *Gazette* had been bitterly anti-federal, and little else. With the presidential canvass then pending, politics had become the absorbing interest of the day; and it seemed to the democrats of Pittsfield essential that the town-newspaper should be of their own faith. To none of them could this have seemed more desirable than to Rev. Mr. Allen; and he invited his young nephew to occupy the office, which the federal *Gazette* had just vacated, or been ejected from. The first number of the *Sun* was issued September 16, 1800, and was printed on a sheet thirteen inches long by eleven wide, beginning on a scale smaller than any of its predecessors, except the *Chronicle*, which was enlarged with its thirty-first number, while the *Sun* remained as at first for twelve years.

The first number was adorned with a rude cut of a rising sun, and bore the motto,

> "Here all may scribble with unbounded sway,
> If they will do it in a decent way."

[1] See vol. I., page 403.

Phinehas Allen

But the motto disappeared after two numbers. In his prospectus the editor gave a glowing ideal picture of what a newspaper should be, which, although widely different from that of Dr. Rush, was excellent in its way. Politics were the predominant element; but they were to be discussed with candor, fairness and impartiality. The *Sun* would defend the republican party; but would eschew calumny, slander and falsehood. The editor seems to have thought that his pledges would be best sustained by the most ardent, undeviating and unqualified support of the republican—or as it began about this time to be called—the democratic party. For sixty long years, he never admitted that there was fault or mistake in any portion of its policy. Whatever it attacked he assailed; whatever it defended, he championed. He advocated the tariff, when Judge Bacon wore homespun clothes in congress, and free trade when George N. Briggs manifested his devotion to American manufactures in the same seat in the same way. He joined with Jefferson in his denunciation of slavery, and with Buchanan, in his warnings against the evil tendencies of anti-slavery politics. But it is only just to him to say that, in following the standard of party wherever it led, his changes of opinion appear to have been sincere, and seemed to him to be called for by altered circumstances. All matters of mere policy, he subordinated to regard for the constitution; and that, as interpreted by the "resolutions of '98." Whatever controverted the extreme doctrines of state-rights, he considered heretical and dangerous. This was his polar star, and by this he steered, let the world go round as it would.

In town-affairs, Mr. Allen took a more zealous and active part than the columns of his paper would indicate. In the earlier efforts to restore the county-seat to Pittsfield, in particular he took an earnest and conspicuous part. Being a member of the state-legislature when this question once came up, he drew upon himself, by his ardent advocacy of the removal, the whole fire of the opposition wit, concerning which a characteristic anecdote is preserved. Discussing the question one day at the hotel-table, he was asked which he really thought was the larger, Pittsfield or London. "Pittsfield, by Heaven!" was the sturdy reply; which pleased his constituents, for it was one of the well-worn witticisms of the neighboring villagers to nickname Pittsfield for the great metropolis, and the representative's way of meeting it seemed happy.

In business Mr. Allen was punctual, methodical and exact, to a proverb; and he would have been more distinguished for integrity and industry, had those qualities been less universal in the community of which he formed a part. In person rather below the medium stature, but lithe, symmetrical and well-knit, no one ever associated with him any idea of weakness or want of dignity.

The influence of such a man laboring persistently in one local journal, in one direction, for over half a century, we need not say, was powerful. In many families the young received almost their whole political education from the *Sun*, and many of them clung to it through life against all the more modern attractions of rival journals. It was the one unchanged thing which reminded them of the past. Itself, as a newspaper, necessarily dealing with ceaseless and often startling mutations in men and nations, it viewed them all from the democratic stand-point of the year 1800, and however essentially they actually varied, gave them color, superficially at least, from the democratic atmosphere of that era.

Jason Clapp, the remaining member of this Hampshire county triad, was born at Northampton in 1783, being the son of Ebenezer Clapp. He removed to Pittsfield in 1802, upon the invitation of his friend Lemuel Pomeroy, by whom he was employed as master-wheelwright until 1809. In that year he purchased the land now included in Clapp avenue and the building-lots adjoining that street upon the west, where he built a shop, around which afterwards grew up Clapp's carriage-factory. Of his business life and character Rev. Dr. Todd thus spoke in his funeral sermon:

> He began life by serving a regular apprenticeship; receiving the almost incredibly small pay of eight dollars per year. But, so economical were his habits that, during the four years of his apprenticeship he expended only ninety-three dollars. On reaching his majority, he immediately paid off the debt of sixty dollars, thus unavoidably incurred, and at once began to assist in the support of his parents. * *
> I have seldom known a man, whom I could hold up with more confidence as a model for our young men to study and copy. He began on a small scale; never asking a man or a bank to loan him a dollar; never asked a note discounted, never asked a man to endorse for him; I doubt whether he was ever sued at law. Slowly, steadily, surely, he

advanced until he stood at the head of his business; the man whose name was a warranty, whose workmanship was as perfect as care and labor could make it; and whose production it was an honor to possess.

It may be added that, at the head of a great manufacturing establishment, Mr. Clapp had the too rare virtue of remembering that his workmen occupied the same station from which he had himself risen; and from which, very much through his example and encouragement, some of them were surely rising. It was with heart-felt truth that Dr. Todd said, "It was a melancholy but a beautiful sight, when some of these men gathered around his coffin and were his gentle pall-bearers—as if lifting the remains of a father."

The great intellectual leaders of the two political parties in the early part of the century in Pittsfield were John W. Hulbert and Ezekiel Bacon, both men of decided ability and more than ordinary eloquence. Mr. Hulbert was born at Alford, and was admitted to the bar about 1794. He commenced practice at Sheffield, but removed to Pittsfield about 1800. He was a man of brilliant intellect, of keen wit, of genial temperament and fascinating manners. His eloquence was polished but pointed, effective, and very apt to excite the ire of his opponents. His fellow federalists, who placed no bounds to their admiration of the talents of their champion, styled him "the silver-tongued," and "the Hamilton of Massachusetts:" and, in their view, this latter phrase included all that was excellent in political character.

Ezekiel Bacon was born at Boston, September 1, 1776. His father, Hon. John Bacon, had been one of the pastors of the old South church, but differing, on some theological points, with his colleague and a majority of his people, he resigned in 1775, and removed to Stockbridge, where he afterwards held many honorable places; among them those of chief-justice of the common pleas and representative in congress. He was accustomed to say that "Ezekiel went to Boston to be born;" his mother being at his birth on a visit to her old home. When the family returned to Stockbridge in the following summer, it was in the first "pleasure-carriage" that ever crossed the Hoosac mountains.

Ezekiel entered Yale college at the age of fourteen and graduated in 1794. Having read law at the law-school of Judge Reeves, in Litchfield, Conn., and in the office of Hon. Nathan Dane, he commenced practice at Williamstown in 1798; but removed to Pittsfield in 1806. His father was a democrat of the straightest sect, and he inherited his principles in full measure. At the law-school he won the sobriquet "le petit democrat;" and in "The Mirror of the Berkshire Bar" he is enrolled as "Young Democrat Bacon." In 1799, he delivered a Fourth of July oration at Williamstown, which had the honor of being printed by his friends and burned by the federal students of the college; although there was nothing in it specially to provoke their ire, unless it were a scornful allusion to the tory-element in the federal party. Mr. Bacon's addresses and speeches, many of which are preserved in print, are, although earnest and decided, moderate and courteous; especially for the era at which they were delivered.

In 1806 he was chosen one of the state-senators from Berkshire, his colleague being Dr. Timothy Childs. In 1807, upon the resignation of Hon. Barnabas Bidwell, he was elected to congress, receiving every vote in Pittsfield, and almost every vote cast in the district. The federalists had no candidate, and seem to have refrained from voting. Mr. Bacon continued in congress until 1813, serving on the committee of ways and means, and being its chairman during the first year of the war of 1812. He was not a fluent speaker or very ready debater; but his speeches, as reported in the Annals of Congress, and in the newspapers of the day, are distinguished for fullness of information, sound logic and clear thought, which gave them great weight. He was on terms of confidential intimacy with President Madison, and numbered among his chosen friends Albert Gallatin, James Monroe, John Quincy Adams, Henry Clay, DeWitt Clinton and the other great leaders of the early democratic party; with whom he maintained correspondence long after he left congress. And it is proof of the life-long constancy of his friendships that so late as 1844 he delivered and published a lecture eulogistic of Gallatin, Madison and others of his early political associates; a tribute which was pronounced by Judge Story to be "eminently just." With Story, his associations were especially intimate and friendly, and continued to the death of the former. It is creditable to Mr. Bacon's judgment that, both being young men together in congress, he recognized the great qualities which afterwards rendered his friend the most eminent jurist of his day, in America at least, and by his influence with the president secured his appointment to the supreme bench, before Story knew that he was a candidate.

Ardent as was his devotion to democratic principles, he was no blind follower of political leadership. He sympathized with Madison in his efforts to avoid a war with Great Britain, and thereby incurred the distrust of the French faction of the democracy. Not insensible to the rights and interests of New England, he favored the embargo of 1807 only as a temporary measure; to him primarily, Jefferson attributed its repeal, and he shared with his friend Story the denunciations of that most arbitrary of political leaders for their course in that matter. He opposed in a vigorous and manly speech the proposition to arm the whole militia of the country at the expense of the national treasury, because under a previous law, Massachusetts and most of the northern states had supplied their troops fully, while most of the southern states had neglected to do so. That he did not continue longer at the head of the committee of ways and means was probably due to the fact that he could not be relied upon to go all the lengths which party exigencies might require. With pure, unselfish and patriotic aims; of sound and independent judgment; well read in the principles of government, and guided by full and accurate information, Ezekiel Bacon ranked high among the very best class of American legislators.

"His temperament," says a biographer, "was poetic, and he was familiar with all the standard literature of that class, and he largely indulged himself at one period of his life in poetic composition, mostly, however, tinged with deep melancholy—the *suspiria profundis* of a depressed spirit and an aching heart." It should be added that this was not the affectation of sensibility, at one time fashionable; but, although deepened by ill health, was the genuine sadness of a heart seeking earnestly for religious truth, and finding it not; for it was not until his latest years that he was able fully to recognize the truths of Christianity. In 1842 he published a volume of poems entitled "Recreations in a Sick Room," and dedicated to his old friend, Story, who acknowledged them in a touching note.[1]

There were, in the excited and busy period of the town's history which we are now considering, other men whom we can see to have been of note and influence equally with some of those whom

---
[1] Life and letters of Joseph Story.

we have mentioned. Some of these are sketched in other connections. Of many it is impossible now to recover more of their story and character than the reader will gather from the statement of their official positions and their places upon committees. The memory of their cotemporaries, or rather those who remember them as men when they were children, describes them with monotonous indefiniteness. "A fine fellow," "A smart man," "A good man, farmer, or trader," are phrases which, when applied to half the town grow obscure. "A glorious old fellow," "A sharp one," "One who knew what he was about, I tell you," have a little more meaning; but, at the best, the judgments of childhood in such matters, unless illustrated by incidents—and incidents personally observed by the narrator—are very liable to be false, or exaggerated.

Of the generation as a whole, we have, however, a very graphic characterization, which, although it refers to a period a few years later, applies with perhaps greater force to the men of 1800-10. It is from an historical sermon delivered by Rev. Dr. Humphrey in 1857, and describes the Congregational society as he found it in 1817:

"The fathers of that day, as I knew them, were a stalwart generation, who had come over the hills from the fat valley of the Connecticut, and settled down here, to clear up the forests, trace these broad highways, and lay the foundations of society upon a stratum of the old Plymouth Rock. They were such men as Fairfield, Larned, Danforth, Childs, Williams, Ingersol, Root, Strong, Fowler, Lancton, Lawrence, the Wards, Merrill, Dickinson, Chapman, Francis, Stevens, Sacket and others."

"They were as a generation staunch, enterprising men—somewhat set in their ways, if you please; but who, despite their shibboleths, would, had the occasion called for it, have united, shoulder to shoulder, as their fathers did, in fighting for liberty to the death."

As the occasion did not require it, they did not stand shoulder to shoulder, but, in quite another attitude, face to face, employed their vigor and their valor in taking care that the liberties of the republic received no detriment from its internal enemies, as they mutually classed each other.

We should be too hasty, if we denounced their political wranglings as altogether profitless; and although they doubtless withdrew much mental energy from more economical employment, and although the material interests of the town must have suffered from the lack of local harmony, still individuals and the community increased in wealth and business activity.

In the chapter specially devoted to agriculture, manufactures and mercantile affairs, it will be seen that farming was prosperous, and growing more skilful, that new branches of manufactures were introduced and became the germ of the present greatness of that interest in the town; that the merchants showed signs of thrift by building new and better stores. The carding-machines and fulling-mills were busy in preparing and finishing the products of the household-looms. The manufacture of carriages was prosperously begun. The iron forges were turning out tons of tough malleable iron, which to a great extent was converted by the smiths of the town into anchors, gun-barrels, plowshares, chains, and other products of their craft. A gun-factory was established, which contributed largely to the arming of the troops of the state and the Union. The seed of the flax which had furnished material for the linen-looms, fed the oil-mills; the ashes from the fires that cleared the fields became precious in the potash crucible. Tanneries, for which bark and hides were then more abundant than now, enriched their owners. Beef-packing, as well as the potasheries, was a profitable source of income to the merchants. The breeding of mules and horses for the West India market was a lucrative branch of the farmer's business. Plows, scythes, nails, carding-machines, looms, silver-ware, drums, hats and combs, made up a goodly number of small manufactures. And, finally, the printing-press was in constant motion, sending out not only newspapers, but political and religious pamphlets, primers, blanks and all the multifarious issues of the job-printing office.

We have thus, in the Pittsfield of 1800–1810, a thriving agricultural, manufacturing and mercantile town of from 2,000 to 2,500 population; agitated by religious and political feuds which extended in a remarkable degree into the affairs of business and social life; but which, although they were to be deplored, did not absorb all activity of thought, or prevent a great advance of material prosperity. We may add that, sadly divided as society was, it did not hinder—and perhaps by its rivalries encouraged—an exceedingly genial social life, in which "merry England" cropped out very perceptibly above the "stratum of Plymouth Rock."

CHAPTER VI.

POLITICAL FEUDS, AND DIVISION OF THE FIRST PARISH.

Political rancor of the age—Exaggerations of tradition—Illustrative anecdote—State of American politics—Sources of political bitterness peculiar to Berkshire—Berkshire federalists and democrats characterized—Elder Leland, Theodore Sedgwick and Rev. Thomas Allen—Obnoxious sermons preached by Mr. Allen—Woodbridge Little's letter of complaint—Mr. Allen's reply—Action of the dissatisfied—Advice of the Berkshire association of Congregational ministers—Mr. Allen annoyed by newspaper scandals—The Berkshire *Reporter*—Letter from Mr. Allen to Mr. Little—Union parish incorporated—Difficulties in organizing a new church solved by an ex parte council—Church of Union parish instituted—Names of members—Proposals for the resignation of Mr. Allen—Ordination of Rev. Mr. Punderson over Union church—Health of Mr. Allen; he preaches an election sermon at Boston; writes a historical sketch of the town and county; his death; monuments to his memory.

WHILE, as we have seen, and shall see, Pittsfield during the first fifteen years of the nineteenth century was characterized by substantial prosperity, advance in the industrial arts, and great improvements in those branches of agriculture subservient to them, and while it numbered among its citizens an unusual proportion of able men, those years in its history have become widely known in tradition for an excessive political bitterness which bisected the town in its social and business relations—and especially in those of religion—into two hostile camps, with passions more malignant, if their weapons were less fatal, than those of the battle-field.

There is a little exaggeration in all this; but tradition has here shown less than her usual proclivity to pervert facts. Her misrepresentation lies chiefly in what she has forgotten. She has neglected to preserve for us the causes which inevitably rendered this feud exceptionally personal and malignant, and has left us to believe that an excess of political rancor was more peculiar to Pittsfield than it really was. Other towns suffered nearly as much from this baleful strife. Other religious parishes were so divided that harmony was restored, if it was restored at all—except by the healing influence of time—only by the resignation of their pastors. Indeed personal malignancy in political strife was characteristic of the times, and of all classes, from the chief-magistrate of the nation—at least during the first eight years—down to the lowest wrangler in the village bar-room. Nor was this unworthy manifestation of feeling confined to America. "How savage," exclaims Thackeray, speaking of English political writings of the same period, "how savage the satire was, how fierce the assault! What garbage hurled at opponents! What foul blows were hit; what language of Billingsgate flung!" The village-discords of Pittsfield in 1800–1815 were therefore not altogether exceptional.

And again, there was evidently a much larger proportion of the population than the sweeping generalities of tradition would indicate, who were in a greater or less degree uninvolved in the prevailing feud; with whom politics were not an all absorbing, or controlling, consideration. Families were rarely divided by political lines; as the father, so generally were the sons. But the children of democratic and federal families sometimes inter-married, and there is no intimation of any resultant troubles like those which befell poor Romeo and Juliet. A venerable lady tells a story of her younger days, illustrative of the rancor of political feeling, to the effect, that she with her sisters—all staunch federalists—one evening accepted an invitation to accompany certain young gentlemen to a dancing-party at some distance from their home; but reaching the scene of festivity, and finding it the house of a democrat, they sturdily refused to enter, and insisted on returning. This certainly shows a pretty intense feeling on the part of the young ladies; but, on the other hand, we must infer that either they had been receiving the attentions of democrats, or that the gentlemen, in their love for parties of pleasure, were indifferent to their relations with parties in politics. The same lady well remembers the delight with which the visits of the arch-democrat, Parson Allen, were received by the young federalists of her father's house; although that was doubtless not during the more violent paroxysms of the prolonged quarrel.

We are then not to believe that for any long time, or that through the entire community for any time, all the courtesies of life, and all social intercourse were suspended, and that the people of Pittsfield met each other on the street only to scowl and pass by on different sides. Such a state of things would be incredible on much better authority than that of tradition; and it is disproved by abundant testimony.

Nevertheless, although the political quarrels of Pittsfield in these years were not so exceptional, nor quite so absorbing, as tradition represents, they were sufficiently lamentable, and did possess painful peculiarities. It is true that they impeded the material progress of the town, engendered family feuds, and rent in twain the Congregational church and parish, which then comprised by far the larger portion of the population. Under their incitement malignant slanders were invented and circulated; those who ought to have been in private life united in the warmest friendship, became the bitterest enemies, and those whose abilities and influence ought to have been combined for the good of the community, wasted their powers in denunciation of each other. For it was the men of strongest mind and warmest heart, who were most deeply involved in this vain and wasteful strife.

A gentleman of sharp and just thought[1] afterwards collected some of the partisan pamphlets of the Pittsfield presses of that era, and had them bound together under the quaintly-significant title: "The Age of Folly." And, in some of its phases an age of profound folly it surely was, when passion obscured the judgment of the wisest and perverted the conscience of the most pure-minded.

There is, however, another aspect in which it is possible to view the asperities of that era. It must be remembered that there was then raging the most stupendous conflict of arms and of opinions, that ever shook the world; a conflict upon whose issue the world's whole future seemed to depend. Not only did it sway the capitals and the battle-fields of Europe, but the most remote jungles of the east trembled to the thunder of its cannon, and the inmost hamlet of civilized men in the west was agitated by the jar of its debates. It was not a question of mere territorial conquest; of the balance of national power; of commercial policy. It concerned the very basis of all government every-where. The issue was between the divine right of legitimate

[1] Hon. Ezekiel R. Colt.

kings, and the right of the peoples to establish, alter or amend their constitutions. These antagonistic ideas, the world over, were contending for the mastery in a contest so desperate, and so nicely balanced, that the champions of each felt, not without reason, that the slightest aid gained or lost, might be of decisive effect. The great powers which led in the struggle adopted therefore the most unjustifiable measures to force the weaker nations from a wise neutrality. In the United States the same quarrel, translated indeed from English soil, had been so recently fought out, that when the French revolution revived it on so grand a scale in Europe, each side found a great party ready to sympathize with it. And, as the conflict had originally been more bitter and more clearly defined in Berkshire than perhaps in any other locality; so there the revived animosities were correspondingly fiercer. At first, few were willing to avow themselves in favor of actually involving the country in the war. Probably few were so minded. Peace was too precious; the friends of England, who held power, were pre-eminently prudent, and the Gallic party had no object in precipitating a crisis until they had obtained possession of the government. But in the arena of politics there went on the same conflict between old and new forms of thought and action which was fought in the campaigns of Europe; with this essential difference, that what in Europe was still revolutionary, had come in America to be simply progressive, while conservatism, if it assumed the European type or allied itself with it, was reactionary.

At bottom, indeed, among the masses of the American people, the difference of aims and opinions was much less than mutual jealousies, and the expressions of extreme but representative men, made them appear. But so long as each party earnestly believed in the evil intentions of the other, it did not matter how just that belief might be, so far as its effect on the virulence of the times was concerned. Or rather, the more erroneous the belief, the more exasperating were its effects; for each party, true to the instincts of human nature, oblivious to its own injustice, perceived and resented only that of which it was the object. Such, in general, was the state of public feeling in America during the whole period covered by the political feuds of Pittsfield, from 1790 to the close of the second war with Great Britain; varying, of course, in intensity with the varying incitements of public events. And what was true of the general conflict, was often more intensely so of the little hand-to-hand local encounters.

But in order to show how legitimately and inevitably the dissensions we are about to relate were the outgrowth of the times, a little more than a general statement is requisite.

The fact is familiar to the reader that the constitution of the United States, as framed by the convention of 1787, was not in all its provisions acceptable either to the progressive or the conservative elements in the proposed union; and that its final adoption was secured only with great difficulty. Concessions which had in convention been reluctantly yielded, by one side or the other, to the necessity of compromise, had to be argued anew before the people,—a more unyielding tribunal; and, after all, the work, as a whole, was only accepted by the states, with the hope strongly held out that the amendments, of which most of them proposed several, would be obtained in the near future. In the state conventions the radical democracy—then known as anti-federalists—continued unconditionally to oppose the ratification.[1]

The conservatives, on the other hand, while they distrusted the new form of government as without sufficient powers for its own preservation, yet saw in it an immeasurable advance upon the old confederacy, and the only escape from impending anarchy. They therefore warmly advocated its adoption; gaining thereby the name of federalists, and with it much popular favor when the successful working of the new institutions seemed to prove their superior wisdom. Their enemies, however, charged that they favored it as a cunningly-prepared stepping-stone towards a monarchical or an aristocratic state. The government was organized under the new constitution in March, 1789, and happily being administered with the same wisdom which created it, its effect upon the prosperity and happiness of the country was so manifest that all parties hastened to declare their allegiance to it. The federalists, however, continued to distrust it as too weak

[1] In that of Massachusetts Pittsfield was represented by Capt. David Bush and Valentine Rathbun, both ultra-democrats, and on the final vote Mr. Rathbun gave the voice of the town against its ratification, doubtless in accordance with the wish of his constituency. There were at that time some very able and earnest federalists in Pittsfield, and the question of the adoption of the constitution evidently excited no little ferment; but it seems to have been far less violent than the political agitations which preceded and followed it; and we have no details regarding it, even in tradition.

to meet any violent storm; the democrats still proclaimed that it was necessary to keep a vigilant watch upon its aristocratical and monarchical tendencies, and as soon as possible, to introduce into the constitution itself a check upon them. That instrument was, indeed, literally but a frame; and a frame capable, in the hands of perverse builders, of becoming a very different structure from that which was actually developed. Much depended upon the construction which might be put upon many articles by judicial and legislative decisions; much sometimes upon what the practice of the people acting through political parties should make custom.[1]

Distrust as to the practical working of the constitution arose, then, not only from the uncertainty which overhangs all experiments of this nature, however honestly conducted; but also from dread of the interpretation which those in power might choose to place upon some of its clauses. "Other constitutions," said the democrats, "have been wrested from meanings as plainly worded as this, to the utter perversion of their intent; why should not ours?" And it must be confessed that this jealousy was not without reason; but it is to the credit of the federal judges and the federal majorities, that their decisions and practice were generally just, and almost always leaned to the liberal side.

The dominant party were prudent, just and moderate; the minority were for the most part men of sense, and although perhaps morbidly jealous of their liberties, had no disposition to disturb a public tranquillity which they perceived indispensable to individual as well as national prosperity; and, although, doubtless, under any circumstances the wholesome conflict between conservative and progressive ideas would have kept alive healthful political action, there is no reason to believe that the early years of the republic would have been disturbed by party quarrels of more than ordinary violence, had no incitement come from abroad, and had not the people honestly believed that the rights and liberties of America were involved with those of Europe.

Questions as to the development of natural resources, the

---

[1] The case of the change in the functions of the electoral college from what the framers of the constitution plainly intended it to be, furnishes a good illustration, although the subversion of a plain meaning is exceptional. Judicial, legislative and popular interpretation ordinarily took effect only where the original language was equivocal.

encouragement of manufactures, the extension of commerce, concerning the respective powers of the state and national governments, and the like, often appeared sharply; but so clearly was domestic tranquillity essential to individual and national prosperity, that even politicians of extreme views were, at least at the north, content to postpone abstract constitutional reforms until "practical inconvenience" should prove their necessity. Thus even a man of so extreme views as Theodore Sedgwick, in a letter to Peter Van Schaack, dated November, 1791, declines to agitate for a change in the judiciary, "because, if it should be attempted to reform the system by proposing an amendment, it may excite all the agitations of federal and anti-federal passions, which now seem to be dormant through all the northern and eastern states."

But, simultaneously with the organization of the federal government, the French revolution began to take definite form by the meeting of the States General and their speedy resolution into "The National Assembly." In America this first act of the grand drama was hailed with almost universal joy, as the substitution of a free constitution for an arbitrary and often grossly-tyrannical despotism. The proclamation of a French republic, although attended by excesses that awakened the fears of the more observing, was generally welcomed as bringing into closer sisterhood with the Union, the great nation which had been its ally in the war of independence; while it flattered the national pride by the sincere homage of imitating our example. Soon, however, the hideous atrocities of the reign of terror, exaggerated by report even beyond the frightful reality, excited the horror and dread of the more timid and conservative classes. In the example of France they saw the realization of their own predictions concerning the results of popular rule. All had witnessed, some had experienced in their own person, the rigors of committee-rule in the times of the revolution. It needed, they considered, only the absolute powers which similar bodies had attained in France, for the committees, or the party in which their spirit, and much of their personnel, survived, to re-enact upon American soil the tragedy which was desolating France. Jefferson, the great leader of the anti-federalists, just returned from Paris, imbued with the most radical Jacobinism, was, they averred and sincerely believed, assaulting not only the administration, but the very foundation of the government. His success involved their ruin. When, therefore, England became the champion of public order and established institutions throughout the civilized world, the federal became an Anglican party.

On the other hand, the anti-federalists—who soon shook off that name for the more popular appellative of republicans—while they must have shuddered at the tales of horror which every ship that crossed the Atlantic brought from Paris, Lyons, or La Vendée, were taught to believe them the inventions, in great part, of the English press; and, bad as the truth was confessed to be, to offset it with the cruelties of kings and nobles which had been endured for ages. The excesses of the republicans, they were told, were but the ebullitions of a newly-enfranchised people avenging itself for the oppression of generations; they would soon subside into a healthy tranquillity. "A few months of the Temple and the Conciergerie," said the more violent, "are not too much to atone for centuries of the Bastile." The slaughters by which the republic sought to exterminate its enemies, revolting as they were confessed to be, it was said—and said to Protestants of the strictest sect—were no worse than those which, by royal edict, sought to extirpate Protestantism in France. The sensual orgies and debaucheries of Robespierre, Le Bon and their fellow-fiends, devilish as they were, it was said, were no more so than those of the Parc-aux-Cerfs, or the palace of the Regent Orleans; and this was said to the sternest of republicans, who prized the honor of the simplest citizen's wife or daughter, at least equally with that of the noblest lady. And thus, while they personally sympathized with sufferings endured by the victims of the revolution, if that sympathy affected the political opinions of the republicans at all, it was to increase their detestation for that system of government, whose prolonged tyranny had rendered so terrible a retribution inevitable. The right and the duty of the French people to reform their government, at any cost, they not only did not question, but vigorously upheld.

At home, they found the loyalists of the revolution giving the most ardent support to the federal administration, while many who had been the truest patriots in that struggle boldly avowed, or unmistakably showed, their distrust of republicanism, and their preference for the British constitution. It was easy, therefore, to revive in the democratic masses the scarcely-dormant hatred of England, which had been engendered by a cruel war, whose story was now sedulously revived, and the more so as the British government was at the moment vigorously endeavoring to suppress free thought on her own soil. When Great Britain placed herself at the head of an alliance of despotic powers, whose avowed object was to protect the divine right of kings against all revolutions, it was easy to attribute to her an intention, should the holy alliance triumph in Europe, to give its purpose a retroactive scope for her own benefit on this side of the water; and to attribute also to the American conservatives the intention of restoring, under her protection, either the old order of things, or a new kingdom, with perhaps a cadet of the house of Brunswick on the throne. Thus ruin to themselves and their country which the federalists feared from the triumph of France, the republicans anticipated in case England and her allies, by victory in Europe, became arbiters of the world's destiny: and so the Anglican party in America was matched by a Gallic.

The usurpation of Napoleon made but little change in the relations of these parties to each other. Military despotism was not more pleasing to the conservatives than democratic license; and with the republicans the emperor's victories over the objects of their hatred more than atoned for his treachery to the republic of their hopes.

There was, to be sure, a third party, or rather a third class of minds, which included some of the greatest leaders of the early federalists, and whose wiser statesmanship foresaw, what actually happened, that when the European conflict should end, victor and vanquished would have so exhausted each other that they would be compelled to leave the rest of the world at peace to pursue its own way to its own better future. Their policy was, under the protection of a strict neutrality, to augment the wealth and harmonize the government of the country, to organize a sufficient naval and military force to protect the coast against sudden and desultory inroads of either belligerent, and patiently wait the event. Happily for the country this policy ruled in the administration of Washington, and measurably in that of John Adams. The insolence of French ambassadors and emissaries was rebuked, and the piracies of the French fleets resisted, with dignity and effect, while entangling alliance with England was avoided. Commerce flourished, manufactures increased, and agriculture found a lucrative market in the ports of both belligerents.

There were few politicians of name, so hardy as to advocate direct interference in the European quarrel at the expense of war. Still the deep sympathy of the federal party with England could not be mistaken. It was constantly manifested in the comments of its journals on foreign affairs, and in the remarkably hearty support which its members gave to the enforcement of the neutrality laws, as against France. And even less could the partiality of the republicans for the French cause be concealed, while they did their best to make those laws a nullity in its behalf, and while their journals constantly denounced Washington and Adams as tyrants and despots, for the most necessary measures in support of the dignity and independence of the government. These journals, by-the-bye, were often edited by foreigners, banished from their own country for the extreme radicalism of their teachings, who infused into their columns the vindictiveness of exile in addition to the bitterness of party spirit. The hatred of Great Britain cherished by the most unrelenting revolutionary whig was tame compared with the rage of the radical just driven from his home for a too ardent expression of his opinions.

But it would lead us too far from our purpose to enumerate all the elements which went to envenom the seething caldron of political hatred between the outbreak of the French revolution and the close of the war of 1812. What concerns us here are the causes which gave to the political contests of Pittsfield and Berkshire county an acrimony, exceptional, at least at the North, even in that era.

Of these the smoldering feuds, which had come down from the days of committee-rule, have already been mentioned. Even before the close of the war, it will be remembered, the conservative whigs and the tories had fraternized in behalf of what they considered law and order. The same community of sentiment afterwards combined the same elements still more intimately in the federal party, and elevated to office some who had been most obnoxious during the war. An instance which excited the warmest indignation of the republicans was the appointment by President Adams of John Stoddard, a son of the tory Israel Stoddard, postmaster of Pittsfield, in place of Col. Joshua Danforth, a gallant officer of the revolution, who had been appointed by Washington when the office was established in 1794.

The treatment of the old soldiers was indeed in the minds of the masses a source of grievous complaint against the federalists, who numbered among their ranks few who had seen active service, except when the militia were called out on some sudden emergency. The discharged soldier, returned from camp with the vices contracted in long service far more conspicuous than the virtues for whose display no opportunity now offered, appeared much less a hero than he did when the terror-stricken community begged his services. The man who had passed the best years of his life in the service of a bankrupt country was a far less respectable person than he who had seized the opportunities of the war to enrich himself. And the federal party cared for none but respectable persons.

The affectation of a social superiority and contempt for the masses on the part of some of the federal leaders in Berkshire, furnished a source of constant irritation, and the democratic writers retaliated by enlarging upon the vulgarity and coarseness of active members of that party, upon the meanness of their parentage, and the sources from which they derived their birth. "A beggar's brat" was the pleasant epithet applied to a man of wealth and culture; and another was delicately characterized as "a coarse, vulgar and illiterate fellow who sought position by clinging to the coat-tails of men who made use of and despised him." When there was a spice of truth in these assaults they were not soon forgotten or easily forgiven.

Hon. Theodore Sedgwick of Stockbridge was the great leader and representative man of the Berkshire federalists, and we present a portrait of him, drawn by the hand of his daughter, the distinguished author, as giving a vivid idea of the politics and political sentiment of his day.

I was a child at the period of the great ferment occasioned by the decline of the federal party and the growth of the democratic party. My father had the habit of having his children always about him, and we had so strong a sympathy with him that there was no part of his life which we did not partake. I remember well looking upon a democrat as an enemy to his country, and the party as sure, if it prevailed, to work its destruction. I heard my father's conversation with his political friends, and in the spontaneous expressions of domestic privacy, and I received the impression then (and looking back I feel assured of its correctness) that the federal party loved their country, and were devoted to it as virtuous parents are to their children. It was to my father what selfish men's private affairs are to them, of deep and ever-present interest. It was not the success of men, or the acquisition of office, but the maintenance of principles on which, as it appeared to them, the sound health and true life of their country depended. They dreaded French influence—they believed Jefferson to be false, the type of evil—they were a good deal influenced by old prestiges—they retained their predilections for Great Britain. They hoped a republic might exist and prosper, and be the happiest government in the world, *but not without a strong aristocratic element;* and that the constitutional government of Britain was the safest and happiest government on earth, I am sure they believed."

"But firm to the experiment of the republic, they had no treasonable thought of introducing a monarchy here. Their misfortune, and perhaps the inevitable consequence of having been educated loyal subjects of a monarchical government, was a thorough distrust of 'the people.' I remember my father, one of the kindest-hearted of men, and most observant of the rights of all beneath him, habitually spoke of the people as 'Jacobins,' 'sans-culottes,' and 'miscreants.' He—and in this I speak of him as the type of the federal party—dreaded every upward step they made, regarding their elevation as a depression, in proportion to their ascension, of the intelligence and virtue of the country. The upward tendencies from education, and improvements in the arts of life were unknown to them. They judged of the people, as they had been, as were the greasy unwashed multitude of Rome and of Shakspeare's time—as they are now for the most part in Europe—utterly inexperienced in government, incapable of attaining to its abstractions, or feeling its moralities."[1]

This portraiture of the political character and sentiments of Judge Sedgwick, drawn by the loving hand of a daughter, well qualified to comprehend and describe them, are precisely such as were attributed to him and his associates by the Pittsfield republicans of 1800; and it is not strange that they believed that men with such views would seize the first opportunity, or make one, to establish here the form of government which they deemed the "happiest and safest on earth." It is barely possible that some chivalrous sense of honor might have held a man like Judge Sedgwick "firm to the experiment of a republic;" but it is clear that he would have been a most unsafe person to decide when

[1] Life and letters of Miss Catherine M. Sedgwick.

that experiment had failed. Probably no party ever numbered among its leaders a larger proportion of men distinguished for honor and integrity than the federal; but they were politicians for all that; and it would have been strange indeed if, finding themselves strongly entrenched in power, they had not availed themselves of it, to substitute their ideal of a perfect constitution for the democratic institutions which they held to be so fearfully dangerous to all that was good in government, society and religion. The most impartial judgment must concede that the Pittsfield republicans had good reason to consider their opponents as the enemies at heart of free institutions.

Nor could the masses of the people be expected to cherish the most amicable feeling towards gentlemen who held them in such estimation as Judge Sedgwick did. It doubtless seemed to Berkshire men an unjust thing to be characterized by those who had lived among them all their days, not by their own lives and actions, but by an ideal picture of the people of other times and countries—and exaggerated even as to them—which Shakspeare had placed in the mouths of some of the least admirable of his public characters. Possibly had the federal leaders studied their neighbors a little more candidly, they might have understood them better, interpreted Shakspeare more correctly, and led their party to a less ignominious fate.

To the flax of such a party as this, the Pittsfield democracy was the natural fire. Those who have followed us in our account of Rev. Thomas Allen, and his associates, from the opening of the revolution, will readily conceive that they had little toleration to bestow upon opponents like these. Hating the name of king with a fiercer hatred than Brutus ever did, they believed, and had good reason to believe, as Miss Sedgwick's testimony shows, that the federalists desired to erect a monarchy in America, and it would have been too much to expect them to trust to the personal honor of the leaders, that they would not seek to gratify that desire. Nourishing even morbid memories of the wrongs done their country by Great Britain, they found their adversaries cherishing an almost fanatical affection for her. Looking forward with the hope of an even more liberal constitution, they found themselves confronted by efforts to establish a still "stronger" government.

Indoctrinated early by the grand republican writers of the

English commonwealth; in later years stimulated in their love of a liberal government by the pamphleteers, the orators and the events of the revolution; in age their blood was fired by the flaming columns of the Jeffersonian newspapers, and by sympathy with the great conflict between legitimate and revolutionary rule in Europe. Veterans of a third of a century, the older leaders were as ardent, as inflexible and as unforgiving as they had been in youth, firmly believing that they upheld the same good old cause against its old enemies.

In 1791 the democracy of Berkshire received new inspiration and vigor by the return from Virginia, where he had resided for several years, of Elder John Leland, of Cheshire, a Baptist clergyman of unusual powers and of vehement feeling. Mr. Leland was in many respects a remarkable man. Of bold, clear and original thought, he reasoned unflinchingly upon all subjects, religious and secular, from the evidence in his possession, to logical conclusions, whatever they might be. And whatever he fully believed, he proclaimed with a rugged and sometimes quaint eloquence, which was exceedingly convincing to such audiences as he addressed. In Virginia he had become the intimate friend of Jefferson and other great leaders of the national democracy, by whom he was highly esteemed; and on his return to Berkshire he formed a link of more immediate connection between his confreres in that county and the central councils of the party. And this communication was maintained by his frequent friendly and professional visits to the Old Dominion. The injustice done to the Baptists and other dissenting Christians by the laws of Massachusetts, to which the great body of the democrats were opposed, still further embittered him against the federalists who—with a few exceptions, principally Episcopalians—strongly supported them. This grievance was a frequent theme of his discourses.

Mr. Leland spoke often in Pittsfield both upon religious and political subjects, and, his liberalism, in regard to both church and state government being about as extreme as it well could be, the effect of his teaching in this form, as well as in his constant correspondence with the *Sun*, may well be imagined. One result to which they largely contributed was perfect harmony in the Baptist and Methodist churches, which was secured by making their members nearly or quite unanimous on the democratic side.

In the Congregational, or town, parish, unhappily, no such harmony was attainable. A majority of the church, and a very large proportion of the wealthier members of the parish, were federalists, and had long sat uneasily under their pastor's introduction of political subjects into his "pulpit discourses." In common with other clergymen of the revolutionary era, and as effectively as any, he had preached the gospel of liberty. From the pulpit he had also denounced the non-constitutional government of Massachusetts previous to 1781, and afterwards the Shays rebellion. He had also, in the same manner, doubtless opposed the adoption of the federal constitution; for in 1788, we find his "interesting himself in his official capacity in political affairs," alleged as one of the causes of the dissensions in the town and parish."[1]

A reconciliation by formal vote of the town, and a covenant of peace for the future, averted at that time the threatened disruption of the church and parish, and Pittsfield partook of that rest from federal and anti-federal passions, noted by Theodore Sedgwick as existing in 1792. These halcyon days continued—although they began to be much disturbed during the presidential candidacy, and first years of the administration of John Adams—until the smoldering passions were roused in more than their original fury by the famous "resolutions of '98," passed by the legislature of Kentucky, and, in a still more startling form, by that of Virginia.

These resolutions, which had been drafted by Thomas Jefferson, immediately became the corner-stone of the democratic party, while they excited the utmost abhorrence of the federalists. Mr. Allen received them as the old war-horse hears the sound of a trumpet. From the date of the declaration of independence, he had been among the most devoted of Mr. Jefferson's admirers and adherents. He regarded him as the champion of civil liberty, whose cause, in 1798 as in 1776, he considered identical with that of religious freedom and protestant Christianity. Federalism, aiming at monarchy, he held to be the arch-enemy of the one, and consequently of the other of these chief objects of his devotion; and to do battle valiantly against this foe of human rights, he thought the first of duties towards both God and man.

[1] See vol. I., page 418.

Bold attacks upon this political monster with him covered a multitude of sins, leading him to condone the avowed deism of Thomas Paine, and indignantly deny the infidelity which was one of the favorite charges of the federal press against Mr. Jefferson.

Holding these views, Mr. Allen was unwilling to relinquish the right to discuss, or at least to express his opinion upon, public affairs, in the pulpit. This was a privilege which had always been conceded to, and held dear by, the New England clergy, from the days of the Pilgrims down; and it was in Mr. Allen's time freely exercised by most of his clerical brethren, federal as well as democratic; and in regard to many subjects— such as slavery and temperance, is constantly used by the clergy to this day.

And, if it was, and is, justifiable and praiseworthy for the pulpit to advocate what the preacher deems right, and to denounce what he believes wrong, in matters such as these; then it was certainly at least excusable in Mr. Allen that he, "in his official capacity," took ground against a party which considered the elevation of the people as a misfortune greatly to be deprecated, and which might be reasonably expected to defeat it so far as it had the power. In the light of the present day, we suspect that there are many who would agree with him in counting such an organization, as to that particular, "oppugnant to the gospel of Jesus Christ," however eminent its members might be for piety. And there are few who, if they could find a political administration, the corner-stone of whose policy was the elevation of all men, would think it blasphemy to style it a Christocracy, as Mr. Allen is said to have characterized the government of Mr. Jefferson.

We do not, of course, here pretend to decide whether Mr. Allen's estimate of the rival parties of his day was correct or otherwise, but merely to show that he endeavored zealously to perform his duty, as a citizen and a Christian minister, as from his stand-point it appeared clear to him; and that his opinions were not the result of prejudice, or of old feuds, but were reasonably warranted by the character and utterances of the leading men of the antagonistic party, at least in his immediate vicinity. Nor do we undertake to judge of the abstract propriety of introducing political matter into the pulpit; but simply to remind the reader that such has been almost the uniform practice of all religious denominations in New England, with the exception of the Episcopalians. There was nothing therefore out of the usual course, in the merely preaching of politics by the Pittsfield pastor. The ferment which arose from it, seems to have been occasioned by the fact that the doctrines which he preached were not those of the wealthier portion of his people, or of the great majority of the churches of New England, who looked upon Mr. Jefferson as the foe of religion as well as of sound government.

Another source of dissatisfaction with Mr. Allen on the part of the federalists was his intimate relations with the Pittsfield *Sun*, which were described in a previous chapter. His printed articles were more pronounced in their partisan character than his sermons, and his federal parishioners, not unnaturally, when the phraseology was similar, interpreted many paragraphs in the Sunday's discourse, which would otherwise have had only a general application, by the light thrown upon them from the columns of the *Sun*. Unfortunately, also, as his articles usually appeared editorially or over a *nom de plume*, some, whose authorship he afterwards disclaimed, were ascribed to him.

In this feverish state, affairs stood with the parish of Pittsfield and its pastor, on Thanksgiving day, 1802, when the first of four sermons of which special and formal complaint was afterwards made, was preached. In this production, the administration of Mr. Adams was most unfavorably contrasted with that of Mr. Jefferson. The federalists also charged it upon the preacher as a sort of blasphemy, that he had "likened the latter to the Savior of the world, in that, 'being reviled, he reviled not again;'" although it would be difficult, since all men are required to form themselves upon the likeness of the Redeemer, to detect the sin in believing and declaring that one man, even though the head of a party, had in a single particular, in some degree, modeled himself in that likeness. That Mr. Jefferson had reached this state of Christian and non-resistant meekness is more to be doubted.

The second of the specially-arraigned sermons was preached in April, 1803, upon the fortieth anniversary of Mr. Allen's settlement in Pittsfield. This discourse, like the first, contrasted the administrations of Adams and Jefferson, representing, as the friends of Mr. Adams alleged, that the former "was opposed to the gospel and to the happiness of the people; and thanking God that the preacher had lived through it to the present glorious period" of democratic triumph and rule. "He declared," said the federal pamphleteer, "that our government was a Christocracy, and that oppugnation to it was oppugnation to the gospel of Christ; adding: 'We are not party-men but opposed to aristocratic domination.'"

Rev. William Allen, in his pamphlet defense of his father printed in 1809, claimed that the expressions quoted had reference to republican institutions generally, as established by the American constitution, and that the application of them to particular parties or politicians was an unwarrantable assumption of jealous minds. The federalists sustained their interpretation by citing the context, and the author's opinions "as openly and plainly expressed in conversation, and in the columns of the *Sun*."

Mr. Allen's sermons were written in short-hand, and not always fully even in that. Often in the heat of delivery, he introduced glowing extemporaneous passages, and it is probable that in the sermons of which complaint was made he may thus have used language which he avoided in the calmness of his study. But we have noted his habit of identifying political with religious heresy, and the tenacity with which he clung to the old privilege of the Congregational clergy, of rebuking one as well as the other in the pulpit. This is the simple key to his whole course in this controversy; and, however carefully his words may have been chosen, there can be little doubt that his hearers made the proper application of them. If he erred in any of his dealings with his parishioners, his true and sufficient apology must be sought in the intense ardor and earnestness of his devotion to free institutions and whatever tended to the elevation of his fellowmen.

The third sermon of the offensive series was preached by Mr. Allen upon the death of his son, Thomas, whose life is sketched in the preceding chapter. It was printed, and does not seem to bear out the character ascribed to it by the federalists; but, on the contrary, to have been a most solemn and touching funeral discourse, such as might have been expected from a father mourning his first-born and well-beloved son.

In March, 1807, the dissatisfied members of the parish and church appointed a committee consisting of Woodbridge Little,

Joseph Fairfield, Ashbel Strong and Eli Maynard, who addressed to their pastor a "letter of remonstrance," setting forth their grievances arising from these sermons. It was written by Mr. Little, and shows that his pen had lost none of its sharpness since he employed it in behalf of his brother-loyalists in the early days of the revolution.[1]

The following extract contains the gist of all the complaints against Mr. Allen:

"In the sermon delivered soon after the death of your son, as it was preached, you appeared more disposed to deliver a political harangue, calculated to affect the approaching election, than to afford consolation to his afflicted relatives and mourning friends, or instructions from such an instance of mortality, to the congregation at large. Your sermon next preceding the April election in 1806—the text of which was, "And no man laid hands on him, for his hour was not yet come,"—was plainly an offensive political and electioneering discourse, in the improvement of which you alluded to the idea that our wicked rulers were permitted, in this state, to be continued over us because at the previous election their hour for dismission had not yet come; yet you urged to perseverance to the end, and foretold that the coming election would effect the looked-for change. Though in this discourse your language was not explicit, yet it was clearly understood by the audience.

Your discourses generally from February, 1806, to the time of your going to Boston in May, were constantly interlarded with politics. Your sermon on the Sabbath next after the last New Year's day was most pointedly irritating and insulting, and has caused very general uneasiness in the town. Your conduct on the 4th of March current, and the toast you then gave and repeated—" No compromise with federalists, no concurrence with neuters,"—we consider as drawing the sword against us and throwing away the scabbard. Your sermon on the Sabbath after, we view as a pointed declaration that your future conduct should comport with that sentiment; for you then knew of our complaints against you, and our uneasiness on that account, yet you asserted that, for forty-three years past, you had preached nothing but

---

[1] Mr. Little stated at this time, that "he had always been the friend of Mr. Allen and his family;" but Hon. Ezekiel Bacon, a competent witness, wrote to Hon. H. C. Van Schaack as follows: " Mr Little was a lawyer by profession, I believe of quite respectable standing, and I think king's attorney for the county when the revolution came on. His town and county were mostly very zealous whigs, particularly the clergyman of the parish, Rev. Thomas Allen, who then, and also in the federal and democratic times, pursued Mr. Little, as he and his friends, at least, thought, pretty warmly and inexorably. However that might be, *there was no love lost between them.*"

Christ and Him crucified, or truths and doctrines therewith connected; and that you should pursue the same line or manner of preaching in future, notwithstanding the menaces of your opposers : which clearly imports, either that you had been menaced on account of preaching such doctrines, or that you consider all your political preaching as consonant therewith; neither of which is admitted." * * * "It gives us no little uneasiness that, while our feelings are thus harassed up and lacerated by your public discourses—while many of your own political adherents are dissatisfied with such sermons, and some of them have told you so—while too many of the uncandid and injudicious are indecently grinning their smiles of approbation, to the disturbance of public worship, and while it is not an unusual thing to hear them, leaving the house, declare that 'the parson has given the federalists a proper dressing to-day,'—you are declaring that you do not preach on political subjects, yet at other times with a strange inconsistency, you have boldly declared that you considered republicanism, or democracy, as exhibited in the administration of Mr. Jefferson, to be the very essence of the gospel of Jesus Christ. We complain of your publications in the *Sun*, and more particularly that 'on the death of Hamilton,' and also that 'on the execution of Wheeler.'[1]

"We complain of your giving public notice in the meeting-house, on the Sabbath day, that the 4th of March would be celebrated in this town as a day of thanksgiving and praise, etc., and of your introduction at a conference-meeting on the evening of the 3d of March, of the political song which was to be sung by your party on the day following."[2]

This extract will give a vivid idea of the temper of the times,

[1] The article upon the death of Hamilton was exceedingly severe in its criticism of that greatest leader and idol of the federal party, and represented his death to have been a divine judgment. The article upon the execution of Wheeler, who was hanged for rape committed upon his own daughter, bitterly censured the federal governor of Massachusetts for not commuting his sentence to imprisonment for life. Rev. Wm. Allen does not expressly deny his father's authorship of these articles ; but he states that of six articles in the *Sun*, including these, which were attributed by the federalists to him, three, at least, were not written by him. He maintains, however, his father's right to have written them, and explains with regard to the Wheeler article, that he was, with thousands of others, strongly opposed to the punishment of death except for murder. In regard to the amelioration of the laws, the Pittsfield minister was, from the first to the last, an earnest reformer.

[2] This charge was reduced by Rev. Wm. Allen to the fact that his father gave permission to rehearse the piece in the school-house, where the meeting was held, after the congregation had been dismissed, and that he invited those who wished to remain and listen.

as well as of the complaints made against Mr. Allen. He replied in the following letter:

PITTSFIELD, March 31, 1807.

To Woodbridge Little and Ashbel Strong, Esquires, Mr. Joseph Fairfield and Mr. Eli Maynard, committee from the aggrieved part of my flock:

GENTLEMEN: Woodbridge Little has drawn up, with the assistance of Mr. Williams and others, a paper containing false and malevolent charges against your pastor, which you have signed as being true.

Two things I request of you.

1. That you would lay said paper of charges before your constituents whom you represent, and that they do not condemn me as guilty of them, unheard; nor scourge a man that is an American, uncondemned.

2. You say in your paper, that you shall be ready to accept of me adequate and reasonable satisfaction, corresponding with the nature and equity of the case; but have left me wholly in the dark as to what you shall be pleased to deem adequate and reasonable satisfaction. If I do not know what my people want of me, how shall I be able to gratify their wishes? You will, therefore, be pleased to tell me what satisfaction will be agreeable to you. Do you desire any *pecuniary* satisfaction? If so, how much will satisfy you? Or do you desire a confession from me? You will dictate one for me and send it to me. Otherwise I shall not be able to ascertain what will satisfy you. Or do you want a promise in respect to my future preaching? You must express to me the nature and extent of such promise—for you may call anything and everything political.

You will, therefore, expressly and clearly define the restraints you design to put me under in my preaching, and substitute your *consciences* and mandates in the room of mine. Be pleased to satisfy my mind on these topics in order to enable me to give you that adequate and reasonable satisfaction, for my manifold offenses, which you demand.

I can do nothing on that subject 'till I hear from you again.

I am, gentlemen, with due respect, your sincere friend and affectionate pastor, THOMAS ALLEN.

A full meeting of "the dissatisfied" voted this reply "unsatisfactory," and appointed Mr. Little with four others to request Mr. Allen to call a church-meeting, and, if they could agree, unite with him in calling a mutual council to hear and advise the conflicting parties; otherwise to take the proper measures for calling an *ex parte* council.

Mr. Allen declined to unite in calling a council "the way not being properly prepared for it,"[1] and the dissatisfied, through a committee of which Mr. Little was again chairman, asked the advice of the Berkshire Association of Congregational ministers, which met at Lenox on the third Tuesday of June. This body made the following response:

"GENTLEMEN: This association feel it a very delicate matter to give advice in the case you have stated to us, because the official character of the pastor of the church in Pittsfield is concerned in it; but, reflecting on the present unhappy and threatening state of the church, we have been influenced to converse together on the subject, and now communicate to you the result of our deliberations.

"We are of opinion that for any members of the church to unite together, or with any others, in measures which implicate the character of your pastor, either as unchristian or imprudent, is an unjustifiable step. If any of the brethren have done this we recommend it to them to embrace the earliest opportunity to acknowledge to the pastor their fault. If, however, difficulties threatening the peace of the church and the town should still subsist, it is our opinion that the brethren should act agreeably to the rule prescribed by the Head of the Church in the eighteenth chapter of Matthew, and take the private steps of discipline with their pastor. If these steps should not produce the desired effect in bringing about a reconciliation, we advise the aggrieved brethren to take no other steps in a matter of so much importance, without having the counsel of able and wise men.

DAVID PERRY, *Moderator.*
ALBERT SAMUEL SHEPARD, *Scribe.*
Lenox, June 17, 1807.

Mr. Allen's friends took exception to this paper on the ground that it was so expressed as "to lead the seceding members of his church to think that he was worthy of discipline," thus in fact condemning one of their ministerial brethren unheard, and without even a statement in writing of the things laid to his charge. On this latter ground, indeed, Rev. Mr. Perry of Richmond, although a federalist, and although he signed the proceedings as moderator, protested against them. The complainants, on the contrary, maintained that their irregularity in failing to take the preliminary gospel-steps of discipline was merely technical, and that they had been led into it by Mr. Allen's own request that the committee should make their communications to him in writing.

[1] This phrase alludes to a technical difficulty, which will appear in the progress of the controversy.

To this again it might well have been replied, that the mode of procedure enjoined in the gospel, according to St. Matthew, contemplated as the essential first step, the private action of an individual, and that the very existence of a committee pre-supposed a violation of covenant obligations in forming a union for combined action; thus destroying the privacy which the Head of the Church had ordained, in order to prevent the obstacles which the publicity of a quarrel inevitably interposes to reconciliation. Mr. Allen and his son laid great stress upon this irregularity of procedure, and the former based his refusal to submit the matters in controversy to a church-meeting, on the ground that their introduction was barred by a by-law requiring that there should be first filed a certificate that the prescribed gospel-steps had been taken without effect.

Mr. Little had always considered it improper to deal with the pastor of a church, in a case of alleged misconduct, as with a private member, and " after careful deliberation had formed the opinion that it was regular and expedient to confer with Mr. Allen through a committee; " a view which seems also to have obtained with a minority of the Berkshire Association, repugnant as it is to the genius of Congregationalism.

The expediency of such a course seemed, however, much more apparent than its regularity; and whatever rightfulness pertained to it arose from the circumstances of this particular case, rather than from any distinction recognized in Congregational usage between pastor and people. Variation from the ordinary method of procedure was justified, if at all, by these facts: First, that the original affront was given to a party, and not specially to any individual, however much resentment for it might have rankled in individual breasts. Secondly, the offense was publicly given, and the anger which it aroused was immediately as publicly manifested; and thus, while the combined action of those aggrieved was natural, the privacy enjoined in the first of the " gospel-steps " was in the nature of the case impracticable. It was only an obstacle to the amicable adjustment, which all professed to desire, that one party sought to enforce, and the other pretended to comply with, precepts which, if they had ever, in some remote stage of the controversy, been applicable, had long ceased to furnish a guide in the pursuit of peace; precepts which, whatever may have been the letter of the law, could no longer be enforced or obeyed. The very attempt to hold communication under the fraternal forms and affectionate phraseology of Christian brotherhood, seems a mockery, if not a profanation, when the whole substance of the correspondence proves that—however honestly the parties may have persuaded themselves to the contrary—the relations of pastor and parishioner, of Christian with Christian, had long been lost and absorbed in those of democrat and federalist.

The awkward attempt of Mr. Little to put himself right on the record, in accordance with the advice of the Berkshire Association will illustrate the absurdity of the position. He thus relates the manner of his confession to his pastor:

"In my conversation with Mr. Allen I intimated no regret that I had engaged in the affair [the withdrawal from attendance on his preaching] but informed him that it proceeded from pure and honest motives, from regard to the peace and unity of the town, and to prevent a division; not from any malice or ill-will towards him. That I had always been friendly to him and his family. But I finally told him that, *if* the *particular mode* of proceeding which was pursued gave him offense, I was sorry for it and asked his pardon; that it *might* be erroneous—not that I was convinced of it—but did not pretend to be infallible. Indeed I meant to convey the idea, that a party might be honest in his purposes, and yet take erroneous measures to obtain them. If I had done so, I was sorry."

In this statement, while Mr. Little lays down some very sound general truths, it is clear that he does not consider himself to have been at all in the wrong. Mr. Allen was quite right in regarding his acknowledgments, guarded as they were with qualifications from beginning to end, as in no sense a confession of injury done his pastor. Yet it was all that he could truthfully and conscientiously have said. Here, as throughout the prolonged controversy, it is apparent that the parties had removed themselves to such widely-separated stand-points, in the all-absorbing questions of politics, that unity, even in the church, was simply impossible.

While this diplomatic correspondence was passing, rumors and suspicions, taking the form of assertion, and even malicious stories, the product of pure invention, found their way into the town-newspapers, were gravely believed by the partisan-readers on each side, and sadly increased the malignancy of the strife.

One of the grosser and more unfounded of these calumnies will serve to illustrate their character. In July, 1808, Governor Gore, making the tour of the state, with much pomp and circumstance, reached Berkshire, and visited its principal towns; Pittsfield twice. On his second visit he was honored with a salute of seventeen guns; the buildings on Park square were illuminated, and the leading gentlemen of both political parties paid their respects to him personally. But, during the night, some democrats of the baser sort prepared effigies representing him, which were burned on the square. This "wretched transaction," as it was rightly termed by Rev. Wm. Allen, was severely and sincerely reprobated by his father; but the next number of the *Reporter* declared that, "after strict enquiry" it had "found that three persons were the instigators and managers of this infamous riot," and that, of these, Rev. Thomas Allen was one. Descending to particulars, the *Reporter* said : " It is presumable that one of the effigies was furnished by Parson Allen; it is *certain* and *we aver* it as an undeniable fact that two of his boots were burned upon one of them. The parson was unfortunate in one circumstance. He ordered his son to take an old pair of boots, which he said 'would do;' but the son, in haste to execute the commands of his reverend father, took, in the dark, one of an old, and one of a new, pair, and they were burned."

Rev. Wm. Allen, whose word is unimpeachable, declares that there was not one particle of truth in the whole story. His father went to bed that night at his usual hour, and knew nothing of the affair until the next day. No article for an effigy was taken from his house. One of Mr. Allen's sons demanded from the editor of the *Reporter* the name of his informant, but it was refused. Mr. Allen, himself then wrote to him, requiring a retraction of the whole story; but this too, the editor, after consulting his friends, refused, and declined to print the letter, on the pretense, that it contained a charge that the paper had, from its establishment, followed the writer with personal abuse, slander and falsehood.

Many of the newspaper-attacks upon Mr. Allen were, like the above, pure fabrications. Others were perversions and exaggerations of things actually said and done by him.

Mr. Allen being now sixty-six years old and in broken health, believed that the enemies which he had made in his more vigorous days were taking advantage of his age and infirmities to avenge their old griefs; a supposition in which he was strengthened by the fact that the leaders of the opposition were many of them men, or the sons of men, whose "handling" as tories he had approved, or perhaps incited; and that writers in the *Reporter* went back to the time of the revolution to find cause of complaint against him. Under these provocations, and the "dissatisfied" having already left his ministry and set up a separate place of worship, Mr. Allen addressed the following letter to Woodbridge Little, shortly after the latter's "confession:"

PITTSFIELD, July, 1807.

Sir—To reclaim a brother who is in fault, to promote the cause of religion, and support the honor of God, is the end of church-government. In a late conversation we had together, you made known to me your disapprobation of the part you had acted in forming a combination in town to forsake my ministry and set up a separate worship, and so to perpetuate a division among us. I enquire whether the honor of religion and the nature of the case do not require that your sense of this matter should be made known to the public; for it is a matter that has not been done in a corner, but has long since been before the public. It is not your degradation that I seek—it is the glory of man to retrace a wrong step he has taken and recover himself from every wrong way. I hope you will not be disposed to justify, or unreasonably to extenuate the part you have acted by persuasion, and under the influence of Doctor James and Mr. Pomeroy over you, to the wonder of all your friends who are new-comers into town, and warm political partisans. Whatever declarations are extorted from men which do not flow from conviction and a temper of mind corresponding with them can do them no good, nor the cause of religion. I wish you, sir, to take a full view of the case before you, and seriously consider what of duty is lying on you to perform towards me whom you have greatly injured and grievously wounded; and above all, for the wound you have given to religion in this place, which may not be soon, if ever, healed. The following statement, which I deem just, I wish you seriously to reflect on, and answer a well-informed and impartial conscience on it:

1. You have drawn up and set on foot for circulation through this town, by subscription, a paper illiberal and very much wanting in candor, and which I consider as false and libelous.

2. You have drawn up a second paper containing criminations against your pastor, which are false, seditious and very malevolent. You was not under the influence of love to me, but of hatred and enmity, when you drew that paper. For which I demand of you personal Christian satisfaction.

3. You have attended the meetings of the inimical part of my flock and been an active partisan at them, taking counsel with them against your pastor as their head and leader.

4. You have acted as the head of their committee, and chief-manager of their evil designs against me, and the whole body has been swayed by your example and counsel.

5. You have been the life and soul of this confederacy against your pastor: giving countenance to it by your pen, your name, property, example and advice, by which many honest people have been induced to unite in it.

6. You acted as their committee-man, delegated to the association of ministers, while I was absent on a journey, improving that opportunity in hopes of prevailing against me in your malevolent designs.

7. By your charge against me of introducing the Jefferson song at a prayer-meeting, you gave authority to a false and very malevolent publication, in the *Reporter* of April 25th last, and which was, no doubt, the cause of it, and some of your party were the authors of it, and various other libelous publications in that paper. Every step you have taken as a leader in this whole business, appears to me to be the fruit of deep-rooted malice, flowing from political motives and enmity to my person, usefulness and family, and design at my extermination. You drew up those false charges against me, not in the spirit of love, not from those pure motives you suggest, but from hatred and enmity and with a view to scandalize me and run me down in my character and usefulness. And lastly, in respect to myself, your greatest offense is your present buoying up your conscience with vain pretensions of friendship to me, and of being influenced by the purest motives in this whole malevolent career. The dimmest eye will readily discern the futility of such a pretext; all your works in this whole matter stand in full proof against any such suggestions.

But, what is unspeakably worse than any personal injury you have sought to do unto me, is, the dishonor you have done to God, and the irreparable wound you have given to religion in this town by setting up such a separate worship, and so perpetuating a division in this church and town. You have signed your name to withdraw from my ministry, and consequently from all communion with this church, and to set up a separate worship, and to call in and to withdraw from my ministry and consequently from the communion with this church and to set up a separate worship, and to call in another minister, for you could hear me no longer: such a minister of whatever order as the majority of the malcontents should appoint. You have raised money for that end and appointed your treasurer; and all this before you had taken one gospel-step for conciliation, which might easily in the first stage of the business have prevented your after-conduct, so disgraceful and injurious to religion and so fatal to the peace and unity of this church and town.

In fine, I am under a great mistake if you have not gone in the way of Cain, who hated his brother, and in the gainsayings of Korah who excited and fomented a combination against Moses and Aaron. Divers members of this church have been fully persuaded that the times will fully justify them in letting all these matters rest till the irritation of the public mind, on political subjects, should subside; which is now the case, and nothing occasions any further delay in order to a final settlement of them, in the church, but my ill state of health.

I thought it needful to make the above statement for your reflection, and that you may fully know my expectations from you; and that whatever you may see fit to do may be the result of conviction and sober judgment and not of restraint. It is now the evening of life with both, and it cannot be long before we shall meet each other at the judgment seat of Christ. I am fully persuaded your plea of friendship and brotherly love to me in this your conduct and your benevolent motives to prevent evil, not foment it, will never stand the test of that impartial tribunal. Wishing you every blessing,

I am, sir, your humble servant,
THOMAS ALLEN.

The following curt note from Mr. Little closed the correspondence:

REV. SIR:
I have received your angry, unfounded and abusive letter.
Yours, etc.,
WOODBRIDGE LITTLE.

P. S.—Matthew, VII, 1-5.

We must now go back a few months in our story to the first definite steps towards a division of the parish. In consequence of the sermon preached on the next Sunday after New Year's, 1807 (January fourth), a paper was drawn up on the second of the following month and signed by a large number of persons, who agreed to pay the sums subscribed by them to Ashbel Strong, Esq., for the support of such a minister as the majority might choose. In accordance with the terms of this agreement an Episcopalian clergyman was engaged and preached once or twice a month in the town-house—which stood where the present Episcopal church does—where regular services were held every Sunday, either with or without a clergyman. From the early part of March, most of the aggrieved party—"except a few church-members"—withdrew from Mr. Allen's ministry and attended the new place of worship.

Some of the seceders went so far as to profess great devotion to Episcopacy; and, for a time, it seemed not improbable that a parish of that order would be formed. But the scruples of "the few church-members" proved invincible; and all, or nearly all, of the disaffected, in calmer moments, finding their Congregational sentiments and principles more deeply rooted than in their angry haste they had perceived, finally held fast to the faith and discipline of their fathers.

They nevertheless did not return to the congregation of Mr. Allen, but, the alienation becoming more and more complete, soon after the date of the letters last quoted, which seemed to close all hope of reconciliation, measures were commenced for the incorporation of a new parish; and in the winter of 1808–9, John Chandler Williams managing the application before the legislature, Woodbridge Little and one hundred and eight others were incorporated as the UNION CONGREGATIONAL PARISH OF PITTSFIELD.

In the act of incorporation as drafted, clauses were inserted giving to the new parish a joint interest with the old in the meeting-house and other property of the original organization; and also releasing the members who transferred their connection from the payment of taxes which had been assessed but not collected. These provisions passed the house of representatives unchallenged, but they did not escape the keen eye of Dr. Timothy Childs, an ardent democrat and zealous parishioner of Mr. Allen, who happened that year to be one of the senators from Berkshire; and he opposed them as an invasion of the vested rights of the old parish and a violation of uniform precedent. It might have been said with truth, that there was no precedent strictly applicable to the case, inasmuch as, whatever it may have been in form, the act was not a mere permission for a colony to offshoot itself from an overgrown parent organization, but rather the separation of co-equal parts, which were entitled in equity to an equal partition of the property to whose accumulation they had jointly contributed, and which, from no exclusive fault of the seceders, they could no longer enjoy peaceably in common. The legislature, that year was, however, strongly democratic and was not likely to take this view of the case. Indeed, the objectionable clauses were not strongly urged, and they were stricken from the bill, having had no other effect than to increase the irritation of the old parish.

The new parish was thus left to its own pecuniary resources, which were indeed ample, as it contained a very large proportion of the wealthy men of the town, whose liberality was stimulated to its utmost by what they deemed the injustice and overbearing conduct of their opponents. They had also the lively sympathy of their political friends in Boston, although it is not stated that they received any considerable sum in money from any of them, except Hon. Oliver Wendell, who was a summer resident of Pittsfield and a zealous member of the new parish.[1]

One difficulty still perplexed the seceders. The legislature was competent to create a new parish, and to form it of members previously connected with another; for the parish was a merely human institution. But the church—each independent, Congregational church—was subject, and subject only, to the laws established by its Divine Founder, as interpreted by itself, and to by-laws made in conformity to the same sacred guide. No human authority outside itself, could release its members from the covenant obligations into which they had entered with God and with each other; obligations the most awful which man can take upon himself.

By the Congregational theory, the independence of the church organization was, and is, absolute. But practically it is very much modified by the moral influences which the great body of the denomination exercises over each of its members; and, for the preservation of Christian comity and a decorous uniformity, as well as that each may have the benefit of the wisdom of all, the churches have submitted generally to mutual oversight and advice; which, however, were only exercised, at the request of the parties immediately interested, and through councils selected by them, or made up of clerical and lay delegates sent by churches invited by them to do so. But to what extent the parties having submitted questions to a mutual council are bound to abide by its decision is still a matter of controversy. Had the

[1] There is still among the plate of the First Congregational parish a baptismal basin of silver presented to Union Parish by Judge Wendell, which was used until the introduction of a stone font.

disputes in the Pittsfield church been submitted to a mutual council, it was evidently, however, the opinion of both parties that its advice, whether authoritative or not, would have had decisive weight.[1]

Such a council the dissatisfied members of Mr. Allen's church earnestly endeavored to obtain, while he as resolutely refused to join in calling it, and as moderator of church-meetings declined to put motions looking to such a measure, or reflecting upon his own official conduct. His defense of this course was that the means of redress and reconciliation prescribed by the gospel had not been exhausted. He had also, it seems, an objection to the system of councils in the abstract. "There was," says his son, "on the part of the seceding, an eager desire of calling in an ecclesiastical body; but Mr. Allen, who never was very fond of an extraneous collection of ministers and delegates in the affairs of an independent church, was entirely opposed to such a measure. He had a perfect right to prevent it, took proper steps to prevent it, and was successful. As to a dissolution of the meeting that he might not be compelled to put the motion, he did dissolve it." A reason, not mentioned, why one party desired and the other opposed the calling of the council, doubtless was that the class from which the clerical portion of it would necessarily have been taken, was almost unanimously of federal politics, and, however earnestly they might endeavor to divest themselves of prejudice, would have hardly been able to do so thoroughly.

The somewhat arbitrary exercise of authority, which Mr. Allen considered necessary for the defense of his pastoral rights was successful in maintaining them, and in defeating the project for a mutual council. There still remained, however, to the dissatisfied, a recourse provided by the custom of the New England churches, by which, although they could not reach Mr. Allen and his adherents, they could procure in regard to their own conduct, the advice of pious and judicious representatives of the neigh-

[1] There are also permanent organizations connected with the Congregational order—such for instance as the Berkshire Association of Congregational ministers,—which are occasionally appealed to for advice, although they strongly disclaim any ecclesiastical authority over the churches. They can, however, undoubtedly discipline members who have voluntarily submitted themselves to their jurisdiction; and would certainly denounce as an imposture any church in their vicinity, which, calling itself by their name, was scandalously loose in doctrine or discipline.

boring churches, and the recommendation of such a course as would secure the recognition of a new church formed under it.

It was in their power to call an *ex parte* council and thus, should its fraternal approval justify them in dissolving their connections with the church to which they had formerly belonged and forming a new one, their own conscientious scruples would be relieved, and they would ward off the odium of proceeding with rash self-confidence under the incitement of personal or political feeling.

On the first of August, 1809, an ecclesiastical council was therefore convened "by letters missive from a committee of Christian professors and others;" the following pastors and delegates being present:

Lanesboro, Rev. Daniel Collins, Andrew Squire.
Hinsdale, Rev. Theodore Hinsdale [not a settled minister although ordained and held in high esteem].
West Hampton, Rev. Enoch Hale, Deacon Samuel Edwards.
Goshen, Rev. Samuel Whitman, Deacon Oliver Taylor.
New Marlboro North, Rev. Jacob Catlin. Elijah Sheldon.
Middlefield, Rev. Jonathan Nash, Col. David Mack.
Lee, Rev. Alvin Hyde, Deacon Oliver West.
Washington, Rev. Jonathan L. Pomeroy, Hon. Ezra Starkweather.
Lenox, Rev. Samuel Shepard, Deacon Nathaniel Isbell.
Dalton, Rev. Ebenezer Jennings, Jacob Chamberlain.

A large majority of the council, if not all its members, were federalists, and some of them were very vehement in their political feelings. During the war of 1812, Doctor Catlin preached a "peace" sermon on a fourth of July. Mr. Collins had at the opening of the revolution rebuked Mr. Allen for meddling with affairs of state, and been censured for it by a Pittsfield town-meeting.[1]

Still Rev. William Allen declared that "no objection could be made to any of the ministers on account of their political sentiments." He impeached the fairness of the council on the ground that those who called it had carefully selected those whose opinions on the questions at issue had already been plainly indicated; so that they knew precisely what advice they were to receive: that it was a packed jury. But whatever extraneous influences may be supposed to have biased the judgment of the

[1] Vol. I, page 198.

clerical portion of the council, they were certainly men who left behind them pure and honored memories, while of some of their number, it may be truly said, that "their praise is still in all the churches."

This body met on the 1st of August, at the house of Dr. Daniel James, who was the federal physician of the town, as Drs. Timothy and Henry Childs were the democratic. Rev. Mr. Collins was chosen moderator, Rev. Mr. Shepard, scribe, and Rev. Mr. Hyde, assistant scribe. The committee of Union parish produced their charter, and the council took the following action, which we give in full from its minutes:

The council having carefully, and as they trust in the fear of God, and with a sincere desire to promote the real interests of religion in the town, attended to the statements made to them; having also deliberately and impartially heard a discussion of the several questions proposed to them in relation to the circumstances of said parish, passed the following votes unanimously:

Voted, 1st. That the council find by documents laid before them that Union parish in Pittsfield is legally incorporated by the general court, and that we as ministers and churches, do recognize it as such.

It having been represented to the council that a number of members of the church in Pittsfield belong to Union parish; that several persons also who are members of neighboring churches have moved into said parish; that others who have hope of a present interest in Christ have never publicly professed religion, but are desirous of doing it; it also having been represented that certain persons have been laid under censure by the church in Pittsfield, as appears by a vote passed to that effect, February 7; it having further been made to appear that suitable exertions to obtain a mutual council have failed.—THIS COUNCIL having deliberately considered all these statements with their attendant circumstances,—

Voted, 2d, That, in their opinion, it is expedient and consistent with gospel rule that a church be organized in Union parish.

Voted, 3d, That as the general court have incorporated a number of the members of the church of which Rev. Mr. Allen is pastor, with Union parish, it is expedient in view of the existing circumstances of the church and town, that they be considered as proper candidates for membership in the new church.

Voted, 4th, That the censure passed February 7, 1809, as already noticed, on certain brethren of the church in Pittsfield, notwithstanding we admit there were some irregularities in their proceedings, *is not a sufficient bar* to their reception with others into a church, as regular brethren of the family of Christ.

Voted, 5th, That "a number of ministers" be appointed in conformity with a written request of the committee of Union parish to proceed, in due time, to organize a church in said parish.

Voted, 6th, That the Rev. Theodore Hinsdale, Rev. Daniel Collins, Rev. Alvan Hyde, Rev. Samuel Shepard and Rev. Jacob Catlin [the Berkshire members of the council] be appointed for that purpose.

The council have been deeply impressed with the magnitude of the difficulties which have arisen in this town, in view of which they have given their best advice, having a solemn regard, as they think, to the general interest of the Redeemer's kingdom. They now heartily recommend to all concerned in these matters the exercise of the Christian spirit; commending them to the care and keeping and guidance of Almighty God.

On the 22d of August, the committee, named by the council, met for the organization of the new church. The selectmen— Joshua Danforth, Robert Green and Oliver Robbins—having refused the use of the meeting-house, service was held in the town-house, Rev. Mr. Hyde preaching the sermon. In the afternoon the committee met the candidates for admission to the church at the hall over the academy, when the following persons presented themselves: Charles Goodrich, Nathaniel Fairfield, Zebediah Stiles, Timothy Caldwell, Timothy Haskell, Joseph Fairfield, Nathaniel Tremaine, Woodbridge Little, Daniel Chapman, Jonathan Weston, Richard Barnard, Charles Goodrich, Jr., Isaac Tremaine, John Chandler Williams, Benjamin Newell, Elisha Ely. Males, 16.

Hannah Goodrich, Abigail Barnard, Hepzibah Whitney, Sally White, Mary Newell, Deliverance Blankenship, Olive Tremaine, Huldah Colt, Sarah Colt, Roxana Allis, Lovina Case, Mary Strong, Amelia Goodrich, Eleanor Newell, Martha Gold, Hart Pomeroy, Fanny Hinsdale, Mehitable Kitteridge, Abigail Root, Sarah Peck, Elizabeth Fairfield (widow), Mary Strong, Elizabeth Pepoon, Mercy Merrick, Lucy James. Females, 25; total, 41.

The council having already decided that the censure of the First church, under which most of the candidates lay, was no bar to their uniting in a new one, it only remained to carefully examine them in their views of gospel truth and experimental religion, and the reason of their hope in Christ. All the candidates passed their ordeal to the unanimous satisfaction of the committee, after which they proceeded to the town-house "to make their doings publicly known." Here, the congregation having re-assembled, the names of the candidates were read, and they gave their public assent to the Confession of Faith. Rev. Mr. Collins administered the rite of baptism to Benjamin Newell and Roxana Allis, and the candidates having in the presence of many witnesses entered into a solemn covenant with God and each other, were "declared to be a regularly-organized church of Christ, and in fellowship with the other Congregational churches of this vicinity."

The division of the church and parish of Pittsfield was thus recognized and sanctioned by the higher ecclesiastical, as well as the legislative powers.

On the 21st of August, Rev. Thomas Allen addressed a long letter of remonstrance to the committee, denouncing the proceedings of the *ex parte* council and the institution of the new church, which was to take place on the following day. Among the objections which he made was that such bodies, before proceeding to act, usually recommended a mutual council, to which he and his church had for some time been willing to agree, although at the meeting of the Association at Stockbridge in February, he did not deem it expedient, or likely to result in a reconciliation; things not then being ripe for that measure; and in this opinion he reminds the committee that they agreed with him.

Before the meeting of the council there had indeed been an effort made in July to avert the consummation of the separation; but the correspondence upon the subject between Hon. John Chandler Williams and Hon. Ezekiel Bacon, in behalf of their respective parishes, showed no great desire to that end on the part of the seceders, on any terms except the unconditional submission of the other party. It seems that the family and friends of Mr. Allen, convinced that his strength was no longer adequate to his parochial duties and to the struggle in which he was engaged,—and indeed that death would be the penalty of persistence,—urged him to retire, and that he assented. The members of Union parish, learning something of this, appointed Messrs. Little, Daniel Chapman, Charles Goodrich, Jr., and Capt. Tremaine, a committee to meet such as the old parish might choose " to promote an event in which the happiness and interest of the town were so much involved—a happy union, etc."

To a letter from Mr. Little, informing him of this action, Mr.

Bacon replied that Messrs. Danforth, Griswold, Hubbard and Crofoot had, with himself, been appointed to receive such written communication as the committee of Union parish might see fit to make, "being at no time indisposed to a union of the two parishes, on fair and honorable terms." In rejoinder, Mr. Williams intimated that there was a misunderstanding as to the purport of his first letter, and that the resignation of Mr. Allen was a condition precedent to any negotiation. Mr. Bacon explained that his committee were well apprised that Mr. Allen's retirement would be made one of the first conditions of the proposed union; but that they had expected that the proposal of this would be "accompanied by such other propositions as the members of Union parish would be willing to comply with in case a union could be effected on that basis." Some of that parish, and even some members of its committee, he added, had individually expressed a willingness to contribute an equal share of any sum which it might be necessary to raise for procuring a settlement for Rev. Mr. Allen. The proposition thus suggested was emphatically rejected. Assailing Mr. Allen with some pretty strong phrases, Mr. Williams declared that there were not many of his associates who "were willing to deprive their own families of their property to build up the family of a man who was not an object of charity, being, they thought, the richest clergyman in the county." In closing, Mr. Williams said: "Were the estate of Mr. Allen so small and embarrassed that it would not afford him a very decent fund for the support of his very excellent lady, his amiable daughter and his other children, the case would be very different; but we all know that he holds a very valuable estate, and, compared with the families of the first settlers of the town, who were here when he came, there is not one, happy and prosperous as they are, which is in so eligible a situation as his own."

Mr. Williams expressed a wish that the correspondence should close with this letter, but Mr. Little, apprehensive that he had stated his case so strongly that an erroneous impression would be left, on the 15th of August, wrote to Mr. Bacon, explaining that it was not intended by the committee "to convey the idea of an absolute refusal on their part to contribute to a compensation to Mr. Allen, if any was necessary or proper, although, all things considered, they thought him entitled to but little, if any." He regretted the ceremony and jealousy which had marked the correspondence, and had never favored a negotiation in writing. He believed that a mere nominal union could not be desirable for either party, and thought that if they could not cordially agree in their feelings and sentiments regarding the settlement of a gospel minister, it would be better for them to remain as they were.

Some explanation is perhaps necessary of the "censure" which was visited by the First church upon its seceding members, but was not considered a bar to their admission to the new organization. It is thus recorded:

"At a meeting of the Church of Christ in Pittsfield, duly notified, held February 7, 1809, voted unanimously: That the members of this church, who signed a paper of separation from this church near two years ago and have withdrawn from our communion, and those who have of late joined with said separation by signing a petition to the general court for a poll parish, and with whom the gospel-steps to reclaim them have been taken in vain, are disorderly walkers, have violated their covenant vows to walk with us in a church-state and are suspended from communion with us, until they give us gospel-satisfaction."

The notice of the meeting by which this vote was passed was given on a stormy Sunday, and it was held on a stormy Tuesday. It was attended by only seven persons,—one of whom, a minor son of Mr. Allen, did not vote,—although the deacons had agreed to notify members in different parts of the town. Those who were placed under censure charged the six voters with unchristian presumption, as well as violation of the rules of the gospel in pronouncing judgment upon them without a hearing and without notice of proceedings pending against them for an offense which, if it existed at all, had done so for nearly two years. The offense had, however, been recently revived and aggravated by the petition cited, and, small as was the number present at the church-meeting, subsequent proceedings showed that they fairly represented the democratic members—about one-half—of the church. Still this, and other acts on both sides, more nearly resembled the anathemas hurled upon each other by rival ecclesiastical authorities in older ages, than the mild and wholesome discipline of New England churches.

This view doubtless had weight in determining the council to admit the branded members to Christian fellowship, and recognize them as proper constituents of a new church, although they also based their decision upon the frivolous and technical nature of the reasons alleged, in test-cases, for refusing letters dismissory: such as the objection that the church of Union parish, at the the time of the application, was only *in posse*, not *in esse*.

At whatever door the sin of dividing the church and parish of Pittsfield may be rightfully laid—and it does not appear that it could exclusively be laid at any—it would be unjust not to admit that Messrs. Shepard and Hyde, and their colleagues in the council, exercised their delicate functions, on the whole, for the best good of all, as little biased by prejudice and passion, as it was possible for them to be, under the circumstances.

The mad dissensions and evil passions which had been aroused had already long passed the stage when benefit could be hoped from the methods of treatment prescribed in less violent cases. A stringent application of discipline and church by-laws could only irritate and inflame. Time, and the calming events which time is sure to bring, were needful before any direct measures of healing could be effective. In the meanwhile whatever prevented the contact of those who could not meet in harmony, was a blessing and a balm, which helped to hasten the day when reconciliation and re-union should be possible. Until that day should arrive, it was in the very spirit of that religious liberty which is the proudest boast of Congregationalism—due to the seceders, that they should not be excluded from the fellowship of the churches, which confessed the same faith and walked in the same discipline, because they desired to worship God in a frame of mind and heart befitting His holy temple, undisturbed by political irritation. To have denied them this would have been unpardonable ecclesiastical tyranny.

But it was not to be expected that the matter would present itself in this light to those engaged in the struggle of that day, and blinded by the dust of its turmoil. The portion of the church which remained with Mr. Allen was, on the contrary, much disturbed by the proceedings of the council of August. They may fairly be supposed to have felt as a church of more recent days would have done, had a portion of its members—disturbed by sermons in favor of political anti-slavery, political temperance, or whatever else in the opinion of the pastor, was entitled to legislation on behalf of moral right—had unceremoniously withdrawn from its communion, formed a new ecclesiastical organization, and been cordially received into fellowship by the neighboring churches. Indeed, they felt this more keenly than it would have been felt in later times, as the democrats seem not yet to have learned that the liberalism which, under their teachings, had begun to characterize the government of the state, was also making its way in that of the church.

They therefore determined to call a counter council, which met on the 10th of October, and consisted of pastors and delegates from the churches in Sheffield, Great Barrington and Richmond, Mass., Green River and Lebanon, N. Y., and Bennington, Vt., including among its clerical members the venerable Mr. Judson, the democratic minister of Sheffield, and Rev. David Perry of Richmond, Mr. Allen's personal friend, although political opponent.

Statements were made to this council by both parties—although only the seceders had been heard by that of August. Both were found guilty of the irregularities mutually charged, and were mildly censured; although the council declared that they discovered in Mr. Allen and his church a commendable zeal to maintain the discipline of Christ's house, and intimate no objection except to the manner in which it was enforced. Their decision closes with the following exhortation :

> When the walls of Zion are broken down, all her cordial friends mourn; and it is characteristic of all who love her prosperity to unite their exertions to build up her waste places ; and when the people have a mind to work, the ruins will be repaired, and God will appear in His glory.
>
> Under these impressions, we exhort Mr. Allen and the church to exercise brotherly love and to let it continue; to worship the Lord in the beauty of holiness, unitedly seek the advancement of the Redeemer's kingdom, and be vigorously employed in bringing forth much good fruit, by which their Father who is in Heaven will be glorified and they prospered.

The decision of the council was not entirely what those who called it expected ; but they accepted it, complied with its advice, and placed it in full upon their records, adding, however, a long apology or explanation of their course in regard to their suspension of the seceders, admitting that their process was irregular in form, but denying that it worked, or was intended to work, any deprivation of a hearing, or resulted in any injury to the delinquents, who were supposed to know, although not from official sources, of the proceedings against them, and had in previous cases contemned the summons of the church, and proclaimed their intention of continuing to do so.

The second council had no practical effect upon the division of the Pittsfield Congregationalists. It did not assume to revise the action of its predecessor, nor to pronounce upon the status of the church established by it; but with propriety confined its action to the body which had asked its advice, including those members who, although they had seceded from it, had not taken the steps essential to a dissolution of their connection.

Its admonition to the latter was heeded in a few instances, but not in a manner to materially affect either the old parish or the new. The First church, having acknowledged the error of their mode of procedure at the February meeting, resolved that it "did not vacate the censure; and that, if it did, still said members were regularly under discipline, and complaints against them were regularly before the church; the first and second steps of discipline having been regularly taken with them, and complaints lodged in the church against them." And having passed this vote on the 16th of October, the church cited Charles Goodrich, Jr., Timothy Haskell and Jonathan Weston to appear for trial on the 24th.

Mr. Goodrich appeared, but refused to acknowledge any allegiance to the First church. The others disclaimed its jurisdiction by paying no attention to its citation. Whereupon it was "voted, that Mr. Charles Goodrich, Jr., a member of this church, has violated his covenant engagements to walk with us in a church state, and, as he confesseth, has used his influence to induce others to do the same; and the gospel-steps having been taken with him to no effect, he is hereby excluded from all Christian communion with us, without repentance, after three months." Similar votes were passed concerning Messrs. Weston and Haskell. Proceedings were also instituted against other seceders, but not until important events had transpired in both parishes.

On the 22d of August, after the institution of Union church, the church and parish concurred in the choice of Rev. Thomas Punderson, of New Haven, to be their pastor, and he was installed on the 25th of October, there being in the council convened for that purpose, besides the Berkshire members who took part in the council of August, Rev. Mr. Perry, of Richmond, and Rev. Moses Stuart, of New Haven, afterwards the distinguished theological professor of Andover. The latter preached the ordination sermon. Rev. Dr. Todd in his Historical sermon describes Mr. Punderson as "moderate in his mental movements, kind in his feelings, faithful and diligent in his duties, and, if he had not the magnetism to make warm personal friends, he certainly had no power to make enemies." He seems to have sustained himself well in the trying position in which he was placed, and to have given satisfaction to his parishioners.

Three months after Mr. Punderson's installation, an event occurred which might well have given pause to the angry passions that ruled the hour: an event no less solemn than the death of the pastor who had ministered to the town in holy things for almost forty-six years, and to the church from its foundation; of a man who had been foremost in the secular, and prominent in the ecclesiastical, affairs of the county through its most trying years; who indeed descended to the grave while yet the leader of an embittered strife, but whose genial and benign disposition, and evident sincerity of purpose, while they could not temper the violence of his oppugnation to what he believed wrong, nor, in the heat of conflict, mitigate the odium incurred by that violence, yet in death, clothed his memory with associations which endeared it to many even of those who could not review his pastoral course with entire satisfaction.

When before the dawn of day, on the morning of February 11, 1810, the solemn tolling of the bell whose silver tones had been so dear to him in life, stirred the frosty air of the Sabbath morning, announcing to all within its sound that Thomas Allen had passed away; it broke upon the ear of some, who in the fervor of youth had joined with him to form the first church of Christ in Pittsfield, of many whose youthful studies had been encouraged and aided by him, of many to whom he had ministered in the saddest, as well as in the most joyous events of their lives, of some whose pride it was that they had followed his leadership to victory in those stormy town-meetings which placed Pittsfield on the side of freedom in the revolution, had shared with him the glories of Bennington field, and suffered with him the toils, dangers and disasters of Ticonderoga and White Plains. And whether they had adhered to, or become estranged from, him in later conflicts, there were few in whose hearts that solemn knelling, as it came to them through the darkness did not waken the most tender and thrilling memories.

Mr. Allen had been in frail health for several years. At one of the most exciting of the church-meetings—that held in April, 1808 —" his infirmities," says his son, " were so great that in presiding, he desired to have the aid of his friend, Mr. Judson of Sheffield;" but the meeting refusing his request, he did not give way for the choice of a moderator *pro tem.* as he supposed his opponents desired, in order to render him powerless to prevent a council— " but encountered the whole burden and fatigue of the meeting while he could hardly, by the aid of a smelling-bottle, keep himself from sinking to the floor."

The excitement and fatigue of this occasion left him much enfeebled; still he visited Boston in May and preached a vigorous and well written "election-sermon" before the governor and legislature, which had, to his intense gratification, became democratic. During the winter of 1808-9 his health began to decline more rapidly, and in the spring, " brought down to the very brink of the grave, he resolved on a visit to Boston for the benefit of the sea-air, although, on taking leave of his family he had little hope of ever seeing them again, and his friends had little hope that he could live to return. He reached Boston in a state which did not afford much prospect that his debilitated frame and enfeebled mind would be again invigorated."[1]

While in Boston he wrote the short pamphlet entitled " An Historical Sketch of the County of Berkshire and Town of Pittsfield" for which he was censured by the federal press. " It was written," says his son, " in a state of very great infirmity and without any labor or care in preparing it for the press. If the charge had been for a literary offense, perhaps the author would have plead guilty." It is nevertheless, although brief, a valuable contribution to the history of the town, in spite of some inaccuracies and a shade of partiality in his statement of political matters.

While at Boston "his mind seemed to be engrossed by but two subjects: Death, and the church of which he was pastor. He left it divided; with a number of its members, who had with-

[1] Rev. William Allen's account.

drawn from his ministry, under censure; yet these members, he understood, were to be formed into a new church and to be formed, too, by his Christian brethren. In apprehension of this event, and in his debilitated state of mind, he wrote several letters to ministers who were of the council, in which he censured them with plainness and pungency. Considering the separation as originating in unworthy motives, he declared those who encouraged it to be engaged in a wicked work."[1] Not being aware of the infirmities under which the writer was laboring, Messrs. Shepard and Jennings permitted the letters addressed to them to be published in a pamphlet-review of Mr. Allen's course, which appeared in the summer of 1809, and whose writer,[2] it is to be hoped was also ignorant of Mr. Allen's condition; reduced to the extremest state of debility, and with the danger which threatened his church continually preying upon his mind. It would seem that if this state of things had been known to the seceders, a little more forbearance might have been shown to the infirmities of a dying pastor, and that there could have been no serious detriment to the cause of religion had the formation of a new church been postponed yet a little while.

Mr. Allen returned to Pittsfield about mid-summer, and a short time before the meeting of the council of August; having derived no permanent benefit from his brief and agitated trip. It was at this time that, in deference to the wishes of his alarmed family, he consented to resign his pastorate, if thereby peace could be restored to the church. The negotiation for this end failing, he remained at his post. The record of a church-meeting held August 7, after his return from Boston, was made by him, and other entries up to the 12th of January, and his handwriting appears fair and firm as at any previous time. But his decline is betrayed by the wording and orthography; points in which he had rarely failed before. A meeting of January 12, 1810, cited Zebediah Stiles and Isaac Tremaine, to answer on the 19th to a charge of having "joined the separation;" and, following the transcript of the citation is an unfinished entry erased by lines drawn through it: "*Friday, January 12th. Church-meeting was held, being opened by prayer. Proceeded to act on charges—*" These are the last words in the records of the First

[1] Rev. William Allen's statement.
[2] Said to have been Hon. John Chandler Williams.

church, written by its first pastor. His pen failed him before he could complete the sentence.

The next entry is as follows :

Friday, February 9, 1810. The church met at the house of Rev. Mr. Allen, and, as he was very dangerously sick, instead of attending to any business, " employed the meeting in prayer for him."

Then comes the following inscription :

The Rev. Thomas Allen,

The first pastor of this church who was ordained, April 18, 1764, died in the peace, hope and triumph of the Christian, at 2 o'clock on the morning of the Lord's day, Feb. 11, 1810, aged 67 years.

Thus died Thomas Allen, the Christian, the philanthropist and the patriot; his end hastened and embittered by the agitations and vexations in which his sense of duty had involved him, in spite of a natural disposition as kindly and benignant as it was earnest and truthful.

His funeral-sermon was preached by his faithful personal and political friend, Rev. Mr. Judson, from the text: " And Jacob said unto Pharaoh, The days of the years of my pilgrimage are an hundred and thirty years; few and evil have the years of my life been, and have not attained unto the days of the years of the life of my fathers in the days of their pilgrimage." Genesis 47 : 9. It is said to have been a very pathetic and affecting discourse, well adapted to the occasion. The other clergymen who took part in the exercises were Rev. Mr. Marsh, of Bennington, and a Mr. Hall, who was preaching as a candidate for the pulpit left vacant by Mr. Allen.[1]

Many of the neighboring ministers were, however, present.

Nine years after the death of Mr. Allen, an article was inserted in the warrant for the annual town-meeting, " To see if the town will erect a marble monument with an appropriate inscription at the tomb, and to the memory, of their late beloved and lamented pastor, the Rev. Thomas Allen;" and the consideration of the subject was referred to Samuel Root, Jonathan Allen, 2d, Henry

---

[1] It would appear by the presence of a candidate of this kind on this occasion, that had Mr. Allen lived he was intending to resign his pastorate as soon as a suitable successor should be found.

H. Childs, Oren Goodrich and Simeon Brown, who made the following report at the May meeting :

With respect to the propriety of public acts designed in commemoration of public benefactors, your committee are perfectly satisfied in consequence of the beneficial effects they are calculated to produce upon society.

In the character of our late beloved pastor, the Rev. Thomas Allen, we discover that strong attachment to the principles of our free government, that love of country, that benevolence, that charity, that zeal for the temporal and eternal welfare of his fellowmen which are the true characteristics of the patriot, the philanthropist and the Christian ; and which eminently entitle him to some commemorative act of the citizens of this town.

And whereas, a free voluntary contribution will best comport with the object proposed, we would recommend the town the appointment of a committee whose duty it shall be to open a subscription book for the purpose of raising a sufficient sum to defray the expense, which your committee have estimated at $175; and whenever such sum shall be subscribed, it shall be the duty of said committee to prepare and place, at the tomb of the late Rev. Thomas Allen, such monument together with suitable inscriptions.

This report was adopted and a committee consisting of John B. Root, Henry H. Childs and Phinehas Allen was appointed to carry it into effect ; but, for some unexplained reason, the monument was never erected. On the erection of a new church in 1853, a handsome mural tablet of white marble was placed over the pulpit, and bears the following inscription :

In Memory of Thomas Allen,

First Minister of Pittsfield, born at Northampton, January 7, 1743. Ordained First Minister of the Congregational Society of Pittsfield, April, 1764. Preached in this place forty-six years, and died February 11, 1810. *Fortiter gerit crucem.*

Mr. Allen's remains were first deposited in his tomb in the first burial-ground near the church. Afterwards they were removed to the grave-yard on First street, from which they were transferred to Pontoosuc Hill in the Pittsfield cemetery, upon which his grandson and namesake has erected a monumental obelisk.

CHAPTER VII.

THE METHODIST AND BAPTIST CHURCHES—CONGREGATIONAL ZEAL FOR THE RELIGIOUS INSTRUCTION OF THE YOUNG.

[1800–1812.]

Inequality of the Massachusetts laws—Re-organization of the Baptist church—Rev. John Francis—Charter of the Methodist parish of Pittsfield and other towns—Secession of reformed Methodists—Dissenters from all churches—Philosophical religionists—Obstacles to the new churches—Rev. Mr. Hibbard—Congregational plan for the instruction of youth in religion.

WHILE the Congregational church and parish were rent by the political dissensions described in the last chapter, the Baptist and Methodist churches, composed mostly of substantial, well-to-do farmers, but comparatively few in numbers and inferior in wealth, grew and flourished; obtaining a foothold in the town which they have never lost. Both were deeply inspired with the zeal peculiar to early religious reformers, each believing undoubtingly that it held tenets essential to the full faith of the gospel, but which had long been lost sight of by the rest of the Christian world. Both, also, felt keenly the injustice done themselves and other dissenting denominations, by the laws of Massachusetts, and the members of both clung with the more ardent love to the church of their faith for the unequal burdens which they were compelled to bear for its sake, and the impediments thrown by the laws in the way of their mode of worship. We have already somewhat fully discussed the nature of these laws,[1] but we quote a portion of a paragraph from a local work showing a Baptist view of some of the chief grievances complained of.[2]

---

[1] Vol. 1, chapter 25.

[2] History of the Baptist church in Pittsfield, Mass., from its organization in 1772 to October, 1853. Prepared by its present pastor, Rev. Lemuel Porter, Pittsfield, 1853.

After speaking of the original laws of the province and the ameliorations and exemptions, granted from time to time, by the General Court, Dr. Porter says:

All these exemptions were loaded with unjust and humiliating conditions. Look at some of them: The person wishing to attend and aid a Baptist church, of which he was a member, must pay taxes to the Congregationalists, unless he lived within five miles of his place of meeting. This, of course, to many, was impossible. Then every Baptist church must, yearly, give into the county-clerk a list of all who professed to be *Ana*-Baptists, and attended their meeting. Then this certificate would be good for nothing unless three other churches should each give a certificate that they esteemed this church to be of their denomination and conscientiously believed them to be *Ana-Baptists*. Here insult was added to injury. You might as well demand that Congregationalists should call themselves *Ana-Baptists*. Then Baptists, etc., must pay their money into the treasury at any rate. On showing that their names were on the certificate, they might draw it out again—if they could. Then no one could draw out his money unless he belonged to a society incorporated by law. Baptists would not get incorporated for various reasons; among which was the very good one, that every incorporated society must always have a minister. If in any six months they were without a minister three months, they should pay, for the first offense, not more than $60 nor less than $30. For every succeeding offense, not over $100 nor less than $60.

With the exception of the misnomer of Ana-Baptist, applied by law to the Baptists, all denominations of Christians, who dissented from the Congregational faith were subject to the indignities and burdens named. Under these and other depressing influences, the Episcopalians, after the removal of their leader, Mr. Van Schaack, to Kinderhook, disappeared. But to the vigorous young life of the Methodists and Baptists, they added new fire.

It will be remembered that the first Baptist church organized in Pittsfield, after an existence of twenty-six years, was by request of its pastor, Elder Valentine Rathbun, and his sole remaining deacon, dropped from the roll of the Shaftsbury Association, and probably entirely dissolved, in 1798. But a brief interval elapsed, however, before, on the 27th of October, 1800, it found a successor, fifteen persons entering into a covenant to form and maintain a Baptist church. Their names, which are held in much veneration by their successors, are Josiah Francis,

John Francis, Josiah Francis, Jr., Oliver Robbins, James Hammond, Daniel H. Francis, Mr. Beckwith, Backus Boardman (colored), Anna Francis (wife of John), Abigail Powers, Anna Chapman, Mahala Chapman, Mrs. Beckwith, Ruth Marvin and Polly Francis.

On the 22d of March, 1801, the body thus constituted was, after due examination of its members, recognized as a church in full fellowship with the Baptist denomination, by an ecclesiastical council, consisting of Elders Ebenezer Smith of Partridgeville—now Peru and Hinsdale—and James Barnes of Canaan, N. Y., with Brothers Jacob Moon and Allen Matterson of Stephentown, N. Y. Their first communion was administered Sunday, August 3, 1801, by Elder Barnes, and their first baptism was on the 15th of August, in the same year, when Elder Smith went down into the waters of the pond at Parker's saw-mill on Churchill brook, with Reuben Brooks and his wife. This pond, situated in one of the most romantically-beautiful regions of the town, was for many years the baptismal font of the church in Pittsfield, and cannot even now be visited without reverential memories of the solemn scenes which it witnessed in the days when the name of North Woods was not a misnomer of the locality in which it lies. Near it stood the homes of Josiah Francis and his sons John and Josiah, Jr., of the Parkers, the Powers and other intelligent, thoughtful and prosperous families, in whose spacious, gambrel-roofed houses—most of which still stand, moss-covered and embrowned by time—the young church planted her most thrifty vines and gathered her richest fruitage. In one of them, that of John Francis, the church was organized, and the council of recognition was held. In it, on the 19th of September, 1801, occurred the first death in the little flock—that of Anna Francis, the wife of its owner.

For the first five years and four months of its existence, the church settled no pastor, but met regularly for united worship, at the houses of its members, the exercises being conducted by such of their own number as had gifts in that direction, except when they received an occasional visitation from the neighboring clergy; of whom, be it remembered, John Leland was one—and one with a large missionary spirit. It is proof that the ministrations of these early pastorless years were not without power, that in them twenty-six members were admitted to the church by baptism, and three by letter, which—one being dismissed and two dying—left their number forty-two.

It seems certain, however, that, although nominally without a minister, the church, during, at least, the latter part of this time, had what may be called a pastoral leader; for when they came to choose a pastor, he was taken from their own number, having doubtless already shown a special capacity for the office.

The member thus honored was John Francis, at whose house the church had been organized, and who, in accordance with the recommendation of a council of advice held a few days previous, was, on the 26th of June, 1806, ordained by a council called for that purpose. The services were held in the Congregational meeting-house, the use of which was granted by the selectmen, it being then town-property.[1] Elder Lemuel Covell offered the introductory prayer and preached the sermon; Elder Leland gave the right hand of fellowship; Elder Justus Hull delivered the charge; Elder Joseph W. Sawyer offered the ordaining, and Elder Ebenezer Smith the concluding, prayers.

Mr. Francis was born at Wethersfield, Connecticut, in the year 1759. At what time he removed to Pittsfield is not certain, but it was probably early in 1780; for in that year he attained his majority, and we find his name enrolled in Capt. Rufus Allen's company of matross, which, in some alarm, "marched forty miles, and served from October 13 to October 17." We next find him mentioned in the town-records in 1789, as one of those whom an investigating committee reported to be unquestionably Baptists, and attendants upon Mr. Rathbun's preaching. In the same list appears the name of his father, Josiah Francis, who, according to the family tradition, came to Pittsfield two or three years after his son. These two were the only members of the new church, which the records indicate to have been members of the old. Josiah, Jr., who was probably also connected with it, is not

---

[1]Several years afterwards, when the federal members of the First church, for political reasons, separated from it, and formed the Union church, they petitioned for the use of this meeting-house, for the installation of Rev. Mr. Punderson as their pastor, stating that a similar courtesy had been granted the Baptists. The selectmen, who were all democrats, refused the petition, on the ground that the Baptist church was organized from an honest dissent from the Congregational faith, while the Union church originated in hostility to that from which it separated.

mentioned in the list, for some unexplained reason ; perhaps being absent that year.¹ But, at whatever time the family or its different members came in, they brought their Baptist principles with them, firmly and religiously fixed in heart and mind. " Here was Baptist stock, root and branch, fiber and tissue, seed and fruit,"² and here it has been transmitted ever since.

Elder Francis remained pastor of the church, preaching in the old North Woods school-house, for seven years and three months, and died in office, September 28, 1813. During his ministry, harmony prevailed, twenty-one members were added by baptism, and one by letter ; three were excluded, and one died, leaving a membership of sixty-nine. In 1807, the Shaftsbury Association welcomed the Pittsfield church back to its fold, and, in the announcement of its pastor's death to the meeting of 1814, placed upon its record the following honorable memorial : " We announce the death of the truly pious pastor of the Baptist church in Pittsfield, Elder John Francis. His highest encomiums are an ardent thirst for the welfare of souls, a pious grief for all sin, and an unblemished character."³ The *Sun* in announcing his death, said :

For a number of years he has been the worthy and highly esteemed pastor of the Baptist Church in Pittsfield, and was a zealous and faithful preacher of the gospel of salvation, uniting in his Christian character, the strength of divine grace with the beauty of spiritual proportions.

Called suddenly to lay down his armor, he calmly bade adieu to the scenes of earth, trusting to that salvation he had preached to others. When asked, a few moments before he expired, what message he would leave behind, he replied, " Remember the words which I have spoken to you while I was yet with you."

Of the introduction of the Methodist church into Pittsfield, we have already given some account,⁴ but something more of

---

¹In the records, John Francis is mentioned as three years on the school committee and holding other town-offices. Josiah, Jr., was also several years on this committee ; was selectman in 1817, and held other offices in town.

²Centennial sermon at the dedication of the remodeled church, April 6, 1873, by the pastor, Rev. C. H. Spalding.

³Rev. Mr. Spalding's sermon.

⁴Vol. I., pages 455–6.

detail is due to the results which have followed the labors of the early apostles of that faith in this vicinity.[1]

In forming the Pittsfield circuit, which then included a large extent of territory, Rev. Lemuel Smith preached the first Methodist sermon in the town, at the house of Zebulon Herrick in the East Part. This was probably in the year 1789,[2] and the appointment was continued at that house until the ensuing fall, when it was transferred to Nathan Webb's, about two miles distant, in Dalton. Here it was continued for several years, after which it was again changed to the school-house, near William Z. Herrick's, in Pittsfield, near the Dalton border. Soon after the first sermon, a class was formed with the following members: Thomas Hubbard, Enoch Hubbard, Zadock Hubbard, Joshua Luce, Ira Gaylord, Henry Durkee, Edward Roberts, senior, Oliver Allen, Nathan Webb, senior, Nathaniel Kellogg, senior, Joshua Arnold, Solomon Clark.

Shortly after his first sermon at Mr. Herrick's house, Rev. Mr. Smith preached at the residence of Col. Oliver Root in the West Part, and made some converts. In the winter following, Rev. Robert Green, being detained by a storm at the house of Captain Joel Stevens, on West street, close under the Taconic mountains, made so good use of the tempestuous hours, in preaching, that a number of converts[3] were made and a class organized with the following members: Josiah Wright, Mr. [probably Joel] Stevens, Joshua Whitney, John Francis, David Ashley, Selah Andrews.

The meetings were held for a while at Capt. Stevens's house, then at the school-house, and finally at the meeting-house, which was erected on West street about the year 1800, and continued to be the principal place of worship for the Methodist society until 1827.[4]

"In 1801, Pittsfield was made the head of a district, embracing all the territory which lies from Connecticut on the south, to the Canada line on the north, and from the Green to the Adirondack mountains east and west; or including what are now known

---

[1] Rev. Dr. Carhart, pastor of the church in 1864, prepared a brief sketch of its history from which we gather many of the facts here stated.

[2] Dr. Carhart thinks 1790-91.

[3] Bishop Asbury mentions in 1792, "a melting time among the people of Pittsfield, where the Lord was at work."

[4] Dr. Carhart's History.

HISTORY OF PITTSFIELD.   141

as the Cambridge, Burlington, Plattsburg, St. Albans, and part of the Troy districts of the Vermont and Troy conferences, besides portions of territory now within the bounds of the New York and New England conferences."[1]

In the year 1804, the following persons, with such as might be associated with them, were incorporated as the Methodist Religious Society of Pittsfield, Hancock, Dalton and Washington:

Gideon Allen, Loyal W. Allen, David Ashley, Allen Barnes, Solomon Clark, John Clark, Seth Coe, John Dighton, Oliver Fuller, Ira Gaylord, Robert Green, Leonard Goff, Enoch Hubbard, Zadock Hubbard, Thomas Hubbard, Malcolm Henry, Nathaniel Kellogg, Jr., Joshua Luce, Richard Osborn, William Pomeroy, William Roberts, Jr., Aaron Roberts, Aaron Root, Amasa Smith, Samuel Stanton, Eliphalet Stevens, Jonathan Stowe, Lebbeus Webb, Nathan Webb, Jr., John Ward, Joshua Whitney, Joseph Ward, Josiah Wright.

Many of the corporators named, we recognize as residents of Pittsfield, and a majority of them were undoubtedly so; but we are unable to point them out. The descendants of some of them still hold a place in the church.

Eli Root, Esq., was designated as the magistrate to issue the warrant for the first meeting of the corporators, but he dying before he had performed that duty,[2] the organization was delayed until the next year, when a supplementary act was passed, authorizing the warrant to be issued by Joshua Danforth, Esq., or any other justice in the county.

In 1807, an important addition to the act of incorporation was passed, providing that

Any person belonging to either of the towns of Pittsfield, Dalton, Washington or Hancock, who may hereafter desire to join said Methodist society of Pittsfield, and shall declare such as his or her intention in writing and deliver the same to the clerk of the town, and a copy of the same to the minister of the parish in which he or she may reside, on or before the first day of March in the year when such application shall be made, and at the same time produce a certificate of their being united with, or having become a member of, said society, signed by the minister or clerk, and two of the committee of the said

[1] Origin and Progress of Methodism in North Adams, by Rev. T. A. Griffin.

[2] Died, October 28, 1804, Eli Root, Esq., aged 74, for 50 years a resident of this town. *Mortuary Record, First Church.*

Methodist society, such persons shall from and after the date of such declaration, with his or her polls and estate, be considered a member of said society. Provided, however, that such persons shall be holden to pay his or her proportion of all moneys [already] legally assessed in said parish to which such person formerly belonged.

Another section of the act required a similar course to be taken by those desirous of relinquishing their connection with the Methodist society.

This addition to its charter went far towards placing the Methodist society upon an equality with the "standing-order," and relieving its members from the vexatious yearly renewal of certificates; giving it a decided advantage over the Baptists, who were unincorporated.[1]

In 1806, a general and interesting revival of religion began under Methodist auspices, and extended throughout the town.

In 1810, the annual New York Methodist conference held its session with the church in Pittsfield.

In 1812, a schism occurred which somewhat retarded the progress of the society; about thirty of its members, at the West Part—a portion of the town, whose inhabitants were always much given to independent thought and action—seceding, and styling themselves "Reformed Methodists." In what their tenets differed from the church from which they separated, does not appear; but the "folly and wickedness," of which they are accused, seem to have consisted of disregard of the constituted ecclesiastical authorities of their sect. Rev. Mr. Hibbard, who was stationed on this circuit in 1813, says that public opinion was in their favor, fearing that they had been unjustly treated, and were a persecuted people. Upon Mr. Hibbard's arrival in Pittsfield, they sent a committee to him, requesting to be formed into a class according to the Methodist discipline; to which he consented on condition that they should conform to that discipline

---

[1] In 1795, Valentine Rathbun, Daniel Rathbun, John Remington, Jonathan Kingsley, and John Bryant, were incorporated as the Baptist Religious Society of Pittsfield with the rights and immunities usually enjoyed by dissenting parishes; but the society died with Mr. Rathbun's church; and for the reasons specified by Dr. Porter, no parish was incorporated in connection with that formed in 1800. Nor to this day is there any parochial organization distinct from the church, which was in 1849 incorporated with parochial powers, having previous to that year, held its property through trustees.

and receive him as their minister. This they did, and appear to have conducted themselves blamelessly through the usual probation of six months. But when, at the expiration of that term, they expected to be fully re-instated, Mr. Hibbard told them that although their motives in withdrawing from the church were, as he believed, pure, yet he considered the act wrong, and that their error had arisen from a mistaken notion of conducting class-matters. He therefore required of them a confession of their error in this respect. To this four or five assented; the others withdrew in displeasure. Mr. Hibbard gives the following account of the end of the schism :

> I found they would neither receive me nor the discipline to govern them, unless we would govern according to their opinions. But my sufferings and labors with them were so well understood, that it changed public opinion, and their congregation left them; this vexed them, and they accused me heavily. They said, "You meant to break us up." I said, "Yes, that is true, and I am only sorry that I did not succeed in making you good Methodists."
>
> These schismatics formed a coalition with others, on different circuits, and made zealous struggles to establish themselves as a church, under the name of "Reformed Methodists." But Wisdom was not "justified of her children" among them; therefore they have not prospered. Confusion was in their counsels, and in many places they dwindled away. Professing themselves to be spiritually wise, when they were not, they became bold in their boisterous preaching, and, having the name of Methodists, they were in good repute for a while. But some have since joined the Shakers, and some the Christians, so that their number is now (1826) small.' [1]

These schismatics, who have long ago passed away, and left no defenders, should not be judged too harshly. The solitude of farm-life in our retired highland valley, palisaded by great hills, favored much erratic religious and theological thought. In the loneness of his forest-hemmed fields, nature, life, few but deeply-conned books, and the Sabbath sermon pondered through the week, propounded to the farmer awful questions, for which no wide reading had furnished him either an answer, or an excuse for setting them aside as beyond answer. A resolute and inquiring mind, with a deep sense of personal responsibility for error, forbade him to avoid or to meet these questions lightly. Had he attempted

[1] Hibbard's Memoirs, page 321.

to shun them, they would only the more persistently have haunted him. He met them, therefore, manfully, and the result was, doubtless, in a great majority of instances, a deep and abiding conviction of religious truth. But often, instead, there came of his meditations, fanaticism on the one hand, deism on the other; or, perhaps more frequently than either, a personal creed more or less approximating to those of the neighboring sects, but doing away, either by explanation, modification or absolute denial, with some of the points which interposed stumbling-blocks in the path of his faith. Every town had marked men of this class, who, by earnest and prolonged thought, however little guided by learning, had wrought out for themselves a philosophy of religion, in various degrees divergent from the orthodox beliefs of the day; some making but a slight reservation, at which the conservators of the church might wink, in their assent to the Articles of Faith; others maintaining heresies so rank that they were deemed infidels.

Fanaticism rarely manifested itself — unless some extreme opinions among the Methodists could be so considered—in regard to either public or private morals; but generally in pushing disproportionately and to undue limits, points in ordinarily-accepted doctrinal theology, or by the perversion of obscure but startling passages of Scripture, which had been morbidly pondered. Thus, much brooding over St. Paul's admission of the possibility of an unpardonable sin, haunted more than one unhappy religionist to madness: a fact which has furnished a theme to the greatest American author who has presented truth under the guise of fiction.

A favorite subject for these lonely thinkers among the hills was found in the mystical prophesies of Daniel and St. John regarding the latter days of this earth; and some of them deemed that they had solved the inspired mysteries.[1]

---

[1] William Miller, known as the Second Advent Prophet, but only professing to be a divinely-commissioned interpreter of prophecy, may be considered as one and the most noted of this class—and the only one who, so far as we know, fixed upon and believed himself to be commanded by God to proclaim a certain year as that in which the Fifth Monarchy would commence. For, although he removed from Pittsfield almost in infancy, his father's family had long been residents of the town, and, in his new home, he was surrounded, among similar scenes, with the same influences which prevailed in the old.

William Miller was born February 15, 1782, at a farm-house which stood on

Occasionally a few persons in Pittsfield, and perhaps some of the neighboring towns, uniting upon an erratic creed, formed a little schismatic sect, of which, if the representations which have come down to us are correct, the Reformed Methodist was one. But, generally even sooner than in their case, the majority returned to the communion which they had left, while the remainder, for the most part, gravitated to the Shakers; whose boast, indeed, it was that, in the bosom of their peaceful church, all troubled spirits found rest; a boast which, after the first few years of their establishment in Berkshire and Columbia counties, had at least the semblance of truth.

If deism, less frequently than other forms of error, resulted from morbid religious studies and meditations, it had, from other causes, become in the mass of community more prevalent than any other. Rev. Mr. Hibbard, writing of his experience on the Pittsfield and Litchfield circuits in 1797-99, says: "I was kindly received by many; but deism was prevailing. Mr. Thomas

the south side of West street, about one mile from the park. In 1786, his parents migrated to Low Hampton, Washington county, New York, where he remained until he was twenty-two years old, when he removed to Poultney, Vt. He was a captain in the war of 1812, and was engaged in the battle of Plattsburg, conducting himself with credit. From his youth he was a devoted student of the Bible, and early became convinced that the second coming of the Redeemer would take place in the year 1843. In 1833, he believed that he received a command from Heaven to go out and proclaim the approaching end of time, that all men might be prepared to meet their Judge. After the mental struggle and pleading with the Lord usual in such cases, he yielded to the impulse—divine or otherwise—and, for ten years, with voice and pen, taught men that the second advent of the Saviour would be witnessed in the year named. And so evident was his sincerity, and so plausible were his arguments—aided by the excitement that such an announcement would create in a certain class of minds—that a great multitude, said to number fifty thousand souls, embraced his doctrine, and, after their fashion, prepared to ascend with their Redeemer and King. And, although the passing of the year 1843 disproved his predictions, and the great mass of his followers left him, yet in the following y⸺ he published an "Apology," acknowledging, of necessity, an error in his omputation, but maintaining that it could be only slight, and that all the signs continued to proclaim the end nigh at hand. In this faith, having returned to the home of his youth at Low Hampton, he died in 1849. A remnant of his disciples still believe in his modified prediction, but year by year, diminish in numbers. All who knew him, agree in pronouncing him a sincere and truthful man, of the utmost purity of character, and earnest in his love for his fellow-men.

Paine's 'Age of Reason' was highly thought of by many who knew neither what the age they lived in, or reason, was." But not only were Paine's theological works "highly thought of" by many persons of superficial thought and attainments—to many of whom they had been introduced by sympathy with his political utterances—but the more learned and subtle reasoning, and the keener and more polished wit, of Voltaire found a favorite place in the libraries of cultivated and able men. The influences which, extending from Paris, Berlin and Ferney, infected the whole civilized world, did not leave remote Berkshire untouched. Many openly denied the truth of the Christian religion; many more secretly doubted, or disbelieved. Even hatred of France could not protect all the federalists from the power of the great French philosopher; and men who would have scorned to yield to the vulgar missiles of Thomas Paine, were almost proud to fall before the knightly lance of Arouet Voltaire. It was the fashion of the day.

Against this fashionable deism, and every other form of infidelity, the Methodist church set itself to war; and not only against these. It was emphatically a church militant. It boldly attacked the theological tenets to which other religious denominations clung most tenaciously. It denounced as sinful many of the pleasures in which, not only the world at large, but most "professed Christians," delighted to indulge. And, in return, it found itself and its doctrines bitterly assailed on every side. As men at that period were intensely partisan in their politics, so they were intensely sectarian in religion. Each sect held most obstinately, and made most pronounced, those tenets which were most peculiar to itself. That is, it concentrated its attention, as it did its defenses, at the points most likely to be assailed. The Baptists being of the Calvinistic branch of their denomination, and adhering to the Congregational church-polity, differed little from the "standing-order," except in requiring baptism by immersion as essential to true membership in the Church of Christ, and in denying that ordinance altogether, to infants. But in these points there was matter enough for sharp theological controversy. Their oppugnation to the prevailing creed was, however, of little moment compared with the attacks made upon it by the Methodists, who acknowledged a hierarchy of bishops, presiding elders, priests and deacons; who boldly denied the doctrine of election and reprobation; averred the possibility of a "fall from grace;" and in other particulars impugned the traditional theology of New England as unscriptural. Little advance had then anywhere been made towards genuine toleration of opinion upon points like these; and with a very large class errors of belief concerning them were considered as fatal to the holder's hopes of Heaven; while many of those who did not deny that those who taught them sincerely, might be saved, yet deemed their offense a very serious one, and dangerous to the souls of others. The result was, on both sides, an immense amount of polemical, doctrinal, preaching and writing, for the public; of angry controversy and uncharitable judgment in private life. And in this storm the Methodists were, as far as numbers and social position was concerned, the weaker party.

But, not content with assailing the favorite theological tenets of the Calvinistic churches, the Methodists entered upon a crusade against the most cherished pleasures of the world. However pertinaciously the Congregational church clung to the doctrinal teachings of the Puritans, its discipline as to social pleasures had, whether for good or evil, become greatly relaxed. Saving a little ascetic observation of the Sabbath, and a few like points, it was, in Berkshire, hardly less tolerant of the genial pleasures of life, than was the English Church. This, the Methodists attributed to the prominence generally given to the notion that good works—if not absolutely, as held by some, a hindrance—were not essential to salvation. It was perhaps in quite as great a measure, due to the liberalizing influence of increasing wealth and culture, and to the position of the Congregational, as a quasi state church. But, whatever may have been the cause, the old Puritanic view of the wassail and the dance, as exceedingly sinful, had almost entirely disappeared. Never was there a people more given to, or more unrebuked in, those pleasures, than those of Pittsfield and Berkshire in the earlier part of the nineteenth century; with few exceptions, and those chiefly from Methodist influence. The numerous taverns were haunted by revelers of all grades; and the social glass, with its associated merriment, was found every-where from the bar-room to the clergyman's sideboard. Festal suppers were frequent: clubs, like the Woronoko, held them at regular intervals at the houses of their members; all public festivals were celebrated by them, or by dinners; they followed the squirrel-hunt, the military election or whatever else afforded an excuse for the jovial spirit of the day. But dancing was the passion of the young, and, while certain tavern-revelries of the coarser sort, were frowned upon by staid elders, the "civil dance" was approved, or at least not greatly discountenanced. Clergymen sometimes defended it as innocent, or at least but a venial transgression, although some lingering trace of older opinions was found in the idea that dancing was not to be indulged in while they were present. But, with this exception, the practice was as universal and as passionately followed as among any European peasantry. In all respects, the people of Berkshire were a genial, pleasure-loving race; often, indeed, it must be confessed, pursuing it too grossly and to too great extremes.

Against all this—including gaming, light conversation, jesting, and of course profanity—the Methodists waged uncompromising warfare; some of the more zealous, indeed, occasionally pushing their opposition to what, in a less primitive state of society would have been deemed impertinent. It may be imagined that while in this conflict they won some friends and converts, and in time largely influenced public opinion and manners, they roused against themselves a hostility which manifested itself in divers ways, and in various degrees. But this, as well as the opposition which they encountered from other denominations, they counted only the persecution which crowned their faith. Nothing of the kind, however, seems to have manifested itself until some years after the first introduction of the Wesleyan Church into Pittsfield; and it could never have been very general. The Methodist preachers first held forth in the houses of Congregational church-members, who hospitably entertained them, and took great pains to gather the people to hear their exhortations; and this was often the case through all the earlier years of the nineteenth century. Nay, even deistical tavern-keepers invited them to exhort in their dancing-halls. And, in return, the preachers, at least in the earliest years, generally left their converts, uninfluenced, to unite with the churches to which they were attracted by circumstances; often the Baptist or Congregational. The courtesies of the deists, of course, could not be returned in that way.

When, however, opposition to the new faith was awakened by its progress, neither sharp denunciations for heresy, nor the unpopularity of its ascetism in morals, proved so great an obstacle to its success—and to that of the Baptists as well—as the opinion in community that these denominations were "not respectable," inasmuch as their preachers, with few exceptions, had not received a collegiate education. They replied, to be sure, that "as these were, so were the Apostles." But they gained little by this retort except a new charge of irreverent presumption. Nor, with the mass of community, did it avail to do away with this prejudice, that many of the Baptist and Methodist clergy showed themselves, not only eloquent and persuasive exhorters, but able to cope with the best in logical argument and theological learning. Massachusetts laws had from the first required a learned, as well as a pious, clergy, and learning was judged only by the standard of Harvard and Yale. Without that learning duly certified by diploma, the clergymen upon whom the new sects—to which not many learned had yet been called—were obliged to depend, could not reflect "respectability" upon their flocks. It did not matter, that in Massachusetts, at that time, infants almost imbibed theological lore with their mother's milk; that, at the least, few grew to man's estate without listening to innumerable theological lectures, so that many laymen were almost as well versed in matters of belief as the majority of clergymen. Nor did it matter that the chief deficiency of the unlearned clergy—inability to consult the Scriptures in their original tongues—was practically shared by many of those nominally learned, but who had little critical nicety of scholarship. He who lacked collegiate training, or at least a collegiate diploma, however little it detracted from his ability as a religious teacher, could bestow no respectability upon his people, whatever else he might bestow. Nor was it altogether respectable to belong to any other denomination than that which was favored by the state, and to which most of those distinguished for wealth or place belonged. And as those who could boast but little education themselves, were often most careful to shine in the light of an educated ministry; so those who were most doubtfully struggling through the debatable ground of society, always clung in the church, as elsewhere, most pertinaciously to association with those whose position was assured. The dread of not being classed with "the respectable" was therefore a powerful obstacle to the spread of new sects; and, not only were those possessed of an uneasy anxiety regarding their place in society, influenced by this prejudice; but ardent and impressible youth, who might be touched by the fervid eloquence or convinced by the masculine logic of the new teachers, were sensitive to the ridicule which was sure to fall upon those who avowed themselves converts. This point of respectability was the weapon which Rev. Mr. Hibbard's father used, and for years effectually, to prevent his avowal of the Methodist faith. "I wanted to be a Congregationalist and to be respectable," said he in his graphic description of his mental struggles, "but I wanted the love and seriousness of the Methodists."

But, however the Baptist and Methodist preachers may have counted secular learning as of secondary importance in their calling, the greater and best part of them were far from holding it in contempt. If it could have been had without detriment to what they regarded essential gospel-truth, they would, as ardently as any, have desired an educated ministry. Some of those whose native abilities best enabled them to dispense with its aids, most deeply regretted their deficiencies in this respect, and among them was Rev. Mr. Hibbard, the only one of the early Methodist pastors of whom we are able to give a sketch.

Mr. Hibbard was born at Norwich, Connecticut, February 24, 1771, his father being Nathan Hibbard, a tanner and shoemaker. His mother's maiden-name was Mehitable Crosby. He was unfortunately christened, not William, but Billy, a circumstance which, coupled with a certain quaint wit which he manifested in common with most men of mark in his day, has led to an underestimate of his ability and character. As we have had occasion to observe in other instances, tradition, an inveterate preserver of distorted and misplaced facts, is sure to keep in memory every anecdote of piquant wit and quaint humor which it can lay hold of in the life of a noted individual; leaving them in grotesque prominence when the solid ground-work of his ordinary life and conversation is forgotten. It is far easier to remember a happy retort or a pointed allusion than to retain the logic, or even the conclusions, of a labored discourse. But, fortunately, Mr. Hibbard has left an autobiography distinguished by an evident truthfulness, and told with a simplicity and earnestness, which make it charming reading—at least for those who do not peruse it with a controversial spirit.

From his earliest years, almost from infancy, he was distinguished by the most unqualified faith in the Holy Scriptures, implicit reliance upon the efficacy of prayer, and a painfully-sensitive conscience. But, unqualified as was his faith, it was not unquestioning; and, even before he had heard or known of doubts concerning any of the articles of the Congregational faith, in which he had been educated, he had reasoned out for himself a creed very similar to the Methodist. In his autobiography the conflict in his mind between old and new ideas is described with much power, and is often deeply interesting; for whatever the reader may think of their grounds, to him his fears of eternal misery were a vivid reality, and his remorse for sin was apparently as bitter as it was in the nature of man to endure. Some of the incidents of this early experience were also amusing to himself in his later days. And all is told with simplicity. From his childhood, too, he was visited by remarkable dreams, and evidently put considerable faith in them, as in other similar modes of communication from the Deity. When he was four years old the revolutionary war began, and his father and four uncles went to take part in it, as soldiers. For years they were absent in the field, and nightly he united his infant-voice in prayer for their safety, with that of his tearful step-mother. He was encouraged in these prayers by a dream. While he was yet a child, his father removed to Hinsdale—about nine miles east of Pittsfield, where his religious experiences were continued and occupied a great part of his attention, although he endeavored to conceal them. His visions continued and were not confined to his sleeping-hours. The doctrine of predestination oppressed him with fearful power. On one occasion, as he was riding, it so affected him that he nearly fell from his horse. "As soon as I had gained strength," said he, "I cried most earnestly to the Lord in these words: 'O Lord, does everybody believe so?' That moment an answer was suggested to my mind, as plain as it could have been spoken to my outward ears: 'No! There is a people in England that teach clearly from the Scriptures, that any poor sinner, who has not committed the unpardonable sin, may be saved if he will repent and turn to the Lord in the time of his probation and day of grace; which God gives to every man. But, if he will not obey the calls of God's Spirit, but resists and grieves him by the sin he willingly commits, then he ought to be damned.'"

"This was good news to my mind. I knew it was power from the Lord. * * * I then cried unto the Lord to spare my life until I should find this people." At this time he had never heard of the Methodists or their doctrines. At least such was his recollection in his later years. Soon afterwards, while still a youth, he received in the same manner a promise that the love of God should inspire him, and that he should be called to preach, and, if faithful, be the instrument of the conversion of many souls. He feared that *this* whispering came from the devil, especially as he had heard his father say that he did not intend to send any of his sons to college. Then, in answer to his prayer for a sign, came "the sweet impression: that the people I should find did not consider a college education as the essential qualification for a minister; yet that all who ministered must study to know the Scriptures, and other books, whereby they may have knowledge of men and things sufficient to teach men the will of God."

There were many visions of this sort vouchsafed him, on which it is not our place here to pass judgment; as we also do not upon any of the views in theology held by him or others of whom we here speak. There are, however, we suppose, but few men who have thought deeply and anxiously upon any subject, and especially upon religion, but who have found impressed upon their mind thoughts, often seemingly expressed in words, coming from without themselves. Mr. Hibbard did not doubt that they had a divine origin. It was some time after this, that a Methodist itinerant preacher came to his father's house, and young Hibbard first heard of the sect. By consent of Mr. Hibbard, senior, the preacher held service, and the son exerted himself to gather an audience. From this time his destiny seemed to be fixed—that he should become a preacher of that order—although it was not fulfilled until after many struggles which are vividly depicted in his autobiography. Finally it was settled in a characteristic way, by an appeal to the Divine oracle. The "impression" came upon him powerfully while he was at work in the field. We omit many simply and powerfully told descriptions of the soul's conflicts with itself, as not within our province, but quote Mr. Hibbard's account of the method by which he finally decided upon his line of duty, because it is illustrative of the simplicity of heart and earnest belief in direct communication with the

Deity, which characterized the members of the new sects, as well as some of those who adhered to Congregationalism. He writes:

One day, when at work clearing up my fallow ground for a crop, having, as in days past, no strength to work, I thought, 'this will never do. I cannot work, and I am not happy in it as in former days. I ought to be submissive to the will of God. If the Lord does call me to preach, I ought to be submissive to the will of God. If the Lord does call me to preach I ought to say, ' Here, Lord, am I, send me.' But how shall I know that this is of the Lord and not a delusion?' It was then suggested to my mind, ' You have fasted and prayed, but you have not opened the Bible, and asked for direction from the Word of God.' Then I kneeled down and prayed that the Lord would direct me by his word; that if my impressions to preach were from Him, I might open the Bible on some text clearly expressing the duty of one called of God to preach. But if not, that I might open on a text expressing the danger of running before I was sent. I then went to my house to open my Bible solemnly; but, I must confess, with a secret desire that I might be delivered from the impression to preach. When I took up my Bible I shut my eyes and said in my heart, 'Now, Lord, let it be a fair lot.' I opened and found my finger on Ezekiel iii. 17, 18, 'Son of man, I have made thee a watchman unto the house of Israel: therefore hear the word at my mouth and give them warning from me. When I say unto the wicked, thou shalt surely die; and thou givest him not warning, nor speakest to warn the wicked from his wicked way, to save his life, the same wicked man shall die in his iniquity, but his blood will I require at thine hand.' I read no further, but shut up the book and left the house in haste, blaming myself for taking this measure, because now I had less ground to excuse myself than before. I got to my field again, but a gloomy horror overspread my mind more than ever. I sat down and wept, and wished the Lord would take my life. For two hours I was but a little from distraction. How can I discharge my duty and be a minister? I must pay for my farm and get something for my wife and children to subsist upon, or it will be said, I am worse than an infidel, if I provide not for my own household. But to feel as I do, I cannot work. I fear, if I preach, I shall not do my duty; and I fear, if I do not, I shall be damned after all. O, if Calvinism were true, that I could not fall from grace, I would easily overcome this distress by leaving all to the irresistible grace of God, and say, ' Once in grace always in grace.' But I am torn and racked in every way.

Thus I struggled, until, exhausted with fatigue, I went and lay down on the damp ground, praying the Lord to take my life and have mercy on my soul. I was in hopes I should take cold and die. I dared not go into the house, lest my wife should ask me what was the matter, and I should have to tell her my exercises. I slept about an hour and a half on the damp ground, and awoke much refreshed in body; and, like a child that had been whipped, more soft and docile in temper. I prayed, and begged the Lord to forgive my refractory temper. I felt ashamed of what I had done. I went to my work, but I could not work; then I again prayed; and at this time I resolved to go to the house and ask my wife to open the Bible with her eyes shut, and put in her finger, and read the verse her finger was upon, and if it was a call to the work of the ministry, I would receive it; I would no more resist, nor, Jonah-like, run from the Lord. I went in and informed her of my distress, the first time I had ever spoken to her about it, and how I had resisted the impression until, like Jonah, 'I was in misery and could do no work. I have fasted and prayed for an answer that would solve the doubt, and now I have come in to have you open the Bible, shutting your eyes until you place your finger on a text, and read the text your finger is on.'

She took the Bible and opened it in a hurry, without shutting her eyes, on John x : 13, and read, 'The hireling fleeth because he is a hireling, and careth not for the sheep.' I said, 'My dear, you knew where that text was, and you opened it to reproach me for not having yielded to my duty; besides, you did not shut your eyes, and it is not a fair lot.'

She smiled to see me so earnest. I said, 'How dare you smile so before God? Why, this is an awful solemn time—you ought not to smile.' I took the Bible and said, 'Now let there be a fair lot; shut your eyes.' She did so, and opened on Luke ix: 60, and read, 'Jesus said unto him, let the dead bury their dead; but go thou and preach the kingdom of God.' I said, 'Why, my dear, there is no such text in the Bible; you have made it.' She burst into tears, reaching me the Bible, saying, 'There, read it.' While I was reading it, to my utter amazement, she said: 'I knew you would have to preach; I have given you up a long time ago.' I said, 'Well, this is of God; let us pray.' So we kneeled down, and all my horror of mind was gone in a moment —my soul was now again happy in God; though I mourned that I should have been unyielding to the impressions that had so long followed me. I prayed the Lord to forgive the stubborness I had been so long guilty of. I said I will preach as well as I can; I will not refuse again if I am called upon.

Next, after his doubts whether his call to preach was of God or a delusion of Satan, the obstacle to his becoming a traveling preacher which most affected Mr. Hibbard was the consideration of his duty to provide for his family. "The economy of the Methodists," he writes, "left all in entire uncertainty respecting the support of their preachers. The utmost that was promised was a bare supply of necessaries, and this uncertain; so that I must reconcile myself to be poor all the days of my life, without the least prospect of ever obtaining the conveniences of this life." But, his wife assenting, he took up the burden which he believed God had imposed upon him; and, although his "difficulties were many, by reason of ignorance and poverty, left all," and, by direction of the presiding elder, in 1797, went with Rev. Mr. Stebbins on to the Pittsfield circuit, where he continued until June of the following year. In 1813, he was again stationed on this circuit, and met the trouble with the "Reformed Methodists" which has already been recounted. In 1814, being strongly in sympathy with the government, he volunteered to supply preaching for the army, and when a regiment of militia were called from Berkshire for the defense of Boston, Colonel Chamberlain appointed him his chaplain. On his return to Pittsfield he visited the prisoners at the Cantonment. After a long service in the cause which he had chosen, he died August 17, 1849, at Canaan, N. Y.

We have given a somewhat prolonged sketch of Mr. Hibbard, believing him to have been a representative man of his denomination in its earliest days in Pittsfield, and that a better idea would thus be presented of its state and struggles, than by any general statement regarding it as a whole. It is not often that a man reveals himself so fully to the reader as Mr. Hibbard evidently does in his memoirs.

The Methodists, as we have seen, were ardently zealous in the reprobation of those amusements and indulgences which they believed, in however remote a degree, to tend to excite the passions or to dissipate "serious" thought; the terms "serious" and "truly religious" being with them synonymous. In this they agreed with the Congregationalists of Puritanic days, and to a great degree with those of more recent times. But the members of the "standing-order" in the beginning of the nineteenth century held that there was a time to dance, and to be merry. In their views of social amusements, they did not widely, if at all, differ from the churches which are usually styled liberal.

But the Congregationalists, as a body and as individuals, were keenly alive to the irreligious, demoralizing and disorganizing tendencies of the age, which it must be remembered was that of the French republic, and of the scarcely less corrupt empire.

And no one would suspect the Congregational churches of Massachusetts of being lukewarm in their oppugnation of any sin which found its root in that soil. There were minds indeed — even among those who professed themselves members of the church— whose faith had been deeply undermined. But, as a mass, the community, which—so slight was the dissenting element in numbers—might be characterized as Congregational, had by no means lost its respect for religion either as the conservator of whatever is good in this life, or as the only true foundation for hope with regard to that life which is to come. Doubtless many of the clergy and the more serious minded of the church, held with the Methodists in regard to amusements; and, if the majority viewed them with a more lenient eye, it was from a sincere belief that they were not inconsistent with a religious life. It was no proof that all were not zealous in the performance of their duty as they understood it. To what degree that zeal extended may be judged by the action of the Association of Ministers in the county of Berkshire and the Northern Presbytery in the state of New York, at a joint meeting of those bodies, held in Berkshire county in the year 1800, when they recommended a plan for the better inculcation of religious truth upon the young.

This plan was in substance as follows: The Association and Presbytery advised that each of their ministers, and, where the churches were destitute of ministers, the deacons or some other meet persons selected for the purpose, should collect the children and youth, in a body or in divisions, as local circumstances might dictate, as often as he might judge expedient, and impress upon them the serious and weighty things of eternity by catechising, instruction and counsel; beginning and closing with prayer. The shorter Westminster catechism was recommended for use, as containing "a compendium of all the leading and most important doctrines and duties of religion, expressed in an easy and plain manner, sanctioned by long custom, and, by people in general, best known and understood."

A significant recommendation was that ministers and "serious" people should use their influence to have the catechism taught in schools; "a practice which of late had grown into great disuse;" and also that the Holy Scriptures might be read, at least once a day, in the schools.

It was also recommended that the family-concert of catechising and prayer, already suggested to some churches and congregations by individual members of the Association and Presbytery, should be warmly supported.

There were some further suggestions as to the methods of carrying the plan into effect, and that a report of its operation should be made by each minister to the body to which he belonged at the first meeting after September 1, 1801.

The plan was printed at Stockbridge in 1800, together with an address full of pious and fervent exhortation regarding the duty of parents and ministers towards the young. They say that many of the pious lament the growing neglect of catechising and instructing the rising generation; but after a strong presentation, according to the manner of that day of the fearful consequences of the neglect by parents of the souls of their children, they add: "It is now a time in which God is pouring out His Spirit in plentiful showers. Awake, and attend to your children. There is a shaking in the tops of the mulberry trees. God has gone forth. Bestir yourselves. Many people, some old, some young, have been brought into Christ's Church. * * * * Should the present favorable moment be neglected, the opportunity in a measure may be lost. Say not that nothing can be done. Attempts, with the blessing of God, may be followed by great and good consequences."

And, with other pious and eloquent exhortation and encouragement to faithfulness, the address closes.

The authors of this address will not be suspected of lukewarmness in their Master's cause.

CHAPTER VIII.

EARLY WOOLEN MANUFACTURES.

[1800-1812.]

State of American manufactures in 1800—First woolen mills in America—Arthur Scholfield—Birth, parentage and education—Emigrates to America—Commences business at Byfield—Removes to Pittsfield—Makes broadcloths, carding-machines, spinning-jennies and looms — The first Pittsfield factory — James Strandring's manufacture of comb-plates — Elkanah Watson's efforts for Berkshire woolen manufactures—Statement of his manufacture of broadcloth from his own merino wool—A woolen manufacturing company formed—It fails—Scholfield establishes a woolen manufactory—His difficulties—The Pittsfield Sun's statement of manufactures in 1809—Close of Arthur Scholfield's life.

PERHAPS the most galling grievances which Great Britain inflicted upon her American colonies — saving the blows aimed at the foundation of constitutional government—were the crippling restrictions imposed upon their manufactures, avowedly designed to crush them out of existence. And, in proportion as this injustice was bitterly felt by the colonists, was their desire to exercise their long-pent-up energies, and develop their natural resources, ardent and hopeful when independence made them masters of themselves and their country.

This desire was, however, not gratified until the new states had been taught by painful experience that internal dissensions, selfish rivalries, and enactments by which each little legislature sought, with unwise cunning, to obtain advantage over its neighbor, were even more fatal to their common—and not less to their individual—industrial interests, than it was possible for the most jealous foreign domination to be.

With the organization of the federal government in 1789, this experience terminated, and a brighter era dawned. Under the fostering action of the first congress, and the grand financial policy of Hamilton, manufactures began to thrive; commerce received new vigor; and agriculture, which—from an overplus of production in proportion to the consumers of her products—had grown poor in the midst of her abundance, once more received an adequate reward for her labors.

The branches of manufacture to which attention was first directed were those described in a previous chapter, in which material that cumbered the fields, the hides left by the beef-packers, and other waste raw material, were transmuted into articles for which commerce offered a profitable market. But the opportunity to utilize otherwise valueless and incumbering substances was not the only circumstance which led to the large production in America, of iron, potash, leather and similar articles; while as yet the making of woolen cloth was confined to the narrow hand-loom; and cotton, which had little or no place, found a substitute in home-made linen. The difference was farther, and perhaps chiefly, accounted for by the comparative simplicity of the processes and machinery required by the branches of manufacture first prosecuted; the cheapness of the raw material rendering possible a profitable return from work every way wasteful, while, for the manufacture of fine woolen and cotton goods, skilled labor, delicate machinery and a refined fleece—neither of which was yet possible in America—were indispensable. The laws of Great Britain jealously prohibited the emigration of artisans and the exportation of machinery. The penalties for the infringement of these statutes had been greatly increased at the close of the revolutionary war; and they were executed with a success which seems less surprising when we remember that the agents of the government were aided, and their vigilance stimulated, by a rich and powerful body of men striving to retain a monopoly of the world's most lucrative trade. For years it proved impossible to obtain correct models of the great inventions by which Hargreave and Arkwright had given to England almost the exclusive manufacture of cotton. Nor did it prove less difficult to obtain proper machinery for the profitable manufacture of the higher classes of woolen goods. Possibly ship-owners and ship-masters trading to English ports, intimidated by severe penalties incurred by a violation of the statutes alluded to, and fearful of disturbing the commerce in which they were absorbed, aided in the enforcement of the laws against smuggling out machinery and machinists, just as the same class of New Englanders, engaged in later days in commerce with the southern ports, aided in the recovery of slaves attempting to escape in their vessels. At all events, these laws were enforced, to the exclusion at least of the English improvements in machinery.

Another impediment, nearly as fatal, was found in the poor and costly character of the raw material used in the cotton and woolen manufactures of America, as compared with that employed in Great Britain. The latter country in 1787, imported about 33,-000,000 pounds of cotton, mostly from the West Indies, East Indies and Turkey, whose markets she controlled, and in which the cheapness of labor enabled the planter to cleanse his produce more perfectly than could be afforded in the United States under the rude hand-processes then used. Indeed, in 1791, when the first successful cotton-mill in America was established, the whole crop did not exceed 2,000,000 pounds; and that, almost all, of an inferior quality, imperfectly cleansed.

But Whitney's gin, invented in 1793, rendered the process of cleansing cheap and perfectly effective. The Sea-island cotton, introduced into Georgia in 1786, was soon found to surpass every other variety for making the finest goods, and was grown wherever the climate and soil permitted. Better upland varieties were obtained. And the southern states of the Union became the cotton-growers of the world.

These happy changes at the south enabled the northern states to enter into a not altogether hopeless competition with England in the manufacture of cotton, at least for their home-market. Some years of the nineteenth century had, however, passed before this condition of things was well established. But then a desire to take advantage of it spread over New England; and we find Pittsfield joining with her successful projects for woolen manufactories, others for cotton-mills, which did not succeed.

In making the ruder fabrics, there was less difficulty with American wool than with cotton; but it was coarse and of a loose fiber, entirely unfit for even moderately-fine goods. There had been some efforts to improve the breeds of sheep by the introduction of English stock; but there probably was not a single merino in America until the year 1802, when Col. David Humphrey, who had been minister to Spain, and Chancellor Livingston, who had held the same position in France, brought home from those countries flocks selected by themselves with great care.

The patriotic zeal of these gentlemen was imitated throughout the country; and—as we shall find in our account of the Berkshire Agricultural Society—with peculiar spirit and success in Pittsfield. In fact, she may fairly claim to stand among the foremost towns of the Union in refining the American fleece by the introduction of the merino. In the early improvement of woolen machinery, there can be no doubt of her pre-eminence.

The first woolen-mill in America, was erected at Hartford, and the Pittsfield *Chronicle* of October 12, 1789, states that it made between September 1, 1788 (probably the date at which it commenced operations), and September 1, 1789, five thousand yards of broadcloth, some of which sold at five dollars a yard. A writer in the Boston *Centinel*, quoted in the *Chronicle* of April 12, 1789, says that John Adams had received an elegant suit from this mill, in which he appeared as vice-president of the United States. Washington, when president-elect, visited the same mill in October, 1788, and ordered from it the suit of broadcloth in which he was inaugurated. He speaks of its product as "good, but not yet of the best quality, as were also their coatings, cassimeres, serges, and everlastings. * * * All the parts of the business were done at the mill, except the spinning. This was done by the country-people, who were paid by the cut."

About the same time, a woolen-factory was started at Stockbridge;[1] but of what character we are not informed.

The imperfections in the Hartford cloth, mentioned by President Washington, were probably due to the coarseness of the wool, to the inequalities which would inevitably arise from the mode of spinning; and perhaps also, to unskillful dyeing. In the process of spinning, performed by the country-people, the carding was included.

This mill was in operation in 1791, and its fabrics were commended by Secretary Hamilton, in his celebrated report upon American manufactures, as having "attained a considerable degree of perfection, certainly surpassing anything which could be expected in so short a time under so great difficulties." Our information regarding this factory and its product, is, neverthe-

[1] Bishop's History of American Manufactures.

less, very indefinite; as none of those who speak of it were desirous, or perhaps even capable, of being critical, or technically accurate. President Washington's opinions are the most clearly expressed. We know nothing of the subsequent history of the enterprise; but it seems not to have had the influence anticipated for it, as a pioneer in American woolen-manufactures;[1] and their career rested until the introduction of finer raw material about the year 1800. Precisely with what justice absolute precedence can be claimed for Pittsfield in the revival of, and impulse given to, this great industry at that time, it is difficult for us to determine. A mill for the manufacture of fine broadcloth, established by Chancellor Livingston at Poughkeepsie, was in successful operation in 1808. At what date it began operations we are not informed, but there is strong probability that a portion, if not all, of its machinery was manufactured by Arthur Scholfield at Pittsfield.

The name of Mr. Scholfield is so intimately connected with the claim of Pittsfield to priority in the foundation of the woolen-manufacture of the country, that a brief sketch of his life before his removal to this town, will not only be proper here, but will afford a convenient starting-point for the narration which succeeds it.

Arthur Scholfield, the son of a clothier of the same name, was born in 1757, at Saddlesworth, a town of Yorkshire, England, noted for its woolen-manufactures; and was apprenticed, at sixteen, to James Wrigley, another clothier of that town. Arthur's

---

[1] Mr. James B. Hosmer, of Hartford, whose 94th birthday occurred September 27, 1875, while the present volume was in press, was, from his earliest youth, familiar with the manufactures of Hartford, and was connected as a clerk with the first woolen-factory. Before the text was written we attempted to obtain his evidence; but he was then very ill. A friend, Hon. Lucius M. Boltwood, has since obtained it for us, in the following statement: The company was formed April 28, 1788. The mill, which stood on the west bank of Little river at the foot of Mulberry street, was burned a few years ago. The wool-house is still standing on Gold street. The mill made excellent cassimeres, but the business did not pay, and was, Mr. Hosmer thinks, not continued beyond 1795. His memory is, that the mill used better wool than some of the present day do, and that it was spun harder. But this is very doubtful unless the wool was imported, and the testimony of Washington as to the mode of spinning incorrect. Possibly it may have been true, however, as to a brief portion of its later years, as Mr. Hosmer's reputation for accuracy is high.

signature to the indentures shows him to have received the rudiments of a common education ; and it was provided, in the articles of agreement, that he should still have two weeks " at Christmas to go to school :" not a very liberal allowance, to be sure, but enough to enable a quick-witted lad to refresh his school-learning.

That he was well-taught in the clothier's art is quite certain.

His father appears to have been of the better class of English artisans, and to have reared his family so that they might rise in the world by their own efforts. His son, Abraham, who died at his native place in 1826, and styled himself "merchant," in his will, by which he bequeathed property of very considerable value in mills, tenements, etc. The family still occupy respectable positions in Saddlesworth and other Yorkshire towns.

In the year 1793, Arthur, then at the age of thirty-six, sailed from Liverpool, on the 24th of March, in the ship "Perseverance" bound for Boston. He was accompanied by his brother John, who was married; he himself being a bachelor. On their arrival, in their search for a tenement, they fell under the notice of Mr. Jedediah Morse, author of the then popular Geography and Gazetteer, who befriended them, and afterwards interested himself largely in their behalf.

Their first venture, after a few weeks' examination of the ground, was in June, when in company with John Shaw, a spinner and weaver, who had accompanied them from England, they began the manufacture of woolen-cloth, by hand. John, on the first day of the partnership, expended from his own funds, for wool seventy-one pounds, three shillings and six pence; for lumber, to build the machinery, two pounds, eight shillings and eight pence. John built the first machinery himself; completing a hand-loom, a spinning-jenny, etc., by the first of August, and charging the company twelve pounds and three shillings for his labor. The first product of this loom—twenty-four and a half yards of broadcloth—was sold for sixteen pounds and sixteen shillings ; and twenty yards of mixed broadcloth for twelve pounds.

"Mr. Morse was an interested observer of all this work, which was carried on in John's house in Charlestown, and, seeing that broadcloth could be made in this country to advantage, and finding that Arthur and John understood the construction of the most important machinery, used in England for that purpose, he introduced them to some persons of wealth in Newburyport, and they were by them persuaded to remove to that place for the purpose of starting a factory, with improved machinery, to be constructed under their immediate supervision."

Their first work in Newburyport was a carding-machine, which was put together in a room in "Lord" Timothy Dexter's stable, and there operated by hand, for the purpose of showing its operations to parties whom it was desired to engage in the enterprise of the factory.

This factory was started at Byfield, complete in 1795, the building being three stories high, and one hundred feet long. The first carding-machine was made single. Afterwards two double machines were placed in the factory. Arthur was employed as overseer of the carding, John as overseer of the weaving and agent in the purchase of wool. John Shaw was employed as a weaver.[1]

"The business at Byfield was conducted prosperously, and was the first successful manufacture of woolen-goods in the United States; all previous attempts having been conducted by hand, and rendered unprofitable by reason of imperfect machinery."[2]

John Scholfield, in one of his wool-purchasing tours, found a mill-privilege in Montville, Conn., which in 1798, he hired for fourteen years, and with his brother established a woolen-factory upon it. Here Arthur remained two years, in which he married Miss Amy Crafts. In the year 1800, he removed to Pittsfield.

Here he found the clothier's business in a flourishing condition, but confined to the fulling and finishing of cloths, includ-

---

[1] The machinery of this mill, although built under the direction of the Scholfields, is stated in the History of American Manufactures, to have been made by Strandring, Armstrong and Guppy, of Newburyport, the senior partner being probably James Strandring, afterwards manufacturer of comb-plates and spindles in Pittsfield. Byfield is a village of the town of Newbury. The owners of the factory were William Bartlett & Co , of Newburyport.

[2] We quote this paragraph from an elaborate article upon The First Woolen Mills in America, published in the Boston Commercial Bulletin of October, 1873, and prepared from original papers, and oral information, furnished by a son of John Scholfield. From the same source we have collected most of the facts concerning the life of the Scholfields, at Charlestown and Byfield. Another authority—Bishop's History of American Manufactures — states that, having proved unprofitable in their hands, the shares of the Scholfields were, one by one, transferred to William Bartlett, and by him to John Lee, one of the original company, who in 1806, converted the mill into a cotton-factory.

ing sometimes, but not always, the dyeing. Carding, spinning and weaving were done in private families and with primitive machinery, with tedious labor and imperfect product. Even the processes left to the professional clothier were conducted with machinery that, although improved from that placed in Elder Valentine Rathbun's fulling-mill in 1770,[1] was still exceedingly imperfect. Rathbun's mill, after lying idle for awhile, had been purchased in 1800, by Dan Monroe, who supplied it with improved machinery. Deacon Eli Maynard, who had succeeded James Ensign in the Water street mill, had made a similar change. Deacon Barber, in the mill at Wahconah, built in 1776, used the best machinery of that period.

With the growth of the neighboring country, business increased, and the clothiers found abundant employment. But while in the manufacture of homespun woolen-cloth, the fulling and finishing were done with tolerable economy and fair excellence, the product on the whole was inferior, and the processes by which it was obtained were slow, laborious and imperfect. This, Arthur Scholfield undertook to remedy. What qualifications he had for the task the reader may judge from the foregoing account of his experience. "His memory," says Mr. Clapp, "was remarkably tenacious, and being a good mathematician, he was able to enter into all the nice calculations required in such a labor."

The processes to whose improvement he addressed himself were carding, spinning and weaving. Heretofore the wool had been prepared in rolls by the primitive little hand-cards, a tedious proceeding, whose product was apt to be uneven, and sometimes flimsy. The spinning upon the old-fashioned hand-wheel was liable to the same defects. The weaving was done upon a narrow hand-loom, which made a coarse cloth, generally twenty-three inches wide. And, for all these machines, Mr. Scholfield undertook to introduce the labor-saving and more efficient inventions which were in use in England.

He completed his first carding-machine, November 1, 1801. Its advent was thus modestly announced in the Pittsfield *Sun*:

---

[1] Described by Thaddeus Clapp, in his Historical statement before the Association of Berkshire Manufacturers, as "none of your new-fangled German inventions, but an old-fashioned, double-action crank-mill, driven by a three-foot open-bucket water-wheel, only warranted to run in a high freshet, or a long spell of weather."

Arthur Scholfield respectfully informs the inhabitants of Pittsfield and the neighboring towns, that he has a carding-machine half a mile west of the meeting-house, where they may have their wool carded into rolls for 12 1-2 cents per pound; mixed 15 1-2 cents per pound. If they find the grease, and pick and grease it, it will be 10 cents per pound, and 12 1-2 cents mixed. They are requested to send their wool in sheets, as they will serve to bind up the rolls when done. Also a small assortment of woolens for sale.

Pittsfield, November 2, 1801.

This machine was set up in the building erected on the dam a little north of the West street bridge over the Housatonic, and dignified by the title of "the Pittsfield Factory," a building which may well be called the cradle of Pittsfield manufactures; for here, as Mr. Scholfield informs us in an advertisement of May, 1802, "were carried on, under different firms, dyeing of wool of various colors, making of chairs of various kinds, cut and wrought nails, marble monuments, Rumford fireplaces, common stone for building, hulling and perling of barley, etc., etc." After such a list one would like to know what the double *et cetera* indicated.

But, to return to Scholfield's carding-machine: the good housewives were at first rather shy of the innovation, and Mrs. Jared Ingersoll,[1] who sent the first fleece, confessed that she did so with great doubts as to the result. But the experiment proved successful. The rolls were more firm and even than those made by hand; the cost was not great, and the saving of time was considerable. Others gave the carding-machines a trial, with the like result, and soon one of the most frequent sights in the streets was a wagon wending its way to the Pittsfield factory with a load of wool, or returning with the rolls nicely wrapped in linen sheets, pinned with thorns.

Capt. Hosea Merrill was an early friend of Scholfield and furnished lumber to him for his machines; but his good wife thought it prudent to risk but little in her first trial of his carding. When the rolls came home there was a little domestic scene, in which the characteristics of the different ladies of the family were exhibited. Mrs. Merrill and her two daughters brought out their spinning-wheels to try the rolls prepared for

---

[1] Readers of our first volume will remember this lady as the intrepid widow of Colonel John Brown.

them. After working silently for awhile, one of the young ladies remarked, with a satisfied air, "This is good." "Yes," said her mother, after waiting a little longer, and with a little more emphasis, "it *is* good." The other daughter spun steadily on, and when she had finished, said quietly: "Mother, I can do twice as much spinning with these rolls as with the old hand-carded things!" And it actually proved that, one and a half runs of yarn having been an average day's spinning with the hand-carded rolls, three could be easily spun after Scholfield's carding.[1]

In May, 1802, Scholfield advertised that he should give no credit; that if the wool was not properly "sorted, clipped and cleansed," he should charge an extra penny per pound; and that he would make no abatement for wool that was greased, as "he made use of none but good grease, and that at his own expense." He had learned something and become independent enough to profit by his experience—had he not been of too easy and generous a nature to adhere to his wise determination.

The carding-machines were not made personally by Scholfield, but by carpenters and machinists, working under his direction, from models and drawings prepared by him. He soon, in the same manner, began the manufacture of machines for sale; and in 1806—to the great satisfaction of other carders—he abandoned the carding of wool altogether, in order to devote himself exclusively to this business and to perfecting models for looms and spinning-jennies, the making of which he shortly after added to it. His immediate successors in the carding-business were Alexander and Elisha Ely; but the carding of wool with machines manufactured by him was entered into as a business by several persons in the county. For some years the greatest obstacle which he encountered was the necessity of himself, or by his workmen, preparing the comb-plates by hand; punching and filing the teeth one by one, and with very rude appliances. But in 1814, his friend, James Strandring, succeeded in smuggling out from England, a teeth-cutting machine, with which he established, at Pontoosuc, a small manufactory of comb-plates, to which he afterwards added the making of spindles. It was probably the smuggling exploit of Strandring that gave rise to the tradition that Scholfield returned to England to refresh his memory by an inspection of the machinery which he was intend-

[1] A run was twenty knots, and a knot forty threads.

ing to imitate. In fact he never returned to his native country after he first left it; for the excellent reason that the British government, through the vigilance of its consul at Boston, was sure to be well informed of his infringement of its jealously-guarded monopoly, by his proceedings at Charlestown and Byfield; and would have been sure, had he set foot in his majesty's dominions, to oppose a very effectual *ne exeat* under the law forbidding the emigration of artisans and machinists.

When Strandring's tooth-cutting machine reached Pittsfield, it was placed in the attic of a little shop near the river, at Pontoosuc, to which the only access was by a ladder, and through a trap-door which was always closed to Yankee curiosity; none being suffered to pass it except Strandring, Scholfield and Wrigley. The machine did its work rapidly and well, and Strandring not only prepared the comb-plates for Scholfield's carding-machines, but made various kinds of saws, and re-cut old ones which were brought to him from a wide range of country. Of course this mysteriously-concealed biter of iron was an object of the most intense curiosity—not always of an entirely disinterested character—to all the region roundabout. Among other incidents illustrating this thirst for forbidden knowledge, Mr. Phillips Merrill, relates the following: He was one day in Strandring's shop, when a Shaker entered with a saw to be re-cut; and as the machinist turned to mount his ladder, offered him five dollars to be permitted to see the operation. "Not for five hundred!" replied Strandring, who, even if he had been off his guard before, would have had his suspicions aroused; for, however moderate a sum five dollars might be for some purposes, it was rather more than the Shaker brethren were wont to pay for the gratification of a profitless curiosity. But, turning to young Merrill, he beckoned him into his dusty arcanum; remarking, "There, Phil! you're the first Yankee that ever saw that machine." Strandring carried on his little manufactory for some years, adding spindles to its product, but he died in middle age, a somewhat frail constitution being unequal to the demands of the free living which prevailed among the Yorkshire artisans in Pittsfield.[1]

---

[1] James Wrigley, mentioned above in connection with Scholfield and Strandring, in like manner fell a victim to the fashionable dissipations of the day. He was probably a son of Arthur Scholfield's old master in the cloth-

Scholfield's carding-machines had a wide reputation and were sold all over the country. Several, as we have said, were set up in Berkshire. The price of those made the first year is said to have been over thirteen hundred dollars. In 1806, he advertised double machines for two hundred and fifty-three dollars each, without the cards, or four hundred dollars including them; and picking-machines at thirty dollars each. The prices were afterwards still further reduced. His annual manufacture amounted probably to from twenty to thirty double machines, at fair prices.

But he was not without his troubles. Some of his customers turned out to be rogues; in two or three instances representing themselves as belonging to places which, when they were sought for payment, denied all knowledge of them. Others, ruined by the financial disasters of the day, were unable to pay. His losses from bad debts were considerable, and he was also annoyed by competition.· In an advertisement of 1804—after informing the public that he continued to card wool on the old terms, and hoped to give general satisfaction, as he "had been to great expense for machinery both in quantity and quality," he adds:

He has carding-machines for sale, built under his immediate inspection, upon a new and improved plan, which he is determined to sell on the most liberal terms, and will give drafts and other instructions to those who wish to build for themselves; and cautions all whom it may concern to beware how they are imposed upon by uninformed speculating companies, who demand more than twice as much for machines as they are really worth.

The disjointed political condition of the times also troubled Mr. Scholfield; and, just after the act laying the embargo on foreign commerce, he wrote thus to his brother John at Montville:

PITTSFIELD, July 11, 1808.

BROTHER JOHN: Yours of the 4th of June is received. You say you hardly know how you are doing; for there was an Imbargo laid last December, and it still continues. The Imbargo is here too, and

---

ier's art. He was certainly associated with him at Byfield and Pittsfield, to some extent, in his business undertakings. He was a man of fine personal appearance and of intelligence. In the procession of the first cattle-show of the Berkshire Agricultural society, he was drawn upon a gaily-decorated platform, neatly dressed in black broadcloth and small clothes, and wearing a cocked hat, while he busily worked at one of Scholfield's looms: affording one of the most striking and best-remembered features of that occasion.

likely to stay, for what I see. It has swindled me out of about $1,500 —for besides what I shall lose by failures, I have twenty-two machines on hand, besides pickers. They were all engaged last summer, and if times had not turned, I should have had the money for them now. If I had left business the spring before last, it would have been much to my interest; but at that time the Imbargo was not thought of, except by King Jefferson and his party, and as they can't do wrong, we must put up with it. I have often thought you might have done better by moving back into the country; but, as things are now, there is no doing anything anywhere. ARTHUR SCHOLFIELD.

Mr. Scholfield's advertisement of a small quantity of woolens for sale in 1801, leads us to believe that he commenced weaving soon after his removal to town; but we have no distinct mention of broadcloths until 1804, when he offered a few pieces of gray-mixed to several merchants of the village, who were all afraid to purchase. The goods were, however, sold in a larger market, and a few weeks afterwards Josiah Bissell, a leading store-keeper, brought home from New York two pieces of cloth which he had purchased for the foreign article. Scholfield was sent for to give an opinion upon them, and had the pleasant triumph of exhibiting to Mr. Bissell the private mark, which proved them to be the same goods which he had so lately rejected.

Still, Mr. Scholfield's labors and successes must have been little known to, or have made little impression upon, his townsmen; for, in April, 1808, a correspondent of the *Sun* wrote as follows:

MR. ALLEN: Some have doubted the practicability of our success in the establishment of woolen-manufactories; and others have foolishly held in derision the importation and the value of fine wool of the Spanish breed. To such I request that you would hold up the following advertisement from an Albany paper: * * * G. W. & I. POR-TER, *Merchant Tailors, No. 66 State street, Albany*, have just had come to hand from the manufactory at Poughkeepsie, best superfine broad-cloth, made of the wool of the Spanish merino breed of sheep, imported by Chancellor Livingston. This cloth, for quality and beauty, is not exceeded by any imported.

A still more marked oversight of Mr. Scholfield occurred about the same time. While the English clothier was perfecting the machinery and minor details of his quasi factory, some improvement began in American wools; and in 1807, Elkanah Watson brought to Pittsfield the merino ram and ewe, whose exhibition in the fall of that year, under the old Elm on the park, proved the germ of the Berkshire Agricultural Society's cattle-shows.

The next June, Mr. Watson had the wool of these sheep made into a piece of blue broadcloth, by "artists" whom he styles "the best in the country." "It far excelled," he says, "any (American) fabric which has yet appeared." Samples of it were exhibited in the principal cities, and among the letters which he received, concerning them, was one from Chancellor Livingston, in which that eminent and judicious friend of American industry wrote: "The samples you have sent me of your cloth are full and satisfactory proofs of our ability to manufacture as good cloth as we should wish to wear, as well as of the great importance of cultivating the merino breed in preference to any other."[1]

A detailed account of the manufacture of this cloth, and of its expense per yard, written by Mr. Watson to Rev. Dr. Shepard, of Lenox, was printed in the *Sun*, of November 12, 1808, and widely copied. The essential portions are given below:

> I am happy in being able to answer correctly your queries respecting the width and cost of the superfine Berkshire broadcloth in which I am now clothed; having been very exact in the first essay made in this county.
>
> On the 10th of June last, my Spanish ram and ewe were sheared, and yielded, including tags, eight pounds and four ounces of wool.
>
> I received in rolls, ... 6 lbs. 11 oz.
> Tags and cuttings, ... 1 lb.
> Waste 7 per cent.,
> _____
> First weight, ... 8 lbs. 4 oz.

This was spun and wove in a superior style *by the Shakers*, who delivered me nine and a half yards of cloth, one and a quarter yards wide. The cloth was dressed by Mr Maynard, who delivered me, after fulling, dyeing and finishing, seven and a half yards of cloth full thirty inches wide. The whole cost was as follows:

> Carding 6 lbs. 11 oz. wool, ... $1 09
> Spinning and weaving, ... 3 98
> Fulling, dyeing, etc., ... 2 85
> _____
> Total cost of cloth, ... $7 92

The cloth, as it is finished, is considered by competent judges to be

---

[1] Watson's Men and Times of the Revolution.

worth three dollars and fifty cents a yard; and, allowing this to be just, the following is an estimate of the profits:

8 lbs. 4 oz. wool, unwashed, at $1.50 per pound, . .	$12 37
Neat cost as above, ...	7 92
Clear profits, 25 per cent., ...	5 96
7 1-2 yards at $3.50 per yard, ...	$26 25

Hence it is unequivocally ascertained that my wool, in the state it was shown, is fairly worth one dollar fifty cents a pound; besides leaving a handsome profit for the manufactory. Or in other words, the value of $26.25, in seven and a half yards of cloth, cost me seven dollars and ninety-two cents, exclusive of the wool as shorn, or two dollars and twenty-two cents a pound, putting profits out of the question. The value of the cloth, as estimated above, is considered low; for imported broadcloth is about fifty-six inches wide, exclusive of list, or twenty-eight for the half. Mine is thirty. This difference I have not noticed.

Watson continued this manufacture of broadcloth by proxy, and in 1812, took the Berkshire Agricultural Society's premium upon it. Before the latter date he became acquainted with, and complimented, the merits of Mr. Scholfield. It is singular that he should not have done so still earlier.

It was certainly a remarkable and very happy coincidence which brought together in Pittsfield, independently of, and unknown to, each other, two men, each in his specialty so essential to the building up of its woolen-manufacture.

In the year 1809, several companies for the manufacture of woolen-goods—frequently connecting with it that of cotton-cloth—were formed in the interior of Massachusetts. Among them were one at Pittsfield, and one at Stockbridge. The organization at Pittsfield originated in a meeting held, January 4th, at Captain Merrick's inn, when Colonel Joshua Danforth presided and Theodore Hinsdale, Jr., was secretary. This meeting

Resolved, That, whereas, from the exertions which have already been made by a few individuals, and from the indications that many others will zealously engage the ensuing season, in the introduction and general spread of the invaluable merino sheep in this county, this meeting are fully impressed with the opinion that the establishment of an extensive woolen-factory for fine cloths and stockings, in this town, will greatly promote the interests of this county by manufacturing a new and valuable raw material within the same, in preference to its future exportation.

Resolved, That the introduction of spinning-jennies, as is practiced in England, into private families, is strongly recommended by this meeting to the attention of the public; since one person can manage by hand by the operation of a crank, twenty-four spindles, or more, at one time; and it is by these labor-saving machines that the American people will successfully rival the Europeans in many important articles; and the establishment of an extensive factory under legislative patronage will always go hand and hand with private enterprise, to the great benefit of individuals.

To carry the objects of the meetings into practical operation, Elkanah Watson, James D. Colt, Jr., and Simon Larned were appointed to apply to the legislature for a charter and to take such other measures as they deemed proper in the premises; Colonel Danforth and Captain Merrick were requested to receive proposals for a suitable mill-site, sufficient land for the erection of the necessary buildings and "such hydraulic works as might be necessary."

The legislature incorporated Simon Larned, Elkanah Watson, Joshua Danforth, James D. Colt, Jr., Jared Ingersoll, Oren Goodrich and such others as they might associate with themselves as "The Pittsfield Woolen and Cotton Factory," and at a meeting of the corporators, in September, 1809, James D. Colt, Jr., was chosen clerk; it was determined that the stock of the company should consist of one thousand shares of the par value of twenty dollars each. The meeting was adjourned until the second Wednesday of the following November. A communication in the *Sun* of January 24, 1810, denies a statement in the *Reporter* that "The company had completed their machinery, and had actually gone into operation under the able management of Mr. Scholfield." The writer says that no assessment had ever been paid on the shares, but that Mr. Scholfield "had commenced manufacturing on a small scale, and entirely at his own risk, without any kind of assistance from the said company."

About this time a New York gentleman wrote to one of the corporators, that there could be no more favorable opportunity for commencing operations; British cloths having risen enormously, a whole cargo being sold by the bale at Philadelphia, in December, 1809, at fifteen dollars a yard. But the company proceeded no farther, being crippled by the failure of the Berkshire bank, of which the principal members were either directors or large stockholders.

Mr. Scholfield, however, having experienced an effect from the "Imbargo" different from that which he contemplated at the date of his letter in 1808—although it did not restore to him a monopoly of the manufacture of machinery—was encouraged to enter into the woolen-manufacture upon the small scale alluded to by the *Sun's* correspondent.

This enterprise of 1809, was, like most of the establishments up to that time, not in all respects what we now commonly understand by a "factory;" i. e., an establishment in which all the processes of manufacture are carried on in immediate succession, under one head and ordinarily under one roof.

In 1806, as we have said, Mr. Scholfield, in order to devote himself more exclusively to the making of carding-machines, spinning-jennies, and looms, sold his wool-carding business to Alexander and Elisha Ely, who carried on the manufacture of marble monuments, fireplaces, "etc." in the same building—the old mill of multitudinous uses. But, notwithstanding the lively demand for American cloths caused by the exclusion and high prices of English goods, the market for machinery did not recover from the glut mentioned in Mr. Scholfield's letter of 1808. And as Alexander Ely, the surviving partner in the carding-business, was also disheartened by bad debts which he had allowed to accumulate during the scarcity of cash in the two preceding years, Scholfield repurchased it; and, encouraged by the increasing demand for American cloths, made changes and improvements in the "Pittsfield Factory," which made it more worthy of its name.

The spinning-jennies and looms, which were both run by hand, were placed in a building newly-erected for the purpose, on the east bank of the river just below the bridge. It was afterwards known as "the old red mill." The carding-machines were retained in the original mill which stood on the same side of the river just above the bridge. The stone-banking, built along the river to receive the building, still remains. In the pressure of business during the war, a few looms were afterwards placed in an addition which was built to the cottage where Scholfield lived and died, and which is still standing on the south side of West street next to the west side of the river. There were few houses in town where there were busier thoughts or merrier hours.

The fulling and finishing of the cloth manufactured by Scholfield in this cluster of little factories, were done at the clothier's works on Elm street, carried on successively by Eli Maynard, Maynard and Allen, and Jonathan Allen, 2d, — the distance between which and the factories was a little over a mile.

But, while the continued improvements in machinery and raw material were tending toward the combination of all the processes of manufacture in a proper factory, the clothiers' business, in its old form, had grown to an importance which it did not lose for years, and which proved of great value to the country in the second war with Great Britain.

In 1805, "a brother-clothier," proposed, through the *Sun*, the organization of a society of his fellow-craftsmen "for the laudable purpose of investigating chemical liquids, and to improve in making and dressing cloth :" which, in his opinion, "would be as useful and honorable to the county, as a missionary, or any other society whatever." And such a society seems to have been formed, although it did not long continue. So far as the art of dyeing was concerned, the necessity of improvement by some means was undoubted. That their colors were not fast, was long the prevailing defect of American cloths. White edges were the distinguishing mark by which their nationality was detected. Daniel Webster long remembered his sorrow when a boy, and crying with vexation, because the blue, on a rainy day, washed out of his new outer garments, and into his shirt. And Hon. Phinehas Allen used to boast with humorous zest of his patriotic persistence in wearing Scholfield's earlier Pittsfield blues, although they crocked him as though he had been dipped in an indigo-pot.

While Scholfield was, as a matter of business, pushing his improvements in machinery, and Watson, as a matter of personal pride and of patriotism, was urging, by example, instruction, and argument, the improvement of Berkshire wools; other citizens of more or less prominence joined them heartily in their efforts. It was justly considered, by almost all the more intelligent part of the community, that there was no act of more true or more effective patriotism than to establish a new branch of manufactures, or to introduce some improvement in husbandry. The newspapers recorded every attempt and every achievement of this kind, with abundant praise, and were profuse in teachings and theories; which were more correct, and less visionary, than could have been expected. Indeed, considering that almost every enterprise in cloth-manufacture was as yet an experiment untried in America, and was to be undertaken by men of little experience, urged on by those of less; it is wonderful how few errors there were as to general principles and long results, however much they may have underestimated immediate difficulties, and overlooked their deficiencies in skilled labor. This may be, perhaps, accounted for by the fact that some of the writers and speakers upon these subjects had been for years residents in Europe, and close observers, under favorable circumstances, of the agriculture and manufactures of its most prosperous nations. Others were diligent students of the best books upon those subjects. In Pittsfield, Mr. Watson, in particular, was remarkably well qualified to be a teacher in these subjects, having long been a resident of France, in close contact with its manufactories, and having visited England, Holland and Belgium, studying with keen and envious eyes, their highly-cultivated farms, their superb flocks and herds, and their factories, where skill in the useful arts was carried to the highest perfection then attainable. Thomas Melville, who succeeded Mr. Watson as the leading advocate of patriotic effort in this direction—a little after the period of which we write—had almost an identical experience. Both these gentlemen were frequent contributors to the columns of the *Sun*, whose antipathy to England gave an added zest to its zeal in building up rivals to its manufactures. Rev. Thomas Allen, and his son Jonathan, paid great attention to this subject, and gave it the aid of their pens. Ezekiel Bacon, and indeed all the capable writers among the democrats, manifested their interest in the same way.

The loss of the files of the *Reporter* prevents our knowledge of the contributions of federalists to this class of literature; but David Campbell, James D. Colt, Lemuel Pomeroy and others certainly gave very valuable practical aid to the movement.

In November, 1809, the *Sun* published a long and carefully-prepared article upon Berkshire manufactures, from which it appears that an attempt had just been made to ascertain the extent and progress of manufactures in the county. And, although the responses of those to whom application had been made for information was not so general as was desired, they afford a pretty satisfactory idea of the facts in the case. Returns

HISTORY OF PITTSFIELD.

were received from ten towns, showing the following production of woolen goods for the year 1808:

Lenox, 3,030 yds.,
Lanesboro, 5,000 yds.,
Hinsdale, 2,000 yds.,
Sandisfield, 5,441 yds.,
Cheshire, 6,960 yds.,
Pittsfield, 15,270 yds.,
Gt. Barrington, 4,400 yds.,
Stockbridge, 3,250 yds.,
Tyringham (estimated), 5,450 yds.,
Alford (estimated), 4,400 yds.
Total, 55,212 yds.

Of the amount credited to Pittsfield, about five thousand yards were dressed at a shop near Richmond—Daniel Stearns, at Barkersville—and were manufactured, in a "good measure, in that town." There were twenty other towns in the county, and although some of them were small, and some had no fulling-mills, it was supposed that the total product of the Berkshire looms was at least a hundred thousand yards. The cloths were made mostly of the common wool of the county, three-quarters of a yard wide; and were estimated to be worth rather more than a dollar a yard.[1]

From this the writer in the *Sun* draws a lesson:

Here then is a single branch of manufacture, carried on principally in private families, at a very trifling expense, and interfering very little with the great business of the farmer, which yields to this small county—consisting by the last census of about 33,000 souls—more than $100,000, being more than three dollars to each person, of all ages and sexes. It is easy to see how greatly the wealth, comfort and happiness of our county are promoted by pursuits of this sort, and how far they tend to increase and invigorate the solid sinews of national wealth. It is equally obvious, how easy it would be for our farmers to double the amount of this branch of manufactures in *quantity*, even by the increase of the common wool of our county; and equally so to quadruple it in *value*, by cultivating the finer species of wool which is now happily brought within the reach of every one.

Statements and arguments like this were frequent in the Pittsfield newspapers during the first quarter of the present century, and, although we may have space to copy, or even allude to,

---

[1] In 1811, Scholfield advertised his prices as follows: for carding, twelve and a half cents per pound, for common or quarter-blood wool; for half-blood, sixteen cents; for full-blood, twenty-five cents per pound; for manufacturing, thirty cents to one dollar twenty-five cents per yard according to quality for 5-4 cloth delivered at the loom. Broadcloths, double that price.

only a few of them, we must bear testimony to their great efficacy in advancing the cause of domestic manufactures. The product of 1808 was certainly a very creditable one, and a noble testimony to the industry of Berkshire households; but it was considerably less than Berkshire looms, under a more perfect organization of labor, and with more perfect appliances, now often send out in a single day; while, although the quality of the goods is greatly improved, the cost to the consumer is but slightly, if at all, enhanced.

The hopeful condition of the woolen-manufacture in 1809, is attributed by the *Sun's* correspondent " very much to the carding-machines now in general use, and the newly-constructed spinning-jennies lately made by the ingenious Mr. Scholfield." The conclusion of this article is full of information, and we quote it:

These machines [the spinning-jennies] go with from twenty to thirty spindles, upon which a single woman can spin from twenty to thirty runs[1] of fine yarn per day in the best manner. A few of them are already in successful operation in this vicinity, and can be conveniently worked in any private family. The cost of them is about fifty dollars, and one of them is sufficient to do the spinning for a number of families, who can join in the purchase.

The cost of foreign cloths of fine texture is already so high that few can afford to wear them. And a number of pieces have been made in this town which sell readily for three dollars per yard—three-quarters wide—which are in every point equal to foreign broadcloth which costs eight dollars; leaving to the manufacturer a profit of more than a dollar a yard. The gentleman before-mentioned is engaged in getting into operation a manufactory of fine cloths, which there is no doubt will succeed with equal advantage to the undertakers and the public. * * *

We have not time to notice as they ought to be noticed, several other valuable branches of manufacture which have grown up among us, within two years past, particularly the *valuable and extensive one of sail duck and cotton bagging,* now in operation in this town, at which it is understood more than twenty thousand yards of the former, and a large but unascertained quantity of the latter have been made the year past; affording a vast profit to the enterprising undertakers, consuming a great quantity of the raw material of flax, and thus encouraging its growth and increase, and employing a great number of the poorer classes of people in its operations.

---

[1] It will be recollected that, under the old system, one and a half runs was considered a good day's work in spinning wool prepared by the old-fashioned card, and three for wool carded by Scholfield.

Many of the same remarks might be applied to the manufactory of muskets and small-arms, which has been pretty extensively carried on here for the year past, and at which more than a thousand have been made, and sold by contract to the state of New York.[1]

In the year 1809, then, a very interesting period was reached in the history of Pittsfield woolen-manufactures. A deep and practical feeling had been created in favor of improvements in the breed of sheep for the purpose of refining their fleece. Some very creditable cloths had been produced; and a very remarkable advance had been made in other essential particulars. Arthur Scholfield had brought his carding and picking machines, his spinning-jennies and looms, to a high degree of perfection; and was manufacturing them, largely, for sale at home and abroad. He had also established a small factory for the manufacture of fine broadcloths. Under the impulse of his improved machinery, and encouraged also by the political state of the country and the world, the clothier-business was exceedingly prosperous. A number of the most prominent business men of the town had been incorporated as a cotton and woolen manufacturing company; and, although the enterprise had been checked by the pecuniary embarrassments resulting from the failure of the Berkshire bank, it was only for a time, and it was succeeded very shortly by two successful projects of a similar kind.

We here intermit our account of this branch of industry, to give place to the early history of the Berkshire Agricultural Society, which had at this stage of its progress an important influence upon it.

But, as Arthur Scholfield's operations, after this date, were mostly in connection with other persons, we will here finish the general story of his life.

After the war of 1812, the extreme depression of manufactures rendered his affairs unprosperous; and, in 1818, he was advised to apply to congress for relief in consideration of his early services to the American woolen-manufacture. He was, however, although in great need, distrustful of the project; and, the changes

---

[1] The *Sun* containing this article has the following paragraph: The Hon. Mr. Bacon left town on Monday last, for Washington. And it is with great pleasure we add, that he was dressed in a full suit of HOMESPUN, manufactured in this town, and a part of it by his amiable and patriotic lady.

of representation in the congressional district operating against him, it appears to have been abandoned.

Mr. Scholfield kept up his efforts to sustain himself, bravely; but he never achieved pecuniary success, or even recovered the position he had lost. He gave up his interest in the "Pittsfield Factory," and in June, 1821, the following advertisement points him out as doing business on a small scale at Goodrich's mill, which occupied the site of the present Wahconah flouring-mill:

UNCLE ARTHUR,

At Goodrich's factory, one mile north of the meeting-house, will card or manufacture, either by the yard or on shares, either in the flannel or finished. And for carding, if it will accommodate customers, I will take half in such produce as I shall want for my family. The other half must be cash when the rolls are delivered; for oil is a cash article, and must be paid for.   ARTHUR SCHOLFIELD.

Pittsfield, June 3, 1821.

In such humble manner was the father of the Pittsfield woolen manufacture struggling for a livelihood in his old age. And thus he struggled on to the last.

Mr. Scholfield died, March 27, 1827, at the age of seventy years and six months, and was buried in the old first burial ground in the rear of the Baptist church. When that ground was secularized, his remains were removed to the new Pittsfield cemetery.

CHAPTER IX.

BEFORE THE WAR.

[1800–1812.]

Business-activity—Establishment and failure of the Berkshire bank—Other business-losses—Building of a democratic hotel—Names of prominent democrats—Park square and its business-surroundings—Drum-factory—Jonathan Allen, 2d—Pomeroy's gun-factory—Ordination of Rev. William Allen.

ABOUT 1806, banking institutions were springing up, in most of the towns of New England where a little capital had been accumulated; and, in February of that year, Gov. Strong signed the charter of the Berkshire bank; the corporators named being Simon Larned, Timothy Childs, Joshua Danforth, Daniel Pepoon, David Campbell, Jr., James D. Colt, Jr., Thomas Allen, Jr., Theodore Hinsdale, Jr., Ebenezer Center and Joseph Merrick. The capital stock was fixed at seventy-five thousand dollars, all to be paid in gold and silver coin previous to October 6, 1806, and the issue of bills was restricted to one hundred and fifty thousand dollars. The bank was organized July 5, 1807, by the choice of the following directors: Simon Larned, John W. Hulbert, Joshua Danforth and Daniel Pepoon of Pittsfield, Joseph Goodwin of Lenox, Andrew Dexter of Boston, and James D. Colt, Jr., of Pittsfield. Simon Larned was chosen president, and Ebenezer Center cashier. The influence of political feeling was indicated by the fact that here, where a harmonious co-operation was essential, democrats and federalists were carefully made to alternate in the board of directors; while the president being a democrat, the cashier was selected from the federalists.[1]

---

[1] This happy spirit of conciliation was imitated in the management of the high-schools, the water-works and the library, and might with profit have been followed still further.

Messrs. Hulbert and Larned, the two directors first named, were not specially distinguished for business-talent, but they were leaders on opposite sides in politics, and were both high-spirited, genial gentlemen, ambitious and popular. The other members of the board, resident in the county, were among its most thorough, systematic and capable business men; but none of them had any practical knowledge of banking. For this they relied upon Mr. Dexter. This person was still a young man, but was in the flush of his fame as a successful financier; and his brother-directors placed in him the most implicit confidence; a confidence which led to their ruin. Mr. Dexter was engaged in operations gigantic for that period: among others, the building of the Boston Exchange, which required the expenditure of large sums of money. To procure this, he became connected with several country-banks, which he dextrously made to contribute largely to his necessities. The methods by which this was effected seem to have been among those cases in which illegal irregularities become so common as to be condoned by public opinion until the inevitable ruin excites public indignation.

But, perhaps, in the case of the Berkshire bank, something stronger may be said. Mr. Dexter was carrying on a business in Boston, which required a deposit of a certain amount of money in bank-bills. In order to meet this obligation, he made an arrangement with the Berkshire bank by which he received two hundred thousand dollars in their bills, with the agreement that they should be kept in the original packages, and not put in circulation. They were merely to be held to satisfy the requisition of the law in regard to private bankers. In making this deposit with Mr. Dexter, the directors clearly violated the provisions of their charter, however innocent their intentions may have been; and they suffered the consequences.

In the year 1809, the bills of the bank, like those of many others, began to be discredited; and were returned for redemption in such amounts that the institution was seriously embarrassed. Finally, so hard was the run upon it that, in one day, more of its bills were placed in the hands of John Chandler Williams for collection, than appeared from its books to be in circulation.

In February, 1810, the legislature appointed a committee to investigate its affairs, together with those of the Northampton bank, which was involved in similar trouble. Their report was somewhat confused; but it clearly says that "there is a considerable demand for Berkshire bank-bills, which the directors state are fully secured; but, of the probable payment of these bills it is difficult to judge."

The directors did indeed fully believe that their bank was perfectly secured. That much of confidence in Andrew Dexter, Jr., they still retained. But it appeared, on examination, that his property was entirely absorbed by mortgages prior to theirs: and the crash could no longer be postponed. Col. Larned, writing to Dr. Timothy Childs, shortly after the report was submitted to the legislature, says:

Under all the circumstances, I cannot say but that it was as favorable as we could reasonably expect; but it will not appear too much so without explanation. We should be willing to have the report lie over to next session. We do not hesitate to acknowledge that, by placing too high confidence in A. D., we are bankrupt to a considerable amount; but we are making an attempt to compromise at twenty-five cents on the dollar, which will take nearly or quite all our several properties: though, could the report be suffered to remain on the table until next session, we should by that time have so far proceeded in our attempt at compromise as would bring the issue within the reach of probable conjecture.

The matter was practically postponed in the legislature for one year; but the charter of the bank was finally vacated, and, the directors being personally responsible, their property was seized for the payment of its debts. This not proving sufficient, in accordance with the custom of the day in regard to imprisonment for debt, all the Berkshire directors were committed to jail at Lenox. When they were liberated, six gentlemen who, a few years before, were accounted among the most prosperous in Berkshire, returned to their homes pecuniarily ruined.

Most of them, however, afterwards recovered their prosperity; and the loss of fortune does not seem to have in the least diminished their influence or the respect in which they were previously held. An attempt was made to obtain the removal of Col. Larned from his office of Sheriff, but it miserably failed, and he held the position until he was appointed to a command in the army. Mr. Hulbert was, soon after, elected to congress against unusual odds, although the *Sun* cited his connection with the Berkshire bank against him.

The neat little banking-house built for the Berkshire bank in 1806, afterwards harbored more successful financial institutions— the Agricultural bank and then the Berkshire Mutual Fire Insurance company. It was removed in 1874, to give place to the Berkshire Athenæum.

Ebenezer Center, the cashier of the bank, was a merchant doing business on Bank row. He afterwards removed to Hudson, but before his death, he returned to Pittsfield. He was an upright and excellent man, with many popular qualities, but was unsuccessful in business.

James Buel, clerk and teller of the bank, was born at Litchfield, Connecticut, in 1787, and removed to Pittsfield in 1807 or 1808. From 1810 to 1812, he resided in Hudson, N. Y. In 1812, he began business again in Pittsfield, with David Campbell, on Exchange row, as successors to S. D. and J. D. Colt. From 1814 to 1816, he was treasurer and general agent of the Pittsfield Cotton and Woolen Manufacturing company. He afterwards spent some years in New Orleans and Connecticut, but returning to Pittsfield, entered into partnership with Ezekiel R. Colt, with whom he continued in business on Bank row, for twenty-five years. He was commissioned notary public by Governor Brooks in the year 1820, and held the office by successive re-appointments until 1870. Pittsfield never had a citizen of more perfect uprightness, and scrupulous integrity, than James Buel.

The affair of the Berkshire bank was not the only one in which large sums were abstracted from the capital of Pittsfield by wrongdoing abroad. In June, 1806, Thompson J. Skinner, of Williamstown, who had represented the Berkshire district in congress, from 1797 to 1799, was chosen treasurer and receiver-general of the commonwealth; and among his bondsmen for the sum of one hundred thousand dollars, were Ezekiel Bacon, Dr. Timothy Childs, Simeon Griswold, and perhaps other citizens of Pittsfield.

At the close of Mr. Skinner's first term, the usual committee to examine the accounts of the treasurer were prevented from reporting by an early adjournment of the legislature, and a second committee appointed nine months later reported them all correct; although afterwards, in the course of legal proceedings, it appeared that they had made no personal examination of the funds in the treasury.

In June, 1809, however, it was discovered—a new treasurer

having been elected—that Mr. Skinner was a defaulter to the amount of sixty thousand dollars, while the assets to be obtained from his estate were only twenty thousand. The deficit of forty thousand dollars, his bondsmen were called upon to pay; and, refusing, were sued for that amount. They defended on the ground that the treasurer was solely the servant of the state-government, and in nowise amenable to his sureties, who had no means of bringing him to account; but that this was the duty of the legislature, by whose neglect to perform it at the usual and proper time, and by the false statements of whose committee, the fraud was concealed until Skinner was able to convey and actually did convey, a large portion of his property out of the state, thereby greatly increasing the burden imposed upon the bondsmen. This apparently just plea was rejected by the courts, and afterwards by the legislature, to which body application was made for relief in equity. Executions were issued against each of the sureties for the sum of ten thousand dollars, and they were put in force in the year 1812. Several other citizens of Pittsfield suffered in smaller amounts as endorsers of Skinner's private paper.

Drains like these upon the resources of the most enterprising and public-spirited citizens—small as the amounts absolutely involved may now appear—could not fail to have a sensible effect upon the material progress of the town; and some valuable citizens were led by them to seek their fortunes elsewhere.

There would seem to have been at all times an abundance of hotels in Pittsfield; and in the earliest years of the nineteenth century, the section about the park seems to have been particularly well supplied. Captain Campbell's coffee-house on Bank row, was a handsome and commodious tavern. The gambrel-roofed inn on the corner of North and West streets, was popular under the charge of Captain Joseph Merrick. Captain Merrick's popularity as a landlord was even so great that the democrats were accustomed to hold their public dinners with him, although he was known to be a moderate federalist.

In the year 1808, however, political feeling had grown so warm that it was alleged that Captain Merrick had refused to furnish the usual Fourth of July dinner for the democrats. Great indignation ensued, and the excluded party celebrated the Fourth with more spirit than even they had ever before exhibited; "although the morning was threatening, and the latter part of the day extremely inclement." The latter circumstance decidedly marred the festivities; for the dinner being prepared by Captain Jared Ingersoll, the elder, who had ceased to keep a public house, was spread in his orchard,[1] within a rustic bower, which had been handsomely constructed with evergreen boughs and beautifully decorated with flags, mottoes and flowers. It was extremely pretty and very romantic; but it was unhappily but ill-adapted to the protection of the guests from the torrents of rain which fell while they honored "with fervor and unanimity" seventeen patriotic toasts each followed by the booming of cannon.

The result of this experience was a determination which, formed under such circumstances, was not likely to fail, that the republicans of Pittsfield would no longer depend upon federalists for a place for their patriotic festivities.[2] For this purpose substantial members of the party contributed freely; and in October, 1808, Rev. Thomas Allen sold to them a piece of land on the south-west corner of his home-lot, with a front of eighty-two feet on East street, and twenty rods deep. The price was sixteen hundred dollars, and the property was conveyed in four hundred and forty-five undivided parts, of which individuals held from one to five each. The following are the names of the purchasers: Simon Larned, Joshua Danforth, Ezekiel Bacon, John B. Root, Jared Ingersoll, Phinehas Allen, Simeon Brown, Oramel Fanning, Septemius Bingham, James Brown, Timothy Childs, John Dickinson, Henry H. Childs, Charles Bishop, Robert Merriam, John Chamberlain, Seth Montague, Daniel Sackett, Oren Goodrich, James Root, Joel Stevens, William Stevens, Timothy Hurlbut, Simeon Butler, John Eells, David Pierson, Jr., William Francis, Jr., Oliver Root, Jesse Goodrich, Seth Moore, Elijah Bagg, Horace Allen, Eldad Francis, Joshua Baker, Oswald Williams, Samuel Williams, James Hubbard, Richard Robbins, William D. Robbins, Elijah Robbins, Jonathan Yale Clark, John Churchill, 2d, Silvester Robbins, James Hubbard, Jr., Robert

[1] This orchard covered the space west of North street between Railroad street and Depot street.

[2] "Our friends can have no cause of present or future regret, that the doors of public houses of entertainment where they usually resorted on similar occasions have this year been closed upon them; and they trust that before another anniversary of this joyful day returns, they shall have provided themselves with more lasting habitations than they have hitherto relied upon."—Report of celebration, in the *Sun*.

Francis, Ichabod Chapman, Stephen Hurlbut, Josiah Francis, Jr., Thomas Stockin, Amasa Jeffords, Daniel Stearns, Simon Langworthy, William Janes, Ethan Janes, Silvester Langworthy, Avery Welch, Alpheus Weller, Enoch Weller, Constant Luce, William Griswold, Uriah Lathrop, Linus Parker, Tertullus Hubby, David Bush, Royal Millard, Gideon Gunn, William Brattle, Appleton Tracy, Joseph Shearer, James Moseley, Zebulon Herrick, Ludowick Stanton, Oliver P. Dickinson, Simeon Griswold, Elias Keeler, Hosea Merrill, Sr., Robert Stanton.[1]

The *Sun* was disappointed in its expectation that before the fourth of July, 1809, its party would be provided with a hotel of its own; and that year the democrats dined at a small tavern kept by William Clark on East street, nearly opposite the head of Pomeroy avenue. But, the next summer "The Pittsfield Hotel," built by the above-named democratic gentlemen, was opened by Simeon Griswold. It was a large three-story building, and in his advertisement, Mr. Griswold justly boasted that it had as airy and convenient rooms as any country-hotel in New England. He further stated that it was "supplied with most of the principal American newspapers of all political parties;" and that "no exertions would be spared to render the stock of liquors of the very best quality."

The Pittsfield Hotel was really a superior house for that day, and Mr. Griswold intimated that he relied for its support rather upon general than partisan patronage. It was, however, chiefly resorted to by democrats. In the war of 1812, the officers and soldiers of the Cantonment flocked to it, while the British officers on parole took their ease, and their wine, at Captain Campbell's coffee-house. When the "era of good-will" put an end to the partisan-divisions of the town, the Pittsfield Hotel felt the effect of an excess of hotel accommodations—as the Union church did of religious—and it maintained a languishing existence until 1822, when it was sold to the trustees of the medical college.

Between the years 1800 and 1812, the appearance of Park

[1]The lot thus purchased is now a portion of the grounds attached to the residence of Hon. Thomas Allen, and lies in the angle formed by East and School streets. Upon it stood the gambrel-roof cottage, occupied by Phinehas Allen as a dwelling-house. The office of the *Sun* had been removed in 1807, to "Mr. Griswold's elegant new building on the corner west of the meeting-house."

square had been greatly changed, although it was still an open, ungraded space, through which roads dividing at the head of East street ran to West street, and to the corner of North street. The old Elm had but a single companion, which stood in the south-east corner of the square. When the first soldiers for the war of 1812 entered Pittsfield, they found a moderately-compact central village with a brisk country-business. The north side of the square, in addition to the church and the town-house, had on the corner of North street, the "elegant store" built by Simeon Griswold: a plain wooden structure which long held its place; being occupied by Josiah Bissell & Son, and by John C. West and Brother. The Pittsfield Hotel had taken the place of the printing-office on the east side. On the south, next to the grounds of John Chandler Williams, stood the Female Academy. Then came the Berkshire bank building, the "bookstore" of J. and R. Warriner, and the "medicine-store" of Henry James & Co., Captain Campbell's coffee-house and the two-story (Stoddard) store occupied by Nathan Willis and son. David Campbell and James Buel had succeeded J. D. and S. D. Colt, in the store built by them on the west side of the square. North of this, on the south corner of West street, still stood the gambrel-roof cottage owned by John W. Hulbert who had collected upon the premises materials for a handsome stone-mansion, when the failure of the Berkshire bank dissipated this, with many another pleasant Pittsfield hope. North of West street, stood Captain Merrick's inn, and the Bush building, with its two tenements occupied respectively by a shoemaker and a goldsmith.

It will thus be seen that the four sides of Park square were pretty closely surrounded with buildings chiefly devoted to business-purposes. But the business of the town was far from being confined to Park square. Colonel Danforth still continued his store on East street, and John B. Root and James McKnight occupied that built by Colonel Larned. Elder Robert Green having recently purchased the stock of Ahab Jinks, kept quite an extensive assortment on Elm street, as Horace Allen did on West street.

Early in 1809, Abner Stevens removed the drum-making business, which he had for some years carried on at Hancock, to Pittsfield, where he built a shop on North street, between Fenn street and the Boston and Albany railroad. Under the militia-laws, which then existed in all the states, every town had at least one military company; and the most essential of all its equipments was the drum. The captain's sword or the private's musket might be supplied by some imperfect substitute; but a drum, and a passably good one, could not be dispensed with. Mr. Stevens made a good rattling instrument, and his business could not but thrive. The war added the national government to the number of his patrons; and, being industrious and economical, he made a handsome fortune. Under the perpetual incitement of the martial music of his own manufacture, he was of course an ardent war-democrat.

Another valuable accession to the ranks of the democrats, was Jonathan Allen, 2d. This gentleman was born at Northampton, September 26, 1786; his father being Elisha Allen. In 1801, at the age of fifteen, he walked from Northampton to Pittsfield, where he learned the clothier's business as an apprentice of Deacon Eli Maynard, with whom he entered into partnership, on attaining his majority, in 1807. Deacon Maynard retired in 1810, and the firm became Allen and (Roswell) Knight. Mr. Knight left the firm in 1811; after which, Mr. Allen carrying on the business alone, accumulated a competent fortune. In 1812, he married Clarissa Arms, of Conway. Mr. Allen, besides being a good business man, possessed some literary taste and was a good writer. Many of the best articles contributed to the *Sun* in its first half century were from his pen. He held many town-offices, and was active in town-affairs as well as in national politics. He died October 17, 1866.

Before 1812, there had grown up in Pittsfield, a manufactory of muskets, which, although not so extensive as it afterwards became, was of essential service in supplying some of the states with arms. In 1806, Jason Mills, from Springfield, purchased the old Whitney forge, and established upon the site a small gun-shop for the manufacture principally of fowling-pieces and other custom-work, for the neighboring country. In 1808, Lemuel Pomeroy purchased the place, of the representatives of Mills, and extended the works to the manufacture of muskets, for which he had contracts with Massachusetts and other states. The extent of the production was about two thousand stand annually.

In 1816, Mr. Pomeroy obtained a contract for supplying the United States government with two thousand stand annually for a term of five years. This contract was renewed for terms of five years, until 1846, although the amount of production was reduced in 1839, to fifteen hundred stand, but of a more expensive quality. In addition to the muskets made for the government, Mr. Pomeroy supplied two hundred stand annually to the trade.

In 1846, the government introducing the percussion-musket, the manufacture of which would have required changes in Mr. Pomeroy's works costing twenty-five thousand dollars, he declined any further contract. He would, however, have made the necessary expenditure, and continued the business, if it had not been that the government about the same time placed the armory at Springfield, which had previously been conducted by civilians, in charge of the war-department, who subjected it to strict military rule. Mr. Pomeroy was satisfied that this course would render the national armory so efficient as to place private competition out of the question. This opinion Mr. Pomeroy expressed to the board who had the question of the change under consideration, and it had great influence upon their decision. The officials were greatly astonished that Mr. Pomeroy should give evidence so detrimental to his own pecuniary interest; but they did not know the man.

While the business was in the full tide of success in 1823, Mr. Pomeroy erected, for its better prosecution, a brick-building fifty feet by forty in size; and in 1828, he added a brick trip-hammer shop; these were called the water-shops, the machinery being driven by the water-power. since used by the Taconic factory. The muskets were finished at a wooden-shop, two stories in height, on the corner of East street and Pomeroy avenue. In 1846, the brick water-shop was burned, and Mr. Pomeroy abandoned the manufacture of muskets; but for about ten years longer the trip-hammer shop was used for the manufacture of iron-axles.

The armory, which employed about thirty gunsmiths, was very profitable from the first, both to its proprietor and the town. From it Mr. Pomeroy obtained a portion of those resources, which under adverse circumstances, enabled him to lay the foundations of his woolen-manufactures. The trade of the gunsmith was hereditary in the Pomeroy family; the muskets manufactured by Mr. Pomeroy's grandfather, General Seth Pomeroy, having been famous throughout New England and the Canadas in the French and Indian wars. Those manufactured by the grandson were even more extensively scattered, having been distributed by the general government to the several states. One of them—a genuine old flint-lock of the date of 1825—was picked up by a Massachusetts officer on the battle-field of Newbern, N. C., and sent as a relic to Rev. Dr. Todd, by whom it was presented to the historical cabinet of the Berkshire Athenæum.

Among the most important events in the years immediately preceding the war of 1812, was the installation of Rev. William Allen, in the place of his father, as pastor of the First church, which occurred October 10, 1810. The story of Mr. Allen's pastorate is told in another chapter. To the citizens of the town he was the democratic minister; and he acted, indeed, as a sort of chaplain to the party on all occasions when the presence of a clergyman was decorous and desirable. He inherited from his father a firm faith in democratic principles and a true love for the party and its leaders ; but his tastes were rather scholarly and literary, than political. The dissensions in the church were painful to him as a Christian minister; and when the feelings excited by the contest in which he was the champion of a father disabled by ill-health, had subsided, his partisanship was not very pronounced. His Biographical Dictionary, the first edition of which, published in 1809, was a work of much original research—although inferior to that of 1832—had made him many friends in all parts of the country, and among all classes of intelligent citizens. And he doubtless longed for the quiet to pursue similar work. His peculiar notions as to requiring a strict compliance with the letter of the law, led him, however, to an enforcement of church-discipline, in a manner which might wisely have been tempered, and which made him many enemies. And a similar unyielding temperament, or judgment, followed him with disastrous results through a great part of his active life, especially in his relations with Dartmouth and Bowdoin colleges.

CHAPTER X.

WAR OF 1812—CANTONMENT AND DEPOT FOR PRISONERS OF WAR.

[1811–1815.]

Politics and political influences in Pittsfield—Names of prominent politicians—News of declaration of war received, and its effect—The Cantonment established—Barracks erected—Troops arrive—Dinners for the soldiers—Social intercourse and officers' balls—Recruiting and drilling—Major Melville as organizer and manager of the post—Slanders against him met and refuted—The 9th and other regiments called to the front—The Cantonment a depot for prisoners of war—Major Melville as agent for prisoners and deputy marshal—Escape of prisoners attributed to federalists—Stables converted into prisons—Incidents—Unruly prisoners—Prisoners released at close of the war and unwilling return to Canada—Berkshire regiments in the war—Pittsfield officers—Dinner to General Ripley.

THE act of congress, approved by President Madison, June 18, 1812, declaring that the long impending war with Great Britain had come, was printed in the *Pittsfield Sun*, June 27, together with the president's message, upon which the declaration was based. The news was received by the democratic majority with joy; while the federalists, after a brief hesitation on the part of some, joined their voice with that of their brethren at the East, in denouncing the war, as needless, and fraught with all manner of evils and dangers to the people, both from their own government, and the enemy. It was a signal for yet another increase of virulence in the political feuds of the day.

The grounds upon which a majority of the people of New England, especially of the more wealthy and conservative classes, began early to hate the administrations of Jefferson and Madison, have been considered. In the years immediately preceding the declaration of war, they had rapidly multiplied, and become more definite. A sense of personal wrong and injury succeeded to the vague fears arising from dangerous theories of government. The evil which they feared, had come upon them. The embargo and non-importation acts, with the irritating and vexatious supplementary laws by which government sought to enforce them, seemed to the importers of Massachusetts and Connecticut—who saw them enforced through favoritism, sometimes with needless severity, and sometimes with scandalous laxity—to be the very essence of tyranny. It was not now so much that government favored France against Great Britain. The new laws seemed aimed less against Old England, than at the very life of New England; for trade, navigation and fisheries were to her, the source of all prosperous life.

"You take my life
When you do take the means by which I live."

All Massachusetts, especially from the eastern slope of the Hoosac mountains to the sea, drew the breath of life through the ports of Boston and Salem; and to the majority of its people, the acts restricting navigation and commerce seemed but another Boston port-bill, quite as malignant as the first, and more comprehensive. Their opinion of the radical tendencies of Jeffersonian democracy was more than confirmed by the effect of democratic measures upon their fortunes. Twice, indeed, in the fourteen years next following the election of Mr. Jefferson to the presidency, the state elected democratic governors; but in both instances it was due to temporary and exceptional causes, which indicated no radical change of political sentiment. For the rest, the federal majorities had varied from 1,000 to 14,000—rarely falling below 3,000—in a total vote of from 100,000 to 104,000.

Berkshire continued to show the result of her mountain isolation from the rest of the state; uniformly, from 1801 to 1815, choosing democratic members of congress; and state-senators of the same political complexion, except in a single year, when a different result was secured by throwing out the votes of two democratic towns, for informality. The territorial position of the county, acting upon a basis of character derived from the Puritans, had made its people in an unusual degree, independent thinkers: independent, at least, of almost all external influence, however biased by traditional prejudice and well-preserved feuds.

All assertions of this sort of independence, must nevertheless, be qualified; and perhaps the best that can be claimed for the people of Berkshire, in this regard, is that their peculiar freedom from the intellectual authority of their state-capital, enabled them to judge with more candor of the arguments and reasonings which reached them from other sources. For, as to the most self-contained man—the most repellent of intruded counsels: so to the most secluded people—the most jealous of teachers claiming authority—influences from without will come, and must, whether consciously or otherwise, be entertained.

And, of these influences, however little the people of Berkshire, as a mass, were inclined to be submissive to the opinions of their metropolis, no small portion were received from the town of Boston. It was impossible that, every year, some of the most active minds of the county—some with liberal culture, and nearly all with abundance of shrewd common sense—should pass weeks among the people of Boston, and some of them in its most attractive social circles, without a very considerable effect upon their personal feelings, as well as upon their views of the measures which were the ordinary topics of conversation. It would be a too curious question fully to consider here, what the effect of these influences was upon different classes of minds; but it is certain that, as a rule, the federalists returned, charmed by the social fascinations of their metropolitan compatriots into a new devotion to the party of whose leaders they had found so pleasant an experience; and that the democrats were nerved by their legislative combats for sterner conflicts at home.

The legislature is always a valuable school, and a medium which can hardly be too highly prized for the diffusion of the culture of the capital throughout the most secluded districts of the state; and it was so especially when intercommunication between city and country was as restricted as it was in the earlier years of the nineteenth century. Many were the respectable gentlemen in Berkshire who marked with white, and perpetually recurred to, the year when they were chosen to the legislature; and with reason, for it probably added twofold to their intellectual ability.

But, considerable as the influence of Boston upon Berkshire opinion was, it was nevertheless not a preponderating power. It was more than counterbalanced by that which arose from the intimate business-relations between the county and the states of New York and Connecticut. Even the federalists drew their inspiration quite as much from Hartford as from Boston.[1]

---

[1] Perhaps less from either than from the old county of Hampshire, of which several of the leading Pittsfield federalists were natives.

A more definite and decided influence came, though Rev. Messrs. Allen and Leland, from the leading intellects of the democratic party in the nation. From the era of 1776, Mr. Allen, until his death, followed Thomas Jefferson, as the great apostle of liberty; and taught men so. Elder Leland, early familiar with the mighty men of his party, in Virginia, and renewing his intercourse with them by repeated visits to the Old Dominion, communicated their spirit in its freshness, as he passed from house to house; and what was thus told and taught, became a mighty power—a power which is felt to this day.

In combining the influences named, and bringing them practically to bear upon the politics of the day, each party had in Berkshire, able leaders. Of those resident in Pittsfield, we may name as active and prominent on the federal side, Woodbridge Little and Capt. Charles Goodrich, who were still active combatants, although of a previous generation; John W. Hulbert, John Chandler Williams, Thomas Gold, Deacon Charles Goodrich, Joseph Merrick and Dr. Daniel James. Among the active young politicians on the federal side, were Lemuel Pomeroy, Theodore Hinsdale, Jr., James D. Colt, Butler Goodrich, David Campbell, the Warriners, Jason Clapp, Joseph Bissell and James Buel.

Among the democratic leaders in chief, were Ezekiel Bacon, Simon Larned, Jonathan Allen, 1st and 2d, Dr. Timothy and Dr. H. H. Childs, John B. Root, Capt. John Dickinson, Phinehas Allen, Elkanah Watson, and Joseph Shearer.

The democrats had also a reserve corps of men, who, although not professed politicians, took a decided and constant interest in political affairs; and a stern, hard-working phalanx it was, always to be relied upon, whatever the emergency and whatever the obstacle to be met. Neither storms nor the imperious calls of private business, ever kept them from the polls. Jackson might have learned from them his famous watchword, "Eternal vigilance is the price of liberty." Among them were to be counted all the influential farmers of the West Part, Oliver Root, Joel Stevens—pronounced by Major Melville "the best farmer in Berkshire county"—William Francis, Josiah Francis, and the long list which bore the honored name of Francis, the Churchills, Hubbards, Parkers, Jesse Goodrich, and indeed almost all the names which appear in the roll of the West Part militia.

So in other parts of the town; at the east, the Bushes, Gunns,

Fairfields, Footes, Nobles and Herricks; at the north, the Merrills; in the center, the Ingersolls, the Hollisters, Oramel Fanning, William Clark, Simeon Griswold, and others.[1]

In the ability of their leaders, the two parties in Pittsfield were nearly equal. The democrats owed their great preponderance at the polls, in part to the sturdy and unwavering phalanx, of which we have just given a few names, and in part to traditionary opinions. But they were greatly indebted, also, to circumstances then recent; and which continued to increase in power, through the war.

And, first, manufactures had, during the preceding twelve or fifteen years been assuming a new importance in the business of the town, and, still more, in the esteem of its citizens; creating among them interests diverse from those of the rest of the state. East of the mountains, manufacturers were either so trifling in extent as to be completely overshadowed by the greater concerns of commerce, or their productions were of a class which looked chiefly to a foreign market; while agriculture found its customers either in the same distant trade, or among those who were engaged in carrying it on.

But Pittsfield had already become, to a good degree, a manufacturing town; not, indeed, so much in what had already been accomplished—although that was considerable, and of a promising character—as in the spirit which had been infused into its people by its newspapers, and by public-spirited men like Elkanah Watson, and his associates in the Berkshire Agricultural Society. The comparison must be made, not between the absolute amounts of manufacturing capital in the two sections, but with regard to its proportion to that otherwise invested, and also with an eye to the connection of the several classes of business-occupations with each other.

In Pittsfield, many of the well-to-do citizens were directly interested in the manufacture of woolen-goods for home-consumption. Each political party — or members of each — had its factory. There was quite an extensive manufactory of looms, spinning-jennies and carding-machines. The farmers were introducing large flocks of merino sheep, and they looked to the

[1] It is obviously impossible to make lists like the above full. The reader will himself add to it from the names of the proprietors of the Pittsfield Hotel, and others mentioned in this volume.

success of the mills to furnish a profitable market for the wools which they were zealously endeavoring to improve, and for their other farm-products. All classes were looking to the new manufactures as the most promising source of the future prosperity and wealth of the town, as well as the nation; and it was easy to see that a war, acting in the nature of a stringent protective tariff—as a war with Great Britain especially would—must greatly encourage them. On the other hand, among the most effective arguments which Mr. Watson used in his advocacy of Berkshire manufactures and improved wools, was the necessity for the country to supply itself with the better class of fabrics from its own looms in the event of a war, which, without any startling manifestation of the spirit of prophecy, he was able to predict as one of the events of the near future. The love of country and the hope of gain thus operated reciprocally upon each other, and harmoniously together, in the encouragement of manufactures. It thus happened, also, that there were not the same economical reasons which prevailed in the eastern part of the state, to restrain resentment for the insults and injuries of Great Britain. Here whatever opposition to the war there was, arose from party affiliations and prejudices, or personal opinions regarding its justice, or its expediency as affecting the whole country. In fact, the war promised to be, and was, most favorable to some of the citizens of Pittsfield who most bitterly denounced it. It furnished the best customer to Lemuel Pomeroy's gun-factory. It was full of promise to those federalists who, like Mr. Pomeroy, James D. and S. D. Colt, David Campbell and James Buel, were just embarking in the manufacture of cloths. It was certainly not private interest which dictated their political course.

But, irrespective of personal interests, there was much to provoke a wide difference of political feeling and opinion. It was far easier for either party to find an excuse for much of its own action in the errors and mistakes—national and state—of its opponents, than to defend it by sound reasoning upon any principle of abstract right.

From a New England point of view, the measures of government which led to the war were liable to the severest criticism; and of its partisanship for France no one now doubts, although no one now imagines that it was of a corrupt character. The puerile jealousy of a regular army and navy which characterized the administration of Jefferson, and the ludicrous expedients by which it sought to defend the country without them, were fair subjects for sneers. Even the absurd underestimate of the expenses of the first year of the war, submitted by Ezekiel Bacon, as chairman of the committee of ways and means in the house of representatives, must be given up as one of the rare instances in which that gentleman allowed the necessities of party to overcome his own good judgment.

It was apparent enough that those who brought on the war were strangely negligent of preparations for it. There is great truth in the assertion of Mr. Hillard, the federal historian of the period, that "never was an unfortunate country precipitated into an unequal and perilous contest, under circumstances more untoward."

But the federalists, on their part, made the greater mistake, when war was declared, not only of refusing it their support, but of going to the very verge of treason in their efforts to thwart the government in its measures for carrying it on; by their votes in congress, by the acts of state-legislatures in which they had control, by discouraging enlistments, and throwing ridicule upon the army and its officers. The democrats complained that, "whatever difficulty or distress arose from the extraordinary circumstances of the times, when great difficulty and distress were inevitable, was aggravated and magnified to the highest degree for the purpose of inflaming the public passions; that from the moment when the war was declared, they (the federalists) clamored for peace, and reprobated the war as wicked, unjust and unnecessary. They made every possible effort to raise obstructions and difficulties in its prosecution; and yet reprobated the administration for their imbecility in carrying it on. They reduced the government to bankruptcy, and then reproached it for its necessities and embarrassments. In a word, all their movements had but one object—to enfeeble and distract the government."[1]

The indictment was a true one. Whatever may have been the impolicy of plunging into the war; however a wiser statesmanship might have led to some other course, it could hardly be disputed that the acts of Great Britain had been such as to justify a resort to arms; that, as regarded *her*, the war was just. By their efforts to impede its successful prosecution, the federalists

[1] Carey's Olive Branch.

committed the fatal error which made their name a stigma and a by-word for generations.

But, although their great leader, John Adams, his son John Quincy Adams, Samuel Dexter, and other men of note, abandoned the party on the first intimation of this policy, it was not until after the close of the war, that its effects were fully appreciated. While hostilities continued, the federal party was not, at least sensibly, weakened from what it was when they commenced.

While its issue was uncertain, while mistakes in the camp and the council offered constant themes for censure of the government; while taxation and high prices bore hard upon the people, without, in most sections, adequate compensation by increased rewards for industry; and, above all, while the heat of party-violence had no time to cool, it was easy to maintain a respectable opposition to the war; but when it closed under circumstances which threw around it a brilliant halo of glory, and with the ends for which it was undertaken substantially attained, although not definitely recognized in the treaty, the reaction came with double power, and the federal party had to sustain, not only the obloquy of its errors, but of many heinous political offenses which were far from its thoughts. Many faithless Peters, who had been among the most hot-headed of its adherents, not only denied it in its fall, but found high places in the hostile camp by maligning their old associates, who, wrapping themselves in the mantle of their pure and patriotic intentions, maintained a dignified silence.

But to return to the opening of the war in 1812, Pittsfield soon had a reason to be reconciled to it—in addition to those already mentioned—in the establishment there, of a cantonment of United States troops, followed in 1813, by a depot for prisoners of war; from both of which, as well as from the purchase of general supplies for the army, there resulted a large expenditure of money in the town and county, with a profit to the people which would have been welcome at any time, but which was specially grateful after their recent losses.

On the passage of the act of January, 1812, for raising 25,000 additional United States troops, a general rendezvous for recruits was established at Pittsfield, Captain A. J. Bucklin of Cheshire, being placed in command. During the first ten days, thirty men were enlisted, and Lieut. Jared Ingersoll was stationed at Sheffield, Lieut. David Perry at Adams, and Ensign Wm. Browning at

Pittsfield; all being of Pittsfield and recruiting for the ninth regiment. Lieut. Ralph B. Cuyler was also stationed at Pittsfield, beating up for the 6th regiment.

On the 25th of April, the advertisements of these officers, in the *Pittsfield Sun*, began to call upon "all true and patriotic Americans, who were determined to vindicate the rights and maintain the independence of their country," "to rally to the standards" of their respective regiments; and the recruiting sergeants began to penetrate into every town in the county.

On the 23d of May, Rev. Wm. Allen deeded to the United States, for $800, one acre of land on the east side of North street, next above the present location of the Boston and Albany railroad. Upon this site stood the gambrel-roofed cottage, so often mentioned in previous chapters, which had been removed from East street to give place to the Pittsfield Hotel. This was now fitted up as a residence for the commandant of the post, and continued to be occupied for that purpose until Pittsfield ceased to be a military station.

On the 30th of May, the town was honored by a visit from the revolutionary veteran, Henry Dearborn, who had, in the previous February, been commissioned senior major-general of the United States army. General Dearborn was received by a national salute, and visited by many of the prominent citizens. He left, the next morning, for Springfield; but, short as his visit was, it resulted in the purchase of thirteen acres of level ground about one hundred rods north of the Park—which were subsequently increased to twenty-six acres and ninety-three rods. [1]

[1] The Cantonment grounds covered the land since occupied by Maplewood Young Ladies' Institute, St. Joseph's church and pastor's residence, and also about seven acres east of First street. There are some facts concerning the purchase not perfectly explained. It is stated in the *Sun*, of June 20, 1812, that government had purchased fourteen acres of land, and there is no doubt that it was correct in stating that buildings for the Cantonment had been commenced. But the land was part of the estate of Rev. Thomas Allen, and the probate court did not grant a license to sell it until June, 1814, soon after which date it was advertised, and sold at public auction, as required by law, the United States being the highest bidder. The other estate advertised with it, was the remainder of the home-lot, a few shares in the Hotel and the Female Academy, and the "meadow lot" on Wahconah street; and so much was to be sold as would raise the sum of $5,400, for the payment of debts and legacies. The executor's deed of the first thirteen acres is dated October 25, 1814, and the price was $1,170. The deed of the

After an interval of twenty-six years since its occupation by General Lincoln's little army in the Shays rebellion, Pittsfield now again began to assume the peculiar bustle of a military post.

The northern part of the thirteen acres purchased by General Dearborn was covered by a beautiful grove. A few rods south of the edge of this wood, on the spots since occupied by the chapel and two boarding-houses of Maplewood Young Ladies' Institute, were ranged the barracks: three plain wooden buildings, each three stories high, and one hundred and thirty feet long, with piazzas along the fronts of the different stories.

The west building was the officers' quarters; the east that of the non-commissioned officers and privates. The middle was used for various purposes. This was the arrangement for the first year. Subsequently some changes occurred, incident to the use of the Cantonment as a depot for prisoners of war. In the rear were two barns of the same length as the barracks, and two stories high; it being in contemplation to form here a regiment of cavalry.

The necessities of the service were pressing; operations on the northern frontier and in Canada were among the earliest proposed; it was hoped that troops for this purpose would be rapidly enlisted; and it was desirable to complete the buildings for their rendezvous as soon as possible. Capt. John Dickinson took the contract to have them ready in sixty days, and fulfilled it; although his health was so infirm that it was necessary for his daughter—now Mrs. C. T. Fenn—to drive with him daily in his chaise from their residence on the corner of East and Second streets, to the Cantonment grounds, in order that he might superintend the work. All the town came together at the raising of the frames, and in return for their aid enjoyed a merry and patriotic hour.

Afterwards, a plain two-story building was erected, for a hospital, in the south-west corner of the purchase of thirteen acres. And, on North street, the thrifty politician, as well as thrifty farmer, Joseph Shearer, built his sutler's shop.

seven acres and ninety-three rods, east of the first, is dated January 27, 1815, and the price $680. [Berkshire Registry of Deeds.] It seems probable that the United States took possession of the ground under an agreement with Mr. Allen, and an understanding with the general public, whose interest it was that the government should have the land.

Before the buildings were well under way, there were received two thousand stand of arms, with a full complement of camp-kettles, uniforms and other military equipments for the northern army.

On the 24th of June, a detachment of seventy fine-looking men from Captain Harris's company of light dragoons—the advance of the regiment which it was intended to gather here—came proudly marching into town. They were not yet mounted, and had marched, in eight days, one hundred and forty miles, from Boston. After a midsummer day's tramp across the Berkshire hills, they must have been somewhat dusty and way-worn; but, before entering the village, they had a little furbishing and refreshing, and, as they marched up East and North streets, "they made an excellent appearance: of good size, young, healthy and active." The sight thrilled the hearts of all, save the most inveterate partisans of England. The democrats had been told by their newspaper of the preceding week, that these gallant youth came "for the glorious purpose of defending the rights which had too long been trampled upon with impunity;" and they welcomed them with wild delight.

The school-teachers, with due instruction as to the significance of the spectacle, released their broods, to gaze upon, and salute with their childish greetings, the gay troopers whom they looked upon as the successors of Marion's men and Harry Lee's Lighthorse; for the patriotic old pastors who, in many households, had taught the fathers the political gospel of Virginian statesmen, did not fail to delight the children with stories of southern heroes. Old men, who were children then, relate with animation their emotions at the sight presented by Lieutenant Wheelock's dragoons; and, often, afterwards, when they were released from their tasks, as detachment after detachment of troops for the northern army passed through the town from the east; or large squads of prisoners, after the victories on the lakes and on the northern frontier, marched down West street. Such spectacles were frequent in the streets of Pittsfield, from that date until the returning tide of war, in 1815, brought back the victors of the Niagara frontier. But there is something which is never afterwards experienced, in the first peal of the trumpet, the first flash of serried arms in the streets, and the first array of men ready to do battle for their country, which, in each new war, breaks the stagnation of long-accustomed peace; and the Pittsfield people of 1812 never, probably, greeted another corps with precisely the same emotions as those excited by the appearance of the light-dragoons. The peculiar nature of this branch of the service, by far the most fascinating to the imagination, and the fact that it was the only corps of the kind to be raised in Massachusetts, also added to the effect.

South of the unfinished barracks, the Cantonment grounds covered a beautiful level area of eight or nine acres, which had been Rev. Mr. Allen's meadow; and upon this the dragoons encamped —as other detachments afterwards did, from time to time, when the barracks were insufficient. Lieutenant Wheelock was complimented as an able, spirited and humane [1] officer, and the soldier-like appearance, and orderly conduct of his men, were much applauded. The troop remained at the Cantonment several months, and continued to maintain the good opinion of the citizens, with whom the soldiers mingled as freely as was consistent with good discipline, especially on occasions of patriotic rejoicing. And a brief account of one of these instances in the *Sun* confirms our belief that, however party-feeling and party-organization, stimulated and guided by extreme men, may have led the federal party to an unwarrantable opposition to the government in its conduct of the war, still the sympathies of the mass of its members were always with the national arms: "On the receipt of the news of the splendid and glorious victory of Commodore Decatur (the capture of the frigate Macedonian), the bells (both of the Union and the First parish) were rung, and the company of dragoons under Captain Harris assembled with the citizens, on the green (afterwards the Park), and with two pieces of artillery, fired a national salute, and *without distinction of party*, gave the officers and crew of the United States frigate three cheers." There was not much affection for Great Britain in that spontaneous outburst of feeling.

Before the arrival of the dragoons, seventy men had been enlisted for Capt. Bucklin's company in the 9th regiment of infantry. The pecuniary inducements then offered for enlistments for a term of five years were a bounty of sixteen dollars, and, at the expiration of the term of service, three months' extra

---

[1] He proved in active service far otherwise, as to spirit at least.

pay, and one hundred and sixty acres of the public lands, "to be designated, laid off and surveyed at the expense of the government."

Recruiting can hardly be said to have been very brisk, as on the 1st of August, the number reported in the barracks, including the seventy dragoons, which Lieutenant Wheelock brought with him from Boston, was only two hundred; but these must have thought that their lines had fallen to them in pleasant places. They were surrounded by a population, the great majority of whom looked upon them as the defenders of their most sacred rights; while, among the declared opponents of the war, there were many ready to welcome companions so genial and intelligent as most of the officers at the Cantonment proved.

The ladies, as ever in such cases, were full of patriotic enthusiasm, which manifested itself in various ways, from providing stockings and dinners for the privates, to marrying the most gallant and distinguished of the officers. In this early stage of the occupation of the town, the first exhibition of this feeling was in the old and natural mode of extending hospitality: by feasting the honored guests. And, on the 4th of July, 1812, "the bountiful hand of female benevolence spread the table of festivity and enjoyment for the soldiers, who were regaled by the republican ladies in a style which reflected honor upon their patriotism."

On the 30th of the same month, the ladies of Cheshire—Elder Leland's town, ten miles north of Pittsfield—went down, laden with a collation upon which the editor of the *Sun* dilated with evident admiration: "An elegant and sumptuous dinner, served up in the best manner by their own fair hands—under a handsome bower erected for the occasion at the encampment—and consisting of every variety of the season: beef, ham, lamb, pigs, turkeys, fowls, green-peas, string-beans, new potatoes, puddings, pies, and indeed everything requisite for an entertainment of the first order, which in truth it was." Lieutenant Wheelock presided at the table, and many of the officers of the 9th regiment were present, and tendered their acknowledgments with a pledge of "their ardent devotion to the service of their country, and an assurance of the most inviolate protection of the American fair." They could hardly have done less: and one cannot help agreeing with the editor of the *Sun*, in his opinion, "that the man who had partaken of the feast thus provided, must be an ingrate indeed, who did not exert himself to the utmost in vindicating the rights of his insulted country;" especially as, by way of giving a more piquant flavor to the sumptuous viands, the soldiers were informed that they were tendered as a testimony of "the respect and approbation of the ladies for the vigorous measures now pursued by our national government for the redress of the insults and injuries heaped upon their country for a long time previous, by the *eternal* enemies of liberty."

On the 4th of August, the whig[1] ladies of Dalton gave a dinner to the officers and soldiers of the 9th regiment, which was provided for them at the tavern of William Clark, on East street. "What gave particular zest to the occasion was the appearance of the patriotic fair ones, who had prepared the entertainment and attended the tables personally." Many of the "whig" citizens attended, and in all nearly three hundred were seated at the table, at which Simon Larned, who had been appointed colonel of the regiment, presided, assisted by Thomas Aspinwall, its major.

Nor were these public and general banquets the only occasions upon which the soldiery at the Cantonment enjoyed social intercourse with the people of the village. The officers, and some at least of the soldiers, were welcomed to the best houses; and it need hardly be said, that none found difficulty in forming pleasant friendships. In return for these hospitalities, the officers began early, and kept up until the close of the war, a round of balls, which, if gallantry and beauty could make them so, were, beyond doubt, brilliant; although gay calicoes were far in excess of muslins, and silks were rare indeed. But the music was good, the suppers were excellent, the dances—thanks to the teachers of the art, who were plentiful—were skillful and graceful, and all were ready to please and be pleased. After the lapse of more than sixty years, the memory of those glad hours, is still grateful to the few now living who joined in those measures, and maintain— rightly we believe—that Pittsfield has never seen balls to equal those at the old Cantonment.[2]

---

[1] The administration-party at this time preferred the name of republican, but claiming to be the successors of the revolutionary whigs, affected their name as a synonym for their own.

[2] Mrs. C. T. Fenn was one of the ladies at these balls. Colonel Aspinwall of the 9th, who lost an arm at Niagara, and is now the oldest graduate of Harvard college, was one of the most pleasant of the dancers.

But we must turn from the pleasures which alleviated the irksomeness of barrack-life at the Cantonment, to the details of its practical work. There was, with recruiting, drilling, and studying the manuals of military science, in which most of the officers had much to learn, an abundance of it.

The dragoons, who were soon recruited to a full troop, and mounted upon horses purchased to a considerable extent in the vicinity of Pittsfield, were daily drilled in the tactics of their branch of the service, and, often, upon the neighboring roads glimpses of their uniform and glances from their arms enlivened the beautiful scenery, while their bugles echoed among the hills.

The 9th regiment—Berkshire's own—grew apace, although not so rapidly as its officers hoped. Colonel Larned was popular, and so, in spite of his severity in drill and discipline, was Lieutenant-colonel Aspinwall. Early in September the regiment had three hundred men in the barracks, all good material for soldiers, and drilling industriously.

The Cantonment was also the rendezvous for the 6th, 21st and perhaps other regiments.

On the 1st of July, Thomas Melville, Jr., who had just returned to his father's home in Boston, after a residence of twenty-one years in France, was appointed commissary and superintendent of supplies for the army, with the rank of major.

At a later period of the war he was made United States deputy marshal and agent for prisoners of war. In fact, although sometimes outranked by regimental commanders at the station, Major Melville was the organizer and superintendent of the post; having his official residence at the gambrel-roofed cottage purchased of Rev. William Allen.

The establishment of a commissary station and a depot for prisoners of war in connection with the Cantonment, furnished a cash-market for almost every kind of surplus product which the county or the neighboring region could supply, and contributed much toward making Pittsfield a local business-center. Major Melville's advertisements, commencing June 17, 1812, with "six or seven hundred yards of yard-wide tow-cloth," called, before they ended, for every variety of cloth, for leather, iron, beef, pork, grain of all kinds, vegetables, hay, wood, wagons, horses, and whatever else the county could produce, or an army consume or use; and they were answered from a wide circuit of country.

But, beneficial as the Cantonment and station for supplies were to the people of their neighborhood, they had hardly been established before the baser sort of the opponents of the war began to impede their operations, by inventing and circulating in the surrounding towns stories of altercations among the officers, and frequent desertions by the new recruits. It was to be expected, therefore, that the coming of Major Melville would be followed by even more violent attacks; and he was, in fact, obliged to publish a card of denial, which appeared in the *Sun* of September 17, 1812, in which he says, that several malicious reports had been spread, since his residence in town, which, being of a *personal* nature only, he thought it advisable to pass unnoticed; but, attempts having been made within a few days, to propagate a report which did not permit him to remain longer silent, viz.: that he was not furnished with funds to meet the obligations of the United States government in Pittsfield, and—what was more infamous—that, in his official capacity, he had borrowed, or attempted to borrow, money of a person here, he took the first public opportunity to "publish the author as an infamous liar."

This vigorous form of denial, which was quite in keeping with the custom of the day, proved effectual for a time. But, in the spring of 1813, the old calumnies were revived under apparently corroborating circumstances. A change occurring in the head of the quartermaster-general's department at Albany, the secretary of war directed that the payment of all debts incurred under his authority should be suspended during the adjusting of his accounts. Upon this foundation, various reports concerning the financial affairs of the station at Pittsfield—some of them gross misrepresentations, and others palpable falsehoods—were put in circulation.

Greatly disturbed by these reports, Major Melville went to Albany, and there addressed a letter to the new quartermaster-general in that city, Robert Swartwout, in which he said:

Sir: Entrusted with the creation of the military post at Pittsfield, Mass., and clothed with the confidence of the late quartermaster-general, I have been enabled to call forth the resources and energies of a considerable and interesting part of the county of Berkshire and vicinity.

Firm and undaunted in my measures, candid and open in my political sentiments, jealous for the welfare of the army and for the interests of the government, I dare flatter myself that I have merited the approbation even of those who may differ from me in political opinion.

It is painful for me to be obliged to anticipate that the measures necessitated by the new organization of the quartermaster-general's department may paralyze, or diminish, the confidence I have labored to establish—and it grieves me to reflect that those persons who have exerted themselves, and put forth their funds for the execution of contracts, for the account of the government, should meet with even a momentary delay in the receipt of their just dues.

In conclusion, Major Melville expressed fears lest the secretary's order might lead persons unaccustomed to the forms of public business to attribute delays in payment to a want of confidence, on the part of the government, either in his own integrity or capability. In reply, General Swartwout, under date of May 8, stated that the suspension of payments was temporary, and under a general order in which the station at Pittsfield was only incidentally included. He added that he had already taken such measures as would shortly enable Major Melville to pay all dues; and added: "I am perfectly satisfied that you have diligently and faithfully discharged your duty in the various important trusts confided to you."

Major Melville published both his own letter and the reply, in the *Sun*, accompanied by a note, which closes with the following warning, alluding to the stories which had been circulated, to the detriment of the post: "Should these reports be again revived, I shall conceive it a duty to the government and to myself, to take such notice of the authors and their abettors as will not, perhaps, be agreeable to them."

We hear no more upon this subject, and probably no more palpable slanders against the post were discovered.

While the commissary and quartermaster of the post were thus prosecuting their duties for the benefit of both the town and the country, the routine-work of the Cantonment also went on well. The buildings were finished according to contract. William Hollister and Oramel Fanning took the contract for the supply of the local commissariat, and executed it satisfactorily. Their first advertisement appeared July 9, 1813, and offered a fair price, in cash, for fifty barrels of good prime pork, one hundred bushels of good rye, with beef-cattle, lambs, and calves, *ad libitum*. It was one of the daily pleasures of the village-children to watch

Mr. Hollister's great hay-cart, with its huge rack piled high with loaves of excellent bread, wending its way to the Cantonment.

Healthful as the location of the barracks was, changed habits of life, and unaccustomed diet, gave hospital-work; and death sometimes anticipated the harvest of the battle-field. In this connection, a new excitement arose. Pittsfield was not yet the seat of a medical college; but it was not without ambitious young doctors, and Joseph Childs, a soldier in Captain Grafton's company of infantry, being interred in the town burial-ground, some evil-disposed persons, not having a due sense of the sacred rights of Christian burial, on the night of the 20th of September, disinterred his body and carried it away for dissection. Colonel John L. Tuttle, commanding the Cantonment, offered a reward of fifty dollars for the detection of the resurrectionist; but although there was little doubt of his identity, no legal proof against him could be obtained. The excitement died away; but, it being revived by a similar occurrence, a guard was at first stationed over the graves, and afterwards, a plot in the Cantonment grounds was set apart for burial purposes.

Among the camp-followers which the Cantonment brought to Pittsfield, was the first elephant which ever crossed the Berkshire hills. It was exhibited, on the 6th and 7th of October—the 6th being cattle-show—in the open space east of Captain Campbell's coffee-house on Bank row. The advertisements headed "Now or never," informed the people that that generation might never again have an opportunity of seeing an elephant; as this was the only one in America, and this might be its last visit to Pittsfield. "The elephant," it was further explained, "is not only the largest and most sagacious animal in the world, but from the peculiar manner in which it takes its food and drink, with its trunk, is acknowledged to be the greatest natural curiosity ever offered to the public."

Troops, by companies, or in detachments of recruits, continued to arrive from the east, and—after longer or shorter intervals, varying from a single day to several weeks, as rest, re-organization, drill, or other exigencies of the service required—to move on towards the seat of war.

About the first of September, news of General Hull's disastrous surrender at Detroit spread gloom over the little camp. But the *Sun*, in announcing the misfortune, was able to lighten the picture by printing, side by side with it, the news of the brilliant affair of the Constitution and Guerriere. The glory of one Hull relieved the disgrace of the other; which was not the only time in that year when naval victories came opportunely to mitigate the sting of defeats on land.

The capture of Hull's army leaving the northern frontier exposed, all the available forces in the department were hurried to the front; and although the 9th regiment had only three hundred and fifty men, it went with the rest; Colonel Larned going in command, but Major Aspinwall remaining in charge of the recruiting-service for western Massachusetts.

One entire company of the 9th regiment, and a portion of the others, were raised in Berkshire. All had, by their good conduct, won the esteem of the citizens of Pittsfield; and they left the Cantonment, already a favorite corps. They marched, on the 4th of September, "well armed and uniformed, and provided with every necessary supply for a campaign; both officers and men in high spirits." A number of Pittsfield gentlemen escorted them as far as Lanesboro, where they were met by a delegation from New Ashford, in which town the patriotic citizens spread for them a plentiful entertainment. Reaching Williamstown at evening, they were again furnished, "by its republican citizens," with every necessary refreshment. The next morning, they proceeded by way of Vermont, to Lake Champlain.

About two weeks later, Lieutenant-Colonel Ripley, of the 21st regiment, who had reached Pittsfield in August, with a hundred and fifty recruits from Portland, Maine, followed Colonel Larned to Whitehall, with two hundred and twenty men for the 9th and 21st regiments. Captain Harris's dragoons remained until December 28.

Early in December, the northern army were ordered into winter-quarters; and it was so confidently expected that the 9th and 21st regiments would return to Pittsfield, that the *Sun*, of December 3d, announced that they might be expected in ten days. The whole army, however, wintered in the vicinity of Plattsburg. The *Sun*, after mentioning this change of plan, which must have been a sore disappointment to the republicans of Pittsfield, requested the patriotic ladies, who had been diligently knitting socks and mittens for the soldiers, to send them to the house of Colonel Larned. In response, four hundred and eighty-seven pairs were sent in, and immediately forwarded to the army by Major Melville. The contributions were: "From Pittsfield and a part of Hancock, 193; Cheshire, 143; Lanesboro, 51; Williamstown, 30; Dalton (six families only), 19; and a few pairs from a couple of patriotic ladies in Lenox."

The winter passed quietly, at the Cantonment.

On the 20th of April, 1813, Jonathan Allen was appointed deputy quartermaster-general, with the rank of captain, and detailed for service at Pittsfield. The expenditures by Captain Allen, in his department, were of course, in addition to those made by Major Melville. Indeed, they formed a large part of the money which the war brought to Pittsfield. His estimates for the year 1813, in which the requirements were much less than in the succeeding year, were twenty-four thousand four hundred dollars; the items being for horses, wood, straw, powder, transportation, provender, and contingent expenses. For the month of December, 1814, the estimate for the same items, with the exception of the purchase of horses, was seven hundred and sixty-six dollars; and for the month of January, 1815, the estimate was eight hundred and fifteen dollars; for the month of February, 1815, sixteen hundred and ninety-two dollars.

These are the only estimates of which we have obtained copies; but they sufficiently indicate the expenditures at the post, by the quartermaster's department.

Captain Allen experienced the same difficulty which Major Melville did from the impoverished condition of the national treasury. He appears to have been left unprepared to meet pressing demands. But his first embarrassment was from claims for taxes upon the Cantonment grounds and buildings. The federal legislature of the state had refused to cede the site to the United States; and the democratic authorities of the town pressed for the payment of taxes upon the land and buildings.

Lieutenant Wheelock, also, on his march from Boston, left several of his men sick, without any descriptive list, or written order for their support, and when some of them died, those who had cared for them applied to Captain Allen for payment, which he had no legal right to make. In January, 1814, he was ordered to forward, as soon as practicable, one thousand blankets, one thousand coats, one thousand vests, one thousand overalls, and thirty-six pairs of stockings, to Boston; but was unable to do so, from lack of funds, "not having had a dollar of public money since the previous September." He adds: "To keep the troops on this Cantonment (four hundred and fifteen now present) with fuel and such other expenses, as they could not do without, has exhausted all my resources, of which I also notified Mr. Monroe [1] by my accounts, and by letters, at least half a dozen times, since September; but have not received the mark of a pen from him, except to make monthly summary statements. * * * I shall have the clothing for New York packed and ready to start immediately after I am in cash."

In another letter, a few days later, he says: "My estimate of expenses for this Cantonment, in my department, exceed eight hundred dollars per month, and no money here to be had: all of which I have notified the secretary of war several times, and, unless I am shortly relieved, I must *stop*. The article of wood alone, which the men *must* have, costs about four hundred dollars monthly."

The energetic remonstrances of Captain Allen seem to have been successful in securing a proper attention at the war-department to the pecuniary necessities of the Cantonment.

With the opening of the campaign of 1813, the movement of troops westward recommenced, and their arrival and departure, in larger or smaller detachments continued to enliven the town, and afford food for conjecture as to future operations.

About the 1st of August, 1813, most of the troops having been withdrawn to the front, it was determined to concentrate the prisoners of war, from several other depots, at Pittsfield, under the charge of Major Melville, who was appointed deputy-marshal of Massachusetts. On the 13th of August, Captain Allen received orders to prepare the barracks for the reception of six hundred men of this class, which he did by surrounding one of the buildings previously erected with a fence ten feet high, and building a guard-room properly furnished with arms, handcuffs, fetters and chains for the restraint of the unruly, and with proper furniture, in the other rooms, for the use of the peaceable.

Four hundred prisoners were expected immediately, but only two hundred were in charge on the 1st of December. Seventeen British officers of militia, magistrates and prominent citizens,

---

[1] James Monroe, acting secretary of war.

arrested near Niagara, for some special reason, reached town on the 11th of August, and were paroled at Cheshire.

From this time to the close of the war, most of the officers resided at Cheshire on parole; smaller numbers at Stockbridge, and a few at Pittsfield. General Riall, captured at Lundy's Lane, boarded at Captain Campbell's coffee-house.

Dr. Timothy Childs was appointed visiting-physician to the prisoners confined at Pittsfield and Cheshire; and in his official statement at the close of the war, he reports that the whole number of private soldiers and non-commissioned officers confined at the Cantonment between September 12, 1813, and the close of the war, was over fourteen hundred; and the average, over six hundred. In addition to these, there were a proportionate number of officers, besides a hundred on parole at Cheshire and Stockbridge.

Captain Allen reported above two hundred prisoners at the barracks in December, 1813; about one thousand, December 1, 1814; and nearly fifteen hundred, January 1, 1815. The *Sun*, of February 2, 1815, states that there were then fourteen hundred prisoners, and that three or four hundred more were expected that week. Rev. Mr. Hibbard, writing loosely from memory in the year 1840, mentions "several thousand;" and other memories, as well as tradition, are equally liberal: but there is no reason to doubt that the official statements, quoted above, are correct.

The first-coming prisoners were quartered, as has been stated, in one of the barracks. But, on the 26th of December, 1814, Captain Allen received a requisition from Major Melville to take immediate measures for fitting the two barns in the rear of the Cantonment for the reception of fifteen hundred prisoners of war on the 15th of October. These barns were two hundred feet long each, and the probable cost of remodeling them as prisoners' barracks, was estimated at between two thousand and three thousand dollars; and Captain Allen having no public funds in his possession for that purpose, and no expectation of any, declined the task; but consented that Major Melville should undertake it, although it belonged more properly to the quartermaster's department.

Major Melville, the next morning, repaired to the house of Captain Hosea Merrill, who was an extensive lumber-dealer and builder—and, moreover, an ardent democrat and supporter of the war—and urged him to undertake the task at once. But it happened to be Sunday; and Captain Merrill would not so much as talk upon the subject; his many years of service in the revolutionary army having not in the least weakened his New England scruples concerning labor on the Sabbath. On Monday, however, without questioning the probability of pay from the government, he began work in earnest.

The specifications required for two of the rooms, windows protected by heavy iron-gratings; and, around the entire building, a plank-fence two inches thick, twelve feet high, and with stout hemlock-posts sunk five feet in the earth. The plank was as yet all in the log, and some of the logs were standing in the forest. The iron was at Boston; and the workmen were nearly all yet to be engaged. But loggers were briskly set at work; the saw-mill at Pontoosuc ran night and day; the prisoners already in barracks were pressed into service; the iron was received and the gratings made by blacksmith Ezekiel Bates. The last stroke of the workman's hammer was heard just as the first squad of new prisoners marched into the barracks.

Justus Merrill, a son of the builder, returning from his brief campaign in Boston, was appointed steward of the prison made of one of the barns, and William Janes of the other. Mr. Janes's brother, Ethan, then a lieutenant in The Blues, was already steward of the prison in the barracks.

During the first year of the depot, there was no especial trouble with the prisoners. To be sure, although a mounted patrol constantly made the circuit of each prison during the night, in addition to the sentries who were always on guard, there was occasionally an escape, which the republicans were fain to attribute to the aid of the political opponents of the war, and the friends of Great Britain in the town; as they did the very moderate number of desertions which took place. But there is not the slightest evidence that any aid was given, in either case, by any reputable member of the federal party; or indeed by anybody except such as, whatever political faith they professed, would have been tempted to a more serious offense by a handsome bribe. The first escape was that of two spirited young officers, Lieutenant Walter Kerr and Ensign Alexander Greig, who are known to have bribed the sentry. A reward of a hundred dollars was offered, without effect, for their capture; and, although no federalist of repute would have probably aided in their escape, it is not unlikely that there were many who, if they had met them in their flight, would not have considered it an imperative duty to detain them.

Many of the prisoners during the first year were Germans, and it was noticed that, although, when exchanged, they returned often for the third or fourth time, yet the fortunes of war did not seem to depress them. They explained that, having observed that the German regiment was always assigned to the most exposed points, they preferred life in a comfortable prison to hard life in camp, and death in a war which did not concern them. The kindness which they received, thus met a probably not altogether unexpected return.

The prisoners were also permitted to avoid the irksomeness of confinement, and earn an honest penny by "hiring out" to parties responsible for their return. The labor dearth was thus relieved; and few, if any, seized the opportunity to escape.

In the fall of 1813, and still more in the summer of 1814, the number of the prisoners increased, and their character was changed, by the victories on the lakes and on the northern frontier; and, although the system of kind treatment was persisted in, more caution was required in the management and guarding of the depot.

Among the prisoners there was now a much larger proportion of native-born British subjects; and these, frequently, of a class not easily touched by kindness. Many of them were habitually unruly; and, on two occasions at least, plots to escape in a body and by violence, were formed, and it became necessary to cover the prisons with the cannon, of which the post had four nine-pounders, with a threat of firing unless order was restored. At other times the small-arms of the guard sufficed.

The least troublesome of the prisoners were the Germans. The most unruly and dangerous were about one hundred and seventy marines and sailors—the survivors of a picked detachment sent out from the lake-fleet, who had been enticed up one of the rivers in pursuit of a body of militia, which, when it reached the desired point, turned upon its pursuers, killed a large number at the first fire, and captured the rest.

This party was full of the spirit usually attributed to the British tar, and kept the prison in a perpetual turmoil by their mischievous pranks, or more serious misdemeanors. When the news of peace came, forty of them were confined in the guard-room, upon a diet of bread and water, as ringleaders in breaking into the hospital store-room, and stealing the wines and liquors prepared for the sick, upon which they became uproariously intoxicated and openly revolted. They were in the guard-room house, when General Weinbold of the British army, who was making the tour of the depots for prisoners, arrived; and to him they made grievous complaints. But the general, who was not inexperienced in such cases, only replied very quietly, " Oh, yes, you're as innocent as sucking doves. You only robbed a hospital of supplies provided for your own sick, and threatened to kill those who wanted to treat you kindly. It's my opinion, you are only too lightly punished."

It is a curious fact that the most earnest desire, and the most serious attempt, to break prison, were after it was known that peace was declared, and that the prisoners were shortly to be given up at the nearest and most convenient British post, which happened to be, as regarded Pittsfield, the famous Isle-aux-Noix, at the foot of Lake Champlain. Many of the prisoners were reluctant to return to Europe at all, especially in the character of soldiers. So determined were they, in fact not to do so, that it would have been impossible to get them into Canada without a strong guard, had not General Weinbold promised that, as soon as possible after their exchange, they should be paid off and discharged, with an additional gift of land in that province.

There is no reason to doubt that, in making this promise, General Weinbold was sincere. The wars which had so long agitated Europe were supposed to be ended; England and her allies victorious; and Napoleon crushed and helpless in the Island of Elba. There seemed to be no better use to which England could put her superfluous soldiers in America than by transforming them into loyal colonists. Still, many of the prisoners were distrustful, and the task of taking them to the Isle-aux-Noix, to be delivered up, was not considered a desirable or safe one. The stewards of the other prisons declining it, Mr. Justus Merrill went in charge of all; and, with the exception of some unavoidable losses by desertion, he accomplished his task successfully, and delivered up his charge to the satisfaction of the British agents. When the first detachments marched, it was yet in early spring, the ground alternately freezing and thawing; and the soldiers, whose feet were tender after their long confinement, suffered much. They were also troubled with doubts as to what would be done with them at the end of the journey; and these doubts proved to be well-founded. No sooner had the last detachment reached Canada, than they learned, to their dismay, that the great Emperor, escaping from Elba, was again in France, and at the head of an immense army, ready for a desperate and doubtful struggle.

Many of the prisoners, just released from Pittsfield, might have cared very little for this, except that from it resulted a "military necessity," which compelled the British government, instead of leaving them as peaceful, and as they hoped prosperous, settlers in Canada, to send them across the ocean, to again engage in conflict. They declared with imprecations that if they had known this before, they would never have crossed the lines. But there was now no help. They were marched rapidly to Quebec, placed upon transports, and reached the seat of war in season for Waterloo. These and other soldiers released by the peace from service in America, may have turned the scales which so long hung suspended upon that eventful field.

The treatment of the British prisoners of war at the Pittsfield depot, as at others, was distinguished by marked kindness and humanity; this having been a matter of pride and honor, as well as of feeling, with all grades of the officers who had charge of them. Mr. James Prince, marshal of the district of Massachusetts, writing to Dr. Timothy Childs, at the close of the war, said: "I cannot fail to observe to you, on this occasion, the very great consolation I experience from reflection on the general conduct of all the gentlemen who have had any agency with prisoners in this district; by which, not only has the condition of a class of unfortunate men, placed in our power by the fortunes of war, been ameliorated, as far as depended on them, but it enables us to present these good offices in contrast with, and as the counterpart of, the conduct to our citizens detained as prisoners of war,—ours, the splendid tablet of mercy and kindness to conquered foes, imitating the benevolence of Deity; theirs, the ferocity of demons."

With regard to Dr. Childs's own services, in a letter concerning the final settlement of accounts, the marshal writes:

That your services would have been constant, arduous and successful was to be expected from your well-known character for patriotism, zeal and professional skill; and it was from these considerations that, when I proposed the appointment, I felt peculiarly gratified that you signified your acceptance.

When the establishment at Pittsfield took place, both its extent and its duration were uncertain, as it respected me, who, although the medium to introduce it, was known to be a subordinate character; and that every officer placed there, as well as the management of its concerns, was dependent upon the will and control of the commissary-general of prisoners. A minute statement of my doings at Pittsfield, was, therefore, transmitted to Washington, immediately upon my return from that place, in which your appointment and terms were made known. Here my agency ended. If, therefore, the number of prisoners has exceeded what was calculated upon at the commencement of the establishment, and, from the great number of wounded men, your duties have been more than ordinarily severe, I cannot for a moment doubt that a representation on your part, certified by Major Melville, the officer charged with the execution of the instructions of the commissary-general, will be received with candor at Washington, and rewarded with liberality.

The representation was forwarded to the commissary-general, John Mason, and that officer, in response, and also, " taking into consideration the high testimonies in Dr. Childs's favor, adduced by the marshal of Massachusetts," determined to comply with his request to be placed on the same footing with a hospital-surgeon in the United States army; the compensation to date from the time the increase in the number of prisoners took place.

As the residence of some of the prisoners at Cheshire, and others at Stockbridge, rendered it impossible for Dr. Childs to attend to them at all times personally, and as he frequently required aid at Pittsfield, especially after a severe battle at the north, he was also allowed the pay of a surgeon's mate; and compensation for medicines furnished. He actually received as follows: For the months of September and October, ranking as surgeon's mate, and including commutation for servant, forage for horse, and rations, $158; from November 1, 1813, when the increase of prisoners began, until May 30, 1815, when the service ceased, ranking as hospital-surgeon, and including pay at the rate of $75 per month, assistants' pay at $45 per month, with servant's pay, rations, etc., $3,892. For medicines dispensed, $325. A total of $4,375. Dr. Childs's assistants were his son, Dr. H. H.

Childs, Dr. Daniel Barker, of Adams, and Dr. Isaac Hodges, of Cheshire.

Probably he had other occasional aid; but we are not informed by whom it was given, nor what compensation he paid to any of his assistants.

Both the British prisoners and the soldiers at the Cantonment, had the proclivity usual in such cases, to sell the clothing and blankets provided by their respective governments; and, especially as the close of the war approached, the officers at the Cantonment had great trouble in executing the law against that practice. In fact, many English blankets were left in the town, and became treasured heir-looms in some families. But, in the enthusiasm for supplying the soldiers of the Union in the civil war of 1861-5, some of them were drawn from their hiding-places; and, after the repose of half a century, found themselves again in the turmoil of camp and field.

It could not be expected that in a war like that of 1812, the soldiery of Pittsfield would perform such conspicuous service as distinguished them in the revolution. But, nevertheless, their record was distinguished and honorable. The two regiments of infantry—the 9th and 21st—in which the town was most largely represented, became noted, in the army of the northern frontier, for their gallantry, their efficiency and their losses.

We have not the means of following them through their several campaigns; but whenever they are alluded to, it is in the most honorable terms. The 9th acquired its sanguinary sobriquet previous to the campaign of 1814, being so styled by Captain Ingersoll in his call for recruits in the spring of that year. "None but gentlemen, and gentlemen's sons," says his advertisement, "need apply for admission to the ranks of the Bloody 9th." The standard of gentility is very sensibly defined, by inference from the context, to be "honesty and sobriety;" under which test it is to be hoped the gentry of Berkshire were not a very circumscribed circle.

Both regiments did grand service, whenever they had opportunity, throughout the war; but they won their brightest laurels in the series of sanguinary conflicts and glorious victories at Chippewa, Lundy's Lane, Niagara Falls and Fort Erie; in some, or all, of which Captain Harris's dragoons also performed brilliant exploits, and contributed the most essential aid in critical emergencies. In all these battles, the 9th and 21st were with the foremost in sacrifice and achievement. The brave 9th, 11th and 25th—the remnants of Winfield Scott's veteran brigade, which had suffered terribly in the previous battles — we are told by Lossing, were hurried into the battle of Niagara, without warning or preparation. All day they fought valiantly; and at ten o'clock at night, the shattered remnants of the brigade, commanded by such officers of the 9th as remained, rallied round the tattered colors of the 11th, and kept the field.

It was at this battle, also, that the 21st performed an exploit which ranks in history with the charge of The Six Hundred at Balaclava, although it has not yet found its poet. "The action," says Salma Hale in his brief story of the war, "was a succession of engagements; in one of the earlier of which the Americans were sorely annoyed into whatever part of the field they might drive the enemy, or be driven, by the British artillery, stationed on a commanding eminence, near Lundy's Lane. 'Can you storm that battery?' said General Ripley to Colonel Miller. 'I'll try, sir!' was the laconic answer. Giving the word of command to his men, they, with steady courage, ascended the hill, advanced to the muzzles of the cannon, killed with their muskets several artillerymen on the point of firing their pieces, and drove the remainder before them. Both parties were instantly re-enforced; and the enemy made a daring effort to regain their cannon. They were repulsed, but quickly repeated the attempt. Nearly all the opposing forces gathered around this position; and to possess it was the sole object of both armies. Again the enemy were repulsed, but again they renewed the effort. After a violent conflict, they were, a third time, driven from the hill. The firing then ceased, the British troops were withdrawn; and the Americans were left in quiet possession of the field."

In these latter charges, General Ripley led his brigade in person; and some of the most remarkable hand-to-hand conflicts on record, were witnessed. Bayonet interlocked with bayonet, the blaze of opposing muskets crossed each other, and sometimes, the rare spectacle of officers measuring swords was seen.

Dr. Elisha Lee Allen of Pittsfield, was assistant-surgeon of the 21st; and, in a letter to his brother, Captain Jonathan Allen, giving a glowing account of the battle, he says that one officer of that regiment was killed and six wounded; and that, in the 9th all, but two, officers, were either killed or wounded.

In the defense of Fort Erie, on the 15th, what was left of both regiments was again desperately engaged, and suffered severely. The same occurred in the famous sortie from that fort, on the 17th; and, while near the head of the 21st, General Ripley received a painful and dangerous wound.

General Ripley, when taking leave of the 21st, upon his promotion, enumerated, as the engagements in which they had taken part, under him, in the early part of the war, York, Chrysler's Farm, Fort George and Sackett's Harbor. And in most, if not all, of these, the 9th also took part.

When the army was reduced to a peace basis in 1815, the following officers from Pittsfield were retained: Captain Reynolds M. Kirby, aid to General Ripley, Lieutenant Thomas Childs, Captain David Perry, First Lieutenant William Browning, First Lieutenant (captain by brevet) Benjamin F. Larned, Surgeon's Mate E. L. Allen. There were also two officers retained who had married Pittsfield ladies, and made Pittsfield for a time their home, General Eleazer W. Ripley and Captain (major by brevet) Benjamin F. Watson.

Captain Thomas Childs, son of Dr. Timothy Childs, was born in 1795. During the war he served in the heavy artillery. He continued in the army, serving with credit in the Seminole and Mexican wars, and at his death, held the rank of brigadier-general.

Captain Larned was the son of Darius Larned, and Eunice Williams Larned, daughter of Deacon William Williams, the noted Dalton loyalist. He continued in the army through life; and, at his death in 1862, held the post of paymaster-general. He was buried in the Pittsfield cemetery.

Dr. Elisha Lee Allen, son of Rev. Thomas Allen, was born in 1783, and died at Pas Christien, Louisiana, September 5, 1817; falling a victim to his conscientious and zealous performance of duty in attending upon soldiers suffering from yellow-fever, even when his professional associates assured him that he needed rest and medical assistance for himself.

A few weeks before the death of Dr. Allen, on the 23d of September, his brother, Solomon L. Allen, was killed by falling from the roof of a college-building, which was unfinished, at Middlebury, Vt. Professor Allen graduated at Middlebury, in 1815, and was elected professor of the ancient languages, a short time before his death.

Still another son of Rev. Mr. Allen, Samuel L. Allen, died at Ogeechee, near Savannah, Georgia, August 10, 1816. He was born in 1784, entered the United States army at the commencement of the war of 1812, and served with fidelity and reputation; being engaged in nearly all the hard-fought battles on what was then the western frontier.

Lieutenant William Browning, before entering the army, was a hatter. He is described by those who knew, as possessing unusual accomplishments, and a very laudable ambition.

Captain David Perry was a lawyer, who removed to Pittsfield from the east—from Boston, it is said; but our information of him is scanty.

Captain, afterwards Major, Reynolds M. Kirby, was also a lawyer in Pittsfield, and married Harriet, daughter of Colonel Simon Larned. In the nullification-excitement of 1832, he was in command of the guard stationed at the state-arsenal in Charleston, which was removed, at the request of the governor of South Carolina, to Fort Moultrie.

Eleazer Wheelock Ripley, born at Hanover, N. H., in 1782, was the son of Rev. Sylvanus Ripley, first professor of divinity at Dartmouth college, and grandson of Rev. Dr. Eleazer Wheelock, the founder and first president of that institution. He was also a lineal descendant of Miles Standish. He graduated at Dartmouth in 1800, and settled, in the practice of the law, at at Fryeburg in Maine. Being a member of the Massachusetts house of representatives, when, in January, 1812, Joseph Story resigned the speakership on his appointment as judge of the United States supreme court, Mr. Ripley was chosen to fill the vacancy. In 1811, he married Miss Love, daughter of Rev. Thomas Allen, a lady to whom tradition attributes unusual charms of mind and person; with whose family that of her husband was already connected by the marriage of Rev. Dr. William Allen to the daughter of the second President Wheelock.

At the breaking out of the war, Mr. Ripley received a commission as lieutenant-colonel in the 21st regiment: of which, Mr. Hildreth says: "A lieutenant-colonelcy was given to Eleazer W. Ripley, a young democrat from Maine, who had succeeded Story as speaker of the late democratic house of representatives. Ripley's subsequent conduct justified this appointment." Lieutenant-Colonel Ripley came back to Pittsfield, where he had married the previous year, at the head of a fine detachment of men which he had raised in Maine. His conduct in the field was so creditable that, in March, 1814, he was promoted brigadier-general in company with Scott, Gaines and Macomb. In the campaign of the following summer he served gallantly; and at the sortie of Fort Erie, on the 17th of September, while at the head of the 21st regiment, then engaged at close quarters with the enemy, received a very dangerous wound in the neck, from which a tedious and painful confinement resulted, during which he was faithfully attended by his young wife.

In November, congress voted to Generals Brown, Scott, Gaines, Miller, Porter and Ripley, the thanks of the nation; and, to each, a gold medal. That of General Ripley bore on one side, his bust, in profile, his name and military title; on the other, a figure of Victory, hanging upon the branches of a palm-tree a tablet inscribed with the names Chippewa, Niagara, Erie. New York, Massachusetts, South Carolina and Georgia, also voted thanks, and "visible tokens of approbation" to General Ripley.

When he returned to Pittsfield, in February, 1815, the citizens honored him with a public dinner "for the great services which he had rendered the country since the commencement of the war." Most of the prominent democrats of the town, with many from other parts of Berkshire, and from the army, were present. The venerable Dr. Timothy Childs presided at the table, assisted by Generals John B. Root and Nathan Willis. The dinner was upon the 20th of February. The news of the treaty of Ghent had been received two days before, and intelligence of its ratification reached Pittsfield the next morning. It was doubtless anticipated by all the guests; and one of the points which the proceedings brought out was the readiness of the democratic mind to turn at once to the old antagonism with British manufactures.

Among the toasts were the following:

Peace: We bid thee welcome; and, as the only means of preserving thee, may we be always prepared for war.

The bayonet and the shuttle: Let us learn to manage the latter in peace as well as we have the former in war, and we shall soon be rid of British goods and British influence.

The 9th and 21st regiments: The dread of the enemy, they have achieved imperishable glory.

The memory of our heroes who have fallen in battle: Pike, Covington, Backus, Lawrence, Ludlow, Allen, and other gallant spirits. They are embalmed in the hearts of their countrymen; and the sod which covers them shall ever be moistened with tears of American gratitude.

The first volunteer toast was by General Ripley:

Massachusetts: May her energies be combined in that course of policy which shall give her an influence commensurate with the valor of her sons in war, and their enterprise in peace.[1]

The following volunteer toasts were given:

By Dr. Childs. Brigadier-General Ripley: He has bravely defended the injured rights of his country; unfading laurels are his reward.

By Colonel Simon Larned. A soldier's honor; his all. His precious heritage must never be wrested from him by force, nor contaminated by the finger of malice or the tongue of duplicity.

By Lieutenant Browning. Brigadier-General Ripley: The hero of Massachusetts, and the savior of the army at Niagara Falls. May his glory never be tarnished by secret enemies.

The peculiar undertone of these sentiments arose from a quarrel then existing between General Ripley and General Brown, his commander in the invasion of Canada; where the latter, after having been severely wounded and carried from the field, claimed the right still to command; which General Ripley, the officer next in rank, denied; and in violation of Brown's express orders, prudently recrossed the river.

Ripley was finally sustained by the government; and his friends emphasized their approbation by the various tokens we have enumerated.

Hildreth thus shrewdly explains the philosophy of the disagreement between Brown and Ripley:

Brown and Scott, inflamed with a strong passion for military distinction, desired anxiously to show that there were officers and men in the American army with courage to face the enemy, and skill and determi-

---

[1] Notwithstanding the unpopularity of the war in that region, and especially in Massachusetts, that state furnished during the year 1814, over fourteen thousand troops Indeed, Massachusetts furnished more recruits than any single state; and lukewarm New England more than all the hot slave-states, who were ever clamorous for war, put together. Lossing, War of 1812.

nation enough to beat him in any equal battle. * * * Brown obtained leave to undertake a new invasion of Canada. Ripley, an able officer, but without any enthusiasm for mere fighting for the sake of it, thought the expedition Quixotic, the force much too small, and, should the enemy obtain the command of the lake, likely to be cut off and obliged to surrender.

General Ripley was one of the four brigadiers retained in the reduction of the army to a peace-basis; the others being Scott, Gaines and Macomb. In 1816, he was assigned to the command of the military district whose head-quarters were at New Orleans. In 1820, he resigned, but remained in that city in the practice of the law; and in 1836, was chosen representative in congress, which office he held until his death in 1839.

Maj. Benjamin Watson was born at Newport, R. I., in 1789, and entered the army, in 1812, as second lieutenant in the 24th infantry, and in the following year was successively promoted first lieutenant and adjutant, with the rank of captain. In 1814, he was breveted major for gallant conduct at the battle of Niagara Falls. In the reduction of the army he was retained as major in the 6th infantry. In August, 1820, being then in command of the post at Pittsfield, he married Miss Elizabeth Marsh of that town, a granddaughter of Dea. Wm. Williams of Dalton. He died Oct. 4, 1827, in the house of his friend, Gen. E. P. Gaines, at Newport, Ky., and was buried in the private burying-ground of Gen. Zachary Taylor.

Captain Jared Ingersoll was the son of a well-known earnest democrat of the same name. His mother was, before her second marriage, the widow of Colonel John Brown, of revolutionary fame. Captain Ingersoll, the younger, was born in 1787. Like his father, a very ardent democrat, he entered the army at the commencement of the war, and served with conspicuous bravery. Even in the Bloody 9th, his gallantry was considered exceptional. His name and that of Major Kirby were frequently mentioned with the highest commendation in the dispatches of commanding officers. The citizens of Pittsfield recognized his merits by the presentation of a costly sword with a scabbard of solid silver. After the war he was for many years deputy-sheriff and coroner, holding the latter office at his death in 1871.[1]

[1] It is extremely difficult to obtain information of the officers and soldiers of Pittsfield in the war of 1812. Even the fallen heroes, who were promised such lasting gratitude at the Ripley dinner, are so forgotten that we can learn the Christian name of only one: Hiram Backus.

CHAPTER XI.

THE WAR OF 1812—POLITICAL EVENTS CONCERNING IT—THE MILITIA—PEACE.

[1812-1815.]

Opening of the war, and position of parties concerning it—Resolutions of Pittsfield in support of the national government—Washington Benevolent Society — Celebration of Washington's birthday — Election of John W. Hulbert to congress—Spies arrested and prisoners of war escape—Critical position of the country—Massachusetts militia called out—The question of their command-in-chief—Patriotic action of Pittsfield—The militia-system and Pittsfield militia — Berkshire militia marched to Boston — Chaplain Billy Hibbard's account—News of peace received with joyful demonstrations.

THE establishment of a military post at Pittsfield could not fail to increase the number and ardor of the supporters of the war; and therefore the violence of their antagonism to the friends of peace. This must have happened wherever, in any community politically divided upon the rightfulness of the conflict, the Cantonment had been placed. But the sources of irritation were multiplied by the location of the town in a state which openly set itself in opposition to the war, and threw all the obstacles it could, in the way of its successful prosecution by the general government.

The federalists of New England, with singular forgetfulness of the teachings of their fathers, and of the traditions from which they derived their name, refused any genuine acquiescence in the declaration of war, by the authority to whom the constitution entrusted the war-making power. If they did not, in arms or by furnishing supplies, afford aid and comfort to the enemy, they hung upon the rear of the armies of the republic with all their great moral force, and with all that could be effected through the state-governments in their control; who, for that purpose, made use of every power which they could wrest to themselves by any interpretation of the constitution.

In Massachusetts, especially, those who had emphatically proclaimed their desire for a stronger government of the Union than was provided by the federal constitution, now avowed their belief in the extreme doctrines of state-rights. The position of the commonwealth was almost that of Kentucky in the civil war of 1861. She was willing to aid, in her own way, in the defense of her own territory, if it should be invaded; and to labor, also in her own way, for the return of peace, without regard to its terms; but not to join in the offensive operations of the national government, or in the defense of other states by her militia, or by encouraging recruiting within her borders. She even, at first, refused to place her militia under the command of the officer assigned to the department by the president, although it was to be employed within her own borders, and for her own defense: thus creating two rival military authorities in the same territory. Passively, and by necessity, submitting to the establishment of recruiting-stations in her towns, she attempted to neutralize their effects; discouraging enlistments by the solemn declarations of her governor and resolutions of her legislature that the conflict, they were asked to engage in, was unnecessary, unjust and wicked. By petty acts of legislation, she did her best to embarrass the federal officers within her limits. Finally, in 1814, while a doubtful war was waging with a powerful enemy, she called a convention of other disappointed states, at Hartford, to change the constitution of the United States, which "had failed," she said, through her legislature, "under the administration of those now in power, to secure to Massachusetts and to New England generally, those equal rights and benefits, the great objects of its formation, and which cannot be relinquished without ruin." "The method of procuring amendments—the probable necessity of which had been foreseen —provided for in the constitution itself, was too slow of operation for the present crisis."[1] And, therefore, she called together the delegates of neighboring states in secret convention, to radically change the fundamental law of the nation, hastily, and in violation of the method which had been agreed to by the great convention,

---

[1] Hildreth's History of United States, vol. vi, p. 532.

over which Washington presided. It can hardly be charged upon the opposition, as an excess of jealousy, that when a convention met and conducted its business in profound secrecy, with an object like that which had been declared in the above quotation they attributed to it, a design to destroy the Union, and even to form an alliance between Old and New England. Some indeed, even went so far as to charge upon the federal party a purpose to return to the original colonial state, or to erect a kingdom, with some scion of the house of Brunswick on the throne. Many defenses of the course of the commonwealth at this era have been published, and there were many pretexts for the acts cited. Her best excuse is the heat of party-passion, and the sense of wrong suffered, in the precipitation of the war, and in the anti-commercial measures by which it was preceded.

But whatever of defense or excuse there may have been for the federalists, the existence of a war with the old enemy, and the adhesion of what were left of the tories of the revolution to the peace-party, served to awaken all the old ultra-whig feeling in Pittsfield; and the democratic leaders spared no effort to fan the well-preserved embers. Nor did the violence of the enemy and the imprudence of the federal orators render this a hard task. The employment of Indian allies by the British commanders, the massacre of Frenchtown, the tales of suffering told by American soldiers, returning from British prisons, to those who daily witnessed the kindness with which those of the enemy at the Cantonment were treated; all sufficiently inflamed the popular mind against those politicians who in the slightest degree favored the enemies of the country. Governor Strong's unfortunate utterance that America was warring against "the Bulwark of the Protestant religion," was derisively quoted in connection with each new outrage of the British soldiery.

But the war-feeling in Pittsfield did not wait for these incitements before it unmistakably manifested itself in opposition to the peace-sentiments of eastern Massachusetts.

When the news of the declaration of war reached Boston, on the 23d of June, 1812, the legislature was in session; and Governor Strong, who had just been elected by a small majority over his democratic predecessor, Elbridge Gerry, immediately transmitted to it the exciting document. The house of representatives, in which there was a decided federal majority—nearly two to one—promptly adopted an address, regretting the declaration, and expressing their sense of its inexpediency. The democrats, however, by means of the famous "Gerrymandering" process, had retained a majority in the senate; and adopted an address of a precisely opposite tenor to that of the house. It set forth the long array of outrages committed upon American commerce and citizens, and declared that the constitutional authorities of the country had been driven by them to submit their cause to the God of battles. This address was a well-directed appeal to popular sentiment, and especially calculated to inflame the passions of the partisans of its authors.

The action of the federalists in congress and the legislature, however injurious its effects may have been in checking the co-operation of the whole people in the support of the war, was in its tone calm and dignified, and suggested no overt acts in opposition to the government. But many town-meetings in eastern Massachusetts were less cautious. Several held in Boston were particularly intemperate in their language. One held on the 6th of August, recommended a convention similar to that which actually met at Hartford as late as December, 1814. This resolution was earnestly opposed by Hon. Samuel Dexter, one of the most prominent members of the federal party, who said that such a convention as was proposed was unconstitutional, and that the government had the inherent power to put it down. Defining his own position and that of the other war-federalists, he declared that it was now too late to speculate upon the various causes which may have tended to produce the rupture with England; and, however he might deplore the existing state of things, he, nevertheless, considered it his duty, since war had been declared, to aid the government to the utmost of his power in maintaining it; that, in his opinion, Great Britain had afforded sufficient ground to justify the declaration; but that, at any rate, the president and congress of the United States were constitutionally the only competent judges upon that point; and that, having sworn as a citizen to support the constitution and laws of the Union, he should consider himself nothing more nor less than a perjured traitor, were he now, since the question of war had been by them determined, to oppose, or hesitate to support, the measure.

The majority of the citizens of Pittsfield entertained views similar to those of Mr. Dexter, and expressed them in the old way; passing the following resolutions, by a very decided majority, in a full town-meeting held for that purpose on the 27th of August, there having first been a very spirited discussion:

PREAMBLE AND RESOLUTIONS.

Whereas, the inhabitants of the town of Boston have, at sundry meetings of said inhabitants lately held, passed sundry resolutions, and recommended a system of measures to be adopted and pursued by such other disaffected towns or voluntary associations in this commonwealth as shall show a disposition to concur with them therein, which, under pretense of *aiding the civil authorities of the state* "in the suppression of tumults, riots and unlawful assemblies," which have neither arisen or been threatened, have obviously in view the organization of an *armed force* within the bosom of the commonwealth, for some *unavowed* and *illegitimate* purpose—and have also appointed delegates to a convention of the state, unrecognized by the constitution and the laws—to be convened by no public or lawful authority—composed of persons deputed in no regular or authorized manner—and for the effecting of objects neither specified nor known to the good people of the commonwealth at large. And certain other towns and associations of disaffected individuals, having also adopted various measures of a similar import, tendency and design. And whereas, the aforesaid proceedings, when taken in connection with the refusal of the governor of this commonwealth, and of the state of Connecticut, to order out such detachments of the militia of these states as are deemed necessary by the president of the United States, for the defense thereof against the invasions or depredations to which they are exposed on the part of a foreign nation with whom the United States are engaged in a just and necessary war. And whereas, the sentiments now openly propagated and avowed through the medium of the public newspapers printed in the town of Boston, and elsewhere, indicate an intention of withdrawing from the service of their country, at this most interesting crisis, the military force of the state, and arraying the people and civil authorities thereof against the authority of the United States, and against the just cause in which our country is now contending. And it is therefore deemed necessary, that the most prompt and efficient measures should forthwith be adopted on the part of such of the inhabitants of this commonwealth as are resolved to *stand* or *fall* with their country, for the purpose of meeting all such events as may be brought upon them through the agency of such alarming and unjustifiable combinations, as well as for the upholding of the constituted authority of the Union in all lawful measures which they may adopt to vindicate the just rights of the nation abroad, and to maintain its authority at home. *Therefore,*

Resolved, as the sense of this town, That we have all that confidence in our national government, which flows from an attachment to its principles and an approbation of its measures. That we will obey its laws, execute to the utmost of our ability its constitutional requisitions, suppress and defeat all unlawful combinations against its authority; and in despite of all *open* or *insidious* attempts to withdraw our allegiance from our country—*will stand or fall in its common cause.*

Resolved, That we have seen with much regret, but entirely without dismay, sundry resolutions and proceedings of the town of *Boston*; which, *under the pretense* of suppressing tumultuous and unlawful assemblies of the people, appear designed to arm one portion of them against the other, and to array the local and state authorities against that of the United States, instead of turning them to their proper and legitimate objects—the arrogance of its declared enemies.

Resolved, That the plan of organizing a state-convention, not recognized by the constitution or the laws of the commonwealth—called by no legitimate authority, and for effecting of no specified or avowed object, is either an idle and wanton attempt to alarm and vex the public mind with vain and nugatory projects; or to usurp unconstitutional and lawless powers, by a body having no regular title or claim to the exercise thereof—a procedure which, on the first supposition, merits our *contempt*, and the second demands, and shall receive, our *unqualified resistance.*

Resolved, That we will with equal promptitude, devote ourselves and substance to maintain the just rights of the nation against foreign aggression, and to put down *domestic usurpations* under whatever pretense they may be attempted, or under whatever local authorities they may be countenanced and supported.

Resolved, That although we have as sincere a detestation of all riotous and tumultuous proceedings as the town of *Boston* has, or would *appear* to have; yet we will not *affect* terrors which we do not feel, nor will we exhaust that spirit and that indignation with which every American bosom ought, at this moment, to beat against our foreign foes, in extravagant and passionate denunciations against our fellow-citizens of other states, who, if guilty, are amenable to their own laws, and punishable by their own civil authorities.

Resolved, That it will conduce much to the quiet of the state, if the inhabitants of the town of *Boston* would attend more to *their own concerns*, and cease to harass the good people of the commonwealth with their impracticable "*notions*" and their ambitious and illusory projects.

Resolved, That the governor of the commonwealth having refused to call out those detachments of its militia, which were deemed necessary by the president of the United States to aid in the defense of its vulnerable points, is justly responsible for the safety of the state, and its proection against all foreign annoyances, depredations or invasion.

Resolved, That it be earnestly recommended to every citizen capable of performing military duty, to furnish and keep on hand suitable arms and equipments, and stand ready to aid the government of the United States, either in the repulsion of foreign enemies or in the suppression of unlawful combinations and usurpations against its authority and the constitutional powers of the state, *whether* under the form of conventions, or any other organized associations whatever.[1]

The town, also, by vote, instructed the selectmen to purchase, in addition to the usual stock of ammunition, six casks of powder and two hundred pounds of ball; and offered a bounty of ten dollars to each of its citizens who should voluntarily enlist: to be paid within one year after the recruit was called into service.

The last clause in the last of the resolutions was aimed at the Washington Benevolent Society. This was a national secret organization, within the federal party, composed of several state societies; which in their turn were divided, and sub-divided, into county and town branches. Its political character was not concealed—although an endeavor was made to direct public attention to its social and benevolent features—and it seems to have been a formidable and efficient agency, loved and cherished by all good federalists, and cordially detested by the democrats, who saw all manner of treasonable plots concocting within its mystic circles. The power, which its opponents often experienced in unexpected and inexplicable defeats at the polls, was not to be questioned; and the democracy of 1812, after the fashion of dominant parties in war-times were slow to recognize the distinction between opposition to their measures, and treason to the country: with how much excuse in this case, the reader must judge.

The *Berkshire Reporter*, of March 11, 1813, says: "The Washing Benevolent Society of Berkshire has been established about twenty-one months, and consists of more than two thousand three hundred members. It is a most animated and interesting spectacle to behold so many good men united, like a band of brothers, solemnly pledged to inculcate and maintain the true principles of our happy constitution; to adhere to the political maxims which distinguished the glorious administration of their beloved Washington; to relieve the unfortunate; and to promote and spread as

[1] The italics in these resolutions are those of the *Pittsfield Sun*.

far as they possibly can, peace on earth and good will toward all mankind."

Each member, on his initiation, was required to sign the following pledge, which is similar in its terms to the *Reporter's* statement of principles:

We, each of us, do hereby declare that we are firmly attached to the the constitution of the United States, and to that of the state of Massachusetts [or to that of such other state as the branch society might be located in], to the principles of a free republican government, and to those which regulated the public conduct of George Washington; that we will, each of us, so far as may be consistent with our religious principles respectively,[1] preserve the rights and liberties of our country against all foreign and domestic violence, fraud or usurpation; and that, as members of the Washington Benevolent Society, we will, in all things, comply with its regulations, support its principles, and enforce its views.

The new brother, having signed this pledge, received a small volume, which contained a certificate of his membership, an engraved portrait of Washington, Washington's farewell address to his countrymen, and the constitution of the United States. This volume he made his *vade mecum*. Such were the principles held, and the obligations taken, by those who joined the Washington Benevolent Society: an organization which embraced a large portion of the citizens of the county most eminent for probity and talent, and very few with whose names it is possible —even for those who consider them to have been most mistaken in their views of duty—to associate the idea of treason or falsehood. It was, however, very possible, in the heated days of the war, for their opponents to believe the entire organization guilty of these wrongs; and the secrecy in which it enveloped its operations rendered it impossible to disprove the charges against it. Discouragement of enlistment—a practice which was common to the whole party—was not denied. And, from an act which treads so very closely upon the confines of overt treason, it is but a step to the inducing and aiding of desertions from the army; and but one more, to assist and harbor escaped prisoners of war— and even to aid in their escape.

It is, therefore, not surprising, that the democrats, including

---

[1] A clause inserted for the benefit of Quaker and other conscientiously nonresistant members.

most of the United States officers in garrison at Pittsfield, should attribute the escapes, desertions, malignant stories and other troubles which beset them at the Cantonment, to the secret cabals of the Washington Benevolent Society. The long and spotless lives of many of its leaders enable us to credit their denial of these charges; but to the democrats of 1812, they were not venerable fathers whose patriotism had been long proved, but active and bitter opponents of their much-loved party; often guilty, as men at such periods are apt to be, of indiscreet speech capable of an interpretation that would prove them guilty of much which their better second thought would condemn.

Still, the very existence of a secret organization of opponents of the war in the immediate vicinity of a military post and prison, rendered the strictest watchfulness on the part of its officers not only excusable, but imperative. But, whether justifiable or not, the jealousies, hatreds and assaults of the democrats were, in a great measure, concentrated upon this society. They denounced its political aims and action as treasonable, and its secrecy as intended for the most pernicious uses. They declared its benevolence to be a hypocritical pretense, and scouted its fraternal kindness.

On the other hand, there has rarely been a political organization, whose members were so thoroughly conscious that in joining it they were governed solely by the purest and noblest motives; and there was, probably, not one of them who did not consider that in the Washington Benevolent Society, he was in the best of all possible good society—at least, on this side of the Atlantic. He proudly preserved his certificate of membership while he lived—if he did not become a violent Jackson democrat, after the war—and when he died, he transmitted it, as proudly, to his children, as a testimonial that he had well-served his country; and served it, too, in company—nay, in fraternity—with the most respectable people in the county.

In the same proud spirit he walked in the procession and took his seat to listen to the oration and to eat the dinner, with which it was the delight of the society to honor the birthdays of their country and of its father. *Pater Patriæ* was their patron saint; and to him was accorded the excess of honor usually bestowed upon such personages. It is even related that on one unusually cold 22d of February, rather than forego, mar or shorten the parade, they heroically sacrificed their ears; every one of which in the procession was frozen, while their owners moved on without flinching.

In illustration of what these celebrations were, which the people of Pittsfield in the earlier years of the century deemed so important, and enjoyed with so much zest, we print an account of one which, although among the more splendid, must represent many; and those of the democrats, or republicans, as well, for there was no essential difference in their external characteristics.

The anniversary to be celebrated was Washington's birthday— February 22, 1814. It was announced as early as the 8th of February that the "Washington Benevolent Society of the county of Berkshire, would celebrate the day at Pittsfield, with an oration by Daniel Noble, Esq., of Williamstown;" and "that every effort would be made to render the occasion splendid and agreeable." In its issue of February 17th, the *Reporter* printed the programme displayed attractively; and we copy it that the reader may, in his imagination, reproduce the scene of that cold winter-holiday:

CELEBRATION

OF THE ANNIVERSARY OF THE BIRTHDAY OF WASHINGTON, BY THE MEMBERS OF THE WASHINGTON BENEVOLENT SOCIETY OF THE COUNTY OF BERKSHIRE.

The members of the fociety will affemble at nine o'clock, A. M., at Wafhington Hall, in Pittffield. Each member will appear with his badge. The meeting will continue open until half paft ten o'clock, for the initiation of members. The proceffion will move at eleven o'clock, A. M., under the direction of the marfhal, to the Union parifh meeting-houfe. Citizens who are not members are invited to unite with the fociety in the celebration.

ORDER OF PROCESSION.

Marfhal, Deputy-marfhal, Artillery in uniform, Infantry in uniform. Citizens: 1ft, young men; 2d, middle-aged men; 3d, aged men; two officers in uniform, Wafhington Standard, two officers in uniform, members of the fociety, two abreaft, in thirteen divifions, each divifion preceded by a banner, each banner attended by two of the cavalry; vifiting members of other Wafhington Benevolent Societies; Stewards and other officers, Secretaries and Treafurers ; Standing Committee ; Committee of Arrangements ; Orator and Chaplain. Vice-prefidents : the oldeft Vice-prefident with Wafhington's Farewell addrefs ; 2d Vice-prefident with the Declaration of Independence ; 3d Vice-prefident with the Conftitution of the United States ; Prefident and an officer in uniform ; Band of mufic, two officers in uniform.

When the proceffion fhall have arrived at the meeting-houfe, the line will halt, open to the right and left, and fo continue until the proceffion, counter-marching, fhall have paffed into the meetinghoufe—the band playing at the door until the proceffion fhall have moved into the houfe, and taken their feats. The Prefident, oldeft vice-prefident, the orator and chaplain, will enter the pulpit. The members will take the body pews, the military the wall pews, the ladies will be accommodated with feats in the gallery. The band of mufic will take the high pew in front of the pulpit. Citizens and vifitors will be feated by the marfhal and affiftants.

EXERCISES.

1ft, An Ode ; 2d, Prayer ; 3d, An Ode ; 4th, Oration ; 5th, Anthem ; 6th, Benediction ; 7th, Wafhington's March, by the Band.

At funrife a National Salute and ringing of the bell. The proceffion will move under the difcharge of cannon. The clergy of the neighboring towns are moft refpectfully invited to attend. All military officers are requefted to appear in uniform.

Jofiah Biffell, John Garfield, Eli Enfign, Butler Goodrich, Eliphalet Reddington, Gerfhom Buckley, Samuel Jones, Jafon Clapp, Henry James, Chauncey Hulbert, *Committee of Arrangements.*

The Washington Banner, for years the pride of the society, is now in the Historical Cabinet of the Berkshire Athenæum. It is of the richest white silk, bordered with gold and fringed with blue ; and in size, about two yards wide by two and a half long. On one side it bears a fine portrait of Washington, surrounded by a profusion of warlike insignia ; on the other, the national coat of arms. The badge of the society was a strip of white parchment upon which winged Fame was blowing a trumpet and placing a wreath upon the head of Washington. It was inscribed with the words, "Washington Benevolent Society" and "*Pro Patria.*"

According to the *Reporter's* account, the celebration was all that its grand heralding promised. Colonel Colgrove was chief-marshal, and his assistants were Ralph Warriner, and Henry Taylor. Colonel Azariah Root carried the grand banner, and thirteen smaller ones were borne by other "true disciples of Washington;" and all were guarded by members of the cavalry, "mounted on elegant grey horses." The procession moved to the firing of cannon and the ringing of the bell—only one bell unfortunately. The silvery tones of that which weekly summoned democratic Christians to the First church could not be expected to join in the federal peal. But "the procession made a grand and interesting appearance." The exercises at the meeting-house were equally satisfactory. There were two chaplains: the "excellent" —but rather eccentric—"patriot and Christian, Rev. Mr. Jennings, of Dalton," and Rev. Mr. Punderson. Of the oration, by Daniel Noble, Esq., the *Reporter* says:

> The sentiments and opinions expressed by the speaker were worthy of a statesman. They displayed a depth of political knowledge and an independence of mind, which excited the admiration of the audience. The orator, in the language of truth and eloquence, called to the recollection of his hearers the happiness and glory enjoyed by our country under federal administrations. He contrasted these blessed times with the present days of gloom and despair. He showed that our present disgrace and wretchedness originated in a hatred of the character, and a departure from the principles of our beloved Washington; and he unveiled and exposed, in their true colors, the guilty authors of our nation's ruin. Deep and lasting will be the impression made on those who heard it, by this oration.

After the oration, the procession marched to Major Morgan's inn, on Bank row, where over four hundred persons partook of a dinner, with appetites sharpened for the substantial viands by the keen winter air, and for the piquant toasts by Mr. Noble's pungent eloquence.

That was the age of rhetoric, and a favorite mode for its exercise was in the elaboration of epigrammatic toasts; the most condensed form in which ideas could be expressed. A sharp and rapid discharge of these glittering, and often envenomed, points followed every public dinner; and, as the drinking of toasts was not then a mere form, but a substantial honoring of the sentiment proposed in a draught of veritable wine or some stronger beverage; and as the best hits were always received with bumpers, the company was generally in a condition, by the time the regular toasts were disposed of, to give and applaud volunteer sentiments without severe criticism.

On this occasion John W. Hulbert, the most famous wit in Berkshire tradition, sat at the head of the table, as president of the society, and guided the "flow of soul;" which, in the volunteer toasts, is said to have been of a more than commonly spicy, pointed and exuberant character.

We are able to quote, however, only a few of the regular toasts, which, with the *Reporter's* account of the oration, will show the spirit of the federal party in February, 1814:

The militia of Massachusetts: Under their lawful commander-in-chief, may they stand on our constitutional limits, and say to foreign and domestic enemies, "Hitherto shalt thou come, but no further."

Our country: Once happy and honorable, now sunk by democracy to the lowest depths of wretchedness and disgrace.

"O how fearful and how dizzy 'tis
To cast one's eye so low."

Our war with England: The prosperity of Bonaparte occasioned it; may his adversity speedily end it.

Free trade and sailors' rights: They have found their worst enemies in our own government.

Peace: May our spears be beaten into pruning-hooks, and our swords into plowshares; and wisdom into the heads of our national rulers.

Bonaparte: The master behind the curtain, who dances the puppets of our administration.

Our navy: It has finally conquered its worst enemies, the democrats.

The memory of Moreau, and his last words: "The scoundrel, Bonaparte."

The World's best friend: The Emperor Alexander.

These toasts were drunk with the warmest applause, followed by the discharge of cannon, and they aid us to comprehend the intensity of the terror inspired in the more conservative classes by the horrors of the French revolution and the subsequent sanguinary career of Napoleon. It must have been deep indeed when a considerable body of the most intelligent and patriotic citizens of Berkshire held up Alexander of Russia, as "the world's best friend."

At this depressing period of the war the spirit exhibited in this Pittsfield celebration, was the same which governed the party then dominant in New England. It had, a fortnight before, manifested itself in the Massachusetts legislature, by an act which brought a number of British officers into close confinement at the Pittsfield Cantonment, by excluding them from the jails of the commonwealth. Mr. Hildreth gives the following account of the immediate cause of this act:

> Dearborn's expedition against York and Fort George having placed a number of British officers in his power, the president, under the act authorizing retaliation, had ordered the close confinement of twenty-three of them intended to abide the fate of the Irishmen taken at Queenstown and sent to England to be tried for treason. Prevost, in consequence of a special dispatch from Lord Bathurst, responded by the close imprisonment of twice the number of American officers and non-commissioned officers; with a threat, if this system of retaliation was carried out, of "unmitigated severity against American cities and villages." Madison replied by shutting up a like number of British officers, and with threats to retort any further severities, in which the British might indulge; whereupon Prevost ordered all his prisoners into close confinement, an example which Madison hastened to follow. In New England, and among the federalists generally, this policy of exposing our own citizens to imprisonment and death, for the sake of a set of foreign renegades, as they were bitterly described, met with little countenance; and the escape of some of the imprisoned British officers from the jail at Worcester *gave very general satisfaction.* The democrats, indeed, complained that, while American prisoners in Canada, and at Halifax, were often subjected to very harsh treatment and gross indignities, the British officers taken by us were sure of every attention and kindness at the hands of their federal friends.

A number of prisoners confined in the Lenox, Worcester, and other Massachusetts jails, were transferred to Pittsfield; but congress soon authorized the marshals of states whose jails were closed against their prisoners, to select other places of confinement; and the penitentiary of Pennsylvania, being offered, was chiefly used.

It was a sad and apprehensive party which set out from Pittsfield, when several carriage-loads of British officers, guarded by a detachment of cavalry, left the Cantonment, as they supposed, for a prison in Kentucky. In the temper which had been manifested by both governments, there was great reason to fear that they were going to a place of military execution. As the carriages were driven off, the private soldiers, left behind as prisoners, followed them with a perfect shower of old shoes: their mode of wishing them good luck.

Among these officers was General Riall, and a few others who had made many friends in Pittsfield, who followed them with their best wishes expressed in other forms. Many years afterwards, Dr. Robert Campbell met some of these officers in London, and they expressed to him their grateful memory of the kindness of his father and other citizens in that day of danger.

Great Britain, however, soon practically abandoned her attempt to deal with natives of Ireland naturalized in the United States, and fighting in the American army, as traitors; and the system of mutual retaliation ended.

The democrats, however, did not soon permit naturalized citizens to forget that the federalists had stigmatized Irish soldiers fighting in our army as "renegades." Nor were they unmindful of the general joy expressed by federal papers over the escape of British prisoners of war. Their disgust culminated when the Hartford convention met with closed doors. And, in Berkshire county, to meet the operations of the Washington Benevolent Society, they organized the Sons of Liberty; but this organization never attained the efficiency of its antagonist.

In the summer of 1814, the Washington Society showed its power by the election of its president, John W. Hulbert, to fill the vacancy in congress, caused by the resignation of Judge Dewey. The opposing candidate was Hon. William P. Walker, of Lenox.

Both these gentlemen were of much more than ordinary ability, and their availability as candidates, although different, was very nearly equal as to the aggregate of probable result. In eloquence and popular manners, Mr. Hulbert was much the superior of his antagonist; and in legal and scholarly attainments, at least his equal. But the democrats accused him of exceeding even the license permitted by that period, in morals; a fault which not even political malice could impute to Mr. Walker; and, while the latter was an exceedingly correct, and quite prosperous businessman, the federal candidate had to bear the unjust opprobrium caused by the failure of the Berkshire bank, of which he was a director, although not a prominent one; as well as the pecuniary embarrassment—amounting, indeed, to poverty—into which he had been brought by the same misfortune. In addition to all this, was the prestige operating against him from the chronic political character of the district, which had not elected a federalist to congress since the choice of Theodore Sedgwick, in 1795, and, after Mr. Hulbert, never elected another.

The contest was animated, and Mr. Hulbert was chosen by a majority of only a hundred votes. His election at all, under the circumstances, was a marked triumph, and was doubtless due in a great measure to the personal popularity of the candidate. The *Sun* scolded the people bitterly for electing " a favorite " to a post of which the editor did not deem him worthy. And, while rebuking its own political friends for their " remissness in duty," being especially severe upon those in Pittsfield, it hastened— " lest the friends of the administration abroad should look upon Berkshire as a real apostate "—to assure them that the result of the election indicated no change of political sentiment.

But, while the personal popularity of Mr. Hulbert contributed greatly to his success, and even his personal friends in the democratic party were induced by the coarseness of the attacks upon him in the *Sun*, either to withhold their votes or cast them for him; it is also true that the perfect organization of the Washington Benevolent Society—stimulated by the admiration and love which he had inspired in its members, while its presiding officer —was powerful enough to turn the scale at the polls. Had no such organization existed, Mr. Walker would have almost surely been elected.

In the election for the full term, held in November, 1814, Mr. Hulbert was again chosen, and by a considerably increased majority.[1]

While the friends of the war in general were exasperated by the national and state action of its opponents, minor events operating in the same direction, happened in Pittsfield. On the 3d of February, 1814, Major Melville published in the *Sun*, an advertisement regarding the escape of prisoners of war from the barracks

---

[1] At the expiration of his term, in 1817, Mr. Hulbert removed to Auburn, N. Y., having become so deeply impoverished by his connection with the bank, and by his devotion to his public duties, that he was compelled to borrow money of a friend to defray the expense of removal there. But at Auburn his talents were at once recognized. He soon rose to a lucrative practice, notwithstanding the laws then just enacted by the New York legislature in its jealousy of the legal profession, and was repeatedly elected to the state legislature and to congress. He died at Auburn, in 1831.

at Burlington, Vermont, and charged that their escape was aided "by evil-disposed and corrupt citizens who preferred the interests of the enemy to their country." He warned them of the consequences of such traitorous conduct as giving counsel or aid to a public enemy; and called upon all good citizens to be active and zealous in counteracting *internal*, as well as external, enemies. He also offered a reward of two hundred dollars for such information as should lead to the conviction of traitors.

In May, one hundred and fifty exchanged prisoners arrived at the Cantonment and remained in town long enough to incense the citizens by their recital of the atrocities practiced in the British prisons; which presented a strange and shocking contrast to what they constantly witnessed in the treatment of British prisoners in Pittsfield.

In August and September, there was a panic concerning British spies and emissaries. In the first week of September, two persons, one of whom was represented to be a British lieutenant, "who had been traveling extensively about the country," were arrested at Cheshire. The next week, a Canadian Frenchman and an Indian were brought to the Cantonment, handcuffed together, as spies.

Nothing was ever proved against these persons except a violation of the order of August, 1812, requiring British subjects resident in western Massachusetts to report themselves to Colonel Danforth, one of the United States deputy-marshals. Nevertheless, it is not improbable that their object in prowling about military prisons, was to aid the escape of their inmates.

In the summer of 1814, the dangers which began to thicken around the country, produced results which, although they seem natural enough in our present comprehension of American character, were surprising to those who had observed it only in its imperfect development during the formation years of the republic. Locally, among the most interesting of these results, was the proof furnished that Pittsfield federalists were thoroughly loyal to their country; however they may have thought themselves justified in discouraging its government in the prosecution of a war which they deemed unnecessary and wicked.

Their evidently sincere joy over the early victories of the American navy might, perhaps, be quoted to the same effect; but the federalists regarded the navy as their own creation: built up by the administration of John Adams against the most violent opposition of the democrats. In its triumphs, they read as much their own glory as that of their country. In 1814, they sacrificed the pride of party to their love of country. The impending of a great and common danger left, indeed, no excuse for any party which should withhold its aid from the common defense; but the heartiness and enthusiasm with which the federalists of Pittsfield united for that purpose with their fellow-citizens of other opinions, showed that they sought none. And this union, although in its terms its immediate object was only state defense, extended a promise of future aid for all parts of the Union. Had the war lasted but another campaign under similar pressure, the federalists would probably have been found, shoulder to shoulder with the democrats, in its prosecution.

What would have been won by such a union, had it been general throughout the country, we may not now determine; but we may be sure that, however splendid its achievements might have been, it would have cost America that which she could ill afford to spare, except as the price of national existence. The British provinces might have been annexed. British capital might have lost the power to ruin the young American manufactures by competition. The verdict of Waterloo might have been reversed, and Napoleon restored to the leadership of Europe: possibly, as the federalists had once feared, then to extend his empire across the seas.

But the possibilities which, at midsummer in 1814, confronted the people of Massachusetts, and the whole country, were something very different from this. Dangers encompassed them on every side. Ever since the spring of the preceding year, British armed vessels of every class—the cumbrous, but terror-striking, seventy-four, the dashing frigate, the midge-like tender and cutter, the ubiquitous and lawless privateer—swarmed along the whole coast; keeping up an annoying blockade to the serious although not total interruption of both foreign and coastwise commerce. This flotilla, however, committed few depredations on land until the spring of 1814, when it destroyed some villages on the coast of Connecticut, and laid others, as well as detached farm-houses, under heavy contributions. In June, the enemy began to ravage the coast of Massachusetts, inflicting damage chiefly upon vessels lying in harbor or on the stocks.

The coast of Maine received similar visitations, and the territory east of the Penobscot was seized with the avowed purpose of retaining permanent possession. All these proceedings, of course, raised the utmost resentment in the breast of every American citizen; and were especially adapted to destroy whatever attachment there might have been to Great Britain.

Almost simultaneously with the arrival of fresh ships of the enemy, and his first attacks on the coast of Massachusetts, came the news of the abdication of Napoleon; leaving England, not only released from the fear of her great enemy, but at the head of the nations of Europe. She was now free to end the contest in America by a sharp and vigorous campaign. And, hard upon this intelligence, followed the information that the enemy was collecting, at Bermuda, a very formidable armament, of men and ships, which rumor, after exaggerating its numbers, destined, by turns, for New York, the Chesapeake, Washington and other points, not excepting Boston.

The most serious and agitating alarm pervaded the whole Atlantic coast; and every seaboard state hastened to give vigorous aid in the preparations for its own defense. And now Massachusetts was no exception. It was felt to be no time to raise any, except the most essential, points as to the limits of national and state authority over her militia. Both parties, for a while, seemed willing to waive, until the danger was past, all differences which stood in the way of harmonious and efficient action. It was but little that the general government asked the commonwealth to yield, and that little for the purpose of better defending her own state capital.

Brigadier-General Cushing, temporarily in command of the military department which included Massachusetts, informed Governor Strong that the regular troops at his disposal for both the forts in Boston harbor were barely sufficient to garrison one; and he proposed that the militia of the state, to be called out in compliance with an expected request of the president, should occupy the other. To secure the governor's assent to this plan, he agreed that the whole detachment, asked for the defense of Boston and other exposed points on the coast—amounting to eleven hundred men—should be subject to no officer of the general government except the commander—superintendent, the governor insisted upon calling him—of the district; retaining only so much authority over the militia as would insure harmony of action between them and the regular troops.

Governor Strong, on his part, "although he did not suppose that in ordinary cases the militia were liable by the constitution to do garrison-duty in the forts of the United States, yet as the defense of the town of Boston was a primary object with the government of the state, and as no other method of strengthening the garrisons was suggested, he accepted the proposal. The requisition was made on the 18th of July, by General Dearborn, who had returned to the command, and confirmed the agreement made by Cushing.

A general order making the detail was issued by the adjutant-general of the state, on the 18th of July, and was obeyed by the militia with alacrity. It included no Berkshire company, and from an article in the *Sun*, of September 15th, announcing a second call, under the heading, "Massachusetts in arms at last," it seems to have attracted no attention in Pittsfield. Striking as was the indication which it afforded of impending danger, and a changed policy of state-government, no mention was made of it in the *Sun*. The *Reporter* was, perhaps, not so silent.

On the 4th of July, President Madison made a requisition upon the several states for ninety-three thousand five hundred militia; of which the quota of Massachusetts was ten thousand. The call was communicated by General Dearborn to Governor Strong, on the 4th of September, and startled him by the number of men required. It appeared also, that, notwithstanding the readiness with which the militia responded to the call of July, the agreement made by the governor with the department-commanders had given dissatisfaction to his party-friends; and that he had met many difficulties and complaints in the execution of the detail.[1]

Both the requisition for troops in July and that in September, came to Governor Strong in a shape essentially different from that received in 1812; to which he returned a refusal which can hardly be condemned by those who applaud a similar maintenance of the rights and dignity of the commonwealth by Governor Andrew in the case of the two regiments raised—one of them in Pittsfield—by General Butler, in 1862. Governor Strong's

[1] Governor Strong's message, October 5, 1815.

refusal, in 1812, was based, according to the *Boston Advertiser* of 1814, upon several grounds. *First,* The requisition was insolently made; its style being essentially different from that made upon Governor Tompkins of New York, and other democratic governors, who were only *requested* to furnish the troops. *Secondly,* Governor Strong judged there was no necessity for the draft. *Thirdly,* The requisition was unmilitary and degrading to the militia; the call being for twenty *companies,* which excluded the detachment of any officer of higher grade than captain—leaving all the field and other officers to be appointed by the United States government. *Fourthly,* A part of the troops were required for service out of the state; contrary to the provisions of the federal constitution. And, *fifthly,* neither of the events had occurred which authorized the calling forth of the militia. No invasion had taken place; there was no insurrection; and the execution of the laws was not obstructed.

The call of 1814 was very different from this. The request was decorously and properly made. The troops were to be employed in the state; and to be commanded by their own officers, except in the single case agreed upon. The danger was more apparent than that of 1812; and one of the events contemplated by the constitution as authorizing the calling out of the militia— invasion—had actually occurred.

Nevertheless, Governor Strong, appalled by the magnitude of the call, and perplexed by the objections of his political supporters, did not see his duty so clearly in September as he did in July. He therefore repaired for advice to the executive council; and in accordance with their opinion, issued on the 6th of September a general order, calling out ten thousand militia; but placing them under the immediate command of a major-general. The refusal of the governor to extend the arrangement of July to the troops now called out, seems not to have attracted much attention in Berkshire at the time. The militia were only rejoiced to receive, on any terms, the long-desired order to join in the defense of their country; and that at a moment when her danger was most imminent.

In this crisis, the action of both parties was most honorable, and fully sustained the patriotic fame of the town. We quote the account printed in the *Sun,* of September 22d, the week following the marching of the Berkshire regiment.

PITTSFIELD TOWN-MEETING.—PATRIOTISM.—UNANIMITY.

With proud satisfaction, we present to the public the proceedings of the town-meeting of Pittsfield, on Monday last, at which Joshua Danforth presided, as moderator. All parties came forward *unanimously*, and sacrificed at the shrine of their common country, all their animosities and dissensions, in support of true American principles. We trust that every town in the county and state will do likewise. We shall thus present an impenetrable phalanx of patriots to the enemy, which will command her respect, obtain for us an honorable peace, and, with it, the admiration of the world.

REPORT OF THE COMMITTEE.

Whereas, a town-meeting has been convened at the request of a number of inhabitants, for the purpose of taking into consideration, "*what they in their corporate capacity ought to do to aid the constituted authorities of our country in repelling the invasion of our territory, and also to enable them in future to protect the other parts of our country from invasion.*"

And whereas, at the meeting so convened, the following persons have been chosen a committee to propose resolutions expressive of the sense of this meeting on the subject for which it is called, viz.: Oliver Root, Thomas Gold, Theodore Hinsdale, Jr., James D. Colt, Elkanah Watson and Thomas Melville, Jr.; and the committee having met, have adopted and present to their fellow-citizens the following preamble and resolutions :

Preamble. That as we have arrived at a crisis which requires the individual and joint exertions of every citizen; and that as the sacred charter of our Independence, and the safety of our country is at stake.

It has become the duty of every American to risk his life and property, to preserve the sacred inheritance, for which our fathers fought and bled. If incentives are necessary to rouse us to a true sense of our danger, and our duty; let us consider that not only our state is invaded, but our enemy has declared it to be her intention, to take possession of, and to re-annex to the crown of Great Britain, all the territory east of Penobscot river; that she has, besides, officially declared, that she will lay waste and destroy such towns and districts on our coasts as may be assailable. And if this is not sufficient, let us cast our eyes on the depredations committed in the south, as well as those more recently committed in the District of Maine.

Those acts, whilst they demonstrate to us most unequivocally the intentions of our enemy, admonish us to shun dissensions; and to keep constantly in view, that *united we stand, and divided we fall.* If the enemy counts on our internal divisions, we trust that the patriotism of Americans will prove to her, and to the world, that no difference of opinion exists among us, on the great questions of self-defense, or our existence as a nation. Let each and every one of us, therefore, in this solemn hour of danger, bring forward and deposit on the altar of our country, every passion, every feeling, every prejudice that may tend to awaken resistance, or impair exertion.

Let us, as a united people, come forward in defense of our common country. Let us take efficient measures to learn the duties of the soldier. Let us be prepared, and in constant readiness, to take the field and meet the enemy.

Let us, like the sages of 1776, pledge our lives, our fortunes and our sacred honor, for the maintenance of our National Independence; and our enemy will soon learn that the cause of America is the cause of each of its citizens.

To these sentiments your committee flatter themselves there cannot be a dissenting voice; and therefore, propose with confidence, the following resolutions :

Resolved, 1*st*, That as an extraordinary occasion exists for putting the whole military force of the town into a condition for active and efficient service, the selectmen are instructed forthwith to provide such arms, munitions of war and camp-equipage, as the law has required of towns; and to have the whole ready for immediate use.

Resolved, 2*d*, That the selectmen be empowered to give liberal aid to the families of such militia as are, or hereafter may be, called into service, who may need assistance; and that the selectmen be charged with that duty.

Resolved, 3*d*, That we will use our utmost endeavors to increase the number of the militia, to discourage and prevent all evasions, or neglect of duty, that we may ensure to the country, an active and efficient force.

Resolved, 4*th*, That it be recommended to all exempts, to enroll and form themselves into a company, to equip and prepare themselves for active service.

Resolved, 5*th*, That we will honestly and sincerely exert ourselves to promote *union, energy* and *public spirit* among all our fellow-citizens; and we appeal with confidence to our fellow-citizens of the county of Berkshire, and elsewhere, on this trying occasion, and we trust they will rise in their native strength and majesty to defend their country and to repel all invasions.

Signed, Oliver Root, Thomas Melville, Jr., Thomas Gold, James D. Colt, Elkanah Watson, Theodore Hinsdale, Jr., Committee.

The preamble and resolutions were unanimously adopted; and one thousand dollars appropriated to carry them into complete effect.

The committee who drafted the resolutions was equally divided, politically: Messrs. Root, Watson and Melville, being democrats; Messrs. Gold, Colt and Hinsdale, federalists. While all censure of previous action was avoided in the resolutions, it will be observed that, by joining in their passage, the federalists went far beyond a mere approval of such niggardly concessions as Governor Strong made in July, and revoked in September. Both parties seem to have been governed by a common desire for united action in defense of their country. The action of the town was as cordial, and free from mutual upbraidings and recriminations, as though it had come together on the first invasion in a fresh war.

It might have been hoped that the spirit manifested by the federalists on this occasion would, for the future, have disarmed all suspicion of their loyalty. But Governor Strong's revocation of his concession of July, and the preparations for the Hartford convention which went on almost in the presence of the enemy, furnished plausible grounds of accusation; of which the democratic editors and orators were not slow to avail themselves. And the democrats were not alone in expecting treasonable action from the convention. The retailers (of ardent spirits) and taverners of Springfield, at a meeting in the house of Eleazer Williams of that town on the 19th of December, 1814, "deemed it expedient to defer the payment of the (National) duties until after the close of the next session of the Massachusetts legislature." They further determined to call a meeting of the retailers and taverners of the counties of Hampshire, Franklin, and Hampden, at Northampton, December 26th. This meeting was held, and

Resolved, Unanimously, that it is expedient to postpone the payment of any taxes which may have been assessed upon us respectively by the government of the United States, until after the proceedings of the convention now sitting at Hartford, and the doings of the legislature of this commonwealth thereupon, shall have been promulgated, and that we will conduct accordingly.

Resolved, That we feel confident that the legislature of this commonwealth will interpose for our relief, and rescue the resources of the people for self-defense and self-protection.

We find the report of these proceedings in the *Federal Republican*, published at Georgetown, D. C., which credits it to a "Massachusetts newspaper." It is headed: "Beginning to Act." "Temper of old Hampshire." When a considerable number of the citizens of the federal counties of western Massachusetts publicly expressed expectations like those quoted above, it can hardly be deemed unreasonable or ungenerous suspicion in the majority of the people in the one democratic county, that they attributed treasonable designs to the Hartford convention. The rather lame and impotent conclusion of its consultations justified neither the hopes of its friends, or the fears of its enemies; but that does not prove that either were without reasonable foundation.

At any rate, so jealous was the democratic public sentiment, that, whatever was alleged against the federal leaders—no matter how exaggerated, or in the nature of things, impossible—found believers. The credulity of the democratic masses in this respect, was indeed often ludicrous. We shall soon meet an illustrative incident.

The militia of Massachusetts, as reorganized under the law of 1810, embraced all citizens between the ages of eighteen and forty-five; with the usual exceptions on account of conscientious scruples and official position. In the organization of this body, it was required that each battalion should contain at least one company of grenadiers, light-infantry or riflemen; and that, in each division, should be included at least one company of artillery, and one troop of dragoons.

The artillery, the dragoons, and generally several companies of infantry in each division, consisted of volunteers. These volunteers, or as they were commonly styled, "independent companies," existed under special charters, which, if granted prior to the year 1810, were protected, both by act of congress and by the state law, from abrogation or change, except as a penalty for misconduct. And, not to create invidious distinctions, the charters granted after 1810, were, in practice, held equally sacred.

These privileged corps, as the élite of the citizen-soldiery, aimed at considerable excellence in drill, discipline and deportment. Membership in them involved some expense, as each man was required to furnish his own arms and uniform; and, if in the dragoons, his horse. But it was the only mode in which those liable to militia-duty could, without the payment of fines, avoid being marched through the streets on parade-day as part of a very questionable array. And this fact, together with the martial spirit which still pervaded the community, sufficed to keep the ranks of the volunteer-companies full.

If the strict letter of the law had been enforced, the ordinary militia would have still been a formidable body. For each man was required to provide himself with arms and equipments which were minutely specified; and to appear with them for parade and training four days in the year, besides the annual review, or "general muster" in autumn. It was provided that their uniform should be of dark blue, turned up with such facings, and completed with such hats and caps as the majority of the field officers of each regiment should determine for it.

But in fact, none but the officers ever wore any uniform at all; and not always they. The case of a man "armed and equipped as the law directed" was rare. The vast majority made the whole system of drills and reviews a matter of sport. Being composed of what was left to the current after the better timber for soldiers had been culled for the independent companies, the ununiformed militia obtained the significant sobriquet of "Flood-wood."

And village-wit—which had always a malignant genius in that direction—having blasted it with a nickname, it defied all the power of the Great and General Court to restore it to respectability. If any of the better classes of society appeared in the Flood-wood ranks, it was for one of two opposite reasons. They were either willing to show their indifference, or contempt, for the entire militia-system; or they were ambitious to secure, by the election even of such a rabble-soldiery, the title of captain, with the possibility, through it, of reaching that of the higher military grades, even up to that of general.

Sometimes this ambition was a matter of personal vanity. There was living, very recently, a gentleman who, having, many years ago, in this way obtained the title of general, was, up to the time of his death, seriously offended, if it was omitted even in the direction of a newspaper. But, more often, the title, with the opportunity afforded by the military command for courting popular favor, was sought as an extremely efficient aid in reaching civil office. There was, for many years, hardly a politician of note, who was not addressed by some military title.

There were many serious evils attending the old militia-system, even from the times immediately after the revolution. The elections, even in the independent companies, were always followed by a succession of "treats," which left many in a state of intoxication; and parades were never conducted on temperance principles. But the same fault could be found with many other occasions to which the same license is not usually so readily accorded; and some regard was generally had by the uniformed soldiery, for their own reputation and that of their corps. The Flood-wood was without this restraint, and also contained most of the class who were habitually lawless; and their excesses were correspondingly great. But, although there were frequent exceptional instances of good conduct and comparative sobriety on the part of individual soldiers, and sometimes of entire companies, yet, as a rule, company elections and "trainings" were occasions of disorder and drunkenness; and "general muster" was the very carnival of riot. On training-days, after the parade—which was preceded by a "treat" from the officers—it was the custom, for the Flood-wood at least, to make the round of the town, firing volleys of musketry before the houses of prominent citizens, who responded to the not unexpected, nor unprovided-for, honor, by alcoholic hospitality. And, often, the final volleys were reserved for the distillery of whiskey and cider-brandy at Luce's mills; with what result need not be told.

The preparations for the general muster were not made without the aid of stimulating beverages; and the arduous duties and labors of that great day of all the year, were sustained by copious draughts from well-filled, and frequently replenished, canteens; a portion of the militiaman's accouterments which was never missed by the inspecting officer, whatever else, from fire-lock to priming-rod, might be lacking. Indeed, it was well if that officer, after duly examining these tin prime-requisites of the military service through a single company, was able to distinguish whether the others carried "Queen's arms" which had seen service at Ticonderoga, in the French and Indian wars, or Lemuel Pomeroy's latest style of flint-lock musket.

This description of the militia of Massachusetts will answer, in its essential particulars, for any period from the close of the revolution until the active militia was reduced to a few small and controllable corps. Whatever good it accomplished was accompanied by an overwhelming flood of evil. It was demoralizing, as well as burdensome, to the community. Instead of making good soldiers, well trained and submissive to discipline, it taught an incontrollable body of armed men to handle dangerous weapons awkwardly. The office of regimental-surgeon was far from a sinecure in time of peace; and the provision made by the state-law for those wounded, and for the families of those killed, at parades or musters, was not unnecessary. It is startling to read in the papers of that day, the frequent serious and fatal accidents caused by ramrods fired from the guns where the fuddled militia-men had left them; by the bursting of muskets in which the owners had unconsciously accumulated several charges of ammunition before they could persuade the obdurate flints to take effect; and by numerous accidents of a similar character. Even when some capable and zealous officer succeeded in forming a somewhat creditable corps, there were inevitable circumstances which gave it the appearance of the mere affectation of military pomp and pride; and, as the village-wags had inflicted a fatal nickname upon the Flood-wood of the militia, so such satirists as Irving and Paulding made the whole system the victim of their irresistible raillery; and it fell into contempt with the more intelligent classes.

The approach of the war of 1812, however, and still more its actual existence, served to rescue the militia, for a time, from the obloquy into which it had fallen. The democratic leaders, in their opposition to a standing-army, had always affected to place great reliance, in the event of war, upon the efficiency of the militia—the bone and sinew of the country. Experiment showed it to be a very fragile reed; but, before it was put to the proof, as war became more and more imminent, patriotic officers entered enthusiastically into the work of rendering the militia efficient defenders of the country. Nor were these efforts confined to the democrats. In Massachusetts, where the governor refused to surrender the command to the officer assigned to the district by the President, the federalists cherished the citizen-soldiery as, in contrast with the regulars, peculiarly their own; and the legislature made liberal grants—at one time $100,000—to arm, equip and fit them for service, in defense of the state. In Pittsfield there were two companies of ordinary militia—one at the West Part, and one in the East and Center. There was also an independent company of light-infantry; and, in connection with other towns, one each of cavalry and artillery.

In May, 1810, anticipating the war, the town instructed its assessors to abate all the poll-taxes—except those for the support of the minister—of every militiaman who produced a certificate from the commander of his company, that he had, for the year preceding, or from the date of his enrollment, attended all the trainings and reviews, completely armed and equipped according to law, and dressed in the uniform prescribed by the proper authority. In the following year, an article was inserted in a warrant for town-meeting, "to see if the town will *explain* the above vote." The town would not; and the democratic selectmen and treasurer, left to their own discretion, if they acted like themselves, construed it liberally in favor of faithful militiamen. The spirited action of the town in September, 1814, regarding its militia, has just been narrated.

Under the fostering influence of the vote of 1810, and by the efforts of competent and zealous officers, the ordinary militia were brought into a very creditable state of efficiency; and the independent corps were greatly improved. When the Cantonment was formed, the militia had the advantage of the example, instruction and encouragement of the officers stationed there, especially when employed as a guard for the prisoners. So that at last when, in the fall of 1814, they were called to more active service, their condition was much in advance of that of peaceful times; and, to some extent, superior to that of the state-militia.

In the work of preparation, the Berkshire Blues, a light-infantry company, under the command of Captain Richard S. Chapell, was distinguished. As soon as news of the declaration of war reached Pittsfield, Captain Chapell ordered his men to provide themselves with arms, equipments and uniforms, within seven weeks; and the order was promptly obeyed. During the entire war the company was kept in a rare state of discipline. Its uniform consisted of dark blue coats turned up with red; pantaloons of the same style; and the tall grenadier cap of leather, —intended for protection against saber-cuts—surmounted by the inevitable plume of black and red.

In the militia-system of that day, positions on the flanks of each regiment, were assigned to independent companies. And, under the order of September 16th, calling out ten thousand of the Massachusetts militia, two flank [1] companies and a regiment of ordinary militia were called from Berkshire. The flank com-

---

[1] The word flank is used in the order as a synonym for independent. Colonel Ward's regiment, to which the Blues were attached, was made up entirely of such companies.

panies selected, were the Berkshire Blues from Pittsfield, and Captain Hunt's company of light-infantry from Stockbridge. The Blues marched on the 11th, and were escorted several miles on their way by " Captain Elisha Allen's company of infantry, and a large concourse of citizens, who cheered thèm lustily as they separated; the company returning the salute and marching off in high spirits."

The full regiment of seven hundred men, commanded by Lieutenant-Colonel Solomon H. Chamberlin, of Dalton, marched from Lenox, for Boston, September 15th.

Rev. Billy Hibbard was chaplain of this regiment, and we quote from his autobiography some quaint paragraphs which graphically illustrate some of the feelings and beliefs of the day; and give the only account we have of the Pittsfield militia's " campaign at Boston."

At our annual conference, in 1814, I intimated that I felt it my duty to volunteer my services to supply the army with preaching in all cases where I could; and if the militia should be called out where I traveled, and wanted a chaplain, I should offer to go with them. This matter was talked over ; and it was thought right to aid the government, and especially to do all we could to prevent wickedness increasing on account of the war. * * * * * * * * * * * *

These were times which tried men's souls. It was im ortant that every man friendly to the general government should show himself and avow his principles. I did not hesitate a moment. Therefore, when the militia was called out to go to Boston, I volunteered my services; and Colonel Chamberlin appointed me chaplain. All was hurry. Orders were given to march forthwith.

Governor Strong had been requested by the President, to call out the number of troops assigned by congress as the quota of Massachusetts, in order to defend Boston from an attack which was threatened by a fleet, and an army of twenty thousand men under the command of Lord Hill.

But Governor Strong, knowing that if he called out these troops by the order from congress, the chief command of them would devolve upon General Dearborn, who commanded the regular troops in Boston; therefore, he called them out by his own order, that he might keep the command in his own hands. I saw by this disobedience that there might be a secret design against the general government. I believed that if Lord Hill should come, Governor Strong might join him and so separate New England from the other states and make himself a king in the land of steady habits. As soon as I had an opportunity, I opened my mind to the officers of the regiment, and some of them were of my opinion. The colonel declared that the moment he discovered that the governor did not defend the place in case we should be attacked, he would command his regiment to turn their arms upon him.

Our men were in high spirits. I had been ordered to join the regiment on the third day's march. * * The day I started I heard of the defeat of the British at Plattsburg and Baltimore. So, when I overtook the regiment in Ware, and informed them of the news, they gave six cheers, which rent the air.

When we arrived at Boston, we were ordered to encamp at Cambridgeport. This was a wet, sunken place, calculated to give our men remittent fevers. However, our good surgeon, Dr. (Asa) Burbank, succeeded in curing all that were attacked. Our regiment was called out every morning to attend prayers, and we had some solemn seasons. I generally prayed six or eight minutes; and would sometimes exhort them about ten minutes. Sometimes many were in tears, while I was pressing home the duty of the soldier to fear God and serve his country in the midst of war. * * * Our government is of God. * * * Let there be no profane swearing; no passions indulged that would violate the decorum of Christian soldiers; but show to all that we fear God and honor our government. After some such short discourse I would close with prayer.

Some of them expressed an opinion that it was needless to have chaplains in an army; but from what I have witnessed, I think, if ministers can do good anywhere, they can in the army, if they are men fearing God, themselves. * * * I believe I was instrumental of some good to the officers and soldiers. * * * Not long after I returned home I had the satisfaction to hear of forty-three, who were in our regiment, who had experienced religion, and joined our society. I met with no abuse either from soldiers or sailors, while with them. But, such was the habit of speaking evil of the president and congress, that I met with several insults from gentlemen of those habits. One instance of insult happened on parade. A gentleman, who often attended prayers outside the hollow square, came to me while I was waiting for the regiment to form; and the invalids were also standing near me. He came to make some acquaintance; he asked my name, and whether I was educated at Cambridge college, etc. He remarked that " our country was once flourishing, but now it is wretched, and all by our damned rulers." I said, " Sir, our rulers are not damned." " Yes," said he, " they are damned rulers." I said, " Sir, you insult me. No man that is acquainted with me, will treat me with vulgarity, nor curse the rulers of our land in my presence; it is written, thou shalt not curse the rulers of thy people." He said: " If I have hurt your feelings, I am sorry for it. I meant *Madison.*" I said, "I feel myself insulted by you, and I owe you no conversation." He steered off without another word. At a proper time I made my complaint to the officers of the staff. I told them I could not hear the rulers of our land cursed, without resenting it. There was such an interest taken in my behalf by the officers and soldiers, that soon it was noised about that the chaplain had been insulted; and it became the subject of much conversation. Some concluded, by way of apology, that the gentleman would not have made so free in my presence if he had not supposed that I was a chaplain of the same political sentiments of the clergy in general, of New England. If so, what an account will those clergymen have to give who have encouraged the people in cursing the rulers of our land. Verily, this has been the cause of this war, and of all the blood which has been shed. *O Tempora! O Mores!* * * * * * Colonel Chamberlin sent word to the governor, that his regiment was ready for service; or to march down to Castine, to drive off the British.[1]

I was requested also to inform those members of the assembly then sitting in Boston, who came from that part of Maine in which the British troops lay, that our regiment was waiting for orders to march down and drive them off. And they petitioned Governor Strong for a suitable force of volunteers for that purpose. But our pious governor loved our enemies so well, that he would not have them hurt or disturbed. So he advised neutrality, and preached peace with all but republicanism: I did not hear of his preaching any peace with that.

It will be observed that these opinions were recorded by Mr. Hibbard, as though still held by him, nearly forty years after the close of the war. If a man so shrewd and well-informed as he, could entertain for such a period suspicions such as he expresses, it is difficult to conceive of any charge against the federal leaders which would not have found credence among the less intelligent masses of the democratic party.

The militia remained at Boston three months, no doubt learning something of the art of war; and certainly seeing as much of metropolitan life as was good for them. If they did not see any active service it was clearly from no lack of inclination. And if they had met the enemy in fight, there is every reason to believe that they would have maintained the reputation which Berkshire soldiers have kept unsullied in all the wars in which they have taken part.

[1] There was the old impatient Berkshire spirit of revolutionary times.

The war had hardly commenced before there were rumors of negotiations for peace or of mediation proffered by neutral powers. But, while both the belligerents constantly declared their desire for peace, no terms were ever suggested by the one which the other would even consider. Finally, however, in the winter of 1813-14, the United States appointed commissioners to treat concerning peace, who met the commissioners of Great Britain in August, 1814, at Ghent. The first news from this commission came in October. Great Britain, rendered arrogant by the splendid success of her arms in all parts of the world, presented terms, which hardly the most devoted of her partisans in America would have consented to accept. Almost the whole body of the people applauded the course of their commissioners in rejecting them; and resolved to fight out the war at any cost rather than to submit to such insolent demands. They were simply these:

Great Britain insisted on retaining that portion of Maine already in her possession; upon excluding Americans from the fisheries to which they had been admitted by the treaty of 1783; and that the United States should agree never to construct or maintain any armed vessels on the lakes, nor hold or erect any forts on their American shores, or on the rivers that ran into them. She demanded, moreover, not only that her Indian allies should be included in the treaty of peace, to which the United States was willing to consent; but that there should be ceded, and secured, to them forever, all the territory now included in the states of Michigan, Indiana and Illinois, with a part of Ohio.

This news, of course, put the expectation of peace far from the thoughts of both government and people; and, although the commission at Ghent was known to be still continuing its labors, they nerved themselves at once for a desperate struggle with that vast power which Great Britain, having crushed with it the greatest soldier in Europe, was now able to concentrate upon them.

There were many reasons why both political parties should seriously regret this necessity. The federalists, of course, as an original peace party; the democrats from the embarrassments which they experienced in conducting the government; and both, from the alarming dangers to which every one perceived that the country was exposed. And the state of the war was not such as to relieve this depression; although we now see that it had just developed officers capable of command, and although the brilliant victories on the Niagara frontier somewhat cheered the gloom. There were great fears as to the result of the invasion of Louisiana. A large portion of Maine was still held by a British army ready to extend its conquests in the spring. Canada, still intact, was the rallying ground of a constantly increasing force. The brilliant series of American naval victories, which distinguished the opening of the war, had ended, and the ships whose names had become a synonym for victory were either lost or hopelessly shut up in port, by fleets which effectually blockaded the whole coast of the Union. The slave-holding states were agitated by perpetual alarms; for the enemy—although his own position as a slave-holding power, by virtue of his West Indian possessions, restrained him from openly encouraging insurrections and arming the blacks—made frequent landings, incited escapes from servitude, and committed other acts which were deemed suggestive of a servile outbreak. The northern commercial states were threatened with the plunder and destruction of their maritime towns and villages, while the almost-impervious squadrons of the blockade completed the ruin of their commerce.

The desperate struggle which seemed inevitable was, doubtless, even under these depressing circumstances, to be accepted, without hesitation, as the alternative of a dishonorable peace; and, in the light of after events, we can confidently believe, that, with much suffering and sacrifice, it would have been brought, by a united nation, to a successful issue. But even with this assurance, it was not a contest to be courted; and in the autumn of 1814, victory at New Orleans was uncertain; the course of the federal party was not well assured, and the Hundred Days of Napoleon could not have been even remotely anticipated.

The intelligence which came in February, that the protocol for a treaty of peace upon honorable terms—although no definite mention was made of some important matters in dispute—had been agreed upon by the commissioners at Ghent, ratified by the prince regent at London, and forwarded to Washington for ratification there, was well fitted to excite the universal and exuberant joy with which it was received.

The news reached Pittsfield on the afternoon of February 13th, in the form of a small handbill of twenty newspaper-lines; which had been issued at five o'clock the preceding afternoon, from the office of the *Albany Argus,* and which was immediately reprinted by the *Sun*, and distributed broadcast. It merely stated the general facts, and that the news had been received in Albany, at the moment of the date of the *Argus* handbill, by Governor Tompkins, to whom it had been dispatched by J. Barker, Esq., from New York. But there was no doubt of the essential facts, and the public joy was unbounded. The *Sun*, of the same week, says: "On Tuesday, the artillery at the Cantonment, and in this village, repeatedly fired salutes; a large number of citizens, and a fine body of regulars, paraded on the green, and fired continued volleys of musketry through the day. It was a scene of rejoicing in which the loud music of the bells, and the roar of artillery and musketry, were but outward demonstrations of the joy which animated every patriot breast."

In its issue of March 2d, the *Sun* again says: "The nation is alive with the welcome news of peace. This town, and almost all the cities, towns and villages throughout the Union, so far as heard from, have given testimony of their joyous feelings by discharges of cannon, ringing of bells, illuminations, etc."

In Pittsfield, there were illuminations, bonfires, public dinners, and—most notable among them—a ball at the assembly-room in the second story of the old yellow Female Academy on Bank row; on which joyous occasion the belles were indeed happy who could appear in a robe of blue calico, covered with innumerable scrolls inscribed with the word PEACE; a style of dress-pattern of which Josiah Bissell & Son could procure but a limited supply for the Pittsfield market; although cargoes had been sent out from Liverpool, almost simultaneously with the ship which brought the treaty of peace—so close upon the withdrawal of the British armies, followed the invasion of British manufactures.

The *Sun*, in announcing the ratification of the treaty by the American government, warned its readers that the peace had been forced upon Great Britain, "who still rankled with commercial jealousy," and that the United States "must be prepared for a second Punic war;" and, with other newspapers of the same political faith it for years cultivated a hostile feeling towards England, and affected to consider the assent to peace as wrung from her. But, although the softening of the terms offered by her between October and December was doubtless in some measure due to a growing perception that her preponderance in Europe was not fixed on so impregnable a basis as in the first flush of victory she imagined, yet it cannot be fairly claimed that she consented to peace from dread of the American arms. Peace was a blessed boon to both countries, neither of which could, by any possibility, have gained from the prolongation of hostilities, anything at all commensurate with the cost; and it was the glory of the American commissioners at Ghent, that they succeeded in convincing the representatives of Great Britain that this was true as to her interests.

Still, although the people of Pittsfield, like those of the whole country, were relieved of many burdens and anxieties by the advent of peace, and although the joyous greeting with which they met it, was not without wise reasons, yet the cessation of hostilities was far from favorable to their immediate material interests. The stoppage of the national expenditure, to a great extent, diminished both the mercantile and manufacturing business of the town: and the abundance and cheapness of the British fabrics with which the whole country was flooded, threatened to complete their ruin.

This, the town soon began to feel bitterly; and it was the opinion of the veteran Britain haters—and, like most of their opinions, not altogether unsupported by at least presumptive proof—that the English manufacturers, unable to protect their monopoly either by preventing the extension of their improvements in machinery, or to crush their rivals by force of arms, had determined to effect their destruction by a free use of their unlimited capital; even a wasteful temporary use of which could be wisely made, if it succeeded in driving their American rivals from their own market. In what manner they acted, on the basis of this opinion, will appear in another chapter.

CHAPTER XII.

THE DIVIDED PARISH—PASTORATES OF REV. WILLIAM ALLEN AND
REV. THOMAS PUNDERSON—REUNION.

[1810-1817.]

Divorce of town and parish affairs—Temporary change in the mode of supporting public worship—Ordination of Rev. William Allen—The town appropriates moneys for a school-fund—Misapplication of the same to the purposes of the First Parish, and controversy concerning the same—The First Church continues the discipline of its seceding members—Measures looking towards reunion, and obstacles to them—Death and benevolent will of Woodbridge Little—The fathers of the church characterized by Rev. Dr. Humphrey—Rev. Messrs Allen and Punderson propose reunion, and resign to facilitate it—Their dismission—The churches agree upon a basis of reunion—It is consummated under the auspices of an ecclesiastical council.

WE resume the history of the Congregational parishes of the town, at the point where it was interrupted on the death of Rev. Thomas Allen, in 1811, and shortly after the establishment of the Union Parish. For seven years after the death of Mr. Allen, religious worship in Pittsfield was supported in a manner then almost, if not entirely, anomalous in the country-towns of Massachusetts.; there being no appropriations of money by the town for that purpose.

Practically, perhaps, this change may be said to have been effected in October, 1809, when the town voted "that the sum of four hundred dollars shall be raised for the support of the ministry; which, together with the expense of assessing the same, shall be assessed exclusively on the polls and estates of those persons who are members of the First Parish in Pittsfield, and be paid over to such uses as they shall appoint." While, to comply with the statute, the town thus voted that the sum which would fall to the members of the First Parish, to be paid for religious purposes, by the assessors' books should be raised, they remitted to them the payment and expenditure of the money; thus virtually dissolving the connection between the town and the parish.

This, and other votes of the town, confirming and perpetuating the separation of town and church and producing very nearly an equality of the parishes before the law, was probably the result of a union between the federal voters in the Union Parish and the democrats among the Methodists and Baptists, with the aid of a few Episcopalians; for there was a considerable democratic majority in the town, taking all denominations together.

After this vote of October, the members left in the First Parish after the secession of those who were incorporated into the Union Parish, were organized as a religious society; but it was not incorporated, such a step not being necessary, as it retained the vested rights of the original town-parish. It must not, however, be confounded with the present First Parish, which, although its successor, is that of the Union Parish as well. On the 10th of August, 1810, the First Church chose Rev. William Allen to succeed his father in the pastorate, and, the parish concurring, he was duly installed; Rev. Joseph Eckly, D. D., of Boston, preaching the sermon.

There is no statement anywhere of the amount of Mr. Allen's salary; indeed all the knowledge we have of the financial affairs of the First Parish during his ministry, is afforded by the record of the town's action concerning the unwarranted payment to him, by Capt. John Dickinson, the town-treasurer, of certain funds which had been appropriated to the support of schools; both the treasurer and the minister probably deeming the vote illegal and void. We give an abstract of the town's action.

On the 5th of November, 1810, the following preamble and resolution were adopted, in pursuance of the policy indicated by the vote already quoted as having passed in October, 1809 :

Whereas, the principal part of the avails of the ministry-lands, which have been sold by the town, and all the avails of the school-lot, sold to Ebenezer White and others, have been appropriated to the building of a meeting-house, now in possession of the Congregational society, of which the Rev. William Allen is pastor, and is now held for their use ; and whereas, it appears that the town did raise by tax, and appropriate, other moneys to build that meeting-house—to the amount of more than six thousand dollars : Therefore, voted, that moneys owing this town, secured by note, bond, mortgage, or other security, and payable with annual interest, be, and the same hereby are, appropriated as a fund, the interest of which shall be annually appropriated to defray the expenses of the schools in the several school-districts of this town.

In the warrant for a town-meeting held in November, 1814, was the following article relative to a violation of the above vote :

To see if the town will choose a committee to ascertain whether the treasurer of the town has paid six hundred dollars—more or less—to the use of the First Parish in Pittsfield, or their teacher of piety, morality, and religion, out of the moneys derived from the debt which the late Rev. Thomas Allen owed the town, and which moneys the town had voted should be put out permanently on annual interest, and the annual interest be applied to the use of schools in said town ; and to pass such votes upon their report as the exigency of the case may require, to effect the purposes of the town in their said vote, and in preserving said fund, and the faithful application of it to the use of schools.

The consideration of this article was postponed to the March meeting of 1815; and the hearing of the report from the usual annual committee appointed in the previous year to settle with the treasurer, was deferred to the same time. When the March meeting came, the hearing of the auditing committee's report was again postponed until April, and then to May. In May it was not read; and the choice of a new committee to settle with the treasurer of the year then ensuing, was indefinitely postponed. Nothing was done by either meeting in regard to the alleged use of the town's funds in contravention of its express vote ; but John Dickinson, who had been treasurer since 1812, was re-elected in 1815, and also chosen representative in the legislature. It is evident that the democratic majority in the town, now become very large, had determined, without rescinding the vote of 1810, to sustain their treasurer in his non-compliance with it. It was not until March 11, 1816, that the report of the committee to examine the treasurer's accounts, bearing date, November 7, 1814, finally obtained a hearing. The following are the closing paragraphs :

"Your committee find that said treasurer has opened an account current with the First Parish in Pittsfield, which he has exhibited to us, and in which he charges himself with the sum of $886 69, collected of the town's debtors, as follows, to wit:

The whole debt due on the note of the late Rev. Mr. Allen, [Being the principal and interest of the note for $87, reported as found in the treasurer's hands after Mr. Allen's death.]	$112 17
Debt of the late Deacon Hubbard,	97 35
Debt of Robert Stanton,	193 61
Part of debt of E. Tracy,	355 00
Part of debt of Isaac Ward,	128 50
	$886 63

And, in the same account, said treasurer charges that parish with the sum of $971 83, as paid by him to the Rev. William Allen, on account of his settlement with them as their minister: by which it appears that the said treasurer considered it his duty to pay the same, and deemed himself legally entitled to be idemnified, out of the debt of Erastus Tracy, for the balance. Signed, JOHN B. ROOT,
JOHN C. WILLIAMS,
JOSHUA DANFORTH.

Messrs. Root and Danforth were active members of the First Parish, Mr. Williams of the Union parish; so that the substance of their report must have been familiar to every citizen, soon after it was prepared: and probably its details also. It is certain, therefore, that the information contained in it—of a nature so interesting to the excited politico-religious factions of the day —was the subject of animated discussion. In town-meeting, especially—although the majority for two years refused to permit it to be formally communicated—it could not have failed to excite vigorous debate.[1]

The report of the committee having, at last, then, in 1816, obtained a hearing, the treasurer's account as to ordinary town-charges, was allowed; but it was voted, "that Thomas Gold, Esq., Deacon Samuel Root, and Mr. Thomas Hubbard, be a committee to settle with Mr. John Dickinson, the town-treasurer, respecting the sum paid by him to the Rev. William Allen, and, if he does not settle with them, that they be, and hereby are, appointed agents, in behalf of the town, to bring an amicable suit on the bond of the said John Dickinson and his sureties."

No satisfactory settlement with the treasurer being effected,

---

[1] No inference to the contrary can be drawn from the silence of the record, where neither discussions, nor abortive motions, were ever mentioned.

suit was commenced as directed, in the court of common pleas, the declaration alleging the wrongful payment by Captain Dickinson, to Rev. Mr. Allen, in the year 1814, of sums amounting to $1,121.80, and a debt due from him to the town, including this sum, of $1,500. The defendant demurred to the declaration as insufficient in some legal point, in which he was sustained by the court.

The town thereupon, by its attorney, Thomas Gold, appealed to the supreme court, in which the case was brought forward at the April term of 1816, and the First Parish requesting to be joined, as a party in the suit, with the defendant, permission was granted, and the case continued to the next term; and then still further, to the September term, 1817.

In the meantime, at the March town-meeting of 1817—four months after measures for the reunion of the two parishes had been initiated, there was an article in the warrant:

To see whether the town will pass a vote to notify the attorney employed by the town to institute a suit against the First Congregational Society in said town for moneys alleged to have been made use of by said society for the settlement of Rev. William Allen, belonging to the school-fund of the town, to withdraw the prosecution.

No action upon this proposition is recorded, but the reunion having been perfected, and it being desirable that all causes of difference between those who had been members of the late parishes should be speedily removed, the following was submitted to a meeting, August 14th:

To see whether the town will agree to refer by rule of court, the suit now pending against John Dickinson, together with all demands subsisting between the town and the *late* First Parish thereof, so that all disputes between the town and parish may at once be decided, under this rule. And that the said Dickinson may have the benefit, by way of offset, or otherwise, under the same, of any claims which the said First Parish may have against the town.

This proposition was adopted; and it was further voted, that "the town consents that the Hon[ble] William Walker of Lenox, the Hon[ble] Ezra Starkweather of Worthington, and the Hon[ble] Joseph Woodbridge of Stockbridge, be the referees," and that "the agents of the town, appointed at a former meeting, be hereby directed to act accordingly."

These agents were Jonathan Allen, Henry H. Childs and John B. Root, all democrats, and members of the defendant parish; who had been substituted for the previous committee, two members of which were federalists and members of Union Parish.

At the September term of the supreme court, the above action of the town was submitted to it, and ratified by the appointment of Messrs. Walker, Starkweather and Woodbridge as referees; and at the same term the award of these gentlemen, "that neither party should recover or pay anything, either debt or costs," was returned, and declared final.

This is the last we hear of this remarkable transaction, or series of transactions, except a vote passed by the town, October 19, 1819, appointing the selectmen, together with Colonel Danforth and Phinehas Allen, to make a proper allowance to Thomas Gold for his services, and for money advanced by him in commencing and prosecuting the suit against the parish. We learn of no protest by the members of Union Parish against the apparent injustice of the town's action. Probably in the era of good feeling which attended the reunion of the parishes, there was no disposition to keep alive any of the old dissensions.

But before the happy era, consummated by this settlement, there had been obstacles to overcome of a more serious and delicate character than that which arose from the misapplication of a few hundred dollars of the town's money, in a manner which was not likely to be used as a precedent. The measures of discipline, commenced, before the death of Rev. Thomas Allen, against the members of the First Church, who had left it to connect themselves with that of Union Parish, were resumed on the 28th of February, 1810—only seventeen days after his decease. At the meeting of the First Church on that day, although only seven members—Deacon James Hubbard, James Hubbard, Jr., Captain Daniel Sackett, George Butler, Amos Delano, Josiah Lawrence and Daniel Foote—were present, it was unanimously voted that Woodbridge Little, Joseph Fairfield, Nathaniel Fairfield, Zebediah Stiles, Charles Goodrich, Captain Nathaniel Tremain, Timothy Cadwell, Deacon Daniel Chapman, Isaac Tremain and Richard Barnard, should be suspended from their communion for the space of six months; and then, still remaining unrepentant, suffer excommunication. A similar vote was passed concerning Charles Goodrich, Jr., Timothy Haskell, and Jonathan Weston. The time allowed for repentance was afterwards extended to September 25th, on which day—two weeks before the ordination of Rev. William Allen—the sentence of excommunication was made absolute.

On the 25th of the next month, eight of the persons excommunicated tendered the following confession:

To the Church of the First Parish in Pittsfield:

We, the subscribers, do voluntarily and cheerfully confess that, IN THE MANNER OF OUR LEAVING YOU, "we are chargeable both with error in judgment and irregularity in practice" (*agreeable to the opinions of the two ecclesiastical councils which have been convened in this place, and which have attended to our difficulties*). *This acknowledgment, which we consider ourselves as having made to you on the 23d of October last*, we *again* frankly make, and ask, not only the Divine forgiveness, but also yours, and that of every person who has been offended thereby.

A confession differing from the above only in the omission of the words printed in italics—was signed by Messrs. Tremain, Stiles, Haskell and the Goodriches. Upon this confession, the First Church pronounced the following decision:

* * * We should have been glad if the confession had been more precise and definite ; yet, considering the circumstances of the case, remembering that the confession followed the sentence of excommunication which had been passed upon them, we must think that by " the manner of their leaving us," they mean the irregularity in departing from us for which they have been disciplined.

A majority of the above-mentioned persons have said in their confession of October 23, 1809, that " the course which they have pursued did not originate in any disaffection to the church." We are fully sensible that the church gave them no just occasion for their secession from it; and that their conduct has been irreconcilable with gospel rules and contrary to the gospel spirit. They "acknowledge that, in the manner of their leaving us they are chargeable both with error in judgment and irregularity in practice (agreeable to the opinion of the two ecclesiastical councils, which have been convened in this place, and which have attended to our difficulties.)" Whatever may have been the opinion of the first council, whose result has never been presented to us, there can be no doubt respecting that of the second, with whose result a compliance is professed. This council declared, that the censured members, above-named, "had violated their covenant engagements with the church"—that " the manner of their withdrawing was irregular, and not according with the gospel rule," and that they had not

" made Christian satisfaction to the church for withdrawing from them." If the confession of the persons referred to, relates, as they say, to the irregularity pointed out by the council, then they confess that they have violated their solemn covenant engagements with us. In this light, we must view the confession of all the above-named persons; and it is only in this light that we are disposed to view it with any complacency.

We believe that, in order fully to discharge their duty, they are under obligation to return to our communion. But, although they at present neglect to return to us, yet, as they express their penitence for the irregular manner in which they left us, we trust that our Congregational churches will not censure us as abandoning the wholesome discipline of the gospel, if, on account of their professed repentance, we take off the sentence of excommunication. This we now do. We can not, however, adopt this measure without explicitly declaring our belief that the foundation of the church with which they have connected themselves, was laid in error and irregularity.

We are still ready to restore these persons to our communion, and receive them into the church, if they should return to us, declaring that they take upon themselves again their former covenant.

With this rather forced construction of, and decidedly ungracious response to, the humble admission of their fault, the gentlemen named were left for five years, in the course of which Mr. Little and Captain Goodrich died, and the country passed through a war, and much political commotion. The confession " of twenty-one females, members of the (First) church," who had joined that of Union Parish was rejected " as equivocal—although it was not charged to be designedly so "—inasmuch as it did not expressly declare their penitence for the faults which they admitted. But, in June, 1815, sixteen of these ladies signed a paper similar to that of the male seceders in 1810; and met with a similar response. At the same meeting in which this action was taken, it was voted unanimously " that we are ready to restore to our communion those members of the church of Union Parish who were formerly members of this church, and to renew with them our covenant; and also to receive into our fellowship all the other members of the church of Union Parish, if they will unite in the same covenant."

In its terms this proposition was but a small advance upon that with which the action of the First Church in 1810, closed. But the hindrances which had obstructed reunion, were slowly giving way; and, twenty-five days after this last vote, the following declaration was adopted by the First Church; and, if still ungracious in tone, it shows a marked advance towards the conciliation which was a necessary preliminary to the consolidation of the Congregationalists of Pittsfield upon the old basis.

Whereas, several years ago, certain members of this church were, in violation of their covenant, in a hasty and irregular manner, without dismission and without necessity, embodied into the church of Union Parish in this town, being a majority of said church of Union Parish;—and whereas, they have presented to us a written confession of their faults acknowledging that they *have done wrong*—we have taken the same, with attending circumstances into serious consideration. We think that the offending members would more fully observe the rules of ecclesiastical order, and discharge their duty, by returning to the church from which they have departed; especially as they are generally convinced that but one religious society is required in this village.[1] Yet, as they consider themselves bound by their new covenant, by which they are connected with others never belonging to this church, and as they profess repentance of their sin in leaving us in an irregular manner; Now, therefore, although retaining our persuasion that " the foundation of the church of Union Parish, was laid in error and irregularity," yet influenced by the desire of promoting the interests of the gospel of peace, we think ourselves allowed to vote, and we do hereby vote, that we will hereafter overlook, in our measures of discipline, the offense which has been acknowledged, and that hereafter we will treat the church of Union Parish as a Christian church.

From the beginning of the rupture, both parties made the strongest protestation of their desire to prevent a division of the parish; and, after that had become an accomplished fact, each was vehement in proclaiming its willingness to take any steps which could reasonably be required of it, toward reconciliation and reunion; but each unfortunately held that the terms proposed by the other were inadmissible; and, indeed it was true, that what each required was very like an unconditional surrender of the very point upon which the other had set its heart. But the protestations were none the less strong on that account. It was to emphasize its professions of a desire for harmony that the new parish assumed the name of Union. The adherents of the

[1] The ignoring of the Methodist and Baptist societies in all the action regarding religious matters during these troubles is noteworthy and suggestive.

First Church retorted that the seceders adopted a strange method of manifesting their desire for union when they drew a fixed line of separation, and set up, behind it, a new organization with all the elements of permanence which it was in their power to provide.

The latter portion of this retort was, however, not strictly true; for, while the Union Parish included among its members, Woodbridge Little, Oliver Wendell, Charles Goodrich, John Chandler Williams, Lemuel Pomeroy, and other of the wealthier citizens, and thus had abundant means for the erection of a meeting-house, immediately upon its organization, it actually delayed that measure for more than a year; either in the sincere hope that a reconciliation would render it unnecessary, or else to avoid the odium of being first in assuming that reunion was no longer to be hoped for.[1]

With the exception of the ordination of its minister, and the building of its meeting-house, we have no positive information of any act of Union Parish during the seven years of its existence. One event, nevertheless, of permanent interest to both parishes, after their reunion, occurred during this period. Woodbridge Little died on the 21st of June, 1813, and by his will left five hundred dollars for the purpose of establishing a fund of which the interest should be "yearly appropriated toward the salary of the Congregational minister in Union Parish;" recommending that it should be placed in the care of trustees. To this request, he added the following provision: "And, as it has ever been my sincere and ardent desire to prevent the causes, and avoid the consequences, of the unhappy division which has taken place in the Congregational church in this town, and which has issued in the establishment of Union Parish; so, if at any time, a union shall be effected between the two societies, on principles of Chris-

---

[1] In the winter of 1810-11, Union Parish finally determined to build a house of worship; and, a liberal sum having been subscribed for that purpose, the town was asked, not to give, but to sell for a suitable consideration, a site "north of the printing-office of Phinehas Allen," on what was then the burial-ground, although as yet unoccupied by graves. The democrats being in majority, this request was refused, and the new house of worship was built, where the South Congregational Church now stands, on South street. It was a neat, tasteful and convenient structure, with a rather graceful spire, and was supplied with a bell. After the reunion of the parishes, it served a good purpose as a lecture and school room.

tian charity, and they become in fact one society and church, then said sum should be given to the united parishes."

After making liberal legacies to several friends and giving one hundred dollars to the Congregational Missionary Society, Mr. Little's will provided that his property should be sold within twelve months after his decease; and what remained after the payment of legacies, and the cost of erecting a monument at his grave, should be paid to the president and trustees of Williams college; to be added to the fund.created by him in 1811, for the purpose of aiding indigent young men in their preparation for the ministry. The amount of Mr. Little's gift in 1811, was twenty-five hundred dollars; and, as residuary legatee under the will, the college received thirty-two hundred dollars. These were the first donations which the college received after it commenced its corporate existence.

Mr. Little's bequest to the Congregational parish did not become available until the year 1818, when his earnest prayer for its reunion had been answered. At a subsequent period his suggestion regarding its committal was heeded; and it became the nucleus of the fund for the support of the Congregational ministry in Pittsfield. Mr. Little was buried in the old First burial ground; but, after two disinterments, his grave is now in the "Pilgrims' Rest," at the Pittsfield cemetery. For four years after his death, the divided parishes struggled on; wrangling almost to the last. But, all along, a restless feeling that neither was altogether in the right, possessed the best minds in both. As time wore on, this consciousness extended and increased in power; and they looked and prayed longingly for the moment which would give them the opportunity to mingle once more in a common fold.

No one ever pretended that the number of Congregational worshipers in Pittsfield was such as to require two parishes of that order in town; nor was their wealth so abundant that the burden of a superfluous establishment could be disregarded. In the heat of conflict, indeed, men subscribed, without hesitation and without stint, for the support of whatever institutions seemed essential to the maintenance of their rights and privileges, or to the honor of their party; but when the conflict was in some measure past, and the necessity arising from it had become at least doubtful, all naturally began to look about for some honorable method of relieving themselves from a useless and wasteful expense.

And, more than this, no one could fail to see, that two churches of the same denomination of Christians, existing side by side—in a temper perpetually hostile to each other, and constantly bandying accusations of unfaithfulness to covenant vows, and of contempt for the directions left by the Head of the Church for its governance—were bringing disgrace upon the whole order with which they were connected, and dishonoring the great name they had taken upon themselves. Every one perceived that such an antagonism was an evil second only to that of a perpetual contention between brethren in the same church.

This evil had, from its beginning, been felt and deplored by Christians throughout Massachusetts, and in the adjoining states; for the scandal had become wide-spread, and concerned all. Nor was it more deeply and sincerely lamented by any than by the pious fathers of the Pittsfield church, who, nevertheless, subject to human frailties, suffered their passions and prejudices to thwart their own earnest purpose to terminate it.

Those who remember the fathers of Pittsfield as characterized by Rev. Dr. Humphrey will readily conceive how such a generation might be long kept divided upon a point which a succession of exceptional circumstances, morbidly contemplated, had magnified beyond its due importance; and it is still easier to comprehend how surely and firmly they would unite, when once convinced that the aims in which they agreed were altogether paramount to the points upon which they differed.

That conviction began to dawn upon the minds of the opposing political factions among the Pittsfield Congregationalists, as soon as the termination of the war of 1812-15 permitted the heated passions, which had accompanied and preceded it, to cool. With the return of peace, the political issues of the previous quarter of a century, and the heated debates which they had elicited, became little more than a troubled dream; a haunting and an annoyance still, but with little real substance. The era of good feeling did not fully dawn, but the light of its coming had began to break; and, under its influence, men began to perceive that many things which they had mistaken for demons and monsters, were but ugly and unsubstantial phantoms of the night. And, with the advancing day, even the most obdurate of feuds—those of neighborhoods and small communities—began to give way.

In the June, following the return of peace, the First Church passed its earliest vote looking— with hesitation, it is true,— toward reconciliation with that of Union Parish. There was unhappily apparent in this vote, and in that following it, an effort, by a forced construction of the language used by the seceding members in their confession, to magnify their acknowledgment of guilt ; and also a repulsive assumption of superiority; by which their invitations were rendered nugatory. But the desire for reunion continued to increase among the people, and found nothing to check its growth, except bitter memories, which time and death had already much abated ; and excepting also the existence of two distinct churches, each with a pastor to whom it was, with good reason, devotedly attached.

To these ministers therefore it fell, to take the initiative in measures which would, of necessity, be painful to themselves, and, for a time at least, derogatory to their temporal interests. This sacrifice, Mr. Allen, in a spirit of noble self-forgetfulness and devotion to the good of his people, was the first to make,[1] by presenting to his church the following paper :

To the First Church and Parish of Pittsfield:

The subscriber, who has been, for the last six years, your minister, with many proofs of your attachment, has often deplored the unhappy effects of the division of the town into two religious societies, and wished that they might be reunited. To facilitate the attainment of this object, he has made some exertions, particularly in respect to a settlement of the difficulty between the churches. The great obstacle of the communion of the two churches having been for some time past removed, and other circumstances appearing to him to be at the present moment more favorable to a union than they have ever before been, the subscriber deems it his duty earnestly to recommend, to the people of his charge, an effort to combine harmoniously the two churches and parishes into one. For the accomplishment of this object, which he thinks is important both to the interests of religion and to the tem-

[1] One tradition has it that, before Mr. Allen took this course, he had a friendly interview with Rev. Mr. Punderson, at which both pastors agreed to recommend to their respective churches and parishes, a reunion upon the ancient basis, and to tender their resignations on condition that this advice should be adopted. It is very probable that this natural course was pursued ; but the record indicates that the contrary was the fact.

poral prosperity of the town, he hereby expresses—what he has often declared to individuals—his readiness to be dismissed from his pastoral office. WILLIAM ALLEN.

PITTSFIELD, November 12, 1816.

This communication was laid before the church on the 13th; and "a disposition to comply with its recommendations," say the records, "was unanimously expressed by the members present;" a committee consisting of Deacons Crofoot and Maynard—who had always been somewhat favorably disposed toward Union Parish—Messrs. Daniel Foot, James Hubbard, and Ebenezer Burt, was appointed to confer, on the subject of union, with any committee which might be appointed on the part of the church of the other parish.

Mr. Allen's letter and the proceedings of the First Church thereon, were communicated to Rev. Mr. Punderson, through Hon. John Chandler Williams, and by him laid before a full meeting of the church of Union Parish, on the 18th of November, together with the following paper, signed by himself:

To the Church of Christ in Union Parish, Pittsfield:

The subscriber, being apprised that much is said at the present time with regard to a union between the two churches and societies in this place, and having learned what has been done by the other church and its pastor, in reference to this object, feels it incumbent upon him in this way to express his desire that it may be clearly and distinctly understood by all parties concerned, that he wishes not to be considered a barrier toward the accomplishment of the proposed union.

Could the two churches and societies become cordially united into one, it is his deliberate opinion, that it would be greatly for the interests of religion, and for the prosperity of the town; and he shall heartily approve of any attempt that shall be made to accomplish so desirable an object.

He feels indeed that, in leaving a people with whom he has ever lived in such perfect harmony, to whom he has so long broken the bread of life, a people who have so warm a place in his affections, from whom he has received so many tokens of friendship and esteem, and from whom he can have no worldly inducement to be separated, he will have to make no small sacrifice of feeling, if not of interest. Still, this sacrifice he is ready to make, should it be thought that the interest of religion, and the good of this people, require it.

THOMAS PUNDERSON.

These papers having been laid before it, the church voted that it was sincerely disposed to make an effort for the harmonious combination of the two churches and parishes; and for that purpose, appointed Hon. J. C. Williams, Deacon Daniel Chapman, and Captain Tremain, a committee to confer with that of the First Church. The joint committee thus constituted, agreed upon the following basis of union:

First. That the male members of each church, living in town, should express their readiness, to fellowship all the members of the other church, who might be in regular standing.

Second. That the members of the two churches should have a separate vote in the choice of the first minister of the united society; and that a majority, consisting of at least two-thirds of the members of each church, present, should be necessary to the settlement of said minister.

These terms were promptly accepted by the First Church, and it immediately took measures to carry them into effect by voting,

First. That, as all the male members of this church, living in town, excepting two, have expressed their readiness to fellowship all the members of the other church who are in regular standing, Mr. James Hubbard be a committee to inquire of the said two members whether they also can fellowship the members of the other church, and that he report to the moderator.

Second. That, for the purpose of union, we are willing that our pastor should be dismissed at such a time as may be mutually agreed upon by him and the parish; and that Deacon Maynard be a committee to act with a committee of the parish in calling, if it should be found necessary, a mutual council for the dismission of our pastor, and the completion of the proposed union.

The church of Union Parish—apparently not quite so well prepared for action—voted, that "in accordance with the spirit of the report, Deacons Goodrich and Chapman and Nathaniel Tremain be a committee to converse with all the members of this church, and to inquire of them whether they have any objection against any of the members of the church in the First Parish in this town, so that they should be unwilling to have the two churches united into one."

On the 23d of December, this committee reported that, "although they found universally expressed a strong reluctance to the dismissal of their beloved pastor, yet all would consent to the union of the churches on such terms as the brethren of Union Church should think proper."

Upon this the church unanimously voted to fellowship that of the First Parish; and, as the excepted two members of the First Church waived their objections, if they had any, the terms of treaty on that point were complied with.

On the 15th of January, the Union Church voted to meet for worship, as soon as the joint committee which had been appointed for that purpose should procure a person to preach to the united society, in the meeting-house of the First Parish; and that they would then consider Rev. Mr. Punderson released from his parochial duties.

The confessions of faith and convenants of the two churches were found to be substantially and verbally nearly the same; but being thought too long, they were condensed into what was considered a faithful summary.

The council for the dismissal of Rev. Mr. Allen met on the 5th of February; and, with the highest expressions of esteem and affection for the retiring pastor, and of deep sympathy in the regret of his people, consented to it solely as a measure indispensable to the proposed union, which they viewed with the warmest approbation and congratulation. The 25th of February was fixed for the termination of Mr. Allen's pastorate.

Among the papers of Dr. Timothy Childs, we find a letter which affords some hints as to Mr. Allen's feelings in this emergency; and from which we may fairly infer that the First Parish was less prosperous than the Union, financially. It is as follows:

HONORED SIR:—In answer to your favor, received this morning, I would observe, that in the short conversation I had with you some time ago, it was far from my intention to suggest anything that would impede the proposed union. The consideration of an incompetent support had, I believe, no more than its just weight in influencing me to pursue the course which I have taken. I was satisfied that I could not long remain in Pittsfield and endeavored to select such a time for the negotiation respecting union as would be most advantageous to my parish. I am highly gratified with the result. Believing that any obstructions to the union on the part of our parish would be very injurious to the interests of the parish, tending to divide and perhaps destroy it, I trust the agreement will be carried into effect. With respect to myself, it would not be honorable to my character to remain after what has been done. Much has been said respecting the probability of my having a call to Hanover. Whatever may be the event, it can make no difference respecting my continuance in Pittsfield.

I propose, being previously dismissed, to remove my family to Hanover, the 17th or 18th of February, and should esteem it a kindness in my friends, if they will make some exertions to procure for me, a few days previous, a part of my salary, that I may make arrangements for removal. I am, with great respect, yours very sincerely,

WM. ALLEN.

PITTSFIELD, January 16, 1817.

It will be remembered that Mr. Allen had married a daughter of President Wheelock of Dartmouth college.

A council called by Union Church, met on the 5th of May, and with like terms of respect and affection, consented to the dismission of Rev. Mr. Punderson, to take effect "whenever the General Court should incorporate the two Congregational societies into one." And, like the previous council, it expressed its approval of the union and its pleasure in the promised restoration of harmony to the Congregational fold in Pittsfield.

No legislative incorporation was had as contemplated by the council. But it was only necessary for the abnormal bodies which had held the field in Pittsfield, to terminate their corporate existence in some legal manner, when, by force of law, the old town-parish would revive, and all persons in its precinct not set off by certificate to a dissenting society, would instantly become members of it. By what formula this was accomplished is immaterial.

There is no record of any meeting of the Union Church, for business, after the council of May; but the First Church, on the 3d of July, passed the following resolution:

Whereas, the religious societies in this town *are now* united into one, and as it has long been wished that the two churches become united, * * * and as it is extremely desirable that this union be made complete without further delay: therefore voted, that Deacon Maynard and Vivus Osborne be a committee on the part of this church to unite with a committee of the church of Union Parish, to call a council consisting of three ministers with their delegates, viz.: the Rev. Messrs. Collins of Lanesborough, Shepard of Lenox, and Jennings of Dalton, to declare us one church by mutual agreement.

We do not know who were the committee on the part of the Union Church; but the council assembled on the morning of July

7th, at a private house; and after a session with the committees of the two churches, repaired to the First meeting-house which was filled with a great assembly. Here they made public their action by reading the following minutes:

At an ecclesiastical council, convened July 7, 1817, at the house of Josiah Bissell, Esq., in Pittsfield, by letters missive from a joint committee appointed by the two churches in Pittsfield, for the object of uniting the two churches into one, agreeably to ecclesiastical order, the following pastors and delegates were present:

From Lanesborough, Rev. Daniel Collins and Wolcott Hubbell, Esq.
From Lenox, Rev. Samuel Shepard and Deacon Stephen Wells.
From Dalton, Rev. Ebenezer Jennings and Deacon Ashley Williams.

Mr. Collins was chosen moderator, and Mr. Jennings scribe, and the council was opened by prayer.

The council had the records of the two churches so far as they related to the union contemplated, and discovering a pacific and uniting spirit in the several steps which were taken to promote a cordial union, they are satisfied of their sincere intention to unite together as brethren in the common faith of our Lord and to walk together in fellowship and to sit together at the same table.

These minutes having been read, the moderator proceeded: "The committee of the churches exhibited before us, the Articles of Faith and the Covenant which the two churches have proposed to make and which we cordially approve, and which, if now adopted by the church in our presence, we are prepared to declare."

At this point the Articles of Faith and Covenant were read and all the members of the united church gave their assent by rising. The council then proceeded as follows:

We are now ready to declare you a united church according to ecclesiastical order, and we acknowledge you as a church in regular standing, and will hold fellowship as with other Congregational churches in this Association of Ministers.

We congratulate you on your union and beseech the Great Head of the Church to cement it with that love which suffers long and is kind. Be forgiving toward one another, bear each other's burdens, and so fulfill the law of Christ. We commend you to that Grace which is able to make you wise unto salvation, and you an inheritance among them that are sanctified. Amen.

And thus the two parishes between which the Congregationalists of Pittsfield had, for nearly seven years, been divided, ceased to be; the ancient parochial organization revived, and one church held the field.

The event was accompanied by other appropriate religious services and thanksgiving, and appears to have created general joy in the town, to whose temporal as well as spiritual welfare it was—as Rev. Messrs. Allen and Punderson had discovered—essential. Much was yet to be done to cement the union, and to some it was doubtless distasteful, and by some distrusted;[1] but the fraternal prayer of the council was fully answered, and soon and permanently, the Congregational Church and Parish in Pittsfield, became as distinguished for peace and harmony, as it had long been for the reverse.

[1] It is singular that no mention can be found in the columns of the *Sun* of events so marked and important as the council of July, and the acts of the churches which led to it.

CHAPTER XIII.

PASTORATE OF REV. DR. HUMPHREY.

[1817-1823.]

Changes in the mode of transacting parish-business—Rev. Heman Humphrey chosen pastor—Sketch of Doctor Humphrey—His installation at Pittsfield—State of the Pittsfield parish—Doctor Humphrey's fitness to harmonize its conflicts—Pastoral work—Catalogue of Bible-class—Sunday-school—His release of dissenting-members of the parish from the payment of taxes—Condition of the dissenting parishes—A remarkable revival—Its effects on morals and feuds—Fourth of July, and St. John's day — Mr. Humphrey is invited to the presidency of Amherst collegiate institute—Opposition to his acceptance—His own doubts—Accepts under the advice of a council—Farewell to Pittsfield—His return—Residence and death there—Interesting incidents.

ALTHOUGH the town-parish system of supporting public worship was revived in 1817, the six years' experience of poll-parishes was not without its effect, which was manifested afterwards upon various occasions; and, first in a change of the manner in which parochial business was transacted by the town. It was resolved in 1796, that only Congregationalists should vote upon the disposition of taxes assessed exclusively upon members of that order; but previous to 1810, business concerning the support of public-worship was acted upon in ordinary town-meetings, to which all persons qualified to vote in town-affairs were "warned," and in which the ordinary secular municipal affairs were discussed and determined.

But in 1817—no parochial business having been transacted by the town for the preceding seven years—such business began to be confined exclusively to meetings warned for that special purpose; the warrant still being issued by the selectmen and directed to the constable, but requiring him to summon only those qualified to vote in the affairs of the "Congregational society" in said town.

This society having no officers, organization, or other means of independent action—being served by the selectmen, assessors, clerk, treasurer and constable elected by the town—a proposition to organize a parish by the choice of a special board, was, in November, 1818, referred to a committee consisting of John Chandler Williams, Josiah Bissell, and Joshua Danforth,—who on the 23d of that month submitted the following report:

Your committee, on enquiry, do not find that there is more than one town, situated as this town is, in the whole commonwealth, in which the parochial concerns for the support of public worship, are managed and conducted by officers chosen for parish-purposes exclusively. Your committee are satisfied, that hitherto the support of public worship by the Congregational society, has been so managed, and we believe always will be, as that no part of the expenses made for its support has been, or can be, paid out of any money except that which is voted and granted for that purpose solely; and assessed on, and paid by, the inhabitants of that society only. Your committee are of opinion that a majority of the parish would not be disposed to adopt any new arrangement, at present, for the purpose contemplated.——We therefore would add, that we do not deem it expedient at this time to elect parish-officers. We would, however, advise that the town-treasurer should annually exhibit to the selectmen, at or before the March meeting, an account current of the money raised for the support of public worship, and the manner in which it has been expended; in order that any person, belonging to this town, may, if he pleases, examine the same, and in that way insure those who do not belong to the Congregational society, that no part of their money is used for the parish's purposes.

The report was accepted, and the matter of further organization of the parish rested until 1834.

The united Congregational church of Pittsfield, now reassuming the name and rank of the First Church, voted September 1, 1817, to invite Rev. Heman Humphrey, of Fairfield, Connecticut, to settle with them in the gospel ministry. It is not stated that a separate vote of the First and Union churches was had, according to the terms of their agreement. Perhaps their harmony had already become so ripe, or the choice of Mr. Humphrey was so unanimous, that this ceremony was deemed superfluous.

The parish, on the 17th of September, concurred in the choice by a vote of sixty-eight to eleven, and tendered Mr. Humphrey a salary of nine hundred dollars per annum, on condition that he should relinquish all claims to the ministry-land or other property of the town.

Heman Humphrey was born in West Simsbury, now Canton, Hartford county, Connecticut, March 26, 1779. His father, Solomon Humphrey, was a descendant of Michael Humphrey, who emigrated from England to Massachusetts before 1643. In the long line of ancestors between Michael and Heman, were many honorable and reverend men. Solomon, the father of the latter, was born in 1747, and married, a second wife, Hannah, daughter of Capt. John Brown, of West Simsbury, who died while an officer in the war of the revolution, at Harlem Heights; and from whom also descended that other Capt. John Brown, who died at Harper's Ferry. Heman, the oldest son of this marriage, was the pastor selected by the First Church and Parish of Pittsfield, in 1817. His father was a substantial farmer, and is described as "a man of good common-school education; of a more than ordinary taste for reading; of good sense and unblemished moral character, temperate, industrious, and frugal." The mother was a woman " of uncommon mental capacity, and an eager reader of such books as could be obtained; the number of which, however, was very small." Heman's early education was of the character usually bestowed upon children of such parents in Connecticut, at that time. He thus describes what it was when, at the age of seventeen, he supposed it finished : " I knew almost nothing of geography as taught by globe and maps, was but indifferently versed in the higher rules of arithmetic, and knew nothing of English grammar, except a little found in one of the earlier editions of Webster's spelling-book." He was fond of reading, but his course of study of that kind was confined to The New England Primer, Robinson Crusoe, and The Pilgrim's Progress, with an occasional stray number of the *Hartford Courant*. Shortly after he had graduated from this course of study, the village-pastor succeeded in having a small neighborhood library collected, of which Heman made excellent use, often, by the aid of pine-torches or of the kitchen-fire, extending his perusal of its contents far into the night. After his education, in this fashion, was "completed," he spent five summers, as " hired man" on farms in various towns, devoting winters to school-teaching. Fortunately, his fourth summer was spent with Governor Treadwell of Farmington, "a Christian and an exceedingly able theologian, as well as an able judge and an incorruptible statesman;" whose library and conversation gave a new impulse to Heman's intellectual progress. Two years later, being left at leisure by an accidental failure to secure a re-engagement with Governor Treadwell, and being encouraged by his pastor, Rev. Jonathan Miller, with the suggestion that he might one day become a minister, he began, under his instruction, the study of the Latin language; and with an intermission of two months, spent in the harvest-field for the sake of health, devoted the season to study. With alternations of farm-labor, teaching and study, Mr. Humphrey went on until the spring of 1803. At that date, he was advised to make an effort to enter the junior class of Yale college the next autumn; and by the most assiduous devotion to study, he succeeded in doing so; in that time reading Horace, mastering algebra, learning the rudiments of the Greek language—even from the alphabet—and enabling himself to pass an examination in two books of the Iliad and the whole of the Greek testament. He passed a creditable college course, and by dint of school-master's work, and that of the librarian of the Linonian Society, graduated without debt; and possessed of a small sum with which to enter upon his professional studies.

Mr. Humphrey's earliest life may be well said to have been of a religious character. So strict, indeed, was his regard for religious duty, that once, having wandered during the forenoon of a Fast-day, with a companion, over the fields and woods, instead of going to meeting, his conscience so smote him that he never tried it again. His biographer, however, considers that it was not until the winter of 1798–9, that he had any marked religious experience. The record of that experience shows it to have been such as that to which the Calvinistic Faith, especially in that earnest time, subjected the strongest natures. "If I was then born again," he writes, "I was born a Calvinist, 'not of flesh nor of blood, nor of the will of man, but of God, who hath mercy on whom he will have mercy.' I then fully embraced the doctrines of the shorter Catechism, and from this platform I have never swerved."

When he entered upon his classical studies, it was with the view to prepare himself to preach the doctrines so emphatically declared, and at the close of those studies, others of a purely theological character naturally followed. There being then no theological seminary in the country, Mr. Humphrey, after remaining a few months in New Haven, in charge of a school and at the same time commencing his theological studies under the direction of President Dwight, entered a theological class conducted by Rev. Asahel Hooker in Goshen, Connecticut, in the spring of 1806. In October following, he was licensed to preach by the Litchfield North Association. His first permanent settlement was at Fairfield, Connecticut, where he was ordained March 16, 1807, and remained until May, 1817.

On the 20th of April, 1808, one year after his settlement in Fairfield, Mr. Humphrey was married to Sophia, only daughter of Deacon Noah Porter, of Farmington. His ten years of labor in that town were pleasant but full of effort. Among his successes there, were the doing away with the half-way covenant in the church, and a temperance reform effected by very bold and novel utterances in which he took what was then the unheard of position of total abstinence.

After leaving Fairfield, and preaching a few Sundays in Hartford, he accepted an urgent invitation to visit Pittsfield; the result being the call to settle over the united churches, which we have recorded.[1]

This call, Mr. Humphrey hesitated to accept. We quote again from his memoirs, which after recording the coming together of the two congregations under the old roof, proceed thus:

The difficult process of organic reunion was now to be promoted. Mr. Humphrey was invited to undertake the task. He shrank from it. He feared the effect of the severe climate of the Berkshire hills upon his family. His "politics" might be regarded with suspicion. But some one must become their pastor. "I did not wish to go to Pittsfield. Not that I had any objection to the people. They were an intelligent congregation. There was a good degree of active piety in the church, and they had treated me kindly. But the congregation was spread over the whole town—six miles square. They were united but not amalgamated. A good deal of the old leaven remained. Some of the prominent families stood aloof. And, to increase my perplexity, I was strongly solicited to return and to be resettled over the church and

---

[1] The foregoing sketch of the life of Dr. Humphrey, before his settlement in Pittsfield, is condensed from an eloquently written volume published by J. B. Lippincott & Co., Philadelphia, in 1869, and entitled Memorial Sketches of Heman Humphrey and Sophia Porter Humphrey, by Rev. Drs. Z. M. Humphrey and Henry Neill, their son and son-in-law.

congregation in Fairfield. I was assured of a competent support. But my convictions of duty at length overcame my objections. I became convinced that the call was from a higher source than the voice of the people, and it was not for me to *choose*, but to *obey*."

Such was the man who was invited to become the first pastor of the Congregational church in Pittsfield, after its reunion; and such were the circumstances, and his own personal feelings, under which he accepted the invitation. And with this thorough comprehension of the situation, he was installed on the 26th of October, " in the presence of a numerous and solemn concourse;" Rev. Dr. Shepard of Lenox, delivering the sermon, Rev. Dr. Hyde of Lee, delivering the charge, and Rev. Mr. Jennings of Dalton, giving the right-hand of fellowship.

By what special human agency, the church and parish were led to so happy a choice of pastor, we are not told; but probably the whole range of the New England clergy did not afford another minister so peculiarly fitted to do the work which lay before him. A thorough scholar, a forcible and correct writer, and a speaker of more than common eloquence, he commanded admiration, as well as respect, by his talents. His earlier associations had rendered him familiar with the modes of thought, the humors, the prejudices, and the mental capacity — natural and acquired — of rural populations, such as that of Pittsfield then was. He was also practically acquainted with all that pertained to agricultural pursuits, and ready at need to skillfully perform any of the labors of the farmer. This, to be sure, was not unusual with the clergy of that day. Most of his clerical brethren could do the same; but few of them had the tact to avail themselves of it in ingratiating themselves with their parishioners, not only without derogating from the dignity of their profession, but, as he did, adding to the respect inspired by it.[1]

He had, moreover, the advantage of a most instructive pastoral

---

[1] Many anecdotes of Mr. Humphrey's skill and prudence in winning the disaffected or the indifferent are still related by his parishioners. One of those oftenest repeated is that of his conquering the heart of a farmer who had steadily refused to attend the Sabbath services, by visiting him in his harvest-field, and, without a word of professional exhortation, engaging him in conversation upon farming, and then taking his "cradle," cutting a swath of grain, as if he had been used only to a farmer's life all his days. Memorial Sketches, p. 72.

experience in Fairfield, where he succeeded in moulding a parish very much to his own ideal from very crude materials; doing away with much erroneous practice to which his people had been wedded, and introducing, by degrees more or less insensible, means of good to which they had been strangers.

With all these advantages of education and experience, Mr. Humphrey had also the quickest appreciation of character, a keen insight into the springs of human action, a calmness and equanimity which left all his faculties habitually at command, and a shrewdness which applied them with rare adroitness to the management of affairs.

All these high qualities of a governing and organizing mind were in him imperatively ruled by a sense of duty which admitted no stint of his labor, and forbade him—for the attainment of any end, however plausible—to swerve one iota in his interpretation of the doctrines which he believed embodied in "the faith once delivered to the saints," or to falter in his administration of the discipline established by the Head of the Church.

All these qualifications were called for in full by the task which awaited Mr. Humphrey in Pittsfield; and, with them all, it was one from which he might well shrink, as he did. But, having once accepted it, he was a man to put all doubts and fears and shrinkings behind him, and to press forward with all his powers to its accomplishment. His method in this is thus partially detailed in the "Memorial Sketches:"

When he assumed the charge of the congregation, "very few of its leading men, such as lawyers, physicians and merchants, were professors of religion." They were, however, regular attendants of public worship. The first object of the new pastor was to win the respect of all for the pulpit. But little pastoral visiting was, therefore, attempted during the first winter. The effects of careful study being realized, systematic visitation began in the opening spring, and was vigorously conducted through the succeeding months. The old methods, so successful in Fairfield, were adopted. A weekly lecture was established in the out-districts. The Sunday-school, which then began to take a recognized place among the institutions of the church, received much attention. The baptized children of the church were collected, once in three months, for public catechetical instruction. A Bible-class of young women was also established.[1]

[1] The agreement for the formation of this Bible-class is preserved, and shows that it was not exclusively for young women. It is as follows:

In 1821, Dr. Humphrey addressed the annual meeting of two female charitable societies of the village. Our information regarding these organizations is meager, but their charity appears, by the address, to have been chiefly applied to religious purposes. Dr. Humphrey

BIBLE-CLASS—We, whose names are annexed to this paper, feeling it to be a duty, as well as a privilege, to gain a more intimate knowledge of the Bible, hereby agree to associate for the purpose of attending such recitations, once in a fortnight, as our pastor may assign us, and also to hear such explanations and instructions as he may give. * * * * * * *

PITTSFIELD, May, 1823.

Henry Strong, Dr. H. H. Childs, James McKnight, James H. Kellogg, Samuel Colt, Uriah Lathrop, John Mason, Edward P. Humphrey, David White, Robert Colt, George A. Peck, Samuel Crocker, Elbridge G. Frisby, Nelson K. Strong, George R. Whitney, Eliza Lathrop, Ann Childs, Julia Porter, Frances Danforth, Maria Allen, Amelia Simpson, Mary Ann Porter, Martha Gold, Eliza Luce, Sarah Ann Weller, M. Clark, Fidelia Clark, Aurelia Johnson, Ann Burge, Martha Root, Sarah Ann Colt, Mary Ann Brown, Julia Colt, Elizabeth Campbell, Clarissa Colt, Loisa Adams, Louisa Merriam, Aurora Eells, Amelia Danforth, Caroline Allen, Salome Danforth, Mary Bissell, Eliza Brown, Harriet Allen, Caroline Colt, Minerva Kittridge, E. M. Seeley, Olivia Porter, Martha D. Bramin, Catherine Smith, Sarah Moore, M. Castle, Charlotte Cady, Abby Warner, Mary Ann Kellogg, Climene Woodworth, Eunice Pomeroy, Parthenia L. Pomeroy, Mary Ann Dickinson, Mary Brown, Mary Dorrance, Elizabeth Jackson, Adelia Merrick, Sarah Chapin, Eunice Rossiter, Nancy Ingersoll, William Goodrich, Christiana Van Valkenburg, Cornelia Dubois, Hannah M. Tyler, Maria Clapp, John Day, James Warriner, Amelia Goodrich, John Ayres, Horace Bissell, John B. Eldridge, William A. Kittredge, Lemuel Pomeroy, Jr., George McKnight, Justin Chapman, William W. Ward, Edward Goodrich, Daniel Goodrich, George Colt, Thaddeus Clapp, Peleg Blankinship, Mary Colt, Sophia Warner, Ann D. Childs, Mary W. Childs, Clarissa Lathrop, Cordelia Johnson, C. Colt, Elizabeth Goodrich, Huldah Goodrich, Edith Powell, Chester Woodworth, Levi Thomas, Charles J. Fox Allen, Aurelia Hollister, Newell, Clarissa Strong, Sophronia Kitteridge, —— Beebe, Maria Center, Abigail Ayres, Cordelia Blankinship.

There is no mention of the establishment of a Sunday-school in the church-records, but the following paragraph occurs in an article upon "The Sabbath-school in Pittsfield," published in the *Sun*, of November 15, 1820: "This is the fourth season of the Sunday-school in this town, and in view of the exertions which have been made, and the good success which has attended them, all who wish well to the rising generation, who seek the welfare of society, or who pray for the prosperity of Zion, have abundant cause to thank God and take courage. It is a pleasant part of our duty to give a short abstract of the doings of the school. The whole number of verses, from the Bible, committed to memory, is thirty-three thousand three hundred and fifty-nine; verses of hymns, eight thousand six hundred and twenty-eight; and of answers in catechisms, twelve thousand seven hundred and twenty;

expressed peculiar satisfaction with the Young Ladies' Benevolent Society, which consisted of eighteen or twenty members, who had for more than two years devoted one afternoon or evening in each week to labor, principally with the needle, for charitable purposes; the product of the year 1820 being more than one hundred dollars. The treasurers' reports of both societies were such as to call for the speaker's congratulations.

Soon all was working smoothly, and success crowned every form of pastoral labor. Old wounds began to heal, and the congregation became organically one.

Among the measures adopted by Mr. Humphrey in doing away with prejudice against the church and parish of which he was the pastor, two are especially noteworthy, as illustrative of Mr. Humphrey's knowledge of men, and as showing how little his sense of right and expediency was obscured by the prestige of law or custom.

Shortly after his installation, discovering that several persons who did not attend upon his ministry—members of his parish by the law, but not by their own will—were assessed for his support; he directed the treasurer to remit their taxes, and charge the deficiency which would arise to his own account. He thus relates the incident in a discourse preached in 1855, and entitled "Pittsfield forty years ago:"

Not only were they taxable, but they were actually taxed, whether they ever attended worship with us or not. Some of their taxes may have been abated by the society's committee; although, if they were, I believe it was not till after I had called on the treasurer, Mr. Dickinson, when my salary became due at the end of the year, and requested him to strike off some twenty or thirty names from his tax-book, and charge me with the amount of their parish-taxes. I did this by no man's request, or suggestion; but because I thought it unwise, to say

making together fifty-six thousand seven hundred; which, supposing the number of scholars to be one hundred and seventy, gives an average to each of three hundred and twenty-nine. The greatest number committed by any one of the pupils is six thousand two hundred and seventeen; the next greatest is two thousand six hundred and eighty-three.

During Dr. Humphrey's pastorate there was also established the New Year's morning prayer-meeting, in which, to this day, the people of all the Protestant denominations in Pittsfield, unite at sunrise on the first day of every year, in the First Congregational Church, and which is always an occasion of the deepest interest.

the least, for the parish to press the collection. The sums were generally small, to be sure, but large enough to give plausibility to the complaints which some, who did not attend our meeting were sure to make. In this way, I believe, everything on that score was kept quiet throughout the town.

A similar disposition is shown in the following letter, which we copy from the town-records:

To the Congregational Parish in Pittsfield—Gentlemen:
In consideration of the scarcity of money, together with the contemplated extra expenses of the society this season—and to give you a new proof that I "seek not yours, but you,"—I hereby tender you the relinquishment, for the current year, of *seventy-five* dollars of my stipulated salary. I should have said *one hundred;* but I thought it would be doing more good with a little, to reserve *twenty-five* dollars, for the benefit of such as may be unable to pay their parish-tax ; and for this last sum I shall hold myself accountable in my annual settlement with your treasurer.

Wishing you every temporal and spiritual blessing, I am, gentlemen, with great respect, your servant in the gospel of Christ.
HEMAN HUMPHREY.
PITTSFIELD, April 16, 1821.

By acts like these, Mr. Humphrey secured among the people a large measure of added respect both for himself and his office. The assessment of taxes for the support of public worship upon non-attendants, had long been a source of complaint and vexation ; and their relinquishment, in 1818, by the new minister, must have contributed not a little to the harmony of the town, while, by removing the odium which attached to their collection, he broke down a barrier which would have obstructed the approaches by which he hoped to bring back some to the fold from which they had strayed.

The other religious parishes in Pittsfield had not profited, as might have been expected, from the troubles of the Congregationalists. They were indeed proportionately more feeble than they were at the opening of the century. At one time, indeed, in the course of the controversy, it seemed likely to result in the establishment of an Episcopalian parish, but the opportunity passed; the return of Mr. Van Schaack to New York, left that denomination without a local leader, and some who had been prominently associated with him became members of Union Parish, and through that door, finally entered the First Congregational Church. The Methodists, who had flourished for a time, had been weakened by dissensions among themselves; and, although they had begun, under the pastorate of Mr. Hibbard and others, to recover their prosperity, had not fully regained their strength. The Shakers do not seem to have obtained any considerable number of proselytes since 1796, to compensate for their natural decrease.

Doctor Humphrey, in the address before mentioned, describes the condition of the several religious denominations of the town, as follows:

Of the Baptists there was a respectable society in the west part of the town; but Elder John Francis had been dead four years, and they remained vacant about nine. Having no meeting-house as yet, of their own, they commonly worshipped in the school-house, and sometimes in the Methodist meeting-house, which stood not far from where Mr. Josiah Francis then lived.

There was a considerable number of Methodist farmers, residing chiefly in the West Part. Then, or soon after, there were two branches of that church: the Primitive Wesleyans and the Independents.[1]

The former worshiped in the meeting-house I have just mentioned, and the seceders in another place farther on towards the mountains. Methodist meetings were also held from time to time, by appointment, in the old school-house, at the east end of the village.

The great body of the people were Congregationalists. In the *village*, there was not, so far as I could find, a single Episcopalian, or Baptist. As well as I can now remember, Elder Green (who lived near the corner of Newell and Elm streets) was the only Methodist; and he could hardly be said to live in the village.

Such were the little parishes to which Mr. Humphrey was neighbor, in his ministry of six years with the Congregationalists of Pittsfield.

In that period, some material changes were made in the condition of those parishes, and events of surpassing interest occurred in the history of his own church. The chief among the latter was the first and most remarkable general revival which was ever known in the town. We condense an account from the "Memorial Sketches."

[1] Rev. Mr. Hibbard, who must have been well informed, states that the division of the Methodists took place prior to 1812, and began to be healed as early as 1814, at least.

In the spring of 1820, revivals occurred in neighboring villages, and the church in Pittsfield was roused to special prayer. The sacrament of the Lord's supper, in May, was celebrated with unusual solemnity. A deep religious interest prevailed during the summer, and resulted in the addition of forty members to the church, in autumn.

The next May, Rev. Asahel Nettleton, the celebrated evangelist, worn down by his exhausting labors, sought rest in a visit to Mr. Humphrey. A general desire to hear him, arose, of course ; and, finally yielding to it, he saw such signs of encouragement as brought his rest to a speedy end. Says Dr. Humphrey:

In two or three weeks we had unmistakable evidence that God had begun to revive His work. Our lecture-room was crowded; men were there who had not been wont to attend our evening meetings, and there was a very marked solemnity in the congregation on the Sabbath. Through the whole month of June, the interest increased among all classes; toward the close, very rapidly. By the middle of July, the work was at its height. It pervaded all classes, and extended to all parts of the town; but principally affected heads of families, and particularly the prominent men of the village. The whole face of the community was changed. Religion was the all-absorbing topic of conversation. The revival continued all summer. On the first Sabbath of November, the harvest was gathered in ; and a glorious harvest it was. Between eighty and ninety, the rich and the poor, the high and the low, stood up together in the long, broad aisle, and before angels and men, avouched the Lord to be their God, and were received into the Church. Never had such a scene been witnessed in Pittsfield. The joy of the Church overflowed in tears and thanksgiving. I am sure there must have been great joy in Heaven.

" Great care," say the authors of the sketches, "was taken in the instruction of the converts of this revival; and they, with their children have been among the most honored members of the church, to the present day."

Among the results of the deep religious feeling at this time, and of the teachings which it inclined the people to receive favorably, was a very marked change in the tone of society, producing a great restriction of the latitude previously allowed in manners and customs, especially those relating to social life and amusements. In the excitements and new emotions arising from the intensity of this revival, there was also lost the last traces of those feuds which had agitated the church in Pittsfield for half a century, and which otherwise might have lingered for years.

One incident occurred in connection with this revival, which is curiously illustrative of prevailing modes of thought, and of a peculiar antagonism of opinion, which was also developed in another form in the constitutional convention which had just closed its session.

Dr. Humphrey believed that it was essential in order to continue and deepen the religious interest which prevailed, that all secular excitements should be suspended, and that so far as possible, the town should maintain the solemnity and quiet of the Sabbath. He was indignant that this favorable condition was, against his remonstrance, interrupted by a spirited celebration of the Masonic Festival of St. John the Baptist, by Mystic Lodge, on the 26th of June, when an eloquent address was delivered by Rev. Hooper Cumming, D. D., of Albany, after which the Lodge marched in procession to Center's coffee-house, where they dined with the usual festal accompaniments. He determined, however, to substitute for the ordinary celebration of the Fourth of July, solemn religious services. Among the subjects of the revival were most of the elder citizens, whose influence had hitherto been preponderating; and through them, and by his own efforts, Dr. Humphrey was able to induce the committee of arrangements to assent to his proposition. In the *Sun* of June 27th, therefore, the following announcement appeared:

Information having been communicated by the committee of arrangements for the celebration of the NATIONAL JUBILEE, that the celebration will this year be dispensed with, the public are informed that the day will be devoted to the worship of ALMIGHTY GOD. The ringing of the bell at sunrise will be the signal for a prayer-meeting at the lecture-room. At two o'clock in the afternoon, public worship will be attended at the meeting-house, where a sermon will be delivered. Our fellow-citizens of the adjacent towns are affectionately invited to Pittsfield, to join in the exercises. As this joyous anniversary has never returned to the free inhabitants of our beloved country under more auspicious circumstances, whether we regard the civil or religious aspect of things, and, as the lapse of another year has been replete with the manifestations of Divine favor to our own town, it is confidently believed that every grateful heart will be disposed to pay its thanksgiving to God for past mercies, and to pray for the continuance of them.

This announcement was not at all agreeable to a considerable number of the citizens of the town. The celebration of Independence Day, was at that era invariably observed in all towns of the size and character of Pittsfield; and the programme of exercises was almost as well fixed by custom as those of the Sabbath. The ringing of the bells, and the salutes of artillery at sunrise and sunset, the procession, the reading of the Declaration of Independence, the oration, with the accompanying prayer and singing, never failed. The orations were frequently published, and the toasts always. In fact, selections from the most brilliant of these intellectual scintillations at the celebrations in different towns and cities sparkled in the columns of the newspapers for weeks after the great day. To the younger portion of the community, the Fourth of July afforded the happiest hours of the year; and by many of the older generation, with whom the traditions of the revolution were yet fresh, it was observed as their political Sabbath. In June, 1821, the press throughout the country expressed a pleasing expectation of unusual spirit in the approaching celebration of Independence Day; and it held up as a good example, the city of Washington where John Quincy Adams was to read the declaration, and William Wirt was to pronounce the oration. A large number of the citizens of Pittsfield were unwilling to forego the realization of these pleasant anticipations, and notwithstanding the assent of the regular committee to the request of Dr. Humphrey, they resolved to celebrate the anniversary, as the *Sun* put it, "with those demonstrations of joy which become a truly free, patriotic and grateful community."

There were the usual salutes and bell-ringing at sunrise; and at 12 o'clock, a procession with martial music and a military escort. The exercises were at the meeting-house, but Mr. Humphrey declined to act as chaplain, and Rev. Robert Green " made an appropriate and patriotic address to the Throne of Grace," Major S. M. McKay read the Declaration of Independence, and Henry K. Strong, principal of the academy, pronounced an oration, after which the procession returned to the hotel.

"As the hour for the celebration of a solemn and religious character was to commence," said the *Sun* in its report, "had arrived, the committee of arrangements gave notice to their elder fellow-citizens, many of whom had joined in the procession, that the dinner would not be served up until after the religious exercises were closed; so that all who might wish should have an opportunity to attend without interruption." The exercises in the church were attended by a solemn and reverent congregation. Mr. Humphrey made an impressive introductory prayer and delivered a sermon of remarkable power from the text, "If the Son, therefore, shall make you free, ye shall be free indeed." John viii : 36.

Unfortunately the meeting-house was situated upon the little public square in whose circumscribed space it was the custom for the people of all classes to assemble on all anniversaries and other exciting occasions, and around which were located the three principal hotels of the town—the largest within a few feet of the meeting-house. It was especially the place of assemblage on the Fourth of July, and at cattle-shows. And on this occasion the usual Fourth of July crowd was gathered upon it, making the usual noises with Chinese crackers, drums, and all the instruments which make that day hideous to sensitive ears. Besides this, the Flood-wood company of militia, which had begun to celebrate the anniversary in the manner inevitable before the temperance reform, and not altogether disused since, paraded, and after marching as well as they were able around the square, proceeded, with the insolence of intoxication, to pass with drums beating and fifes screaming through the tower under the belfry of the meeting-house.

The character of the gentlemen engaged in the secular celebration forbids the belief that they gave countenance to these acts; and we have the word of those whose word was never impeached, that they did not. Mr. Humphrey, however, believed that the disturbance was incited by them, and in his indignation prolonged the services to an unusual length; upon which the committee of arrangements, in their turn provoked, ordered the dinner to proceed with the ordinary salutes by cannon, at the close of each regular toast. The cannon were of necessity placed within less than a hundred feet of the meeting-house, and the result was a complication which produced a remarkable and memorable scene within. Doctor Humphrey, fifty years afterwards, gave the following account of it:

The first discharge shook the house. My text was, "*If the Son make you free, ye shall be free indeed.*" It was one of the most appropriate I could think of for the occasion. In two or three minutes, there was another discharge. The shock of the first being over, the second produced a solemnity more profound than the sermon would have occasioned, and gave me opportunity for enlargement which I had not anticipated. I had reached the application of my sermon. By the time of the third discharge, the whole congregation seemed perfectly composed. As the cannonading went on, I took occasion to hold up the contrast of Christ's freemen and the servants of Satan, as strikingly illustrated both without and within the house. By this train of extempore remark I added something like a quarter of an hour to the length of the sermon. Each discharge of the cannon overpowered my voice for a moment, but I went on. When I had finished, I called upon Rev. Dr. Shepard, of Lenox, who was present to lead in prayer. His remarkably heavy voice sounded triumphantly over the disturbance. When we came out, some of the more prominent men, among whom was the sheriff of the county, were very much excited, and proposed to have the leading rioters arrested and punished. I said, " By no means. In attacking us they have shot themselves through and through. They have so outraged the feelings of the whole community that we have only to leave them to themselves, and go on with our Master's work, praying God to give them repentance."

I have never witnessed a more striking example of the moral sublime than on that day and evening. Those who had been foremost in the disturbance hastened away as soon as they could. By eight o'clock there was scarcely a soul left upon the green; whereas, on all former like occasions, a large number lingered there and kept up their "celebration" until late at night. The evening lecture, which had been appointed from the desk under the cannon's roar, was unusually full and solemn. The work went on for some days with more power than ever. We had but to "stand still and see the salvation of the Lord."

A writer in the Charleston (S. C.) *Intelligencer* thus closes a description of the scene :

I sat near the Rev. Mr. Nettleton ; and so delighted was he with the discourse and so accurately prescient, too, was he of the result, that whenever an apt allusion dropped from the lips of the preacher, he would turn round with a holy smile ; and whenever a shot from the cannon pierced our ears he would say—it would involuntarily escape from him—" *that is good—that is good.*" Speaking afterwards of the events of this day he observed to me: "Did you not feel calm ? I thought there was a deep majestic calm overspreading the minds of Christians."

But whatever may have been Doctor Humphrey's views of the importance of preserving this day sacred to religious impressions, and whatever may be now thought upon that point, it must be conceded that the gentlemen who then differed with him, and persisted in celebrating the day as they and their fathers had done, year after year, for nearly half a century, could not justly be classed with the riotous militia which with drum and fife wantonly disturbed the exercises in the meeting-house. They, voluntarily, it will be observed, intermitted their celebration while those exercises were in progress, postponing their dinner until an unusually late hour in order that they might not be interrupted; for the firing of cannon occurred only after the sermon had been protracted to an extreme length which exhausted their patience. The term young men, applied to them, is liable to mislead. The president at the dinner was Timothy Childs, Esq., who shortly after was elected to congress from the Rochester, New York, district. The reader of the declaration, Major S. M. McKay, had represented the town in the legislature, and among those associated with them were Jonathan Yale Clark and Dr. H. H. Childs, two of the three gentlemen whom the town had the year before chosen as its delegates to the convention for the revision of the state constitution, and the latter of whom the next year founded the Berkshire Medical College; William C. Jarvis, who represented the town that year and the three succeeding years in the legislature, who had just won a high reputation as an author by the publication of an excellent treatise upon political economy, and who in 1822, was a leading candidate for congress; Henry Hubbard, who seven years before had represented Lanesboro, Dr. A. P. Merrill of the United States army, and others of like character were also of the party.

It was, they averred, no hostility to religion which impelled them to the course they pursued; but that they regarded such patriotic demonstrations as entirely consistent with it, and unprejudicial to healthy religious feeling. From circumstances not peculiar to Pittsfield, but which pervaded all Massachusetts, many of them were at the time in a mood to vigorously resist what they considered clerical dictation, especially when it called upon them to give up observances which they so warmly cherished. The Free Masons had manifested the same spirit, the previous week, when the orator previously engaged for St. John's day having been persuaded to break his appointment—members of that body went to Albany, and engaging Dr. Cumming, an orator whose eloquence is compared favorably with that of Edward Everett, brought him by fresh relays of horses to Pittsfield, just in season for the hour announced.

The celebrators of the Fourth put their views of it upon record in the toasts which were published in the *Sun's* report of the occasion, which was headed: "*The Day of Jubilee has Come and Flown.*"

Among the regular toasts the sixth reads:

Religion and Patriotism—They are not incompatible, and may the political Sabbath of our country be celebrated, solemnized, as the dictates of good and honest men may incline them. The seventh was: *Religious Liberty*—without which freedom is but a name. Among the volunteer sentiments were these:

By Levi Goodrich—The Rev. Mr. Green, chaplain of the day: may his " last days be his best days."

By Jonathan Yale Clark—Our national birthday: When the sons of America shall neglect to commemorate it, or to celebrate the memory of those who achieved it, then let nettles grow instead of wheat and cockles instead of barley.

By Spencer Clark—Due respect to our brethren not in unison with us this day; may they never cherish a hope to deprive us of a celebration sealed with the blood of our ancestors.

By Henry Hubbard, Esq.—Religion: While it nerved the arm of our fathers to fight for freedom, it cannot silence the voice of praise in their sons.

By Nelson Strong—The celebration of this anniversary: It teaches those tyrants who would clip the wings of our American eagle, we prize our privileges, we love our country.

By Arnold Bentley—Liberty, which was bequeathed to us, sealed by the blood of the fallen heroes of the revolution : may it not be abridged by priest-craft, nor trampled upon by a foreign despot.

By Major S. M. McKay—The fundamental principle of civil and religious liberty: The undisturbed enjoyment of civil and religious opinions.

These opinions are more definitely expressed in a card published in the *Sun*, of July 11th, which reads as follows:

OUR NATIONAL BIRTHDAY.

As our independence was achieved at the risk of everything dear to the American people; and as it has been the advice of our political patriarchs, as well as the undeviating practice of the friends of the American republic, to celebrate the return of its anniversary with decent and suitable demonstrations of rejoicing; it was resolved, at a meeting of citizens of Pittsfield, and the neighboring towns, assembled at the hotel on the afternoon of the 4th current, not to abandon, on any future anniversary, the wise precepts and practice of the best men who ever adorned this, or any other, country.

Influenced by these views, it was resolved by the meeting, that the earliest moment should be embraced to give publicity to its determination to celebrate the next anniversary of our national independence with the suitable and customary demonstrations of joy and national festivity.

To carry this laudable design into full effect, a committee was chosen, of which the following were the Pittsfield members: Henry H. Childs, Joshua Danforth, Samuel M. McKay, Jonathan Yale Clark, John Churchill, Robert Stanton, Jonathan Allen, Jonathan Allen, 2d, Phinehas Allen, Oren Goodrich, William C. Jarvis and John Dickinson. George N. Briggs was the member from Adams.

It will be perceived that a very respectable minority of Mr. Humphrey's parish differed with him in regard to the propriety of omitting the celebration of the Fourth, even in the peculiar season during which that of 1821 occurred. Few of them, however, relaxed their friendship for him on that account, and some of them became members of the church during the revival then in progress.

In addition to his strictly pastoral duties, Mr. Humphrey took a sincere and active interest in the secular well-being of the town and parish. Many of the alterations and repairs of the meeting-house were due to his influence; and so, to some extent, was the improvement in church-music, and the gift by Joseph Shearer of a town-clock. He was active in the management of the common schools, the academies and the library. He was one of the original trustees of the medical college, and gave it his aid in its most trying days. He was also among the foremost in giving to the village those avenues of elms and maples which are now the pride of its finest streets; some of which he planted with his own hand.

In the midst of a life and labors like these, Mr. Humphrey was, in July, 1823, elected president of the Collegiate Institution, which afterwards became Amherst College. This institution was at that time held in the deepest disfavor by the people of Pittsfield and Berkshire county, who had for years been desperately resisting the attempts of its friends to build it up by taking away Williams College from the spot where its founder had fixed it, and joining it with their own school at some point in the valley of the Connecticut; Northampton and Amherst being most prominently suggested. These attempts were denounced by the press of Berkshire as neither honest or generous, and the strongest resentment against their authors prevailed throughout the county. This feeling was intensified when, in 1821, Rev. Dr. Moore, the second president of Williams, and some of its professors were induced to resign their positions to accept similar ones at Amherst.

Dr. Moore died in June, 1823, and the proposition to fill his place by the removal of the able and beloved Pittsfield pastor, from the field in which he was so eminently useful, and in which it would be so difficult to provide a competent successor, roused all the old feeling into full life. Nor even if the call had been to a field upon which they looked with more favor, would the people of Pittsfield have considered the removal of Mr. Humphrey as justifiable. It did not seem that any other could present claims like those of the parish in which he had accomplished, and was accomplishing, so much good. Men of all denominations, who had the interests of the church and the town at heart, learned with unbounded regret that he was considering the question of accepting the call to Amherst. They feared that some of the moral evils which had been checked, but not destroyed, would revive if the champion, who held them in control, left his guard. The Congregationalists, whose union under his ministrations, had imperceptibly become amalgamation, did not feel themselves as yet in a condition to part with the physician who had healed them more perfectly than they knew. An extraordinary number of new converts seemed to have an especial need of, and claim upon, his fostering care, and certainly regarded him with the greatest affection. In the year 1821, fifty members had been added to the church; in 1822, there had been a hundred and twenty, and a few others had been received in 1823. More than a hundred and fifty neophytes in religion demanded his training and guidance. If he should remain, how many more might there be; if he left, how many of these might backslide. "I felt," said he, fifty years afterwards, "that this large increase of new members brought upon me a heavy weight of pastoral responsibility; and I tried,

in my poor imperfect way, to meet it as well as I could. After
that, no people, perhaps, ever enjoyed a greater quietness than
we did. And I said: 'I shall die in my nest.' How could I be
lured from it? Least of all, when there was no storm, how could
I shake myself out of it? But it is not in man to mark out his
own destiny; and when he thinks himself most securely an-
chored, he may be nearest being drawn out to sea."

The position at Amherst, to which Mr. Humphrey was invited,
was not more alluring to him, upon a superficial view, than it
was agreeable to his parish for him to accept it.

The Collegiate Institution was, with many enemies and few
friends, struggling to raise itself to the rank of a college. Its
application to the legislature for permission to assume that character had just been refused. It was barely living on under an
old charter as an academy: doing the work of a college, and giving to its students, so far as its scanty means enabled it, a collegiate education; but with no authority to confer degrees. To
become its official head, was to challenge even more arduous
labors, and more discouraging difficulties, than the president-elect
had encountered either at Fairfield or Pittsfield, and that with
far less assurance of success, and far less of the sympathy of his
brethren in the ministry. But Mr. Humphrey seems to have
found a potent fascination in such encounters; and, moreover,
dreaded that, in declining them, he might be opposing the Divine
will. He was, at all events, not the man to shun, through cow-
ardice, the place to which he believed himself divinely appointed.

The question of duty was nevertheless far from clear, and the
arguments for going to Amherst were very nearly balanced in
his mind by those for remaining in Pittsfield. He thus states
his position in his Half-Century discourse:

> I must either say yes or no, which I did not dare to do on my own
> unsupported responsibility. It might be my duty to go and it might
> be my duty to stay: which, I could not decide, though my friends here
> thought the case perfectly plain. I was greatly perplexed; and more
> and more so, as I tried to weigh the reasons for and against. At length,
> after much and prayerful consideration, I came to the conclusion that I
> ought, in a regular way, to submit the question to an ecclesiastical coun-
> cil for advice. This, my friends strenuously opposed. They still insist-
> ed: It can't be your duty to do any such thing. We can't consent
> to help you off in any way. If you go the burden will be greater than

you can bear, and you will sink into the grave under it. Why should you run such a risk? Why give up a certainty for an uncertainty; or rather for a certain failure?

But neither these nor other reasons urged by his reluctant parishioners seemed to Mr. Humphrey conclusive against his asking the church to unite with him in calling a council. "I did so ask," his account continues, "proposing to submit the whole matter to them and abide their decision. They utterly declined: saying, they saw no reason for it, and I must take the entire responsibility of calling it, if I insisted upon such a reference. This increased my perplexity, but did not satisfy me that I ought to let the matter drop there. I wanted the advice of my brethren in the neighborhood. I called a council, laid the matter before them as well as I could, and was dismissed."

The records of the church do not perfectly accord with this account, and we give an abstract of the story as there given, partly to show what liability to error there is in the memory of the most clear-headed men, earnestly desiring to relate correctly matters likely to impress themselves most deeply and permanently on their minds. Mr. Humphrey's request for the church and society to unite with him in the call for a council was laid before the church on the 27th of August; and action upon it postponed to September 3d, in order to enable the society to take precedence in it. At the adjourned meeting, the parish having declined to join in the call, the church concurred. On the 18th of September, however, Mr. Humphrey renewed the subject by the following communication:

To the Congregational Church and Society in Pittsfield:

GENTLEMEN:—Since my last communication on the subject of my removal nothing has occurred to alter the result of my enquiries and reflections, in regard to the path of duty. I still think that the call from the Institution in Amherst is one which I ought to comply with, provided I can obtain your consent for a dismission from my present ministerial charge. This, therefore, is to request that you will, through your respective committees, unite with me in calling a council of pastors and delegates to dissolve the connection now subsisting between us, according to the usages of our churches in similar cases.

Wishing you the Divine guidance and blessing, I am, gentlemen,
Your Affectionate Pastor,
H. HUMPHREY.

Upon the receipt of this communication both the church and the parish voted to unite in calling the council and appointed a joint committee for that purpose, consisting of Deacon Josiah Bissell, and Capt. Joseph Merrick, on the part of the church, and of Samuel M. McKay, Esq., Hon. Phinehas Allen, and Hon. John C. Williams on the part of the parish. The council met on the 3d of October, and approving Dr. Humphrey's purpose of accepting the Amherst presidency, dissolved his connection with the church in Pittsfield.

"Nothing now remained," says Dr. Humphrey, "but to make arrangements for my removal, and to take those sad farewells, which cost me more anguish of soul than anything in my long life, except the loss of children." These farewells over, he removed to Amherst and was inducted into office, October 15, 1823.

At Amherst his labors were more arduous; and his wisdom and success, if not greater, were more conspicuous than even in Pittsfield. They are too familiar to need repetition here; but a curious instance of his jealous regard for the rights of the college, whose building-up was the crowning glory of his life, is found in the Pittsfield town-records, and is worth preserving. He was taxed upon a little real estate which he retained here, after his removal. The assessment was, in itself, inconsiderable, the aggregate for three years being only twenty-four dollars. But among the persons entirely exempt from taxes, by the laws of Massachusetts, were the presidents, professors, and students of Harvard and Williams Colleges. President Humphrey was struggling to establish a perfect equality of Amherst with the elder colleges; and he conceived that the charter of Amherst, granting to it privileges and immunities usually enjoyed by similar institutions, extended to it their exemption from taxation. He therefore refused payment to the Pittsfield collector, as a matter of principle and precedent. The town, perhaps, still a little vexed at the institution which had robbed it of its pastor, insisted upon the tax; and the matter being referred to arbitrators, it was found that the privilege claimed was strictly confined to the colleges named in the law. The legislature, by some oversight failed to insert it among the immunities specially granted in the charter of Amherst. The tax was therefore paid, and a remedy for the inequality obtained by a supplementary enactment.

While Mr. Humphrey was considering the invitation to Amherst, he received the degree of Doctor of Divinity from Middlebury College. In 1846, Yale College conferred upon him the further degree of Doctor of Laws.

Having resigned the presidency of Amherst College in 1845, leaving it among the leading institutions of learning in the country, Dr. Humphrey showed the strength and permanence of his affection for the people of his old charge by returning to Pittsfield, to spend the evening of his days among them. He was then but sixty-six years old, and for seventeen years he contributed his counsel and aid, with all the ardor, and almost with the vigor of his youth, to every enterprise, religious or secular, which was proposed for the good of the town. Having thus lived, beloved and venerated, until the year 1861, he died on the 3d of April; and, on the 8th was buried in the beautiful cemetery, which from the day when he took part in its consecration, he had loved to contemplate as his last resting-place.

CHAPTER XIV.

CONSTITUTIONAL CONVENTION OF 1820—AMENDMENT TO THE THIRD ARTICLE OF THE BILL OF RIGHTS—ABOLITION OF SEATING THE MEETING-HOUSE.

[1820-1836.]

Opinions and votes of Pittsfield regarding the convention—Equality of religious sects before the law—Amendment of the bill of rights offered and advocated by Hon. H. H. Childs — Rejected by the convention — Senatorial apportionment upon a property-basis—Changes in the political-year—Vote of Pittsfield on the several amendments—Reforms in the constitution finally obtained—Curious advertisement of Sylvester Rathbun as Methodist committee-man—Legislative action upon the amendment of the bill of rights—Proposition to change the pews in the meeting-house into slips and to abolish the seating-system — Doctor Humphrey's description of the old system—Names of seating-committees from 1790 to 1830—Evils of the seating-system—Plans for change—Change effected.

THE old difficulties and discontent caused by the preference given by the laws of Massachusetts to societies professing the Congregational faith, and the taxes laid for the support of public worship, continued to disturb religious harmony in Pittsfield, and through nearly all the towns of the commonwealth until the year 1834. In Pittsfield a considerable portion of the Congregationalists, especially those of the democratic party, agreed with members of other denominations in considering the law unjust and impolitic; inconsistent with American institutions, and detrimental to the true interests of the religion which it was intended to protect. In this view the pastor of the church, in 1818, seemed, at least partially, to concur.

Two years afterwards, in 1820, the question whether a convention should be held to revise the Bill of Rights and Constitution of the State was submitted to the people; and Pittsfield gave a hundred and sixteen affirmative votes, with none in the negative.

Very diverse feelings prevailed in different towns in regard to this subject. Thus in Stockbridge there was little or no interest taken in it, while Great Barrington threw twelve yeas to a hundred and three nays; and a similar diversity appeared in the votes of other towns without any obvious reason for it. In the entire state eleven thousand seven hundred and fifty-six votes were given in the affirmative; six thousand five hundred and ninety-three in the negative. In Suffolk county, the vote was twenty-one to one in favor of calling the convention. In Berkshire two to one. Very different views were also entertained by those who agreed that the convention ought to be held, as to the character of the changes which it ought to make. Thus Boston and Pittsfield, which were among the towns giving the largest affirmative majorities, were governed by precisely opposite opinions in regard to the necessity of making radical alterations in the organic laws of the state. Daniel Webster, who was a member of the convention, thought, with his conservative friends, "that it should have a view to the permanency of the constitution, and it would be necessary to change it only for practical purposes. It has been found, in the practice of forty years, that it had served to protect all the essential rights of the citizens; that the great outlines were so established as to need no alteration."

The majority of the people of Pittsfield, on the other hand considered several provisions of the constitution subversive of natural right, and inconsistent with republican institutions. Chief among the obnoxious clauses whose reform, they asked from the convention, were the third article of the Declaration of Rights—under which the laws providing for the support of public worship were framed—and the article in the constitution which required that the General Court, in fixing the number of senators to which the districts should be respectively entitled should be governed by the proportion of taxes paid by the respective districts.

Under the latter article it was found that the county of Suffolk was entitled to one senator for every seven thousand and five hundred of its inhabitants, while the county of Berkshire had only one for every twenty thousand; which was "deemed a gross and cruel inequality." The *Sun* cited the case of an individual in Boston whose property of one million three hundred thousand dollars, had as much representation in the senate as thirteen hundred independent Berkshire farmers with a property of one thousand dollars each.

The democratic instincts of Pittsfield revolted against these and some other provisions of the constitution which seemed to favor particular classes; and, to carry out their views in the convention the people chose Hon. Nathan Willis, Dr. H. H. Childs and Mr. Jonathan Yale Clark, as their delegates.

The convention met, November 15th; and the question of an amendment of the third article in the Bill of Rights came up for consideration on the 20th of December, when Mr. Phelps of Chester offered a substitute, doing away with all interference on the part of the state with religious affairs other than to protect all sects and persons in the free exercise of their respective modes of worship. Mr. Saltonstall, of Salem, moved a resolution that it was not expedient to make any change in the article except to insert the word "Christian" instead of "Protestant." Between these extremes Dr. Childs proposed to amend the article as follows:

As the happiness of a people and the good order and preservation of civil government, essentially depend upon piety, religion and morality, and as these cannot be generally diffused through a community but by the institution of the public worship of God; and, as it is the inalienable right of every man to render that worship in the mode most consistent with the dictates of his own conscience, no person shall by law be compelled to join, or support, nor be classed with, or associated to, any congregation or religious society whatever. But every person now belonging to any religious society, whether incorporated or unincorporated, shall be considered a member thereof until he shall have separated himself therefrom in the manner hereinafter provided.

And each and every society, or denomination, of Christians in this state shall have and enjoy the same and equal powers, rights and privileges; and shall have power and authority to raise money for the support and maintenance of religious teachers of their respective denominations, and to build and repair houses of public worship, by a tax on the members of any such society only, to be laid by a major vote of the legal voters assembled at any society-meeting, warned and held according to law.

Provided, nevertheless, That if any person shall choose to separate himself from the society or denomination to which he may belong, and shall join himself to another society of the same, or a different, denomination, he shall leave a written notice thereof with the clerk of such society, and shall thereupon be no longer liable for any further expenses which may be incurred by said society.

And every denomination of Christians, demeaning themselves peaceably, and as good citizens of the commonwealth, shall be equally under the protection of the law. And no subordination of one sect, or denomination, to another, shall ever be established by law.

Dr. Childs subsequently stated that the reason why he was the mover of this resolution was that Rev. Thomas Baldwin, D. D., who was a member of the committee, and had proposed making a motion of similar import, was not in his seat when the subject came up in convention. But, Mr. Phelps withdrawing his proposition, the amendment offered by Dr. Childs was vigorously and ably supported by Dr. Baldwin, Levi Lincoln of Worcester, and other gentlemen of liberal views. Dr. Childs, himself, advocated it to the end with characteristic ardor and no little parliamentary ability. He was, however, met by such leaders of the opposition as Daniel Webster, Samuel Hoar and Josiah Quincy, and, with the conservative sentiment of the convention also arrayed against him, his effort was from the first almost hopeless. Although the liberty he asked in religious matters for the people of the country had long been enjoyed by the citizens of Boston, Salem and Newburyport, they feared to extend it to the people of the country. Perfectly efficient and satisfactory as the voluntary system, in their hands, had proved for the support of public worship, the delegates from the favored towns, with some honorable exceptions, and the conservatives of the interior dared not trust the free-will contributions of country Christians for the support of their own institutions of religion. Indeed, the whole tone of the speakers who opposed a change in the third article indicated that they considered the friends of the voluntary system as the enemies of all religion, and believed that the success of their proposition would result in the decay of all the churches, and the spread of infidelity and immorality throughout the state. And they were followed in these opinions by a majority of the delegates from the country-towns themselves; and among the rest by Nathan Willis, who certainly acted in this instance contrary to the wishes of a majority of his constituents.

The discussion was prolonged, and became probably the most excited which took place in the convention. Many amendments to Dr. Childs's propositions were offered; but it was finally submitted to a vote in a new draft made by himself, the variations being hardly more than verbal. It was rejected by a vote of one hundred and thirty-six yeas to two hundred nays; General Willis voting in the negative.

The amendment of the third article of the Bill of Rights which the convention finally submitted to the people, made substantially the same provision as to the mode of supporting public worship as already governed legislation in practice.

Dr. Childs and Mr. Clark united heartily with the other liberal members of the convention in their effort to make persons instead of property the basis of representation in the senate. But here again the conservative element proved too powerful for them. The reform was rejected by a vote of one hundred and forty-seven to two hundred and forty-five; General Willis not voting.

Among the alterations in the constitution desired by Pittsfield, in common with other country-towns, was one making the first Wednesday of January the beginning of the political year, and substituting a single session of the General Court in winter for one in the spring and fall respectively: and this amendment was submitted to the people and adopted.

Fourteen articles of amendment were submitted to the people for ratification; and a committee of twenty-eight members, of whom General Willis was one, was appointed to meet on the fourth Wednesday of May, 1821, to ascertain the result.

In the Pittsfield town-meeting the feeble amendment to the third article of the Bill of Rights received but eight ayes, to a hundred and eighty-five nays. The amendment regarding the basis of representation in the senate, although somewhat modified from its first·extreme inequality, was still so unsatisfactory that not a single vote was cast in its favor, while two hundred and six were cast in opposition.

A similar temper was shown by the votes thrown upon all the amendments submitted.

On the count of the vote of the entire state it was found that the amendment of the third article of the Bill of Rights, and the article in the constitution concerning the appointment of senators were both defeated; those in favor of reforming those articles altogether, voting against the amendments, together with those who were opposed to any change. The amendment regarding the alteration in the beginning of the political year was also rejected; but was finally secured in 1831.

After a while, also, the public sentiment of the state, as usual, overtook that of Pittsfield, in regard to the other proposed liberal reforms. In November, 1833, the following amendment to the "third article," having obtained the requisite majorities in the legislature, was ratified by the people:

As the public worship of God, and instructions in piety, religion and morality promote the happiness and prosperity of a people, and the security of a republican government; therefore the several religious societies of this commonwealth, whether corporate or incorporate, at any meeting legally warned and holden for that purpose, shall have the right to elect their pastors or religious teachers, to contract with them for their support, to raise money for erecting and repairing houses for public worship, for the maintenance of religious instruction, and for the payment of necessary expenses; and all persons belonging to any religious society shall be taken and held to be members until they shall file with the clerk of such society a written notice declaring the dissolution of their membership, and thenceforth shall not be liable for any grant or contract which may be thereafter made or entered into by such society; and all religious sects and denominations, demeaning themselves peaceably, and as good citizens of the commonwealth, shall be equally under the protection of the law; and no subordination of any one sect or denomination to another shall ever be established by law.

The amendment was introduced in the legislature of 1832, by the presentation of sixty-five petitions in the house of representatives, on the third day of the session. A few days afterwards Jonathan Allen, 2d, one of the representatives from Pittsfield, introduced similar memorials from that town, signed by Jarvis C. Nichols, Robert Francis, and others. The amendment passed, after a sharp discussion, on the tenth of February, by a vote of three hundred and forty-seven to ninety, receiving the support of all the Pittsfield representatives: Nathan Willis (who had voted against it in convention), Thomas B. Strong, Jonathan Allen, 2d, and Jirah Stearns. In the senate, it received the requisite two-thirds vote, although the judiciary committee, to whom it was referred, reported, through its chairman, Hon. Leverett Saltonstall, that the change was "neither necessary or expedient."

When, having in like manner passed the ordeal of the second trial in the legislature of 1833, it was submitted to the people in

November of that year—it was adopted by the extraordinary vote of thirty-two thousand three hundred and twenty-four yeas, to three thousand two hundred and seventy-two nays: almost ten to one. So great had been the change in less than twelve years.

In 1840, by another amendment, the anomaly of a property-basis for representation in the senate was abolished and the senators were apportioned to the several districts according to their population.

The defeat of the expected reform of the inequality of different sects before the law created intense dissatisfaction among those who were not members of the standing-order, and they in Pittsfield, were loud in their denunciation of the delegate, who, differing from his colleagues, voted against it. The large number of Congregationalists who favored the change, and the fact that Dr. Childs, its champion on the floor of the convention, was of that faith, prevented the old angry division of the town upon the question. The irritated feeling of the dissenters was, however, manifested in various ways, and among others by the following advertisement, which was printed in the *Sun* of January, 1821, with a rude wood-cut of a man kneeling, with a chain around his neck, before another who held the other end:

To all whom it may concern: Having been informed, that there are many persons wishing to become members of the Methodist parish, and free themselves, as far as possible, from the oppression[1] of a religious persecution, which the intolerants of the late convention still think proper to advise the people to submit to; I therefore take this method of giving notice that I am legally authorized, by said parish, to give the necessary certificates of membership.

January 16th, 1821. SYLVESTER RATHBUN.

Upon the ratification of the amendment of 1833, the corporate connection of the Congregational society with the town of Pittsfield ceased; but under the operation of the law passed by the legislature of 1834, all persons previously connected with the parish continued to be so until they filed with the clerk a notice declaring the dissolution of his membership. It also retained all the rights, privileges and immunities which it had previously possessed, except such as were abrogated by the amendment, and the law explanatory of it.

[1] It will be remembered that the Methodist parish in Pittsfield had some important immunities and privileges by special charter.

While the effort to secure equality before the law for all religious denominations was going on, a similar endeavor for alterations in the First Parish meeting-house, in the interest of equality within that church, was also in progress.

The pews under the old plan were square and huge; "so that the congregation," said Dr. Humphrey, "might stare at one another instead of looking at the preacher; and high, square play-houses along the sides of the galleries above, were the seats of the children. The boys not content to be so shut up made good use of their penknives in opening such communications as suited their convenience." "It is true," he added, "we had tithing-men then, and they occasionally rapped in the midst of the sermon, and once in a while took a boy by the collar and marched him along to the tithing-man's seat, where he sat, casting an occasional stealthy sidelong glance at his playmates, who were enjoying his duress. It was a bad arrangement of the seats, above and below. But it was generally the same in other places; and there was one thing about it I liked: The aged were seated together nearest to the pulpit, where they could hear better than far down the aisles. It was pleasant for the preacher to see them sitting so near, under the droppings of the sanctuary."

But there were other circumstances than that named by Dr. Humphrey, which were considered by the committee in "seating the meeting-house;" and some of them did not command so unanimous an approval. There were taken into account, social standing, official position, professional occupation, wealth, and that indefinable combination of dress, bearing, and manner of living, which, under the name of "style," is peculiarly obnoxious to the jealousy of a large class in every village community. And it would be to attribute to the committees an almost miraculous exemption from human frailties, did we not add to the list of the considerations which might sometimes influence their allotment, favoritism and its reverse.

Embittered feeling and jealous heart-burnings, of course, arose from a custom like this; and would have done so if angelic wisdom and purity of purpose, instead of human imperfection, had made the assignment. Wounded sensitiveness often prevented the attendance of the more susceptible or irascible upon Divine service. The church-records contain many instances of discipline administered — and generally administered in vain — for the reclaiming of those who had abandoned both public worship and the communion, exasperated at what they deemed an unjust assignment of their places in the house of God. Frequently a pew was given to more of the class likely to be thus offended, than could be possibly be crowded into it; the committee remarking, "O, it won't matter, they never go to meeting, anyhow."

In the latter days of the system, however, more attention was given to attempts to satisfy all; and the committee gave notice, through the newspapers, asking all persons desirous of seats to specify those which they preferred. But, however sincere and painstaking in their efforts, it was obviously impossible to place every person where he wished to be, or to avoid giving offense to many.

Another evil arising from the old system was the separation of families; and this was specially connected with the huge square pews of which it was not practicable to give one to each family; as it is with the greater economy of space secured by the division of the floor into slips. Indeed, the old system of pews, and that of seating the congregation by a committee, were so inseparable, that it would have been very difficult to abolish the latter without changing the former.

With this statement of the evils connected with the interior arrangement of the meeting-house, the reader will be able to detect without special mention in each case, the reasons for the votes, and other town-action, by which improvement was sought.

In March, 1824, the votes of the town belonging to the Congregational society were called upon to decide whether they would agree to make sale of the pews in their meeting-house as they then were, or previous to said sale, alter them into slips. The wording of the warrant would indicate that a sale of the pews in some form had already been determined upon; but such was not the fact. That was a question still unsettled; and Thomas B. Strong, John Dickinson, Butler Goodrich, Thomas A. Gold and Samuel M. McKay were appointed a committee to estimate the cost of making the proposed change, to devise a plan for selling the slips, if they were built, for the benefit of the society, and to devise also, if practicable, "*a mode to seat the meeting-house; other than* the mode heretofore adopted — or for selling the pews in their present form."

Two weeks afterward, the committee reported. They submitted a plan for making the pews into slips at an expense which they thought would not exceed three hundred and fifty dollars, and in a manner which would seat a hundred and fifty persons more than could be comfortably accommodated in the old pews. And it was their opinion, if it was the pleasure of the parish to so alter the house, "the slips, or a part of them, should be sold at auction, for a period of five years, for certain sums, payable annually, to be applied toward the support of the pastor." They thought it would be inexpedient to sell the pews in the old form, as there were not enough of them to accommodate separately all the families in the parish.

They found it beyond their power to devise any plan for seating the meeting-house which would, in their opinion, be better than the old; but they thought that the substitution of slips — "even if they were not sold, but seated — would contribute much to the convenience, comfort, and eventually, the harmony of the parish." Still, as the project was new to a majority of the parish, the committee proposed a postponement of its consideration in order that they might become better acquainted with it. Their advice was accepted, and the meeting ordered their report, with the plan attached, to be conspicuously posted.

The next year the subject again came up, but the parish was still unprepared to act upon it, and Phinehas Allen, Hosea Merrill, Charles Churchill, S. M. McKay, and Jonathan Allen were directed to examine into it, and report to an adjourned meeting. The meeting was held; but there is no further allusion in the records to the change of pews into slips until March, 1830, when it was considered with a deliberation that indicates the interest which it excited, and the difference of opinion concerning it.

The moderator, Joseph Merrick, nominated a committee — Josiah Bissell, Phinehas Allen, and Henry Hubbard — who, having been formally approved by the meeting, nominated as a committee to consider the article in the warrant regarding the proposed alteration: Nathan Willis, Simeon Brown, Ezekiel R. Colt, S. M. McKay, Curtis T. Fenn, E. M. Bissell, Solomon L. Russell, and Henry H. Childs.

In September following, the committee reported three methods of disposing of the question. The third, which was adopted by the meeting, is the only one described in the record; and is as follows:

RESIDENCE OF JAMES H. HINSDALE, Esq.

The third method is the one at present in force ; viz.: To seat the house by a committee, under the delegated authority of the parish ; with the merits of which the parish are sufficiently familiar. Should this method be adopted, the committee recommend that the seating-committee be instructed to preserve, as far as possible, the present order of seats and seat-mates. This they believe to be very important; for, should any changes be made, the hazard of producing dissatisfaction will be very great.

And thus, so late as 1830, the parish, although it made a step in advance by changing its square and cumbrous pews into neat and commodious slips, nevertheless deliberately adhered to the antiquated practice of seating the congregation by the allotment of a committee.

Much dissatisfaction, however, continued to prevail, and complaint was made that Pittsfield was far behind neighboring towns which had already adopted the desired change. Dr. O. S. Root, the next year, in behalf of himself and some other young men, annoyed by the bad eminence conferred upon them by their seats in the gallery, made known their grievances through the newspapers, and were assigned places in the pews below.

Finally, in November, 1836, nearly two years after the abolition of the compulsory support of public worship — the practice of seating the congregation by a committee was entirely done away with, and the pews were leased at a fixed price, the precedence of choice being sold at auction ; a method which still prevails.

And thus ended the long contest to do away with arbitrary distinctions of class in the house of God; leaving only such as inevitably and incidentally arise.

CHAPTER XV.

THE BERKSHIRE AGRICULTURAL SOCIETY FOR THE PROMOTION OF AGRICULTURE AND MANUFACTURES.

[1807–1830.]

Agricultural societies in Europe and America prior to the Berkshire—The just claims of the Berkshire society to precedence—Evidence and acknowledgment of its beneficial influence throughout the country—Biographical sketch of Elkanah Watson—His removal to Pittsfield and exhibition of merino sheep under the Elm—He advocates the establishment of an agricultural society and the introduction of merino sheep—Independent cattle-show in 1810—Its influence upon Berkshire sheep-culture—The society incorporated—Its first cattle-show—Premiums, and prophetic address by Elkanah Watson—Berkshire system of agricultural fairs gradually developed—Ingenious device to interest women in them—Organization of the society's work — Plowing-match and viewing-committees introduced — Marked effect of the society's efforts upon Berkshire agriculture—Pecuniary difficulties—Contributions of Pittsfield — Aid granted by the Commonwealth—Efforts to make the shows migratory successfully resisted—Death of Mr. Watson—Ode by William Cullen Bryant.

WHEN in the year 1807, the idea of founding, in Berkshire county, a society for the promotion of agriculture and manufactures, happily occurred to Elkanah Watson, societies for a similar purpose were by no means a new thing in the world. The Society of the Improvers of the Knowledge of Agriculture in Scotland was formed as early as 1723. The Highland Agricultural Society, which afterwards, in 1784, became national as the Highland and Agricultural Society of Scotland, was incorporated in 1777, and early established an annual show of livestock, implements of husbandry and other articles of interest to farmers. In 1777, the Bath and West of England Agricultural Society was organized, and immediately established cattle-shows. The success of these institutions was so remarkable, that similar organizations of a local character soon spread all over

Great Britain; and in due time national boards and societies, formed under royal patronage, assumed the lead in promoting the cause of agriculture in the United Kingdom.

The history of these bodies is still related with just pride, by British writers, and to them is attributed in great part, the marvelous perfection to which the art of agriculture has been brought in every part of their country.

Societies of the same kind were also organized in France, and their annual shows were distinguished by the pomps and splendors characteristic of that nation.

In America, also, state-societies for the same object were formed early. That of South Carolina dates from 1784. The Philadelphia society, formed the following year, seems to have had something of a national character; for the *Pittsfield Chronicle* of March, 1790, states that it had just awarded a gold medal to a Rhode Island farmer. In 1791, the celebrated New York Society for the Promotion of Agriculture, Manufactures and Arts, was organized by Ezra L'Hommedieu, Chancellor Robert R. Livingston, Samuel DeWitt, Alexander McComb, and many other respectable and patriotic citizens of that state. It was incorporated in 1793, and accomplished much in behalf of the interests which it was intended to foster. The Massachusetts Society for Promoting Agriculture was incorporated in 1792, and diffused much valuable and practical information throughout the state, by means of a series of papers known as the *Agricultural Repository*, and afterwards by a publication styled the *Massachusetts Journal of Agriculture*.

These associations labored assiduously to obtain information upon agricultural topics, by the importation of the best European treatises upon farming; by experiments which their members made, often at great personal expense, and by such other means as were within their reach. The results of their reading and experience were compared and discussed in frequent meetings, much after the manner of those recently instituted by the Board of Agriculture in Massachusetts; and their proceedings, published in pamphlet-form, or in the newspapers, were scattered broadcast through New York, Massachusetts, and all the more favored states, conveying a vast amount of instruction.

However it may have been with the masses, these papers show that there were then many educated and clear-headed farmers, whose knowledge of their art, at least as to principles, has been little bettered in those who have had sixty years of added investigation and observation. And, although much jealousy of book-farming was manifested in the great body of practical farmers, thought was awakened, and even among those most prejudiced against innovation, more intelligence was employed in cultivation, and essential improvements gradually won their way to adoption. Since that era, and much through the influence of organized societies, some truths have doubtless been discovered, some fallacies detected and abandoned. Some changes for the better have taken place in matters of practical detail; vast improvements have been made in the implements of agriculture; more valuable breeds of cattle, richer varieties of fruit, grain and vegetables, have been introduced. But the farmer, well-read in the recent literature of his profession, if he should peruse the essays and discussions of sixty or seventy years ago, would be surprised to find how little positive advance has been made in agricultural science; how few questions which were then, or have since been propounded, have been absolutely determined. There are many writers and speakers, at this day, upon agricultural topics who present as many points obnoxious to modern criticism, as are to be found in L'Hommedieu, DeWitt, and other leaders of the New York Society.

For the further advance of the interests committed to their charge, the state-societies awarded premiums, medals and diplomas for superior farms, and for excellence in particular products. Distinguished services to the arts or to agriculture, by discoveries, inventions, importations, or otherwise, were rewarded in the same way.

In 1793, the New York Society recommended the forming of county-organizations, whose members should be *ex facto* members of the parent body. It offered to such counties as adopted the proposition, the nucleus of an agricultural library; but there were few responses. Duchess county, however, certainly formed a respectable society, and held a series of successful cattle-shows,[1]

---

[1] The Kingston *Ulster County Plebian*, in its notice of the Berkshire cattle-show of 1810, has the following paragraph, which seems to claim for the Duchess County Society the honor of having the first cattle-show in America: "The laudable example exhibited by our sister county of Duchess in instituting a society for agricultural fairs, has been adopted in various parts

although both were abandoned after a few years, and the latter were not resumed until 1834.

In Pennsylvania, there were several county agricultural societies which held annual exhibitions. In 1805, "a society for the encouragement of domestic manufactures, economy, and the agriculture of our country" was formed in Orleans county, Vermont, and offered three premiums for woolen cloths "of not less than a coat's cloth to be manufactured that season within the circuit of the society." It also recommended that its members should disuse foreign woolen cloths, especially the fine, as soon as may be; and that, so far as practicable, each member should at the next meeting appear clothed in our own manufactures. It moreover determined that "the spirits to be procured for the future refreshment of the society should be of the distillation of our own country."

An association of Middlesex (Massachusetts) farmers, formed in 1794, was incorporated in 1803, as "The Western Society of Middlesex Farmers."

The Kennebec (Maine) Agricultural Society, organized in 1800, was incorporated in 1801.

Thus it will be seen that, contrary to the tradition which strangely obtained popular credence and long remained uncorrected, the Berkshire was by no means the first agricultural society established in America; nor did it hold the first exhibition of cattle. But these are honors which it can well afford to forego. That in which it justly claims precedence is better than mere primogeniture.

The pre-existing organizations had labored faithfully and wisely. The state-societies especially, had achieved very valuable results; but their membership was limited, and chiefly from the richer and more cultivated classes. Their leaders were often eminent statesmen, merchants or professional gentlemen, although generally farmers as well. They held their meetings at the metropolitan centers of their respective states; working upon, rather than with and among, their fellow-agriculturists. These disadvantages were early recognized by the central societies, which accordingly recommended the organization of county branches in order to diffuse their spirit and generalize their oper-

of the country with a zeal that insures the most extensive benefits. Berkshire was among the first and most active in this praiseworthy competition, and her exertions promise to realize the most sanguine expectations."

ations. But both the state-societies and the county—whether formed under their auspices or independently—failed to obtain any strong hold upon the popular heart; and they accomplished comparatively little in elevating the mass of the farming community intellectually, socially, or indeed economically. They created no great holiday for the people; no fellowship of the farmer's craft; and thus they missed two of the most potent means of elevating the art of husbandry. In the language of the founder of the Berkshire Society, "they depended too much upon types, and did not address the interests and sentiments of the people." Their approaches were too direct. They sought to influence their humbler fellows almost entirely through the cold medium of the press; neglecting appeals to the imagination, to social sentiment, and to that love of pageantry which characterized the period. If they sought to arouse the spirit of emulation by the offer of premiums, they missed much of the additional stimulus which the Berkshire Society provided in the character of these rewards of merit, and the manner in which they were bestowed. It remained for the Berkshire farmers—under the leadership of a gentleman singularly qualified by nature, education and social position—to work out a model which proved so well adapted to its purposes that it has been followed by all the county agricultural societies in America, and has exercised a controlling influence over the operations of the state-organizations.

The obligations of the country to the Berkshire Society, in this regard have, from the first, been freely and gratefully acknowledged. We need quote but a few of the instances in which this acknowledgment has been expressed.

On the Fourth of July, 1815, the following toast was given at Lexington, in Middlesex, in which county the Association of Husbandmen, which has been alluded to, already existed: "The Berkshire Association for the Encouragement of American Manufactures: May similar institutions become the bulwark of our national independence; and, under the patronage of our government, teach Great Britain that American resources and American industry are competent to the exigencies of the United States."

In 1817, the Massachusetts Society for the Promotion of Agriculture acknowledged the value of the Berkshire model, and bore testimony to the esteem in which it was held throughout the state by announcing its first cattle-show as to be held after the plan of those established at Pittsfield.

In 1821, Hon. Jonathan Allen, in his address to the Berkshire Society, quoted the following paragraph from an oration delivered in 1820, before the Hampshire, Hampden and Franklin Society: "The Massachusetts Society for the Promotion of Agriculture, a similar society in Pennsylvania, and a few others, were early organized; but we witnessed little of their effects, and there still existed, among us, an extreme apathy, until our brethren in Berkshire, few in numbers, weak in funds, and apparently feeble in means, by their spirited and well-adapted measures, became the honorable and proximate cause of the interest which is now felt, and of the efforts which are now making, throughout the Union. To that society, we are unquestionably indebted; and let the obligation be forever remembered and acknowledged."

Thomas Gold, Esq., in his address as president of the society, in 1816, said: "The respectable State of New York has adopted the society as their model; and they are forming several institutions resembling this. And, within a few days, we have had an application from the State of Kentucky, requesting our assistance to enable them to form a society like our own."

Thus it will be seen that, in less than twelve years from the first cattle-show under the Old Elm, and the other initial movements, which we are about to relate, the Berkshire Agricultural Society was recognized throughout the country as having inaugurated a new era in organizations for the improvement of American agriculture.

In accomplishing this happy end, the most effective means was the substitution of the festival known as "The Cattle-Show and Agricultural Fair," for the occasional meager and unattractive exhibitions which few witnessed, and for the unexciting system of premiums, for which few contended, and which were offered for a very limited number of products. Interesting and pleasing to all classes from its first establishment, this holiday, by gradual accretions of alluring features, became to the farmer, all, and more than all, that commencement-day is to the college-graduate. Fixed in date and place, the cattle-show and fair, once every year, turned the attention of the whole community to the interests of agriculture. It was the grand harvest-home of a region in which almost every man was to some extent a farmer. In it there was some pleasure and profit for all ages, for every class and for both sexes; and it was enjoyed as no other festival—not even the "Glorious Fourth," or, it is hardly an exaggeration to add, Thanksgiving—ever was.

To the practical farmer, especially, in addition to its delights and excitements, it brought both material and intellectual profit. It collected for his examination the latest importations and inventions in the implements of his art, the best blooded stock, the latest varieties of seeds and plants. It was used to some extent for the purposes of traffic. But, more and better than all, it drew the husbandman out of his seclusion into contacts which enlarged and liberalized his mind. In conversation with his fellows, as well as in addresses and reports treating upon subjects of immediate interest to him, he found abundant food for thought—to be compared, on winter evenings, with books and pamphlets, and to be well digested in his lonely fields. In many ways his autumn holiday made the farmer more proud of his profession, while it rendered the profession more worthy of pride.

The gentleman to whom the county of Berkshire owes the honor of furnishing to the country the model for this most beneficial institution, was Elkanah Watson, a member of the New York Society for the Promotion of Agriculture, Manufactures and Art, who purchased the farm and mansion of Henry Van Schaack, and removed to Pittsfield in 1807.

Mr. Watson was born at Plymouth, January 22, 1758, and was a descendant of Governor Edward Winslow. In 1773, he was apprenticed to John Brown, an energetic and enterprising merchant of Providence, and afterwards the founder of Brown University. Mr. Brown was also an ardent and active patriot, and, having captured and burned the British schooner Gaspee, was arrested and carried to Boston, which was then in possession of General Gates. In connection with this affair, young Watson, although not enlisted in continental service, saw some pretty warm patriotic work. In 1777, at the age of nineteen, he went in charge of treasure to the amount of nearly fifty thousand dollars, sent by the Brown firm to their correspondents in Charleston, S. C.—an eventful journey through a very dangerous country, in which he kept his eyes open and his mind active.

Upon attaining his majority in 1779, Mr. Watson, having engaged in some mercantile affair with the Brown Brothers, went to France, where he remained until 1784. In the greater part of this time he was engaged in commercial -----ess; but he spent two years at Rennes, perfecting himself in the French language, and also found opportunity to travel extensively in Holland, Belgium and Great Britain, studying a-- --y whatever was worth seeing, and especially the nati---- ----stries. In 1784, he returned to America, and after spending more than a year in examining ------nt sections of the country, ---------------- a plantation in North Carolina. Two years of p--------------------- were more than sufficient to satisfy him: of all modes of -------- this was the least adapted to his restless mind; and in 1788, he returned to Providence. In the same year curiosity led him to the old Dutch city of Albany, which in 1789, he made his home. "At this period," says his biographer, "commenced his efforts and labors in projecting and advocating various subjects of local and ---eral improvements of the most diversified character ---- objects, which were continued to the end of his life." He had, from his earliest youth, been an observant and th--------- ----f traveler. He had sought the acquaintance of the n---- men of his time, and had been greatly favored by circumstances in so doing. Washington, Franklin, Adams, Schuyler and Livingston were among the sages who gave him their counsel. And no fact, no opportunity, offered itself in vain, from paving and lighting the streets of Albany up to pr------g the grand system of canals, which had so large a sh---- -n making New York the Empire state, some plan or effort --- the public ------- occupied his thoughts.[1]

When, in 1807, he removed to Pittsfield, his conduct was marked by the same characteristics, varied in their manifestation by the changed ---eld of action. "It was," says his son, "in accordance with a long-cherished desire, that he retired from the city in pursuit of rural occupations and felicity, and, at the age of fifty, commenced his agricultural career. His only error in the adoption of this pursuit, was, as he himself said, that he embraced it at too late a period in life: after his habits and feelings had been moulded by a long residence in cities."

This very fact, however, much as it may have impaired his

---

[1] For most of the facts previously stated regarding Mr. Watson, we are indebted to a very interesting volume entitled Men and Times of the Revolution, or Memoirs of Elkanah Watson: Edited by his son, Winslow C. Watson.

success as a p----ical farmer, rendered him perhaps better fitted to introduce the improvements and reforms which he effected in the agriculture -- -erkshire. Mr. Watson's agricultural learning, his well-co---- experiments, his liberality and enterprise in conduct --- business, may have lacked something to make his farming profitable; but to the tiller of the soil, bred to the plow, family might, and did, afford lessons whose costly tuition ------ elf unable to pay, but whose teachings were of untold v--------m. The enlarged and quickened thought, the fruit of an energetic life and wide observation, which Mr. Watson, and after him, Major Melville, brought from abroad, combined happily with the practical common-sense and homely experience of the Berkshire farmers, who, as we have shown in a former chapter, were also not unprepared to receive it, by some knowledge of --- -cience of agriculture as taught in books.

--- - --w years preceding that in which Mr. Watson removed to Pittsfield, the attention of the New York Society for the Promotion of Agriculture, Arts and Manufactures --- turned specially and very -----ly to the improvement of the breeds of sheep in relation to the ---- of their fleece, and also to its manufacture into cloths. Mr. Watson was a member of that society, was deeply --bued with its spirit in -- respect; and among his first acts a farmer, was the purchase of two fine merinos—a ram, and a ewe,—the first of that breed which were ever brought to New England. They were exhibited in the --ll of 1807, on the green under the Old Elm.

"Many farmers, and even females," says Mr. Watson, "were attracted to this humble exhibition;" and, from this lucky incident, he "reasoned that, if two animals are capable of exciting so much attention, what would be the effect of a display on a large scale, of different animals." "The farmers present assented to this reasoning, and thus became acquainted with the speaker," who, it will be remembered, had been but a few months resident among them. "From that moment," said he in 1820, "to the present hour, agricultural fairs and cattle-shows, with all their connections, have predominated in my mind, greatly to the prejudice of my private affairs."

Mr. Watson quoted the example and influence of the great European fairs and cattle-shows, as an encouragement for the establishment of that which he proposed in Berkshire; but he does not tell us what hints he derived from them in forming it. It would have been strange if he had not learned much, and profited much from them.[1] But whatever transatlantic features Mr. Watson incorporated into his agricultural festival, we shall find to have been thoroughly Americanized; so much so, that it may be rightly considered an independent and original creation. We proceed to a detailed account of the organization of the society.

During the winter following Mr. Watson's little exhibition under the Elm, he addressed the farmers of Berkshire, through the newspapers, "urging the spread of the merino sheep," which he considered invaluable for the hilly districts of New England. In furtherance of the same object, several gentlemen from different parts of the county, met, on the 30th of Januay, by his invitation, at the tavern of Captain Pepoon, and having elected Simon Larned president, and John W. Hulbert secretary, passed resolutions favoring the introduction of the Spanish breeds of sheep, and the establishment of agricultural societies. And, in order to make their work practical, they further resolved that an agricultural society should be established in the county of Berkshire and be called "The Berkshire Agricultural Society." To carry out this vote the meeting appointed Elkanah Watson and Alexander Ely of Pittsfield, William Walker of Lenox, Wolcott Hubbel of Lanesboro, and Nathaniel Bishop of Richmond, to report at a future session the name of a suitable person in each town of the county, to form a committee of correspondence.

The embryo society then adjourned to the ninth of the next

[1] In the *Massachusetts Agricultural Journal* for 1824, Mr. John Lowell, one of the editors, in reply to a correspondent who was indignant that he had intimated in a previous number of that magazine, that the idea of agricultural shows did not originate in Berkshire—said, in substance, " that, although the idea had originated in Europe, he had always admitted that to the Berkshire Society belonged the unquestioned honor of introducing it here. But he had personally seen and read, before any cattle-show was dreamed of in America, the proceedings of English and French shows at Smithfield, Bath, Lewes, Caen, and Paris, exceeding in splendor any of ours at present (1824). The French excel us, on such occasions, in speeches and dancing; but we believe we are the only people who combine religion with these public festivals. Yet we would cling as zealously as any to the usages of our ancestors in this respect." In another article Mr. Lowell styles the Berkshire Society, "the nurse of agriculture in Massachusetts."

May: and we hear no more of it. But, in the *Sun* of May 28th, Mr. Watson published an eloquent "Appeal to the Inhabitants of Berkshire." He stated that, having been a member of the New York State Agricultural Society, where the subject had been agitated by the patriotic Livingston, his mind had been deeply impressed with the practicability, and infinite importance, of introducing the Spanish sheep. When he removed to Pittsfield — "foreseeing a heavy cloud evidently on the point of gathering over our land, and the probability that we should shortly be compelled to seek within ourselves a supply of articles of the first necessity, especially woolens — he made every suitable effort to awaken public attention to that important source of national wealth." He explained the advantages of agricultural societies very clearly; said that several of the states had already experienced great benefits from them; and declared that to such institutions England owed her surprising superiority over other nations in agriculture.

He informed the farmers that, in February, he had obtained the refusal, for a limited time, of sixty-seven full and half-blooded Spanish rams — the whole of Chancellor Livingston's spare flock — intending to give over the refusal to individuals or to an agricultural society in the county, "in the pleasing expectation of seeing extensive woolen-factories rise up in different parts of the county, the basis being first laid in an increasing supply of an improving raw material." But the languor attending the organization of the society so discouraged him, that he had given up his bargain. He announced, nevertheless, that he had hazarded the purchase of forty of the flock, which he offered to any who should make application to Colonel Danforth, postmaster of Pittsfield, before the fourth of July. Colonel Danforth was to retain one dollar from the amount paid for each sheep, and to pass it over to an agricultural society, if one was formed that summer, as the nucleus of a fund for premiums upon broadcloth made in the county from the wool of these sheep, and those bred from them.

Mr. Watson promised that the rams should be delivered to Colonel Danforth's order, on the first of September, and eight or ten more from his own flock on the first of October. This would make two for each town, and he estimated that, with proper management, there would be about five thousand sheep from this source alone, in the county, the next spring; preparatory for a second cross with full-blooded rams, which could probably be procured the ensuing season. The second year sufficient wool for extensive manufactories of superfine broadcloths might be produced in Berkshire. This wool, he thought, would be superior in quality to the imported, as the best of foreign growth was retained for home-consumption. Finally, the product of Berkshire wool would so increase in quantity beyond the means of manufacturing in the county, that there would be a considerable surplus, to be sent profitably to market.

The address, of which the foregoing is an abstract, exhibits the arguments by which Mr. Watson constantly urged his favorite schemes of sheep-culture and a county agricultural society upon the Berkshire public; and they met with great success, although to his ardent mind it seemed to come slowly.

Mr. Watson's biographer states that at this time he stood almost alone in advocating his projects, "exposed to the shafts of ridicule and satire." But he does not seem to have suffered more in this respect than usually falls to the lot of the projector of any new institution. We have, to be sure, seen a newspaper-article in which some correspondent exposed his clumsy wit in an attempt to burlesque Mr. Watson's project, by a proposition to offer premiums for an improved breed of turkeys: a suggestion which has long since been carried out, and which, if it had been seriously made, would doubtless have been welcomed by Mr. Watson. But this article stands almost alone in the columns of the *Sun* and *Reporter*, which were crowded with frequent arguments for, and eulogiums upon, the new scheme.

Mr. Watson had much more to fear from apathy than from hostility or ridicule. Yet even this was far from universal. The gentlemen who participated in the meetings of 1808 were heartily sincere in the feelings which they expressed, and sympathized with him warmly, although with a zeal not quite equal to his own. The people generally of Berkshire and Pittsfield — as is their wont with new projects to this day — turned over his propositions and arguments in their minds for a couple of years, and, when satisfied of their value, entered into his plans with enthusiasm and vigor.

In the *Sun* of August 8, 1810, appeared the following appeal, signed by twenty-six of the most respectable farmers and intelligent gentlemen of the county: —

BERKSHIRE CATTLE-SHOW.

"*The multiplication of useful animals is a common blessing to mankind.*"— Washington.

TO FARMERS.

The subscribers take the liberty to address you on a momentous subject, which, in all probability, will materially affect the agricultural interest of this county. Annual fairs, or shows of cattle, we are informed, are found in many European countries, particularly in Great Britain, of great importance, at fixed periods and places, at which point there is generally a large collection of the most intelligent farmers, exhibiting a show of prime animals. Some in view of obtaining prize-premiums, others in a view of sale or exchange, by which means the breeds have greatly improved, to the general benefit of the community. The same advantages have also resulted from a similar practice in several parts of the United States; particularly in certain districts in Pennsylvania, and in Duchess county in the State of New York. Being fully impressed with the belief that a like practice in this county will have the same good effects, and in a hope of being instrumental in commencing a plan so useful in its consequences, we propose to exhibit on the square in the village of Pittsfield, on Monday the first of October next, from nine o'clock to three, bulls, oxen, steers, and other neat cattle; merino sheep of the different grades, as well as other improved breeds; hogs or swine of different breeds.

Farmers in this county or vicinity are respectfully invited to attend this first exhibition, with such useful animals as they see proper. It is hoped that this essay will not be confined to the present year, but will lead to permanent annual cattle-shows; and that an incorporated agricultural society will emanate from this meeting, that will hereafter be possessed of funds sufficient to award premiums, and thus promote an amelioration of valuable breeds of domestic animals.

Samuel H. Wheeler, Calvin Hubbel, William Beard, Uri Bradley, Josiah Wilcox, Joel Bradley, Peter B. Curtis, Joseph Farnam, Ebenezer Buck, Charles Morse, Daniel Brown, John Wells, Jr., Hicok Hubbel, John Farnam, Wolcott Hubbel, Rosswel Root, Erastus Sackett, Solomon Sackett, Joseph Shearer, Lodowick Stanton, Elkanah Watson, John B. Root, Titus Goodman, Joseph Merrick, Samuel D. Colt, Thomas B Strong.

The last eleven signers of this call were citizens of Pittsfield: Messrs. Morse, Brown and Wells were of Cheshire; the others of Lanesboro. The exhibition took place at the appointed time; and notwithstanding its limited character, and the meagerness of pleasing accessories, it attracted a large attendance of the principal farmers from the surrounding country: and, without the incitement of premiums, the show of animals was respectable; comprising three hundred and eighty-three sheep, seven bulls, a hundred and nine oxen, nine cows, three heifers, two calves, and one boar; a large proportion of which were blooded stock. Among the more valuable exhibitions were a young Holderness bull which Mr. Watson had imported in 1808, and which was accompanied by some of its stock; and there was also some of the small-boned, short-legged pigs, of which the same gentleman had, in the same year, brought a pair from Duchess county, and which gradually supplanted the old slab-sided, plowshare breed which previously rooted in the soil of Berkshire. In the three hundred and eighty-three sheep, there were thirteen entries of exhibitors: Merrick and Colt (Joseph Merrick and Samuel D. Colt), two hundred and eighty-four; Root and Chappell (John B. Root and Richard S. Chappell), thirty-six; D. Humphries (Colonel Humphries of Poughkeepsie), eleven; Root and Willard (George B. Rodney Root and Josiah Willard), twenty-one; Daniel Couch, six; Campbell and Goodwin (David Campbell and Joseph Goodwin), four; Jonathan Chapman, four; Samuel H. Wheeler, two; Arthur Schofield, Charles Morse, Levi Chittenden, Benjamin Luce, Asahel Buck, one each.

Of the exhibitors in the general department — other than sheep — there were, from Chatham, N. Y., one; Canaan, N. Y., one; Pittsfield, seven; Lanesboro, fourteen; Adams, three; Cheshire, one; Richmond, one; Dalton, one. Of the exhibitors of sheep, Poughkeepsie furnished one, Pittsfield eight, Lanesboro one, Richmond one, unknown three.

The announcement of the Pittsfield Fair, and afterwards of its marked success, excited a wide interest, not only in Massachusetts, but in all the neighboring states; especially in New England, where it was the first essay of the kind.

At home, in Berkshire, it had the desired effect of giving a new impulse to the new sheep-culture. Immediately after the show, we find Root and Chappell, Mr. Watson and others, advertising merinos for sale; John B. Root advertising for persons to board from ten to five hundred sheep by the year; and a general interest in the subject of wool and woolen manufactures everywhere manifested.

While the fair was in progress, Hon. Jonathan Allen was in Lisbon purchasing merinos; an enterprise in which he had remarkable good fortune. Spain was at that moment agitated by the intestine wars engendered by the French revolution, and confiscations ruled the hour. Among the property seized were many of the superb flocks which had long been the pride of Andalusia, New Castile, and Estramadura. These, the Juntas administering the government — King Ferdinand being detained a prisoner by Napoleon — sent in immense numbers to clog the markets of Portugal.

From this source many of the finest sheep in Spain found their way to Great Britain and the United States. Among those sent to Lisbon were six thousand from the flocks of the Count of Montaco, of which Mr. Allen purchased one hundred.

Regarding the quality of these sheep, there is still preserved the certificate of the Spanish Consul at Lisbon, stating — on the authority of the secretary of the governmental Junta, of Estramadura — that they were of the fine Transhumante[1] breed, from the confiscated flocks of the Count of Montaco, whose stock was of the highest credit in Spain, and also held in great estimation abroad.

Mr. Allen had a very stormy return voyage, in which he lost many of his sheep, and was himself so very sea-sick that he begged of the captain to throw him overboard. But, of those which he saved, he sold a sufficient number in Boston to defray the whole cost of his venture, some of the bucks bringing one thousand dollars each.

Forty remained, with which he returned to Pittsfield. Here he purchased of Titus Goodman, "vendee of David Campbell," the farm near Coltsville, afterwards owned by Phillips Merrill. Taking up his residence upon this beautiful, valuable and extensive farm, he entered with zeal into the business of sheep-raising, and contributed largely to the introduction of the fine-wool sheep.

In 1809, Samuel D. Colt was appointed agent for the sale of

---

[1] Transhumante, or traveling race; so called because, although carefully sheltered in winter, they were in summer kept almost constantly traveling for pasturage; being distinguished in this respect from the Estantes, which do not migrate, and are of a somewhat inferior quality.

Clermont merino rams for the State of Massachusetts. The animals were to be delivered in Pittsfield on the fifteenth of August, the purchasers selecting from the flock in the order of their applications. The stock of these rams was represented to be imported from France by Robert R. Livingston, who, when minister to that country, selected them from its best national flock. Mr. Colt's large exhibition at the cattle-show of 1810 indicated the spirit with which he entered upon this enterprise. Indeed, it was the foundation of an exceedingly prosperous business in buying, raising and selling of sheep, which was conducted for many years by himself and his son Robert, in which they proved themselves among the most able and successful business men of the county.

Other farmers entered with zest into the raising of the improved breeds of sheep, and many more became interested in agricultural societies. And thus, within three years of Mr. Watson's humble show under the Old Elm, the objects which he there set himself to accomplish were in a fair tide toward success. In fact, if there had been any dispiriting indifference regarding these objects previous to the success of 1810, after it public feeling seemed likely to rush to the opposite extreme. One enthusiastic correspondent, at least, proposed to establish, at Pittsfield, a grand fair, like those of Europe, for all the four states which approach each other at this point. He showed the great advantages of this location as a center, and would even have premiums offered annually for the agricultural and manufacturing products of the whole Union. And, indeed, the premiums offered at the early fairs of the Berkshire Society were, to a great extent, open to competitors outside the county and the state.

While the cattle-show of 1810 was in progress, it was determined, at a meeting of the leading farmers in attendance, that the institution should be made permanent, and, for that purpose, to apply to the next legislature for an act incorporating a county agricultural society. In accordance with this action, the legislature granted a charter to Elkanah Watson, Ezekiel Bacon, John B. Root, and Thomas B. Strong of Pittsfield, Caleb Hyde of Lenox, John Chamberlin of Dalton, and Samuel H. Wheeler of Lanesboro, with such as might be joined with them, as "the Berkshire Agricultural Society for the Promotion of Agriculture and Manufactures." The society was authorized to hold property whose annual income should not exceed five thousand dollars, and was invested with the powers requisite to carry out its objects.

The first meeting was held on the 1st of August, 1811, when a code of by-laws was adopted. One of these required that there should be two meetings of the society annually; one at Lenox on the first Wednesday of the spring session of the supreme court, the other at Pittsfield on the last Tuesday of September. The latter date was also that of the cattle-show and fair, which it was provided, should be held in Pittsfield and should include " an exhibition of neat cattle, sheep, hogs, all kinds of seeds, roots, samples of compost, manufactures, patent-rights, improvements in agriculture, machinery, and useful inventions of all kinds."

Another by-law provided that new members should be elected by ballot, and, under this rule, the following were chosen: William Walker, Jonathan Allen, Timothy Childs, H. H. Childs, Hosea Merrill, R. S. Chappell, David Campbell, Josiah Bissell, Rossell (Roswell) Root, Arthur Scholfield, S. D. Colt, Joseph Merrick, Thomas Gold, Lemuel Pomeroy, James Brown, John Dickinson, and Oliver Partridge Dickinson. In September this rule was repealed, and the secretary and treasurer were authorized to receive members who signed the constitution and by-laws, and paid the admission fee of one dollar.

The officers of the society, chosen at its first meeting, were Elkanah Watson, president; William Walker and S. H. Wheeler, vice-presidents; Caleb Hyde, corresponding secretary; Thomas B. Strong, recording secretary; John B. Root, treasurer; Joseph Shearer, Ezekiel Bacon, and Jonathan Allen, trustees. At a subsequent meeting, Thomas Gold, S. D. Colt, Roswell Root, David Campbell, Arthur Scholfield and James Brown were added to the list of trustees.

In the *Sun* of August 10th, Elkanah Watson as president, and Messrs. Shearer and Allen, a committee of the trustees, announced that the society had determined to hold a cattle-show on an extensive scale, at Pittsfield, on the last Tuesday and Wednesday of the ensuing September. They stated that, should funds be provided in season, premiums would be given; but, in the meanwhile, they advised farmers and manufacturers to select and prepare choice specimens of their respective products, and machinists to have ready models of useful inventions. All members of the society were requested to appear clad in American manufactures.

In the last issue of the *Sun* previous to the days appointed for the show, premiums were offered of ten dollars each for the best bull, and for the best full-blooded merino lamb; five dollars each for oxen, cows, heifers, sheep of mixed blood, common sheep and swine.

The first day of the fair proved one of those delightful days which almost invariably characterize the last week of September in Berkshire. The streets and public square early took on that lively appearance which subsequent cattle-shows rendered so familiar. People from the neighboring regions, in all sorts of vehicles, began, almost with the rising of the sun, to pour into town, mixed with herds of cattle, sheep in wagons or flocks, a few swine, and some mechanical inventions.

The public square boasted but a single tree besides the Old Elm, and around the latter was an inclosure for the live stock. The remaining space and the neighboring streets were soon thronged with an excited and expectant crowd; many of them females, although the ladies did not honor the occasion with so numerous a representation as in later years. Booths for the sale of refreshments and Yankee notions had sprung up like mushrooms. The venders had already learned their trade at general musters and the celebrations of the fourth of July; but neither of these holidays ever brought them so rich a harvest as they found in cattle-shows. The committee had announced that innocent amusements would be allowed, and enterprising geniuses provided them in abundance; especially the "fandango," or, as it was then called, the "aerial phaeton," which has never since failed to offer its dizzy pleasures to the youths and maidens who resort to cattle-shows. In this earlier time it often remained stationary for weeks in the open space adjoining Captain Pepoon's tavern on the south side of the park.

The proceedings and pageants of the day, under the direction of the society, were unique and imposing, and the whole occasion formed one of those gala days in which Pittsfield has always delighted. At eleven o'clock the members met at the town-house, where Mr. Watson delivered a brief but very interesting address. After apologizing for reading his remarks, as he was unaccustomed to extemporary speaking, he argued the value of agricultural societies from the good they had accomplished in many European countries. He dwelt particularly upon their effect in England, where the knowledge which they had collected and diffused, and the emulation which they had excited by the example of successful farmers, and by liberal prizes, had overcome the obstacles which nature herself seemed to interpose to successful agriculture in an island lying ten degrees north of our latitude. There was no country in Europe so generally, so well and so profitably, cultivated as England. To this, and to their numerous manufactories, he attributed the astonishing power which she had recently displayed in the Napoleonic wars; and, although, as a good democrat, he was bound to think that she seemed then sinking, comparatively, with a mill-stone around her neck, yet her energies and endless resources were the theme and the astonishment of mankind. Turning "from blood-stained, guilty Europe, to our more peaceful and more virtuous borders," and particularly to Berkshire county, he found himself in a latitude parallel to that of the most luxuriant countries of Europe, but far behind them, and at least a century behind England, in the profitable product of our soil. The natural vigor of our virgin soil, which had hitherto supplied in some measure the place of artificial manures, was now abated, as was remarkably evinced in the culture of winter wheat, which was once so congenial to our land, but which had in a manner disappeared.

The remedy for this declining agriculture he expected to find in this society whose duty, as a body and individually, was to collect and diffuse useful information, to make experiments, suggest improvements and excite a spirit of honorable competition.

Cattle-raising was then the primary object of the Berkshire farmer, and having a limited experience in that department, he quoted from Lawrence Sickel, president of the Pennsylvania Society : " Although the cattle of the northern states are the best in this country, and make as fine beef as the world can produce, yet there is much room for improvement. Even in England, notwithstanding their successful exertions for the last fifty years, good cattle are extremely scarce and command high prices. The present time is peculiarly favorable for a change in our stock. For the purpose of knowing what cattle of improved breeds are among us, and to give an opportunity for the more easy diffusion of valuable stock, the society have resolved to establish cattle-shows in the vicinity of Philadelphia. This, and giving premiums are the most powerful means of improving cattle in the United States."

Mr. Watson commended this example as apposite to the aims of the Berkshire Society. He had introduced an improved breed of swine which he hoped, by the aid of the society's committees, to extend throughout the county. By a fortunate accident he had also been enabled to introduce a species of wheat lately brought from France, and a superior variety of potatoes, some of which would be delivered, during the winter, to the members of the society in each town of the county. He was cultivating madder—an important dye-stuff previously imported from Europe, although natural to our soil and climate, and easily cultivated. He would be able in the spring to supply a considerable number of sprouts for general cultivation. He called the attention of the society also to the importance of cultivating woad or pastel, a plant similar in its nature to indigo.

Of manufactures, he said:

In my view, there is every rational probability that this county is destined to become eventually, and probably in a much shorter period than is generally imagined, a respectable manufacturing county, in all those branches where the excessive dearness of labor can in some measure be obviated by the powerful application of machinery. And as no branch is so susceptible of this application as the manufacture of woolens, there can be little doubt, especially under the aspect of the times, but the future wealth and respectability of the county of Berkshire will be built on that substantial foundation. Owing to the fortunate introduction of a new and invaluable species of sheep, we shall, to all appearance, be abundantly supplied with a precious raw material to go hand in hand with the increase of our manufactories; thus mutually propping and supporting each other.

Whether Mr. Watson looked with so true a prophecy to the future in other respects, will perhaps be questioned, although many will concede the wisdom of his foresight as exhibited in the following extract:

It is a lamentable truth, to which it has appeared heretofore impossible to apply a remedy, that the excessive use of ardent spirits, and the great increase of tippling-houses, has gained such a dangerous ascendency over the less wealthy part of the community, arising principally from the want of habitual employment at certain seasons of the year. Will not the extension of manufactories open a door for constant and regular employment to all classes and ages ; and thus gradually diminish the inducement to resort to such places—as the saying is—to kill time ? Will it not thus, by degrees, correct this unfortunate habit, so disgraceful to the character, and so injurious to the morals of that unfortunate portion of the community ? May we not also fondly hope that constant employment will tend to infuse into the rising generation more correct morals, habits of industry, and due subordination ?—Will it not also tend to check the spirit of emigration which holds our population nearly stationary ? As the means of subsistence are increased, will it not in the same proportion increase our population and lessen the inducement to enrich distant new regions—for the most part unhealthy to the first adventurers—thus depriving us of those energies to which we are naturally entitled ?

Mr. Watson closed his address, after stating several other encouraging circumstances, with the following paragraphs :

I have received a communication from Dudley A. Tyng, Esq., recording secretary to the respectable Massachusetts Agricultural Society, stating that they, highly approving our infant establishment, have already spontaneously voted for our acceptance a valuable collection of books on agriculture, which I shall deposit with our recording secretary for the benefit of our members.

The determination of our society to hold its exhibitions annually in this place will give them permanent stability and increasing respectability ; and it will be important to unite with our views, all that portion of the commonwealth lying west of the Connecticut river. The community will habitually look forward to enter the list of competitors in various objects ; besides, from the rapid increase of our society, there is no doubt but ample funds will be provided to give out in future with a liberal hand, prize-premiums, as a stimulus.

After this address, in which we must not forget to mention Mr. Watson declared that the society met " under the universal approbation of the community," a procession was formed, at 12 o'clock, which impressed itself more deeply upon the memory and traditions of the towns-people than any other spectacle that the village streets have ever witnessed. Those who enjoyed it as children described it to their dying day with unequaled vividness and enthusiasm.

First in the pageant, came " The Pittsfield Band " whose music, according to the account of the day, was very inspiriting and creditable. After them walked sixty yoke of prime oxen, connected by chains, and drawing a plow held by Charles Goodrich, Esq. The leading driver of the oxen was Nathaniel Fairfield; Captain Goodrich and he being the two oldest farmers in the town; veterans also, it will be remembered, in the French and Indian wars, as well as in the politics and municipal affairs of the town, having been among the first settlers of Poontoosuck plantation in its initial year, 1752. After them, in natural order, followed the farmers of the county, carrying a flag "representing a sheaf of wheat on one side and a plough on the other."

Next, and suggestive of the new era opening in the industries of the town, came a broad platform, drawn by oxen, and bearing a large broadcloth loom, with a flying shuttle and a spinning jenny of forty spindles, all the machinery being in actual operation under skillful workmen. Among the latter was James Wrigley, a man of remarkably fine person, who was dressed in the old fashion then passing out of date, with small clothes, cocked hat, and shoes with silver buckles: his whole costume black, but decorated with an abundance of bright-colored ribbons or "favors." The appropriate following to this was composed of the mechanics of the county carrying a flag representing a saw on one side and a shuttle on the other.

Then came—perhaps in the nature of a triumphal car—a broad platform drawn by horses, and bearing various specimens of Berkshire manufactures; among them rolls of broadcloth, bolts of sail duck, handsome rose blankets, muskets, anchors, leather, etc.; with the flags of the United States and of the Commonwealth displayed above it.

The last division was formed by the officers and members of the Berkshire Agricultural Society, with heads of wheat, the badge of the organization, in their hats; the members having two heads tied with pack thread, the officers three fastened with a green ribbon. High sheriff, Col. Simon Larned, acted as marshal of the day, a post which has generally since been held on similar occasions by his successors in office. His assistants were Deputy Sheriff Theodore Hinsdale, and Messrs. Oramel Fanning, Jeremy Warriner and Elisha Ely. The whole five were mounted on white horses.

Mr. Watson, in his diary, commemorates this procession as "splendid, novel, and imposing beyond anything of the kind ever before exhibited in America." "It cost me," he says, "an infinity of trouble and some cash, but it resulted in exciting a general attention in the northern states, and placing our society on elevated ground."

There appears, from the description, to have been nothing in the display very showy or gorgeous, even for a country-town, but it was sufficiently striking to please the common fancy, and, what was of more importance, it was full of pregnant meanings which impressed themselves with great force upon the popular mind, sharply pointing the facts and logic of Mr. Watson. From that day the society and its objects held a chief place in the hearts of the people of Berkshire. At its meeting on the first day of the fair, the society appointed as a committee to award premiums on the stock exhibited: Major Erastus Rowley, Major Samuel Buffington, Joseph Shearer, Esq., Wolcott Hubbel, Esq., Col. Levi Belding, Dr. Thaddeus Pomeroy, and Capt. Daniel Brown, who, the next day, made the following report: That Erastus Sackett of Pittsfield exhibited the best bull; that Capt. Nathaniel Fairfield of Pittsfield, exhibited the best yoke of oxen, but he not being a member of the society, could not receive the premium, and it was given to David Ashley, Jr., of Pittsfield, who made the next best exhibition of oxen. That Roswell Root of Pittsfield showed the best four-year-old steers, David Campbell of Pittsfield the best three-year-old, Henry Chamberlin of Dalton the best two-year-old. That Benjamin Brown of Cheshire exhibited the best cow; Roswell Root of Pittsfield and Henry Chamberlin of Dalton, the best swine; Jonathan Allen of Pittsfield the best full-blood merino lamb; Arthur Scholfield of Pittsfield the best seven-eighths blood merino lamb; Samuel L. Allen of Pittsfield the best twenty common ewes. And the premiums were delivered accordingly.

This first cattle-show under the direction of the Berkshire Agricultural Society more than satisfied the most brilliant anticipations of its projectors. The *Sun's* report says: "The concourse of citizens was more numerous than has probably ever convened in Pittsfield and, what is of more importance to the real objects of the society, the number of valuable and prime objects brought forward for premiums and exhibition, was undoubtedly greater than was ever before collected in this section of country."

Congratulations poured in from every quarter, and these, with the approbation expressed by leading journals and distinguished patriots in all parts of the country, inspired the leaders of the institution with new courage and vigor. They were, to be sure, still embarrassed, as they continued to be for many years, by the lack of pecuniary means with which to carry out their liberal desires; but they were conscious that the foundation which they had laid, good as it was, would, unless promptly built upon, soon go to ruin, as others had before it. They therefore applied themselves zealously to preparations for the cattle-show of 1812.

Before it came, the country was involved in the war which Mr. Watson had prophesied in 1808. How intimately that event was connected with the interests of agriculture in Berkshire, will appear from the account which we give, in another chapter, of the Cantonment. The second cattle-show took place on the sixth and seventh of October, 1812; or about three months after the declaration of the war. The newspapers, occupied with political wrangling and war news, gave less of their aid than in the previous year; but the managers were indefatigable, and enjoyed the prestige of past success, and also the encouragement of the commandant and other officers of the Cantonment. Premiums to the amount of two hundred and eight dollars, were offered; including one of fifty dollars for the best piece of superfine broadcloth, six quarters wide, not less than twenty yards in length, to be manufactured in either of the counties of Berkshire or Hampshire.[1]

Competition for the premiums in the department of domestic animals, was invited from all parts of the Union. The Fair was again favored with delightful weather, and the town was thronged as in the previous fall. The procession was of a somewhat less marked character; the plow, with its venerable holders and its long string of cattle being missed, while instead of the loom and other machinery in operation, there were borne simply the broadcloths which had been entered for premium. But escort was furnished by a detachment of United States troops from the Cantonment, and the popular interest in these gallant defenders of their country, who were about to march for the northern frontiers, found in them abundant sources of enthusiasm.

Bitter as were the partisan feuds of the day, both political parties took a hearty and harmonious part in the anniversary. An

[1] "Old Hampshire," which was, in 1812, divided into the counties of Hampshire, Hampden and Franklin.

address was delivered in the First Parish (democratic) Church, by Thomas Gold, a prominent federalist. There was a dinner at the democratic hotel; and the day's festivities closed with a brilliant illumination, and a ball at Captain Merrick's federal inn; the latter, the first of a joyous series which for many years gave a crowning zest to the cattle-show and fair.

On the second day, the society met in the Union (federal) Church, where the premium broadcloths were suspended before the pulpit. President Watson — a democrat — made a brief address, and delivered the premiums to the successful competitors, each of whom also received a diploma. The fifty-dollar premium for broadcloth had been awarded to Mr. Watson, himself; but he divided it between James Wrigley, the English weaver, and Andrew Murphy, the dresser and finisher, who was an Irishman.

Encouraged by this continued success, the society, at its meeting in connection with the show of 1812, determined upon a new advance, and one which contributed much to the interest of succeeding exhibitions. "It was considered," says Mr. Watson, "of the first importance to enlist the sympathies and arouse the interest of the females of the county in the operations of the society." Not, we apprehend, that they had shown any lack of appreciation of the pageantries of the procession, or the exercises in the church—and certainly not in the ball. But, as yet, the articles of feminine workmanship upon which premiums were offered, were confined exclusively to a few products of the loom, for which they competed in common with those of the other sex. To say nothing of the innumerable nick-nacks, works of art, taste, elegance and usefulness which have since filled the exhibition-halls; then not even butter and cheese, hosiery or linen cloth, were included in the premium-list.

The backwardness of the ladies in competing for such prizes as were within their reach was, however, attributed by Mr. Watson to their native shrinking from publicity; and he devised a plan to overcome this obstacle. In January, 1812, the society had held a show of cloths, when four premiums, to the value of thirty dollars, were awarded, two of them to ladies: Mrs. Experience Luce and Mrs. R. S. Chapell. It was now determined to hold a similar show in January, 1813, offering sixty dollars in premiums, and two of the society's silver medals: the competitors to be exclusively women, who must receive their prizes in person. We will allow Mr. Watson to tell the remainder of the story in his own words:

The day arrived; a large room (Washington Hall, in Captain Merrick's inn) was prepared. Many superior articles were exhibited, especially woolens and linens; but no female appeared to claim the premiums. This was the crisis, and I was extremely agitated lest the experiment should fail. Native timidity and the fear of ridicule restrained them. No one dared be the first to support a new project. To counteract this feeling, we resorted to an expedient which, in an hour, accomplished our wishes. I left the hall, and with no small difficulty, prevailed upon my good wife[1] to accompany me to the house of exhibition. I then dispatched messengers to the other ladies of the village announcing that she waited for them at the cloth-show. They hastened out. The farmers' wives and daughters, who were secretly watching the movements of the waters, also sallied forth, and the hall was speedily filled with female spectators and candidates. I immediately arose in the rear of the table, on which the glittering premiums were displayed, and delivered a formal address.

At an adjourned meeting in November, 1812, the work of the society was divided into four departments: of agriculture, under the management of Thomas Gold, Ezekiel Bacon and Samuel D. Colt; of manufactures, under the management of Thomas Melville, Arthur Scholfield, and John B. Root; of domestic animals, under the management of Joseph Shearer, Oren Goodrich and David Campbell; of general administration, directed by the president of the society, and the chairmen of the three other departments.

The cattle-show of 1813, although it continued but one day and the procession was omitted, marked a great advance in the character of the festival. The premiums at the ladies' cloth-show in January, just described, were given in silver-plate and the silver-medals of the society, and at this cattle-show, the practice of giving premiums in these articles became general. On woolen cloth, of household-manufacture, the first premium was a silver-bowl (with engravings) valued at twenty-five dollars; the second, a similar bowl worth fifteen dollars; the third, a cup worth twelve; the fourth, a set of tea-spoons worth ten dollars; the fifth, the society's silver-medal worth five dollars. Premiums

[1] Who, it seems, shared the native timidity of the rustic females.

of a similar character from sixteen to five dollars in value were offered for carpeting, flannels, blankets, stockings, linen, flax, leather, clothier's work, madder, woad, and domestic animals. At this time, it will be observed, and at all the earlier shows, the premiums were of much greater cost than were offered for similar articles at the later fairs; rarely being less than four dollars. In the early part of the year, it was arranged that the January cloth-shows should be devoted exclusively to the display of ladies' work; but so effectually had Mr. Watson's ingenious device done away with the obstacle of female timidity, that it was found practicable to consolidate this exhibition with the October cattle-show and fair. "The ladies of Berkshire" were, however, "notified that the assembly-room[1] over the Female Academy would be appropriated exclusively to the display of their industry and ingenuity in exhibiting such articles as they might be disposed to offer in person, for premiums or inspection; in particular, woolens, shirting-linens, blankets, carpeting, stockings, chip-hats, plaids, bombazets, and rugs." They were further informed that the passage leading to the hall would be kept open, and the whole house devoted to their use, and that suitable refreshments would be there provided for them.

Superfine broadcloths from any part of the United States were to be delivered to James Buel on the 11th of October, by noon, and were to be removed on the next day to the assembly-room, in Morgan's coffee-house on Bank row, for exhibition. All animals were excluded from the public square except those offered for premium; and these were to be placed in pens under the direction of Joseph Shearer. Animals, for exhibition only, were placed in North and South streets.

These arrangements were fully carried out, and in the cattle-show of 1813, we find most of the characteristic features which distinguished those of later years. The invitation to the ladies, in particular, was answered by a very creditable display of house-hold-manufactures, mostly cloths; although very far short of that marvelous variety of useful and ornamental products which has since rendered this department so attractive to the spectators, so interesting to the competitors and so honorable to their taste, ingenuity and skill. Only so much of the diffidence complained

[1] "Assembly-room" was the name by which it was then the fashion to call any public hall used for dancing.

of by Mr. Watson, remained to the ladies, as served to make them more interesting. A Virginian letter-writer, in 1822, thus describes the scene as premiums were awarded to them:

The president, from the pulpit, immediately after the address, announced : " As premiums are proclaimed for females, they will please arise in their places, and the head marshal will deliver to each her premium and certificate of honorable testimony." The instant the name of the successful candidate was announced, the eyes of an exhilarated audience were flying in every direction, impelled by the strongest curiosity to see the fortunate, blushing female, with downcast eyes, raising both her hands, as the marshal approached ; with one to receive her premium, with the other her certificate. The effect cannot be described. It must be seen to be realized."

At the show of 1813, the premiums awarded the Pittsfield ladies were as follows: To Misses Ann Maria Chapell and Sarah Spring, silver-bowls, and to Mrs. Betsey Ball, a silver-cup; all for woolen cloth. To Mrs. Keturah Brown, a silver-cup, and to Mrs. R. Watson, a silver-medal, for carpeting. To Mrs. Abigail Backus, a silver-cup, and to Mrs. J. D. Colt, a silver-medal, for flannel. To Miss Jerusha Chapell, for the best blanket, a set of tea-spoons. To Miss Almira Weller, a medal for a pair of stockings. To Mrs. Laura Derbyshire, a medal for chip-hats. To Mrs. Clarinda Luce, a medal for woolen-plaid, and another for bombazete. There were eighteen premiums awarded to women, of which thirteen were taken in Pittsfield. Twenty-five were awarded to men; of which fifteen were taken in Pittsfield, as follows: By Elkanah Watson and Daniel Stearns, on the largest quantity and best quality of madder ; by Jonas Ball and Jonathan Allen, 2d, upon woad, or pastel ; by Joel Stevens, on bulls ; by Richard Campbell, and Jonathan Yale Clark, on grass-fed oxen ; by Erastus Sackett, on four-year-old steers ; by Joseph Shearer, on two-year-old heifers ; by Richard Campbell, on working-oxen ; by Ichabod Chapman, on swine ; by Jonathan Allen, 1st, on full-blooded merino ram lambs ; by Joseph Merrick, on full-blooded merino ewe lambs ; by James and Simeon Brown, on calf-skin leather ; by Jonathan N. Chapell, on the best finished household-cloth ; by Oramel Fanning, on merino-wool hats.

As we have said, the cattle-shows and fairs of the Berkshire Agricultural Society, moulding themselves into more perfect form, year by year, had in 1813, assumed most of the distinctive features which afterwards continued to characterize them. The most marked exception was the plowing-match. Competitive contests of this kind were held at Hartford and elsewhere previous to the organization of the Berkshire Society in 1811 ; but they did not become part of the Pittsfield show until 1818, when premiums of ten and five dollars were offered. Four teams, each of one yoke of oxen, were entered : The competitors being Levi Beebe, Thomas Melville and Charles Goodrich of Pittsfield, and —— Curtis of Stockbridge. Mr. Beebe plowed a quarter of an acre of green sward in thirty-five minutes; Mr. Melville's plowman— name not given—in thirty-nine minutes; Mr. Curtis in thirty-seven minutes; Mr. Goodrich in forty-two minutes. Other considerations than time governing the decision, Mr. Melville received the first premium and Mr. Curtis the second.

The superiority of Mr. Melville's work was attributed very much to the excellence of his plow, which was represented " to cost but little more than those in ordinary use, and to be of so much better model, that the farmer making the change would be the gainer in a single year." The aid which it gave in introducing improved agricultural implements, in place of the clumsy tools of earlier times, was one of the chief advantages of the cattle-shows.

Still earlier than the plowing-match, in 1814, upon the suggestion of Ebenezer Center, a prominent member of the executive committee, another " interesting and novel feature in the practical operation of the society was adopted. A committee of prominent farmers was selected and the duty devolved upon them of traversing the county in the month of July, when the fields are in full luxuriance, and examining and awarding premiums upon the standing-crops offered for competition."[1]

This committee soon became the most important of all, and the reading of its reports was among the most valuable, although the least showy, features of the cattle-show. A southern gentleman, in a letter widely-published at the time, says the most interesting of all the proceedings were the reports of the committees, especially the detailed reports of the visiting-committees. And, from that time down, these reports of the committee on agriculture, since divided into that upon summer, and that upon fall, crops

[1] Watson's Memoirs.

have been prepared with more labor and research than any others, and have been often distinguished for their array of valuable facts and sound thought.

The Berkshire Agricultural Society thus took form as an institution, by degrees, and the general characteristics which we have sketched show, as others of minor importance would, how unlike it soon became to the organizations in New York, Pennsylvania, and elsewhere, which it at first proposed to itself for models. Indeed, the parts of teacher and pupil were reversed, and in 1822, Thomas Gold, the third president of the association, was able to write of it : " Its fame and influence have extended over the entire surface of the United States ; its example followed, its approbation courted, by its extended offspring. It has been recognized, as well in Europe as in America, as an original, novel plan, and the most excellent organization ever conceived to promote the great interests under its patronage."

Nor had the society confined itself to the advancement of agriculture by the premiums and other incitements of its cattle-shows and fairs. Like the older organizations, it had been zealous to disseminate information in books, pamphlets, and newspapers, to introduce new products and new varieties of the old, and to improve the breeds of cattle and other live stock by importations and otherwise. Of course, some of the new products were introduced as experiments, and occasionally proved unsuccessful. Thus woad, which it was hoped would prove a substitute for indigo, was planted under the auspices of the society, which published elaborate directions for its cultivation ; but, although considerable quantities were raised, it proved valuable only as a ferment for the more costly dye, and was given up by the farmers. So with madder, which was found not to be a profitable crop.

Still, most of the action of the society proved of practical value, and Major Melville in his address as president, even as early as 1816, could thus congratulate his asssociates :

Only six years ago, the agricultural concerns of this county were stationary. Few, if any, valuable improvements were attempted. Indifference and unconcern seemed to pervade society. In 1810, the genius of the county shook off the slumbers of its husbandry, and the spirit of improvement commenced. Under the auspices of your association, a career of usefulness was resumed and diligently promoted. The former state of things has given way to a new condition ; unfolding to us improvements, in variety and usefulness surpassing the most sanguine expectations. Every department of rural employment demonstrates an intelligent cultivation, and effectual good management. In the selection and rearing of domestic animals, more correct information prevails, and greater emulation is awakened. The vast increase in variety and excellence of our crops satisfy our warmest desires, and leave us nothing to envy in the most favored regions of the west.

There is, perhaps, something of the rostrum's rose-color in this picture; but, addressed to those familiar with the facts, it could not have been very violently overtinted, and it at least indicates very marked and beneficial effects of the society's operations.

But these effects were more conspicuous in Pittsfield and its immediate vicinity than in other parts of the county, although throughout its whole extent, its good influence had been largely felt. And even in the most favored spots very much remained to be accomplished. In this work we cannot minutely follow the society, nor in its efforts to extend its operations. We return to its early difficulties and the methods by which they were overcome.

And, chief among these difficulties, was the lack of pecuniary means. From 1811 to 1816, the society depended entirely upon its small fee for membership, and upon the voluntary gifts of individuals, which amounted in that interval to over thirty-six hundred dollars, mostly in subscriptions of from five to twenty-five dollars; the larger sums being almost invariably given by citizens of Pittsfield, or obtained by them from friends outside the county. In 1812, Mr. Watson spent a good deal of time, and a hundred and fifty dollars in money, in an abortive attempt to obtain legislative aid for the society, and continued his efforts in the same direction, and with like result, as long as he remained in office. He was much vexed by his ill-success; but his successors in office, with perhaps a more intimate knowledge of the ways of legislators, persevered in their application, and in 1816 obtained a grant of two hundred dollars yearly for three years. In 1818, through the exertions of the Berkshire Society primarily, a general law was passed, providing that every agricultural association in the state, whose field of operations embraced at least one county, and which possessed a securely invested fund of one thousand dollars obtained from private sources, should receive two hundred dollars annually from the treasury of the Commonwealth; and in the same proportion for additional investments. From this time the society was comparatively free from pecuniary embarrassment, although its means were far from adequate to secure all the objects which it desired.

Its course was, however, beset with vexations of a still more irritating character, arising from the jealousy which sprang up against it — especially in the southern towns of the county — as designed for the aggrandizement of Pittsfield, and as manifesting partiality to its citizens in the distribution of offices and premiums. The short-lived apathy which annoyed Mr. Watson, was of little moment; and the labors of organizing the society and developing its system of operations must have been rather an agreeable mental task. Perplexity concerning the means of defraying current expenses was certainly not so pleasant; but, to men conscious of only the most liberal and patriotic motives, it was not so trying, by far, to the temper, as it was to meet the cavilings of those who could not, or would not, rise above the influence of petty village-rivalries.

No sooner did it become manifest, that, while the society was to become an honor and a source of great benefits to the entire county, it would redound especially to the credit and advantage of the town whose citizens had originated it, than appeals to local feeling began to be made, greatly checking its progress and weakening its power for good. It was one of the many instances in which the sedulously cultivated jealousy of Pittsfield reflected serious injury upon the whole county.

This jealousy found vent in efforts to exclude citizens of Pittsfield from the management of the society, and to hold the cattle-show and fair yearly in different towns. It had been a leading principle with Mr. Watson, derived from European example, that the fairs should be stationary in one town; and universal experience has since proved its wisdom. To violate it, would have been to sap the well-laid foundations of the institution; and its leading members in Pittsfield successfully resisted the attempt.

These efforts to disturb the original plan culminated, in 1825, in newspaper-discussions which elucidated how large was the share which Pittsfield had in founding and building up the society. The amount of its contributions prior to the legislative act of 1816 has been indicated. In order to obtain the benefit of this act, the members of the society gave to the treasurer their notes for fifty dollars each, with interest annually; which, as they were all responsible men, was considered such an investment as the law required. In 1825, the society numbered two hundred and three active members, and the fund obtained and invested, as above described, amounted to two thousand four hundred and seventy-five dollars, of which citizens of Pittsfield contributed eighteen hundred dollars. This fund was established in 1819. Previous to that date, the whole amount contributed to the society by individuals was about forty-two hundred dollars, of which the people of Pittsfield gave three thousand and ninety-eight dollars, the remainder of the county eleven hundred and twenty-two dollars. The contributions of the town, in time, influence, and personal effort, were even in much greater proportion. The labors of the president, secretaries, and other officers there resident, were, alone, of value almost beyond computation. The publication of these statistics sufficed to show that the benefits derived by Pittsfield from the location of the cattle-show and fair were not out of just proportion to the support which it had given the society; and, since it was moreover for the best interest of all that the show should not be migratory, all motions to hold them in other towns were uniformly voted down. Every effort was, however, made, to conciliate the friendship of all parts of the county. The leading offices were conferred upon citizens of Lenox and Stockbridge; great care was taken that other towns than Pittsfield should be liberally represented on the committees, and accommodations were provided for the stock brought from a distance to the shows. Local clubs were proposed as a substitute for holding the cattle-shows in different towns, it being suggested that only cattle and other articles which had received premiums at local shows should be entered at those of the county. A local society was actually established at Stockbridge. But perfect satisfaction, it was found, could only be obtained by the division of the large territory of the county into districts, each having its own society.

Vexatious as this controversy was, it proved finally beneficial to the society, and the cattle-shows and fairs rapidly increased in the character and amount of their exhibitions. Something of the splendors of the earlier processions was revived, and the escort of the Berkshire Greys and the music of excellent bands enlivened the display; while the exercises in the church were generally in the highest degree creditable. It was at this time, too, that the proposition was first made, although not carried out for more than a quarter of a century, to purchase grounds for the society's exhibitions.[1]

We cannot here fully enter into all the interesting and curious details of this early history of the Berkshire Agricultural Society; but a few detached incidents must not be omitted. After the first year or two, the semi-annual meetings at Lenox appear to have been discontinued. In 1812, a board of trustees were appointed to whom a great part of the business of the society was for a time intrusted.

In 1814, Mr. Watson declined re-election as president of the society, and was succeeded by Major Thomas Melville, who manifested a spirit very similar to that of his predecessor.[2]

In 1816, he returned to his former residence in Albany; "abandoning," he says, "all those rural scenes which had delighted me — all my flocks and herds, which I had reared with infinite pains for nearly nine years. In the midst of promoting agricultural improvements and domestic industry, I returned to resume the dull and monotonous scenes of a city-life."

The society instructed its president to convey to him its sentiments of regret for his removal, and its " high sense of the important services he had rendered, by his patriotic efforts to promote agriculture and manufactures, and by his perseverance in the establishment of this interesting institution." And it farther voted " to perpetuate its gratitude to its founder by offering annually, as a premium for the best full-blooded merino buck, a silver-cup of the value of $12.00, with the words 'Watson cup' inscribed thereon." Mr. Watson attended the twenty-seventh anniversary of the society in October, 1837, where he received the most gratifying public and private exhibitions of respect and kind recollections, and delivered his last address ; his valedictory to all such associations; "and here," says his biographer, "appropriately terminated his public course." He died at Port Kent, New York, December 5, 1842, in the eighty-fifth year of his age. The

[1] By a resolution offered in 1822, by Thomas A. Gold, Esq.

[2] When Mr. Watson removed from Pittsfield, in 1816, Major Melville purchased and occupied his residence and farm, where he continued until late in life, exhibiting his interest in agricultural affairs in various ways, and among others by establishing in 1822, "a repository for the sale of agricultural implements"—the first in the county.

inscription upon the plain and simple obelisk which marks his grave, indicates the feeling which he retained to the last, concerning his work in Pittsfield:

Here lie the remains of
ELKANAH WATSON,

The founder and first president of the Berkshire Agricultural Society. May generations yet unborn learn by his example to love their country.

 The annual festivals of the Agricultural Society continued to be the great gala-days of the year for the town and the county, and many pleasing incidents regarding them might be related; but no very striking changes in their management took place until their removal to grounds purchased by the society in 1855, which introduced a new period in their history, whose consideration must be reserved for another chapter. We take leave of its earlier era by quoting the ode written for the cattle-show of 1820, by William Cullen Bryant, who was at that time a young lawyer of Great Barrington, and an active politician, serving often as secretary of the federal conventions.

> Since last our vales these rites admir'd,
> Another year has come and flown,
> But where her rosy steps retir'd,
> Has left her gifts profusely strown.
>
> No killing frost on germ and flower,
> To blast the hopes of spring, was nigh;
> No wrath condens'd the ceaseless shower,
> Or seal'd the fountains of the sky.
>
> But kindly suns and gentle rains,
> And liberal dews and airs of health,
> Rear'd the large harvests of the plains,
> And nurs'd the meadow's fragrant wealth.
>
> As if the indulgent power who laid,
> On man the great command to toil,
> Well-pleased to see that law obey'd,
> Had touch'd, in love, the teeming soil.
>
> And here, while autumn wanders pale
> Beneath the fading forest shade,
> Gather'd from many a height and vale,
> The bounties of the year are laid.

Here toil, whom oft the setting sun
  Has seen at his protracted task,
Demands the palm his patience won,
  And art has come his wreaths to ask.

Well may the hymn of victory flow,
  And mingle with the voice of mirth,
While here are spread the spoils that show
  Our triumphs o'er reluctant earth.

CHAPTER XVI.

MEDICAL COLLEGE AND MEDICAL SOCIETIES.

[1784–1875.]

Preliminary action—Dr. O. S. Root—Application for charter—Nature of the opposition to it—Charter granted—Lecture-course before the charter—First faculty and trustees—Purchase of Pittsfield hotel-building—Subscriptions and endowment—Town action and grant—Popular dread of resurrectionists—Exciting cases of "body-snatching"—Anecdote of Timothy Hall—Provisions for anatomical study at the medical college—Doctor Goodhue elected president—Sketch of his life—Lyceum of natural history—Sketch of Prof. Chester Dewey—Death of Doctor Goodhue—Dr. Zadock Howe elected president—Dr. H. H. Childs made president—Connection with Williams College dissolved—Equality of the two medical colleges of Massachusetts recognized by the State Medical Society—Death of Professor Palmer—College-building burned—Relief by grant from the legislature and citizens' subscriptions—New college erected on South street—Dr. H. H. Childs resigns his professorship—Decline of the college—Clinique established—Doctor Timothy Childs—Efforts to restore the prosperity of the college—*Berkshire Medical Journal*—The institution dissolved and the building sold—Lyceums and alumni—History of Berkshire medical societies—Condition of the profession in 1785 and in 1875 contrasted—Pittsfield Medical Society established—Vaccination introduced into Berkshire.

THE year 1822 is marked in the annals of Pittsfield by the practical establishment of the Berkshire Medical Institution, which for many years contributed much to the town's material prosperity, and still more to its intellectual culture. At this date there were already, in New England, seven medical schools, of high repute. Nevertheless, there had long been a desire for a similar institution in western Massachusetts. The first effectual effort in that direction was not made until 1821, when Oliver S. Root[1] returning from a course of lectures at Castleton, Vt., Dr.

[1] Oliver Sacket Root was born at Pittsfield, July 1, 1799, and passed his youth in the family of his grandfather, Col. Oliver Root. In 1821, he com-

J. P. Batchelder, a professor in that institution, having become dissatisfied with it, sent word by him to Dr. H. H. Childs that the favorable moment had arrived to establish a new school at Pittsfield. Doctor Childs seized the hint with avidity, and immediately took steps to avail himself of it. Public-spirited, devoted to his profession, and eager for distinction in it, this movement was one to enlist his warmest sympathies. Prompt, practical, and energetic, he pushed it vigorously and without pause; never, for a moment, suffering the public interest in it to flag.

He first pressed his plans upon the newly organized Berkshire District Medical Society, which appointed Drs. Asa Burbank, of Lanesboro, and Daniel Collins of Lenox, together with himself, a committee, to petition the legislature for a charter and endowment for a medical college at Pittsfield. This petition was presented at the June session of 1822. It was worded with great shrewdness and tact, and placed in a clear and strong light, both the argument for the proposed measure, and the answers to anticipated objections. After demonstrating concisely and forcibly the absolute necessity of public institutions for medical instruction, it presented a cogent argument in favor of the new one. It called the attention of the legislature to the fact that a large proportion of the students in the medical colleges of the neighboring states were citizens of Massachusetts, and concluded as follows:

Your petitioners forbear any comment upon a fact which will become disgraceful, should it be permitted to exist after being brought to the notice of the Legislature. Lest this statement should be thought to affect the high reputation which is so justly due to the distinguished professors in the institution at Cambridge, your petitioners beg leave to state, that an explanation of the fact is to be found in the enormous expense of attendance on a course of lectures at that institution, which amounts to an utter denial of all its advantages to students of mod-

---

menced the study of medicine at Castleton, Vt.; but, after his first course of lectures, he spent a year in Virginia, as a teacher. On his return he resumed his studies at the Berkshire Medical Institution and graduated in 1824. He immediately entered upon the practice of medicine in his native town, and continued in its active duties almost to the day of his death, October 22, 1870. For many years in the latter part of his life, Doctor Root was secretary of the trustees of the medical college, secretary, treasurer and actuary of the cemetery corporation, and an active member of the town school-committee. In the latter position he was especially distinguished, and the children of the public schools attended his funeral in a body.

erate pecuniary means. With this view of the subject your petitioners anticipate that the only question on which your honorable body will deliberate is with respect to the location of the institution. And on this subject it is not, perhaps, presuming too far to expect that the Legislature will concur with the medical society of the county of Berkshire in selecting the town of *Pittsfield*, as offering the most eligible situation. This town is about equally distant from the several medical institutions in the adjoining states, and would afford the necessary accommodations for students on terms as moderate as could be offered in any part of the Commonwealth.

The county of Berkshire has cheerfully paid its due proportion to the treasury of the Commonwealth, and its citizens have rejoiced in the munificent patronage which literature and science have received at the hands of the Legislature ; and they confidently trust they shall not be disappointed, when in their turn they ask that pecuniary assistance, which they have enabled the Legislature so liberally to extend to other institutions. Justice to the inhabitants of the town of Pittsfield compels your petitioners to observe, that in anticipation of an incorporation and endowment by the Legislature, they have subscribed the amount of three thousand dollars, including the grant from the town to be paid to the trustees of a medical institution to be located in that town. Your petitioners therefore pray an act of incorporation for a medical institution to be established in the town of Pittsfield, county of Berkshire, and a grant for the benefit of said institution.

This petition was referred to the Fall session and ordered to be printed in the *Boston Centinel* and *Pittsfield Sun*. When it came up for consideration, it met with no little opposition from the friends of the school connected with Harvard University, and from other gentlemen in the eastern part of the state, who as yet were too little willing to admit the intellectual equality of the professional men of the two sections, and who also dreaded innovation from the teachings of a younger seminary.

The location proposed, and the most active leader in the new enterprise, did not tend to reassure them. The radicalism of Berkshire, and especially of Pittsfield, was proverbial at Boston ; and Doctor Childs was known to be ardently attached to the most ultra school of democratic politicians. Only two years previous to the petition, this feeling had been revived by the doctor's course in the constitutional convention.

It is not strange that many of the eastern conservatives were reluctant to trust the education of youth, even in medicine, to so dangerous hands ; and to place them in a locality where they would be surrounded by so very progressive influences.

The petition was, however, ably and zealously supported in the senate by Hon. Jonathan Allen, and in the house by Hon. William C. Jarvis. Doctor Childs was also at Boston, urging the claims of western Massachusetts with his usual ardor. The charter was finally granted and was signed by Governor Brooks, January 4, 1823; but the people of Berkshire were generously permitted to endow their own college.

This charter authorized the establishment of a medical school at Pittsfield under the title of the Berkshire Medical Institution; and named as trustees, Rev. Heman Humphrey, Dr. J. P. Batchelder, Henry Hubbard, Samuel M. McKay, and Henry H. Childs, together with such others as they might associate with themselves; the number in all, to be not less than seven nor more than fifteen.

This board was authorized to hold real estate of the value of $50,000, and the same amount in personal property. The usual governing and managing powers were granted, but it was provided that degrees should be conferred only by the president and trustees of Williams College, and under the same rules and restrictions which were adopted and recognized in bestowing similar degrees by "the University at Cambridge."

This plan was adopted to assimilate the practice here to that of the Massachusetts Medical College whose head is the president of the University; and with the further view to secure conservatism and uniform practice throughout the commonwealth, to avoid the multiplication of bodies with the power to confer scholastic degrees, and to give greater dignity to, and confidence in, the Berkshire diplomas. The trustees, in their first circular, stated that it was adopted "by agreement" (probably with the trustees of Williams) "sanctioned by the commonwealth;" but it doubtless went far to allay the fears of those who had honestly opposed the charter. It, however, proved inconvenient in practice, and soon came to be unnecessary for the purposes named.

Without waiting the result of their application to the legislature, the friends of the college, on the 16th of August, chose a "board of management" to superintend its affairs. And this board, which consisted of the same gentlemen named in the charter as trustees, announced in the *Sun* of August 22d, a course of lectures to commence on the 18th of September, with the following professors: Theory and practice of medicine, Dr. H. H. Childs; anatomy, surgery, and physiology, Dr. J. P. Batchelder; materia medica, Dr. Asa Burbank; chemistry, botany and mineralogy, Prof. Chester Dewey of Williams College. Obstetrics, by a lecturer not named.

The tuition for the course was fixed at forty dollars; and board at one dollar and seventy-five cents per week, including washing, room-rent, and lodging in the institution.

In 1821, the Pittsfield (democratic) Hotel had become unprofitable, and the pacification of parties rendered it no longer necessary. It was therefore determined to sell it, and Joseph Shearer, Eldad Francis, and Doctor Childs were appointed a committee for that purpose. Of the original three hundred shares into which the property was divided, Joseph Shearer, a strong friend of the proposed college, owned at this time one hundred and sixty-two, and Doctor Childs thirty-nine; and it was, perhaps, in anticipation of that enterprise that a deed of the premises, for the sum of three thousand dollars, was made to the latter gentleman, on the 28th of January, 1822; although this was three months before the vote of the medical society to petition for the charter.

The purchase included the large three-story building described in the account of the hotel, the grounds on which it stood, and the furniture. The furniture was somewhat worn, and the building needed repairs, as well as a few changes to adapt it to its new uses; but little was done in that direction until after the charter. With the aid of the stable for anatomical purposes, very fair provision was, however, afforded for the informal course of 1822.

The embryo college was organized at the time specified; going into operation with twenty-five students, almost before a large portion of the neighboring people knew that it was contemplated. The result of this preliminary course was most beneficial; attracting, by the favorable reports of the students, the attention of the public not only in western Massachusetts, but in the adjoining states; while it greatly facilitated the subsequent labor of organizing the institution.

The first meeting of the trustees was held January 31, 1823, when Henry C. Brown and Joseph Shearer, were added to the board. Jonathan Allen and William C. Jarvis of Pittsfield, Levi Lincoln of Worcester, Daniel Noble of Williamstown, Henry

Shaw of Lanesboro, became members during the same year. Rev. Mr. Humphrey resigned in May. Upon the remaining members, during the earlier years of the school, there devolved a vast amount of labor and anxiety.

The trustees commenced their work with a fund of barely three thousand dollars, mostly in unpaid subscriptions. Measures were immediately taken for the collection of these subscriptions; and in May, 1823, Doctor Childs received fifteen hundred dollars, and gave a mortgage-deed of the "Institution." In May, 1826, the trustees paid sixteen hundred and fourteen dollars more, and came into full possession of the estate.

In the meantime, the town had shown an interest, although, it must be confessed a not exceedingly liberal one, in the institution. In May, 1822, General Nathan Willis, chairman of a committee appointed to consider the petition of Dr. H. H. Childs " for a site on which to locate a medical chapel,"[1] reported that they were "highly impressed with the importance of establishing liberal institutions for the diffusion of science and useful knowledge, and particularly such as will tend to the suppression of quackery." But they relied upon "a minute and able exposition in writing by Doctor Childs, of the benefits which might accrue, from the proposed establishment, to the cause of medical science, and to the pecuniary advantages of the town;" and they recommended the following resolution:

Resolved, that we highly approve the establishment of a medical college in the town of Pittsfield, and that we feel disposed to render it every facility consistent with the interest and duty of the town.

The committee, however, hinted that the resources of the town were limited, and the claims on its liberality numerous. The meeting adopted the resolution; instructed the selectmen to join in the petition for the college-charter; and granted the trustees the privilege of erecting a fire-proof building, thirty feet by forty in area, on the town-land east of the town-house, and as near it as the selectmen might deem safe.

In March, 1823, more ambitious projects were entertained, and a committee of fifteen citizens of note was appointed to consider a resolution offered by Doctor Childs, "to erect an elegant and commodious building for the Medical College." We hear no more

[1] *Sic* in records.

of this committee, but in July, 1824, in response to a somewhat humbler request, the town permitted the trustees, in lieu of erecting the fire-proof structure required by the vote of 1822, to remove the old hotel-stable to the lot east of the town-house, and remodel it for the purposes of the college, on condition that the townhouse was kept constantly insured against fire communicated from the new building.

The stable was removed and converted into a neat building containing cabinet, and anatomical rooms and apartments for other purposes. Some other out-buildings were erected and improvements were made in the old hotel-building to fit it for a "commons house;"[1] the entire expense being thirty-three hundred dollars.

The college had now buildings which compared favorably with those of similar institutions; but the trustees still experienced extreme perplexity in providing for the necessary outlay, and in meeting the current expenses of the school. In 1823, Doctor Childs and Hon. Henry Hubbard were appointed a committee to petition the legislature for an endowment; and they succeeded in obtaining a grant of five thousand dollars, payable in five annual installments. But this was soon absorbed by the imperative demands of the new enterprise, and no further assistance was obtained from the commonwealth, although often asked, until an especial emergency arose in 1850.

For twenty-six years the Institution lived and flourished upon a fund — including the legislative grant and all paid subscriptions—of certainly not more than ten thousand dollars, all of it invested in the college-buildings, furniture and apparatus. During that time it seems never to have been out of debt. Until the last installment of the grant was paid, the amount to be received was anticipated by loans; when that payment was made, debt had become chronic. In 1835, the outstanding claims were reported at four thousand and thirty-eight dollars, most of them dating back to 1825. The legislature refused the aid which was asked from it, and, so far as the record shows, no further effort to free the Institution from debt was made, until 1843, when the number of students having become large, it was voted to appropriate one hundred dollars yearly, from the income of the faculty, as a sinking fund.

---

[1] "Commons" in this instance included lodging, as well as board.

In January, 1825, the too sanguine hopes of the fathers of the college having been somewhat chilled by the coldness of some from whom they expected better things, it was voted, that, "whereas the trustees are without disposable funds for the payment of the salaries of the professors and lecturers, and the contingencies that do not relate to fixtures and apparatus, therefore, the said professors and lecturers must look for their compensation, and for the defrayment of incidental expenses, to the tuition of students;" the fees to be divided among the faculty, in such proportion as they might agree upon, with the right to appeal to the trustees in case of dissatisfaction.

It may well be imagined that the compensation thus derived was often meager; and the more so, that the fees were not unfrequently paid in notes of the students running for indefinite terms; the specification indeed often being, "when the said student shall be able to pay." These notes were duly distributed to the faculty, and many of them, which were left to await payment, were found at the dissolution of the Institution in the deserted office of the dean.

But small and uncertain as the income of the faculty was, it was several times subjected to a sort of forced loan guaranteed to be paid "when the trustees should be in funds for that purpose." Sixteen hundred dollars of this class of debts appeared in the report of 1835, of which four hundred and forty-four dollars were due to Doctor Batchelder, who was dismissed from his professorship in 1828; three hundred and four to Doctor Childs, and two hundred and fifty-eight to Professor Dewey. It does not appear when the trustees came to be in funds to liquidate these claims.

Such in brief is the story of the pecuniary management of the Berkshire Medical College during the first twenty years of its existence. Let us now see what its success was as a scientific school.

On the first of July, 1823, the trustees issued a pamphlet-circular in which they announced the following lecture-course to commence on the second Wednesday of September:

General Anatomy and Physiology, Dr. Jerome V. C. Smith of Boston.[1]

[1] Afterwards well-known as the mayor of that city, and as an author. He married Miss Eliza, daughter of Major Henry C. Brown.

Surgery and Anatomy, and Physiology as subservient to the Theory and Practice of Medicine and Surgery, Dr. J. P. Batchelder.

Theory and Practice of Medicine, Dr. H. H. Childs.

Obstetrics, Dr. Asa Burbank.

Materia Medica and Pharmacy, Dr. John DeLa Mater, of Sheffield.

Chemistry, Botany, Mineralogy, Natural and Experimental Philosophy, Prof. Chester Dewey.

Medical Jurisprudence, by a lecturer to be named.

Reading terms were also promised, in which the same branches were to be taught with the exception of those in Professor Dewey's department.

The following table of fees was fixed: For all the lectures, $40 ; yearly tuition, exclusive of lectures, $50 ; graduation, $12 ; for Professor Dewey's lectures on the natural sciences, $6.

Students " destined for missionary labors" were admitted without charge.

Students were promised "access to an extensive library, a cabinet of minerals consisting of about one thousand specimens, and a museum of valuable anatomical preparations."

One drawback there was to the satisfaction with which the citizens of the town saw a medical college established among them, and especially on the very edge of their principal graveyard. It was the dread of the resurrecting propensities of the students. Those who live when wise and humane legislation has provided unobjectionable means for obtaining an abundant supply of anatomical subjects, can hardly realize the feeling which pervaded the community when the student found it almost, or entirely, impossible to become even moderately familiar with the structure of the human frame unless he resorted to the nocturnal robbery of neighboring graves.

There are many thrilling traditions originating in the popular excitement upon this subject, which in the cities and larger towns often led to fearful riots. In Berkshire there was hardly a village in which one or more graves had not been robbed.[1]

---

[1] Mr. Timothy Hall—afterwards for many years a police-officer of Pittsfield, noted for courage, determination and coolness in danger—once, when a boy of sixteen years, passing a lonely grave-yard in a neighboring town, saw what appeared to be a white figure bowing to him. His first thought was to fly, but his better judgment told him that to do so was to become a ghost-coward for life ; and, with such boldness as he could summon, he approached he mysterious object, which proved to be a shroud that some resurrectionists

In 1820—only two years before the foundation of the Medical College, Pittsfield was thrown into the most violent commotion by the discovery that the body of George Butler, Jr., a respectable young man, with numerous relatives, had been stolen from its grave. Young Butler died in November, 1819, and, during the ensuing winter, his mother constantly dreamed that his grave was empty ; which may, perhaps, be accounted for by the fact that suspicion had been roused in the fall by the appearance of the sod, and the finding of a shroud-sleeve in the burial-ground, although we do not know that she was informed of these circumstances. But, however that may be, when, at her solicitation, one of her surviving sons, early in May, opened his brother's grave, and found that the body had been removed by the usual rude method, the mother's dream conspired with other circumstances to deepen the public horror. Almost every person in Pittsfield— men, women and children — as well as many from neighboring towns, went to gaze, shuddering, into the gaping grave, which was purposely left open all summer, exposing its shattered and tenantless coffin, to remind the spectator of the most shocking circumstances of its desecration.

A town-meeting was called on the 7th of June to consider the case, and to see what method should be taken to prevent in future "the horrid and savage practice" of body-stealing. At this meeting a committee—consisting of Henry C. Brown, Josiah Bissell, William C. Jarvis, Nathan Willis, and Dr. Timothy Childs— reported that, while they "viewed with abhorrence, the violations of the right of sepulcher," they could find no statute of the commonwealth regarding such an offense, and that, in their opinion, the town had no power to raise a tax for the purpose of offering a reward for the detection of the perpetrators. They might, however, be indicted for a misdemeanor at the common law, if

had torn from a recently disinterred body. In this case the coffin had been only partially uncovered and the corpse rudely dragged through a narrow aperture. This indeed was the common practice of the "body-snatchers," who were provided with an iron-hook, which, inserted under the chin of the corpse, enabled them with little trouble to draw from the coffin its tenant,— especially if, as was oftenest the case, he was emaciated by disease. This brutal treatment of the stolen subjects, even before the application of the dissecting-knife, added greatly to the exasperation of the people, who were accustomed to look upon the dead with the most profound awe, and upon the remains of their friends and neighbors with the most tender reverence.

they could be detected by the activity and vigilance of private citizens. Somewhat astounded by this exposition of the law, the town instructed the selectmen to "lay the facts before the governor and council, and request them to take such order thereon as they might deem proper;" but, if they did so, it had no effect, for the first Massachusetts statute for the protection of the repose of the dead was not passed until 1830.

The town further appointed a committee of twelve to collect subscriptions, in order to offer a reward for the detection of any person who had violated or might violate any grave in the town; and also directed Josiah Bissell, whose store adjoined the central burial-ground, to view it occasionally to see whether there were any indications that it had been disturbed.

These occurrences are still vivid in the memory of the elder citizens of Pittsfield; and, as late as 1870, Mr. James Butler, in a debate regarding the removal of the remains of the dead from the First street burial-ground to the new cemetery, alluded with the deepest feeling to the painful memories regarding his brother, which had, for fifty years, haunted him and other relatives.

In 1822, the facts we have stated, were fresh in the minds of the whole community, and it was with good reason that the trustees of the Medical College, in their first circular, strove to allay the apprehensions naturally excited by the location of their institution. "That the repose of the dead had been disturbed" they did not deny; but such outrages had arisen from lack of a seminary where students could pursue anatomical researches chiefly. Compelled by law to obtain a competent knowledge of anatomy, and unable to meet the expense of city-schools, they were driven to expedients as repugnant to their own feelings as they were odious to the public. The new school, therefore, increased rather than diminished the security of the grave-yards.

The trustees even paid great regard to the feeling of "those many individuals of excellent minds who entertained prejudices against the dissection of the human frame" at all, and suggested for their relief that "the great number of anatomical preparations in the museum lessened the necessity for extensive dissection." They even went so far as to add that "comparative anatomy, or the dissection of brute-animals, furnished a substitute for the use of the human body, which would neither be overlooked nor neglected;" which looks very much as though the venerable fathers in medicine were attempting to soothe their fellow-citizens with opiates of very questionable orthodoxy. All the dissection of dumb animals which was ever done or contemplated in the institution—except with distinct reference to comparative anatomy—might, we suspect, have been witnessed in no more solemn ampitheatre than Commons hall. The trustees, however, declared that, the state having imposed upon them the duty of providing the means of instruction in every department, they would faithfully perform that duty, although "with a most sacred regard to private feeling as well as to public sensibility."

And, while thus addressing the public, they showed their good faith by stringent provisions in the college-statutes requiring the faculty to procure their subjects for dissection only from the largest cities; that no student should be concerned in obtaining them; that no private dissection by students should be permitted, and that any who might infringe this rule should be publicly exposed. These by-laws did not perfectly accomplish their purposes.

It is probable that the grave-yards in the immediate vicinity of the college were safer for its establishment, and, perhaps, as a larger number of anatomical students could avail themselves of the same subjects, and as some of these were bought by the faculty in the large cities, there were not so many illegally obtained as before. But there were frequent and generally credited reports of the desecration of burial-grounds in towns at some distance from Pittsfield, by students of the Berkshire Medical College.

Finally, one party was followed from eastern Hampden, and a body which had been stolen by them was recovered at Westfield. In the early part of March, 1830, the bodies of two persons who had just been buried at Montague and Conway, in the county of Franklin, were found to have been disinterred, and were traced to two students of the college, who were arrested. The bodies were recovered without mutilation and restored to their friends. The pursuers found the warmest sympathy among the people of Pittsfield, who, in the height of their indignation, before legal measures proved effective, threatened to take the law into their own hands; Major Butler Goodrich offering to head a party to demolish the college-buildings unless the ghastly prey of the students was given up. A full town-meeting was held on the 7th of March, in which the citizens expressed their "sentiments of unmingled indignation and horror," and pledged the town's best endeavors to aid in the discovery of persons residing among or near us who had been charged with this foul offense; and to place a social ban upon those who were known to be guilty, but who from the difficulty of obtaining direct evidence might escape legal punishment. Acknowledging the necessity of dissection, they held all medical institutions to a strict responsibility in regard to the manner of obtaining subjects, and declared that those permitting students to provide subjects for themselves or the college, ought to be discountenanced and held up to "public censure and public shame." Jonathan Allen, a trustee of the Medical College, was moderator of the meeting which passed these resolutions.

In another case preserved by tradition—but whether occurring before or after that of 1830, is not stated,—the result of the pursuit was not so satisfactory. The officers and the friends of the deceased were permitted to search the college-buildings; but were accompanied by a tall student who concealed, under one of the long camlet cloaks then in fashion, the body of the subject—a slight girl emaciated by long illness.

This last grim story of course rests on not the most unimpeachable testimony; but it is likely enough to have been true, and even if false, its very invention illustrates the popular feeling.

On still another occasion a person employed in Pomeroy's factory, having died, was buried in the north-east corner of the old grave-yard, and when friends from a distance came to disinter and remove it, it was found that the grave had been robbed. This affair created the usual excitement, which was intensified by a horribly ludicrous incident. One of the mourning friends resorting too often to the tavern for consolation, became intoxicated and fell into the open grave, whereupon a student of wicked wit proposed to leave him to fill the vacancy which he had discovered. The wag, however, came very near being rewarded for his indecorous pleasantry, by being himself consigned to the yawning tomb; the spectators, as may be imagined, being in no humor for joking of that kind.

We have dwelt more at length upon this practice of surreptitiously procuring subjects for the dissecting-knife, as it was one which seriously affected the tranquillity of the community, and was by no means the least of many discomforts of which society has been relieved by wise legislation.

By the old law, judges in capital cases had the power to direct the bodies of criminals, executed by their sentence, to be delivered to the surgeons for dissection; but the supply of subjects from this source was too limited and uncertain to supply the wants of students in anatomy; and they were, by courtesy, supposed to procure them "from the largest cities." But even in those cities in 1823, the dead of the criminal and friendless classes were not in such superabundant numbers as now, and the cost of procuring and transporting subjects was beyond the means of country students and physicians. Resort was therefore, almost necessarily, had to the neighboring grave-yards; the practice being almost countenanced by the law permitting physicians to have in their possession dead bodies for the purposes of anatomy, without accounting for the mode in which they obtained them. In 1830, however, simultaneously with the law for the better protection of burial-grounds, an act was passed directing that the bodies of persons dying under certain circumstances should be delivered to surgeons and medical schools for dissection; and this, together with the increasing supply from the cities, has rendered subjects so cheap that for years there has been little temptation to resort to the odious midnight-prowlings of the resurrectionists.

The first president of the college was Dr. Jonah Goodhue, of Hadley; one of the most eminent of those New England physicians, who, with few advantages for early professional education, won high position by dint of strong native talent, close observation of nature, and a very diligent study of books when they became able to obtain them.

His selection as president of the new college was in all respects fortunate. The Institution prospered, the first term opening with eighty students, and the number increasing from year to year.

By their charter the trustees were authorized to promote, not only medical science, but others kindred to it; and for that purpose to organize a lyceum of natural history, with such members as they might deem best. In furtherance of this object, the circular of July announced that the branches of instruction in Professor Dewey's department would be taught in strict reference to the arts of life, and as sources of rational amusement and moral improvement. "The advantages to be derived from an institution like this by a community of mechanics, artisans and practical agriculturists," they say, "cannot be calculated or foreseen. In this respect an importance appertains to the Berkshire Medical Institution which cannot be attached to any seminary of the kind situated in a populous city."

Tickets to Professor Dewey's lectures were, therefore, sold separately, and the general public were expected to attend them. At first a considerable number of persons did so; but it was found less easy than had been expected to create a popular interest in those studies whose advantage to the public it was not at all difficult to demonstrate; an experience very far from exceptional.

The attempt was, however, vigorously made. The lyceum of natural history was organized on the first day of the first term of the college; and the event was distinguished by an address from Rev. Edward Hitchcock, afterwards the eminent geologist, and president of Amherst College, in which he sketched the theory which he afterwards rendered famous, as a mode of reconciling the teachings of geology and revelation. The leading spirit in the lyceum was Professor Dewey.

In 1829, President Goodhue died, and was succeeded by Dr. Zadock Howe of Billerica, who continued in office until 1837, when he resigned, and Dr. H. H. Childs was elected his successor.

Up to this time the Institution had struggled with some vexatious disadvantages, although in spite of all obstacles it had achieved a very gratifying success. Among these impediments, in addition to the financial difficulties which had been mentioned, the chief were the non-residence of the presidents, the dependent connection with Williams College, and the fact that the State Medical Society, in admitting members, discriminated in favor of the graduates of Harvard.

By the election of Doctor Childs, the faculty, always pre-eminently a working body, had its hardest worker at its head, and resident in Pittsfield. In the same year, the legislature dissolved the connection with Williams, and constituted the school at Pittsfield an independent medical college. There was no longer any doubt of the orthodoxy of its teachings, nor of its sound discretion in conferring honors; nor was there any need to borrow prestige from any other academical name to add dignity to its diplomas: its graduates had carried the fame of its own all over the Union.

In 1823, the legislature had conferred upon graduates of the Berkshire Medical Institution the same rights enjoyed by those of Harvard; and now, in 1837, the Massachusetts Medical Society tardily voted that, like them, they should be entitled to admission as fellows of that body without fee or examination. And thus, after a probation of fourteen years, the Berkshire College attained, so far as statutes could confer it, perfect equality with its elder sister at Cambridge.

From 1837 to 1850, no event of general interest occurred in the history of the college, except the sad death of one of its ablest and most beloved professors, Dr. David Palmer, of Woodstock, Vt. In the fall of 1840, Doctor Palmer, in addition to his duties in the college, delivered a course of popular lectures upon geology and chemistry. The course was nearly completed when, on the evening of October 12th, in the presence of a crowded audience, as he was endeavoring to partially fill a glass-tube by suction, the orifice at the lower end having been enlarged by an unobserved fracture, the corrosive fluid rushed into his mouth and throat. He was taken to his room and all that the most unremitting exertions of his professional brethren could do to save him, was done: but, after two days of intense suffering, he died.

On the 5th of February, 1850, the building used as a lecture-room, anatomical theater, and cabinet-rooms, was destroyed by fire, with a considerable portion of its contents. The trustees took immediate measures to replace it with a structure more commensurate with the demands of the day, and in a more suitable location. A grant of ten thousand dollars was obtained from the legislature, very much through the influence of Hon. Ensign H. Kellogg, who was speaker of the house of representatives, as Hon. William C. Jarvis was, when the first legislative grant to the Institution was made. The citizens of Berkshire contributed five thousand dollars. A most commanding and conspicuous site on South street was selected for the new building, which was immediately erected under the special supervision of Messrs. Gordon McKay, George W. Campbell and M. H. Baldwin, with the assistance of John C. Hoadley. The college, which was exceedingly commodious and well adapted to its purpose, was dedicated August 5, 1851, with prayer by Rev. Doctor Humphrey, and addresses by Doctor Childs, and Rev. Doctor Todd.

The advantage of a boarding-house connected with the college had often been questioned, and in its new site was clearly unnecessary. In 1852, therefore, the old hotel-building, which had been used for that purpose for thirty years, was sold to Hon. Thomas Allen, who demolished it, and reannexed the land to the Allen estate, which, by descent and purchase, had come into his possession, and upon which he was erecting a costly mansion on the site of his grandfather's parsonage.

In April, 1863, Dr. H. H. Childs, at the age of 80, although still manifesting much of the nervous energy which had distinguished his youth, and all his early devotion to the college, resigned his professorship, retaining the presidency, although most of the arduous duties which he had so faithfully performed for forty-one years were transferred to younger men.

The trustees passed the following resolution :

Resolved, that the resignation of Dr. H. H. Childs requires from us more than a passing notice. For more than forty years, he has been the active head of the Berkshire Medical Institution, his usefulness having extended to a period almost unprecedented. During these years by his energy and zeal, he has achieved a wide-spread reputation as a medical man, and, by his kindness of heart and courtesy of manner, a no less deserved name as a Christian gentleman. He has ever maintained a high standard of medical honor ; and his pupils must forget or ignore his teachings before they can stoop to anything base or ignoble. With quick appreciation of merit, however modest, and ever ready with a timely word of needed encouragement, his pupils learned to love him, and thousands throughout the length and breadth of the land look back to him as to a foster-father. While we regret the infirmities which compel the retirement of our venerable President from the active duties of instruction, we earnestly hope that the interests of the institution which is so identified with his life and name, may not abate, and that he may long be spared to speak words of cheer to the new generation of students, and give the benefit of his advice and counsel to the faculty and trustees.

The hope expressed in the last paragraph of the resolution was not disappointed. Doctor Childs frequently addressed the students, by their invitation, with paternal counsel and instruction, and also delivered the diplomas at the commencements until 1867. Soon after the close of the lecture-term of that year he went to Boston, where, after passing the winter in the family of his son-in-law, Hon. Elias Merwin, he died on the 22d of March, 1868.

From the year 1823 to 1835, the average attendance of students upon the lectures was about eighty-five. In 1836 it rose to one hundred and five ; but fell off in 1837 to sixty-eight, and the average from that year to 1844 was not more than eighty. From 1844 to 1848,—the most prosperous era of the college,—the numbers for the respective years were 135, 129, 140, 130, 120. The next year, 1849, showed a catalogue of only ninety-five, and thenceforward the decline continued, although not with perfect uniformity, until the term of 1867 attracted barely thirty-five students.

This decadence was not permitted to go on without vigorous and repeated efforts on the part of the trustees and faculty to stay it.

In 1852, Dr. Timothy Childs[1] being in Paris pursuing his medical studies, the trustees purchased through his agency, a very valuable collection of anatomical models and preparations from nature, surgical apparatus, etc.

In 1854, the faculty—to supply the place of the hospitals in whose wards medical tyros in the cities fledge their callow experience — instituted a weekly clinique for the free diagnosis and treatment, in the presence of the students, of such ailments as might be submitted to them. This plan was suggested by Dr. T. Childs,—who had just returned from Europe—and it was successfully initiated under his zealous and energetic management as dean. Patients came in from Pittsfield and a wide circuit of surrounding towns; and, among a multitude of cases more or less simple, there were found an unexpected number of an obscure or obstinate character, which had defied the penetration and skill of the isolated local practitioner, but often yielded to the combined wisdom and varied experience of the college-faculty, occasionally aided by some of the more distinguished members of the District Medical Society.

Men of brilliant professional reputation, many of them young and full of enthusiastic hope of reviving the fortunes of the college, were from time to time added to the faculty: among them

---

[1] Timothy, son of Dr. H. H. Childs, was born at Pittsfield, December 1, 1822, graduated at Williams College in 1841, and at the Berkshire Medical College in 1844. In 1847 he was appointed surgeon of the regiment of Massachusetts Volunteers in the Mexican war; and afterwards was professor of Anatomy, Physiology and Medical Surgery in Pittsfield, and of Surgery in the Maine Medical School at Brunswick, and the New York Medical College. For several years he was also Dean of the Faculty in the Berkshire Medical Institution. He died at Norwich, Conn., in 1865, having shortly before removed to that city.

Drs. Pliny Earle, A. B. Palmer, Paul A. Chadbourne, William H. Thayer, Corydon L. Ford, R. Cresson Styles, William Warren Greene and H. M. Seeley; all of whom gave themselves vigorously to their work; but most of them, soon becoming sensible how hopeless was the task, abandoned it for more promising fields. Little, however, as they were able to accomplish for the college, their influence was very strongly and happily felt in the Medical Society of the county. Doctors Thayer and Styles especially contributed to this result, and greatly intensified the local *esprit de corps* of the profession by the publication, in 1861, of the *Berkshire Medical Journal*, a handsome magazine of forty-eight pages, in which, besides much general medical and surgical matter of interest, there appeared monthly, the transactions of the society, and articles from the pens of its members. Although the magazine was continued but a single year, its influence was lasting.

It did not, however, perceptibly check the decline of the college; and in 1867, the faculty represented to the trustees that expensive additions to the building were needed in order to afford proper facilities for instruction in modern chemistry as applied to the science of medicine. The cost of this improvement, and also of some necessary repairs, they suggested, might be defrayed by a loan, the interest of which would be met by increased receipts from tuition. Upon this suggestion it was voted to raise a sum not exceeding five thousand dollars, for the purposes named, by a mortgage on the real estate of the institution. Three thousand dollars were actually borrowed in this way, of which one thousand dollars were expended for repairs, and the introduction of gas and water into the college-building. Two thousand dollars were applied to the fitting up of a very perfect chemical laboratory, and the purchase of some costly philosophical apparatus.

The desperate expedient of running in debt for the sake of proximately meeting the requirements which the age makes upon this class of seminaries, did not avail. Only thirty-five students attended the lecture-course of 1867, affording a compensation of but about one hundred and thirty dollars to each professor. Salaries like this of course could not procure learned and capable men of established reputation; and, although it would have been easy to collect a faculty of young and ambitious physicians, willing to try their "'prentice hands" as preceptors and lecturers, the trustees had no desire to protract the existence of the college on such terms.

Permission was therefore obtained from the legislature of 1869, to transfer so much of the cabinet, library apparatus, and other personal property as might be deemed best to the Athenæum then about to be established in Pittsfield; and to sell what might not be so desired, together with the real estate, and, after paying the debts of the college, to pay the receipts to the same corporation.

The building was sold, in 1871, to the town, which remodeled it for the use of its High and Grammar schools. The price paid was eight thousand dollars, of which the Athenæum received forty-four hundred, the remainder being required for the payment of the debts of the college. The cabinets, library and apparatus had previously been removed to the Athenæum-building.

So many causes combined to break down the Berkshire Medical Institution that the wonder is that it sustained itself so long as it did. The final and chronic difficulty lay in the fact that it never was free from debt, except for a brief interval at the time of the building of the new college, and that, although the trustees in that halcyon period voted to set apart one thousand dollars, as a nucleus for a fund, the institution in fact never had any such foundation, even to that extent. The sole reliance for meeting the current expenses of the college was upon the tuition of students; a variable and precarious resource, which was sure to fail when most needed.

This was sensibly felt when handsomely endowed and lavishly provided schools sprang up in the western states, retaining at home the students, who before had resorted to Pittsfield in great numbers. The war of the rebellion cut off another region from which the Berkshire school had received many pupils, leaving a very limited section, and that full of rival seminaries, to which it could look for support. And even in this section there was a growing proclivity on the part of young men seeking a medical education, to resort to the great city-schools, which provided facilities for study and observation, with which no country-institution could hope to compete; while, in addition to all this, it was but natural that young men, who upon graduation were for the most part destined to practice in towns and villages more or less retired, should desire to see what they could of metropolitan life in their college-days.

To all this the Berkshire school could oppose little in the way of economy; for, while its tuition was only about one third that of those in the larger cities, board, in consequence of the outgrowth of agriculture by other industries, had come to be as dear in Pittsfield as in New York or Boston, if the students in those cities were content with humble lodgings. While in some of the western schools, like that at Ann Arbor, both tuition and board were cheaper than at Pittsfield.

It was, therefore, wisely determined to abandon an institution which could not be respectably maintained without an outlay, which could be devoted to other purposes with much greater advantage to the interests both of the town and of science.

The Institution thus honorably closed an honorable career. In an existence of forty-four years it had graduated eleven hundred and thirty-eight doctors in medicine, who held a rank in their profession equal to that of those sent out by any college. It had had a large share in the advancement of medical science and the elevation of medical character. It had attracted to Pittsfield in its faculty and others, persons of culture, who had adorned the society of the village while they mingled with it, and left it the better for their presence. And, when it could no longer creditably perform the work which was entrusted to it, it gracefully yielded the place to those who could.

Of one pleasant feature in the life of the college no mention has been made; the voluntary associations—for mutual literary and professional improvement among the students—in which some men afterwards of mark in the world took part.[1]

The early lyceums were ably conducted; and, in 1844, the permanent "Association of the Berkshire Medical College"—a society of alumni—was formed; its object being the promotion of fraternal feeling and unity of action among the students and graduates. The members were of two classes: under-graduates, who had a sort of inchoate position, although entitled to full participation in all the privileges of the society so long as they remained connected with the college; and full members who became so by graduating.

The association had a handsome diploma adorned with a portrait of Doctor Childs, who was *ex officio* its president; although

[1] Among the most eminent were, President Hopkins of Williams College, and Dr. J. G. Holland.

a class-president officiated at the ordinary meetings of the undergraduate members for mutual improvement. The organization flourished until the last commencement in 1867.

The most active students in forming the society were Dr. J. G. Holland, and Dr. Charles Bailey, who wrote the constitution and delivered the first two commencement-orations. After graduation, these gentlemen were associated in practice at Springfield; but Doctor Holland soon abandoned his profession, for that of literature, and Doctor Bailey adopted the Homeopathic, or perhaps Eclectic, practice, and became the leading physician of that school in Pittsfield and Berkshire.

MEDICAL SOCIETIES.

The Massachusetts Medical Society, incorporated in 1781, appointed in 1785, a committee in each county of the commonwealth, "for the purpose of encouraging the communication of all important or extraordinary cases that might occur in the practice of the medical art; and, for this purpose, to meet, correspond, and communicate with any individuals, or any association of physicians in their respective counties, and make report of their doings."

Drs. Erastus Sargent, and Oliver Partridge, both of Stockbridge, were elected for Berkshire, and the secretary, informing them of their appointment, expressed confidence that they would soon be able to form an association that would redound to the honor of the county.

In June, 1787, fifteen physicians, all from towns south of Pittsfield, met at Stockbridge for the purpose of forming such a society; but the "tumults of the times" [the Shays rebellion] prevented any further action, except the choice of officers, until the 12th of June, when articles of association and rules were drawn up and signed by fourteen physicians; among them Dr. Timothy Childs. One of the rules was the following:

No member shall introduce his pupils into the practice of medicine, unless they be first examined by the censors, and recommended by them to the Association, for a certificate of their qualifications, which certificate shall be signed by the president and countersigned by the secretary.

These censors were Drs. Timothy Childs, Erastus Sargent and Eldad Lewis; and at the next meeting of the society, which was held at Pittsfield, in January, 1788, three young men who had been approved by them received the required certificate. Their names were Elijah Catlin, Reuben Backman and Jacob Hoyt; and their diplomas in medicine were the first ever conferred in Berkshire by any authority higher than that of an individual preceptor.

The association adjourned to meet at Stockbridge in June; but it never again assembled: the records closing with the following minute:

But the rebellion in this Commonwealth, raised by Daniel Shays and his associates, proceeding with such rapidity to a crisis, a final period was put to the above-mentioned Association.

There is something not quite clear in this statement. The Shays rebellion in Berkshire county was entirely suppressed during the summer of 1787. Probably the reference is to the bitter feuds which resulted from it. Doctor Whiting, the president of the society was imprisoned and heavily fined for participation in the rebellion, and other members may have been implicated. It was certainly an era not favorable to the fraternal association of any profession.

In November, 1794, a second Berkshire Medical Association was formed, but contained no member from Pittsfield or any town north of it. It continued only two years.

In February, 1818, the legislature granted a charter for the Berkshire District Medical Society, and, in July, 1819, the Fellows of the State Society resident in Berkshire, were called together at Lenox to consider its acceptance. The charter was not accepted at that time; but a committee of which Dr. H. H. Childs was one, was directed to report a fee-table of some kind. The charter was finally accepted in 1820, at a full meeting of the Fellows; and the following officers were chosen: president, Dr. Timothy Childs; vice-president, Dr. Hugo Burghardt; secretary, Alfred Perry; treasurer, librarian and cabinet keeper, Dr. Charles Worthington.

The first business after the organization, was to discharge the old committee upon the all-important matter of a fee-table, and appoint a new one consisting of the president, the vice-president and Dr. Daniel Collins, who reported the following table in June, 1821:

FEE-TABLE 1821.

Visit and advice within one mile (medicine not included),	$1 50
Rate of mileage,	25
Consultation, exclusive of mileage,	1 00
Reducing dislocations and fractures,	$1 00 to 3 00
Venereal cases,	5 00 to 10 00
Amputation,	20 00 to 25 00
Trepanning,	15 00 to 20 00
Operation for strangulated Hernia,	20 00
Extracting and depressing cataract,	10 00
Venesection, or extracting tooth,	25
Emetic or cathartic,	25
Closing harelip,	10 00
Obstetrical cases, mileage after three miles, and a reasonable compensation for long detention,	4 00

Dr. Timothy Childs died February 25, 1821, at the age of seventy-three years, having been in the active practice of his profession until within one week of his death.

Dr. Hugo Burghardt of Richmond, was chosen his successor as president of the Medical Society and Dr. H. H. Childs was elected vice-president.

After the incorporation of the college, the semi-annual meetings of the society were held at Pittsfield on commencement-day; the annual convening, as before, at Lenox. From 1820 to 1834, the meetings appear to have been kept up with considerable spirit; although in the earlier years of that period there was often no quorum.

From 1834 to 1837—owing to a difference with the parent society, which refused to admit graduates of the Berkshire Medical College on the same terms with those of the institution connected with Harvard University—there were no meetings. But in September of the latter year, the State Society having yielded that point, the Fellows of the District Society and other physicians of the county, met at Lenox and revived the old organization. There is no record of any further meetings until March, 1842, when, in response to a call in the county-newspapers, they again met at Lenox, chose the usual officers, and resumed their regular meetings, which have not since been interrupted.

At the semi-annual meeting in November, 1858, it was determined to hold the regular monthly meetings at Pittsfield; and in

1862, the annual meetings were transferred from Lenox to the same place.

In 1871, the Pittsfield Medical Society was formed, its object being the encouragement of social intercourse among the members of the profession and the promotion of scientific culture. The Pittsfield Society entertains the members of the County Society at its monthly meetings; thus, in some measure, equalizing the cost of attendance, they being free, by their location, from traveling expenses.

Since the last-named arrangements have become permanent, the meetings of both societies have been maintained with spirit.

CHAPTER XVII.

DETACHED SUBJECTS.

[1820–1840.]

Population — Business-changes — Agricultural bank — Fires and first fire-engine—First mutual insurance company — Stock-insurance company — Berkshire Mutual Fire-Insurance Company—First grading and planting the park—Abel West—Visit of General Lafayette—The temperance-reformation—Explosion of a powder-magazine.

IT might be supposed that a considerable number of new residents would have been drawn to Pittsfield during the war of 1812, by the business-activity caused by the Cantonment and the office of the superintendent of army-supplies; but the effect of the war in increasing the permanent population of the town seems to have been exceedingly slight, even if it did not actually retard its progress; since the number of inhabitants was only advanced from twenty-six hundred and sixty-five in 1810 to twenty-seven hundred and sixty-eight in 1820.[1]

From 1820 to 1840, when the route of the Western railroad was decided in its favor, the growth of the town was still very slow, although it was more rapid than that of most New England towns not situated upon navigable waters, in those days of excessive western emigration; the census of 1830 showing a population of three thousand five hundred and forty-three, and that of 1840 increasing it to four thousand and sixty. During this period the Pomeroy, Pontoosuc, Stearnsville and Barkersville woolen-factories, and the Pittsfield cotton-factory had been successfully established. The Pomeroy machine-works continued in successful operation, the diminished production of muskets being more than counterbalanced by the introduction of other articles of manufacture. Clapp's carriage-factory constantly

---

[1] In 1800, the population was twenty-two hundred and sixty-one.

increased the quantity and quality of its work. Several minor manufactures had sprung up; but the town had met with losses as well as gains. In 1840 the Housatonic Woolen Company had ceased to struggle against fate and flowage. The Duck factory and the rope-walk had ceased operations; and, since 1832, there had been no fulling-mill; there were few household-looms weaving either woolen or linen in cloths; the cultivation of flax had ceased, and the oil-mills had perished for lack of food. Only a single tannery remained, and there was not a single iron-forge or a potashery left. The cutting of nails, manufacture of looms, spinning-jennies, cards, comb-plates, and spindles, the distilling of essential oils, the making of combs and other small articles, had ended long before. And, whether it was to be counted loss or gain, the temperance-reformation had put out the fires of the distillery and the brewery. As there are gains for all our losses ; so there are losses for all our gains.

But, of those most felt and least compensated, in Pittsfield, during this period, was the constant drain, especially upon the farming-portion of its population, by emigration to the west. Much as had been accomplished by the Agricultural Society, it had not been able to perform the miracle of making the soil of New England rival that of the Genessee valley and Ohio—then the wheat-growing west. Speculating companies, taking advantage of the severe winters and cold summers, about the year 1816, stimulated the western fever by painting the new country as at once the paradise and the El Dorado of the farmer, and, by offering lands upon the most favorable terms. And, as if this were not enough, religious enthusiasm was brought to aid in the depletion of the population of the town. In 1835, while a great revival was in progress at the Baptist church, a preacher from the west portrayed the wants of that region to the assembled crowds, so vividly that one hundred and six of the most valuable members of the church—and it is to be presumed equally valuable citizens—at once emigrated, and were followed soon after by a second migration in such numbers that only three men were left in the organization.[1]

But, however much these drawbacks retarded her increase in population, Pittsfield, between 1820 and 1840 made great and

[1] Rev. Dr. Porter's Historical Sketch of the Baptist Church.

solid progress. The First Baptist and Methodist churches were built in this period; and some of its best secular institutions also date from it. And, to it also belongs the initiation of the first great temperance-reform.

In 1818, the legislature chartered the Agricultural Bank, whose name takes us back to the days when agriculture was still the chief pursuit of the people of Berkshire, and manufactures were struggling for existence. The corporators named in the act were Nathan Willis, Joseph Shearer, David Campbell, John B. Root, Thomas Gold, Theodore Hinsdale, Jr., Lemuel Pomeroy, Henry C. Brown, Samuel D. Colt, Josiah Bissell, Jonathan Allen, Timothy Childs, Henry H. Childs and Phinehas Allen. The capital was fixed at $100,000, and the par value of the shares at one hundred. On the 9th of March, books were opened for subscription to the stock, and the commissioners appointed by the corporators, Messrs. Willis, Gold and Colt, appealed, by advertisement in the newspapers, " to the moneyed interest of the county, to embark in the bank and rear it for the public good." " It is our object," they said, "to concentrate the money-capital of the county, and to render this bank a safe and profitable deposit. It is, therefore, desirable that no shares should be taken on speculation and, at present, not more than fifty by any one person." The time first fixed for closing the books was March thirtieth; but it was afterwards extended to April twentieth; "the season having been unfavorable for traveling;" a statement which indicates the condition of roads in Berkshire; although 'the delay may have been in part due to a lively recollection of a not very remote experience with the Berkshire Bank.

The stock was all subscribed by the twenty-seventh of April, when the stockholders unanimously chose the following board of directors: Thomas Gold, Nathan Willis, Josiah Bissell, Samuel D. Colt and Henry C. Brown; who subsequently elected Thomas Gold president, and Ezekiel R. Colt cashier. Mr. Gold continued president until October 2, 1826, when he was succeeded by Hon. Edward A. Newton. In 1830, Mr. Newton being about to visit Europe, was succeeded by Hon. Henry Shaw, who held the office until 1840, when Mr. Newton was re-elected. Mr. Colt continued to be cashier long past the period we are considering, and, to his financial skill, integrity, industry and firmness, was due, in a very large degree, the remarkable confidence and credit, which the

Agricultural Bank soon acquired and still continues to hold, both with the moneyed and the general public, although his successor has eminent qualifications for the place, and the presidents of the institution have uniformly been men of marked financial ability. The bank purchased and occupied the building erected for the Berkshire Bank.

In the early years of the nineteenth century, the destruction of property by fire, seems, in proportion to the number and value of buildings, to have been more frequent and more disastrous than in later years. Tallow-candles and oil-lamps with their exposed flames and spark-encrusted wicks, open fireplaces and wood-ashes in wooden receptacles, wood-sparks falling upon dry shingle-roofs, and imperfect means of controlling and extinguishing conflagrations, were more powerful causes of this class of disaster than friction-matches, inflammable manufactures, kerosene oil, and fraudulent insurance. In 1819, a committee, appointed by the citizens to consider the subject of mutual insurance, reported that the losses in Pittsfield for the preceding ten years, had been thirty-three hundred dollars, or an average of three hundred and thirty dollars per annum: a considerably larger percentage on the value of combustible property than similar losses for the ten years preceding 1875 would show.

The first recorded movement to check this destruction was at the March town-meeting of 1811, when a proposition for the town to buy a fire-engine was successfully resisted.

In 1812, a movement was made to purchase an engine by subscription. The project lingered, however, until June, 1814, when Major Melville,—who probably had an eye to the protection of the valuable national property in the town—invited those who had subscribed to, or who were interested in, the project, to meet on the 6th of July at Captain Campbell's tavern, to take measures to carry it immediately into effect.

The engine was procured, and the town was asked, at its next meeting, to convert the small dwelling-house which stood where the Baptist church now does — and was occupied by William Smith, the sexton of the old grave-yard—into an engine-house; and to provide buckets and other appendages for the engine, which had no suction-hose; but both these requests were refused, by the votes of that class who always resist town-expenditures for any purpose which does not inure to their own immediate and certain

Five years afterwards, Mr. William Hollister's residence, on South street, near the Housatonic river, was burned, on the afternoon of January 4, 1819, involving a loss of over two thousand dollars—no small amount for that day—and the *Sun*, in its account, says that the lack of complete appurtenances for the engine was severely felt.

The engine and its company, however, seem from the following card, to have done themselves credit:

To the Members of the Pittsfield Volunteer Fire-Company:

Gentlemen:—Permit me to express to you my warmest thanks for your good conduct at the distressing fire yesterday. Even prejudice itself is now awake in your favor. In giving me this new proof of your zeal and abilities, you have confirmed the good opinion I have ever entertained of you.[1]

M. R. Lancton, Director, etc., etc.

There was a general feeling that the protection of the town against fire was insufficient, and a meeting of citizens, to consider the subject, was convened, at Captain Campbell's coffee-house.

At this meeting, William C. Jarvis, H. H. Childs and Josiah Bissell were appointed to consider the expediency of establishing a mutual fire-insurance company. In the March following, this committee published an address to the people, in which they strongly urged such a measure. The address estimated the number of dwelling-houses in the town at two hundred and eighty, worth on an average, one thousand dollars each; making an aggregate of two hundred and eighty thousand dollars of insurable property. They made an elaborate argument for the advantages of the mutual system of insurance; and closed by stating that they had procured from the legislature an act incorporating "The Pittsfield Mutual Fire-Insurance Company." The corporators named in this act were Josiah Bissell, Henry H. Childs, Phinehas Allen, Henry C. Brown, Solomon Warriner, Ezekiel R. Colt, Moses Warner, Jason Clapp, Simeon Brown, Jonathan Allen, 2d, Thomas B. Strong, Calvin Martin and William C. Jarvis.

The company organized, March 29th, by the choice of William C. Jarvis, Josiah Bissell, Oliver P. Dickinson, Oren Benedict and

[1] The services of the engine-company are commended in the newspaper-accounts of several fires during the next fifteen or twenty years, and among the others, at the burning of Ansel Nichols's tavern, a little east of the Dalton line, in 1827, when Capt. [Dr.] Robert Campbell commanded.

John Dickinson, as directors; Calvin Martin, secreta͟ṟ͟ urer. On the 14th of April it gave notice, through the *Su..* it was prepared for business, and that it had been already offe͟ṟ thirty thousand dollars worth of property for insurance. I͟ career was, however, short, and the organization was abandoned after a trial of one or two years. It had made the fatal mistake of requiring no cash-premiums on the issue of its policies; relying upon the collection of assessments when losses actually occurred.

In 1828, Edward A. Newton, Henry Shaw, Theodore Sedgwick, David Campbell, Jr., Lemuel Pomeroy, E. R. Colt and Henry W. Dwight were incorporated as the Berkshire Fire-Insurance Company; a stock-institution with one hundred thousand dollars capital; but it never went into operation.

In 1835, the Berkshire Mutual Fire-Insurance Company was chartered, the corporators named in the act being Nathan Willis, E. A. Newton and E. R. Colt; Messrs. Newton and Colt, who had been engaged in both the previous attempts, having now the gratification of seeing their persistent efforts crowned by the establishment of a permanent and prosperous insurance-company; or one destined to become so.

The new company was organized May 28, 1835, by the choice of the following directors: Nathan Willis, Edward A. Newton, Jabez Peck, Solomon L. Russell, Ezekiel R. Colt, Jason Clapp, Henry C. Brown. The directors chose Nathan Willis, president; and Parker L. Hall, secretary and treasurer.

The succession in the chief offices has been as follows: Presidents, Nathan Willis, elected 1835, died 1849; Thomas B. Strong, elected 1850, died 1855; Ezekiel R. Colt, elected 1855, resigned on account of declining health, in 1860; Walter Laflin, elected 1860, died 1870; John C. West, elected 1870. Secretaries: P. L. Hall, 1835, resigned, 1846, on account of failing health; James Buel, 1846, resigned in 1860, on account of advanced years; John A. Walker, 1860, died 1864; Edwin F. Sandys, 1864, resigned 1872; Albert B. Root, 1872.

The first policy issued by the company was for the rectory of St. Stephen's church on North street, insured by the wardens, E. A. Newton and Hosea Merrill, Jr., for seven hundred and fifty dollars at the rate of one per cent. The number of policies issued by the company during the first ten years of its existence

THE PARK IN 1807.

was seventeen hundred and eight; the number during the last decade — 1865 to 1875 — was eight thousand one hundred and ninety-eight.

The assets in cash, January 1, 1875, were fifty thousand five hundred and eighty-seven dollars; the assets in notes, one hundred and thirty-seven thousand two hundred and thirty-six dollars.

In the year 1815, although the Old Elm had long been held in veneration by the citizens of Pittsfield, nothing had been done to surround it even with a level green, or to protect it from the teeth of the horses which people, trading at the village-stores, or attending church, were accustomed to tie to iron-staples driven into its trunk.[1]

But it happened in that year, that Edward A. Newton visited the town, where he married a daughter of John C. Williams, to whom the town owed its Common; not then known as the Park. Both Mr. Williams, and his wife the savior of the Elm, were then living, and their young son-in-law took a deep interest in it, having heard its story from their lips. It then spread its foliage in full vigor and luxuriance; but Mr. Newton thought it in danger from the practice spoken of; and, to protect it, he with the aid of a friend heaped around the trunk a pile of large stones, which rude device answered its purpose for a while.

The first attempt on the part of the citizens to improve the Common was in the first week of June, 1824; of which we know only what is told in the following paragraph in the *Sun* of the 10th of that month:

> The last week was a busy one in this village, from the vigorous and patriotic efforts which were made to improve the public square and the streets. From the liberality of our fellow-citizens in the town, who cheerfully volunteered their assistance (bringing with them their teams and implements), between three and four hundred days' work were done, to the great improvement of our village, and to the honor of all who participated in the work. * * * We cannot omit noticing the liberality of our friends, the Hancock Shakers, who generously came to our aid.

At its next meeting the town voted its thanks to the Shakers and to gentlemen living outside the central highway-district, for their voluntary service in leveling the public square and grading East street.

---

[1] Some of these were found imbedded in the tree when it fell, in 1861.

In 1825, Mr. Newton made Pittsfield his permanent home, and soon commenced an effort to excite an interest in the improvement of the central square. Many citizens cordially joined in the movement and, in 1826, the town appointed a committee of five, to be joined by the same number appointed by the citizens of the village, to consider certain contemplated improvements. Nathan Willis, Abel West, Jonathan Yale Clark, Butler Goodrich and Charles Churchill, were the committee on the part of the town; S. D. Colt, S. M. McKay, E. R. Colt, on the part of the village.

These committees determined to enclose a park in the center of the square, and to plant it with trees. There was much difference of opinion concerning the form to be given the enclosure, and more as to the amount of land to be withdrawn by it from the highways. Finally, it was decided that the form should be an ellipse; and the size was fixed by a compromise between the largest and the smallest areas proposed. It has since been increased until it equals the largest proposal of 1826.

Nathan Willis, Joseph Merrick and Abel West were made a sub-committee to superintend the planting of the trees. Mr. West, who had for several years been connected with a Rochester nursery, was practically familiar with the work of selecting and transplanting; and, although his own residence was three miles from the square, he was enthusiastically in favor of its improvement. Being also the youngest member of the committee, while General Willis was absorbed in other duties, and Captain Merrick not over sanguine as to the result of the experiment, he was permitted to assume the laboring-oar.

The young trees were planted in the spring of 1827, and although many volunteers came to his aid[1] and the work may be said to have been done by a general "bee" of the people, Mr. West was the master workman; transplanting at least half of the trees with his own hands, and carrying them from the woods upon his shoulders. All passed through his hands. Many were obtained on his own farm; others on that of his neighbor Robert Francis. There being a scarcity of the graceful white elm, and finding a fine clump of the red or slippery elm on the eastern shore of Lake Onota, he intermixed a few of that variety, although well

---

[1] Jonathan Yale Clark was very zealous and efficient. Mr. Clark was born at Lanesboro, in 1782, and died at Pittsfield, in 1866. He was a very active democratic politician.

aware of its inferior quality. Recognizing the beauty and luxuriance of the bass, or American linden, he introduced a few specimens of that fine tree. Only one row of lindens and elms were set, on the outer edge of the enclosure, within the fence; the Old Elm being permitted to stand alone in the center.

In the same year many fine trees were set on South street, where others had been previously planted by Capt. John Dickinson, Thomas B. Strong, Dr. H. H. Childs, William Hollister, Henry C. Brown and others.

Mr. E. A. Newton contributed eighty dollars toward the expense of this improvement of the park; the citizens raising an equal amount. So much of the labor, however, was performed without payment that the expenditure of the whole sum was unnecessary; and, two years afterwards, the surplus was, upon Mr. Newton's suggestion, applied, with an additional subscription raised by Mr. S. L. Russell, to the building of sidewalks on Park square; the first built in town by public effort.

Abel West, to whose energy and public spirit the elms and lindens of the Pittsfield Park, are a monument, was, although not a native of the town, a model specimen of the Pittsfield farmers of his generation. His father, who bore the same name, was born in Vernon, Conn., in 1747. We take the following account of him from the sermon preached by Rev. Dr. Todd, at his son's funeral:

Mr. West was in early manhood when the revolutionary war broke out. The little congregation in Vernon being assembled for worship on the Sabbath, a courier rushed in and announced that the enemy were on hand, off New London, and men and help were needed. The minister stopped services and exhorted his people to take their arms and go. All the men rose up and rushed to their arms, such as each man had. Young West was lame, and had nothing but a single-barreled fowling-piece, but he was there on the ground as soon as his neighbors. Governor Trumbull, seeing his lameness and weapon, assured him that he would do more for his country by going home and raising food for the army than by fighting. He took the advice, and returned home; but the fire of patriotism glowed, and grew in intensity, till, hearing how hard it was for Washington to procure food for his army, he sold his farm, and put the avails in open wagons loaded with food, all he had in the world, and started south. When passing through New Jersey, he met a courier riding and shouting that Lord Cornwallis had surrendered, and the war was over. The provisions would not be needed, and he need not proceed further. The government took all off his hands, paid him down, in Continental money, which was not worth a farthing, and the patriot returned home stripped of all he had, and was a poor man the rest of his days.[1]

It therefore happened that in the year 1800, his son came to Pittsfield, a poor boy. Of his early experience he writes as follows, under the date of April 1, 1870:

Seventy years ago the writer of this was on his way from Washington (Berkshire county) to Pittsfield, with a little bundle under his arm, to work for Col. Simon Larned, seven months, for ten dollars a month; had to make up lost time; four days training and Independence day. Saved thirty dollars of my wages, clothed myself and paid two dollars and eleven cents, parish, town and county taxes. The winter following, I went to school, and did chores for my board. The next year, I worked nine months for the same man at ten dollars a month; and began to get rich. With less than a staff, I passed over the Jordan line of Pittsfield: and now I have become three bands—one in Massachusetts, one in New York, and one in Ohio.[2]

In 1817, Mr. West was able to purchase a farm of eighty acres on West street, in one of the best neighborhoods of the West Part. This he gradually enlarged and improved, and on it he lived until his death, in February, 1871.

Shortly after his removal to the West Part, he was chosen district school committee-man, and was re-elected for many years. He was also representative in the legislature of 1842, the town that year taking the unusual course of sending only one member. But to the office of school committee-man, he devoted himself most assiduously; and conscious that in his own district its duties

[1] He died at his son's house, in Pittsfield, in 1836.

[2] Mr. West married Miss Matilda T. Thompson, by whom he had seven children. The eldest, Prof. Charles West, of Brooklyn, N. Y., was born in 1809, and was educated at Professor Dewey's Gymnasium, in Pittsfield, and at Union College; graduating from the latter institution in 1832. He is at the head of the Brooklyn Heights Female Seminary, and president of the Brooklyn Athenæum. He is widely known as one of the most successful teachers in the country, and as a man of profound scholarship and varied culture. Of Mr. Abel West's other sons, John C., long a selectman of Pittsfield, was born in 1811, and Gilbert, in 1823. They are successful merchants and real estate owners in Pittsfield. William T., born in 1815, Abel K., in 1817, and Thomas D., in 1820, are also successful merchants and real estate owners in Sandusky city, Ohio. Mr. West's only daughter, Harriet, who was born in 1813, married David Campbell, editor of the *Sandusky Clarion*, but is now a widow, residing in Pittsfield.

were performed faithfully and well, he clung to the old district-system of school-management to the last. Indeed, although a whig in politics, he was strenuously opposed to all centralization of political power, whether in the town, the state, or the nation; and held that all assemblies for debate on public affairs, from the district-school meeting up to the houses of congress, were graded schools of statesmanship.

In all respects he was a model of the old-fashioned New England farmer and father; ruling his household with absolute authority, unbounded affection, and a profound sense of his obligation to rear his children in the fear of God, and for the good of their country.

We have given a sketch of Mr. West thus fully, not only on account of the intrinsic merits of its subject, but because he was an excellent type of the men of his class and of his generation, and because his life is otherwise illustrative of the times in which he lived.

In the year 1825—the next after the citizens of Pittsfield had turned their attention to the improvement of their park,—they enjoyed, upon it, one of those pageants for which the town is famed: the reception of the nation's guest, General La Fayette.

When the general was in Albany, in the previous year, a delegation from Pittsfield, of which Col. Gad Humphrey was chairman, had invited him to visit Berkshire; but he was then hastening to Washington to pay his respects to the national authorities at whose solicitation he had crossed the Atlantic. He, however, promised that on his return north he would accept the invitation of the citizens of Pittsfield; and, on the evening of Sunday, June 14, 1825, information was received that he would reach town the next day. Preparations were immediately made to give him a suitable reception, and word was sent through the county of his expected arrival.

On Monday morning, the illustrious visitor left Albany, and was escorted by a corps of cavalry and a numerous cavalcade of gentlemen, to Lebanon Springs, which he reached at half-past two o'clock. After partaking of some refreshment, he proceeded to the state line where he was met by Col. Joshua Danforth, president of the day; chief marshals, Hon. Jonathan Allen and Gen. John B. Root; a deputation from the general committee of the citizens, composed of Messrs. Henry Hubbard, Phinehas Allen,

Henry H. Childs and Thomas A. Gold; High Sheriff Henry C. Brown; Major-General Whiting and staff, with the military escort, consisting of the commissioned officers of the seventh division of Massachusetts militia, in uniform, and a troop of cavalry, under the direction of Majors E. R. Colt and E. M. Bissell, Lieut. Lemuel Pomeroy, Jr., and Ensign Elisha Allen, as marshals of the day.

General La Fayette was welcomed to the county, and the commonwealth, by Sheriff Brown, and after acknowledgments made with his usual grace and courtesy, he took his seat in an elegant coach, provided by Mr. Jason Clapp, which, richly festooned with flowers, and drawn by four spirited greys, bore him pleasantly and rapidly to the village of Pittsfield.

The approach of the cavalcade to the village was announced by bells and cannon, and thousands of citizens from all parts of Berkshire assembled in the park, and neighboring streets, to greet the expected guest, who, at a little before six o'clock, alighted from his carriage, at the door of Captain Merrick's coffee-house, amid the most enthusiastic cheers of the multitude.

On the green, between the church and the Old Elm, a beautiful triumphal arch had been erected; bearing in the center of the front the salutation, WELCOME LA FAYETTE, and on the sides, the names of the American battle-fields upon which he had most distinguished himself. Above the arch hung a well-proportioned national flag, forty-seven feet long, which the ladies of the village had made that morning, and which had been suspended, by Mr. Levi Beebe, from the top of the Old Elm, where, in the favoring breeze of the day, it floated with imposing effect.[1]

General La Fayette, accompanied by the committee, passed between two columns of citizens and soldiery, to the arch, under which he was addressed, by Hon. Jonathan Allen, in a few comprehensive and striking remarks; to which he replied with much feeling, expressing his reciprocation of their affection, and a deep sense of the unequaled honor bestowed upon him. He then proceeded through two lines of school-children to the church, where he was addressed by Professor Batchelder, of the Medical College, in behalf of the ladies of Berkshire, who filled the house to overflowing. The *Sun's* report states that "the brilliant display of

---

[1] The arch was built by Messrs. B. F. Hays and Charles S. Francis.

the beauty and elegance of Berkshire females evidently made a deep impression on the general;" and it may be so, for the Berkshire ladies of that era were widely noted for their loveliness. But, whatever may have been the effect of the spectacle upon the general, who had seen a good many lovely women in his day, from Marie Antoinette down, he certainly addressed those present in a very affectionate and complimentary tone. He was here also introduced to many of the clergy and to a number of revolutionary veterans, several of whom had been his companions in arms.

He then returned to the coffee-house, escorted by the Berkshire Greys—a favorite military company commanded by Capt. Daniel B. Bush — " the citizens crowding upon the procession, anxious to behold, and, all who could, 'to touch the hem of his garment;' among them some of the leaders of the Shakers, who, contrary to their custom, approached the august personage with their hats in hand."[1]

At the hotel, a sumptuous dinner had been prepared; the hall and tables being decorated with evergreens and flowers, mingled with paintings and standards " some of great elegance, which attracted the particular notice of the general and suite, and the admiration of all."

" A blessing was invoked by Rev. Dr. Griffin, president of Williams College, in his usual exalted style ; and the closing benediction was made by Rev. Mr. Bailey, in a very appropriate and elegant manner, with a solemn allusion to the recent catastrophe on the Ohio."[2]

A number of toasts were given; among them, the following by Colonel Danforth : " Our beloved guest, General La Fayette ; the companion in arms of Washington, Greene, Gates and other brave officers of the revolutionary army."

The General responded with the following sentiment : " The citizens of Berkshire, and the people of Pittsfield—may they continue to enjoy, more and more, the benefits of their industry, and the fruits of their republican institutions."

The General's son, George Washington La Fayette, gave as a

[1] *Sun's* report.

[2] The sinking of the steamer Mechanic, by which General La Fayette lost his baggage, including some very valuable mementos—which were, however, subsequently recovered—and came near losing his life.

toast — "The American constellation; the political lighthouse of the world."

M. Le Vasseur, offered — "A free press, the centinel of liberty."

General La Fayette, being on his way to Boston and Charlestown, where he was to assist at the laying of the corner-stone of Bunker Hill monument on the 17th of June, could be detained no longer, and took his leave, accompanied by an escort, and attended by the sheriff of the county to the Hampshire line.

The publication of Doctor Rush's essay concerning the effects of alcohol upon the human system, in 1789, undoubtedly enlightened the public mind upon that subject, and, for a time at least, in some degree checked the excessive use of ardent spirits. Under its influence temperance-societies were organized in various parts of the county; but the only one in Berkshire of which we have knowledge was formed at Adams, in 1789.[1] The pledges conformed to the theory of Doctor Rush that, while distilled liquors, uncombined with other ingredients were ruinous to both soul and body, punch, the cheaper flip,[2] wine, beer, and cider were not only harmless, but beneficial.

When the Massachusetts Society for the Suppression of Intemperance was formed in 1813, it was on the same basis, and it did little but observe an anniversary and listen to a sermon; after which preacher and hearers would repair to tables richly laden with wine.

In 1806, Rev. Ebenezer Porter of Washington, Conn., excited a deep interest among the clergy and people of that section, by a sermon upon the evils of intemperance. Under the influence of this sermon a committee was appointed by the Litchfield Association of Congregational Ministers, to inquire what remedy could be found for the great evil of the day. After deliberating until 1811, they reported that they could find none; when, on motion of Rev. Lyman Beecher, they were discharged, and a new committee appointed, Mr. Beecher being chairman. This was quite

---

[1] *Berkshire Chronicle*, March 4, 1789.

[2] So completely have old customs passed away, that it may be necessary to explain that flip—the usual Sunday drink, on returning from church, and in Pittsfield, at the tavern, between the services—was made of small beer and a glass of spirits, with sugar and nutmeg, made hot by plunging a heated poker into the mug. It was considered a proper beverage for ladies.

a different body from its predecessor, and it promptly reported that a remedy could be found in the agreement of all good Christian people no longer to use spirituous drinks. The idea was scouted as impracticable; but it proved seed that in after years bore good fruit.

In the winter of 1811-12, Rev. Heman Humphrey preached several sermons to his people in Fairfield, in which he practically took the ground of total abstinence from all that can intoxicate; and, much by his influence, the consociation of Fairfield county excluded all spirituous liquors from their own meetings, and in 1812 published an able appeal to the public against the drinking usages of the day; the joint production of Mr. Humphrey and Rev. Roswell Swan of Norwalk.

When Mr. Humphrey removed to Pittsfield in 1817, his interest in the great cause did not diminish, but, before making any special effort in its behalf, in the state of feeling which then existed upon this subject, he deemed it best to thoroughly heal the breach which existed in the church—to do the work which, at that moment, he was specially called to do. The closing years of his pastorate were absorbed in the conduct of the great revival by which they were distinguished, and whose results seemed to him to afford the surest basis for all moral reforms, and so to be preferred before them in effort. And thus, although, no doubt, earnest words upon the subject fell from his lips, both in public and in private, he left the town without having made upon it any recognizable impression as an advocate of temperance.

His immediate successors manifested no marked interest in the reform, and seem to have felt none, other than as good men everywhere had their attention gradually aroused to the public and common danger from the prevailing habits of intemperance. The press, in Pittsfield, was in advance of the pulpit in this matter, and its columns contained frequent warnings and appeals. It was also introduced into the orations upon the fourth of July; and the speakers at the anniversaries of the Agricultural Society dwelt with much earnestness and force upon the harm done to the farmer and his work by the practice of dram-drinking. Indeed, some of the most striking pictures, we have, of the evil, are contained in these addresses; and they affect us the more powerfully that, in general, they are not given in the language of the moralist or of the professed reformer, but in a practical tone, which convinces us how deeply the practice was affecting the business-life of the community.

Still, in all these efforts, there was a certain want of well-defined purpose. The speakers and writers addressed themselves to the task of deepening the sense of an acknowledged danger and evil, with the hope of thus persuading to a restraint in the amount or the character of potations, which they did not dare wholly to condemn. And yet experience had taught them to feel, in the midst of their best efforts, that the hope which prompted them oftenest proved illusory; that the means they were using were altogether inadequate to the great ends they sought to compass.

In the meantime, in a few earnest minds, faith in total abstinence as the only effectual barrier to the flood of intemperance continued to grow; and, in the year 1826, the movement in that direction received a great accession of strength from the organization of the American Temperance Society, and by the publication of some admirable sermons and essays, which set the new doctrine before the country in so favorable a light, that it was taken up everywhere by eloquent tongues and spread through the country like wild-fire; so that in 1831 there were three thousand Total Abstinence Societies, with three hundred thousand members.

The first movement for a temperance-society in Pittsfield,[1] was about the first of January, 1828, when the citizens met at the town-house, to consider the expediency of forming an organization for the suppression of intemperance. The meeting was fully attended, Rev. Eliakim Phelps presiding, and Luther Washburn, Esq., being secretary. After a spirited discussion, it was resolved that a society ought to be formed as soon as possible; and the following gentlemen were appointed a committee to take the preliminary measures to that end: Joseph Merrick, Rev. Augustus Beach, Edward A. Newton, Henry K. Strong and Henry Hubbard.

Rev. Mr. Beach was the leading spirit in this movement; and

---

[1] "Moral Societies," theoretically for the suppression of every species of vice, were common in New England in the early years of the century, and one was formed in Pittsfield in 1814. But in Berkshire, at least, the efforts of these societies were directed almost exclusively to the enforcement of the laws against Sabbath-breaking; and, in all their troubled existence, they did not accomplish so much towards that end as the religious revival of 1822 did in one year.

among his most zealous coadjutors, were Captain Merrick and Messrs. Charles Francis and B. F. Hays, all of whom went from man to man throughout the town, entreating all to sign the pledge.

Mr. Beach, an able speaker, and by temperament an exceedingly ardent and ultra reformer, was, in the discussions which attended the formation of the society, the leading advocate of the extreme doctrines of total abstinence, which some of his associates on the committee were not yet prepared to accept. All, however, except Mr. Newton, did finally accede to them; Rev. Mr. Tappan, a man of a very high order of intellect, who had recently come to Pittsfield with strong opinions against the new doctrines, being, according to tradition, among those whose opinions were reversed by an address of Mr. Beach at an evening-meeting.

We find no record of the organization of this society; nor any mention of it in the public prints, after the preliminary meeting, until May, 1828, when the secretary, Samuel A. Danforth, announced a monthly meeting with an address by Henry Hubbard, in the south lecture-room. Persons now living have, however, a vivid recollection of frequent meetings in the lecture-room, with eloquent speaking and very affecting scenes in connection with the signing of the pledge. Among the speakers were all the clergy of the town, George N. Briggs, then of Lanesboro, Col. Henry W. Dwight, of Stockbridge, Henry K. Strong, and others whose names are not remembered.

The society increased rapidly, and its strong influence, as well as that of the general temperance-sentiment which was spreading through the country, soon began to be apparent. At the election in May, 1828, the town of Pittsfield voted, almost unanimously, that it "disapproved the practice of treating at representative-elections;" and, said the *Argus*, "the representatives-elect went home that night, for the first time for many years, without paying for their honors with rum."

On the 10th of November, 1828, a "highly respectable" meeting of citizens, Rev. Henry P. Tappan presiding, unanimously resolved that it was their wish, that the merchants and others vending and retailing ardent spirits, in the town, should altogether refrain from doing so as soon as it was practicable. The meeting also voted to publish its proceedings in the newspapers, and appointed Jason Clapp, Henry Hubbard and Calvin Martin to communicate its sentiments to the merchants. The latter held a meeting to consider the request and passed the following resolutions:

Resolved, That in common with our fellow-citizens of whatever employment, we deprecate the present excessive use of ardent spirits.

Resolved, That we are disposed to adopt every measure for the suppression of intemperance which may be just and proper.

Resolved, That, in our opinion, the suppression of vice, of whatever description, especially under a free government can only be effected through the medium of moral principle and public feeling. Therefore, while we are willing to meet the feelings of our customers on this subject, we deem it both impolitic and improper, as a class of business, to enter into any combination for the coercive regulation of their opinions or habits.

Resolved, That we cordially approve the institution of the State Society for the Suppression of Intemperance, and rely much upon the moral influence of its operations.

Resolved, That we will so regulate our trade in this article as to check, as much as possible, the evils consequent upon it.

These proceedings were published in the newspapers, signed by Deacon Josiah Bissell, as chairman, and James Buèl, as secretary. Messrs. Bissell and Co., however, a few days afterwards, published an advertisement in which, after quoting the last resolution of the series, they say: "Wishing to carry into effect this resolution, and being satisfied that this branch of trade, with its attendant consequences, is neither pleasant or *profitable;* and, believing our customers generally will approbate the measure, we have determined that from and after this day, we will not sell ardent spirits except for medicinal uses."

Messrs. Buel and Colt also, who had done the most extensive business in this line in the town, totally abandoned it, and most of the other merchants within a few years followed their example.

The reform soon extended to the suppression of the manufacture of ardent spirits, which were no longer distilled, at least upon a large scale.

Of course, in such a state of public sentiment as these proceedings indicate, the old public and social drinking-customs, in a great measure disappeared. Neither wine or spirits were, as a rule, any longer offered to the visitor on casual or formal calls; nor was it the general practice to provide them at private parties, the better class of public balls, or at public dinners. The proportion of those who totally abstained from alcoholic beverages of every class, and those who occasionally, or habitually, indulged in their use, was nearly reversed from what it had been previous to 1828. Within ten years from that date, although there was still a large amount of ardent spirits consumed, the greatest moral revolution that the town has ever known, was effected.[1].

Since 1838, Pittsfield has shared with the rest of the commonwealth the vicissitudes of the temperance-reformation; without any very marked local peculiarities, except such as are incident to a large increase of wealth, and the addition of new and foreign elements to its population. It has had the ordinary succession of temperance-organizations with their several characteristic developments: The Washingtonians in 1841, a tent of the Rechabites in 1846, a lodge of the Sons of Temperance in 1848, and in the same year its first address by John B. Gough, resulting in an earnest movement by the citizens. In 1867, the Mount Sinai Lodge of Good Templars, and the George N. Briggs Temple of Honor were instituted. The Mount Hope Lodge, composed of colored members of the same order, was formed in 1871; and the Noble Lodge in 1874. All the bodies of Good Templars continue to flourish; but the earlier organizations had each only an existence of a few years. The Pittsfield Catholic Total Abstinence and Benevolent Society, was organized in February, 1874, through the efforts of Rev. Thomas Smith, then assistant-pastor of St. Joseph's church, and has had a remarkable influence in checking the prevalence of intemperance. Its pledge is founded upon the extreme doctrines of total abstinence; but it approves only moral suasion for their advancement. It gives a stated amount of aid to sick members and at their death pays a funeral benefit of twenty dollars, besides providing a High Requiem Mass.

One of the most vividly remembered of the minor events in the history of the town was the explosion of the public powder-magazine in July, 1838. This building was located, with singular disregard to public safety, in the north-east corner of the old burial-ground near the center of the village; and, at the time of the explosion contained about seven hundred pounds of gunpowder; of which four hundred pounds, intended for use in testing the

[1] See chapter xviii.

arms manufactured at Lemuel Pomeroy's armory, was owned by the United States government, and the remainder by various merchants.

For several months previous to the explosion the inhabitants of the village had been annoyed by the nocturnal misdemeanors of disorderly young men. Gates were unhinged, signs removed, fences defaced, and other like petty crimes were endured with little resistance by those who suffered from them. Finally, the artillery-pieces belonging to the state were frequently taken out of their house and discharged at dead of night, while the firing of muskets and smaller arms was incessant night after night. Emboldened by the neglect of efficient measures to bring them to justice, the authors of these disturbances, sometime previous to the fourth of July, stole both the cannon and secreted them until, on the night of the seventh of July, one of them was planted in the earth in front of the house of Lemuel Pomeroy, and after being loaded to the muzzle was discharged, ruining the piece and inflicting considerable injury upon the house of Mr. Pomeroy and that opposite to it.

Proceeding to more dangerous practices, the disturbers of the peace several times entered the magazine, by means of false keys, and obtained considerable quantities of gunpowder.

Now, at last, active measures were taken to bring them to justice; and, at the request of Mr. Pomeroy, the Adjutant-General ordered the artillery pieces to Boston. Provoked by this threatened interruption of their discreditable exploits, they threw out menaces to which little attention was paid, that the magazine should be exploded. Even their previous recklessness had not prepared the magistrates or the people to believe that they would perpetrate an act fraught with such danger to life and property, and likely to bring swift and extreme punishment upon themselves. No watch was therefore set over the exposed property, or any other measures of precaution taken. On the night of the 12th of July, however, the threats were put in execution, and at half-past eleven o'clock, the magazine was exploded, the great mass of gunpowder contained in it having been fired by a slow-match.

By remarkable good fortune no loss of life ensued; but the destruction of property was very great. The house owned by Nelson Strong, situated on Fenn street, very near the magazine, was a perfect wreck. Windows, doors, and whatever else could be loosened by the explosion were thrown upon the beds where the family were sleeping. Every piece of crockery in the house was broken. On the opposite side of Fenn street, the house of Mr. Henry Callender was much injured in a similar way, and a brick was thrown entirely through it. The brick school-house on the corner of Pearl and Fenn streets, and a neighboring house lost their windows. The dwelling-house of James Warriner on East street, James H. Dunham on North street, the Medical Institution, the town-hall, the Congregational and Baptist churches suffered severely. Some twenty other buildings suffered considerably, but chiefly from the breakage of glass.

Intense excitement prevailed on the following morning, and at a large meeting of the citizens, after speeches such as the occasion would naturally call out, a committee, of which Edward A. Newton was chairman, was appointed to bring the authors of the outrage to justice. The selectmen also offered a reward of two hundred dollars for their conviction. The committee reported on the 19th of July, that they were "engaged in a course of investigations and suits which promised to bring the guilty parties to justice." But, nevertheless, and although several young men connected with highly respectable families were generally believed to be implicated, no one was ever convicted.

CHAPTER XVIII.

PROMINENT CITIZENS.

[1812-1860.]

Thomas Melville—Henry Clinton Brown — William C. Jarvis — Samuel M. McKay—Thomas Barnard Strong—Henry Hubbard—Edward A. Newton— Ezekiel R. Colt—Nathan Willis—Dr. Robert Campbell—Dr. John Milton Brewster—Solomon L. Russell—Berkshire hotel and incidents.

SEVERAL of the gentlemen who were mentioned as leading citizens of the town during the early part of the nineteenth century, continued in active life, generally with increasing influence, for many years afterwards. Dr. H. H. Childs, Capt. Jonathan Allen, Lemuel Pomeroy, the Campbells, the Colts, and others maintained their position in political life and in town-affairs, with little or no variation in the characteristics which distinguished them in earlier life, while many of their associates of their own generation disappeared from the field; and all of the generation which antedated the century. But the vacancies were filled by men, who, if they did not answer in all respects the description of the earlier Pittsfield fathers, possessed much of their energy and vigor with all their love for the town, while, as a rule, they surpassed them in liberal culture.

Among those who came in especially in connection with the war, were Thomas Melville, Jr., and Henry C. Brown.

Major Melville was the son of Major Thomas Melville, of the Boston Tea-Party, an officer of reputation in the revolutionary war. The senior Major Melville lived to a good old age, and the cocked hat and small clothes, which he continued to wear to the end of his days, were probably the last relics of the costume of the revolution which attracted the admiration of the new generation on Boston streets. Towards the close of the last century, his son and namesake, then about seventeen years old, sailed for

France, where he eventually became a banker at Paris. Here he resided during the stormy closing years of the republic, and the scarcely less stirring era of the consulate and the first empire, until within a year or two of Napoleon's abdication.

In his position as banker, and as an American citizen of polished manners, he had every opportunity to observe Parisian society, and to become acquainted with the leading persons in French politics as well as commerce. Of an enterprising and sanguine temperament, Major Melville engaged in various tempting ventures, for which the wars then convulsing the continent, gave frequent opportunity. And naturally he shared in many fluctuations. Eventually such reverses overtook him, that after an absence of twenty-one years, he returned to his father's roof, bringing with him a wife and two young children; for he had previously married at Paris, a Spanish lady of rare beauty.

Shortly after his return home, the war of 1812 broke out, and he received the appointment of commissary with the rank of Major, and was stationed at Pittsfield. Of his career in that position, and in others of a more or less public character, an account is given in the proper connection.

About the close of the war his wife died, and he afterwards married Miss Mary A. A. Hobart, a granddaughter and ward of Major-General Dearbon, the department-commander.

He finally experienced new pecuniary misfortunes, and, says a relative, "living in the plainest way, became a simple husbandman; though of broad acres, whereof many lay fallow, or in lake and pasture." Nevertheless, to the last, he retained the respect and gratitude of the community, for which he had done much; and for whom he continued to labor, as he had opportunity, with his pen and otherwise. The relative from whom we have before quoted writes as follows:

In 1836, circumstances made me for the greater portion of a year an inmate of my uncle's family, and an active assistant upon the farm. He was then gray-headed, but not wrinkled; of a pleasing complexion; but little, if any, bowed in figure; and preserving evident traces of the prepossessing good looks of his youth. His manners were mild and kindly, with a faded brocade of old French breeding, which—contrasted with his surroundings at the time—impressed me as not a little interesting, nor wholly without a touch of pathos.

He never used the scythe, but I frequently raked with him in the hay-field. At the end of the swath, he would at times pause in the sun, and taking out his smooth-worn box of satin-wood, gracefully help himself to a pinch of snuff, while leaning on his rake : quite naturally ; and yet with a look, which—as I now recall it—presents him in the shadowy aspect of a courtier of Louis XVI, reduced as a refugee, to humble employment in a region far from the gilded Versailles.

* * * * * * * * * * *

By the late October fire, on the great hearth of the capacious kitchen of the old farm-mansion, I remember to have seen him frequently sitting just before early bed-time, gazing into the embers, while his face plainly expressed to a sympathetic observer that his heart—thawed to the core under the influence of the genial flame—carried him far away over the ocean to the gay Boulevards.

Suddenly, under the accumulation of reminiscences, his eye would glisten, and become humid. With a start he would check himself in his reverie, and give an ultimate sigh ; as much as to say, " Ah, well !" and end with an aromatic pinch of snuff. It was the French graft upon the New England stock which produced this autumnal apple ; perhaps the mellower for the frost. * * * * * * *

In 1837, though advanced in years, the Major, yielding to strong inducements, and with a view of ultimate benefit to his children, removed to Galena, in Illinois, there to occupy a responsible position in a mercantile house. * * * He died at Galena, in 1846, and not without the consolation of knowing that his venturous removal so late in life to what was then the remote west, had, in part, already been attended with many happy results to his family.

But enough. He survives in my memory, a cherished inmate—kindly and urbane—one to whom, for the manifestations of his heart, I owe unalloyed gratitude : and, for the rest, pleasingly, though strangely, associated with Tuileries and Taghconics.

In tradition, and in the memory of the older inhabitants of Pittsfield, no man is remembered with higher regard than Major Brown. We give as much as our space will permit of a very faithful sketch prepared by Hon. Alexander Hyde, of Lee :

Among the noble men whom Pittsfield has produced, Major Henry Clinton Brown must stand in the first rank. He is entitled to this position by birth and culture.[1] Good blood flowed in his veins from both his ancestral lines. His father was Col. John Brown, an eminent law-

---

[1] See vol. 1, p. 181. The grandfather of Col. John Brown, whose birth and parentage are there chronicled was Lieut. Jacob Brown, a retired officer of the British army, who was among the earliest settlers of Massachusetts, and established himself at Haverhill.

yer of Pittsfield, and still more eminent for his patriotic services in the revolutionary struggle of '76, in which he laid down his life as a sacrifice, while fighting with the Indians and tories at Stone Arabia. His mother was Huldah Kilbourne, of Sandisfield, Mass., who was left a widow when Henry, who was born at Pittsfield, May 9, 1779, was five months old; and who inspired him with that love of justice and integrity for which the Kilbourne family has ever been distinguished. An intimate friend of Major Brown writes us : " His mind was so constituted that it never entertained the possibility that a Christian could be a dishonest man."

It was the intention of Mrs. Brown to educate her son for the profession of his father, and for this purpose he was early sent to Williams Free School, now Williams College, to prepare for Yale, where his father had been educated. At the age of seventeen, his health becoming seriously impaired, he spent a winter in South Carolina. On his return he was still too feeble to pursue his studies, and deciding that a business-life would be better for his health, he entered the store of his distant relative, Mr. Harry Brown, then a merchant in Stockbridge. Having served an apprenticeship with his cousin, he established himself in the mercantile business in Williamstown, having for a partner, Judge Ezekiel Bacon, late of Utica, and for a clerk, Ezekiel R. Colt of Pittsfield ; and there was ever after a strong friendship between the three. While living in Williamstown he married widow Sutton, a woman of strong character, who lived to bear him two daughters. He afterwards, in 1815, married his cousin, Mary Kilbourne, of Sandisfield, who died in February, 1876.

At Williamstown, he held the office of postmaster, but on the appointment of High-Sheriff Larned as colonel of the Ninth regiment in 1812, he was appointed to the vacancy, and removed to Pittsfield, being then thirty-two years old. We quote again from Mr. Hyde :

The governor was induced, by the very unanimous request of the 'citizens, and particularly by the urgency of those who were contemporaries and fellow-patriots with his father, to tender him this office, for which his courteous manners and systematic business-habits rendered him eminently fitted. This office he continued to hold, to the great acceptance of the people, for twenty-seven years, or till his death, which occurred May 22, 1838.

Many of our older citizens remember Major Brown's high-bred courtesy, manifested not only in the presence of the judges and his peers, but also in all his intercourse with those in the lower walks of life. The boys in the street and the laborers in the field were treated by him with courtesy and consideration. We well remember the urbanity of his manner as he passed the students of Lenox Academy, always bowing to them and greeting them with a pleasant salutation, which tended to increase their self-respect, and more especially their respect for the sheriff. As he drove by us when we were playing "wicket" — the game of ball then fashionable — he did not drive his stylish horse and gig over our wickets, as many took a malicious pleasure in doing, but turned aside, with a pleasant smile, as much as to say, "Boys have some rights which gentlemen are bound to respect."

As an instance of Major Brown's great courtesy toward the most neglected and lowly, we give the following: An aged colored man, named Tip, of whom Miss Sedgwick has given a pleasant sketch, came to his house soon after his death, and poured forth the grief of his grateful heart with a pathos that made every one present to weep. "What a loss! What a loss! Ah, what a friend he was to me!" he continued repeating, while the tears flowed down his cheeks. One of the sons, supposing that his father had conferred some pecuniary benefit upon the poor negro, finally asked him: "What did my father do for you?" "He always treated me like a gentleman, young sir. When I saw him I knew I should be honored. Respect and honor come very blessed to the poor colored man."

Among the duties of his office were some calculated to annoy, if not exasperate, men subject to stern justice, but such was Major Brown's uniform sympathy of heart and kindness of manner in executing the decrees of law, that the poor victims felt that the bitterness of their cup was greatly mitigated. The sheriff not only seemed to share but actually did share their sufferings, and who can estimate the value of such sympathy in alleviating the sorrows of life! Not an instance is known during his sheriffship of more than a quarter of a century, in which his mingled dignity and sympathy did not so far overcome the asperity of convicts and those criminally accused, that they yielded ready obedience to his requests and regarded him as their friend.

* * * * * * * * * * * *

In his church-relations he manifested the same fidelity as in his more public civil office. For many years he was deacon in the First Congregational church of Pittsfield, was superintendent of the Sabbath-school, and took an active part in all causes of benevolence and moral reform. Among other minor offices filled by him was that of president of the Berkshire County Temperance Society.

The title of Major, by which he was so generally known, was fixed upon him by his fellow-citizens, from the fact that the general government once sent him a commission as Major in the United States army. Though he did not accept the commission, his neighbors and friends dubbed him with the title, in spite of his remonstrance.

* * * * * * * * * * * *

As he had lived the life of the righteous, so he died his death peaceably, in the hope of a better life, May 22, 1838, aged fifty-nine; leaving a rich legacy to his family, the town, and the county, in the example of a noble, Christian character.

Hon. William C. Jarvis ranks high among the lawyers and politicians, whose learning and talents have done honor to Pittsfield. He was born at Boston.

In 1811, he was admitted to the bar, and removed to Pittsfield, about the year 1815. He represented the town in the legislatures of 1821–22–23 and 24. In 1825, he was appointed director of the state-prison, and removed to Woburn, which town he represented in the legislatures of 1826–27 and 30. In 1824–26– and 27, he was speaker of the house, receiving at his last election two hundred and sixty-two out of three hundred and thirteen votes. In 1828, he was chosen senator for Middlesex county, on which occasion the *Pittsfield Argus*, which, it will be recollected, was the organ of the conservatives in Berkshire, used the following language: "We believe that he will be a great acquisition to the senate. Mr. Jarvis has always been a friend to the people and an advocate of popular rights. He has done much to liberalize the views of this commonwealth, with regard to civil and religious freedom. We are glad to see a man of his talents and liberal views in our senate, at present the most aristocratical branch of our state-government, founded on the rotten basis of property, and not population."

In 1827, Mr. Jarvis was chosen state-treasurer, but declined. In the same year he received sixty-seven votes for United States senator. For sometime previous to 1829, he held an office in the custom-house, from which he was removed in that year, having opposed the election of President Jackson.

Mr. Jarvis was a clear and thoughtful writer, and in 1820, he published, from the press of Phinehas Allen, a volume of some three hundred pages, 12mo, entitled "The Republican: a Series of Essays on the Principles and Policy of Free States: having a particular reference to the United States of America, and the Individual States." This work attracted considerable attention at the time, and still affords valuable instruction to the political student.

Few, if any, of the citizens who have served the town of Pittsfield well, better deserve its grateful memory than Samuel

Metcalf McKay. Colonel McKay was born at Bennington, Vt., April 3, 1793, and was educated at Williamstown.[1]

He commenced the study of the law at Boston; but at the opening of the war of 1812, he entered the army as lieutenant of cavalry; served with distinction, and rose to the rank of major. In the campaign on the Niagara frontier he did good service as a member of the staff of Major-General Brown.

After the close of the war he removed to Pittsfield, and engaged in farming; but in 1832, entered into the manufacturing business, building the Pittsfield cotton-factory, in connection with Capt. Curtis T. Fenn. He married Katherine Gordon Dexter, daughter of Hon. Samuel Dexter, the distinguished federalist, whose position in favor of the government in the war of 1812, has been related in another chapter.

Colonel McKay was a member of the state-senate in 1829, and represented the town in the legislatures of 1823-24-25-26-28-33-34. He was appointed by Governor Lincoln, commissioner of education; and, in 1827, a member of the first board of Massachusetts railroad-commissioners.

A man of marked earnestness of purpose, Colonel McKay held pronounced opinions and clearly-defined aims; so that he was often brought into conflict, not only with political antagonists, but with those from whom he differed in matters of local policy. But his manners were conciliating and prepossessing. His was one of those happy characters, which compel even political assailants, when about to attack it, to prepare the way by a concession of abundant praise. He died October 6, 1834, of consumption, and was followed by his two elder sons, Samuel Dexter and Eustace, who fell victims to the same disease, both at about the age of twenty-one years. The youngest, Gordon, became a leading man in Pittsfield; built in 1842, the first large iron foundry in the town; and was the first projector of its water-works, to whose success he contributed much. In 1852, he removed to Lawrence, and soon afterwards to Boston. He has accumulated a large fortune, by prosperous manufacturing and shrewd investment in patent-rights.

The widow of Colonel McKay, survived him seven years. She was a lady of elegant culture and fine intellect.

---

[1] He received the honorary degree of A. M. from Williams College, in 1823.

Hon. Thomas Barnard Strong, was born at New Marlboro, in 1780, and graduated at Yale College in 1797. Having read law with his uncle, Hon. Ashbel Strong, by whom he was adopted, he was admitted to the bar in 1800. Inheriting a sufficient fortune, he did not devote himself closely to his profession, but gratified his taste for farming. He was an original corporator and ardent friend of the Agricultural Society, and was actively interested in all institutions for the public good, and especially in schools. Representative in the legislatures of 1827-28-29 and 32. He died May 24, 1863. He employed his leisure largely in liberal studies, which, with fine wit and a keen appreciation of character, rendered him extremely interesting in conversation.

Hon. Henry Hubbard, was born at Sheffield, May 22, 1783. His father, John Hubbard, was a member of the legislature in 1786, and a prominent participant in the Shays rebellion. His grandfather, Rev. Jonathan Hubbard, was the first clergyman of Berkshire county, being settled at Sheffield in 1735; and, through him, he traced his descent to John Hubbard, who landed at Saybrook, Conn., in 1640, and afterwards settled at Hadley, Mass., and became the ancestor of nearly all of the families of the name of Hubbard in western Massachusetts.

Henry Hubbard was educated at Williams College in the class of 1803; but owing to some diffculty between himself and the faculty concerning his commencement-theme, he did not graduate.

He studied law at Sheffield, with his brother-in-law, John W. Hulbert, and, having been admitted to the bar in 1806, commenced practice at Lanesboro, where he continued to reside until 1815; in which year he married Sophia, daughter of Timothy Whitney, a leading merchant of that town. Before the close of the year 1815, he removed to Dalton, and in 1821, to Pittsfield.

In political life he was first a federalist, and afterwards belonged successively to the whig, free-soil and republican parties. He represented the town of Lanesboro in the legislature of 1812, and Pittsfield, in 1838; and was for three years a member of the executive council under Governor Lincoln. When, in the year 1844, the legislature of Massachusetts deemed it incumbent upon the commonwealth to send legal agents to protect its colored seamen in the ports of the southern states, Mr. Hubbard was selected to perform that duty in the courts of New Orleans. He met somewhat more courteous treatment than Mr. Hoar, who was sent on a similar mission to Charleston, experienced ; but the city, and especially the neighboring country, were thrown into intense commotion, and, however politely they expressed it, the merchants and other gentlemen of the city insisted that it was not in their power to protect him. It was clearly impossible to execute the duties intrusted to him, and he returned to Pittsfield. The commonwealth, by not resenting the insults offered to its agents, approved their judgment in withdrawing from the posts to which they had been sent.

For nine years, closing with 1849, Mr. Hubbard edited the *Berkshire County Whig.*

For many years after his removal to Pittsfield, he was one of its most influential political leaders, although somewhat too earnest and impulsive to attain personal success ; frequently advocating unpopular measures : notably in the instance of the famous law forbidding the sale of spirituous liquors in less quantities than fifteen gallons, for which he made a long and powerful argument, in the legislature, which was published in the papers of the county, and drew down upon him the indignation of the opponents of the law who honored him by hanging his effigy on the Old Elm.

Nevertheless, his advocacy of matters of home-policy was esteemed of the highest value, and his speeches contributed much to the success of some of the most important; among them the Medical College, the Hudson and Western railroads, the location of the cemetery, and the improvement of the public schools.

Mr. Hubbard was a high-minded gentleman of the old school. Prominent among his characteristics was a delicate and rare sense of honor which forbade every mean act. With him meanness was the last fault to be pardoned. For every other wrong he had charity. Few men, indeed, whose lives are so pure and who have so high veneration for what is great and good, exhibit so gentle a consideration for those who are the reverse. His mind was of a metaphysical cast, and his deeper thought and study were generally in directions not immediately practical; but his wide and varied reading, his independent thought, and his close observation of men through a long life, made him one of the most interesting conversationalists ; and often enabled him to throw new and valuable light upon subjects, even in common life, which practical speakers had apparently exhausted. He died December 25, 1863.

Hon. Edward Augustus Newton, who was born at Halifax, N. S., May 1, 1785, was the great grandson of Thomas Newton, who came to Massachusetts from England, in 1688, with Governor Phipps, in whose administration he was attorney-general of the province, and comptroller of the customs. The son and grandson of Attorney-General Newton, left Boston upon its evacuation by General Gage, in 1776, and successively held the office of collector of customs for the province of Nova Scotia; the latter holding it at the birth of his son.

His father dying in 1802, Mr. Newton was left without pecuniary provision; and from that time he undertook, not only his own support, but in great part, also, that of his mother and a large family of brothers and sisters. In 1804, he went to Boston and obtained a situation in the commercial house of Stephen Higginson & Co.; by which firm, he was, in 1805, sent out as a super-cargo to the East Indies. Having made a series of voyages in this capacity, both to the East and West Indies, he became a partner in the house; and in 1816, went to reside in Calcutta as their representative. In May of the previous year, he had married Miss Sarah T. Williams, daughter of Hon. John Chandler Williams of Pittsfield. During a residence of nine years in Calcutta, he conducted business with eminent success, and also became deeply interested in the welfare of the neighboring country. Here, also, he became intimately connected with the cause of missions to the heathen; and not only gave much of his time and means to its support—his house being always a home for newly-arrived missionaries of whatever land or creed—but was enabled, by his influence with the native governments, to rescue some of them from prison and probable martyrdom.

In 1825, he retired from business with a handsome fortune; having resisted tempting offers to increase it by remaining longer abroad. When he returned to America, it was his intention to make his residence in Boston; but family considerations inducing him to remain a few years in Pittsfield, he became attached to the place and decided to make it his home.

His father-in-law dying about this time, he purchased the interest of the other heirs in the Williams homestead, in which he continued to reside until his death; identifying himself closely with all the interests of the town.

Chief among the founders of the Episcopal Church, he always had its welfare deeply at heart; but he also sympathized heartily in the growth and prosperity of the other churches of the town, and in all its religious and educational concerns. He was president of the Berkshire County Bible Society, from 1834 to 1844; and of the Agricultural Bank for many years. He was also president of the Agricultural Society for two years, and trustee of Williams College for nineteen. Frequently a member of the town school-committee, he performed its duties zealously.

Although never engaging actively, or at least as a partisan, in political life, he was not at all indifferent to public affairs. Originally a federalist, and by temperament conservative, he generally coincided with the views and measures of the whig party, by which he was elected a member of the executive council, in 1842 and 1843, and presidential elector in 1836. Agreeing with the class of statesmen represented by Messrs. Clay and Webster, in their views regarding the treatment of the institution of slavery in the earlier days of the agitation against it, with the changed circumstances of the country, his opinions became considerably modified, and in his later years he was a warm supporter of the government in the war for the preservation of the Union.

Mr. Newton's first wife died at Rouen, in France, in 1835. In July, 1837, he married Miss Susan C. Tyng, daughter of Dudley Atkins Tyng of Boston, a member of one of the most ancient and distinguished families of Massachusetts. Mr. Newton died August 18, 1862.

On the 8th of May, 1791, before the afternoon-sermon in the little brown meeting-house under the Elm—for it was the Sabbath-day—James D. Colt, son of Capt. James D. Colt, was married, by Rev. Thomas Allen, to Sarah, daughter of Ezekiel Root; and in accordance with the custom, " the marriage-festivities were continued through three days, commencing at the house of the bride's father in the village, and terminating in feasting and joy at the homestead of Captain Colt, on the hill between Stearnsville and the Shaker village. The guests accompanied the wedded pair, all on horseback, in a happy cavalcade from the village to their own home.[1]"

Among the children of this auspicious wedding, was Ezekiel R. Colt, who was born Febuary 9, 1794, and educated at the Pittsfield and Lenox academies. In his earlier youth, Mr. Colt was clerk in the store of his kinsman, John B. Root, and with Henry C. Brown, at Williamstown. He was also clerk in the commissariat of Major Melville at the Cantonment, and at Rutland, Vt. About the year 1816, Mr. Colt commenced the mercantile business in connection with Moses Warner, who, dying soon after, was succeeded by James Buel. This firm continued to do business on Bank row for twenty-five years, maintaining an unrivaled reputation for integrity, and an unusual popularity.

Upon the charter of the Agricultural Bank, Mr. Colt became its cashier, and continued to hold the office until his resignation in 1853. Here he had the opportunity to exercise his peculiar talents, and also some of his marked virtues. In an administration of thirty-five years, no man was ever wronged by him to the extent of a fraction of a penny; while during the whole term, dividends averaging nine per cent. a year, were regularly paid the stockholders, through seasons of panic and through seasons of prosperity. And when at last he left the bank, it was in possession of a large accumulated reserved fund. After his resignation he was appointed state bank-commissioner, and still later, receiver in bankruptcy of the Cochituate Bank of Boston, and performed the duties of both places with ability and with the same probity with which he executed all the offices of trust held by him. The whole range of country-banking scarcely furnishes a parallel to Mr. Colt's career in successful and upright financiering.

During his whole life, Mr. Colt held many offices of honor and trust in the town which none loved better, and to whose good name few contributed so much. Mr. Colt held strong opinions and took a deep interest in politics, but he had little inclination or time for political office. He was, however, chosen presidential elector in 1852.

The prominent virtue in Mr. Colt's character was thorough, unqualified, uncompromising integrity; a love and appreciation

[1]Mr. Colt died at Pittsfield, in 1856, at the age of eighty-eight. Mrs. Colt also died at their homestead, April 8, 1865, aged ninety-four. Some account of Mr. Colt will be found in a previous chapter.

of perfect honesty between man and man, that would not admit the variation of even a penny, when perfect adjustment of accounts was attainable. This, however, was only an indication of character manifested in that relation in which he came most in contact with men. The same exact sense of right governed his actions in all the affairs of life. Neither in word, thought, or deed, would he have knowingly wronged any man. In the greatest material interests of life, in its minutest courtesies, he was alike desirous to render every man all that was his due. For the proprieties of society, he was an earnest advocate, and he enforced them by precept and example. For all the social and moral virtues, he demanded, as he yielded, a strict observance. For every kindly and genial aspect of society, he had a keen and liberal appreciation, but for every violation of propriety which could lead astray, a stern rebuke. The hospitalities of his elegant home were extended to a wide circle of friends from abroad; and here many distinguished visitors to the town, met its most cultivated society. With deep-seated convictions of the realities of religion, although not a church-member, he had for it, and all its institutions, the highest respect and reverence.

Mr. Colt was married December 9, 1819, to Miss Electa, daughter of Capt. David Campbell, who was born at Lenox, May 5, 1793, and died at Pittsfield, June 25, 1875. Mr. Colt died December 3, 1860.

Among the strong men of Pittsfield, in the period we are considering, was Gen. Nathan Willis, who is described in the genealogy of the Willis family, as the son of Nathan; who was the son of Thomas; who was the son of Benjamin; who was the son Benjamin 1st; who was the son of Dea. John Willis, a Puritan of distinction and great respectability, who first appears in 1637, at Duxbury. In 1650, Deacon Willis was one of the grantees of the town of Duxbury, to which he removed the next year, and which he represented in the General Court without interruption for a quarter of a century. Nathan was born in 1763, at Bridgewater, where he spent his early years as a nail-maker and iron-forger. Removing to Rochester in 1790, he became a merchant; and, engaging also in ship-building and navigation, accumulated what was then considered a large fortune.

In 1814, at the age of fifty, he removed to Pittsfield, where he made farming his chief occupation, although engaging sometimes

in mercantile pursuits, and to a small extent in manufactures. "As a business-man," says his biographer, "he was remarkable for exact punctuality; and never, it is believed, during his long life, suffered any one to be disappointed in pecuniary transactions through the non-fulfillment of his promise. Esteemed for his integrity and economy, and confided in for his good sense and judgment, he became the strong man of the democratic party, was repeatedly chosen representative and councilor, and represented both Plymouth and Berkshire counties in the senate." He was, also, twice the democratic candidate for lieutenant-governor, and was delegate from Pittsfield, in the constitutional convention of 1820.

He married in 1787, Sophia, daughter of Col. Benjamin Tupper of Chesterfield, who died in 1790; and in the same year, he married Widow Lucy Dagget, daughter of Noah Fearing of Middleboro, who died in 1860.

General Willis had thirteen children; the best known of whom is Col. George S., who was born at Bridgewater, in 1810, and educated at Union College in the class of 1832. Afterwards he was a merchant and agriculturist in Pittsfield. He was high-sheriff of Berkshire, and several times selectman, and has been otherwise prominent in town-affairs.

Dr. Robert Campbell, son of David Campbell, the elder, was born at Pittsfield in 1796, and graduated at the Berkshire Medical College in 1822, having commenced his studies before the foundation of the Institution. No Pittsfield man, of his generation at least, excelled him in mental power or in liberal culture. The variety of the subjects of which he acquired accurate and practical knowledge was remarkable. His skill in his profession was widely recognized, although he abandoned it in the prime of his life. In the principles and details of the manufactures which were developed in the town during his youth, he became thoroughly versed, although not himself a manufacturer. Placed in command of the primitive fire-engine which served the town until 1844, he made himself acquainted, not only with all that he could learn concerning that class of machines, but with all their appurtenances, with the building of cisterns and tanks, and whatever pertained to the protection of property against fire; knowledge which proved of great value to the town when it came to establish a fire-department. When the subject of building the Western railroad, and of its location in Berkshire, was agitated, it was found that he had quietly become the best-informed man in the county on all points connected with those questions. Even in minor matters, his thirst for experiment and study was ardent; and as an instance, becoming interested in pyrotechnics, he formed a club for their study, which displayed some very brilliant fireworks of their own manufacture, on the park.

He was an excellent connoisseur in the fine arts, and in music was himself an adept; and this, not only from culture, but from a mental organization originally delicate and sensitive.

Another and most distinguishing characteristic of Dr. Campbell, was his extreme conscientiousness, displayed not only in business-integrity, but in all the affairs of life. Neither personal interest or feeling, nor the persuasion of friendship seemed able to swerve him from the course which he believed right and just, as was shown in some notable instances.

With these traits of character, Dr. Campbell could hardly have been expected to prosper as a politician; but he was elected representative in the years 1834 and 1835. He died in 1866.[1]

Among the most active of the early anti-slavery men of Pittsfield, was Dr. John Milton Brewster, a son of Dr. Oliver Brewster, the surgeon of Colonel Brown's regiment at Stone Arabia, and a descendant of Elder Brewster of the Plymouth colony. Dr. J. M. Brewster was born at Becket, October 22, 1789, and in July, 1813, he married Miss Philena Higley, by whom he had ten children. He was educated at the Lenox Academy, and commenced the study of medicine under the instruction of his father. He attended lectures at New Haven in 1810, and graduated in 1812, at the Medical School in Boston, under the charge of Dr. James Jackson. He practiced medicine at Becket until 1821, when he removed to Lenox, where he was a successful physician and surgeon for sixteen years. In April, 1837, he removed to Pittsfield, and continued the practice of his profession with zeal and fidelity for thirty years: making fifty-five years of practice. He died May 3, 1869, at the age of eighty.

Among the citizens who, for the half-century ending with the year 1875, have been the most active and practical in their devotion to public improvement, Solomon L. Russell has been among

---

[1] For further account of Dr. Campbell, see chapter on Railroads.

the most generous, disinterested, and indefatigable. No effort which he believed for the good of the town has lacked his most efficient aid. Mr. Russell was born at Chesterfield, in 1791; his father, Solomon Russell of that town, although blind from the age of seventeen to his death at seventy-nine, rearing a large family in honorable poverty, and proving an especially excellent teacher in morals and religion; his favorite text-book being, "Edwards on the Will." His son, Solomon L., worked on a farm at Northampton, from his nineteenth to his twenty-eighth year, as "hired help." He then removed to Conway, where he cultivated a small farm of his own, and married Wealthy Nash.

In 1826, he removed to Pittsfield with his brother Zeno, an experienced hotel-keeper; and, in the following April, the two purchased the inn on the corner of North and West streets, previously kept by Captain Merrick. In the fall of the same year, the inn was burned accidentally; but the proprietors, new-comers as they were, found themselves among warm-hearted friends. On the adjoining side of Park square, stood the coffee-house, then kept by David Campbell, Sr., who, upon the suggestion of his son, immediately leased it at a fair price to the Messrs. Russell, who occupied it while they were rebuilding their own hotel; making the liberal profit of fifteen hundred dollars. In addition to this, the citizens of the town raised for them a subscription of about six hundred and fifty dollars; the donors stating their desire to aid the Messrs. Russell "in building a house suitable to the public wants, on the same ground as the old one, with barns a suitable distance from the house, and to perfect the whole establishment, and make it such as it should be in our beautiful village."

The house built under these auspices—the Berkshire Hotel—immediately acquired a wide and exceedingly favorable reputation, which it retained for many years. From the date of its erection until the completion of the Western railroad, it was a central station for the several stage-routes, with whose passengers it was constantly thronged. The Berkshire hills, in those days, except under the most favorable circumstances in regard to the condition of the skies, presented few attractions for night-travel; and the hotels, especially the favorite Berkshire, were often so crowded, that they were obliged to seek lodgings for their guests in private houses; while their dinner-tables presented a busy scene, far out of proportion to the size of the village.

After the completion of the railroad, this class of travel very much diminished; but from other circumstances the Berkshire continued a popular and prosperous house, particularly as a resort of travelers for pleasure.

Mr. Russell continued his connection with the Berkshire Hotel for nine years, when he was succeeded in the firm by Lyman Warriner. Afterwards it became Warriner and Cooley; and then, Mr. Warriner withdrawing, Mr. William B. Cooley became sole proprietor, and continued so, until 1866, when he sold the premises, and the Berkshire Life Insurance Company built upon them the finest business-structure in Pittsfield.

In connection with the early story of the hotel, Mr. Russell gives some interesting facts regarding the temperance-reform. Previous to the interest in that cause excited by the addresses of its great apostle, Hewlett, the annual sales of liquors were about one hogshead and one forty-gallon cask of brandy; two hogsheads of Santa Cruz rum; one pipe and forty gallons of gin; twenty barrels of ale; three quarter-casks and a few dozen bottles of choice wines.

It was the practice to place upon the dinner-table a bottle of brandy for each ten plates, from which the guests were privileged to drink at their pleasure, without extra charge. They, however, only partook moderately, and generally not at all. But after Mr. Hewlett's visit, the sales of liquor were diminished fully one half, and the practice of placing brandy upon the table was discontinued.

In 1826, Mr. Russell having disposed of his interest in the hotel, purchased a farm in a beautiful location a little north of the village, where he has since resided; continuing the active interest in town-affairs which he manifested at his very first settlement in Pittsfield. We have already noticed, elsewhere, his valuable services in connection with the first improvements of the park, and the establishment of the cemetery. In many other undertakings for the public interest he was equally zealous; but, perhaps more than any others, in the building of the Western railroad, to which he contributed much as a member of the legislature and otherwise; and in the management of the public schools. In regard to the latter, he was able to effect, shortly after his arrival in town, the reform of an abuse which had gradually grown up in the entire district. It had become the practice, after the school-taxes were assessed, to return to each tax-payer the portion paid by him, which he was to devote to the defraying of the tuition of his own children; so that practically there was no free school in the district. To this custom Mr. Russell strenuously objected, and more with the thought of testing his courage in a contest with the village magnates than with the expectation that he would effect a change, he was elected district committee-man. But he at once refused to draw the customary orders or any other, until schools had been organized as the statute required. Threats of suits at law were made against him, but he was unflinching, and finally triumphant. The illegal custom was broken up.

CHAPTER XIX.

CONGREGATIONAL CHURCHES.

[1824-1875.]

First Church and Parish—Rev. Mr. Bailey—Rev. Dr. Tappan—Rev. Mr. Yeomans — Revivalist preaching, and division of the church — Six ex-pastors of the Congregational churches become college-presidents—Rev. Dr. Brinsmade—Rev. Dr. Todd—Church-statistics—Rev. Mr. Bartlett— Encouragement of sacred music—The first organ and other instrumental music—Trustees of the Ministerial Fund—Parsonage bought, burned and rebuilt — The church hires the Union Parish meeting-house for a lecture-room — Building struck by lightning — Objections to its use—A new lecture-room built—The church of 1794 damaged by fire, sold and removed —A stone-church built — A stone-chapel built — South Congregational Church and Parish—Measures preliminary to colonization—Organization of parish, and first members—New church begun and burned—Rebuilding —Organization of church — Pastorate of Rev. Dr. Harris — Succeeding pastors—New organ—Second Congregational Church.

THE affairs of the First Congregational Church and Parish, after the removal of Dr. Humphrey, flowed so smoothly in the channel in which he had guided them, that its history presents few points of a striking character.

Rev. Rufus William Bailey became pastor in 1824, and continued until 1827; his salary being raised during his pastorate from eight hundred to nine hundred and fifty dollars. He was succeeded in August, 1828, by Rev. Henry Philip Tappan, one of the most profound scholars who ever resided in Pittsfield. He resigned in August, 1831; and was followed in February, by Rev. John W. Yeomans. The salary of both Mr. Tappan and Mr. Yeomans, was eight hundred dollars per annum; but the parish made Mr. Tappan a farewell gift of four hundred dollars.

The latter years of Mr. Yeoman's ministry were disturbed by a difference of opinion in the church, which resulted in a temporary division. The wonderful revival of religion, in Dr. Humphrey's time, under the preaching of the evangelist Nettleton, was remembered by many with an ardent longing for another such outpouring of the Spirit. And this, the more sanguine believed would certainly result from the employment of similar means. The advent of a certain Mr. Foote from Albany—who, although a Congregationalist, preached at Pittsfield in the Baptist Church, was therefore hailed by them with joy; and, for a time, Mr. Yeomans favored the attendance of his people upon his exhortations. Afterwards, however, observing things in Mr. Foote's behavior which he deemed indiscreet and presumptuous, he withdrew his countenance from him. Upon this, those who were styled the "New Measure Men," as favoring the employment of evangelists and other extraordinary means for exciting a popular interest in religion, charged their pastor with obstructing the Gospel work, by neglecting to ask, and even refusing to receive, the class of aid that, gladly welcomed by his predecessor, had been so gloriously effective.

We are not called upon to enter into the merits of this controversy; but having stated the charge against Mr. Yeomans, it is only right to say, that Dr. Humphrey did not sustain the course of those who appealed to his example for support. "Mr. Nettleton," said he, "had many imitators, but not one, that I have any knowledge of, so safe and so helpful to pastors in times of refreshing from the presence of the Lord. They generally insist upon taking the reins, for the time being, out of the hands of the ministers. * * * By so doing, they have unsettled many pastors, instead of strengthening them; weakened and divided many churches."

Whether this was the case or not with Mr. Foote, a large number of the members of the First Church, who favored the "New Measures"—including Deacons Josiah Bissell, S. A. Danforth and T. E. Mosely, with Dr. H. H. Childs, and others—forsook the First Parish and worshiped in the old Union meeting-house, the use of which was tendered them by its owner, Lemuel Pomeroy. The article in the Bill of Rights regarding public worship having been amended, and the legislature having remodeled the statutes in conformity with the change, Mr. Pomeroy and nineteen associates, on the 19th of May, 1834, organized a new religious society, under the name of the Second Congregational Parish of Pittsfield.

There was no formal secession from the First Church, nor was any church formed in connection with the Second Parish; but the professors of religion who joined it—having among them three of the four deacons of the old organization—partook of the communion as though nothing had occurred, except a vacancy in the office of pastor. The new parish settled no minister; but Rev. Samuel A. Allen, and Rev. Professor Chester Dewey, officiated for a time; and Rev. Messrs. Hooker of Lanesboro and Gridley of Williamstown gave their aid. Rev. Mr. Kirk—afterwards celebrated as the eloquent Dr. Kirk of Boston, but then a very popular evangelist of Albany—preached for the new parish two Sundays; and, with this and similar assistance, the advocates of the new measures realized from them their hope for a revival of religion.

But with such a breach in the First Parish, and with many of its remaining members affording no very cordial support to their pastor, it was clearly not a desirable post for him; nor did duty require him to maintain it, when the point at issue was of so little consequence as compared with the harmony of the Congregational body. He therefore resigned his charge, and was dismissed September 9, 1835.[1]

When the statutes passed in conformity with the amendment of the Bill of Rights took effect, in the year 1835, the action of the Congregational Society ceased to form a part of the town-records; and the book in which the doings of the parish were afterwards recorded were destroyed in the burning of the clerk's office in W. M. Root's block, March 4, 1868. Our information regarding them is therefore less full and definite than it otherwise would have been. We believe, however, that the account we give is correct.

Rev. Mr. Yeomans was succeeded in the pastorate by Rev. Horatio Nelson Brinsmade, who was installed in 1835, and con-

---

[1] Mr. Yeomans afterwards became president of La Fayette College, at eastern Pennsylvania. It is a curious fact that five of the nine pastors of the First Church became, after their dismissal, presidents of colleges: viz. Rev. Dr. Allen of Bowdoin; Rev. Dr. Humphrey of Amherst; Rev. Mr. Bailey of Austin; Rev. Dr. Tappan of the University of Michigan; and Rev. Mr. Yeomans of La Fayette. Rev. Dr. Harris, of the colonizing South Parish, also became successively Professor of Theology in the Bangor Theological Seminary, president of Bowdoin College, and Professor of Theology at Yale.

tinued in office until August, 1841, when he resigned, notwithstanding the most earnest endeavors of his people to retain him.

On the 21st of December, 1841, the church and parish elected as Dr. Brinsmade's successor, his friend and classmate, Rev. John Todd; offering him a salary of one thousand dollars, and the use of the parsonage. Mr. Todd commenced his labors January 1, 1842, and was installed on the 16th of the following February. His pastorate, which continued through thirty-one years, embracing the most prosperous era of the town's history, was distinguished by six marked revivals of religion, under the influence of some of which seventy or eighty members were added to the church in a single year.[1]

In the same period, and very much through his influence, a lecture-room of wood, a costly church of stone, and a more costly chapel of the same material were built. The parish grew in numbers so that colonization became necessary and took place. The American Board of Commissioners for Foreign Missions met with it twice. The pastor's salary was raised from time to time, until it became twenty-five hundred dollars, in addition to the use of the parsonage.

In the year 1870, Dr. Todd made a communication to his people requesting to be released, at its close, from the responsibility and

[1] In his historical sermon, February 3, 1873, Dr. Todd gave the following statistics of the church and parish, during their whole existence : " Under the ministry of Rev. Thomas Allen, of forty-six years, three hundred and forty-one members were added to the church ; there were seven hundred and ten baptisms, and four hundred and six marriages ; Rev. William Allen, seven pastorate years, fifty-seven admissions, seventy baptisms, thirty-five marriages ; Rev. Thomas Punderson, eight pastorate years, fifty-six admissions, ninety-seven baptisms, twenty-eight marriages ; Rev. Heman Humphrey, six pastorate years, two hundred and fourteen admissions, one hundred and eighty baptisms, forty-nine marriages ; Rev. Rufus W. Bailey, four pastorate years, ninety-nine admissions, eighty-two baptisms, twenty-four marriages ; Rev. Henry P. Tappan, three pastorate years, one hundred and thirteen admissions ; Rev John Yeomans, two pastorate years, one hundred and forty-one admissions ; Rev. Horatio N. Brinsmade, seven pastorate years, two hundred and eighteen admissions ; Rev. John Todd, thirty-one pastorate years, one thousand and eight admissions, five hundred and two baptisms (three hundred and eighty-seven infants, one hundred and fifteen adults), three hundred and fourteen marriages ; and had those who thought they passed from death unto life at Maplewood made a profession here, I think the number would have amounted to twelve hundred at least."

active duties of the pastorate, but desiring to continue with them as *pastor emeritus*, " so that he might not feel that he was cut off from their sympathy." His request was accompanied also by a very thoughtful and touching statement in detail of the position which he wished to hold.

The church and parish, in acting upon this paper, acceded unanimously and cordially to their pastor's propositions; but with the condition that his resignation should be postponed for two years; to January 1, 1873. But in May, 1872, sudden illness warned him that to persist longer in pastoral labor would endanger his life; and, his request for relief being renewed, was at once granted, with the most fervent expressions of love and sympathy. The parish also voted to continue his salary and the use of the parsonage as when performing the active duties of his pastorate. An additional sketch of his life, regarding matter not especially pertaining to his clerical character is given in another connection.

He was succeeded in January, 1873, by Rev. Edward O. Bartlett of Providence, R. I.; his salary being three thousand dollars in addition to house-rent. He resigned in January, 1876.

THE MEETING-HOUSES.

Liberal appropriations were made, as they were required, to keep the meeting-house, finished in 1794, properly painted and in good repair. Alterations were also made in it, from time to time, to meet the changing tastes of the age; the most important being the substitution of slips for the old-fashioned pews, connected with which was the abolition of the ancient method of seating the people, or " dignifying the meeting-house."

Entries in the record indicate that the parish early began to take an interest in the music of the sanctuary, which has continued to increase to this time. The first appropriation of money for its improvement was eighty dollars, in 1795; the year after the completion of the second meeting-house, when Joshua Danforth, Woodbridge Little, Thomas Gold, and Robert Francis, were appointed to supply a suitable teacher, and see that a suitable number should attend upon his instruction. Similar appropriations were made from time to time, until the organization of musical societies in the town rendered other modes of encouraging the study of church-music more efficient.

About the year 1816, Joseph Shearer presented to the parish its first organ; but the gift, although received with thanks, does not seem to have been highly appreciated. At all events, either through some defect in the instrument, or from inability—perhaps indisposition—to obtain a competent organist, it was suffered to go to ruin, and its pipes became the spoil of the village-boys— the terror, in those days, of all interested in the meeting-house properties.

Until the year 1846, instrumental music in the church was furnished by an orchestra, consisting of a bass viol, violin, and a flute—sometimes two violins, two flutes, a violincello, and the bass viol, played by a performer as bulky as itself. In 1846, an organ was purchased in Boston—a second-hand instrument, whose price we cannot exactly ascertain; but it was insured for one thousand dollars. Miss Helen Dunham, daughter of Deacon James H. Dunham, became the organist, and although having little or no previous acquaintance with the instrument, building upon her skill as a pianist, she soon became an accomplished performer, especially admired for the grace of her voluntaries, and her excellent judgment in accompanying either the choir, or solo-vocalists. Her salary was one hundred dollars per annum.

In 1822, John C. Williams, Nathan Willis, S. M. McKay, Thomas B. Strong, Calvin Martin and Joseph Shearer, were incorporated as the Trustees of the Ministerial Fund in the Town of Pittsfield, with power to superintend the permanent ministerial fund of the Congregational Church. The funds committed to their charge consisted of the legacy bequeathed by Woodbridge Little, as before stated, and of the remaining ministry-lot, reserved in the sale of the "Town Commons," and situated in the northeast corner of the town. It was sold in 1827, to Captain Hosea Merrill, for seven hundred dollars; in 1831, a legacy of four hundred and seventy-six dollars and ninety-four cents was received from Mr. John R. Crocker,[1] which made the amount of the trust-fund one thousand six hundred and seventy-six dollars and nine-

---

[1] Mr. Crocker was a merchant doing business in the brick-store, now No. 3 South street, which he built. He married a daughter of Hon. Phinehas Allen, and died young, of consumption.

ty-four cents; the income from which was paid over annually by the trustees to the treasurer of the parish. Subsequently, in 1866, the fund received an addition of five hundred dollars from a legacy of Deacon Daniel Crofoot, who died in 1832, leaving this bequest, besides others to the American Board of Commissioners for Foreign Missions, and similar institutions, to be paid on the death of his widow, which occurred in 1865.

In the year 1840, the parish bought the homestead of Deacon Josiah Bissell, on South street, for a parsonage, and it was occupied by Messrs. Brinsmade and Todd. But in 1842, it was destroyed by fire; Dr. Todd losing three-fourths of his manuscript sermons, and most of his library. The loss to the parish was two thousand dollars, and the insurance one thousand; but, owing to some informality, the insuring company was able to avoid payment. It was determined, however, to rebuild at once, and on the recommendation of a committee, consisting of Lemuel Pomeroy, S. L. Russell, S. D. Colt, and Elijah Peck, application was made to the trustees for the loan of the Ministerial Fund. The trustees consented on condition that the parish would convey to them by warrantee deed the parsonage, when finished, together with the land attached to it, inserting in the deed a covenant that the parish would keep the building perpetually insured. The pastor being also required to release his right to occupy the premises by virtue of his office.

These terms being communicated to the "committee of ways and means" verbally, the deed required was understood by them to be one of mortgage only, instead of warrantee. Under this natural mistake they gave their assent; and, reporting the facts as they understood them to the parish, they were instructed to erect the building. And it was built by Abraham Burbank, including the painting of both the interior and exterior, for fourteen hundred dollars, it being his first contract after his return to Pittsfield from New Orleans. Papering, fencing, and other incidentals consumed the remainder of the loan of one thousand six hundred and seventy-six dollars and ninety-four cents.

The trustees of the Ministerial Fund gave a perpetual lease of the parsonage to the parish for the interest upon the loan, and as it was incumbent upon them to pay over the income of the fund annually to the parish to be applied to the support of the minister, the accounts of the two parties of necessity balanced each other without any formal adjustment, so long as no addition to the fund disturbed the equilibrium, and no new party was admitted to an interest in the fund.

Until the year 1844, rooms for religious purposes, when other than the meeting-house, town-hall, or the school-houses were required, were provided not by the parish but by the church, which at various times hired the old Union Parish meeting-house, which, on the dissolution of that society, was purchased by Lemuel Pomeroy, and appropriated to many uses, under the name of the lecture-room.

The church occupied it for their prayer-meetings and evening-lectures, and the following memorandum made in its records, preserves the memory of a scene not easily forgotten by those who witnessed it.

SUNDAY EVENING, September 6, 1835.

A pretty full prayer-meeting, supposed to number about three hundred, were in attendance at the lecture-room, when the lightning struck and descended the rod to the eaves. The rod had become detached from the building, and swung loose. There the lightning parted. One portion descended the rod to the earth, and there made a mighty display of its wonderful power. The other portion entered the lecture-room between the first and second windows, carrying in the second window, to the large stove; followed the pipe to the chimney at the west end of the house; descended until it met the stove-pipe in the lower room; thence followed the pipe north to the stove in the north-west lower room, where it tore its way through the floor, and passed out through the underpinning: leaving a visible trace of its irresistible course in the earth outside, and at the north-west corner of the building. Although several were severely injured, yet God's great goodness and mercy were signally manifested in the preservation of the life of every one present.

Efforts were made, from time to time, for the erection of a new lecture-room, or as it was styled in the propositions, sessions-room; but nothing was done effectually until the year 1844–5. The old Union Church was leased for one evening in the week for a religious lecture, while for the others it was used for secular purposes; some of which, in Dr. Todd's view, illy accorded with joint occupancy for religious worship. This feeling on his part was, in the fall of 1844, roused to its fullest extent, when the room was engaged by a traveling dramatic company, for the performance of the play entitled "The Reformed Drunkard." This engagement covered the whole week, except the Wednesday evening reserved for the immemorial religious lecture. But when that evening came, with the preacher's desk surrounded by theatrical paraphernalia, Dr. Todd directed the sexton not to ring the bell; and on the next Sunday declared to his people that he would never again enter that room to hold religious service.

Upon this, vigorous measures were taken for building a lecture-room. The town granted a site adjoining the north-east corner of the meeting-house. Jason Clapp, Elijah Peck, Daniel P. Merriam, Curtis T. Fenn and Amos Barnes, were appointed a committee to erect the building as soon as the necessary funds, which were estimated at fifteen hundred dollars, were procured. It was built in the summer of 1845, at a cost of fourteen hundred dollars. The lecture-room thus erected, was a neat building, fifty-one feet by thirty-six in external dimensions, including an open piazza, seven feet deep, supported by heavy doric pillars. The audience-room was forty-two feet by thirty-four. It fairly served the purpose for which it was designed for nearly twenty-five years; after which it was leased for two years for a district court-room. It was then sold to the town, which removed it to School street, and converted it into a store-house for the fire-department.

At half-past eight o'clock, on the morning of January 9, 1851, fire was discovered in the church, and before it was extinguished considerable damage was done to the interior, including the destruction of the organ; but the bell and town-clock were uninjured, and the latter struck the hour of nine while the flames were still blazing beneath it. There was an insurance of one thousand dollars upon the organ, and of five thousand upon the church.

The injury to the church could have been repaired for twenty-five hundred dollars, which was awarded on the insurance; but a strong desire prevailed in the parish for an edifice of better material, and architecture, and of more ample size; and such it was determined to build. The old meeting-house was therefore placed upon heavy timbers, and raised from its foundation at an expense of four hundred dollars. While it stood thus, a proposition was made that the town should buy it at a price merely nominal, remove it to School street, and remodel it for a town-hall; but an unexpected opposition developed itself. Fears were excited that, if placed upon the proposed site, it would, from its large size and combustible material, endanger the Baptist and Methodist Churches, between which it would stand; and, for this reason, and others of less easy explanation, so strong a feeling was raised, that it was considered useless to call a town-meeting on the subject. The building was then sold at auction to Levi Goodrich for two hundred and seventy dollars; so that the parish was absolutely one hundred and twenty dollars worse off than it would have been had it abandoned the wreck, as the fire left it, to whoever would take it away; and two thousand seven hundred and twenty dollars poorer than it would have been had the building been entirely consumed.

Mr. Goodrich sold his purchase for five hundred dollars to Rev. Wellington H. Tyler, the proprietor of the Pittsfield Young Ladies' Institute, who made some effort to unite the town with him in remodeling it for their joint use. But the location proposed—that now occupied by St. Joseph's Church—was inconvenient for both parties; and that project too was abandoned.

All the town-hall schemes thus failing, and the parish rejecting, by a large vote, a renewed proposal to repair the house for its old purpose, Mr. Tyler removed his prize to the Institute-grounds and converted it into a gymnasium.

The old meeting-house being thus disposed of, Messrs. George W. Campbell, and John C. West, with other gentlemen, whose names we cannot now learn, were appointed to ascertain what amount of money could be raised for a new edifice. The plan adopted was that familiarly known as " dooming," a method of raising money for public purposes then common in Pittsfield. In accordance with it, the committee assessed upon each man of property in the parish, a sort of semi-voluntary tax, proportioned not exactly to what they supposed his resources to be; but based partly upon that, and in part upon his interest in the proposed object, his reputed liberality, and his sense of duty in such matters. In short, they assigned to each individual that measure of contribution which they believed he would voluntarily assume, were he as well-informed in the premises as themselves. Of course the acquiescence of the parties doomed was entirely optional, except in so far as a regard for moral obligation, or respect for public opinion, enforced compliance. In the present case, the members of the parish were divided into classes; the first being asked to contribute six hundred dollars each, the second five hundred dollars, the third four hundred, and so down to one hundred. No assessment was laid upon those who were not considered able and willing to pay the latter sum; but they were left to their own judgment, and many of them contributed very liberally. The result of this plan was a subscription of sixteen thousand and seven hundred dollars.

Before this result was ascertained, Thomas F. Plunkett, Julius Rockwell, Ensign H. Kellogg, John C. West, Gordon McKay, Levi Goodrich, and Moses H. Baldwin, were appointed a committee to superintend the erection of the new church, according to plans and specifications which were to be proposed by them and accepted by the parish before they were acted upon.

Mr. Goodrich soon resigned in order to compete for the contract for building; and Mr. Baldwin, owing to the pressure of his private affairs, took part only in the earliest meetings of the committee. When it organized for business, Mr. Rockwell was in Washington, attending to his duties as representative in congress; Mr. Kellogg was in Boston, as a member of the state-legislature; and Mr. Plunkett was traveling in Europe. Messrs. McKay and West were delegated to examine churches, which had been commended to the committee, in various cities. From these they selected a church in New London, as most nearly approaching their ideal.

Mr. Eidlitz, a New York architect of high reputation, had aided in their tour of observation, and was employed to make plans as nearly resembling the church selected, as the means of the Pittsfield parish would admit. These were submitted to the full committee, from whom they met general and warm approval. But they were still beyond the resources which could then be commanded; and Mr. Eidlitz made yet further modifications, the principal of which were the omission of a tower on the southwest corner, and of a spire which in the first plans surmounted that on the south-east corner; a reduction of the height of the sidewalls; the substitution of less costly windows and less elaborate ornamentation. The auditorium was also made shorter in proportion to its width than the architect, in obedience to the rules of Gothic art, had designed it in his first draft; but this was for acoustic, and not economic reasons. Still the subscription of sixteen thousand seven hundred dollars, with the aid of two thousand five hundred dollars received from insurance, was not sufficient to carry out the reduced plans ; and the questions, what was to be done and how to do it, dragged on from committee-meeting to committee-meeting.

A proposition to restore the old house was renewed before the parish, and rejected, receiving but three votes. A plan for a new wooden church was rejected almost as emphatically. Stone the church must be ; and the question recurred, how to get it. At this point the committee, in the month of May, 1851, advertised for proposals for building the church, according to Mr. Eidlitz's last specifications; the price not to exceed twenty thousand dollars, which the committee, having already nineteen thousand five hundred in their hands, thought they might safely venture. No bids were tendered ; but Messrs. John C. Hoadley and Levi Goodrich offered to take the contract at twenty-one thousand five hundred dollars.

The committee hesitated, but each member added one hundred dollars to his previous subscription ; and Mr. J. C. West, who had become deeply interested in the project, in one day obtained additional subscriptions for the greater part of the deficiency, and the guarantee of responsible gentlemen that the remainder should be paid without loading the parish with debt.

The contract with Messrs. Goodrich and Hoadley was thereupon signed, and work under it was commenced on the 4th of August. During the progress of the building, additions to the plan were made at a cost of fifteen hundred dollars, so that the total sum paid to the contractors was twenty-three thousand dollars. Messrs. Goodrich and Hoadley, finding they were losers by their bargain, a subscription of something over six hundred dollars was raised for the relief of Mr. Goodrich. A tax was assessed for the payment of the deficiency in the original subscription which had been guaranteed, and of the fifteen hundred dollars subsequently added to the cost.

The carpets and the upholstery of the pews were provided by the ladies ; who obtained a handsome sum from a fair, which being invested for them in Reading railroad bonds, by George W. Campbell, who insured them against loss by the decline of those securities in the market, was increased by their rise to fifteen hundred dollars. Still further sums were obtained by the efforts of the ladies. Mr. and Mrs. Jason Clapp, presented a handsome carved sofa and chairs, for the pulpit, which were made from oaken beams taken from the second meeting-house. St. Stephen's Parish (P. E.) presented a costly Bible, in recognition of the courtesy of the First Parish in granting them the use of their lecture-room for divine service while their church was remodeling in 1851. The organ was purchased for three thousand two hundred and fifty dollars, and paid for by subscription. Estimating the gift of Mr. and Mrs. Clapp at two hundred dollars, the entire cost of the edifice, completely fitted for divine service, was a little over twenty-eight thousand dollars, exclusive of the bell, which cost about one thousand dollars, and the clock, which cost six hundred dollars; both of which escaped the fire, and were transferred from the old building to the new.

The corner stone of the church was laid on the 28th of May, 1852, by Rev. Dr. Todd, who made an appropriate address. There were other ceremonies, such as are usual on similar occasions; but perhaps the most interesting feature of the day was the presence, seated on the platform, of respected and venerable citizens who had worshiped in the first humble sanctuary of the parish, and had also aided, sixty-one years before the present ceremonies, in raising the frame of the second meeting-house. They were Butler Goodrich, John Dickinson, Oren Goodrich, Elijah Robbins, and Enoch White.

The church was dedicated July 6, 1853; Rev. Dr. Todd preaching the sermon from the text, Ezra 5:9. "Then asked we those elders, and said: who commanded you to build this house and to make up these walls?"

The church is of the gray limestone of Pittsfield, laid in broken ashlar, trimmed with square blocks of rock-faced Great Barrington blue-stone. The style is Elizabethan, with low walls and a very high roof. The interior is finished in chestnut in the Gothic style, and is opened to the roof. It will seat an audience of eleven hundred.

As the parish continued to increase in numbers and wealth, a desire arose for a chapel, better suited for the use of its Sunday-school and for religious meetings other than the regular Sabbath services. This feeling was cherished by the pastor, and the people gradually grew to adopt his ideal of what such a chapel should be. Finally, in April, 1868, a committee consisting of George N. Dutton, Henry Colt, and Jabez L. Peck, was appointed to report upon

THE FIRST CONGREGATIONAL CHURCH.

the expediency of building a new chapel, or enlarging and repairing the old lecture-room; with some definite plan, including location and probable cost.

At the annual meeting the committee reported that the old lecture-room could not in any way be put in a suitable condition to meet the pressing needs of the parish. They therefore submitted plans which they had procured from Mr. Charles T. Rathbun, for a chapel of the same style and material as the church, to be placed upon the land in its rear, owned by the parish. The cost, they estimated at eleven thousand nine hundred and fifty-one dollars and eighty cents.

The report was accepted, and Messrs. Thomas Colt, Theodore Pomeroy and Robert W. Adam, were appointed a committee, with instructions to erect the chapel at a cost not exceeding fifteen thousand dollars.

At a meeting on the 31st of May, Mr. Colt, in behalf of the committee, recommended that the building should be somewhat larger than was first proposed, and the appropriation was raised to nineteen thousand dollars. And, in November, it was still further increased to twenty-one thousand and two hundred dollars.

The chapel was first occupied in 1870. Its style is Gothic, and the material is the blue limestone of Pittsfield. The interior is finished simply and massively. The workmanship throughout is remarkable for faithfulness and scrupulous care in all its parts. The entire charge of the erection of the chapel and the consideration and advocacy of various important improvements upon the original plans, suggested by the progress of the work, devolved upon Mr. Colt, the chairman of the building-committee, who gave all the details the most constant and assiduous personal supervision, and left as few defects as possible to be discovered by experience.

SOUTH CONGREGATIONAL CHURCH AND PARISH.

We have recorded two instances in which the First Congregational Parish was divided inharmoniously, and in a manner to be regretted; but the time finally came when the growth of the town, and with it that of the Congregational denomination, required more ample accommodations than could be found in the ancient fold. This necessity was anticipated as early as 1844, and led to some measures for gradually extinguishing the parish debt.

In 1847, the proper moment seemed to have come. Several members of the church and parish expressed their willingness to colonize; and Rev. Dr. Humphrey, bound as he was by many tender associations to the old organization, was impelled by a sense of duty to join the movement, and did so with the utmost zeal and cordiality; his labors in its behalf becoming more devoted as their necessity became more and more apparent.

There was not, indeed, perfect unanimity in the belief that absolute separation was the best mode of relief; and Lemuel Pomeroy, constitutionally averse to radical changes except upon extreme need, advocated the employment by the undivided parish of two clergymen, one of whom should preach in the old lecture-room, which he offered to give, and which he thought would prove sufficiently large if an addition of fifteen or twenty feet were made to the length. The proposition was supported by Dr. H. H. Childs, but received few votes in parish-meeting.

In 1848, therefore, some of the gentlemen who had determined to join in the colonization took the initiative by organizing themselves as the South Congregational Parish; not disconnecting themselves, however, at that time from the First Parish, but carrying forward their plans harmoniously within it. Their names were: William M. Ward, Curtis T. Fenn, Charles Hulbert, Welcome S. Howard, Ebenezer Dunham, Henry G. Davis, Charles Montague, Oliver S. Root, Theodore Hinsdale, Avery Carey, William M. Walker, Lewis Stoddard, Wellington H. Tyler, William S. Wells, Merrick Ross, and James H. Dunham.

These were the legal members of the parish-corporation; but the following gentlemen advised with them, and it was understood would formally become connected with the organization when the church was ready for occupancy. They did so in 1850: Heman Humphrey, William L. Peck, Jason Parsons, Josiah Carter, Avery Williams, Bernice Granger, Aaron Clough, Edward Goodrich, Calvin Martin, Amos Barnes, James Dunham, N. J. Wilson, Noah Pixley, William Hubbard, Nelson Tracy, Solomon Wilson, Bradford B. Page, P. L. Page, A. K. Parsons, Charles B. Golden, T. M. Roberts, William Robinson.

The society was organized on the 8th of May, 1844, under a warrant from Calvin Martin, as the South Congregational Parish:

of course only the gentlemen named in the first list taking part. The following officers were chosen: Theodore Hinsdale, moderator; Merrick Ross, James H. Dunham, and Welcome S. Howard, prudential committee; Dr. O. S. Root, clerk; Curtis T. Fenn, treasurer; Theodore Hinsdale, collector.

On the 10th, Wellington H. Tyler, O. S. Root, Avery Carey, James H. Dunham, were appointed to procure a place for a church-edifice; and W. H. Tyler, Avery Carey, Ebenezer Dunham, Lewis Stoddard, Amos Barnes, and Calvin Martin, were chosen a building-committee.

Plans were reported and accepted on the 12th of June, and the building-committee were instructed to advertise for proposals from contractors. On the 9th of July, this committee reported that the lowest proposals received by them exceeded the means of the society to the amount of one thousand or fifteen hundred dollars; and Rev. Dr. Humphrey, Theodore Hinsdale, W. H. Tyler, O. S. Root, C. T. Fenn, and J. H. Dunham were requested to solicit further subscriptions. On the 16th, they reported that they had obtained three hundred and seventy-five dollars.

From the last-named date until April, 1850, by some neglect of the clerk, there is no record of the doings of the parish. Neither is there any record of the measures taken, previous to this date to procure means for the erection of the building.[1] From other sources, however, it appears that after the organization of the new parish, several of its members and friends, and among them Rev. Dr. Humphrey, still favored the purchase and enlargement of the old South-street lecture-room, which was offered to them for seven hundred dollars. It was finally decided to submit the question of accepting this proposition for building a new house to the test of a subscription-paper, which resulted in favor of the latter plan.

The subscription reached the amount of about nine thousand dollars. The old lecture-room was purchased for the sake of the land on which it stood, and which was included in the sale, for fourteen hundred dollars, of which Mr. Pomeroy gave one-half. The site was not so large as was desired, and at the request of the First Parish, it was enlarged by the gift from the Trustees of the

[1] This statement is to be understood as referring to the official parish record. Mr. W. S. Howard kept a full record of the proceedings of the committees, but we have not been able to obtain it, Mr. Howard having removed from town.

Ministerial Fund, of a strip thirty feet wide from the northern edge of their parsonage-garden.

The new meeting-house, which was designed to be a handsome structure of wood, with a graceful spire, was commenced, and had well advanced towards completion, when the old lecture-room, which had been removed a little northward, and was used by the carpenters as a work-shop, caught fire early on the morning of September 15, 1849, and both edifices were entirely consumed. Thus ended the Union Parish meeting-house of 1811–17; scarcely less noted in later years as the "lecture-room;" and in which also the Episcopal Parish of St. Stephen's had its first home. Its companion in misfortune soon arose from its ashes.

Their fellow-citizens of all denominations, and particularly the members of the First Parish, warmly sympathized with the loss and disappointment of those who had expected to soon occupy the new house of worship. This feeling was manifested in many ways, and to give it more full and practical expression, a public meeting was held, at which appropriate resolutions were passed and a committee, consisting of Julius Rockwell, O. S. Root, M. H. Baldwin, Amos Barnes, and James H. Dunham, was appointed to solicit the necessary aid for the re-erection of the burned church.

Some delay arose from the necessity of first ascertaining what sum would be needed, beyond the means at the command of the society; but about the first of November the new building-committee—Calvin Martin, W. H. Tyler, Amos Barnes, Avery Carey, Ebenezer Dunham, and Lewis Stoddard—reported that a new contract had been made with Mr. R. B. Stewart, which would require the sum of twelve thousand dollars, of which the parish was able to furnish nine thousand, leaving three thousand to be raised by subscription. In appealing to the people of the town to supply this deficiency, the citizens' committee said:

> We are quite aware that the chief reliance must be upon those connected with the Congregational denomination; but the generous sympathies and truly Christian feeling, manifested by our fellow-citizens of other denominations, convince us that it will be proper to make our application open to all; in accordance with the friendly relations which so happily exist between all our religious societies and their members. * * * We think it is the general wish of our citizens that this additional fountain of religious instruction should be opened without unnecessary delay. We shall deem it our duty to apply particularly to those

whose means have not been burdened with other enterprises of a like kind. But we respectfully ask the attention of all, and shall in behalf of this object, be happy to receive such subscriptions and donations, large or small, as any of our fellow-citizens may be disposed to give.

The Baptists and Methodists had just rebuilt, or were rebuilding their churches, and that of St. Stephen's Parish had been remodeled at large expense. The contributions from these sources were therefore small. What response was made by the Congregationalists, we cannot, owing to the defect in the record, now ascertain. But the rebuilding of the meeting-house was commenced at once, and it was completed and dedicated November 13, 1850, the sermon being preached by Rev. Dr. Peters of Williamstown.

The church was organized November 12, 1850, by one hundred and thirty members who had been dismissed for that purpose from the First Church. The first pastor, Rev. Samuel Harris of Conway, was installed March 11, 1851; Rev. Nehemiah Adams, D. D., of Boston, preaching the sermon. Doctor Harris was a graduate of Bowdoin College, and of the Bangor Theological Seminary, was a man of eminent ability and of the noblest character. His pastorate was in the highest degree successful; but was terminated in August, 1855, by his acceptance of a professorship in the Bangor Theological Seminary.

Doctor Harris was succeeded in June, 1856, by Rev. Charles B. Boyington of Cincinnati, who was dismissed in July, 1857. Rev. Roswell Foster of Huntington, was installed April 2, 1859. Rev. Samuel R. Dimock was installed September 24, 1861, and dismissed April 24, 1864. Rev. Edward Strong, D. D., of New Haven, and a graduate of Yale College, was installed March 15, 1865, and dismissed November 15, 1871. Rev. Thomas Crowther was installed May 22, 1872, and dismissed May, 1875. Rev. William Carruthers was installed in January, 1876.

The deacons chosen at the organization of the church in 1850, were Curtis T. Fenn, Thomas Taylor and James H. Dunham.

The growth of the church and parish since their organization has been uniform, and their history presents few incidents to be noted.

In 1859, the spire of the church was blown down by a violent gale, which also injured the spire of the Baptist Church so badly that it was necessary to rebuild it. The spire of the South Church was restored at a cost of thirty-five hundred dollars.

In 1873, a new and excellent organ was purchased, and the church so remodeled as to locate the organ and choir in the rear of the pulpit. This change greatly improved the architectural appearance of the interior; and was effected at an expense, including the cost of the organ, of over five thousand dollars. The committee who had charge of the work, were William B. Rice, H. H. Richardson, E. F. Humphrey, W. K. Rice, and James H. Dunham.

SECOND CONGREGATIONAL CHURCH.

In the year 1846, the Second Congregational Church was formed, consisting entirely of people of color. Rev. Dr. Todd, Hon. E. A. Newton, and other gentlemen took a deep interest in the new organization, and with their aid, a neat church was built. Rev. Dr. Garnett of Troy, and other colored clergymen, assisted by preaching and otherwise in gathering a congregation. The first pastor was Rev. Samuel Harrison, who was ordained in 1850, and has been pastor ever since, with the exception of intervals, in which he preached in Springfield, Mass., Portland, Me., and Newport, R. I., and another period, during which he was chaplain of the Fifty-fourth Massachusetts Regiment.

CHAPTER XX.

CHURCHES AND TOWN-HALL.

[1812–1875.]

First Baptist Church — Methodist Episcopal Church — Wesleyan Methodist Church — St. Stephen's Church — Town-hall — St. Joseph's Church — Church of St. Jean Le Baptiste — German Lutheran Church — Synagogue Ansha Amonium — Shaker Society.

FIRST BAPTIST CHURCH.

FOR nine years after the death of Elder Francis, the Baptist Church was without a pastor, and severely felt the deprivation, in the backsliding of some of its members. Still it steadily grew, and the records report many "precious interviews" and "solemn seasons," in the school-house on West street — beyond Lake Onota — to which the Sabbath services had been transferred.

Elder Leland and other neighboring clergymen, often officiated at these meetings; but they were generally conducted by the officers of the church. The people were not insensible to the value of a settled ministry, and the scantiness of their means was painfully apparent in their efforts to obtain it. An examination in 1819, showed that there were only nine members of the church who held property — meaning, probably, real estate — "on which money could be raised for the future," viz: Sylvester Robbins, $1,700; Simeon Lewis, $800; Samuel Root, $4,500; Luke Francis, $2,000; Josiah Francis, $2,500; Oliver Robbins, $4,500; Sylvester Clark, $100; Daniel H. Francis, $1,500; Noble Strong, $4,500. Total, $22,100.

No member of the society was rich; but none were needy, except Backus Boardman, a colored brother, who was supported by the church. The first recorded action for the supply of the pulpit, after the death of Elder Francis, was in 1819,[1] when

[1] Some may, nevertheless, have been made, as the clerk between 1816 and 1819 made no records.

Elder Otis was invited to preach once a month at one dollar per day. He declined. The church next looked to Elder Leland; but he was bold and original, in thought and expression, to a degree which startled some of the more conservative members, and it was voted in September, "on account of the tryals in some minds, not to invite Elder Leland to preach with us at present." The vote was soon rescinded; but Mr. Leland did not accept the call, being absorbed in the revival of religion which was going on in northern Berkshire. He, however, preached in Pittsfield four Sundays in the year 1820.

In March, 1822, the churches in Lanesboro and Pittsfield engaged Elder Augustus Beach to preach in the two towns on alternate Sundays, the Pittsfield church agreeing to pay him on their part, one hundred dollars, and "provide a place for his family." This arrangement continued until 1827, Mr. Beach receiving thirty dollars per annum in lieu of house-rent. About half the pastor's pay was raised by assessment upon the church-members; the remainder by subscription among the members of the society.

Mr. Beach was educated at Williams College, although ill health compelled him to leave at the end of the sophomore year. He was a man of marked character in his profession, being a revivalist in religion and a reformer in morals. Well qualified for a leader in the church-militant, he was ever ready to assail, not only every form of wrong which presented itself, but all which he could seek out; a warfare which, as his people thought, he made too broad, to the neglect of home-duties. But his eloquence being powerful from its earnestness, as well as by its logic, he did not lack success. As a preacher of the gospel, he of course combated indifference, irreligion and sin, in their ordinary manifestations, with all his might; and his achievements as a revivalist were great, resulting in large accessions to his own as well as to other churches. But, as we said, he set himself against all the evil that is in the world; and, as intemperance was then the special wrong to whose enormity reformers were striving to awaken both the church and the world — he made himself a devoted champion against that vice. It was he who first persuaded the friends of temperance in Pittsfield to make total abstinence from wine, beer and cider, as well as from distilled liquors, the corner-stone of their creed. Afterwards he was an equally zealous opponent of slavery. In his later years — long after his removal from Pittsfield — he was, for a time at least, a believer in the near approach of the second advent of the Savior. The reader will hardly fail to note a general resemblance in his character to that of Elder Valentine Rathbun.

Mr. Beach appears to have been the man needed by the Baptist Church when he became its pastor; but for two years it received no accession by baptism, and only four members were added between 1822 and 1827. During the three years next preceding, the religious interest which pervaded all northern Berkshire, extended to Pittsfield, where twenty-three persons joined the Baptist Church; and it may have been that the barren years of Mr. Beach's pastorate were due to reaction. It needed, perhaps, that the field should lie fallow for awhile. But, however that may be, the fruit of the remaining years of his ministry, which extended to September, 1834, fully compensated for those early years of patient waiting, labor and prayer. During the twelve years and four months of Mr. Beach's ministry, the church received one hundred and eighty members by baptism and forty-two by letter. Thirteen died; thirty-seven were dismissed, and thirteen excluded, leaving a net gain of one hundred and fifty-nine. When he resigned its charge it numbered two hundred and forty members.

The pastorate of Mr. Beach was marked by some interesting events. It was upon his motion that several of the Berkshire churches, in 1821, withdrew from the Shaftsbury Association; of which the History of that body gives the following account:

In 1826, Elder Beach, in behalf of some of the Berkshire churches, asked leave to form a new Association, which was granted, although but few of the churches improved the liberty for several years. Only the Adams, Cheshire, Pittsfield, Savoy, Sandisfield and Williamstown churches had left the Shaftsbury Association in 1831, when the Berkshire Association contained fourteen churches. * * * In 1828, correspondence was opened with the Berkshire Association, and Elders Keach, Olmstead, Savory and Marshall appointed delegates to its next session at Pittsfield in May. Thus did the mother give her blessing to the young daughter in her settlement; and finally bequeathed her the whole Baptist territory of Berkshire county as her dowry; though it was a number of years before all the churches in that county could leave the embraces of the mother, even to stay in their own mountain home. It was like the parting of Naomi and her daughters.

"The circular of this year (from the Shaftsbury Association) 'on the Christian Sabbath' is very well written, and is, we suppose, from the pen of Elder Augustus Beach, of Pittsfield, Mass."

In 1831, probably out of regard for the missionary-spirit of the pastor, the sittings in the church were made free; but the experiment did not long continue.

But the most important event in the history of the church during the pastorate of Mr. Beach was the erection of its first meeting-house. The growth of the Baptist denomination in the town, before 1827, rendered a permanent house of worship— and that in the central village — indispensable. As early as the spring of 1825, the town voted to grant a lot of land in the old burial-ground for a site, and appointed the following committee to select the location: John Churchill, Josiah Francis, Jr., Joseph Merrick, Henry Hubbard, Oren Goodrich, Daniel H. Francis, Oliver P. Dickinson.

This committee made choice of a lot, in the north-west corner of the burial-ground, having a frontage on North street of forty-eight feet, and a depth of fifty-six feet. For this selection they gave these reasons to the town: "First, It was best for the town, as it was the least valuable ground on the west line of the burial-ground, and would give an additional value to the remainder,— over and above what any other practicable location would — equal to that of the land given. Second, That, being the most elevated spot in the ground, it is the most eligible as a building-lot; and, being at the greatest possible remove from all the public buildings facing the common, will not increase the danger from fire,[1] or occasion any interruption of any public meeting. Third, The location would require the removal of only two grave-stones, and one of them on an infant's grave. "To be sure," they add, "there are graves without monuments, on this site, but not so many as upon a lot of the same size further south. And as a very general practice formerly obtained of burying the dead under churches, and was only discontinued on account of those who assembled in them to worship, we think that this circumstance can form no objection to the location on that account."

[1] The dread of fire is noticeable in all the action of the town regarding the disposition of the old burial-   om 1796 to 1850.

This reasoning seemed good to the town; the grant was made accordingly; and the first Baptist meeting-house was built with a crypt under it, instead of a cellar. The dead were not removed until the building of the new church; which saved them two changes in reaching their long home.

During the summer, a subscription-paper was circulated to obtain means for building the house; and Eldad Francis called a meeting of the subscribers, at the town-house, October 17th, for the purpose of choosing a committee to propose a plan, fix the location, and superintend the erection of the house. In the record this is described as "a meeting of the Baptist Church and Society, duly notified." Luther Washburn presided,[1] and Daniel H. Francis was clerk. The meeting chose the following committee for the purposes named in the call: Eldad Francis, Luther Washburn, Benjamin F. Hayes, Charles B. Francis and Josiah Francis.

This committee were instructed to further circulate the subscription-paper; which they did to so good purpose, that, on the 28th of November, they were able to report the amount offered as one thousand seven hundred and eighty-three dollars, and a promise of one hundred dollars from Joseph Shearer, Esq. Upon this, they were authorized to proceed to the erection of the house either of brick or wood, at their own discretion; finishing the outside and laying the floor, or "as far as their means would permit." They were also empowered to assign the proportion and class of material to be furnished by those who had made subscriptions, to be paid in that way. After an ineffectual attempt to purchase the old Union Parish meeting-house of Lemuel Pomeroy, the committee proceeded to erect a brick-church sixty feet long by forty-five wide, with a well-proportioned tower and spire. It had sittings for four hundred and fifty persons. Two of the committee, Benjamin F. Hayes and Charles B. Francis, were experienced builders, and under their direction the work was well done. By the terms of the subscription, the material was to be on the ground by April 1, 1825, and the building was completed and dedicated June 13, 1827.

The dedicatory exercises were of a peculiarly interesting char-

[1]Luther Washburn had then recently removed from Lanesboro to Pittsfield. He was an able lawyer, a prominent citizen, and a member of the Baptist Society, although, at least in 1825, not of the church.

acter; and at their close, the large and attentive audience proceeded to the river-side, where fourteen persons received the rite of baptism by immersion.

After the resignation of Mr. Beach, the pulpit was supplied for several years by different ministers, among whom Elders John Leland, S. Remmington and Orson Spencer were prominent. This was a period of great depression with the church, so far as its numbers were concerned. The business of the town was prostrated, and a spirit of emigration to the West prevailed throughout Berkshire. It was at this time that a missionary from the West made known the need in that great region of Christian emigrants to help mould its character, and there went out from this church in one year more than one hundred of its members.

Rev. Edwin Sandys became settled minister of the church in May, 1838, and resigned in December, 1841. Mr. Sandys was born in Worcester, England, December 25, 1798, and was educated at Bradford in Yorkshire. He came to America in 1826, and in 1830 he married Miss Mary Francis, a niece of Elder John Francis. He was a scholarly, pious and discreet preacher; but during his pastorate only four members were added to the church by baptism and eighteen by letter; while eighteen were dismissed and eight excluded, leaving a net loss of four. "The church," says Dr. Porter, "was troubled with many of the delusions which at that period agitated the whole religious community. Perfectionism swept in and bore off some of the most valuable members." In the year after the resignation of Mr. Sandys, however, although there was no settled minister, the church received thirty members by baptism, and seventeen by letter, while only three were dismissed; a net gain of forty-four. Others had entered into his labors.

Since 1842, the story of the Baptist Church has been one of almost uniform progress, with few incidents to be specially noted. Rev. George W. Harris was pastor from January, 1843, to April, 1844; Rev. A. Kingsbury, May, 1843, to December, 1845; Rev. Bradley Miner, April, 1846, to December, 1850. At the close of the year 1847, there were about two hundred members of the church, with a proportional congregation; and the necessity of a larger house of worship began to be apparent. At a church-meeting, December 20th, a committee was therefore appointed to circulate a subscription-paper, and it was resolved to build a house, if the sum of six thousand dollars should be promised. In April, 1848, the committee reported that the required sum had been subscribed, and the following building-committee was appointed: James Francis, George N. Briggs, O. W. Robbins, Olcott Osborne, Robert Francis, S. V. R. Daniels, Henry Stearns, Henry Clark. The committee chose Rev. Mr. Clark chairman.

On the 12th of May the committee reported the plan of a house "sixty feet wide by eighty-three feet deep, containing six rows of slips; supplying, with the slips on each side of the pulpit, a hundred and twenty seats, or six hundred comfortable sittings; also, a singers' gallery, to seat one hundred persons." The committee also recommended that the basement of the house should be so constructed as to admit of two stores in the front, eighteen feet wide by forty deep, and a vestry in the rear of about thirty-seven by fifty-six feet.

On motion of Deacon James Francis, the plan of the committee was amended so as to dispense with the stores, and construct a front with columns and a recess, and to have a properly graded yard in front. In August, the committee presented a design for a church which was estimated to cost eight thousand five hundred dollars; and, after some efforts to reduce the cost by adopting inferior plans, it was determined to build upon that estimate.

This building was of brick, sixty feet wide by eighty-two long, and had a steeple a hundred and sixty-six feet high, surmounted, on the suggestion of Governor Briggs, by a large gilded cross.[1] It was dedicated January 10, 1850, Rev. Rollin H. Neale, D. D., of Boston, preaching the sermon.

Up to this date the church, although acting in the capacity of a parish, had been unincorporated; but, the increasing importance of its business-acts rendering it expedient, it regularly organized under the general statute regarding religious parishes, on the 27th of December, 1849; retaining the name of the First Baptist Church of Pittsfield.

Rev. Lemuel Porter of Lowell, became pastor of the church April 1, 1851, at a salary of one thousand dollars, that of his predecessor having been five hundred. During his residence in

[1] When the spire was partially overthrown by a gale, in 1859, a belfry with somewhat smaller cross, was substituted for it.

Pittsfield he received the degree of Doctor in Divinity. He wrote a brief but very excellent historical sketch of the church. His successor, Rev. Mr. Spaulding, says of him:

> Courtly in his manners, agreeable in his address, with a dignified and commanding presence, genial and scholarly in his work; not profound, but thoroughly imbued with good sense, Lemuel Porter has left an impress upon this church, more lasting in its character, and more potent in its results, perhaps, than any other pastor during this century. Covering a period of eleven years and five months, his pastorate, of a commendable and unusual length, bears upon it, all the way along, marks of great faithfulness and of distinguished zeal in winning souls to Christ. His eye was single to the ministry, and his hands knew no other employment. Souls must have hung heavy upon his heart, or baptisms would have never so filled his hands. Every year but one he was permitted to report baptisms to the Association; and one year, the largest ever reported in any single year of the century— one hundred and two.

Doctor Porter was dismissed August 1, 1862. The later pastors have been Rev. Wayland Hoyt, August, 1863, to August, 1864; Rev. Prof. William C. Richards, January, 1865,—November, 1867; Rev. D. S. Watson, November, 1867,— January, 1871; Rev. C. H. Spaulding, August, 1871,— October, 1875.

In the year 1874–5 the church was very beautifully remodeled under the charge of a building-committee consisting of Deacons James Francis, and Almiron D. Francis, and Mr. S. T. Whipple, assisted by Frederick S. Parker, and D. C. Bedell. This remodeling included an entire change of the front and the interior, making the external architecture of the church very unique and handsome, and the audience-room remarkably attractive. A new organ, placed in the rear of the pulpit, was built at a cost of seven thousand dollars, and its tones are much admired. In connection with these changes, a chapel fifty by sixty feet in size and two stories high was added to the rear of the church, upon land bought of the town for two thousand dollars. The seating-capacity of the audience-room is six hundred, and of the chapel two hundred and fifty. The entire cost of the remodeling, including that of the chapel and organ, was thirty-nine thousand dollars.

The church was re-dedicated on the 6th of April, 1873,—which being within one year of the hundredth after the organization of Valentine Rathbun's church — the pastor, Rev. Mr. Spaulding, preached a centennial sermon, from which we have quoted the passages attributed to him in the foregoing pages.

The architect upon whose plans the church was remodeled, was Charles T. Rathbun, a descendant of the first Baptist minister in Pittsfield.

THE METHODIST EPISCOPAL CHURCH.

The Methodists of Pittsfield, in the earlier years of their history, were notably a frugal, industrious and temperate people, distinguished for their zealous piety even in a strictly religious community. What their character was, in these respects, we have described in a former chapter. What it was among their fellow-townsmen, in the year 1828, will appear from a report of a committee of the town, which included only two of their own number.

In March, of that year, a petition was presented to the town for a grant of land to the trustees of the Methodist Episcopal Society, to aid them in building a church. This petition was referred to S. M. McKay, H. H. Childs, M. R. Lanckton, T. B. Strong, Luther Washburn, Henry Hubbard, Sylvester Rathbun, John Pomeroy and Samuel Root, who, in May, reported in favor of the grant. Their report was recommitted to them, and in June, the committee reiterated their recommendation, sustaining it by an argument, in the course of which they say:

> It is the object of the petitioners to establish, in this place, a station of the Methodist Circuit which embraces the whole county of Berkshire, and a part of the county of Hampshire. The Methodist Episcopal communicants, or church-members, in the circuit, now number six hundred and fifty-nine. It is the opinion of Methodist preachers and class-leaders that a permanent station at this place, where regular and constant preaching shall be maintained, would not only be well attended from abroad; but that it is absolutely necessary to the accomplishment of their system, which has done so much for the interest of religion in the West and South.
>
> It should be explained to the town that this system, throughout the United States, comprises in part the establishment of permanent stations in every circuit, where there are places sufficiently populous and central to warrant the supply of regular and constant preaching.
>
> The petitioners state that they believe that they have resources and wealth enough to construct a suitable house for public worship. They,

therefore, place themselves before the town, and ask the extension to them of that liberal policy which has been extended to other denominations. In this connection, they presented for consideration, the number of their communicants actually resident in the town, which is one hundred and sixteen. They also present their respectable character, both as Christians and citizens, whose civil rights, considered personally, or in reference to the amount of their property, give them some claim upon the town for so much of the public land as has heretofore been appropriated for the accommodation of other religious societies. The number of regular members of the Methodist Episcopal Church (one hundred and sixteen) is exclusive of the Methodist Reformed or Dissenters;[1] and it was stated to the committee that the Dissenters have no objection to the proposed station.

The committee, recognizing the justice of these claims, recommended the grant of a lot "of such dimensions, and upon such terms, as would secure the interest of the public, and at the same time meet liberally, in truth and spirit, the object of the donation." The town granted a lot from the burial-ground, commencing thirty feet north of Allen's book-store, and having a front of thirty feet on North street, and a depth of forty feet. The conditions were that whenever a building should be erected upon the lot — which was not to be occupied by the church — it should be an "elegant brick-structure with marble-trimmings, and at least two stories high;" and that the church should be built within three-quarters of a mile of the Congregational meeting-house, and should be equal in elegance and durability to the Baptist house." In the latter part of November, 1829, the selectmen reported that these conditions had been complied with so far as the erection of the church was concerned, and transferred the lot on North street to the trustees of the Methodist Society: James Foot, William Stevens, John Butler, Lyman Dewey, and Thomas A. Gaylord.

The church was commenced in the spring of 1829, and completed and dedicated November 11th of that year; the services being conducted by Rev. Samuel Merwin, aided by Rev. Arnold Schofield. It was a plain brick-building, with a spire, and cost about three thousand dollars, half of which was raised after the dedication. Rev. Cyrus Prindle was pastor from May, 1829, until the spring of 1831; and in 1867 he stated that the effort to

[1] See Chapter VI.

liquidate this debt was the first great financial struggle of his life; and he went through many for similar ends. The Methodist Episcopal Church worshiped in this humble sanctuary until 1852; but, during the pastorate of Rev. Stephen Parks, in 1851 and 1852 — and very much through his instrumentality — means were raised and a new church of wood built on the corner of Fenn and First streets. The lot cost fifteen hundred dollars; and the church—a respectable building, with an audience-room capable of seating six hundred persons, and with chapel and class-rooms in the basement, cost seven thousand five hundred dollars. The building-committee were Rev. Stephen Parks, Levi Childs, T. G. Atwood, J. M. Holland and J. H. Butler. Mr. D. C. Morey, treasurer of the trustees, acted with the committee, and had the laborious task of collecting the subscriptions, and paying the bills. The house was dedicated in the fall of 1852, Rev. Allen Steele, of Albany, preaching the sermon.

In 1866, the Methodists of Pittsfield were not behind their brethren in other parts of the country in the spirit with which they celebrated the centennial year of their church. But in their offerings for church-extension, they looked forward to the necessity of soon building a church of a costly character at home. During the year, the pastor, Rev. Mr. Brown, preached a glowing sermon, in which he set before the people a high ideal of what such a church should be. Three years afterwards, his successor, Rev. Dr. Wentworth — one of the ablest and most learned clergymen who ever filled a Pittsfield pulpit — having preached a sermon partly upon Solomon's Temple, suddenly changed the subject, and made an eloquent appeal to his people, in behalf of a proper house of worship for themselves.

The seed thus sown lay dormant for awhile in the minds of the people; but in March, 1871, the church occupied by them having been partially burned, the official board resolved to submit the question of the erection of a new house to the church and society; and at this meeting, Rev. Mr. Waters presiding, and E. H. Nash being secretary, it was voted nearly unanimously to proceed with the work at once.

The following committee were appointed to select and purchase a site, and contract for and superintend the building: William Renne, Charles E. Parker, C. C. Childs, Oren Benedict, T. R. Glentz, Charles T. Rathbun, Flavius P. Noble, James H. Butler,

Samuel E. Howe and Henry Noble. Mr. Renne was chosen chairman, and Mr. Howe secretary and treasurer, of the committee.

The committee was clothed with full power to act; but upon important points they consulted the official board, and sometimes the entire body of the church and society. After examining and ascertaining the price of several fine locations, they recommended the purchase of a site on the corner of Fenn and Pearl streets, where, by uniting lots belonging to three different parties, sufficient space could be obtained for an aggregate price of twenty-one thousand five hundred dollars. This recommendation was approved, and the land was bought.

In the summer of 1872, a plan remarkable for grandeur and beauty was submitted by Charles T. Rathbun, and accepted. The foundation and first floor were built in the fall of 1872, the mason-work being done by Haskell Dodge, and the wood-work by James H. Butler; the aggregate price being ten thousand dollars. The contract for building the superstructure was awarded to Mr. Butler, who contracted with Mr. Dodge, and with the firm of Butler, Merrill & Co., of which he was the senior partner, for the wood-work; the aggregate price being fifty-six thousand dollars. This was exclusive of the glass for the windows, the pews, pulpit, heating and lighting apparatus and some other small items.

Steam-heating apparatus was afterwards put in by Robbins, Gamwell & Co., for three thousand dollars. The glass cost fifteen hundred dollars. An organ was built by Johnson & Co., of Westfield, for five thousand dollars. And the cost of the land and foundation, with minor items, carried the entire cost of the work to one hundred and fifteen thousand dollars.

Work upon it was begun in the spring of 1873, and the corner-stone was laid April 22, 1873, Rev. Dr. Wentworth officiating, assisted by Rev. Mr. Clymer. The church was completed and dedicated May 5, 1874, Bishop J. T. Peck, of California, preaching the sermon. During the day, under the persuasive eloquence of Rev. B. I. Ives, D. D., of Auburn, N. Y., a sufficient sum was subscribed to cancel the debt for the construction of the building. The ladies—who had pledged three thousand dollars towards this purpose, and had also defrayed the expense of upholstering, and in part furnishing the church — on

THE METHODIST EPISCOPAL CHURCH.

the day of dedication, entertained hundreds of guests with excellent free dinners in their parlor over the chapel.[1]

The church is built of Philadelphia pressed brick, with rich trimmings of light-drab freestone, from the Amherst, Ohio, quarries. The style is Gothic, and the ground-plan is cruciform, the arms, however, being quite short. The extreme external length of the main building is one hundred and sixty two feet, and its width seventy-two feet. It has three spires; the highest of which surmounting a tower which forms the main entrance, is a hundred and seventy-six feet high. The effect of the grand contour of the building, with its numerous spires and pinnacles, is very striking; much more so than that of any other building in the town.

The main audience-room is one hundred and one feet long, sixty-eight wide, and forty-eight high. The chapel — which opens into the main room by sliding-doors, of its whole breadth — is ninety-six feet long by forty-eight wide. Over it are ladies' parlors and class-rooms. The audience-room is handsomely finished, and is lighted by eight windows of stained glass of elegant designs. It has a seating-capacity of fourteen hundred, and, with the chapel, which can be easily thrown into one room with it, it will furnish seats for nineteen hundred persons. Twenty-one hundred were in the two rooms on the day of the dedication.

The architect and builders were all citizens of Pittsfield, a fact of which the Methodist people were proud; this being the first time that a work of such magnitude had been accomplished without aid from abroad. The architect and contractor were also members of the parish.

The contrast between this noble building and that on East street which the town required to be so "elegant and durable," well illustrates the progress of Methodism in Pittsfield, between 1829 and 1875. The projectors of the East-street church did not exaggerate the harvest which might be expected from the seed sown in it. The number of Methodist communicants in Pittsfield, at the latter date, was six hundred.

The influence of individual-pastors of the Methodist Church upon the town is less than that of some clergymen of other

[1] The largest original contribution to the fund for building the church was Mr. William Renne; who gave eleven thousand five hundred dollars. Mr. Renne's services on the building-committee were also of great value.

denominations, who have filled long pastorates in it. Their brief residence forbids it; but perhaps the aggregate power which they have exercised in molding the character of the place has been as great as that of any other class of preachers. We append a list copied, principally, from a manual prepared by Rev. Dr. Carhart.

PREACHERS ON PITTSFIELD CIRCUIT FROM ITS FORMATION IN 1792 TO 1876.

1792. D. Kendall, R. Dillon and J. Rexford.
1793 to 1795. J. Covel and Zadoc Priest.
1795 " 1797. Timothy Dewey, Cyrus Stebbins and Ebenezer Stevens.
1797 " 1799. Joseph Sawyer, Reuben Hubbard and Daniel Brumley.
1799 " 1801. Michael Coate and Joseph Mitchell.
1801 " 1803. Joseph Mitchell, Oliver Hall, Moses Morgan and Elias Vanderlip.
1803 " 1805. Elias Vanderlip, E. Ward, R. Searl, Elijah Chichester and Nehemiah W. Tompkins.
1805 " 1807. William Anson, Richard Flint, John Robinson and James M. Smith.
1807 " 1809. Noble W. Thomas, Eben Smith and John Crawford.
1809 " 1811. Elijah Woolsey, Phinehas Cook and Seth Crowell.
1811 " 1813. Samuel Cochran, C. H. Gridley, James M. Smith and F. Draper.
1813 " 1815. Billy Hibbard, Beardsley Northrop and John Finnegan.
1815 " 1817. Datus Ensign, John Finnegan, Lewis Pease and James Covel.
1817 " 1819. William Ross, T. Benedict, Elisha P. Jacob and John Matthias.
1819 " 1821. Bela Smith, Daniel Coe, T. Clark and Daniel Kilby.
1821 " 1823. T. Clark, David Miller, William Anson and Smith Dayton.
1823 " 1825. Cyrus Culver, Samuel Eighmey and Robert Jarvis.
1825 " 1827. Gershom Pierce, John J. Matthias, Phinehas Cook and John Nixon.
1827 " 1829. Bradley Sillick, Peter C. Oakley.
1829 " 1831. Cyrus Prindle, Charles F. Pelton and Noah Bigelow.
1831 " 1833. J. Z. Nichols.
1833 " 1835. T. Benedict and Oliver Emerson.
1835 " 1837. F. W. Smith.
1837 " 1839. Henry Smith.
1839 " 1841. Luman A. Sanford.

1841 to 1842.   John Pegg.
1842 " 1843.   Peter M. Hitchcock.
1843 " 1845.   D. D. Wheedon.
1845 " 1847.   Andrew Witherspoon.
1847 " 1849.   Z. Phillips.
1849 " 1850.   Sanford Washburn.
1850 " 1852.   Stephen Parks.
1852 " 1854.   Bostwick Hawley.
1854 " 1856.   H. L. Starks.
1856 " 1858.   R. H. Robinson.
1858 " 1860.   D. Starks.
1860 " 1862.   J. F. Yates.
1862 " 1864.   J. Wesley Carhart, D. D.
1864 " 1867.   William R. Brown.
1868 " ——   C. F. Burdick.
1869 " 1871.   Erastus Wentworth, D. D.
1871 " 1872.   W. G. Waters.
1872 " 1875.   J. F. Clymer.
1875 " ——   David W. Gates.

WESLEYAN METHODIST CHURCH.

When the Methodist Episcopal congregation removed to their new church on Fenn street, some twenty members united to maintain divine worship in the old brick-sanctuary; but the design was frustrated by the sale of the building to T. G. Atwood. Mr. James Foote, one of the original builders and trustees, "feeling a great reluctance to see the house of worship, which had become endeared to him by many sacred incidents, converted to secular uses, purchased it of Mr. Atwood, and immediately it was opened for worship again."[1]

Rev. Cyrus Prindle, who had preached in the church the first year after its erection, visited Pittsfield in September, 1852; and having become a minister of the Wesleyan Methodists, was urged by Mr. Foote and others to remove to Pittsfield, and attempt to build up a congregation of that order. Before the plan was matured Mr. Foote died, but provided in his will that the church be leased for the simple interest upon eight hundred dollars. The enterprise found friends; a few assumed the responsibility of inviting Mr. Prindle to become pastor of a new congregation, and he commenced his labors in October, 1852.

[1] Rev. C. Prindle's statement.

The building was refitted and re-dedicated, Rev. Dr. Harris of the South Church preaching the sermon, and Rev. Drs. Todd and Porter, Rev. Messrs. Harrison and Prindle, taking part in the exercises. The church maintained an existence until the removal of Mr. Prindle from town, and did a great deal of valuable missionary-work. After his removal, it languished, and when the building was demolished, in the year 1867, it had not for some time been used for religious purposes.

ST. STEPHEN'S CHURCH.

"The Episcopal Religious Society of Lenox, Pittsfield, Lee and Stockbridge," which was incorporated in 1805, seems to have become extinct, so far as its Pittsfield members were concerned, on the removal of Henry Van Schaack to Kinderhook. An attempt to establish an Episcopal parish during the political troubles of the First Parish failed; and no further efforts to that end were made until the year 1830. Hon. Edward A. Newton was, however, known to be a devoted member of the Protestant Episcopal Church, although tolerant of other religious denominations, and for several years superintendent of the Sabbath-school of the First Congregational Church. About 1830, circumstances arose which induced him to desire the establishment of a parish of his own faith; and he undertook the foundation of one, with unbounded zeal and untiring exertion.

Whether from his own previous teaching, or some other reason, he found many ready to sympathize with him; and, on an invitation published in the *Argus*, a considerable number of "persons interested in the establishment of the Episcopal Church in Pittsfield, or desirous of uniting with a parish of that communion," met at Pomeroy's coffee-house[1] on the evening of June 25th. Inhabitants of neighboring towns, not already in connection with Episcopal parishes, were also invited to attend, and they were informed that arrangements were completed for carrying the object into immediate effect, "free of any tax for the current year."

As a result of this meeting, on the 6th of July, Hon. Henry Hubbard, a member of the parish, issued his warrant, reciting that Benjamin Luce and twenty-four others had "united to form

[1] The old Campbell coffee-house, then kept by Mr. John Pomeroy, who was himself an Episcopalian.

a religious society according to the doctrine, discipline and worship of the Protestant Episcopal Church in the United States of America, under the title of St. Stephen's Church, Pittsfield," and calling a meeting for the choice of officers at Pomeroy's. coffee-house. No record remains of the action of that meeting; but, under the organization then effected, public worship was conducted for one year, and the first rector was elected. Afterwards, in 1832, a special act of incorporation was obtained.

In the meantime, the lecture-room (old Union Church) was hired by the parish, and here the first religious service was held in the afternoon of August 1, 1830; Rev. Theodore Edson, of Lowell, officiating. Here, too, the first Christmas-eve and Christmas-day services were held; the lecture-room being styled in the public notices, "the Episcopal Church."

In the *Sun* of March 17, 1831, "the committee appointed by the united parishes of St. Stephen's, Pittsfield, and of St. Luke's, Lanesboro, to procure the permanent services of a clergyman for said parishes," gave notice that they had obtained Rev. George T. Chapman, D. D., and that the church in Pittsfield would be open for divine service on the afternoon of Easter Sunday; and that the sacrament of the Lord's Supper would be administered at Lanesboro.

Rev. George Thomas Chapman, D. D., son of Thomas and Charlotte (Carnzu) Chapman, was born at Pilton, a suburb of Barnstaple, Devonshire, England, September 21, 1786; came to the United States in 1795; and graduated at Dartmouth College in 1804. From 1808 to 1815, he practiced law at Bucksport, Me., where he married, in 1811, Alice, daughter of Ebenezer Buck. In 1815, he resumed the study of theology, which he had previously pursued, and was ordained by Right Rev. Bishop Griswold, deacon in 1816, and presbyter in 1818. For several years he preached in various places; among the rest, in the year 1819–20, at Lanesboro, Lenox and Great Barrington; his parish thus covering whatever of Episcopacy there was then in Berkshire county. In July, 1820, he became rector of Christ's Church, Lexington, Ky., and from 1825 to 1827, while holding that pastorate, was Professor of History and Antiquities in Transylvania University. In 1830, he resigned his charge at Lexington, and came to Pittsfield.

Doctor Chapman was a rare man. In the opinion of those best

qualified to judge, the church had few such preachers. A volume of his sermons, entitled "The Ministry, Worship, and Doctrines of the Protestant Episcopal Church," published many years ago, has become a standard work in the literature of the church. Of this book, Rev. George D. Johnson, rector of St. Paul's Church, Newburyport, said in his funeral-discourse: "The multitude of men brought into the church by its simple clearness of argument, is most wonderful. Many prominent clergymen, several bishops, and a host of useful laymen attribute their first clear knowledge of the church and its teachings to Doctor Chapman's sermons; and, not only this, but men of actually godless lives, having no connection with any religion, from an accidental (if we may use the word where God orders all) perusal of his works became Christians and churchmen; giving their time, their money and their lives to show the sincerity of their convictions."

Doctor Chapman also published a volume of twenty-seven "Sermons to Presbyterians of all Sects," and another of sketches of the Alumni of Dartmouth College, which is highly prized for its faithfulness and accuracy. His style, both in the pulpit and in books, was singularly terse and lucid, but not without passages of pathos and sentiment. His logic did not obtrude itself formally, as logic. Choosing as a theme some religious truth or some fact in sacred history, it was his wont to clear away the non-essential incidents which might becloud it; and then to state it with such perspicuity, that, while the listener was unconscious of any process of reasoning, the truth which the speaker sought to inculcate stood out clear, well-defined and self-evident. His discourses were brief, and the unwearied hearer always carried away a distinctly-impressed lesson.

In his varied pastorates, and in his many intervals of detached missionary service, Doctor Chapman saw much of the world and numbered among his parishoners many eminent men; among them Henry Clay, whose memory he most cherished. But, living in the world, he had kept himself unspotted from the world, and maintained a wonderful simplicity of character. No child was ever more free from guile.

These qualities as a preacher and a man, admirably adapted him to the building-up of parishes in those sections where ignorance of the doctrines of the Episcopal Church prevailed, with consequent prejudice against it. And to this class of work, Doctor

Chapman gave a large portion of his life with remarkable success. In Pittsfield, before he resigned the place, in 1832, to the permanent rector, more than fifty families had become connected with the parish. In March, 1831, the parish having determined to erect a new church, the town granted in aid of the project, a lot thirty feet wide and forty deep, lying between Mr. Allen's book-store and the land previously given to the Methodist Society; the conditions being that the new church should be constructed of brick or stone, and that a respectable brick-building should occupy the granted premises.

In December, 1831, the *Sun* stated that the wardens had already contracted for a building of stone in the Gothic style, to be commenced in the following spring. From what the editors had heard, the *Sun* was "disposed to think that it would contribute much to the beauty of the village." A difficulty, however, arose at the very outset. It was the desire of Mr. Newton and his associates, that the church should stand, where it was afterwards built, upon what is now the corner of Park place and School street; and they offered the town five hundred dollars for a lot of sufficient size at that point. But the site was already occupied in part by the town-house, in which the Central school-district claimed an interest by virtue of its occupancy of its lower story for a school-room. For this, and other reasons, Lemuel Pomeroy and other citizens, averse to change in the old order of things, opposed the sale, and the proposition was rejected by the town.

Upon this Mr. Newton announced his determination to erect the church on a portion of the grounds attached to his own residence, and adjoining that of Mr. Pomeroy. And here, in the spring of 1832, the contractors began to collect stone and other material. The danger of a chronic and bitter neighborhood-feud was imminent; but it was happily avoided by a compromise offered by Mr. Pomeroy, who proposed that the difficulty should be surmounted by the erection of a new town-hall, and the purchase by St. Stephen's parish, of the school-district's interest in the old building. This recommendation was submitted to a committee which, on the second of April, through its chairman, M. R. Lanckton, made a report in which they say:

However commodious the present town-hall may have been for the number of inhabitants at the time of its erection, yet, from the prosperity of the town — promoted and occasioned, as it no doubt is by the schools and institutions of learning, and by the liberal spirit of its former and present citizens — such are our numbers that a much larger hall is considered by all a necessary convenience. Your committee are unanimous in the opinion that, if we continue to be guided by the spirit which has heretofore guided and governed us, the day is not far distant when we shall number more than twice our present population and * * * be literally compelled to resort to some more capacious hall for transacting the ordinary business of the town. * * * Whenever a hall is erected, it will be for the interest of the town to finish a room for the town-officers with a vault in the same for the security of the town-records.

The committee were not satisfied that the time had come when the town should tax itself to build a new hall, but they stated that they had received two propositions from Lemuel Pomeroy, Esq., for the erection of a hall, one of which they recommended the town to accept. These propositions, which were appended to the report, were as follows:

In case the town should deem it for their interest to convey to me their present town-house, with sufficient ground for the erection of the Episcopal Church and provide another lot of ground at an equal distance from the two churches, I will erect a town-house at my own expense, conformable to the plan and report of their committee, the house not to exceed fifty-six feet in length and forty-two in width; reserving to myself the whole basement floor, except one room, marked out on the plan, in which I am to place a good fire-proof vault, of sufficient size for the safe-keeping of the town-books, records, etc. The hall above to belong exclusively to the town.

I will also pay the Center School District such a sum for their interest in the present town-house as the selectmen of the town shall adjudge they are entitled to. The expense of insurance and keeping the roof of the house in repair to be borne equally by the town and myself.

A second proposition I will also submit. In case the town should think it more to their interest to build and own the entire house, I will add to the sum of five hundred dollars which Mr. Newton proposes to pay for the site of the Episcopal Church, the sum of three hundred dollars. I will also loan the town, if desired, any sum they may want, in addition to the above, to build the proposed town-house, at the rate of six per cent. per annum, during their pleasure, not to exceed ten years.

And in case either proposition is accepted, I will give the town the use of the lecture-room to hold town-meetings for the term of eighteen months or two years.

All of which is respectfully submitted by your fellow-townsman,

L. POMEROY.

The town accepted the first of these propositions; and it was afterwards agreed that the hall should be sixty-three feet long instead of fifty-six. And on Mr. Pomeroy's suggestion, the deed of the church-site was made directly to Mr. Newton. The following provision was also inserted in the articles of agreement between the town and Mr. Pomeroy:

The building shall be kept constantly insured at the joint and equal expense of both parties. And, if it shall ever be destroyed by fire, said Pomeroy, his heirs or assigns, are to have the benefit of said insurance, provided he or they shall erect another similar building, and give similar privileges to said inhabitants within a reasonable time; but in case said Pomeroy, his heirs or assigns, shall unreasonably delay to provide another similar building and privileges, then the sum insured shall be equally divided between the parties, and the use and occupancy of the land shall revert to said inhabitants.

The hall, a plain brick-building with stuccoed front, was erected according to this agreement. Although the same remarks may now be applied to it which the committee of 1832 applied to its predecessor, it was, for its time, a creditable and convenient building, and it has been the scene of most important town-action. In it have been discussed all the measures of town-policy, which we have recorded, since the date of its erection. Here were held many of the patriotic meetings at which soldiers were raised for the suppression of the rebellion. In it the people of Pittsfield have listened to the most eloquent and eminent orators of the day. In its earlier years every fall saw it filled with the exhibition of household-manufactures at the agricultural fair, and packed with exhibitors and spectators. It has often been used for religious services, and once, for several months as the county court-house. In short, it has served all the multifarious purposes of a New England town-hall; and, for the most part, served them well.[1]

The church to which the old town-house gave place was a modest Gothic structure, of the gray Pittsfield lime-stone, for

[1] For view of town-hall, see view of the park in 1876.

which Mr. Newton might have found a model in some quiet English village. Its dimensions were sixty-seven feet by forty-three; and a tower, eighty feet high, projected from the front. The cost of the building was four thousand seven hundred eleven dollars and twenty-five cents, exclusive of the five hundred dollars paid for the land.

Hon. John Chandler Williams died in 1830, and was buried from the lecture-room, then used as a church; Doctor Chapman preaching the funeral-sermon. His widow now presented to the church an organ, built by Goodrich of Boston, and costing five hundred and seventy-five dollars.

To establish a fund for the support of public worship, Mr. Newton gave four thousand dollars; to which, on his suggestion, an East Indian gentleman, whose sons were educated in Pittsfield, added five hundred dollars. Mr. Newton then added the same amount, which raised the fund to five thousand dollars. Mr. Newton and Mr. Hosea Merrill afterwards presented to the parish a rectory situated on North street. In 1832, the parish having received a new act of incorporation, Edward A. Newton and Benjamin Luce were chosen wardens, and continued in office for two years. From 1835 to 1845, Edward A. Newton and Hosea Merrill were wardens.[1]

The church was consecrated in the forenoon of December 7, 1832, Right Rev. Bishop Griswold officiating, assisted by the rector-elect, Rev. Edward Ballard, and Rev. Samuel Brenton Shaw, then recently instituted rector of St. Luke's Church, Lanesboro. In the afternoon, Mr. Ballard, who had been elected in October, 1831, was instituted rector of St. Stephen's Parish.

In the same year the parish was admitted to representation in the diocesan convention.

Mr. Ballard was born at Hopkinton, N. H., in 1804, and received his theological education at the General Theological Seminary of the Episcopal Church in New York. Without the eminent abilities which distinguished Doctor Chapman as a pulpit-orator, Mr. Ballard was an excellent preacher. His discourses were marked by a pure and classic style and a ripe scholarship. And they were, moreover, well-springs of the purest instruction in morals and of the soundest doctrines in religion.

[1] In return for his gifts to the parish, Mr. Newton received the grant of two pews in fee, exempt from taxation for the support of a rector.

If their waters did not always sparkle, they were always clear and wholesome. But it was not chiefly as a pastor that Mr. Ballard became endeared to the people of Pittsfield, probably more universally and more strongly than any pastor of any denomination ever was. This was due rather to his daily walk and conversation, which won the esteem of every class, and to the gentle and benign manner which charmed all who came in contact with him. Entering heartily into every scheme for the public good which commended itself to his judgment, he never made use of any of them for his personal aggrandizement, or for the gratification of personal vanity. Nor did he ever make submission to his own views of policy, the condition of his support of measures which he believed to be good in the main. He was for many years a member of the town school-committee, and gave to the performance of its duties many laborious hours. In the Bible Society, in the movements in behalf of temperance and good morals, and in every other good word and work, he was a meek and unselfish laborer.

These were qualities to win for him rare love and approbation; but they did not necessarily endow him with power to gain large numbers of proselytes to his faith. The growth of his church was healthful and steady, but it was not so rapid as the impatient founders of the parish craved. And they took measures which, in 1847, ended in his resignation. His farewell-sermon, characterized only by forgiveness and charity, brought tears to many eyes; and, in spite of its mild teachings, filled many breasts with grief and indignation.

After his removal from Pittsfield, Mr. Ballard was, for a time, principal of a school in Connecticut; but in 1858 he was called to the rectorate of St. Paul's Church in Brunswick, Me. Here he was received with warm welcome by the circle of scholars which then formed the faculty of Bowdoin College, or were gathered around that institution. In his new home his abilities were at once recognized. In 1858, he received the degree of A. M. from Bowdoin College, and in 1865 that of Doctor of Divinity from Trinity. In 1866, he was chosen superintendent of the common schools of the State of Maine, and filled that office successfully for three years. In 1859, he became a member of the Maine Historical Society, of which he was afterwards secretary, and to whose objects he made very highly-prized contributions.

He died at Brunswick, November 14, 1870, and his funeral obsequies were attended by the most honorable testimonials of the respect and grief of that community, and of the friends of learning throughout the state.

The unfortunate termination of Mr. Ballard's rectorate in Pittsfield excited great feeling in the parish, and proved a lasting injury to it; and in order to prevent a still larger secession of its members, the wardens and vestry hastened to recall Rev. Dr. Chapman; who returned to the scene of his early labors with some of the infirmities of age, but with an unimpaired intellect. Years had mellowed the genial traits which distinguished his character, and he was welcomed as a father. Within the circle of his own parish, he was soon as tenderly loved as Mr. Ballard had been. To those who were not brought by circumstances into intimate social relations with him, he appeared reserved. His imposing mien, his portly and venerable figure, and often an absent manner, together with his physical infirmities, one of which affected his eye-sight, seemed to repel cordial intercourse. But nothing was further from his real character than contempt or disregard for any of his fellow-men. Under his grand preaching, the parish flourished, and among its congregation were numbered many men of the highest culture.

In 1851, the attendance had grown to such an extent that it was determined to enlarge and remodel the church. Every member of the parish entered enthusiastically into the work, and none more so than the rector. An addition of thirty feet was made to the building. A tower of stone took the place of the old one of wood, and the interior was remodeled elegantly, and in admirable architectural taste. The ladies of the parish furnished a very beautiful chancel-window, and Miss Lucretia Newton presented an organ better adapted to its place than that which had served since 1832. The entire cost of all the changes was something over seven thousand dollars.

The gratification of the parish with the chaste elegance of the remodeled church was very marked, and it looked forward to a most auspicious future. But, unfortunately, a prominent gentleman, in communicating an account of the building to a religious newspaper, added, "that what was now needed to enhance the prosperity of the parish was a younger rector." This paragraph caught the eye of Doctor Chapman, and a slight inquiry showing that a few individuals of wealth and age participated in this sentiment, he promptly resigned. Some stormy passages occurred in parish-meeting before the resignation was accepted; but, under strong pressure, a vote to that effect was finally obtained. The same misjudging ambition which had deprived the parish of its first pastor, robbed it of its second.

Doctor Chapman afterwards succeeded in founding St. George's Parish at Lee; and, while the incumbent there, became reconciled to those who had been the instruments of his leaving Pittsfield. He died at Newburyport, October 18, 1872, aged 86 years.

After the resignation of Doctor Chapman, there was again danger of disruption of the parish, and some members actually withdrew. To prevent farther trouble, both parties cordially united in the election of Rev. Robert J. Parvin as rector. Mr. Parvin was a young man, and did not possess the extraordinary qualifications for the place which had been displayed by his predecessors. But he was a popular preacher, and a most faithful, assiduous, and well-trained pastor. His manner was courteous and pleasant, and the harmony which he maintained with the clergy of other denominations was exceedingly cordial. He was somewhat more determined in the maintenance of his pastoral rights than Doctors Ballard and Chapman had been; but he resigned in 1856, under circumstances similar to theirs. He was succeeded by Rev. William H. Stewart. Mr. Stewart was an Englishman, and a member of an eminent clerical family. He was a logical and able preacher, and a scholar of fine attainments. But he indulged in higher notions of the prerogatives of the clergy than those which prevail in America; and he attempted to apply them to the correction of the evils which existed in the parish. The endeavor was doubtless prompted by pure motives; but, as might have been expected, it failed. And in 1859, Mr. Stewart resigned, and was succeeded by Rev. E. M. Peck.

Before Mr. Stewart's resignation, however, a portion of the parish had seceded and formed the parish of Christ's Church, worshiping in the town-hall; and they were particularly happy in the choice of Rev. James J. Bowden as rector. Mr. Bowden was a man of a somewhat different class of acquirements from those of Doctors Ballard and Chapman; but as a pastor he was worthy to rank with them. Of varied learning and distinguished for polite accomplishments, he was also a fervid and effective preacher, and an earnest and consistent Christian minister. In the difficult position in which he was placed, by a tact which did not include dissimulation, he so governed himself as to command the respect, and finally the affection, of all parties.

Mr. Peck, the rector of St. Stephen's, was an estimable pastor; but the general desire for a union under Mr. Bowden was so apparent that he resigned. Mr. Bowden was chosen to fill this vacancy; and the high expectations entertained of him were not disappointed. While he lived, the parish enjoyed a halcyon season; but in 1862, after a brief illness, he died; his untimely removal from duties which he seemed so perfectly qualified to perform, being deeply mourned by the whole community.

Rev. John Stearns became rector in 1863, and was succeeded in March, 1865, by Rev. E. Livingston Wells, whose pastorate continued until July, 1870.

In December, 1870, Rev. Leonard K. Storrs was chosen rector, and held the office until April, 1875, when he resigned, his health requiring a season of rest. Rev. William McGlathery became rector in October, 1875.

In the course of years all the elements of discord were eliminated, and the parish of St. Stephen's became entirely harmonious, with prospects for the future as bright as its friends could desire. During the pastorate of Mr. Storrs, the church was again handsomely remodeled and decorated.

About 1853, by consent of the donors, the parsonage on North street was sold, and the proceeds applied to the payment of debts. During the pastorate of Rev. Mr. Parvin, a new rectory was built on Broad street, but it had no permanent effect upon the interests of the parish; and it was sold, about 1864.

During the troublous times of the parish, its other endowments were in various ways reduced to thirty-five hundred dollars.

ST. JOSEPH'S CHURCH.

In 1835 there were very few Catholics in Pittsfield; but in that year the first religious services performed in Pittsfield, according to the rites of that church, were held. It happened in this wise. Rev. Jeremiah O'Callahan, who was then stationed at a mission in Vermont, passing through town, was accidentally detained at the Berkshire Hotel, and gladly consented to remain and administer to the spiritual wants of his co-religionists. A Mass—the first in Berkshire county[1]—was celebrated at the house of a Mr. Daley, on Honasada street; Daley, with his wife and seven children, Thomas Colman, and five or six other persons being present. A purse of fourteen dollars was made up by those in attendance, for Father O'Callahan; but the good father hesitated to receive it. Being pressed, however, to do so, a mode of escaping from his embarrassment happily occurred to him. He chanced to remember that the price of flour was fourteen dollars a barrel; and proceeding to the village, purchased a barrel and ordered it to be sent to Daley's house; remarking that, with his large family, he must need it more than he did.

From that time, Father O'Callahan visited Pittsfield yearly, until 1839. In 1841, Rev. John D. Brady began, as a mission-priest, to visit the town once in three months; the services being held, at first in a room given by L. Pomeroy & Sons, in the brick-building erected by them near the depot. Afterwards they were held in a house near the rear of the present church of St. John the Baptist, in which the first collection for building a church was taken up. In 1844, Father Brady bought of Henry Callender, a lot on Melville street for a church and burial-ground; and the church was built the same year. Here service was attended occasionally by Rev. Messrs. Brady, Kavanagh, and Straine. After the death of Father Brady, the church was attended several years by Rev. Bernard Kavanagh. In May, 1852, Rev. Patrick Cuddihy was appointed by Bishop Fitzpatrick, pastor of the church and of all missions in the county of Berkshire. Mr. Cuddihy labored with great zeal and industry; but, in 1852, his constitution not being adequate to the increasing work, he was obliged to call upon his bishop for help; and in the following year Rev. Edward H. Purcell was sent as his assistant. In 1854, Mr. Cuddihy was transferred to Milford, Mass., leaving Father Purcell pastor of the church.

Mr. Purcell has carried out the ideas of his predecessor by building churches in several towns in the county, and especially by substituting for the wooden building in a comparatively obscure location in Pittsfield, a noble edifice of stone on a con-

[1] Unless one may have been performed here in the French and Indian invasions.

spicuous site on the main street. The site for this church, which is next south of the grounds of Maplewood Institute, and comprises three and a half acres, was purchased of Rev. W. H. Tyler, for ten thousand dollars.

The building is a fine specimen of the lighter Gothic architecture in its chastest type. Its chief exterior characteristics are an airy lightness of structure, a simple grace of outline, and perfect unity and completeness. Its extreme length is one hundred and seventy-five feet, including the tower and two low wings in the rear occupied as chapels, but opening into the main building. The breadth is sixty-eight feet. The spire, with the richly ornamented cross which surmounts it, rises to the height of one hundred and seventy-six feet. The walls—and the tower to the height of ninety-three feet—are built of light-gray lime-stone, quarried some two miles north, and are laid as broken ashlar. Standing apart from any other building, the effect of this fine piece of architecture is very pleasing; and, by the purchase of an ample site, care was taken that it should never be greatly impaired.

The interior is distinguished by mellow harmony of coloring, elegance of ornamentation, and a pleasing vista of columns and arches. The nave is one hundred and eight feet long, with a pointed, arched roof, springing fifty-five feet from the floor to the apex; supported on seven arches resting on eight pillars. The church is lighted on each side by seven handsome stained-glass windows; while three of more elaborate art adorn the chancel. The latter are filled with full-length figures of the Savior, the Virgin Mary, and St. Joseph. They are the gifts of the St. Joseph's Mutual Aid Society, the Ladies Altar Society, and Mr. Owen Coogan.

On each side of the chancel broad arches open into chapels designed for the children of the Sunday-school, where they may join in the services of the congregation. These chapels furnish five hundred seats, and, the nave accommodating thirteen hundred, the house has sittings for nearly nineteen hundred persons.

The first ground was broken July, 1864. The corner-stone was laid August 20, 1864, by the Very Rev. John Joseph Williams, then administrator—but, before the completion of the church, Bishop—of the Diocese of Boston.

ST. JOSEPH'S R. C. CHURCH AND RESIDENCE OF PASTOR.

The architect was P. C. Keely of Brooklyn; and the work was prosecuted under the personal supervision of Rev. Mr. Purcell.

The church was consecrated November 29, 1866; Right Rev. Bishops Williams, Conroy and McFarland, with a long array of priests, officiating.

About the year 1869, Rev. Mr. Lemarque, assistant-pastor of St. Joseph's Church, collected the considerable number of French Catholics in the town, into a congregation by themselves, to whom he preached in their own language. He was succeeded by Rev. Mr. De Beuil, and Rev. Joseph Quevillon. When the congregation of St. Joseph's took possession of their new church, the French Catholics purchased the old church, a neat and commodious wooden building, and occupied it under the name of St. Jean Le Baptiste.

GERMAN LUTHERAN CHURCH.

In the year 1858, when the Protestant German population of Pittsfield was about four hundred, arrangements were made by a portion of them for divine service in their own language. These services were at first held in private houses, and with occasional visits by clergymen from the State of New York. But in April, 1859, Rev. Augustus Grotrian, a learned and able minister of Albany, accepted a call and organized the German Evangelical Church of Pittsfield, upon the basis of the Augsburg Confession. By invitation of the First Congregational Parish, the services were held in its lecture-room; but measures were at once taken for the erection of a church. The town granted a pleasant site in the corner of the First-street burial-ground. Rev. Drs. Humphrey and Todd took a strong interest in the enterprise, and the citizens contributed liberally. The Germans gave as liberally as they then had the power. The church was built at a cost of two thousand three hundred and seventy-four dollars, and dedicated September 14, 1865.

Mr. Grotrian resigned in April, 1865. Rev. A. Kretchner was pastor from September, 1865, to April, 1866, and Rev. J. T. Simon from June, 1866, to October, 1868.

All these pastors were "free" or independent, ministers, and—like the church—without ecclesiastical connection. In the cases of Messrs. Kretchner and Simon, the result of this experiment was not satisfactory; and friends of the parish in the State of

New York advised that it should associate itself with some established ecclesiastical body. While this question was pending, Rev. John David Haeger was called to the pastorate, and commenced his duties, December 20, 1868. Mr. Haeger favored the change, and the church voted to place itself under the jurisdiction of the Synod of the Evangelical Lutheran Church of the State of New York; assuming the name of the Evangelical Lutheran Church of Pittsfield. The society is in a flourishing condition, having over fifty male members, and embracing from seventy to ninety families. The German population of the town in 1875, was estimated at eight hundred.

THE SYNAGOGUE ANSHA AMONIUM.

In November, 1869, the Jewish citizens of the town, for the better observance of divine worship, according to their peculiar rites, organized the society *Ansha Amonium*; the officers being Edward Friend, president; Louis England, secretary; Moses England, treasurer. This society, which included some of the most substantial and respectable citizens of the town, numbered, in 1875, eighteen heads of families. And its officers were L. V. Simons, president; H. Goodman, secretary; Isaac Newman, treasurer.

THE SHAKER SOCIETY.

Throughout the century, the united society of Shakers has maintained a respectable position in the western part of the town. They are embodied with the organization known as the Hancock Shakers, which numbers about a hundred members, of whom, perhaps, fifty reside within the limits of Pittsfield. The society includes four families, and has a neat church. It is not numerous, but it forms a picturesque feature in the religious aspect of the town. The respect in which its members are held by the people, presents a strong contrast to the light in which they were viewed in 1781.

CHAPTER XXI.

WOOLEN, DUCK, COTTON, PAPER AND FLOURING MILLS.

[1808-1875.]

State of manufactures in 1812—Effect of Scholfield's machinery—Seth Moore's rope-walk—Root, Maynard & Co's duck-factory—Housatonic woolen and cotton mill—Pittsfield woolen and cotton company—Their mills built; leased to L. Pomeroy and Josiah Pomeroy—Sold to Josiah Pomeroy & Co. —Bought by L. Pomeroy & Sons—Berkshire agitation for protection to American manufactures—Henry Shaw—Pontoosuc woolen-factory built— Hindrances to success—Saxony sheep introduced—Henry Clay's visit to Pittsfield—The Stearns family and their factories—The Barker brothers and their factories—The Russell factories—The Peck factories—Taconic factory —Pittsfield woolen-factory—Bel Air factory—Tillotson & Collins's factory —Pittsfield cotton-factory—Coltsville paper-mill—Wahconah flouring-mills —Shaker flouring-mill—Osceola River flouring-mill.

THE machinery introduced by Scholfield, and the refinement of the Berkshire fleece through the better breeds of sheep brought in from the New York flocks, by Elkanah Watson, John B. Root, S. D. Colt and others, or imported directly from Europe by Jonathan Allen, had, previous to the war of 1812, considerably increased the quantity, and very much improved the quality of Pittsfield woolen-manufactures; but not to an extent which enabled them even proximately to meet the market which was brought to their doors. Much the larger part of the cloth produced was still made upon the household-looms; and, even in the so-called factories, so important a process as the weaving, was carried on by hand.

The same state of things extended through the country. In 1810, information received from every state in the Union, and from more than sixty different places, showed an extraordinary increase, and rendered it probable that about two-thirds of the cloth, including hosiery, house and table linen, used by the inhabitants outside the cities, was the product of household-manufactures. In the eastern and middle states *carding machines*, driven by water, were everywhere established; and others were extended southward and westerly. *Jennies* and other spinning-machines and flying-shuttles were introduced in many places.[1]

From the above and cognate statistics, it is safe to infer that the greater effect of the improvements in machinery introduced by Scholfield, was upon household-manufactures, and by their value, we must measure the benefits conferred by him upon the county, in relieving its necessities during the war. The zeal and capital of Livingston and Humphries, even if unaided by him, were sure soon to overcome the difficulties in the way of supplying their mills with suitable machinery. But it was Scholfield, who came opportunely, at a moment when such relief was most needed, to enable the country to provide for one of its most pressing wants; and, when taxes began alarmingly to increase, to scatter among thousands of families the means of materially adding to the income from their labor. And it was he alone who performed this immense service; for to him must be fairly ascribed, not only the benefits derived from the machinery sent out from his own manufactory, but from that made by his numerous imitators.

Still, valuable as the relief thus furnished was, and much as had been accomplished by the impulse imparted in various ways to American manufactures, they were not able to prevent a considerable scarcity of cloth, when the foreign supply was interrupted by the war. In Berkshire, if the hundred thousand yards of domestic woolens, reported as the product of 1809, had been doubled, or trebled, in 1812, it would, after the necessary reduction for home-wear, have gone but a little way toward meeting the demand which was made upon the county when, in the fall of the latter year, Major Melville advertised, "Cash, Cash, and a generous price, for blue, brown, and mixed woolen cloths, and short stockings."

This demand, however, powerfully stimulated the spirit of manufacturing enterprise. This spirit had indeed not slept, but had already accomplished much, and was ready promptly to accomplish more; so that Elkanah Watson was able to boast, at the

[1] Bishop's History of American Manufactures. If tradition is to be at all trusted, the extent to which homespun goods were used in New England must have been much greater than the proportion given by Mr. Bishop.

Ladies' Cloth Show of the Agricultural Society in January, 1813, that the President of the United States and the President frigate —which he styled "the pride of the American navy"—were clothed from the Pittsfield woolen and duck looms. And, in the same year, the *Albany Argus*, under the heading "Aid and Comfort to the Enemy," alleged that a suit of superfine Berkshire broadcloth had been sent as a present to the Prince Regent of Great Britain. "It is thought," added the editor sarcastically, "that it will prove a good negotiator." And, indeed, whatever may be thought of the patriotism or good taste of making presents to a ruler with whom the nation was at war, there was no prince in Europe so well qualified to judge the quality of the article said to have been sent, or so sure to appreciate it if good.

This story labors under the suspicion of having been invented for political effect; but it bears testimony, even if that suspicion is correct, to the reputation of Berkshire broadcloths. Of the truthfulness of the boast regarding the clothing of the two presidents, there is no doubt. Mr. Watson, himself, after exhibiting in several cities the broadcloth upon which he had, in 1812, taken the first premium of the Agricultural Society, sent it to Mr. Madison and some other statesmen at Washington, and suits made of it were worn by them at his inauguration in 1813.[1]

The frigate President was supplied with a superior suit of linen-duck sails from the duck-factory of Root & Maynard, and her cordage was, in part at least, from the rope-walk of Seth Moore.

Moore's rope-walk was built about the year 1808, in the rear of Maynard & Root's duck-factory, which stood on the east side of Elm street, midway between East street and the river. He carried on the business successfully for several years, making superior cordage and twine, and accumulating some property; but afterwards, depressed by family troubles, he resorted to spirituous liquors for relief, with the usual result; and, in 1814, he committed suicide, by hanging, in his place of business, having made preparations which indicated great deliberation.

---

[1] It is stated in several publications, that Mr. Madison, at his inauguration in 1809, was dressed in a suit of Scholfield's broadcloth. But no mention of anything of the kind is made in the *Sun;* and the *National Intelligencer,* in its report of the occasion, states that the president "wore a full suit of cloth of American manufacture, of the wool of merinoes raised in this country; his coat from the manufactory of Colonel Humphries, and his waistcoat and small-clothes from that of Chancellor Livingston:" presents from those gentlemen.

John B. Root added manufacturing to his mercantile business in the fall of 1808, when he commenced making sail-duck from flax. In 1810, he was joined in the business by Deacon Eli Maynard, who had just sold his interest in the fulling-mill at White's dam, on Water street, to his junior partner, Jonathan Allen, 2d; and the sails of the frigate President were woven by Root & Maynard. Early in 1812, Oliver Robbins became a partner in the concern, which took the name of Root, Maynard & Co. In the fall of 1813, Mr. Root withdrew from the firm, and in 1815, Mr. Robbins also retired; leaving Deacon Maynard, who had from the first been the practical manufacturer, alone. He continued in the business a few years longer, adding to it a grocery-store; but finally the grocery absorbed his entire attention, and the manufacture of sail-duck in Pittsfield ended.

In 1809, Deacon Maynard advertised that he would give a generous price, and furnish directions, for spinning immediately a large quantity of tow; and, in the same year, John B. Root offered to furnish tow for making four thousand yards of such cloth as he should direct.

On the 10th of July, 1810, Mr. Root and Richard S. Chappell,[1] as partners, gave notice that they had for sale a number of merino rams of different grades, "derived from the flocks of Colonel Humphries and Chancellor Livingston," and that—having lately erected a factory for the manufacture of cloths from the merino wool—they would receive in payment well-washed and merchantable merino wool, at the following rates per pound, by the fleece:

Full blood, two dollars; three-quarter blood, one dollar and fifty cents; half-blood, one dollar; quarter-blood, sixty-seven cents. They also offered to buy common wool of the first quality at fifty cents per pound, and inferior qualities at proportionate prices.

Messrs. Root and Chappell were, in 1812, incorporated as the Housato*nuck* Manufacturing Company; the engrossing clerk at Boston substituting the more antique spelling for that previously used by the firm. Their charter conferred power to hold real estate to the amount of thirty thousand dollars, and personal

---

[1]Mr. Chappell was, like his partner, a man of restless business-activity and enterprise. He was also fond of military pursuits, and during the war of 1812 made a very efficient captain for the Berkshire Blues.

property to the value of fifty thousand, for the purpose of making cloth of wool, cotton, flax, or tow. They had also the usual authority to associate other corporators with themselves; but they did not immediately avail themselves of it.

The factory erected by them in 1810, and then styled by them "The Housatonic Woolen Mill," stood at a bend in the east branch of the Housatonic river, about a quarter of a mile south of the crossing of the railroad by Beaver street. The water-power at this point is of a very inferior class; it being impossible to obtain a fall of more than four feet, without flooding a great part of the valuable meadows as far back as the farm now owned by Amasa Rice on Unkamet street. But the manufacturing establishment which grew up around it, however small as compared with those of a later date, was an important enterprise for its time; comprising, as described in an advertisement of 1816, "a large and commodious building improved as a woolen and cotton factory, four dwelling-houses, a store, a large and convenient building used for spinning, weaving, and finishing cloth, a fulling-mill, dye-house, and four acres of land."

The factory proper was of wood, painted yellow, about seventy-five by thirty-five feet in size, one of the four stories being a basement formed by the descending bank of the river.

The machinery was catalogued in the same advertisement as follows:

In the woolen-department, three double carding-machines; three spinning-jennies, containing one hundred and forty spindles; one roping jack; one picker; four broad looms, three narrow looms, and complete sets of loom-tackle. In the cotton-department, four throstle frames, containing two hundred and forty spindles, with the necessary preparing machinery for five hundred spindles.

Also all the factory-furniture, and implements necessary for manufacturing and finishing woolen-cloth, and spinning cotton-yarn, and warp.

No cotton-cloth was made at the factory, but the warp spun here was either sold at the shops, to be woven on hand-looms, or sent to mills in other places to be mixed with wool in satinets.[1]

Even when, in later years, the manufacture of satinet was introduced into the Housatonic mill, although warps were made in the

---

[1] The manufacture of cotton-cloth on household-looms was quite common in the early part of the 19th century.

mill by parties to whom the cotton-machinery had been leased, they were all sent out of town for a market; while those used in the mill were brought from a factory in Valatie, N. Y. It is also worthy of remark that the warps were beamed where they were woven, not where they were spun; being sent to market in skeins.

The first years of the Housatonic mill were prosperous, the war affording a constant and profitable market for its cloth. But, in common with other American manufactures, it suffered severely from the overslaugh of foreign goods upon the return of peace; besides being greatly embarrassed by the inferiority of its water-power.

The proprietors seem, however, to have struggled bravely against adverse circumstances. In February, 1815, Richard C. Coggswell, clerk of the company, called a meeting, for the purpose of making alterations in the by-laws; probably rendered necessary by an increase of the number of stockholders, several gentlemen having taken an interest in the mill, in the hope of sustaining it. They were, however, soon discouraged, as the *Sun* of March 24, 1816, contained an advertisement signed by Nathan Willis, Simeon Brown, and Royal Millard, as directors, offering the whole establishment, as described in the extract quoted above, for sale at public vendue. The sale did not take place, probably from lack of bidders; and the proprietors resorted to various expedients to keep the mill in operation until more favorable times, and in the meanwhile to obtain some moderate income from their outlay.

Richard S. Chappell's name appears in connection with the company, for the last time, in his signature as clerk to a call for a meeting of the stockholders, dated January 24, 1816. The next call of the same kind, which was in the following March, was signed by Nathan Willis, who had purchased Chappell's stock, or a large part of it. Messrs. Root and Willis were, from this time the chief, and finally the sole owners of the Housatonic factory; sometimes leasing it in whole, or in part, and sometimes carrying it on for themselves.

In May, 1816, the company attempted to add to their income by offering to card wool for customers, "having in their employ one of the best carders in the country." In July, Jonathan N. Chappell, and Joseph Wadsworth, "having connected themselves in business at the Housatonuck Factory (east of the meeting-house)," offered to dress cloth, and to take in payment wool, flax, wood, soap, and all kinds of country-produce, for all colors except indigo blue, for which part cash was expected.

Chappell had been the head clothier under the old system, and in August, 1815, advertised to dress cloths at the mill on his own account, in the best European manner. He has in tradition, the reputation of a superior workman. His business-connection with Wadsworth continued only until October 10, 1816.

On the 9th of November a meeting of the company was called to consider its affairs and "raise money." What they did at this meeting is not stated; but work seems to have been continued, as in the following May, the directors, Messrs. Root and Willis, called the stockholders again together, to divide such cloths as were finished, and to provide funds to meet certain demands against the company. In the previous month, Nathan Willis, as agent for the company, advertised that they would card wool for customers, and had engaged Arthur Schofield to take charge of that work.

The Housatonic factory experienced to a moderate extent, the beneficial effects of the tariffs of 1824 and 1828, and continued in operation for some years after that, sharing the vicissitudes of the woolen-manufactures of the country, but generally with a little more of the bad fortune, and a little less of the good, than fell to its contemporaries. By a series of transactions in 1828 and 1829, the factory became the property of William Weller and John Dickinson, for whom it was managed by General Root, who resided on the premises.

The imperfection of the water-power was, from the first, the great drawback to the prosperity of the mill; and it increased as the enhanced value of the meadows above increased the demands for flowage. Finally, a dispute upon this point arose between the proprietors of the mill and the owners of the meadows, and was referred to a board of arbitrators, to determine the compensation to be paid; but upon the very night previous to the day fixed for their meeting, a freshet carried away the dam, and the water-power was not considered sufficiently valuable to warrant its rebuilding. The water-power was subsequently consolidated with that of the Pittsfield cotton-factory, below. Previous to the destruction of the dam, Curtis T. Fenn and Hamilton Faulkner occupied part of the mill for the manufacture of lasts, of which they sent a large quantity to market. On the east end of the dam stood Root's saw-mill, in which John B. Root and Jacob Barton placed a saw of which they owned the patent-right for Berkshire; the improvement in which "consisted principally in hanging the saw in such a manner as to supersede the necessity of using the saw gate or frame, by which a quarter more speed is given to the saw with the same head of water, and the sawing is performed in a more perfect manner, as the saw is so fixed as to operate like sawing by a miter-box." The patent worked well for a while, but the machinery proved liable to get easily out of order. In this mill was also placed the first circular saw in the county, and the first sawed shingles were made by it. The beaming-mill of Simeon Brown's tannery was also on the east end of the Housatonic dam.

By these various operations quite a village had, previous to 1831, grown up around this dam, most of the dwellings in which, and the factory itself, were afterwards removed, chiefly to Beaver street.

The reader will not be surprised to learn that, in the days of feud, during the war of 1812, as there were democratic and federal hotels, ball-rooms, churches, merchants and physicians, so each political party had its factory. The Housatonic mill made its fabrics under purely democratic guidance, and in February, 1814, the following gentlemen, all federalists, were incorporated as "The Pittsfield Woolen and Cotton Factory." (*Sic*:) Lemuel Pomeroy, Joseph Merrick, Ebenezer Center, Samuel D. Colt, David Campbell, Jr., Thomas B. Strong, James Buel and Arthur Schofield. Their charter was subject to the general law of 1809, regarding manufacturing companies, and they were empowered to hold real-estate to the value of thirty thousand dollars and personal property to the amount of one hundred thousand dollars. A meeting of the corporators was held April 8, 1814, and, it having been determined to fix the par value of the shares at one thousand dollars each, the whole capital stock was at once subscribed, as follows: Lemuel Pomeroy, thirty shares; Arthur Scholfield, twenty; Eben. Center, thirteen; David Campbell, thirteen; Thomas Gold, five; Samuel D. Colt, thirteen; James Buel, four; James Wrigley, seven; Joseph Merrick, thirteen; William C. Jarvis, one;

Thomas A. Gold, two; Isaac Scholfield, seven; Jason Clapp, one.[1]

Messrs. Center, Colt, Pomeroy, Campbell and Arthur Scholfield were chosen directors, and James Buel clerk.

The directors lost no time, but immediately purchased from Samuel D. Colt, for two thousand one hundred and twenty dollars, a tract of land consisting of five acres on the west side of the west branch of the Housatonic river, and a strip about six rods wide along the east side. Between the two there was a fine water-privilege—the same now used by the lower mill of L. Pomeroy's Sons—and a dam which had recently been erected for a contemplated powder-mill.

There was no public road; but the most convenient access was by South street, from which a private way extended to the mill, on the line upon which a road was afterwards laid by the town as described below.[2]

James D. Colt was engaged, at a salary of five hundred dollars per annum, commencing April 11, 1814, "to superintend the building of the factory, under the direction of the directors; he keeping an account of lost time, which was to be deducted from said five hundred dollars."

The factory built under Mr. Colt's superintendence was a substantial brick-structure eighty feet long, forty-five wide, and three stories high, besides an attic. It was lengthened, in 1871, to one hundred and twenty-five feet, and is now the lower mill of L. Pomeroy's Sons.

The factory went into operation in the spring of 1815, under

[1] Within two years Mr. Clapp sold his share to T. A. Gold; Isaac Scholfield seven shares to Alpheus Smith; James Wrigley seven to Arthur Scholfield, fourteen to Josiah Bissell & Son.

[2] In 1820, the company offered, if the town would lay a road from the northeast corner of High-Sheriff Brown's land—a little south of the present corner of South street and Danielson avenue—to Luce's mill, to see that it was built free of expense to the town, to maintain a bridge at their factory, and, with the aid of Messrs. Adams and Luce, to build a bridge at Luce's mill. The offer was accepted, and the road and bridges were built, costing the town only land-damages to the amount of ninety-five dollars paid S. D. Colt, and ninety dollars paid Capt. John Dickinson. For some reason, the town-survey of the road extended to West street, although Mill street had been established in 1795. That portion of the new road between the factory and South street, has been discontinued, having been rendered unnecessary by the opening of West Housatonic street.

as competent management as the town then afforded. Messrs. Pomeroy and Campbell had the general conduct of its affairs; Ebenezer Center, a merchant, and Samuel D. Colt, who had for some years been successfully engaged in the sheep and wool trade, were entrusted with the purchase of raw material; Arthur Scholfield had charge of the picking, carding, spinning and weaving; and Richard Lowe, an Englishman and a new-comer, was engaged to carry on the fulling, dyeing and finishing.

Mr. Buel, the clerk and treasurer, was appointed general agent, in addition to his other duties, at a salary of one thousand dollars for all; and he was voted three hundred dollars for his services in his former capacity for the first year of the corporation. The goods to be made were fine broadcloths.

But general business-talent does not always avail to secure immediate success in special enterprises; and it did not in this instance; especially in the face of the altered circumstances which American manufacturers soon encountered. The American portion of the managers of the factory, with perhaps the exception of Mr. S. D. Colt, in his special department, had small knowledge of the details of the woolen-manufacture. Some of them afterwards became eminent in the business; but in 1814, they were, however apt, mere apprentices in their art. Of the two Englishmen, Scholfield was thoroughly trained in his art, so far as it had advanced when he left England; but his business-habits were not of the best, and the era was one of continual improvement in woolen-machinery.

The other, Lowe, proved to be a rascal. It was, moreover, at an inopportune moment, that in the spring of 1815, after the influx of foreign goods had commenced, the new factory went into operation. The proprietors, however, commenced hopefully although economically, as may be inferred by the votes of the directors, in December, 1814, to authorize Lowe to purchase a dye kettle, which had been used at the mitten-factory; and, in January, 1815, to take the set of cards which had been purchased by Isaac Scholfield some time before, and pay him for them, with interest, in April. The weaving was done on hand-looms, and most of the machinery was probably of the Scholfield manufacture.[1]

---

[1]Looms, in all the early factories, were run by hand. A power-loom was projected in 1809, but failed to work. Another was patented in 1812, but did not come into general use. In 1815, F. C. Lowell invented a loom, which,

Not many months after the factory went into operation, it was found that a considerable quantity of cloths which had been put in Lowe's hands, for finishing, had not been returned. More than a reasonable time was allowed him to produce them; and then, when Mr. Buel, whose suspicions had been long aroused, demanded the key of the finishing-room, which Lowe, on pretense of concealing the mysteries of his art, had kept locked, he was refused with defiant insolence. The door was thereupon broken open, and Mr. Buel's suspicions were more than verified. The cloths were found cut and slashed, so that every piece was ruined. It was apparent that the injury was wanton and malicious; and the only explanation which suggested itself at the time, was that Lowe was bribed by foreign manufacturers, who hoped to discourage American competition. This theory accorded with the temper of the day, and was accepted even by the federal proprietors of the mill; but we do not learn that it was sustained by any corroborating circumstances.

Lowe was, of course, discharged; and Mr. Thaddeus Clapp of Easthampton, became general superintendent and manager of all the departments of the mill.

Mr. Clapp was bred to the clothier's trade in his native town, and afterwards perfected himself, so far as was then possible in America, in all the details of the woolen-manufacture, in the factories at Middletown, Conn., and Germantown, Pa. He was the first American-born citizen of Pittsfield, who, by his native talent, thorough knowledge of his art, and general business-qualities, was competent to manage a woolen-factory. Indeed, he was the first of any nationality who was so qualified; for Scholfield, in many particulars, fell far short of that mark.

The Pittsfield Woolen and Cotton Company had thus secured an honest and capable management of its mill; but they had still the most disheartening difficulties to encounter. If British manufacturers had indeed instigated the rascality of Lowe, they had no longer necessity for such low devices. The return of peace had

used in a Waltham factory, enabled the proprietors to make a profit of twenty-five per cent., "although it cost three hundred dollars." But, in the same year, William Gilmore smuggled from Glasgow a Scotch loom, from whose pattern, he made a machine better than Lowell's, which he could profitably sell at seventy dollars. Between 1815 and 1823, a large number of improvements in looms were patented.

put it in their power to overwhelm the infant-manufactures, by means of heavy consignments of goods to be sold at auction, and upon the most liberal credit to merchants. This was even avowed and advocated as a part of the national policy of Great Britain; as when Henry Brougham—afterwards the celebrated Lord Chancellor—declared in 1815, in parliament, "It is even worth while to incur loss upon the first exportations, in order by the glut to stifle in the cradle these rising manufactures of the United States, which the war has forced into existence, contrary to the natural course of things."

The patriotic manufacturers of Berkshire county, in common with their brethren throughout the Union, held opinions regarding the natural course of things widely different from those of the philosophic Mr. Brougham; but, in carrying them into practice, they struggled against fearful odds. The sacrifices which the wealthy manufacturers of Great Britain were called upon to make, could be charged to the ordinary account of profit and loss, without entailing much personal suffering. With the American manufacturer it was often absolute financial ruin. Very shortly, it is true, the resumption of specie-payments in England, by its disturbance of financial bases, somewhat reduced this inequality; but it, at the same time, increased the necessity of sacrifice, and threw more goods upon an impoverished and already glutted market. The resumption of specie-payments in the United States, also created a similar disturbance of values here. A large number of the banks, which in the heated days of speculation, had sprung up in unhealthy luxuriance, failed. All branches of industry and business suffered together. The tariff of 1816, although it was accepted by the manufacturers as a step in advance, fell altogether short of what the times demanded, and did not help matters much. The constant improvements in machinery also, although they contributed much to the advance of manufactures generally, operated to the disadvantage of the earlier mills, which were compelled to adopt them, discarding their old machines, or be outrivaled by younger factories.

We have already described the distress of the Housatonic company under these circumstances. The greater capital of the corporators of the Pittsfield company, and their superior business-capacity, gave them the advantage in contending with the obstacles of the times; but it was probably the fine water-power which prevented final failure, and enabled those of the stockholders who from time to time became discouraged, to sell their shares at a not much greater depreciation in value than most property underwent at this time. And even this would not have availed, had not Lemuel Pomeroy been willing to invest in it the profits of his more lucrative business.

In July, 1817, the company found it necessary to levy an assessment of five per cent. on each share, to pay its debts; and the question arose whether operations should be suspended entirely, or the property leased, "if a taker could be found." Finally, it was leased at public auction, from September 1, 1817, to June 1, 1819, Lemuel Pomeroy taking it at thirty-seven dollars per month.

In this year, 1817, Messrs. Center and Buel having sold out their shares and removed to Hudson, N. Y., Thomas Gold was elected president of the company, and Samuel D. Colt clerk and treasurer.

In March, 1819, the proprietors voted to make a second lease to Mr. Pomeroy for five years, from the first of June, 1819, unless the company should wish to take the works into their own hands at the end of four years; in which case, they should give six months' notice to the occupants. It was provided that the first year's rent should be paid by the erection of a house of that value; and, for the remainder of the time, one half in cash, and the other in salable goods at their market-value. If, in the opinion of Messrs. R. and N. Merriam, and Arthur Scholfield, repairs on the carding-machines should be needed to make good work, they were to be made at the equal joint expense of the proprietors and the lessee.

Mr. Pomeroy associated with himself in the business, his distant relative, Josiah Pomeroy, who resided on the premises, and had the immediate charge of its affairs and the store connected with it; the firm-name being Josiah Pomeroy & Co. In April, 1824, before the expiration of this lease, the proprietors voted to extend it three years, with the privilege to each party of terminating it at one year's notice.

During the five-years' lease, some improvements, valuable for the times, were made upon the property, probably including the bridges, although the proprietors specified simply, "buildings and repairs," for which, in their settlement with the lessee, they allowed one thousand one hundred and fourteen dollars, together with five hundred and sixteen dollars for a dye-house, to be deducted from future rents. From the remainder of the rents already accrued, a dividend was declared of sixteen dollars and fifty-eight cents per share.[1]

Instead of a dye-house, a brick finishing-mill, two stories high, eighty feet long and forty wide, was, in the year 1825, erected on the east side of the river, opposite the main factory.

In 1827, Messrs. Lemuel and Josiah Pomeroy having, by gradual purchases, consolidated in their hands, in about equal proportions, all the shares in the corporation, the corporate-form of conducting its affairs was abandoned, and the business was carried on by them as co-partners until 1839.

During the existence of the corporation, in addition to the original subscribers, the following gentlemen held shares by transfer: Alpheus Smith of Leicester, Josiah Bissell & Son, Josiah Pomeroy and Thaddeus Clapp.

The Messrs. Pomeroy continued the manufacture with vigor and liberality, keeping fully abreast with the constant improvements in all branches of their art. They shared largely in the general prosperity which followed the tariffs of 1824 and 1828, and continued under that of 1832.

Through purchases of adjacent lands, either by one partner or the other, they extended their real-estate for nearly a mile in length, along both banks of the river, south of West street; most of which still remains the property of Lemuel Pomeroy's heirs. Among these purchases were the Luce mill and water-power, with one acre of land, purchased in 1830 by Josiah Pomeroy for five thousand dollars, and the old Pittsfield factory with an acre of land, north of West street, purchased in 1830 by Lemuel Pomeroy for eight hundred dollars.

In 1839, Lemuel Pomeroy purchased the interest of his partner in the concern, including the Luce mill and other real-estate, and took into partnership his sons, Theodore, Robert, and Edward, under the firm-name of Lemuel Pomeroy & Sons.[2]

---

[1] A portion, at least, of this dividend was paid in cash, being the first in the history of the company distinctly so declared; although in April, 1819, it was voted "to receive the balance of the rent due from Josiah Pomeroy & Co., and divide it to each proprietor's share."

[2] Josiah Pomeroy, before this sale, had purchased the water-privilege on

The new firm continued unchanged until the death of the senior partner in 1849, and became widely noted for its business-energy, successful enterprise, and the excellence of its goods. Shortly after the purchase of the Luce mill, about the year 1842, it was converted into a satinet-mill, for which, being a large, brick building, two stories high, it afforded considerable facilities. But, the experiment proving successful, the new firm, in 1852, erected of wood, a large mill of the same class; one hundred feet long by fifty wide, three stories high, besides an attic. The old Luce mill was changed to a dwelling-house in 1852.

Since the death of the founder of the firm, his sons, under the firm-name of L. Pomeroy's Sons, have sedulously conducted the business on the principles and in conformity with the practice of their father; the eldest, Mr. Theodore Pomeroy, being the managing partner, and residing near the mills, where he has erected an elegant villa, upon a beautiful site, which was part of the original purchase of 1814.

Near the close of his life, Mr. Lemuel Pomeroy was accustomed to say that all his experience as a woolen-manufacturer had been a hand-to-hand conflict with obstacles now of one kind, and then of another; and that, for results, he would be glad to exchange all his profits for two per cent. upon his outlay. And those who have read our story thus far, will easily believe that to be a woolen-manufacturer in Berkshire, in the earlier years of this century required a most steadfast and almost heroic courage. Nevertheless, Mr. Pomeroy was the most prosperous business-man of his day in Pittsfield; and, looking to the interest of his heirs, no act of his life more strikingly displayed his wonderful foresight and sagacity, than his purchase and persevering retention of what are now the Pomeroy Woolen Mills, and the lands attached to them. Looking to long results, there was, perhaps, never a wiser investment made in the town. His action in all this business fully accords with the character which we have elsewhere ascribed to him.

A peculiarity in the management of the Pomeroy mills—which they share with that of other old Pittsfield factories—is the long retention of faithful employés. Not to multiply instances, Solo-

Shaker brook, since occupied by the Osceola woolen-mill, and established a grist-mill, which he continued until his death, in 1851, with success, the withdrawal of the Luce mill from that use having prepared the way for it.

mon Wilson, the present superintendent, has been employed in various capacities since 1825, with the exception of five years. Joel Moulthrop, a spinner, for forty years; Henry Dunbar, James Denny and Thomas Rice, finishers, for forty years; Wesley Housen, a fuller, for thirty-five years.

The old brick-factory, when in full operation, now runs seven sets of machinery, employs one hundred and fifty hands, and manufactures weekly, an average of four thousand yards of all-wool and union broadcloth. The satinet-mill runs seven sets of machinery; employs one hundred hands, and makes, weekly, three thousand yards of satinet, and fifteen hundred yards of six-quarter union cloths and fancy cassimeres. Both mills are furnished with steam-power, are heated by steam, and lighted by gas. Their water-supply has also been greatly increased and regulated by the conversion of Lakes Onota and Pontoosuc into reservoirs. Altogether the mills and their accessories afford a fine contrast to their beginning in 1815.

The Pittsfield and Berkshire manufacturers did not content themselves with laboring perseveringly under the depressing circumstances in which they were placed at the close of the war of 1812. In alliance with the more energetic class in all the manufacturing districts of the country, they combated those circumstances themselves. Within a few months after the influx of foreign goods began, a meeting of the proprietors and manufacturers of Pittsfield, in November, 1815, directed its president and secretary—Thomas Gold and Jonathan Allen—"to invite the principal persons concerned in the woolen and cotton establishments of the county, to meet at Pittsfield, for the purpose of consulting on such measures as the condition of the country rendered necessary, to preserve these establishments, and enable them to progress successfully; and especially to prefer petitions to the next congress of the United States for such aids as it may be in its power to grant."

The meeting thus called was fully attended; and a memorial to congress was adopted, in which was detailed the progress already made by the county in manufactures, the causes of their present embarrassment, their hope for the future, and the general nature of the relief which was desired from congress. They did not rest here; but, from that time on, conventions, meetings, and other concerted action of the friends of manufactures in Berkshire were constant. True to its original purpose, the Agricultural Society was foremost in these measures. In October, 1817, on motion of Judge William Walker of Lenox, it expressed its belief that excessive importations were the prime cause of the financial distress of the country; and resolved that, as soon as the convenience of each member would permit, they would clothe themselves and families in domestic manufactures; that they would, by advice as well as by example, contribute as far as was in their power, to their exclusive use; and that in future, none of the premiums of the society should be awarded to any person not clothed in American fabrics. This was an old method of promoting the desired end, but it was not very efficacious; and, in November, the executive committee of the society called a meeting, at Coben's coffee-house in Pittsfield, of all who felt any attachment to these great interests of the country (domestic manufactures), to devise ways and means to promote them. The meeting was held, Thomas Gold being chairman, and John B. Root secretary. A series of resolutions was passed, expressing the sense of the meeting, "that, in the present condition of other nations and their manufactures, and the means of conducting them, through long experience and accumulation of capital, and their legislative provisions for protecting and encouraging them, manufactures in the United States can never be established, or be made to flourish, without adequate protection and encouragement from government;" "that every portion of the United States is deeply interested in the establishment and prosperity of manufactures; inasmuch as the greatest pursuit and employment of the people consists in their agriculture, from which source are drawn the raw material and means of conducting manufactures; that the public good requires of government to restrain, by duties, the importation of all articles which may be produced at home, and to manufacture as much as possible of the raw material of the country." There were a few minor propositions of a similar tenor; and a petition was adopted, in which the memorialists say that they have already stated to congress the extent of the stake which the inhabitants of Berkshire have in woolen, cotton, and other manufacturing establishments. The officers of the meeting were instructed to forward a copy of the proceedings and the memorial to Hon. Henry Shaw, the Berkshire representative, to be used as occasion might require.

Four years afterwards, in 1821, the Agricultural Society determined, in its own name, to petition congress in behalf of American manufactures; and appointed, as a committee to draw up its memorial, William C. Jarvis, William Walker, Lemuel Pomeroy, S. D. Colt, and S. M. McKay. A committee more fully competent for the task, it would, at that time, have been difficult to select from any community. It would have been impossible in Berkshire. Its chairman was distinguished as a political thinker and writer. All the members were men of thought and intelligence, and most of them were familiar with the practical details of the subject entrusted to them. The memorial which they prepared filled six double columns of the *Sun*, and was compact with logic and fact.

We need not chronicle all the numerous meetings in which the citizens of the county assembled to take action in regard to the desired protection of American manufactures. The strongest and best men in the county took part in them, and their action contributed its part to the passage of the tariff of 1824. Chief among their leaders was Henry Shaw of Lanesboro, who represented the district in congress from 1817 to 1821. In brilliant talent and intellectual power, Mr. Shaw was surpassed by few men of his day, although opinions, sometimes erratic, always independent and boldly expressed, unfitted him for success as a politician, and impaired his influence with the masses. Truth to say, democrat though he called himself, Henry Shaw was an aristocrat by nature and by breeding; and could never bring himself to adopt the arts of the demagogue. He went to congress, however, thoroughly imbued with the enthusiasm for American manufactures which then specially characterized Berkshire democrats; although, in Pittsfield, the leading federalists were even then beginning to rival their zeal in that respect. In Washington, he became warmly attached to Henry Clay, already among the foremost leaders of the democratic party, and the acknowledged champion of home-industries. The Berkshire representative was heartily welcomed by Mr. Clay, who at once recognized his great qualities, and an intimate friendship sprang up between the two statesmen which was only terminated by death.

It was perhaps owing to this association, that Mr. Shaw gave the vote in favor of the Missouri compromise, which forever destroyed for him all hope of high political preferment in Massachusetts : although the cast of his own mind was likely enough to lead him independently to the same course. At least he defended it in the columns of the *Sun*, with great ability.

But, however that may have been, Mr. Shaw's associations in congress inspired in him a still more ardent and confident advocacy of manufactures than he had before indulged in, as was manifested by his part in the meetings held for their promotion in Berkshire, and in his personal conversation.

In May, 1824, congress passed the famous tariff advocated by Mr. Clay, as the foundation of his "American system;" and as soon as the success of this measure was assured, Mr. Shaw showed his confidence in its effects by persuading many of his neighbors to turn their farms almost exclusively into sheep-pastures, setting them an example by converting his own broad acres to the same use,[1] and by embarking a considerable portion of his own capital in a factory since widely known as the Pontoosuc; being so styled by its founders from the Indian name of the territory of Pittsfield; not because they were unaware of the true spelling, but to simplify the word for business-purposes, just as another company at a later day preferred Taconic to Taghconic, and the Messrs. Barker dropped their middle initials from their firm-name. The Pontoosuc Woolen Manufacturing Company, by which this mill was erected, consisted of Henry Shaw of Lanesboro, David Campbell, Thaddeus Clapp, and George W. Campbell, of Pittsfield. It was formed in 1825, but not incorporated until 1826, nor formally organized until 1827, when the following officers were chosen: Henry Shaw, president; David Campbell, Jr., general agent; Thaddeus Clapp, superintendent; George W. Campbell, clerk and treasurer.

Of Messrs. Shaw and Clapp sufficient sketches have been given. David Campbell, Jr., was born in Pittsfield in 1782, being the son of Capt. David Campbell, whose business-talents he fully

[1] Berkshire did not prove as well adapted to sheep-culture as the more enthusiastic expected, and those who made it their sole dependence had cause to regret it. In seasons of marked depression of manufactures they bestowed their objurgations freely upon Mr. Shaw. Gradually, under the increasing competition of the more favored regions of the West, the raising of sheep has become a comparatively insignificant item with the Berkshire farmer. It could hardly be called a failure, however, in the first half of the century, and certainly the supply of wool which it afforded was an invaluable aid to the early manufacturers of Pittsfield.

inherited. Engaged in most of the commercial and manufacturing enterprises of the town during his active life, he always held a prominent place on their boards of control, as well as in those of the Agricultural Society. The confidence of his associates in his knowledge, sound judgment and integrity was unbounded, and his contemporaries paint him as shrewd, reticent, a close scrutinizer of men and things, strict in his dealings, but with a warm heart and kindly manner for those who dealt frankly and fairly with him. Previous to his connection with the Pontoosuc mill he was engaged at one time in mercantile business with James Buel. He had also been successful in distilling the oil of peppermint, a drug then in great demand for exportation. He contracted for entire fields of that herb in Lanesboro and Pittsfield; but he foresaw the glut in the market and withdrew from the speculation in season to escape loss. At another time he was engaged in the manufacture of linseed oil at Luce's mill in Pittsfield, and at a mill in Hinsdale. He died June 30, 1835.

George W. Campbell, the youngest son of Capt. David Campbell, was born at Pittsfield in 1807, and graduated at Union College in 1825. He was president of the Agricultural Bank from 1853 to 1861, and represented the town in the legislature of 1839.

The managers of the mill were all unusually competent, and had great advantage in point of experience over those who, eleven years before, had undertaken the control of the Pittsfield mill. Mr. Shaw had business-talents at once keen and comprehensive, and had been called by his position in congress, to make a thorough study of the subject of manufactures; the Messrs. Campbell had enjoyed and made use of an opportunity to become familiar with the details of the woolen-business in the Pittsfield mill. Mr. Clapp had eleven years' experience added to the admirable qualifications with which he entered upon the superintendence of that mill.[1]

The site selected for the factory was a beautiful spot on the outlet of Lake Shoonkeekmoonkeek, or Lanesboro pond, which thenceforward took the name of Pontoosuc lake. It was about equi-distant from Mr. Shaw's residence in Lanesboro and the Pittsfield park; but a mile south of the Pittsfield line. In 1762,

[1] In 1823 the Massachusetts Agricultural Society awarded to Messrs. Pomeroy and Clapp the first premium for satinets exhibited at its fair in Brighton.

Joseph Keeler bought of Col. William Williams, to whom they fell in the partition of "the commons," two hundred acres of land at the south end of the lake and extending forty rods down the outlet. This tract was noted for a remarkably fine growth of pines — of which some noble representatives remained very recently—and in 1763, Mr. Keeler built a dam at the foot of the lake, and a saw and grist mill on the site of the present reservoir-dam. A grist-mill occupied the site as late as 1834. In 1825 this property was owned by Capt. Hosea Merrill and was sold by him to the Pontoosuc company.

Below the Keeler water-privilege, was another upon which, about sixty rods south of the reservoir-dam, had stood the comb-plate and spindle-factory of James Strandring. This was owned by Arthur Scholfield, by whom it was sold in 1816 to John Crane, who converted Strandring's little works into a scythe-factory, which he carried on until the property was purchased, in 1825, by the Pontoosuc company.

The two privileges combined furnish a greater water-power than the company has ever used, and which has been made unfailing by the reservoir of 1866. The factory was placed midway between the two, on a site which is said to have been occupied by a saw-mill in the early days of the town. It is one hundred and forty-five by fifty feet, in ground dimensions, and four stories high, and is built of brick. Work on it was commenced in 1825; but such was the scarcity of skilled mechanics, and so great the difficulty of procuring the desired machinery promptly, that it was not ready to go into operation until 1827.

It is difficult to realize the change which has taken place in the last fifty years in the facilities for transacting business, especially of a manufacturing character. In 1825, nearly a quarter of a century had elapsed since Scholfield set up his first carding-machines, and eleven years since the building of the Pomeroy factory, but still it was no simple task to build and furnish a woolen-mill in Pittsfield. There was not a millwright in the region competent to put in such a water-wheel as was required at Pontoosuc. The shafts—not molded and turned like the work of later machine-shops with a precision which permits no waste of power, space or material—were rudely cast in some neighboring furnace and hammered into some clumsy approximation to the desired shape, with no further aid from mechanical appliances than could be afforded by a trip-hammer, and always with much superfluous metal. This difficulty extended to repairs, but it was remedied so far as the Pontoosuc factory was concerned, by the building of a furnace and machine-shop, near the mill, by William Sunderland, who, in 1832, sold them to the company, by whom they were maintained until the establishment of similar works, on a larger scale, in the village, rendered them unnecessary. Most factories, at that time, had machine-shops attached to them, where heavy work was done, and repairs made upon the more delicate machinery.[1]

But, in addition to this, in 1825, it was necessary to give orders for the more delicate and complicated machinery a much longer time in advance than it now is, and the improvements, which were constantly going on, rendered it indispensable to give close and watchful personal attention to the state of the market, in order to get the best. And, in place of telegraphs and tri-daily mails by railroad to the great centers of business, the stage lumbered three times a week to Boston and Hartford, and Hudson, with the orders sent by post, or the agent to make special contracts, for articles which, when finished, were shipped by water to Hartford, or Bridgeport; or at best, to Hudson; thence to be transported over roads, often of the heaviest, to the factory.

And these disadvantages were quite as sensibly felt after the factories went into operation, especially when in the case of a sudden demand for a special class of goods, or a change in market-prices, it became necessary to send sleighs, sleds, or wagons heavily loaded, in all directions, in all sorts of weather, to the nearest point of water-communication, if not the entire distance to the city. Many were the adventures in flood or storm, that the younger members of the earlier Pittsfield manufacturing companies encountered in thus forwarding their goods to market.

But, to return to the building of the Pontoosuc factory: the brick of which it was constructed was made at a yard on the north shore of the lake, which has been submerged by the successive raisings of the water-level. The lumber was furnished chiefly by Captain Hosea and Mr. Phillips Merrill, who still had good logging-ground close at hand. David Campbell, as agent, made the contracts for material and for work, and superintended

---

[1] Mr. Pomeroy's machine-shop, in connection with his armory, rendered any such attachment to his factory unnecessary.

PONTOOSUC WOOLEN MILLS.

their execution; but Mr. Clapp selected the machinery and other appliances of manufacture.

The factory went into operation in the spring of 1827, and at the cattle-show and fair of the Agricultural Society in October of that year, the committee on domestic manufactures, Ezekiel R. Colt chairman, "noticed, with pride and pleasure, the growing independence of the country of foreign looms, as shown in the exhibition by the Pontoosuc Woolen Manufacturing Company of broadcloths and cassimeres, not excelled by any cloths imported from Great Britain." There was patriotism still behind the interest of the Berkshire public in manufactures.

Although under all the tariffs, cotton and woolen manufactories in the country had increased in numbers, and, it is to be inferred, must have been conducted with some profit to their owners, none of them—not even Mr. Clay's tariff of 1824—was considered by the manufacturers as really protective of their interests,[1] and agitation for a still more stringent policy continued. In Berkshire, under the lead of Mr. Shaw, public meetings favoring and earnestly urging this course, were more frequent and determined than before. At one held December 12, 1827, Mr. Shaw presiding, speeches of unusual force and ability were made by Thomas B. Strong, George N. Briggs, and the chairman; and a memorial to congress, drafted by Mr. Shaw and Henry Marsh, was adopted; the meeting at the same time resolving, that the "interests of the grower and manufacturer of wool were alike in a ruinous condition, beyond their means to retrieve, and only within the power of government to redress." The famous "Black Tariff" was enacted in 1828, and was the first regarded by the mass of manufacturers with entire satisfaction. But, Mr. Clay being secretary of state, it lacked, in congress, his judicious supervision. It contained many provisions which did not meet his approval, and some most obnoxious features, introduced by the opponents of the bill with the hope of defeating it;[2] and which, although they did not accomplish that object, did create, in some sections of the country, a prejudice against all tariffs, which has never been eradicated. Mr. Shaw and his associates in the Pontoosuc company, concurred with their great leader in regard to the imperfections of the bill. We copy, from *Niles's Register* of 1829, an article illustrative of

[1] Bishop's History American Manufactures, vol. II, page 324.
[2] Colton's Life of Clay, vol. II, page 178.

this point, and also containing other interesting information concerning the mill.

The senior editor has received a present of extra superfine cloth, for a suit, from the Pontoosuc Woolen Manufacturers in Berkshire, Mass., accompanied by a letter, more valued than the cloth; but written in terms so kind and complimentary as to prevent its publication entire. Some points, however, may interest the public.

"The degree of perfection reached by this manufactory, will be best displayed by the specimen itself. Wear it out of respect for the motives which prompt the gift. * * * 'The [American] System' cannot be arrested; its march is onward. Trying as are our present embarrassments, the system will survive the misjudged efforts of its friends, and the misjudged opposition of its foes. It needs material modifications. The *effective* protection to woolens under the present tariff, is less than under the old duty of thirty-three and one-third per cent., with fair invoices. The auctions and the frauds combined inflict upon the revenue, not less than upon the manufacturer, a heavy loss. The remedy appears so obvious, that no fair man can mistake it;— repress the auctions and abolish the one-dollar minimum. The duty on wools should be modified. We do not, nor shall we, under the present tariff, raise very fine wools. From more than fifty thousand pounds, all that we could select, suitable for the fabric sent you, was less than seventy pounds; and we believe that the fifty thousand pounds was as fair a lot, taking entire flocks, as could be procured in New England. * * * We also send you a pattern card, containing specimens of the cloths we make. It will show you the manner in which we send them to market. Sales are made by these samples."

The factory appears to be a most prudently managed concern, employing forty men and sixty girls as operators, and making what is equal to one hundred and fifty yards of broadcloth daily. About ninety thousand pounds of wool will be manufactured the present year. The account concludes thus: "We use American wool, we employ American labor, we desire American patronage. Will a wise government permit establishments like this to sink under the combined operations of English frauds and New York auctions?"

Mr. Shaw had reason soon to revise some of the opinions expressed above. Even before the date of his letter, the extremely fine-wooled sheep of Saxony had been introduced into Berkshire, and were bred even upon his own farm. They multiplied without much respect to tariffs, and within a very few years almost entirely superseded, or were very largely crossed with, the merino. The change from the coarser and more oily fleece of the latter breed to that of the Saxony, was almost as great and as beneficial, as that from the native wools to the varieties introduced by Livingston and Humphries, and soon after, 1830, wool of as fine quality as was desired was grown abundantly in Berkshire.

Nor was the lack of protection the sole evil under which the Berkshire and other American woolen-manufacturers labored. There was a lack of perfect skill in their art, which, whatever tariffs might be imposed, required long years to overcome. Of the trouble in obtaining fast colors, we have already spoken; but there was another difficulty which affected the manufacturer, rather than the wearer, of domestic goods. The makers of broadcloths, especially, were ambitious and determined to make their fabrics as firm and as heavy as the best imported goods; and, by dint of crowding an unlimited amount of material into the weaving, and removing the surplus in the process of dressing, they accomplished their purpose; but with an enormous waste of stock, that was fatal to the hope of profit. The foreign manufacturers had a nack and mystery in this particular, which their American rivals were long in acquiring.

There was also an unfortunate custom of American manufacturers which greatly hindered advance in their art. At the present day it is the general practice for each mill to devote itself to the making of a single class of goods; sometimes confining its product to one color, in the manufacture of which it becomes perfect and for which it holds its specific place in the trade. The earlier American manufacturers had not learned the wisdom of this division of labor and concentration of effort. Each little factory set itself to satisfy the varied demands of the universal market; and the advertisements of the first Pittsfield mills read like descriptions of diverse spectra, or an enumeration of the colors of the rainbow imparted to every known fabric of wool.

Thus, before the manufacturer had discovered the source of his failure in one class of goods and devised or learned a remedy, he was called to another, in which he encountered new and mysterious troubles; and so on in an endless circle of tribulations.

Notwithstanding the comparative skill of Mr. Clapp, the Pontoosuc factory met its full proportion of this class of obstacles; which were doubtless augmented by its ambition to excel. Its proprietors were, however, shrewd business-men, and quite as prompt as any of their rivals to detect and reform an erroneous practice; and they struggled through to the day of ultimate triumph, with as little embarrassment as any; and with some moderate profit from the first.

In 1835, George W. Campbell became general agent in place of his brother, David, who died that year, leaving his estate to his sons, George, David and' Edward, and his daughter Caroline, who afterwards married Hon. Ensign H. Kellogg.

In 1841, George W. Campbell sold his interest in the concern to his partners; and his nephew, George, became clerk and treasurer.[1]

In 1841, Henry Shaw sold a portion of his stock to Socrates Squier of Lanesboro, who then became president of the company. In 1846, he sold the remainder, which was divided among his associates. In 1861, Mr. Squier sold his interest to his associates, and Hon. E. H. Kellogg succeeded him as president. In May, 1862, Col. Thaddeus Clapp transferred a portion of his stock to his son, Thaddeus, Jr., who was made assistant-superintendent, and in 1865, became general agent and superintendent.[2]

In 1865, Colonel Clapp died, leaving his share in the Pontoosuc property to his widow and children. In 1864, J. Dwight Francis, son of Mr. Almiron D. Francis, having purchased a portion of David Campbell's stock, was chosen clerk and treasurer; and in 1865, assistant-superintendent.

The goods manufactured at the Pontoosuc mill, in the forty-eight years since it went into operation, have often been varied to suit the changeful moods of the market; but, since 1834, not so frequently as to forego the advantages of devotion to a single product. Indeed, many of the fabrics are of a class in regard to which the market is most fickle; and it has been the pride of the company to meet its phases promptly and profitably, without depreciating the quality of its goods.

[1] George Campbell was born in 1811. He represented the town in the legislature 1857, and was selectman for several years.

[2] Thaddeus Clapp, the younger, was born in 1821, being the eldest son of Colonel Thaddeus and his wife Elizabeth, who was the daughter of James D. Colt, the second of that name in Pittsfield. Familiar with woolen-mills from his infancy, he early acquired an accurate knowledge of all the details of the manufacture, which, together with an unusually correct taste and judgment in styles, and an intimate acquaintance with markets, gave him great success in his position.

RESIDENCE OF THADDEUS CLAPP, Esq.

It commenced, in 1827, upon plain broadcloths and cassimeres, making, as has been said, the mistake of attempting to supply every color, from black to crimson, and all grades of quality. This course continued until 1834, when it began the manufacture of drab carriage-cloth, for which it soon obtained a demand that occupied it exclusively, except at occasional brief intervals when black and blue broadcloths were made. This continued until 1860, when, the fashionable rage for the balmoral style of ladies' skirts commencing, the company made them a specialty; and, not only devoted all the machinery in their mill to this product, but filled several neighboring buildings with hand-looms for the same purpose. Mr. Thaddeus Clapp, having collected in Canada some recently-imported patterns, among which were the plaids of several Highland clans, was able to introduce new designs, distinguished for good taste and brilliant colors. And during the patriotic fervor of the earlier years of the civil war, a few styles in red, white and blue, added to the reputation of the company for adapting its work to the market.

When the balmoral fashion began to pass away in 1865, the company turned its attention to the production of carriage lap-blankets, of which Mr. Clapp had procured an English specimen as a model. The imitation soon equaled the original in splendor of color and beauty of design; and in six years one hundred and sixty-two different patterns of carriage-blankets were sent out from the Pontoosuc looms.

The enterprise of the company in adding this great article of luxury and comfort to the list of American manufactures, was well rewarded, and it also led to the introduction of the sleeping-car blanket, now the leading product of the mill, with which it has supplied many leading railroads, as well as the noted Pullman palace-car company.

In addition to the blankets, the present products of the mill are meltons, cassimeres, repellants, and flannels.

The machinery now comprises eleven sets of cards, the same number of jacks and spinning-jennies, and fifty-eight broad looms. The number of employés varies from two hundred and twenty-five to one hundred and twenty-five. In 1865, the mill turned out, besides blankets and some minor products, one hundred and sixty thousand seven hundred skirts. In 1871, the product was over sixty thousand skirts, sixty-eight thousand yards of meltons and repellants, and seventeen thousand blankets.

There is, perhaps, no more proper place than this, in which to introduce an account of Henry Clay's visit to Pittsfield. Mr. Clay being in Northampton, Sunday evening, November 18th, received a delegation from Berkshire, consisting of Henry Shaw, George N. Briggs and Samuel M. McKay, who invited him to pass through the county, and receive its hospitalities. The next afternoon Mr. Clay, having accepted the invitation, crossed the mountains with his family, and spent the night at Lanesboro, as a guest of his old friend, Mr. Shaw. On Tuesday morning, the county-committee of arrangements waited upon him, and accompanied him to Pittsfield, " escorted by a cavalcade of fifty well-mounted gentlemen, and several hundred citizens in carriages," although the rain fell in torrents. At the town-hall, the guest was welcomed by Colonel McKay, in a speech full of encomiums upon his course regarding the protection of American manufactures, and upon his political conduct generally.

Mr. Clay replied cordially, and with his usual fascinating grace. He alluded to the then recent compromise-act—upon which Colonel McKay had specially dwelt, characterizing them "as the olive-branch with the sword"—in words which are described, by those who heard them, as "a fine specimen of his resistless and incomparable eloquence." "He foresaw," he said, "that his opponents would assail, and some of his friends distrust, him; but he held that no man had a right to refuse to sacrifice himself to his country. He had not been much alarmed by the threats of civil war. He knew the power—or rather the impotency—of the state which threatened it. Yet something was to be accorded to the dangerous tendencies of other states; and, although he did not believe, and would not admit, that the insurrection could ever have been successful against the arms of the federal government; yet the disaffected states themselves, when subdued, would have been left with feelings illy adapted to harmonize with their sister-states of the Union." He concluded by expressing a desire "to proceed without further delay to the more agreeable part of the ceremony of presentation:" the personal greetings.

At two o'clock, Mr. Clay attended a public dinner at the Berkshire Hotel; and when Hon. Henry W. Dwight of Stockbridge, with some eloquent remarks, gave the name and services of the guest as a toast, its enthusiastic reception called from him some remarks full of feeling, in the course of which, he mentioned that, on one occasion, Colonel Dwight was the only member of congress from Massachusetts, who had stood up in defense of that policy of protection to American manufactures, which had since spread prosperity over the whole country.

After the dinner, Mr. Clay visited the Pontoosuc factory, Lemuel Pomeroy's musket-factory, and other points of interest in the town. In the evening he attended a party given in his honor, at the hospitable residence of Ezekiel R. Colt, where he was presented to many of the ladies of the county. When he left town, the next day, there were few men or women in it whose friendship he had not won. Men of all political parties had joined to do him honor, and only those whose souls were wholly encrusted with political prejudice, could entirely resist the fascination of the great statesman's manner.

BARKERSVILLE AND STEARNSVILLE.

The histories of the factories of J. Barker & Brothers, and of D. & H. Stearns, are so intimately connected that they must be told in connection. The factories of the two firms are all located upon the south-west branch of the Housatonic river; stretching along that stream for about a mile, from a point one mile from its issue from Richmond lake.

In opening their story, we must return again to the eighteenth century. Among the first settlers in Watertown, Mass., between the years 1625 and 1640, were some who wrote their names indifferently, Sterne, Sternes, and Stearns. A genealogist of the family has traced it back to an honorable ancestry in Yorkshire, England. Many of its descendants afterwards emigrated to various sections of New England. Among these was the father of Daniel Stearns, who was born in Killingly, Conn., in 1764.

In his boyhood, Daniel was apprenticed to Colonel Danielson of Colchester, Conn., from whom he learned the art of cloth-dressing, and of dyeing cloth and yarn. At the close of his apprenticeship, he established himself in business at Brookline, Conn., where he continued until 1795, when he removed to Hinsdale and purchased the water-privileges now occupied by Hinsdale Brothers and the Plunkett Woolen Manufacturing Company. He removed to

Hinsdale in the fall of 1795, and made preparations to erect buildings for his business; but the winter, proving unusually severe, gave him an unfavorable impression of the locality; and, having an opportunity, in the spring, to sell his property there, he did so, and removed to Lenox Furnace, where he established himself in his business and remained some years. In 1803, he removed to Salisbury, Conn Fever and ague affecting his family in that locality, he purchased the Valentine Rathbun fulling-mill, and removed to Pittsfield.

In 1811, Mr. Stearns built, in the same vicinity, what was long known as the "New Woolen Factory;" a wooden building thirty-one by forty feet on the ground, one story high, besides a basement. In this mill he placed a spinning-jenny of twenty-five spindles, and a double carding-machine, both of Scholfield's manufacture.

In the year 1825, he retired from business, leaving the control of the property to his sons, Jirah, Daniel, Henry, and Charles T.; but retaining the title until his death in March, 1841.[1]

In 1826, the brothers formed a firm under the name of J. Stearns & Brothers, "for the manufacture of broadcloths, cassimeres, satinets, and flannels." In 1826, they built upon a water-privilege with a fall of twenty-two feet, some half a mile below the old mill, a brick-factory, seventy feet by forty in area, four stories high, and an attic. In this they placed two sets of machinery, which were run upon broadcloth until 1849, when two more were added; and the products changed to satinets and union cassimeres.

On the next fall below, the firm, in 1828, built a saw-mill and finishing-shop.

In 1835, Charles T. sold his interest to his brothers, and removed to Michigan. In 1843, Jirah disposed of his share in the same way, and removed to Glenham, and afterwards to Newburgh, N. Y.; when the firm became D. & H. Stearns.

In 1853, the Messrs. Stearns purchased the water-privilege below their brick-mill, a fall of twenty-eight feet, and built upon

---

[1]Jirah was born at Lenox Furnace in 1798, and represented the town of Pittsfield in the legislatures of 1831 and 1832. Daniel was born at Lenox Furnace in 1800, and was representative in 1835. Henry was born at Salisbury in 1800, and was representative in 1864. Charles T. was born at Pittsfield in 1806.

BARKERVILLE.

it a stone finishing-mill of one hundred and twenty-five by forty feet, and a number of operatives' cottages. Upon the water-privilege below, they also built what is known as the railroad-mill, a stone-structure one hundred feet long by forty-two wide, and three stories high. In this they placed eight sets of machinery, which they used for making union cassimeres. In 1861, the brick-mill was burned, and the Messrs. Stearns turned their whole attention to the stone-mills until in December, 1865, they sold them to J. Barker & Brothers.

In 1866, a corporation in which the Stearns brothers were the largest stockholders—the others having been their employés, and a commission-house with which they dealt in New York,—was organized as the Stearnsville Woolen Company, and purchased all the water-power of the firm which had not been sold to the Barkers; comprising a water-privilege with a fall of thirty-three feet, in its entire length, to which were attached forty-five acres of land, with a store, an office, and thirty cottages for operatives. The ruins of the brick-mill stood upon the upper part of the water-privilege: and, lengthening the old canal, the new company, in 1866-7, built, a short distance below them, a wooden mill of one hundred and fifty-six by forty feet, and two stories high, and had nearly furnished it with machinery, when it was entirely destroyed by fire. Owing to the depression of the woolen-manufacturing business, which has since prevailed, only the L part of the factory has been rebuilt.

The brothers Barker, who succeeded the Stearns family in the ownership of the earlier mills built by them, and who have built up one of the most prosperous manufacturing-establishments in Berkshire, are sons of Gardner T. Barker, who was born at Cheshire in 1779, and was married in January, 1806, to Harriet Lyon,[1] who was born in Warrensbush, near Schenectady, in 1790. John V. Barker was born at Cheshire in 1807, and Charles T. in the same town, in 1809. Otis R. was born in July, 1811, at Moriah, in Essex county, N. Y., to which place Mr. G. T. Barker had removed that spring, and where he reared a family of nine sons and three daughters. Mr. Barker was for many years trial-justice and supervisor of the town of Moriah, and an officer in its company of militia at the battle of Plattsburg. On the death of

[1] Mrs. Barker was a daughter of Dr. John Lyon, a physician at Cheshire, both before and after 1790.

his wife, he removed to Pittsfield, where, after residing for thirteen years in the families of his sons, he died in April, 1873, at the age of ninety-four.

His eldest son, Mr. John V. Barker, having learned the wool-carding and cloth-dressing business, came to Pittsfield in 1830, and was employed by Messrs. Stearns until 1832, when, his brother, Charles T., joining him, they formed the firm of J. & C. Barker, the middle initials being omitted for the sake of brevity. Otis R. was admitted a partner in 1834, and the firm became J. Barker & Brothers.

In 1832, J. & C. Barker purchased, of Daniel Stearns, the mill built in 1811, which had been disused for some years. It was then only of its original size. There was a basement, but it was built so low, that in freshets the water was often so deep that the unlucky stranger who, unaware of its peculiarities, stepped incautiously into its door, was completely immersed. This difficulty, the new owners of the mill remedied by lifting it to a proper level. As their means increased, they added to its height, and lengthened it until it was three stories high, and one hundred and eighty feet long. They also added a wing of the same height thirty feet long by twenty wide; and erected near by a boiler-house of one hundred by thirty feet. In 1869-70, the Messrs. Barker, having removed the wing and one end of the old mill, built around the remainder—in which the machinery meanwhile continued in full operation—the walls of a new brick-factory; after which they tore down the old, and completed the interior.

The new mill is one hundred and sixty-five feet long by fifty-three wide. It is three stories high, with an attic, and contains eight sets of machinery, making union and all-wool cassimeres, both broad and narrow.

In December, 1865, the Messrs. Barker bought of D. & H. Stearns, their entire lower establishment, consisting of seventy acres of land; two stone-factories with eight sets of machinery; a wooden weave-shop and wool-house, one hundred feet long and twenty wide; two stores, and a large number of dwelling-houses. The mills continue to make union cassimeres.

THE RUSSELL WOOLEN-FACTORY.

In the account of the manufactories to be given in the following pages—all of which have been established since 1825—we do

S. N. & C. RUSSELL'S WOOLEN MILL.

not deem it advisable to enter into the details which are of interest in the story of those founded before that date; for the sole reason that the later manufacturers have had only to encounter the ordinary obstacles of business; and their enterprise and struggles, however noble, have been so similar in their character, that they would become monotonous in the repetition.

About the year 1820, a small building was erected on or near the site of the Rufus Allen iron-forge on Onota brook, and from that date until 1843, was occupied as a manufactory of carpenters' tools, by Moses Sweet.

In 1843, it was purchased by Solomon N. Russell, who, in the following year, associated with himself his brother Charles.[1]

The brothers Russell, in 1845, converted the little shop into a manufactory of cotton-batting, a class of goods for which they soon obtained a high reputation in the market. The product was afterwards changed to wadding. The mill was burned and rebuilt. Its use for the manufacture of wadding was discontinued in 1860.

In 1856, the Messrs. Russell hired the Wahconah woolen-mill for ten years, and run it for a portion of that term upon army-cloths, and for the remainder on balmoral skirts.

In 1863, they built upon Onota brook, nearly opposite their batting-mill, a handsome and substantial brick-mill; one of the most perfect in the town. It is one hundred and eighty feet by fifty on the ground, and three stories high. Connected with it is a dye-house of seventy-five by thirty feet, and also a house, fifty feet square, for the boiler, picker-room, and dry-room. It has a capacity for ten sets of machinery; and in seasons of ordinary prosperity, employs about one hundred and twenty-five hands. It makes various classes of fine woolen-goods.

Mr. Charles L. Russell, one of the most capable and popular Berkshire manufacturers of his day, died in 1870, and his share in the manufactory was inherited by his father, who divided it among his heirs, Solomon N., Joseph, Zeno, Hezekiah S., and Frank W. Russell, and Mrs. G. L. Weed. Hezekiah and Joseph sold their interest to their co-partners in 1871. Solomon N., who has had thirty-four years' experience as a manufacturer, and Zeno, are the managing partners; Frank being connected with the house of William Turnbull & Co., New York.

[1] Sons of Solomon L. Russell, of whom a sketch is given in Chapter XVIII.

PECK'S FACTORIES.

In the year 1816, the firm of J. & E. Peck hired one end of John B. Root's store on East street, where they commenced the manufacture of tin-ware; the partners alternating in the charge of this establishment, and a similar one, which they owned at Richmond, Va.[1]

In the spring of 1828, they purchased the store and stock of Mr. Root, and added largely to the latter. In both the store and the tin-manufactory, they continued in the same locality until 1864; building up a prosperous business, notwithstanding the tendency of trade towards Park square and North street.

In 1844, Elijah Peck and William Barnard purchased the water-privilege, formerly occupied by Seymour's forge, a little west of that owned by the Messrs. Russell, on Onota brook, and erected upon it what was intended for a batting-mill. Mr. Barnard was the active partner, but before the mill was fitted with machinery, Mr. Jabez Peck purchased his interest and, with his brother, began the manufacture of cotton-warps, the firm name being J. & E. Peck. In 1853, Mr. Jabez L. Peck bought the interest of his father, Jabez, and in 1864, purchased that of his uncle Elijah; since which date, he has remained sole owner.

The warp-mill was destroyed by fire in 1866, and rebuilt the same year; the new structure being a two-story wooden building of two hundred and four by fifty feet. It runs forty cards and four thousand four hundred spindles and, when in full operation, produces, weekly, seventy-five thousand yards of eighteen hundred end warps.

During the war of 1861-5, Mr. Peck engaged with Mr. J. K. Kilbourn in the manufacture of balmoral skirts, with a success which led to the erection, by the firm of Peck & Kilbourn, of a woolen-factory still further up Onota brook, upon the site formerly occupied by the Hicox forge. This mill, which was built in 1864, is a handsome brick-building, two stories high, with a basement. In 1868, Mr. Peck purchased the interest of his partner and has since run the mill with remarkable success on various classes of flannels, for which its reputation in the market has given it an unfailing demand.

[1] Jabez Peck was born at Berlin, Conn., in 1780. In 1781 his father removed with his family to Lenox. Jabez removed to Pittsfield in 1816. Elijah Peck was born at Lenox in 1791, and removed to Pittsfield in 1828.

The flannel-mill runs four sets of machinery and five jacks, making eleven thousand yards of domett flannel weekly, and employing fifty hands; one-half of whom are males. The warp-mill runs forty cards and forty-four hundred spindles; producing, weekly, seventy-five thousand yards of "eighteen hundred yard ends." It employs ninety hands; one-third of them males.

TACONIC MILL.

The Taconic mill was built in 1856, on the water-privilege two miles north of the village, formerly occupied by the Pomeroy armory. It is a wooden structure of one hundred and fifty by fifty feet; four stories high and an attic. It has the usual dye, picker, boiler, wool, and store houses. At the time of its erection no pains were spared to make it complete in all its appointments. Its manufacture was union cassimeres, of which it made four thousand yards weekly, requiring four hundred thousand pounds of wool annually. The original stockholders were William C. Allen, William Pollock, Theodore Pomeroy, Robert Pomeroy, Edward Pomeroy, Charles Atkinson, Edward Learned, Frank Cone, and James L. Baldwin. Edward Learned was the first president of the company, George Y. Learned the first general agent and treasurer, and Charles Atkinson the first superintendent.

PITTSFIELD BEL AIR AND WOOLEN COMPANIES.

The west branch of the Housatonic, from Pontoosuc lake to the Wahconah mills, presents a close succession of water-falls; one of the best of which is midway between Taconic and Wahconah. It is formed by the union of two distinct water-privileges, upon the lower of which, having a fall of only six feet, Spencer Churchill, as contractor, built for E. M. Bissell, in 1832, a four-story brick-factory, of eighty by thirty feet. But the owners of the next privilege above, having some business-controversy concerning the right to the privilege, put in a mudsill-dam, which rendered it impossible to obtain a sufficient regular supply of water; and the mill never went into operation.

The speculation ruined Mr. Bissell financially, and the building remained uncared for, and gradually falling into a ruinous condition, until, when it seemed about to fall by its own weight, it was purchased in 1852, by the newly-organized Pittsfield Woolen Company, who rebuilt the lower story, and thoroughly repaired and remodeled the whole structure.

The new proprietors also bought the water-privilege next above, and combining it with the old, by the erection of a massive stone-dam, obtained a fall of twenty-six feet, instead of six. They placed in the mill four sets of machinery, which had some years before been used for a short time in the unfortunate Ashuelot mill in Dalton.[1]

The first officers of the company were Henry Colt, president; Robert Pomeroy, treasurer; W. Frank Bacon, secretary and general agent. Among the principal stockholders were Theodore Pomeroy, Edward Learned, and Edwin Clapp.

In June, 1861, the upper story of the mill was destroyed by fire; the remainder being saved; very much through the efforts of Company D (the Pollock Guard) of the Tenth Regiment of Massachusetts Volunteers, which was then organizing upon the neighboring grounds of the Berkshire Agricultural Society. The upper story was not rebuilt, and the old mill was converted into spinning and dressing rooms. In 1864, the upper story was again burned off, and it was repaired as a building of two stories.

In the meantime, in 1862, a fine, new brick-mill of four stories one hundred feet by fifty in area, was erected, a short distance up the stream, and supplied with the best and most modern machinery. In 1870, it ran eight sets of machinery, and employed one hundred and fifty hands, one-fifth of them girls; making, monthly, twelve thousand yards of cassimeres, beavers, and doeskins, worth from three to five dollars per yard. Its monthly pay-roll was forty-five hundred dollars.

In July, 1873, the property of the Pittsfield Woolen Company was purchased for one hundred thousand dollars, by the Bel Air Manufacturing Company. President, Hon. Edward Learned; secretary, E. McA. Learned; treasurer, Frank E. Kernochan. This new company has improved the property, put up new buildings, and added new machinery, at a cost of between twenty-five and thirty thousand dollars; and the mill is now turning out, monthly, almost twelve thousand yards of fine, fancy cassimeres, which command as high a price as any similar goods of American

---

[1] Owned by Henry Marsh of Dalton, Asahel Buck of Lanesboro, and M. R. Lanckton of Pittsfield; all of whom were seriously involved in its failure.

manufacture. One hundred and sixty operatives are employed, one-fourth females, and the monthly pay-roll amounts to about forty-five hundred dollars.

THE OSCEOLA WOOLEN-MILL.

The Osceola Woolen-Mill is located near the foot of Mount Osceola, at a point on the south-west branch of the Housatonic, about one mile from its junction with the Housatonic. The fine water-power by which it is operated, was occupied in 1790, by a saw and grist mill, built by King Strong. In 1833, it was bought by Josiah Pomeroy & Co., who built a wooden mill of thirty by twenty-five feet, for grinding plaster-of-Paris, brought from Nova Scotia. Mr. Lemuel Pomeroy, whose policy was to concentrate the investments of the firm about their mill, near the village, yielded reluctantly to this purchase, and when the co-partnership was dissolved in 1839, Josiah Pomeroy took it, and converted it into a grist-mill, for which an opening was made by the disuse of the Luce mill for that purpose.

Upon Mr. Josiah Pomeroy's death in 1851, Noah W. Goodrich bought the grist-mill, and run it mostly on custom-work, until 1862, when the dam was carried away, and work suspended. In 1864, Mr. Goodrich sold the property to Otis L. Tillotson and B. F. Barker, who converted the mill into a woolen-factory. Mr. Barker, before the undertaking was fully under way, sold his interest to his partner, who carried on the business alone for one year, with one set of machinery. In 1865, Mr. Dwight M. Collins was admitted as a partner, and an addition, fifty feet square, was made to the mill; while its capacity was increased to two sets of machinery. In 1866, the machinery was increased to four sets. In 1873, that portion of the mill purchased from Mr. Goodrich was replaced by a building fifty by sixty feet in area, and three stories; while the capacity of the entire establishment was increased to six sets of machinery; making union cassimeres. New boiler, dye and wool houses were built, and the property generally improved. Additions have been made to the real-estate, until it now amounts to one hundred and fifty acres, with sixteen tenement-houses.

Mr. Tillotson died in 1873, leaving his interest in the property to his brothers.

Mr. E. Farnham, previously of the Taconic factory, became connected with the Osceola in 1867.

THE PITTSFIELD COTTON-FACTORY.

The first mill-dam in Pittsfield—built by Deacon Crofoot, some few rods south of the Elm-street bridge—passed, in 1778, into the hands of Ebenezer White, under a lease of nine hundred and ninety-nine years, from the town. It remained in the hands of Mr. White, and, after his death, of his son Enoch, until 1832; Mr. Enoch White continuing and improving the saw and grist mills on the east end of the dam, and the successors of Jacob Ensign maintaining the fulling-mill on the west end; Jonathan Allen, 2d, being the last. Simeon Brown also built a bark-mill, for the supply of his tannery, just below the dam, and obtaining its power from it.

In 1832, the privilege, with the considerable amount of land attached to it, was contributed by Mr. White, as stock in trade, to a firm, to which Col. Samuel M. McKay and Capt. Curtis T. Fenn, the other partners, furnished the cash-capital, for building and running a cotton-factory. This factory, which was built of brick, in 1832, was eighty feet by forty in area; three stories high, besides an attic and basement.[1]

Messrs. McKay and Fenn soon bought the interest of their partner, and continued to run the mill until the death of Colonel McKay in 1839, when the property was sold at auction, and purchased by Thomas F. Plunkett, who, in 1845, removed the dam down the stream, to a point near the factory.

He also added forty feet to the rear of the building, making it one hundred and twenty feet long; and gave it its present capacity of twenty-nine cards, over one hundred looms, and nearly four thousand spindles, producing one million, five hundred and sixty thousand yards of sheeting annually, and employing one hundred operatives.

In the year 1849, Martin Van Sickler, who had become connected with the mill in 1840, as overseer, and Lyman Clapp,[1]

---

[1] Mr. Zalmon Markham put in the water-wheel—a breast-wheel, thirteen feet in diameter, and twelve feet bucket—one of a hundred built by him for mills in the vicinity of Pittsfield.

[2] Second son of Mr. Jason Clapp.

each purchased a quarter-interest in the property, and the firm became Plunkett, Clapp & Company, and, although Mr. Clapp died suddenly at New York in 1853, so continued until 1864; the representatives of the deceased partner retaining his interest. In 1861, at the breaking out of the rebellion, work was suspended at the mill, in deference to Mr. Plunkett's judgment, and Mr. Van Sickler entered into a temporary partnership with Mr. N. G. Brown, for the manufacture of gray flannels, at a small factory on Beaver street, where Mr. Brown had formerly made twine. This business proved profitable; but, in 1864, Mr. Albert Learned purchased Mr. Plunkett's interest in the cotton-factory, —and, with Mr. Van Sickler, that of Mr. Clapp's heirs also—and the firm was again changed, becoming Learned & Van Sickler. In 1867, Mr. Learned sold to Mr. Van Sickler, who has since conducted the business alone.

THE COLTSVILLE PAPER-MILL.

The iron-forge of John Snow, at what is now Coltsville, of which an account has been given in another chapter, was succeeded, in 1826, by a tannery established by Alexander Dorn. The tannery was sold a few years afterwards to John Chase & Brother, who, in their turn, sold it, in 1835, to Royal Weller. In 1837, it was purchased by H. N. & A. P. Dean. Stowell Dean succeeded H. N. in 1840; and, in 1843, Benjamin Dean succeeded A. P.; the firm becoming S. & B. Dean, who carried on the tannery until 1847, when Olcott Osborn was admitted as a partner.

In 1848, the tannery was converted into a paper-mill, and the Deans sold their interest to James Wilson and F. W. Gibbs; the firm taking the name of Wilson, Osborn & Gibbs. In 1850, Mr. Wilson sold to his partners. In 1851, Hon. Thomas Colt purchased Mr. Osborn's interest, and, in 1855, that of Mr. Gibbs.

The old building was insufficient in size, and otherwise illy adapted to its purposes as a paper-mill; and Mr. Colt, from his first connection with it, intended, in good time, to replace it with a building of proper size, and constructed in the best manner. In 1862, the increasing business of the concern seemed to warrant and demand that the improvement should no longer be delayed, but that a mill worthy of the superior water-power at that point, should take the place of the dilapitated old structure. It was accordingly demolished, and in the following year Mr. Colt built, upon its site, a brick-mill, which is one of the most substantial and handsome in the county. Built under his personal supervision, it is finished, in all its details, with the most scrupulous care and faithfulness, and is filled with machinery of a corresponding character.

It is one hundred feet by fifty in area and two stories high, besides a basement and attic; and has, besides, a "lean-to" in the rear, of one hundred feet by twenty-eight. It has two rag-engines of five hundred pounds capacity, and one of one thousand pounds. When working in full, it consumes about three hundred and fifty tons of rags yearly; and employs fifteen men and thirty girls. It is lighted by gas made on the premises, and heated by steam.

The manufacture of paper requires a very large and uninterrupted supply of the purest water; and, pellucid as are the mountain streams of Berkshire, they often—even when not polluted with the refuse matter of the factories, or the sewerage of villages—contain mineral ingredients injurious to the paper. Mr. Colt, therefore, in 1856, bored, near his mill, an artesian-well, two hundred and fifty feet deep. And, this not furnishing an adequate supply, he followed it, in 1868, with another, five hundred and one feet in depth. These wells were the first of their kind in western Massachusetts, and they met the usual obstacles which try the faith and patience of those who make the first experiment in penetrating strata like those of the Berkshire geological formation. Their cost was ten thousand dollars; but they proved successful, affording five hundred and seventy-five thousand gallons of perfectly pure water, daily. And they have been followed by several others, at different points in the Housatonic valley.

WAHCONAH FLOURING AND MEAL MILLS.

A few miles below the Bel Air factory is a water-power of seventeen feet head, upon which, in 1776, Dea. Nathan Barber built his fulling-mill; there being already a saw-mill upon it. The fulling-mill was succeeded, in 1816, by a wooden factory, forty by thirty feet in size, which was erected by Caleb Goodrich and Spencer Churchill; the latter selling his interest to his partner in the following year. Mr. Goodrich used it for turning wood for bedsteads, etc., and leased room and power for various minor manufactures, among which were lead-pipe, wheel-hubs, machinery and buttons. Arthur Scholfield transferred his wool-carding to this mill, in 1827, and was succeeded by his son Isaac, who in turn sold the business to James S. Little. The richly gilt buttons manufactured here by Nicholson & Guilford, and exhibited at the cattle-show of 1832, were very honorably mentioned by the committee upon manufactures. John Webb occupied most of the upper story, for the manufacture of carpenters' planes, from 1837 to September 27, 1849, when the building was destroyed by fire. In 1849, Mr. Goodrich replaced it by a wooden mill, eighty feet by thirty, and three stories high; in which he resumed the turning-business, which he continued until 1859, when he sold the premises, including the water-privilege, to George H. Clark,[1] Charles T. Bulkley, and Otis Cole, Jr.

The new proprietors remodeled and enlarged the building, and converted it into a flouring and meal mill, giving it the name of Wahconah. In 1861, Asahel A. Powell purchased Mr. Bulkley's interest, and in 1864, Doctor Clark sold to his partners, Cole and Powell, who, in 1875, own and conduct the mill.

In 1848-9, Caleb Goodrich built—on the side of Wahconah street opposite the mill just described, and next south of the entrance to the Pittsfield cemetery—a stone-mill, sixty feet by forty in area, and three stories high. It is on the same privilege with the Wahconah flouring-mill; but, standing lower, has nineteen feet head of water. It was first occupied, for a couple of years, by George A. Burnell and Ebenezer Goodrich. The Russell Brothers then hired it, as has been stated, for ten years. Jonathan M. Jones & Sons then run it for one year, on balmoral skirts. In 1866, T. G. Atwood and Lyman Abbee bought it of Cole & Powell, who had purchased it with their upper mill, in 1859, and for several years manufactured flannels, tweeds, and balmoral skirts. In 1871, Messrs. Cole & Powell re-purchased the mill, and removed to it the meal-portion of their business; and it is now the Wahconah meal-mill. The flouring-mill has

[1]Dr. George H. Clark, who had acquired a fortune as partner in the leading drug-firm of Rushton, Clark & Co., New York, retired in 1856 to Pittsfield, where he erected a fine residence, upon the site of the old fort on the southwest shore of Lake Onota, and took a lively interest in the affairs of the town. He died in 1869.

three run of stones, and makes six thousand barrels of flour yearly. The meal-mill has two run of stones, and grinds, yearly, about two hundred and fifty car-loads of corn and oats.

SHAKER FLOURING-MILL.

On the water-privilege next below the factory built by Daniel Stearns in 1810, there was, in 1823, an old oil-mill; but in that year, the privilege was bought by the Pittsfield and Hancock Shakers, who erected a dam, and in the following year a wooden grist-mill, forty feet by thirty, two stories high, and containing two run of stones. The Shakers intended it for their own special convenience, but the excellence of their work soon gained it favor, which continued to increase until, in 1867, it was necessary to almost entirely rebuild it.

The mill then erected is sixty-three by forty-two feet in area, with three stories of wood, and a stone-basement fifteen feet high. It has three run of stones, one of which is devoted entirely to the grinding of wheat.

OSCEOLA RIVER FLOURING-MILL.

In 1865, Charles Morgan built on the south-west branch of the Housatonic, a quarter of a mile below the Barkers' Railroad-mill, a wooden factory fifty feet by thirty in size, in which he made satinets for about a year. It was then sold to George W. Adams, who converted it into a grist-mill, with four run of stones. In 1869, it was bought by George W. Sprague. One run of stone is devoted to wheat; the others to different grains. About four hundred bushels of grain are ground daily.

CHAPTER XXII.

TURNPIKES AND RAILROADS.

[1797-1875.]

The turnpike-system—Third Massachusetts, or Worthington, turnpike—Pontoosuc turnpike—Favorable pass through the mountains—Obstacles to the plans of the company—Final success, and opening excursion to Springfield—Proposed canals—Railroad from Boston to the Hudson river—Explorations for a route made—Theodore Sedgwick—Discussion of the railway-system in the newspapers—Public meetings—Patent railroad from New York to Pittsfield proposed—Further prosecution of the project for a railroad from Boston to Albany—Hudson and Berkshire railroad constructed—Peculiar charter of the Western railroad—Books of subscription opened—Contest and decision concerning the route through Berkshire—The road completed and opened—Depots in Pittsfield—North Adams railroad—Stockbridge and Pittsfield railroad.

WHEN the business of the country began to revive during the last quarter of the eighteenth century, greater facilities for intercommunication between different sections were imperatively required; while the poverty of the towns, especially in rocky and mountainous districts, where the building and maintaining of roads were most difficult and costly, rendered it impossible for them properly to meet the constant demands for new and improved routes. And it seemed the more unjust to impose this burden upon them, since the straight highways which facilitated the through-travel between rich and populous centers, were really not so convenient for local intercourse as the old winding roads, which turned aside to every farmer's door. In this dilemma the first resort was to a multiplication of turnpike-corporations, authorized to collect tolls upon certain lines of road, which they were required to improve and keep in good condition.

Investments in turnpikes did not finally prove very remunerative; but they were, for a time, great favorites with public-spirited men. And in a few years, there was a continuous line, interrupted only at Pittsfield from the Connecticut river to the Hudson; and thence four hundred miles into western New York. In Massachusetts, at least after the year 1795, it was not the practice to grant charters for turnpikes, except in sparsely populated, mountainous, rocky, or otherwise difficult, districts. It thus happened that, while some of the great highways in the eastern part of the commonwealth were turnpiked under old charters, the turnpikes in western Massachusetts, where the system began later, were interrupted in populous towns where the surface was not difficult. The turnpikes west from the Connecticut valley began at the western boundaries of Northampton and Westfield; and there were none in Pittsfield, except where the Pontoosuc turnpike entered the east part of the town for a very short distance.

Still, the great lines which terminated at her western and eastern borders, and were connected by her main streets, were of great interest to the town, whose citizens were large stockholders in them, and whose intercourse with the outer world was, to a great extent, dependent upon them. They were, indeed, essentially Pittsfield institutions.

The first of these lines was the Third Massachusetts turnpike,[1] for building which, a company was chartered, in 1797, the following citizens of Pittsfield being among the corporators: Timothy Childs, Joshua Danforth, Josiah Dickinson, Thomas Gold, Simon Larned, Henry Van Schaack and John Chandler Williams. The route extended from the west line of Northampton, through Westhampton, Williamsburg, Chesterfield, Worthington, Partridgefield (now Peru and Hinsdale) and Dalton, to the east line of Pittsfield, where it connected with Unkamet street. By an act of 1798, the line was extended from the west boundary of Pittsfield, across the town of Hancock—a distance of two and a half miles—to the New York border.

In the year 1800, Simon Larned and J. C. Williams of Pittsfield, and Ezra Starkweather of Worthington, a committee of this corporation, represented to the legislature that it had expended thirty thousand dollars upon its turnpike, and had been able to declare no dividend; the cost of care and repairs swallowing up all the receipts. They therefore asked that the towns through which it passed might be required to expend more

---

[1]The name was changed, in 1814, to "The Worthington Turnpike."

upon bridges than they had done, and that they should turn out in deep snows to break out the roads. They also asked that the toll upon wagons and pleasure-carriages might be slightly increased. It does not appear that their prayer was granted.

The Eighth Massachusetts Turnpike Corporation, incorporated in 1800, was authorized to turnpike a road from Russell in Hampden county, through Blandford, Norwich (now Huntington), Chester, Becket, Washington and Dalton, to the east line of Pittsfield, at Honasada street. This road, which essentially covered the route afterwards occupied by the Pontoosuc turnpike, was built only as far as Chester, and the charter for the remaining portion was repealed in 1818.

A large portion of both the third and eighth turnpikes was of the most forbidding character; difficult of construction, and to be kept in repair only by constant and costly care. But, soon after 1818, it became known that a very easy grade existed, along the banks of the Westfield river, to Becket; and thence, over Washington mountain, to Pittsfield.

For more than twenty years before there was any continuous road through the Pass of the Westfield, it excited the deep interest of all who became aware of its wonderful facilities, and especially, "of frequent exploring parties of careful and judicious men from Pittsfield, Springfield, Westfield, Middlefield, and Chester." But when even such witnesses reported that a road might be built through these rugged and frowning gorges, that would be more level and more easily traveled than that from Chester to Springfield, their testimony was received by the general public with incredulity.

Eight, however, of these "judicious and cautious citizens" of Pittsfield, Southwick and Springfield, were so well convinced of the grand advantages of the route that, in 1825—although, with few exceptions, turnpike-stocks were then notoriously worthless—they obtained a charter authorizing them to avail themselves of it, as the Pontoosuc Turnpike Company. Their names were, Jonathan Allen, Lemuel Pomeroy, Joseph Shearer, Joseph Merrick and Thomas Gold of Pittsfield; Henry Stearns of Springfield, and Enos Foot of Southwick.

These gentlemen declared that, although they did not doubt that the stock of the proposed turnpike would prove remunerative, they much preferred that a free road should be built. But, when the charter was granted, the law required that all public roads should be built at the sole expense of the towns through which they passed. The portion of the proposed route which lay along the rivers, was remote from the villages, or centers of population, and some hundred feet below them; and it would have been grossly unjust to tax their inhabitants for a free road which would benefit only the large towns at its termini, and the through travel between Boston and Albany. Before the company organized, however, the road-laws were modified so that the commissioners of highways[1] might, at the expense of the counties, lay and make such roads as the general convenience required.

It seemed very clear to the corporators of the Pontoosuc turnpike, that the road proposed by them was of this class; and they postponed action under their charter, in the hope that the commissioners of the three counties, through which it would run, would build it. Every effort was made to induce them to do so; but embittered parties arose upon the question, and other elements than ease of grade entered into the consideration of the route. The Worthington turnpike, although the grade was somewhat more difficult than that of the Pontoosuc, was fifteen miles shorter. It also terminated at Northampton, while the practical terminus of the new road would be Springfield. The effect of the Pontoosuc route, if it should prove as successful as its friends anticipated, would be to carry the great current of eastern and western travel through the latter town instead of the former. This was one of the earliest of those struggles, which have made the city of Springfield the great center of travel which it now is. In it, of course, Springfield and Westfield on the one hand, and Northampton on the other, were governed by local interests. Pittsfield was divided into violently antagonistic parties; Jason Clapp with his associate, Mr. Rice of Albany, had a well-established and successful line of stages, which they had long run upon the Worthington turnpike, and they opposed the proposed rival route with all the influence, and all the strategy, which they could bring to bear upon it. The Pontoosuc corporators were quite as active and strenuous on their part. Lemuel Pomeroy, in particular, made himself their leader, and entering into the pro-

---

[1] Boards appointed by the governor for each county, and having powers as to highways and bridges similar to those now vested in the county-commissioners.

ject with his whole soul, he prosecuted it with his accustomed determination and energy; being in close league with Henry Stearns and other friends of the proposed line in Springfield.

This statement will explain why, when the commissioners were asked to build a free road, those of Berkshire and Hampden were favorable to the project, while those of Hampshire positively refused to make the portion which came within their jurisdiction; rendering it useless for the others to proceed. It was supposed, however, that, if the connecting link in Hampshire was built by private enterprise as a turnpike, the exterior counties would extend it to their respective termini; and the corporators of the Pontoosuc turnpike asked the legislature, in February, 1828, for an amendment to their charter, so that they might be permitted to build in Hampshire county only. The amendment actually made, allowed them to extend their road over the whole, or a part, of the towns originally named, viz.: Chester, Middlefield, Becket, Washington, Dalton, and Pittsfield. This modification was probably made on the suggestion of the petitioners. At least, it was happily introduced, as the opposition succeeded in defeating the expectation that free connecting roads would be laid by the commissioners in Hampden and Berkshire; and the company were compelled to build the whole line.

The new charter also changed the western terminus from the south-eastern to the eastern part of Pittsfield; so that the turnpike, instead of entering Pittsfield, as was first intended, by way of Honasada street, entered by Elm street, which, through the efforts of its friends, was opened a few years afterwards.

In the meantime, while the petitions for the free roads in Berkshire and Hampden were still pending, Messrs. Allen, Shearer, Merrick, and Pomeroy of Pittsfield, Stearns of Springfield, and Fowler of Westfield, published in the *Sun* of November 13, 1828, a long and well-argued appeal to the citizens of the towns most interested, urging liberal subscriptions to the stock. In this address, they entered quite elaborately into the statistics and philosophy of transportation as affected by the grades of roads; and dwelt particularly upon the facilities of the new route as developed by the first surveys for the Western railroad, which had positively demonstrated "that the route of the Pontoosuc turnpike presented, of all others, the most level passage from the Hudson to the Connecticut, and that a railroad might be wrought on this route, which would be but eight feet a mile steeper, in its hardest places, than the Quincy railway in its steepest sections.

In response to the appeal of the corporators, citizens' committees were appointed in the towns interested; and, sufficient stock having been taken to warrant an organization, Samuel M. McKay was chosen president, and Matthias R. Lanckton clerk and treasurer.

Eight thousand dollars of the stock was subscribed before the 22d of July, 1829; the whole amount estimated to be necessary to complete the work being ten thousand dollars.

The turnpike was completed in October, 1830, and a correspondent of the *Pittsfield Argus* (Hon. Julius Rockwell) gave an account of the opening, from which we extract the essential portions:

We have long been told that Springfield was one of the most beautiful towns in New England, and have long wished to visit it; but could not bring our minds to the determination to undertake so long and perilous a journey. We knew, indeed, that nature had pointed out a passage through the mountains, and were confident that the enterprise and energy of New England character, would not suffer it to remain forever unimproved. We knew that, twenty-six years ago, a route for a turnpike had been surveyed ; but the project had slept so long, that we feared it would never again be wakened in our day. It was, therefore, with the greatest pleasure, that we learned, last week, that the "Pontoosuc Turnpike Corporation" had actually constructed a road through the formidable range of mountains which had so long separated us from the beautiful and magnificent valley of the Connecticut. * * * Availing ourselves of the liberal proposals of Messrs. Clapp and Tuttle, stage-proprietors, we started, in company with twenty-five gentlemen from our village, upon an excursion to Springfield over the new turnpike. We entered upon the new road about three miles from this village, and soon accomplished the ascent of the only hill of any importance on the route. We soon found ourselves at the residence of Captain Deming, in Washington. The ascent was easy, as the elevation is in no place more than five' degrees ; and the declivity upon the eastern side is still more gradual. From this place to Colonel Henry's, in Chester, a distance of about twelve miles, the road is as perfectly level as the most fastidious traveler can wish. The labor and expense of constructing the road, and the wildness and peculiar beauty of the scenery, can only be estimated by those who have passed over it. The ravine was previously penetrated by a small and rapid rivulet, and the only way of passing it on foot, was by resorting, in many places, to the bed of the stream. In several sections, where the road was laid out, the stream was walled in, upon both sides, by precipices almost perpendicular, and the foundations of the road were laid in the bed of the brook, and the passages cut through a rock almost solid.[1]

We were agreeably surprised, about midway in our passage, to find the log-hut of an old settler. He had occupied his almost inaccessible residence for thirty years. * * His only visible means of communication with the world, was a narrow foot-bridge terminated by a flight of rude stairs, made of rock and stones, leading over the precipice. For miles beyond his house, the scenery is as wild and romantic as any which the great novelist of Scotland has described in that land of mountain and of song. The views are sufficient richly to repay the time and expense of the whole journey.

We reached the termination of the Pontoosuc turnpike, at Colonel Henry's in Chester, about one o'clock, where we found an excellent dinner, to which we did ample justice. There were no complaints of dyspepsia or want of appetite. We here mingled our congratulations upon the completion of the road. We had no immediate interest or agency in the enterprise; but we rejoiced at the gratification of the proprietors present, and particularly of our respected fellow-citizen,[2] to whose efficient direction the turnpike owes so much, and whose animated sociality contributed greatly to the spirit and pleasure of our excursion. * * * * * * *

We were kindly welcomed on our arrival at Springfield, and, after a fine supper at Mr. Russell's, retired and slept well upon the recollections of a pleasant and active day.

High as were our expectations, upon rising in the morning, we were surprised at finding ourselves in so large and pleasant a village; presenting so many indications of wealth, enterprise, and elegant taste. We spent most of the day in visiting numerous points of interest in and about the town, to which we were politely directed, and accompanied by a large number of citizens. * * * *

We wished for a much longer time to enjoy several splendid views of the river, and the country adjacent. We paused, also, to admire the situation of several private residences. The taste displayed in their architecture, and the arrangement of their grounds, is worthy the natural beauties with which they are surrounded.

We have given more space to the account of this excursion than we otherwise should, as, besides being exceedingly well written, it indicates the beginning of that intimate connection

---

[1] The traveler over the Boston and Albany railroad will recognize the picture.

[2] Lemuel Pomeroy.

between Pittsfield and Springfield, which has ever since continued and increased; although, as between the more prominent citizens, this connection had commenced before. So intimate has the intercourse between the two places become, that to speak of a ride to Springfield as "a wearisome and perilous journey," seems now, at first glance, a ludicrous exaggeration. But it must be remembered that, previous to the opening of the Pontoosuc turnpike, the most direct and convenient routes were by the Worthington turnpike and Northampton, or through Lenox, Lee and Blandford, by the Housatonic turnpike; on each of which hills were encountered which had become famed for stage-accidents. On either route the journey consumed the better part of two days. In short, one can now travel to Bangor, in Maine, on the east, or to Chicago on the west, with greater ease and safety, and in about the same time, which was required in 1829 for a trip to Springfield: the traveler at the later date, however, riding night and day, and at the earlier, as the custom was, only by day.

And yet the advance from "the covered, or the open cart"—probably springless wagons—described by the Duc de la Rochefoucault Liancourt in 1796, and the rude mountain-roads of that period, to the smooth Pontoosuc turnpike and Jason Clapp's comfortable stage-coaches, was hardly less agreeable—although less wonderful—than that from the stages to the steam-car.

The completion of the Pontoosuc turnpike was an occasion of pride and congratulation to its projectors and builders; but it had already come to be considered by them as only a way-station in the progress of a far mightier enterprise. The whole state, or at least the more intelligent and spirited portions of it—especially Berkshire—was pervaded by a deep interest in the improvement of its internal communications.

This feeling was not, indeed, new, but was the result of healthy growth. We have spoken of turnpikes as its first fruits. Canals came not far behind; but various circumstances forbade their rapid extension. Gen. Henry Knox proposed a canal from Boston to the Connecticut river, as early as 1791, and surveys were made the next year. Then the project slept.

The successful completion of the Erie canal in 1823, however, roused an earnest spirit of emulation. It was a too tantalizing sight for the spirit of New England trade, to witness the teeming products, and the lucrative commerce of the great west, which the canals brought almost to the borders of Massachusetts, suddenly turned aside by the easy highway of the Hudson river, to enrich the city of New York. This divergence from the more direct path to Europe, through Boston, was not to be endured, and, in their eagerness to do away with the mountain-barriers which turned from them the rich flood of commerce, the people of Massachusetts would recognize no obstacle as insurmountable.

The most remarkable result of this feeling was the revival of the project for a canal from Boston to the Connecticut, with an extension to some point on the Hudson, near the terminus of the Erie canal. Governor Eustis mentioned the scheme with some favor, in his message of January, 1825, and, upon his suggestion, the legislature appointed three commissioners and an engineer, to ascertain if it were practicable. The commissioners were Nathan Willis of Pittsfield, Elihu Hoyt of Deerfield, and Henry A. S. Dearborn of Boston. The engineer was Col. Laomi C. Baldwin.

Their report, submitted to the legislature in January, 1826, gave the results of the exploration of several routes between the Connecticut and Hudson rivers. One of these routes had its summit-level in Pittsfield. But water was to be supplied at this point for the canal as far east as Middlefield or Chester, and as far north as Cheshire or Adams. The commissioners thought that the lakes of Pittsfield and vicinity, together with the head-waters of the Housatonic, might possibly, by the building of reservoirs, be rendered sufficient for that purpose. But this could only be ascertained by actual survey, which there was no inducement to make, as the altitude was greater than that of a route through Vermont; and moreover, "the rugged features of the country, the whole distance from Blandford to the borders of Pittsfield, being a succession of rocky hills and interminable ledges, imposed most formidable and forbidding obstacles to the construction of a canal." Besides all this, the route finally recommended was twenty-eight miles the shorter. So the danger was not very imminent that Pittsfield would find its water-power absorbed, its lakes robbed of their graceful outlines, and its rich valleys submerged, in order that transportation between Boston and the Hudson might be cheap.

The route recommended as feasible, lay across northern Worcester, up the Deerfield river, through the Hoosac mountain, and, by the valley of the Hoosac river, to the Hudson, near Troy. The plan included a tunnel—nearly at the same point where a similar work has been constructed for a railroad—to be four miles long, twenty feet wide, thirteen and a half high; total of excavation two hundred and eleven thousand two hundred cubic yards. The elevation of the mountain-ranges which still remained was to be overcome by a stupendous series of locks, whose total rise and fall was three thousand, two hundred and eighty-one feet.

The boring of the Hoosac Tunnel has since furnished us some clue to what the actual cost would have been; and enables us, in some measure, to appreciate the magnitude of the undertaking. The commissioners estimated the entire cost of the canal, of one hundred and seventy-eight miles length, at only six million, twenty-four thousand and seventy-two dollars, including that of the tunnel, which they put at nine hundred and twenty thousand eight hundred and thirty-two dollars.

The estimates of the commissioners were gravely impeached in influential quarters; and a writer in the *Boston Courier* showed that upon their own data, it would take fifty-two years to finish the tunnel. It is to be doubted, nevertheless, whether an attempt to carry out the project would not finally have been made, so strong was the public desire for cheap intercommunication between Boston and the west, had no other means of satisfying that desire presented itself. But, not long before the assembling of the legislature, news arrived that engines for the use of steam as a motive-power, which had for some little time been in use upon the English railways, had been carried to such perfection, that a locomotive upon the Stockton and Darlington road had drawn a train of ninety tons at the rate of ten miles an hour. It was not yet supposed that steam could be made available on a route like that between Boston and Albany, without resort to stationary-power at the mountain-grades; but a discussion of the comparative merits of railways and canals sprang up in the English newspapers, and extended to those of America, with a result largely in favor of the railroads.

In the Massachusetts legislature, five days before the commissioners' report in favor of the grand canal, an order passed both houses directing an inquiry, "whether any practical and useful improvements had been made in the construction of railways, and of steam-carriages used thereon, so as to admit of their being successfully introduced into this commonwealth; and, if so, whether it is expedient to extend thereto the aid and encouragement of the legislature."

A resolve was also reported, in response to a petition from Boston, authorizing the governor to appoint a commission to make surveys for a railway between that city and Albany; but, after passing the senate, it was indefinitely postponed in the house, on motion of Henry Shaw of Lanesboro, who was, from the first, a bitter enemy of all railroad-projects.

At the June session, however, a committee, consisting of Dr. Abner Phelps, and George W. Adams of Boston, and Emory Washburn of Worcester, were appointed to inquire, during the recess, into the practicability and expediency of constructing a railway from Boston to the western line of Berkshire county, with a view, if leave could be obtained from the State of New York, of extending it to the Hudson river. The committee worked with great fidelity, and "their chairman, Doctor Phelps, was from that time ardently devoted to the object."[1]

Berkshire furnished to the same cause a champion equally zealous, able and influential; Hon. Theodore Sedgwick, of Stockbridge. Mr. Sedgwick early informed himself thoroughly upon all that was then known concerning railways; and, becoming convinced of their unspeakable value to the commonwealth, and especially to his native county, he devoted himself to their advocacy before the people and in the legislature, both by his pen and his voice. A long series of articles, published at first in the *Berkshire Star*, and afterwards condensed into a pamphlet which was scattered throughout the commonwealth, had, in particular, a powerful effect.

The first time that the citizens of Berkshire were formally addressed upon the advantages which railroads would bring to themselves, appears to have been in a communication of Mr. Sedgwick to the *Pittsfield Sun* of May 4, 1826, briefly introducing a long letter from John L. Sullivan of New York. Mr. Sullivan's letter exhibits much familiarity with the achievements which had been made in the science of building, equipping, and managing railroads, and is remarkable for its clear foresight; but it forcibly illustrates how crude that science yet was.

[1] Historical Memoir of the Western Railroad, by George Bliss.

Mr. Sullivan's immediate object was the building of a railroad from New York to Pittsfield, "and perhaps to Bennington." But it was to be of a peculiar construction, which he thus describes:

The "American railway," invented by Colonel Sargent, is called "elevated and single," because, to avoid the expensive foundations requisite on the parallel English railway, posts or pillars of wood, stone, or iron, are substituted to support *one* rail, which, by its elevation allows of carrying two loads, balanced, or nearly so—on each side one—below the rail, suspended by stiff bars from strong cross-bars; so that the whole machine is inflexible, and moves on two wheels following each other on the rail, which is wholly of iron or, for the sake of economy, of the most durable wood, with a plate of wrought-iron, four inches broad.

A road of this class had been constructed in England, and operated with some success; but Mr. Sullivan considered the invention peculiarly adapted to the American climate, and to the economical requirements of long routes through our sparsely populated country. He knew of no route to which it could be applied with more probability of success and profit, than that between Pittsfield and New York; a distance of one hundred and forty-two miles.[1] He estimated the cost of building it at one million, seventy-eight thousand, two hundred and six dollars, or less than half that of a canal. But, if they were of equal expense, he contended that the railway, by its continuity of operation, its capability of branches, its little liability to interruption, and its three-fold speed, ought to have the preference. The imperfection of railway-engineering, at the time, is shown by the fact that he considered it necessary to overcome elevations, one of fifty-four feet, and another of eighty-four, by obliquing the track, or by stationary-power.

He was in advance of the Massachusetts Board of Commissioners, in regard to the use of steam. "Although" said he, "horse-power is used with advantage on railways, it is the combination of the steam-engine with the railway, which has given it a decided preference over canals, in England." He found it necessary to argue the advantages of railways to the interior country on account of the saving of time and expense in bringing their prod-

[1] A railroad of similar description is now in operation in California, and one each in England and Turkey.

ucts to market. "This mode of producing like effects at less expense will," he said, "when fully explained and investigated, strike every section of our country with equal surprise and pleasure; because it will be seen that those districts which are without the means of water-carriage, have an equivalent in the railway." * * * * "Suppose a railway constructed; if horses be used, seven days' travel will transfer loading from Pittsfield to New York; if steam-engines, two and a half days, without traveling by night; to which, indeed, there is no objection with steam-engines." * * * * * "I am aware of the elevation of the country, and that deep snows are to be provided against. The elevation of this railway is above the general level of the snow. While other railways would be buried in it, this would be high enough for continued operation. A machine to move on it and clear away the drifts, is easily contrived."

The proposition thus plausibly stated, seems not to have attracted general attention. Mr. Sedgwick was too cautious to positively commend it. Indeed, two years later, he was found, with the great majority of the friends of railways in Massachusetts, basing his calculations upon the use of horses. And this, although the *Lenox Star* of March 30, 1826, after recounting the achievements of the locomotive in England, prophesied that within five years, there would be a line of intercourse over the Berkshire hills, between Boston and Albany, with merchandise and passengers traveling each way at the rate of ten miles an hour. It is possible that Mr. Sedgwick may have been the author of the *Star's* article; for many who, in the enthusiasm created by Stevenson's successful experiments in England, anticipated the immediate triumph of steam in America, soon, under various influences, abandoned, or pretended to abandon, that hope. It is hardly probable, however, that he made such a prediction, as he must have been well aware of the obstacles, both physical and moral, which would render its fulfillment impossible.

In 1828, the Massachusetts Railroad Board, having thoroughly examined the subject, concluded that the cost of railroad-transportation, in this country, by horse-power, would be less than it would be in England, either by horse or steam power; but, that horse-power would be the more economical of the two, in America. All the earlier plans for railroads, in Massachusetts, were based upon this opinion. That this should be so, in the face of English experience, is in part accounted for by the rude condition of the manufacture of machinery, and by the lack of skilled engineers (engine-drivers). But one cannot help suspecting that the opinions of leaders in these enterprises were modified in order to quiet the clamors of a large class of farmers, who cried out that the market for horses, then a favorite farm-product, would be destroyed if the new method of transportation should prevail. It was necessary to build the railroads, if they were built at all, by the aid of legislative grants; and the legislature was largely composed of, and still more largely elected by, a class which it took years to educate up to the desired point. It is to be noted, in this connection, that none of these roads were actually equipped for horse-power. Their managers were all converted to the use of steam as soon as it became expedient.

The early idea of the construction of a railroad was as faulty as that of its equipment. The *Boston Advertiser*, in 1826, thus described the Quincy road:

The road is constructed in the most substantial manner. It rests on a foundation of stone, laid so deep in the ground as to be beyond the reach of frost; and, to secure the rails on which the carriage runs against any change in their relative position, they are laid upon stones eight feet in length, placed transversely along the whole extent of the road, six or eight feet apart. The space between these stones is filled with smaller stones or earth, and over the whole, between the rails, a gravel-path is made. The rails are made of pine timber, on the top of which is placed a bar of iron. The carriages, run upon the top of the iron-bars, are kept in place by a projection on the inner edge of the tire of the wheel. The wheels are considerably larger than a common cart-wheel.

When, in 1829, the state-board recommended the building of a railroad from Boston to the Hudson, the plan of construction was similar to the above; requiring for its substructure a greater outlay than now suffices to obtain much greater security.

The Berkshire fathers of 1826–30, in their efforts to introduce railroads, only looked to transportation at a very moderate speed, by horse-power, over a track solidly, but faultily, constructed. The greatest benefit which they anticipated was cheap and sure carriage of their ponderous wares and natural products to markets from which their weight had before practically excluded them. Some, doubtless, indulged in more brilliant visions; but this was all that the more prudent leaders deemed it wise to promise. The usual means of affecting the popular mind were employed: pamphlets, newspaper-articles and public meetings, followed each other in rapid succession. What the writers and speakers had to teach is briefly summed up by Mr. Sedgwick: "first, the effects of internal improvements generally; secondly, the peculiar benefits arising from facilitating communication with the market, and the superiority of the railroad to every other method of accomplishing this object; thirdly, the mechanical effects of railways, and their application; and, lastly, their peculiar local advantages."

The discussion of the turnpike-system had, in some sort, prepared the minds of the people for the consideration of the first of these topics; but in the others, the teachers, often themselves but imperfectly informed, were obliged to commence their lessons with the very rudiments; and, moreover, to meet in many instances inveterate prejudice and obdurate regard for selfish interests. While large masses of the people readily received the lessons of the day, and entered heartily into the spirit of the new enterprise, other large masses, less intelligent, opposed it bitterly, and found able and learned leaders in doing so.

The strenuous efforts of the early friends of railway-enterprise in Berkshire were, therefore, necessary; if not to secure a majority of the people in their favor, at least to make that majority as large as was desirable: especially when it came to the matter of subscriptions for stock. In these efforts, two classes of men took part; one with minds better adapted to the establishment of general principles, and to scientific instruction regarding the matter in hand; the other capable of practically judging of the best methods and the best routes, and influencing their adoption. Both were equally necessary, and occasionally an individual combined the qualities of both classes.

Stockbridge has the honor of being the first town in the county to move in favor of the introduction of railroads; others of its citizens, besides Mr. Sedgwick, becoming deeply interested in the subject.

In the legislature of 1826, a petition, originating in Stockbridge, and signed by James Whiton of Lee, and others, was presented, asking for the incorporation of a railroad from Berkshire to Boston, taking the Housatonic turnpike for its western beginning, and passing through Stockbridge, Springfield, and Worcester.

During the next summer and fall, Richard P. Morgan of Stockbridge made a volunteer survey from the Connecticut to the Hudson, which he presented to a meeting held on the 21st of September. The line, he proposed, ran from Springfield, up the Westfield and Little Westfield rivers, to Otis; thence through Lee, Stockbridge and West Stockbridge. The highest summit was in East Otis, being thirteen hundred feet above the level of the Hudson. Although the distance by turnpike from Springfield to Albany was only eighty-four miles, this route was ninety miles long; and yet ten miles shorter than that finally adopted.

Mr. Morgan had an original device for overcoming the formidable grades to be encountered. He would divide the line into a succession of levels, and raise the loads from one to the other by water-power; for which an abundant supply was generally provided in frequent lakes and streams. When the water-power was deficient, he preferred horse-power to steam; and oxen to either. Representations of the required machinery accompanied the report.

The meeting thanked Mr. Morgan for his spirited and patriotic efforts in making the survey, and instructed their representative, Samuel Jones, to communicate the information contained in it to the legislature, and urge the most efficient measures for the necessary surveys and estimates; that the people might be enabled to judge of the expediency and practicability of a railroad from Albany to Boston.

Throughout the commonwealth, railways gained greatly in favor under the judicious discussions of 1826. In Berkshire, many individuals declared "that they never were acquainted with a subject which so well bore investigation; and that, although a railway from Boston to Albany at first appeared quite visionary, they now looked upon it, as not only extremely desirable, but as a work which would elevate the public and private interests of the whole state." [1]

At the opening of the legislative session in January, 1827, the committee appointed the previous year reported that they were unanimous in their opinion that it was practicable to construct a railway from Boston to Albany. They did not undertake to des-

[1] *Western Star*, January 11, 1827.

HISTORY OF PITTSFIELD. 523

ignate any route; but, referring to the labors of Mr. Morgan, they said: "Upon one route at least, a survey has been made by an intelligent and enterprising citizen of Berkshire, and by him a railway has been pronounced, not only practicable, but highly expedient." At the June session of 1827, resolves were passed for the appointment of two commissioners and an engineer, "to cause the necessary surveys, plans, and estimates, to be made on the best practicable route from Boston to the New York line, and thence (with leave obtained) to the Hudson river at or near Albany;" and ten thousand dollars were appropriated for the purpose.

Nahum Mitchell of Boston, and Col. S. M. McKay of Pittsfield, then one of the governor's military-aids, were appointed commissioners, and James F. Baldwin engineer.

The commission made explorations through two entire routes. The first, which was then called the southern — but which afterwards, by the prominence acquired by the route through Lee and Stockbridge, became the northern — was substantially that now followed by the Boston and Albany railroad. The "northern," of this report, extended from Troy *via* Adams to the Connecticut at Northampton. Instrumental surveys were made only upon the southern route; and that only between Springfield and Albany, and for twelve miles west from Boston. The length of the entire road was stated at one hundred and eighty miles. The length, as since built, is two hundred miles; the difference being all east of the Connecticut.[1]

The highest summit—that in Washington—was given as having an altitude of fourteen hundred and seventy-eight feet above tide-water.[2]

The extreme southern route appears to have been left to what Mr. Morgan's report could do for it. The labors of the commission were based "exclusively upon the use of animal-power, as better adapted to the transportation of the endless variety of loading, which a dense and industrious population requires."

The evident favor shown to the route through Pittsfield led Mr. Sedgwick and other gentlemen interested in a more southern location, to aid in the change, which was made in the following year, from a board of special commissioners upon the Boston and

[1] Bliss.
[2] See vol. I, page 8.

Hudson River railway, to one of nine directors of internal improvements for the commonwealth; of which Colonel McKay was not one.

The change was, however, proposed by the commissioners themselves; and the committee on roads and canals, in submitting their report to the legislature, pay a high compliment to its authors when they say that the railroad, as applicable to Massachusetts and New England generally, has, since the making of said report, assumed a new and greater importance; that it will prove a new creation of wealth, power and prosperity to the state. Colonel McKay soon afterwards had an opportunity, as president of the Pontoosuc Turnpike Company, to make his influence felt in favor of the Pittsfield route.

During the year 1827, the railroad-agitation continued to increase in Berkshire and the adjoining New York counties. On the 25th of January, hundreds attended a meeting at Canaan, when the enthusiasm ran so high that, if a corporation had been authorized, all the stock for a railway from the Hudson to West Stockbridge would have been taken on the spot. A large meeting at Lee, April 30th, adopted a strong memorial in favor of the road from Boston to the Hudson. All the members of the committee which drafted it were residents of southern Berkshire; but it favored no particular route.

The first Berkshire county railroad-convention was held at Lenox, November 16th, Hon. William Walker presiding; and, although the weather was inclement, it was fully attended; some gentlemen riding twenty miles in order to be present. Henry Hubbard of Pittsfield, addressed the meeting especially upon the effect which railroad-communication would have upon the business, political and social relations of the people of Berkshire with the citizens of the commonwealth east of the mountains. The *Star* says that his remarks upon this point were peculiarly interesting, and in unison with the sentiments of all present. Richard P. Morgan of Stockbridge, treated the subject in all its important bearings, giving the meeting the full benefit of his laborious investigations. Theodore Sedgwick gave a general and striking view of the whole argument in favor of the road.

Messrs. Sedgwick and Hubbard, with William Porter of Lee, were appointed to report a series of resolutions to an adjourned meeting at Pittsfield, December 12th. The attendance at this

HISTORY OF PITTSFIELD. 525

meeting was large and respectable; Pittsfield, Stockbridge, Lenox, Lee, West Stockbridge, Dalton, Lanesboro, and Adams, being represented. Hon. Edward A. Newton presided, and Mr. Morgan exhibited models of the different forms of railways, and also of an ingenious railway-carriage, invented by himself, and designed to lessen friction. The descriptions were animated; and resolutions, reported by the committee, were adopted, expressing in the strongest terms, a sense of the value of the projected road, and of its special importance to Berkshire; a decided approbation of the measures of the legislature in its behalf; and an approval of such farther appropriations as might be necessary. The *Star* says of the meeting:

> Nothing could be more satisfactory than its spirit. It was an earnest of the public sentiment of the whole county. We have never doubted as to what that opinion would eventually be. It is advancing in favor of the project as fast as its discreet friends could desire. The railroad-system is a novelty in this country, and the people of Massachusetts will not adopt it till they understand it. This information, they are seeking; and the friends of the contemplated movement will, in due time, and not remotely, realize what a little while since they thought far distant.

In April, 1828, the New York legislature passed an act to facilitate the construction of the railroad, pledging itself that if Massachusetts should build it from Boston to the New York boundary, the State of New York would continue it thence to the Hudson river, or authorize the State of Massachusetts, or some incorporated company, to do so.

In the winter of 1829, the commissioners of both states reported surveys and explorations, to their respective legislatures. The New York surveys were for two lines: one from Troy through Pownell to Adams; the other with two branches, one starting from Hudson and one from Albany, uniting at Chatham, and continuing to West Stockbridge. The Massachusetts commissioners considered three lines. Two of them ran north of Pittsfield, and, as stationary-power would have been required upon either, the commissioners preferred the southern, which was in general the same that was recommended by their predecessors.

Some local surveys were made in Berkshire with a view, if possible, to vary the route in the interest of certain towns south of Pittsfield. One of these variations ran from West Stockbridge, through Stockbridge, Lee and Lenox, to Pittsfield; but was found to be too circuitous. Another ran from Lee to the summit in Becket; but this summit was two hundred and forty feet higher than that in Washington, and would require stationary-power. In other respects both of these local surveys presented favorable points.

Upon the route through Pittsfield, the commissioners, therefore, recommended "the construction of a double railway, with a flat, iron-rail, laid upon a longitudinal rail of granite; the rails of each track to be five feet apart, with a space between them graded for a horse-path; the elevation in no case to exceed eighty feet per mile. Generally one horse only to be used; but two upon the higher grades. An alternative upon the higher grades was the introduction of stationary-power, on inclined planes, rising at an angle of five degrees, and operated by water or horse power. Two horses would be required for about two-fifths of the way for a load adapted to a single horse on the level portions."[1]

The governor repeatedly advised action upon these recommendations; but, in spite of this and other pressure, it was four years before the legislature again moved in the matter, and five before anything practical was done towards extending the road beyond Worcester. The delay, however, proved fortunate, as much unnecessary expenditure was saved by the experience dearly bought by other routes. Pittsfield was, perhaps, also favored by the delay, as she was, by means of the Pontoosuc turnpike, better able to thwart the local attempts to turn away the road from the route which successive boards of commissioners and engineers had, with remarkable unanimity, pronounced the most feasible. During the delay, also, steam came to be recognized as the only proper motive-power; which still further favored this route, by making stationary-power comparatively less economical, and high grades, therefore, more objectionable. The postponement of action then, however disagreeable to the ardent friends of the railroad, and, whether prompted by the timidity or the wisdom of the legislature, is not now to be regretted.

The inaction of the legislature intensified instead of calming railroad-agitation in Berkshire. Discussion was more animated than ever; both sections of the county being earnestly in favor of the road, and each ambitious to secure its location within its own

[1] Bliss.

limits. The local trade was of far greater consideration in building the road, than it has since become in running it. Indeed, in the popular mind of Berkshire, the primary object was to open a way to market for the heavier productions of the county; and, in this, as the resources of the two sections were then developed, the south had a great advantage. A meeting at Great Barrington, in January, 1828, put the argument thus:

Resolved * * That such railroad, as particularly connected with the middle and southern sections of the county of Berkshire, ought to pass through the towns of Lee, Stockbridge, West Stockbridge, Great Barrington, and Egremont, towards the city of Hudson. Such location being best calculated to accommodate the transportation of the great mass of agricultural products of those sections, and particularly the heavy article of marble from the extensive quarries in West Stockbridge, Great Barrington, and Sheffield; such location being also best calculated to encourage the transportation of heavy articles from the extensive iron and other manufactories in Salisbury and Canaan, Conn.

The authors of this resolution had evidently heard of the report of the first board of commissioners, which aroused great indignation throughout all the southern towns;[1] and the meeting was very much in earnest; but its members had a clearer comprehension of their local resources than of the exigencies of railroad-engineering. Still, in the fall of 1875, an engineer of the Massachusetts Central railroad, reports that he has found a perfectly feasible route across southern Berkshire, at Great Barrington, making the western terminus at Poughkeepsie, which would have very well satisfied the Great Barrington meeting of 1828.

But while northern and southern Berkshire disputed regarding the Boston and Albany road, there was one line in whose support they cordially agreed. It might be long, they well knew, before the railroad would give them communication with Boston. Even if it were immediately undertaken, years must pass before it could be completed. But a short and easily constructed road would speedily enable them to follow the old familiar track of trade to Hudson, and thence, by steamer, to New York. And nobody then thought of preferring the railroad to the steamer.

[1] This indignation displayed itself at the next election in the defeat of Colonel McKay for state-senator. The feeling against him, however, rapidly passed away, and he was elected the next year by a fair majority.

The first action in favor of this route was taken by a meeting held at West Stockbridge, January 31, 1828; the citizens of Hudson having just before sent delegates to the Berkshire towns principally interested. This meeting was fully attended by leading citizens of Berkshire and Columbia counties, who resolved to present a joint petition to the legislatures of New York and Massachusetts, for the incorporation of a railroad from Hudson to West Stockbridge, and—there dividing—through Richmond to Pittsfield, and, through Stockbridge and Lee, to Lenox Furnace. On the 12th of February, the Pittsfield delegation to the West Stockbridge convention, reported to a meeting of their constituents; which strongly approved the action taken, and appointed the following committee of Vigilance and Correspondence—a name savoring of revolutionary earnestness:—Joseph Merrick, Henry Hubbard, Butler Goodrich, Jonathan Allen, Dr. William Coleman, Jonathan Yale Clark, Thomas A. Gold, Jonathan Allen, 2d, S. D. Colt, Hosea Merrill, Jr., M. R. Lanckton, Ephraim F. Goodrich, E. R. Colt, E. M. Bissell, C. T. Fenn, David Campbell, Jr., Lemuel Pomeroy, and Jirah Stearns.

The charter for the Hudson and Berkshire road, with a capital of five hundred thousand dollars, was granted by the New York legislature, May 1, 1828. In the Massachusetts General Court, after two postponements, it was refused in January, 1829. It might have been supposed that this action arose from reluctance to add to the already too great facilities for intercourse between Berkshire and New York city; but the bill providing for the construction of a railway between Boston and the Hudson, was also defeated in the house of representatives by a majority of one hundred and twenty-three.

Disappointed in their efforts to secure railroad-communication with the metropolis of their own state, the people of Berkshire became more earnest to secure it with the city of New York; and a meeting was held, October 6, 1831, at West Stockbridge, to consider the interest which Berkshire had in the construction of a railway to the city of Albany. In this meeting, Col. S. M. McKay, Hon. Henry W. Dwight, Ralph Taylor, and other prominent citizens of the county, were appointed a committee to respond to any movement which might be made, across the line, for a railroad from New York to Albany, by the valleys of the Croton and the Housatonic.

On the 10th of October, a convention of several north Berkshire towns, Lemuel Pomeroy presiding, adopted a preamble and resolutions, of which the following are the significant portions:

Whereas, the citizens of New York and Albany, with their characteristic enterprise and intelligence, already appreciate the wonderful advantages which, *within a few months,* have been practically developed by the railway-system, and are now about to make a railroad from the city of Albany to the city of New York :

And whereas, it is well understood to be the true policy of the cities of New York and Albany, if it shall be found practicable, without materially increasing the distance, to establish a road so far east of the Hudson as to avoid competition with the steam-boat and sloop-freightage thereon ; but at the same time to secure to the railroad all the travel and transportation which demand greater expedition than can be obtained on the river ; and also to open to those cities the rich resources of the county of Berkshire, parts of the counties of Hampden and Hampshire, and all the western counties of Connecticut—and that such a route will combine much greater resources than one on the banks of the Hudson.   *   *   *

Resolved, that measures of co-operation should be spiritedly and cordially adopted by the citizens of Massachusetts and Connecticut.

On motion of Thomas A. Gold, the meeting passed a resolution urging the next legislature to incorporate the road from Pittsfield, to connect at West Stockbridge with the Hudson and Berkshire road chartered by the State of New York. On motion of Henry Hubbard, it was resolved cordially to co-operate in procuring a charter for the other branch of the road; through Lee to Lenox Furnace. Mr. Hubbard strenuously advocated the division of the road, at West Stockbridge into two branches ; not only as a matter of justice and fair dealing, but because it would provide a rich feeder for the road from Boston to Albany, if that should run through Pittsfield; and would also do away with one of the strongest arguments for a more southerly location, by providing an outlet for the heavy freight of that section. The meeting also appointed S. M. McKay, Henry Hubbard, and T. A. Gold, delegates to a county-convention to be held at Lenox on the 17th of October. This convention passed a long series of resolutions similar in tenor to those of the preliminary meetings; but the only remarkable portion of them is the first distinct recognition in Berkshire of steam as the proper motive-power; although the recent experiments in England are obscurely alluded to in the Pittsfield resolutions.

Nothing definite was done with regard to the proposed railroad from Albany to New York; but it was held in reserve as a probable resort in case of the final abandonment of that from Boston to Albany.

The movement for a road between Berkshire and the city of Hudson was, however, persistently pressed. The high grades did, indeed, discourage the building of the branch from West Stockbridge to Lee; but, in 1831, the Massachusetts legislature granted a charter for a road from West Stockbridge village to the New York line; and, in 1832, S. M. McKay, Lemuel Pomeroy, and T. A. Gold, were incorporated, with a capital of two hundred and forty thousand dollars, as the Pittsfield and West Stockbridge Railroad Company. These charters expired before any action was taken under them; but in 1836, they were renewed; the capital of the West Stockbridge road being increased to seventy-five thousand dollars; and that of the Pittsfield and West Stockbridge company, of which Lemuel Pomeroy, M. R. Lanckton, and Robert Campbell, were now named as corporators, to three hundred thousand dollars. Provision was made in the charters of both companies that the Western railroad might use their tracks upon specified terms.

It being determined, in 1837, that the Western railroad should pass through Pittsfield, and over the route of the Pittsfield and West Stockbridge company, Mr. Pomeroy and his associates, who had become deeply engaged in the former road, deemed it useless to continue their separate efforts upon a small section of it. The West Stockbridge company were in a somewhat different position; and, although maintaining a separate organization, built and ran their road in connection with the Hudson and Berkshire; which was put under contract in the fall of 1835, and opened for travel September 26, 1838.

The completion of this road was celebrated at West Stockbridge by a reunion of the citizens of Berkshire and Columbia counties, which was largely attended from Pittsfield. Jason Clapp immediately began to run a line of fine coaches from Pittsfield, to connect with the cars at West Stockbridge; and continued to do so until they were superseded by the trains of the Western railroad.

The Hudson and Berkshire road was a poor enough affair, as compared with what it has since become. It had grades, for four miles, of from seventy-one to eighty feet. It was laid simply with flat, iron bars, five-eighths of an inch thick, resting on longitudinal wooden rails; and the whole construction was so frail, that when it was necessary for the Western Railroad Company to use it for a time, while their track was building, they found it extremely difficult to procure locomotives so light that the superstructure would not be crushed by their weight. The cars were short, box-like structures, resting upon springs so unelastic, that the jolting, which would enable the traveler to count every joint in the rails, made every one of his own ache, until he often looked back regretfully to Mr. Clapp's luxurious coaches. Nevertheless, in the matter of speed, and especially in the transportation of freight, the road was an immense advance upon the old modes of transportation.

We return to the story of the early struggles for a railroad from Boston to the Hudson river.

Although the legislature of Massachusetts would do nothing in aid of this project as a whole, it chartered, in June, 1831, the Boston and Worcester Railroad Corporation, whose line covered the proposed route as far as the city of Worcester; a division which afterwards proved a source of almost unlimited trouble. In 1833, the legislature, in its wisdom, provided other sources of vexation and delay, which, although they were not tolerated so long, were annoying while they lasted. It incorporated the persons who were then directors of the Boston and Worcester company, *individually*, as the Western Railroad Corporation, with authority to construct a railway from Worcester to the western boundary of the state. The stock was to consist of not less than ten thousand, nor more than twenty thousand, shares of the par value of one hundred dollars; and, should the subscription exceed twenty thousand shares, the subscribers who were for the time being stockholders in the Worcester company, should be entitled to the preference.

The Boston and Worcester company were thus entrusted with the entire control of the matter of a railroad from Boston to the Hudson; and, of course, managed it with exclusive reference to their own interests. No response was made to the earnest request to have the books opened for subscription, until November, 1834, and "even then," says Mr. Bliss, "the efforts were confined to Springfield and the towns between there and Worcester. There was an entire want of confidence in the enterprise as a financial undertaking—and very many doubted the practicability of its execution."

There seems, however, to have been no good reason why this lack of confidence should have restricted the opening of the subscription-books to the towns east of the Connecticut; for nowhere was there such thorough faith in the practicability and expediency of the work as in Berkshire; and, although the subscriptions of its citizens could not be expected to compare with those of the richer regions of the east, the managers of the scheme, when it was undertaken in earnest, were anxious enough to get them.

And, through all the years of delay, until the road was finally located in accordance with their wishes, the citizens of Pittsfield were planning enterprises, to be undertaken in connection with it; or independently if it failed them. Of some of these schemes we have already spoken; but there was one other, which specially interested them, and which slightly antedated the quasi opening of the subscription-books of the Western railroad, in November, 1834. This was the railroad chartered by the legislature of New York, in May, 1834, as the "Castleton and West Stockbridge," to run between the towns from which it took its name; but which was, in 1836, changed to the "Albany and West Stockbridge," with a corresponding change of route, and also the same which— its franchise being transferred to the Western Railroad Corporation—finally became the New York portion of the Western road.

The corporators of the West Stockbridge and Castleton road were chiefly citizens of New York; but it was looked upon as an integral portion of the great Massachusetts railroad, and the people of Berkshire watched the proceedings of its managers with intense interest; and it was in co-operation with them that Lemuel Pomeroy and his associates obtained the charter for the Pittsfield and West Stockbridge railroad in 1836.[1]

---

[1] The petitioners for this road were Lemuel Pomeroy, Luther Washburn, Phinehas Allen, Levi Beebe, Elijah M. Bissell, William E. Gold, Thomas Moseley, Simeon Brown, John Brown, Butler Goodrich, Levi Goodrich, Parker L. Hall, John Pomeroy, Curtis T. Fenn, Jonathan L. Hyde, Elijah Peck, Solomon L. Russell, Lemuel Pomeroy, Jr., Nial Bentley, Ira Platt, Michael Hancock, Merrick Ross, Charles B. Francis.

In February, Mr. Pomeroy presided at a very large convention of the friends of the Castleton road; and at this meeting the stock was duly subscribed; so that the company was organized on the 23d. Statistics concerning the business of Berkshire, presented at this meeting by C. B. Boyington[1] of West Stockbridge, and others which he subsequently collected, afforded valuable aid in the prosecution of railroad-work in Massachusetts and New York.

A gentleman better informed than any other, concerning the action of Pittsfield at this time, says:

Mr. Pomeroy pursued the object in a way that nobody else did. While others were full of good feeling, and were willing to attend meetings at home, it was he who got out a delegation at every meeting abroad, and saw it carefully attended to. But little would have been done, it seems to me, without this pressing enthusiasm on his part. * * * Dr. Robert Campbell was better acquainted with the subject than anybody else. He and one or two others went with Major Whistler and Captain Swift in making the preliminary observations. * * * Mr. Hubbard was always enthusiastic on the subject, and made many speeches in town-meeting and elsewhere.

Throughout the struggle, the friends of the road had the best aid which Pittsfield and its most capable citizens could give them. In particular, the town took care to send to the legislature men of influence and ability, and fast friends of the enterprise. Hon. Julius Rockwell especially, then a young but influential member of the house, of which he was twice speaker, was looked upon by the advocates of the route through Pittsfield, as one of its most effective champions. He was also their most active agent as well as a highly-valued counselor. Whatever was to be done in behalf of the route, they felt at liberty to call upon him to do it, with a certainty of zealous service. Wherever his powers as a debater could avail, they were freely used; and so also was his scarcely less valuable influence in personal conversation. Some of his minor labors, and something of the position held by Lemuel Pomeroy, are indicated by the following letter:

PITTSFIELD, July 18, 1835.

DEAR SIR:—We have lately examined the different routes for the railroad from our village to the line of our state, to meet the Albany

---

[1] Afterwards pastor of the South Congregational Church of Pittsfield.

railroad, and we find that we can improve the Baldwin survey very much. We are determined to have a railroad from this place to the state line, and that *forthwith*. I have not the pleasure of an acquaintance with N. Hale, Esq., and as he seems to be the man more prominent than any one else, in giving direction to our railroads from Boston to the line of the state, I wish you to see him, and urge him to attend a day or two, in person, while Mr. Ellison (the engineer) is on the route from this place to West Stockbridge.

We expect the directors of the Albany and West Stockbridge railroad will be on the ground; and it is of great importance that our Boston railroad-friends should know much more of this part of the country than they now do, in reference to the proposed road. We have no fears on the subject of the final route of the road. Nature has so formed the earth, that when the instruments are applied, it will be apparent that no other route can be found except upon the Pontoosuc road; the summit-level of this route being two or three hundred feet lower than that which would pass through Lee and Stockbridge.

The great variety of matters and things connected with the railroad, and the taking of the stock, renders it exceedingly necessary that Mr. Hale, or some other gentleman from Boston, should be at Pittsfield and at Albany, at or about the time the books are opened for the stock. The location of this road will have great influence upon gentlemen in our part of the country in taking the stock. * * * *

Truly Yours,
L. POMEROY.

JULIUS ROCKWELL.

It is beyond our province to narrate the struggles by which a line of railway from Worcester to the Hudson river was finally attained, except as they are of special local interest. The story is well told by Mr. Bliss. But in order that the local story may be intelligible, some portion of the general history of the road must be briefly told.

Early in 1835, there were movements at Hartford and Worcester in favor of a railroad directly across the country between those cities, to connect with the road from Hartford to New York. The friends of the Western railroad in Springfield were naturally rendered uneasy, when they remembered to what hands the legislature had entrusted the destinies of the Western railroad; and they took energetic measures which resulted in the opening of books for subscription to the stock of the Western railroad at Boston, New York, Springfield, Worcester, Albany, Hudson, Pittsfield, and Lee. Among the conditions of the subscriptions was one "that the work should be commenced in such manner as to complete at the same time the road from Worcester to Springfield, and from the boundary-line of New York—there connecting with such railroad as shall be made to that point from the Hudson river—either to Lee or Pittsfield, whichever of those towns should be ascertained, on the completion of the definitive surveys, to be the most eligible route for the railroad from the Hudson to Springfield.

The ten days, for which it was announced that the books would be opened, elapsed; and still seven thousand of the required twenty thousand shares were not taken. The books were, therefore, re-opened on the 9th of October, with the additional conditions, that the corporation should not be organized until stock to the amount of two million dollars was subscribed by responsible parties; that the subscription should be void unless the whole number of shares were taken prior to the first day of April, 1836; and that the construction of the road should not be commenced until the sum of ten dollars had been assessed and paid on each share.

To meet these conditions, the friends of the road, all along its line, strained every nerve. Public meetings were addressed by some of the most eloquent and influential speakers in the state. The newspapers published able articles upon the importance of the enterprise. The friends of the road were unwearied in their personal efforts; and we know that the labors of those in Pittsfield were as untiring and energetic as any other. The *Argus* had been removed to Lenox, and became hostile to the Pittsfield route. Indeed, when that route was finally adopted, it opposed granting state-aid to it. The editors of the *Sun* were personally among the foremost friends of the road; but editorially, politics, which were always the primary consideration with them, and fealty to party at that moment, forbade them to give the aid of their paper to a project condemned by the democratic creed of the hour. We, therefore, rarely find in the *Sun* more than a bald paragraph chronicling the progress of the Western railroad. It did not report even the meetings called by advertisement in its own columns. Meetings were, however, held, and the people were addressed, through the press, with excellent result.

In the whole state, the two million dollars required to warrant the organization of the company, were subscribed prior to December 5, 1835, and the directors were chosen on the 4th of the following month; all being residents of Boston, except George Bliss and Justice Willard of Springfield. In March, it was found that a million dollars more were needed, and the legislature, by nearly a unanimous vote, agreed that the state would take that amount of the company's stock.

The work was now entered upon in earnest; and, in the summer of 1837, it became necessary finally to locate the route across the county of Berkshire; a question of infinite moment to the town of Pittsfield, whose citizens were instantly alive to its importance. The people of the towns along the proposed southern route, and particularly those of Stockbridge and Lee, were equally sensible of the influence which its determination would have upon their fortunes. Each side, therefore, brought forward its strongest facts and arguments; and the directors of the road were most thoroughly informed when they made their decision. In regard to their action, we quote Mr. Bliss, who was a member of the board:

The surveys and reconnoissances for ascertaining the best route from the Connecticut river to the New York line, were very extensive. The range of mountains which forms the summit between the Connecticut and the Hudson, was thoroughly examined from Washington on the north, through Becket and Otis, to Tolland, near the line of Connecticut,—twenty-two miles northerly and southerly. Every important depression and every considerable stream, passing down the mountain, was fully surveyed. The north line, essentially as surveyed by Mr. Baldwin, in 1828, had appeared the most favorable, and an approximate location was made upon it by the engineers of the Western company, under the supervision of Mr. John Childe, in 1836-7. But numerous friends of a southern route, through Stockbridge and Lee, thought that a preferable one; and, to concentrate the results of a vast number of experimental surveys, an approximate location was ordered, and was made in the spring of 1837, by Richard P. Morgan.

This route was, from the village of Westfield southerly, ascending the slope of Sódom mountain, to Loomis Gap and Mount Pisgah, by the valley of Little Westfield river to Cobble mountain, with a tunnel of six hundred feet; thence to the Blandford line, and, by Bush Hill, to Spruce Swamp Summit, fourteen hundred and seventy feet above the bench mark on Connecticut river, and about thirty miles from it; then descending through East Otis, by the outlet of Great pond, to Nichols pond, near Baird's tavern, past Green Water pond into the valley of Hop brook, through a corner of Tyringham, to Stockbridge plain, and to West Stockbridge and the state-line; sixty-two and thirty-eight hundredths miles from the Connecticut river; all reducible to a grade not exceeding eighty feet per mile.

On comparison of the north and south routes, thus approximately located, it was found that the measured distance differed but sixty-six hundredths of a mile, though the equated lengths gave about five miles in favor of the north route. There were five summits on the south line, and four on the north. The average of grades was in favor of the north.[1]

The estimated cost of grading and bridging the north line was one million, two hundred and fifty-nine thousand one hundred dollars and eighty-seven cents; of the south line, one million, two hundred and thirty-two thousand, nine hundred and five dollars and forty-five cents; in favor of the south line, twenty-six thousand, one hundred and ninety-five dollars and forty-two cents. The engineers had reported in favor of the north line. But before this was known to the parties, the board, at their request, gave the friends of each route a hearing at Springfield, June 25, 1837.[2]

Gentlemen from the south urged the board to postpone all proceedings west of the Connecticut river till the next year; but claimed that if the location was through Pittsfield, the parties there should assume the stock subscribed in Stockbridge and Lee.[3]

After full consideration, and an examination of both routes, by a part of the board, they, August 10, 1837, decided in favor of the northern route, through Pittsfield, and ordered it to be definitely located.

Thus far Mr. Bliss; but the contemporary accounts in the *Sun* do not quite concur with him. On the 15th of June, 1837, we read in that paper:

The directors of the Western railroad were to meet at Springfield, yesterday, to decide upon the location of the road at its western termi-

[1] The approximate location on the northern route gave one grade eighty-two and eighteen hundredths feet per mile, at North Becket. On the final location, this was reduced to eighty feet, as the maximum grade on the route. When that part of the road was nearly graded, and the masonry finished, a severe freshet raised the stream so much above what had been known before, that it was deemed prudent to raise the grade from eighty-one to eighty-three feet, varying at different points. About a mile and a quarter is at eighty-three feet per mile.

[2] Pittsfield was represented by Lemuel Pomeroy, Phinehas Allen, Robert Campbell, and Julius Rockwell, to whose influence upon the decision their contemporaries ascribed great weight.

[3] Subsequently, after one or two payments, the company assumed the stock subscribed in those towns.

nation. It will probably be known here to-day, whether it is to run through this town, Lee, or by a route still more southerly. A delegation from this and one or two of the neighboring towns, left on Tuesday, to be present at the meeting, and to represent the interests of the citizens in this vincinity.

THURSDAY, June 22.—We state, with much gratification, that the directors of the Western Railroad Corporation, at their meeting in Springfield, last week, decided upon the northern route, by way of the Pontoosuc turnpike, for the location of the railroad. * * It is expected by the directors, that stock to the amount of twenty-five thousand dollars, at least, more than has been subscribed by the citizens of Berkshire, will be taken without delay. That the just expectations of the board, now that the route has been decided upon, will be fulfilled, no one acquainted with this community will doubt. The directors are to meet in this town on the 6th of July next, and, if the amount mentioned is subscribed, will probably make arrangements for the immediate commencement of operations at this village.

It seems, therefore, that, although the *Sun*, on the 22d, announced the location as permanently made, and a salute was fired in honor of the event, it was really contingent upon the success of the subscription. But of this, neither the editors or the people seem to have doubted. The town held a meeting on the 24th of June, and voted to take fifty shares in the railroad, "on the conditions mentioned in the letter of George Bliss to Lemuel Pomeroy, and others, dated June 15th." It was also voted to grant a right of way through the north part of the new burial-ground.[1]

The citizens at once set to work to secure the remainder of the subscription. There was no need of organization. The books were at the bank, and every public-spirited citizen constituted himself a committee to see that the names of all, who had the necessary means, should be placed in them. Nor were the people of the other towns along the road, behind Pittsfield in their spirit and liberality. Hinsdale, Dalton, Richmond, and the rest, subscribed generously; and so did Lanesboro, although not directly on the road: so that the *Sun* was able to announce that

---

[1] These are the only votes of the town at any time, in aid of railroads; except one, in June, 1835, when it appointed Lemuel Pomeroy, Oren Goodrich, and Robert Campbell, commissioners to superintend the survey of a route from Pittsfield to West Stockbridge, and appropriated three hundred and fifty dollars to defray the expense.

HISTORY OF PITTSFIELD. 539

the directors had, upon the 10th of August, met at Pittsfield, and "decided upon the route through the town for the construction of the Western railroad, the expected subscription having been promptly taken."

We have not ascertained the amount of stock taken by the citizens of Pittsfield at this time; but shares were held by them in the year 1840, as follows, one share being understood when no number is mentioned:

Jonathan Allen, Phinehas Allen & Son two, Dennis C. Baker, Amos Barnes two, John V. Barker, Charles T. Barker, Otis R. Barker, Augustus F. Belden two, Andrew Boyd, Horatio N. Brinsmade two, John Brown, Henry C. Brown three, Josiah Butler, Simeon Butler, Robert Campbell two, George W. Campbell, Avery Carey, Griffin Chamberlain, Martin Chamberlain, R. M. Chapman two, Henry H. Childs two, Samuel Churchill, Jason Clapp two, Ezekiel R. Colt two, Samuel D. Colt two, Richard Coman, Henry Daniels, Stephen P. Day two, Oliver P. Dickinson, Ebenezer Dunham, James H. Dunham, Thomas Durant two, Caleb W. Ensign two, James Foot two, Luke Francis, Robert Francis, Jr., William W. Goodman two, Caleb Goodrich two, Butler Goodrich, Timothy Hall, Parker L. Hall, Austin Hayden, Welcome S. Howard, Daniel L. Hubby, Matthias R. Lanckton, Uriah Lathrop two, Moses A. Lee, Constant Luce, Oliver Luce, Calvin Martin, James Martin, Grove P. May, Obediah McElwain, Albert Merriam, Daniel Merriman, Philips Merrill, Hosea Merrill, Jr. two, Addison Merrill, Ansel Nichols, N. & J. Noble, William Noble, Linus Parker, Elias Parker, Abijah Parks, Lysander F. Parks two, Lemuel Pomeroy thirty-three, Theodore Pomeroy, Pontoosuc Manufacturing Company ten, Nathan Reed, Amasa Rice two, William Roberts, L. Pomeroy, Trustee for the Shakers fifteen, Henry Robbins two, Elijah Robbins & Son two, Julius Rockwell two, Merrick Ross four, Franklin Root, James Root two, Henry Root, Peter Roy, Solomon L. Russell, Joseph Shearer five, G. & S. Spencer, William Stevens, Henry Stevens, Thomas B. Strong, P. V. R. Taylor, Nelson Tracy, Appleton Tracy, Town of Pittsfield fifty, Franklin Wadhams three, Otis Wardwell, Isaac Ward, Lyman Warriner, Robert Watts, Jr. two, Joseph Weatherhead, J. & W. Webb, Weeks, Belden & Co. three, John Weller two, Abel West, Samuel Williams two, Frederick J. Wylie.

Among the subscribers who afterwards became citizens of Pittsfield were George N. Briggs, and William D. B. Linn, both then residents in Lanesboro; and among the notable stockholders, outside of Pittsfield, was Hon. Henry Shaw of the same town, who, although he had been an early opponent of the road, in the legislature, held five shares.

It is probable that this list contains the names of some who were not among the original subscribers to the stock, and omits some of those who were. Indeed, we know that Jason Clapp subscribed for ten shares, of which he had sold eight before 1840. And, in the same interval, had occurred the great financial crisis of 1837, which rendered many of the subscribers to the stock, everywhere, unable to fulfill their obligations. Still the list is substantially that of the early stock-takers.

In March, 1839, Lemuel Pomeroy was chosen one of the directors of the road on the part of the state; a just recognition of his great services, and a wise addition to the strength of the board.

In 1839, the road had still to encounter formidable obstacles; and Mr. Pomeroy was able to use his efforts to as good purpose as before;. especially in overcoming the delays in the extension of the road to Albany. The track between Chester Factories and the New York line was put under contract in May, 1838, and the grading commenced at once. Work was pressed vigorously eastward of the Connecticut. But the spring of 1839 came, and as yet nothing had been done by the parties in the State of New York, who held the charter of the Berkshire and Albany railroad. This was a source of great anxiety to the Massachusetts directors, who, in April, delegated Messrs. Pomeroy, Bliss and Quincy, "to visit Troy, Albany, Hudson, and Catskill, confer with persons interested, and make such arrangements as they deemed expedient, to secure at either of those places a western terminus for the Western railroad." The committee succeeded in reviving, to some degree, the interest in the road at Albany, and procured an act of the legislature, authorizing the city to borrow four hundred thousand dollars, for the purpose of subscribing for,. or purchasing, the stock of the Albany and West Stockbridge company. But nothing definite was accomplished that year towards the desired end. In 1840, a large delegation of the Massachusetts stockholders, of whom Mr. Pomeroy was one of the most prominent, visited Albany, to advocate the speedy construction of the extension. But it was found that the Albany and West Stockbridge company proposed to lay their road with a flat rail only; and it was, moreover, "feared, even if it were built in a more substantial manner, that it might, in process of time, fall into the hands of parties more partial to a free intercourse between New York and Albany, than between Albany and Boston." An arrangement was, therefore, made, by which the road was to be built and managed by the Western company.

New difficulties constantly arose in the path of the directors. Additional state-aid was asked and obtained. Questions as to the use of the Hudson and Berkshire track, and similar matters of policy were to be considered. Long embankments sank. We must leave those desirous of learning the details, to seek them in the Historical Memoir of Mr. Bliss.

The road advanced steadily towards completion; the gaps between the several sections, as they grew more and more narrow, being supplied with connecting lines of stages. The section between Pittsfield and West Stockbridge was finished; and a locomotive with a single car, belonging to the Berkshire road, reached the Pittsfield depot at half-past one o'clock, on the afternoon of May 4, 1841. This was the first railroad-train which had ever entered the town, and crowds assembled to witness the novel spectacle; but, striking and auspicious as the event was, there was no formal celebration of it. The train which had crept into town rather cautiously, returned with more speed and confidence. The first accident on the road, in Pittsfield at least, occurred on the following Saturday, when a locomotive, with several passengers, ran out a couple of miles east of the depot, and an old man named Berry, jumping off, as it approached his house, was severely injured.

The bridge across the Connecticut was not finished until July 4th; but a locomotive and cars having been conveyed over the river, a train began running between its western shore and Chester Factories (now Huntington), twenty-eight miles, May 24th. On the 9th of August, trains ran from the summit-section in Washington to Pittsfield, and from Chester Factories to the east end of those sections, September 17th; and through them on October 4th. The whole road from Worcester to the line of New York was now completed; and, by the aid of the Boston and Worcester road at the east, and the Hudson and Berkshire at the west, railway-communication was continuous between Boston and the Hudson.

The portion of the road between Albany and the junction with the Hudson and Berkshire, at Chatham Four Corners, was so far finished as to be ready for use on the 21st of December, and on that day trains ran from Albany to Boston. The independent track between Chatham and the state-line was opened September 12th, enabling the Western road to dispense with the further use of the Hudson and Berkshire road.

During the four years it had been in the course of construction, the money expended by contractors and workmen, and the market provided for produce and labor, had given a great impetus to the business of Pittsfield, and had materially increased its population and capital. The communication opened with the great market-centers, also materially increased the value of the manufacturing establishments, and of the water-privileges upon which others might be established. Every species of property in the town, including men's property in themselves, felt the beneficial effects of the road, even before it was opened. Many of those who early took stock had declared, when subscribing for it, that if they never received a dividend, they were sure to be the richer for their outlay; and their prophetic hopes were realized long before the road declared a dividend. The *Berkshire County Whig*, commenting on the arrival of the first train in May, 1841, says: "The village feels sensibly the genial influence. The smith, the carpenter and joiner, the mason, the merchant, the tailor, the coach-maker, drayman, and hackman, are all alive with busy employment."

Still, when compared with the Boston and Albany railroad of to-day, the Western road of 1842 was, indeed, but a small beginning. Two passenger-trains each way passed through Pittsfield daily, and one freight-train. Two large locomotives had been purchased—the Massachusetts and the New York—but even the most sanguine friends of the road doubted whether freight enough would ever be offered to test their full capacity for drawing it over the mountain. On many days this single train was not half filled. Wood was used for the locomotives; and of coal, which now employs a vast number of trains, not a pound was brought to Pittsfield for several years; the first being a small quantity which was sent to Mr. Levi Goodrich as an experiment, and after lying a long while near the depot, was finally carted away by some unknown persons. The regular trade in coal was commenced in the year 1847, by Messrs. Seth W. Morton and Gerry Guild, who sold, that year, fifty tons. Four firms now deal in this article, and, including that purchased by the cargo for manufacturers who use steam-power, twenty-five thousand tons of anthracite are annually discharged at the Pittsfield depot. Besides which, over twenty-one thousand tons of bituminous coal are brought for the use of the locomotives of the road, and over twelve hundred tons for the gas-works. When the first freight-train arrived at the depot, Mr. Gerry Guild waited upon it with a single horse and dray, with which, for a considerable time, he did all the freight-cartage to and from the depot; but continuing the business to his death, in connection with his trade in coal, he acquired a considerable fortune. His son and successor, in 1875, employed in it twelve men and fourteen powerful draft-horses.

In 1843, the agents employed at the Pittsfield depot were S. H. P. Lee, master of transportation, at a salary of one thousand dollars;[1] W. H. Powers, depot-agent, six hundred dollars; and Seth W. Morton—who was afterwards, for many years, station-agent—ticket-clerk, at a salary of five hundred dollars.

The first depot, which was a wooden imitation of Egyptian architecture, stood over the road on the west side of the bridge on North street. The passengers were landed in a damp and smoky cellar-like recess, and climbed by a tedious flight of stairs to the upper regions of the waiting and refreshment rooms. This depot took fire from locomotive-sparks at noon on the 5th of November, 1854, and was entirely destroyed. The flames presented a beautiful spectacle, as they swept through its large, hollow, wooden columns, and no regret for the loss of the building checked the enjoyment of the scene. It was never so much admired as during the last half-hour of its existence.

A neat, convenient, and rather elegant depot of wood, one story high, was next built, a short distance west of the North-street bridge. It was sufficiently spacious for its time; but in less than ten years, its capacity was outgrown by the increasing business. There were also other reasons which demanded a change. The depot of the Housatonic road, as the streets then were, was about half a mile from the Western, and that by a somewhat hilly route. Ever since the Housatonic road had been opened, this had been a source of great vexation, and considerable expense, to passengers passing from one road to the other. Much complaint was also

[1] This office was abolished February 1, 1843. Mr. Lee had held it from the opening of the road.

made that the public were unnecessarily incommoded by the failure of the companies to agree upon proper connections between their respective trains. Some ill feeling had thus grown up between them; but, before the year 1866, it began to be apparent to both that more harmony of action was desirable, and that a union depot would contribute towards it.

To this end, the representatives of the parties agreed upon a plan of action, including the location of a depot; which, having been embodied in the form of a statute, was submitted to the legislature of 1866 and, by its enactment, became a law. This statute required the closing of West street, by the erection of the depot across it, at a point about a quarter of a mile west of North street. It also required that the county-commissioners should lay a new street around the south end of the depot, and under the tracks of the two roads; this street to be built by the railroad-companies, to the satisfaction of the town. For some reason the commissioners laid this road farther south than was necessary, making it more expensive to the company, and less convenient to travelers. But it was built, and accepted. The line of the street having been thus changed, the eastern side of the hill by which it previously passed over the railroad, was reduced to the level of the track; a location was prepared for the station-house, at a point which affords some view of the town and the neighboring scenery; and here one of the most convenient and beautiful depots in the country was built by the Boston and Albany Railroad Company; the Housatonic Railroad Company having an equal use of it as tenants.[1]

The legislature, under the terms of its contribution to the stock of the Western railroad, elects five members of its board of directors, who hold office for terms of two years. The following citizens of Pittsfield have been elected to this position: Lemuel Pomeroy, 1838 and 1840; Parker L. Hall, 1842; Thomas Plunkett, 1843 and 1870; Robert Campbell, 1845; William H. Murray, 1874.

Robert Campbell, shortly after the expiration of his term as state-director, was chosen to the same place by the corporation,

[1] We have used the name of the Western railroad throughout our story, as it was not until after the last event in their history, which it comes within our province to record, that the Western and the Boston and Worcester companies were consolidated as the Boston and Albany.

UNION RAILWAY STATION.

and was annually re-elected until his death in 1866. Hon. James D. Colt was then elected to fill the vacancy, and held the office until his appointment as judge, in 1868, when he was succeeded by Henry Colt, who, in 1876, still retains the place.

Of the Pittsfield directors, Parker L. Hall was a native of Pownal, Vt. He graduated at Williams College in the class of 1818, and was admitted to the Berkshire bar in 1822. He was a successful lawyer and a prosperous business-man. He died in 1849.

Henry Colt, the youngest son of James D. Colt 2d, was born in 1812, and educated at the Berkshire gymnasium. He was originally a farmer, but has for many years been an extensive dealer in wool. In September, 1839, he married Elizabeth Goldthwaite, daughter of Hon. Ezekiel Bacon. He was representative in the legislature of 1859–60, and was selectman for several years; among them those of the civil war.

Great as were the advantages which accrued to Berkshire and Pittsfield from the Western railroad, two short, local roads were afterwards built, which have done more to bind the county together as a unit, and have contributed nearly as much to its wealth and comfort. They are known as the Pittsfield and North Adams, and the Stockbridge and Pittsfield railroads.

When the Western road was completed in 1842, a strong desire arose in the towns of Adams and Cheshire to participate in its benefits; especially in Adams, which needed railroad-communication for the development of its great natural resources. A charter was, therefore, obtained in 1843, for the Pittsfield and North Adams railroad; but the corporators had a like experience with other projectors. They found popular enthusiasm not to be synonymous with capital-producing confidence.

The charter expired before anything was accomplished; but was renewed in 1846, when the road was constructed under the direction of the Western Railroad Company, at an expense of four hundred and fifty thousand dollars, which was paid by the Pittsfield and North Adams Corporation. Before work was commenced, an agreement was made by which the road was leased to the Western company, at a rent of six per cent. per annum upon its cost, for a term of thirty years; at the end of which it has the right to either buy the road at cost, or renew the lease for ninety-nine years, at five per cent. rent.

In order to induce this arrangement, the citizens of North

Adams raised a guarantee-fund of thirty-one thousand dollars, which was to be drawn upon yearly to make up to the Western company any deficiency between the earnings and expenses of its Pittsfield and North Adams branch. This guarantee-fund was exhausted about the year 1855, soon after which the road became renumerative.

The last rail on the road was laid at eleven o'clock, A. M., October 6, 1846; and at half-past eleven, the locomotive Greylock, with a passenger-car conveying a party from Pittsfield and Cheshire, entered North Adams amid the ringing of bells, firing of cannon, and other demonstrations of public joy. After an entertainment, the party returned to Pittsfield with several citizens of Adams and Cheshire, as their guests. The time occupied in making the trip of twenty miles and a half, was less than an hour. The next two days were those of the cattle-show and fair, and more than four thousand passengers were carried over the road.

The Stockbridge and Pittsfield railroad is the terminal link at the north of the chain of railroads commonly known as the Housatonic. In 1842—nearly simultaneously with the opening of the Housatonic railroad proper, which extends from Bridgeport to the north line of Connecticut at Canaan—an extension of that road, under the name of the Berkshire, was made through Sheffield, Great Barrington, and the village of Van Deusenville in Stockbridge to West Stockbridge. In 1842, it received, from the Massachusetts legislature, authority to connect with the West Stockbridge road; and in 1847, to make a like connection with the Western at the state-line.

By this line of roads, together with the Hartford and New Haven, from Bridgeport, a moderately direct route was thus offered from Pittsfield to the city of New York, which was of much value, especially when the Hudson river was closed by ice. Still it was seen to be very desirable that a road should be built from Pittsfield down the Housatonic valley, through Lenox, Lee, and Stockbridge Plain, to unite with the Berkshire at Van Deusenville; and, in 1847, Charles M. Owen and Charles C. Alger of Stockbridge, and George W. Platner of Lee, obtained for this purpose, a charter for the Stockbridge and Pittsfield railroad. Doubts, however, existed among the local capitalists, whether the road would be remunerative. The project lingered until 1848, when Thomas F. Plunkett, accidentally meeting W. D. Bishop, president of the Housatonic road, mentioned that he thought the proposed branch could be built for twenty thousand dollars a mile, and that if the Housatonic company would take a perpetual lease of it at seven per cent. on the cost, the capital could be at once subscribed. The plan struck Mr. Bishop favorably, and an arrangement was soon effected. Ground was broken in 1849, and the road was opened for business in 1850. It is generally well built; but, as the cost was restricted to twenty thousand dollars per mile, the contractors, Messrs. Schuyler and Miller of New York, who were permitted to appoint the engineer, avoided expense by making curves and retaining high grades, at many points, where excavations would have rendered the road shorter, straighter, and more level.

CHAPTER XXIII.

FIRE-DISTRICT AND WATER-WORKS.

[1795-1875.]

Old fire-department—Organization of fire-district—Purchase of fire-engines—Housatonic and Pontoosuc engine-companies—Greylock hook-and-ladder company—List of engineers—Steam fire-engines—Fires—Early water-works—Ashley water-works—Sidewalks, sewers, and main drains.

PREVIOUS to the year 1844, the only means provided in Pittsfield for protection against fire, were the rude box-engine purchased by subscription in 1812, with two others of a similar character, one owned by Lemuel Pomeroy & Sons, and one by the Pontoosuc Woolen Company; which were stationed at the factories of their owners. All were of small capacity, and neither was supplied with suction-hose. At fires, water was passed in buckets through long lines of citizens, who, when occasion required, were aided by their wives and daughters.

Even this imperfect organization, and these rude appliances, were often of great service; and this early fire-department received many encomiums from the press, and from its official head. In 1844, however, it had become utterly inadequate for the needs of the town. Indeed, for fourteen years before that date, efforts had been annually made to induce the town to purchase a new engine; and as often defeated. As early as 1834, the old machine was reported in town-meeting not to be worth the cost of repairing. Its captain, Edwin Clapp, maintained that he could put it in good order at a small expense, and, being directed to do so, he made it able to do some further service. Nevertheless, it was a superannuated affair after all, and the town frequently suffered for lack of something better.

In 1844, the growth of the central village, and the additional amount of exposed property caused by the opening of the Western railroad, stimulated a renewed and determined effort to pro-

HISTORY OF PITTSFIELD. 549

vide an efficient fire-department. And when the annual proposition to purchase a new engine came up in town-meeting, a little more strongly worded than usual, Thomas F. Plunkett, Henry Stearns, Robert Campbell, E. H. Kellogg, and George S. Willis were made a committee to consider the protection of the town against fire. And on the 29th of April, they submitted a report, in which they said:

The committee think it unnecessary to direct the attention of the town to the danger which hangs over its property from year to year, from the want of the necessary means of protection. Fire after fire, and loss after loss, remind us but too often and too painfully of the almost wanton indifference of our citizens to the subject. The committee think that there is not another town in the state, of the size, and whose property is so much exposed as that of Pittsfield, which is guilty of failing to provide itself with security against fire.

The committee, therefore, recommended the organization of a fire-district, under the general statute enacted in the previous March. Under this law the town might establish the district, or it might be organized by its own inhabitants, under a warrant issued by the selectmen, upon the application of seven legal voters; but the second course could not be pursued until a petition for the adoption of the first had been presented and rejected in open town-meeting. For this reason, they appended to their report, a petition for the establishment of the district by the town, which was promptly rejected.

This action seems to have been merely *pro forma*, as a necessary preliminary to the alternative mode of procedure. The other votes of the town show that it indicated no spirit of hostility to the new project.

The committee reported, that while the fire-department would chiefly benefit the district, the whole town would, to a certain extent, enjoy its protection; for all its citizens were joint owners in the churches, town-house, and other public property; and the department would always proceed to any part of the town where it might be needed. And if it could not save buildings in which fires originated, might prevent them from spreading to others: It would, therefore, be only an act of justice for the town to furnish the land requisite for engine-houses, and pay six hundred dollars towards the purchase of apparatus. The town made the grant of land and money, increasing the amount of the latter to one thousand dollars.

With this encouragement, the center, east, and west center districts, on the 3d of June, 1844, organized as the Pittsfield fire-district.

The territory thus incorporated is about two miles square, the park being nearly in the center. But its boundaries are very irregular, those of the school-districts having been arbitrarily followed, and having been originally fixed on the principle of equalizing and distributing population and property in different districts rather than of centralizing them. Thus, sometimes a man's residence lay just within the borders of one district, while his farm naturally extended far into another; and the land followed its owner. Or, again, for the convenience of a family, their home was set off from the district in which it was originally placed; and often, to aid a poor district, a wealthy farmer's land was set off to it from a richer.

At its first meeting, the fire-district taxed itself twenty-one hundred dollars; the town's grant being on condition that it should raise two thousand. The following committee was appointed to report upon the proper number of officers for the department, and recommend candidates to fill them: Thomas A. Gold, E. H. Kellogg, Phinehas Allen, Lemuel Pomeroy, E. A. Newton, Jabez Peck, Richard C. Coggswell, Nathan Willis, Levi Goodrich, Merrick Ross, Oliver S. Root, Ezekiel R. Colt, H. H. Childs, Robert Campbell, George S. Willis, Jared Ingersoll, and S. H. P. Lee.

On the 8th of June, this committee reported the following nominations, which were confirmed: chief engineer, Levi Goodrich;[1] assistant engineers, Robert Campbell, Jason Clapp, Jared Ingersoll, George S. Willis, Henry Callender, and William G. Backus. Ensign H. Kellogg was afterwards added. Prudential committee, Phinehas Allen, Edward A. Newton, Ezekiel R. Colt.

[1] Levi Goodrich was born at Wethersfield, Conn., in December, 1785, being the son of Josiah Goodrich, a cousin of Capt. Charles Goodrich, the noted early settler of Pittsfield, to which place, when Levi was six years old, his father also removed. In February, 1826, Levi Goodrich married Miss Wealthy Whitney, a daughter of the proprietor of the iron-forge at Taconic. Mr. Goodrich was an energetic and prosperous citizen, and was, throughout his life, after he reached the age of manhood, prominent in town-affairs. He died August 8, 1868.

Under the recommendation of the committee, an engine-house was built, on what is now School street, at a cost of five hundred and forty dollars. It was thirty feet square, and two stories high; containing apartments for the two engines, and the hook-and-ladder cart, as well as rooms for the meetings of the several companies.

Two engines, both made by Henry Waterman of Hudson, and as nearly alike as possible, were purchased at a cost of six hundred and eighty dollars each. The first, which afterwards became the Housatonic, was described as a seven-and-a-quarter-inch hydraulion, complete, with suction-hose, drag-ropes, and the necessary tools. It was at first furnished with three hundred and twenty-eight feet of hose, at a cost of two hundred and twenty-eight dollars.

The Housatonic Engine Company was formed in October, 1844, the following names being signed to the by-laws:

John C. West, foreman; Edwin Clapp, first assistant; Martin Blunt, second assistant; Thomas Colt, clerk; James H. Anderson, Thomas G. Atwood, Julius Bannister, Henry P. Barnes, William W. Barrows, Daniel Bodurtha, Joseph H. Brewster, Henry S. Briggs, Horatio N. Brooks, Crowell Brooks, Leland S. Burlingham, George Burlingham, Matthew Butler, Only Carpenter, Horace Carrier, David Chapman, Joseph B. Cunningham, Henry G. Davis, Daniel J. Dodge, Joseph Gregory, Perry G. Holdridge, E. P. Little, H. M. Millard, Amasa Rice, Cyrus Shaw, Moseley W. Stevens, Frank E. Taylor, William H. Teeling, William M. Walker, William A.Ward, William H. Warren, Charles H. Watrous.

The company thus formed has had a remarkable permanence of organization. Several of the members who first manned its brakes being still actively connected with it; while most of the others were dropped from the rolls either on account of death or removal from town. Mr. West, after serving as foreman eighteen months, declined re-election, and was succeeded by Edwin Clapp, who is still in command. Thomas Colt then became first assistant, which office he held until his temporary removal from town in 1849, when he was succeeded by the present incumbent, William H. Teeling. Daniel Sprong succeeded Mr. Teeling, and remained second assistant until, in 1875, he was appointed to the charge of the district's hose-tower and apparatus.

During all this period, the company has maintained unbroken

internal harmony; and never, in any excitement of active service, public parades, or festive meetings, has offended public decorum; while it has never lacked promptness, spirit, or efficiency, in the discharge of its duties. Its *esprit de corps* has been almost unparalleled even among firemen, and like its other good qualities has been due very much to its singular permanence of organization.

In the fall of 1844, the Western Railroad Corporation sent to Pittsfield the fire-engine "Union," to be stationed near its depot; but it was not formally accepted by the district until after a second machine had been purchased; whence it ranks as number three.

The engine Fame, the mate of the Housatonic, was received in June, 1845, and was equipped like its companion; the hose-carriage being built by Jason Clapp & Son. William H. Power was foreman; but the company was disbanded in 1848, and a new one formed with the following officers: S. W. Morton, foreman; Gordon McKay, first assistant; H. L. Pope, second assistant; Charles Hurlbert, clerk; James D. Colt, 2d, assistant clerk; Newell Bliss, treasurer. The engine and company now took the name of Pontoosuc. Mr. Morton continued foreman until 1855, and was followed in succession by John Lane, Charles Pitt, John E. Dodge, Wesley L. Shepardson, A. H. Munyan, George W. Smith, Edward Dunham, P. E. Morton, and Henry Hurlbert.

Owing to the destruction of the records by fire, it is impossible to give a list of the other officers prior to 1864. Since that date the first assistants have been E. B. Mead, Seymour Gardner, Benjamin Evans, George S. Willis, Jr., and Warner G. Morton. The second assistants,[1] George S. Willis, Jr., Seymour Gardner, David Campbell, Anthony Stewart, Louis Blain.

The company has always been distinguished for dash and enthusiasm; and, in its latter, as well as in many portions of its earlier, history, it has rivaled the Housatonic in the excellence of its discipline.

In 1853, the railroad-company put in place of the old Union a better engine, which was first known as the Eagle, then the Taconic, and afterwards as the S. W. Morton. It is still in active service, and often fills a place which could not be supplied

[1] By the later custom of the department, the second-assistant foreman, instead of the first, is *ex officio* captain of the hose.

by an additional steamer. It has been manned mostly by employés of the railroad, and other mechanics doing business near the depot; so that the company has been subject to frequent changes. The records are preserved only since 1869, since which date the officers longest in service are Foreman Michael Fitzgerald, First-Assistant Terrence McEnany, Second-Assistant Michael Doyle, Treasurer James Mannion, Clerk John Ready.

The Greylock Hook and Ladder Company has always been a valuable portion of the department, and has maintained a high character for discipline. Henry Groot was its foreman for many years, and until his removal from town. The records prior to 1867 are lost. Since that date, the officers have been: foremen, George Burbank, William Leslie, Benjamin Smith, Robert Francis. First assistants, William Leslie, S. D. Milliman, Andrew Palmer, J. W. Fuller, H. H. Smith, R. E. Crandall, C. H. Hopkins. Second assistants, Benjamin Smith, William Leslie, George W. Burbank, J. H. Granger, E. E. Cole, C. H. Hopkins, P. J. Roberts. Clerks, W. H. Coleman, E. E. Cole, F. H. Breckenridge, Charles B. Watkins. Treasurers, S. D. Milliman, E. E. Cole, B. F. Robbins.

The following gentlemen have been

ENGINEERS OF THE PITTSFIELD FIRE-DEPARTMENT.

1844. Chief, Levi Goodrich; assistants, Robert Campbell, George S. Willis, Jason Clapp, Henry Callender, Jared Ingersoll, William G. Backus, E. H. Kellogg.

1845. Chief, Levi Goodrich; assistants, Robert Campbell, George S. Willis, Jason Clapp, Henry Callender, Jared Ingersoll, William G. Backus, Ensign H. Kellogg.

1846. Chief, Robert Campbell, assistants, E. H. Kellogg, George S. Willis, Phinehas Allen, Jr.

1847. Chief, Robert Campbell; assistants, E. H. Kellogg, T. F. Plunkett, Phinehas Allen, Jr.

1848. Chief, Thomas F. Plunkett; assistants, E. H. Kellogg, P. Allen, Jr., John C. West.

1849. Chief, Thomas F. Plunkett; assistants, William H. Power, Phinehas Allen, Jr., John C. West.

1850. Chief, Gordon McKay; assistants, Abraham Burbank, J. C. West, Thomas G. Atwood.

1851. Chief, Gordon McKay; assistants, A. Burbank, J. C. West, T. G. Atwood.

1852. Chief, John C. West; assistants, A. Burbank, Thomas Colt, David Campbell.
1853. Chief, John C. West; assistants, A. Burbank, Thomas Colt, David Campbell.
1854. Chief, J. C. West; assistants, Thomas Colt, David Campbell, Robert Pomeroy.
1855. Chief, J. C. West; assistauts, S. W. Morton, F. E. Taylor, Austin W. Kellogg.
1856. Chief, Seth W. Morton; assistants, Frank E. Taylor, George S. Willis, J. L. Peck.
1857. Chief, S. W. Morton; assistants, J. L. Peck, Daniel J. Dodge, C. Burnell.
1858. Chief, S. W. Morton; assistants, J. L. Peck, William M. Walker, L. Scott.
1859. Chief, Jabez L. Peck; assistants, William M. Walker, Lebbeus Scott, A. Burbank.
1860. Chief, J. L. Peck; assistants, William M. Walker, L. Scott, Charles M. Whelden.
1861. Chief, J. L. Peck; assistants, William M. Walker, L. Scott, C. M. Whelden.
1862. Chief, J. L. Peck; assistants, William M. Walker, L. Scott, William R. Plunkett.
1863. Chief, J. L. Peck; assistants, Lebbeus Scott, William R. Plunkett, John Feeley.
1864. Chief, Lebbeus Scott; assistants, William R. Plunkett, John Feeley, Henry Groot.
1865. Chief, Lebbeus Scott; assistants, William R. Plunkett, John Feeley, F. F. Read.
1866. Chief, A. Burbank; assistants, John Feeley, F. F. Read, H. Groot.
1867. Chief, Abraham Burbank; assistants, John Feeley, F. F. Read, Henry Groot.
1868. Chief, A. Burbank; assistants, John Feeley, F. F. Read, W. H. Murray.
1869. Chief, John Feeley; assistants, William H. Murray, William C. Gregory, George S. Willis, Jr.
1870. Chief, John Feeley; assistants, William H. Murray, William C. Gregory, Seth W. Morton.
1871. Chief, John Feeley; assistants, William H. Murray, H. S. Russell, S. W. Morton.
1872. Chief, John Feeley; assistants, S. W. Morton, H. S. Russell, George S. Willis, Jr.
1873. Chief, Jabez L. Peck; assistants, George S. Willis, Jr., H. S. Russell, Seth W. Morton.

HISTORY OF PITTSFIELD. 555

For twenty-five years the Pittsfield fire-department, thus organized, maintained a high reputation for efficiency: but the time came when the increase of property exposed to danger rendered it desirable, and the progress of invention made it practicable, to provide more powerful defense against fire. In 1865, Chief-Engineer Lebbeus Scott, recommended the purchase of a steam fire-engine; but no action was taken in the matter. And the same fate befell similar propositions in 1868 and 1870.

It was twenty-seven years since the town had granted a little aid in land and money for its own protection against fire. Meanwhile, the fire-department had rendered valuable service outside of the district. Property beyond the fire-limits had vastly increased, and its safety would be greatly enhanced by steam fire-engines, even if they were located in the neighborhood of the park. It seemed, therefore, no more than just, that the town should contribute something to the expenses of the department: the next effort for the purchase of steam fire-engines, was made in that direction, in the spring of 1871. In that year, when the article relating to this subject was reached in the action of the town-meeting, a letter was read from Assistant-Engineer S. W. Morton, recommending its reference to a committee of leading manufacturers.

This suggestion was adopted, and the committee then appointed, reported at an adjourned meeting, calling attention to the frequent difficulty, at even moderately-protracted fires, of procuring men to work the engines; and stating that one steamer of the fourth class is equal in effect to three of the best manned and best managed hand-engines. They, therefore, recommended the purchase of two steamers of this class. These machines were to be drawn by the firemen; and the only expense anticipated, more than from the use of the hand-machines, was one hundred dollars yearly, for the pay of each engineer, and fifty dollars for the firemen of each machine.[1]

The town adopted the report, and appointed Jabez L. Peck, Charles T. Barker, H. S. Russell, John Feeley, George S. Dunbar, H. W. Morton, and Jarvis N. Dunham, a committee to purchase two steamers, with the necessary apparatus, at a cost not exceeding eight thousand dollars.

[1] Finally, the steamers were provided with horses, and the engineers received a salary of one hundred and twenty dollars each, and the firemen eighty.

The Clapp & Jones Manufacturing Company of Hudson, N. Y., sent a fourth-class steamer to Pittsfield, to be used as occasion might require, until the committee should decide in regard to purchasing.

The committee made a very thorough trial of this machine, and in order to compare it with others of different manufacture, visited several cities and had a competitive trial at Pittsfield. The result was the purchase of both the steamers from the Clapp & Jones company: a decision the town has never found cause to regret.

The contract was for two fourth-class steamers, to differ in no particular, except that No. One was to be painted red, and No. Two blue, these being the colors adopted respectively by the companies to whose charge the engines were committed.

On motion of Mr. Morton, the committee voted that No. One should be called the Edwin Clapp; and on motion of J. N. Dunham, the name of Pontoosuc was agreed upon for No. Two. The Pontoosuc company, however, changed its name to the George Y. Learned, in honor of a liberal and popular manufacturer; and, at their request, the committee made a corresponding change in the name of its machine. The Housatonic company, while gratefully accepting the compliment to its foreman, in the designation of its steamer, decided, as an organization, to adhere to the name which was associated with their honorable history.

The steamers were received January 19, 1872, and proved all that had been promised of them. They were immediately transferred to the fire-district, upon which the vote of the town devolved their care and the cost of their maintenance. The expenditures under the town's appropriation were: for the two steamers, with one hundred feet of rubber leading hose for each, six thousand seven hundred and fifty dollars; for three hundred feet of leather leading hose, nine hundred and four dollars and fifty cents; for expenses of the committee, one hundred and forty-six dollars and thirty-three cents; total, seven thousand eight hundred dollars and eighty-three cents. The district afterwards expended seven hundred dollars for the purchase of a hose-carriage for steamer No. Two; to which the company added two hundred and fifty dollars for the addition of ornaments. The No. One had already a handsome carriage, made by George Groot, a Pittsfield carriage-manufacturer.

The first active service of the steamers was at Lanesboro, February 27, 1872, when the coal-sheds of the Briggs Iron Company, containing about three hundred thousand bushels of coal, were consumed. A violent gale blowing from the north-west, at that time, there was great danger that the furnace and the south village would be destroyed, as it is probable they would have been had it not been for the assistance rendered by the two Pittsfield steamers.

The efficiency of the steamers could hardly have been subjected to a more severe test than it was by this fire at Lanesboro. But their value for the protection of home-property was more fully proved by a fire which occurred on the 21st of the following March, on McKay street, which, but for their aid, would have probably destroyed some of the most valuable buildings on North street.

The first fire after the establishment of the fire-district was in September, 1845, and between that date and July, 1875, the department was called out, wholly or in part, by fire or alarms, one hundred and seventy-one times. Seven of these fires were outside of Pittsfield, and ten others were beyond the limits of the fire-district; thirteen occurred in the larger manufactories, or in buildings connected with them.

WATER-WORKS.

The township of Pittsfield, as a whole, is remarkably well watered by lakes, streams and springs, generally of great purity. But the soil of considerable tracts, in the central section, is composed, to a great depth, of sand and gravel, in which it is difficult to obtain water by digging, except where it happens to be underlaid by basins of clay or some other impervious earth, forming what is known, in the New England dialect, as "hard-pan." And where it is so underlaid, the result is often a swamp. In addition to this, in the districts where wells are easily made, the water is often so charged with lime that a thick calcarious deposit soon coats the interior of vessels in which it is boiled; indicating its unfitness for domestic purposes.

This scarcity of pure water, in some sections of the town, while abundant sources of supply lay near, led to a succession of efforts to diffuse it by means of aqueducts.

The first enterprise of the kind was that of Capt. Charles Goodrich.[1] The next projectors of water-works were Simon Larned, John Chandler Williams, William Kittredge, Joshua Danforth, who were incorporated, in 1795, as "The proprietors of the water-works in the middle of the town of Pittsfield." This company contracted, in April, 1795, with Joel Dickinson, and David Blackman, to convey the water to the town in pipes; and, as the contractors were capable men, and gave security for the faithful performance of their work, it was probably done in the following year. But the company soon began to discover the difficulties of their undertaking; for, in 1803, we find them advertising for some person who will contract to repair their works and keep them in order, "for a fixed sum to be paid by each member of the company:" meaning, probably, that he should collect his pay of the water-takers. In 1804, the company had become so disorganized that a special act of the legislature was necessary to authorize any three members to call a meeting, and empowering the officers last previously elected to act until others were chosen.

In the year 1808, Hon. Ashbel Strong conveyed to the company, by deed, the right to take water from the springs upon his farm,—a little north-east of what is now known as the "Springside" estate—and about a mile and a half from the park—the consideration being the right to take as much water for his house on South street as was allowed to any member of the company, and also for a watering-trough at the farm. From what source the company obtained its supply, previous to this date, we cannot absolutely determine; but probably Mr. Strong's springs were used under an unrecorded permission. Earthen tile-pipe, in which the water was conveyed and distributed, is frequently dug up on the line from that point, to and through North street, and in the neighborhood of Park square; but nowhere else in a position where it can be supposed to have been used for this purpose.

The insufficient depth, less than four feet, at which the pipes were laid, affords a sufficient explanation of the bursting of the pipe.

The next distinct proposition for water-works in Pittsfield, of

---

[1] See vol. I., page 142. Later owners of the farms around Wendell square found excellent water, but at a depth of ninety feet.

which we have knowledge, was in 1819; and the only information regarding it is the following advertisement:

NOTICE.

At a meeting of the citizens of Pittsfield, the undersigned were appointed a committee to receive proposals for delivering water at their respective houses, about sixty in number, at an annual rent (or perhaps on contract), east, to Mr. Simeon Brown's house [facing the foot of East street]; north, to Captain Ingersoll's [opposite St. Joseph's church]; south, to Maj. H. C. Brown's [a point below Broad street], and west to Doctor Childs's [opposite the railroad-depot]. As many families will need two outlets, the whole number that will be required may be ninety. Rent shall be required only while the water is furnished; and each occupant shall be under suitable restrictions in the use of it. The water from either the East or the West river will be preferred—whence it is proposed to have it taken by means of a force-pump, and thence conveyed in logs, or taken out and conveyed by a canal. Proposals to be received during all this month.

L. POMEROY,
H. C. BROWN,

January 11, 1819. T. A. GOLD.

This movement originated in the excitement caused by a fire; but nothing came of it.

In November, 1827, three buildings opposite the Baptist church were burned, in part from the lack of water, and the *Sun* warned the citizens to provide against a similar deficiency in the future. In 1828, John Dickinson and Oren Goodrich undertook to supply this pressing need by an aqueduct fed by a cluster of springs about a mile from the park, and situated upon Captain Dickinson's farm. The natural outlet of these springs fed a reservoir on Onota street.[1] From this reservoir, the water was conveyed in two-inch lead-pipes to a brick distributing-reservoir, near the south corner of North and Melville streets. The fall of the water was only eleven feet, which was not sufficient for the successful working of the aqueduct; and it was soon abandoned. The failure seriously embarrassed both of the enterprising proprietors, and, coming at a crisis in Captain Dickinson's fortunes, was sufficient to turn the scale against him.

[1] This reservoir was afterwards the mill-pond which furnished water-power for a button-factory, run by a Mr. Kilbourn, as it now does for the brewery of Gimlech and White.

Until 1855, the locomotives of the Western railroad were supplied with water from the Dickinson springs—the level of the depot being some thirty feet lower than that of North street—but they finally became insufficient for the increasing demand, and resort was had to the town water-works. About 1853, the Ashbel Strong springs, of 1795, were also again called into use by an aqueduct for the supply of Springside—then the residence of Abraham Burbank,—and the Young Ladies' Institute.

These repeated efforts to furnish the Central district with pure water, indicate the popular sense of its great necessity; which was also shown by the suggestion of many unexecuted plans. Among others, Gordon McKay, in 1842, urged various schemes upon the citizens of the town; but, failing to meet with any encouragement, he postponed his efforts to a more favorable season. This seemed to come in the year 1850, when Thomas F. Plunkett called Mr. McKay's attention to the abundant and convenient supply of excellent water in Lake Ashley, a pond of some ninety acres extent, lying upon one of the summits of Washington mountain.

The existence of this lake was, of course, well known, as it was laid down upon the state-map, and was often visited by sportsmen, wood-cutters, and like classes of observers; but little was known accurately of its qualities as a source of water-supply. Mr. McKay was much impressed by Mr. Plunkett's suggestion; and, after visiting the lake, he brought the subject before the newly organized Library Association. The association at once became interested; and, at its request, Mr. McKay, with the aid of John C. Hoadley and Thomas Colt, during the summer of 1850, made careful surveys, and prepared elaborate estimates of the cost of an aqueduct.

A report, drawn up by Mr. Hoadley but embodying the opinions of all the explorers, was submitted to the association on the 19th of September. It strongly recommended the introduction of water from Lake Ashley,[1] which they described as "a beautiful sheet of water lying in a basin of white sand-stone (granular quartz), near the summit of Washington mountain; its elevation, above the surface of the ground in the park, being not less than

[1] So styled upon the state-map, although in accordance with the local custom of changing such names as ownership changed, it was known in Washington as Lanckton pond.

seven hundred feet, and its distance about six and a quarter miles. * * * The outlet is at the westerly end, and runs down the mountain, almost exactly towards our village; so that a point may be selected for taking the water from the stream at a sufficient elevation at about two-thirds the distance of the pond."

No actual analysis of the water had been made; but, from the testimony of families living in the vicinity, and from their own observation, they believed it quite soft, and free from every impurity. Upon the same authority, they believed that the supply would never be less than one million two hundred and fifty thousand gallons of water daily, or sufficient for fifty thousand inhabitants at the rate of twenty-five gallons each, daily. They also decided that a fall of three hundred feet, and a pipe of six inches in diameter, "would best unite the conditions of adequacy, economy, and convenience;" and they believed that iron-pipes of this size would furnish a supply for the wants of the village as long as they should endure: and that, in case of fire, it would be sufficient to keep four hydrants playing with such force as to send the water to the roofs of the highest buildings in town, without interfering with its ordinary use. The cost of the pipes from the reservoir, through Elm and East streets to the east end of the park, and thence through North street to Maplewood; through West street, nearly to the point now occupied by the depot; and through South street, below Broad, would be twenty-seven thousand nine hundred and eighty-two dollars. The cost of distribution through twelve other streets, in four-inch pipes, three-eighths of an inch thick, was placed at nine thousand three hundred and fifty-seven dollars. The total cost of construction, including land-damages, superintendence and incidental expenses, was estimated at thirty-nine thousand eight hundred and thirty-nine dollars; and the committee stated that they had a proposition from responsible parties to contract for the entire work upon this basis.

The whole number of houses which were already built, that might be supplied from the pipe thus distributed, was three hundred and sixteen. The number of hydrants to be put in and supplied was forty-one.

The estimates of probable revenue were: From the Western railroad, three hundred dollars;[1] water-rents, seventeen hundred

---

[1] The interest of five thousand dollars which the railroad-company offered

dollars; amount properly chargeable to fire-department, eight hundred dollars; total, twenty-eight hundred dollars.

The annual expenses were estimated as follows: Interest on forty thousand dollars, at five per cent., two thousand dollars; cost of superintendence, collection, and repairs, four hundred dollars; total, twenty-four hundred dollars.

The committee believed that the charge of eight hundred dollars to the fire-department, would be fully compensated by the relief from other expenditures, which the water-works would afford; but that the amount would constantly decrease with the growth of the village, and consequent increase of water-takers.

Their plan of carrying out their recommendations was for the fire-district to petition the legislature for the necessary powers, and then to construct the works by a loan, bearing five per cent. interest, and payable in thirty years. In regard to the loan, the committee say:

The constant growth of the population, and the more rapid increase of wealth, would make the burden comparatively light, even if the stock had to be paid at maturity by direct taxation; while the same causes will inevitably insure such an increase of revenue, as to provide for the extinction of the debt by a sinking fund. Nor is it visionary to suppose that the very enterprise here recommended, will aid materially in advancing the growth and prosperity of the town. The great deficiency of water, and the wretched quality of nearly all we have, are serious objections to Pittsfield, either as a place of residence or business— particularly of business requiring steam-power. But fortunately these objections are easily removed. When, to the numberless advantages which nature and art have bestowed in our soil, climate, location, and scenery, our enterprise shall have added the pure and abundant supply of water which Providence seems to have prepared and held in reserve for us, we may safely challenge the most favored towns in the state to hold out greater inducements than our own, for residence or business.

The saving to individuals in the reduction of premiums of insurance, and in diminished risk from fire, would be very great, but wholly unsusceptible of calculation; and the diminution of those diseases which are thought to be induced by the use of impure water, would be an inestimable blessing.

The committee recommended a public meeting, which was held, and appointed the following gentlemen to prepare a petition

towards the construction of the works, in consideration of a free supply of water for their locomotives.

regarding the water-works: E. H. Kellogg, Robert Campbell, John C. West, Charles Hurlbert, N. S. Dodge, John C. Hoadley, and George Brown. This committee made their report to a legal town-meeting, January 11, 1851, generally concurring with the opinions expressed by the Library Association's committee, but suggesting that the supply-pipes should be laid by the district, which would involve an additional outlay of seven thousand dollars. Still, they thought fifty thousand dollars would cover the whole cost.

No perfectly unobjectionable boundaries could be fixed; but it was agreed that the fire-district was the most convenient section of the town to undertake the enterprise; it being already a body corporate, with defined limits, for purposes not unlike those which it was proposed to add. The district, however, being a corporation somewhat novel to the laws, and with whose character for responsibility the general public was not familiar, it was proposed that the town should be the nominal borrower, with power to idemnify itself for its liability, by taxing the polls and estates of the district.

The committee appended to their report the form of a statute, embodying their recommendations; and the town instructed the selectmen to petition the legislature for its enactment, whenever they should be requested by the district to do so. And at a meeting of the district, January 1st, a motion that such a request should be made was offered; but met with so strong an opposition, led by Hon. E. A. Newton, that resolutions were substituted, postponing the subject until November, and appointing a committee to make a thorough examination of the quantity and quality of the water of Lake Ashley; and also to inquire concerning other sources of water-supply. This committee consisted of John C. Hoadley, Wellington H. Tyler, Robert Campbell, Thomas F. Plunkett, Walter Laflin, M. H. Baldwin, John Brown, George S. Willis, C. B. Platt, and N. G. Brown. The meeting passed a vote "thanking Messrs. McKay and Hoadley for their public-spirited efforts in behalf of supplying the village with pure water."

In November, the committee reported very strongly in favor of Lake Ashley, both in regard to the quantity and quality of its water. Observations made monthly from January to November, and after every heavy rain or thaw, showed that Ashley brook, the stream issuing from the lake, was never turbid or discolored; and that five-sixths of its natural flow was derived from springs.

The natural minimum flow of the stream would be sufficient for the ordinary wants of the village; but the committee justly thought "that any system of water-works, to be worth constructing, should be adequate to meet the exigencies of fire, and provide for an increase of population. Recourse must, therefore, be had to a reservoir." Upon this point they say:

Fortunately the lake affords an ample and excellent reservoir, available at a small cost. It appears, by measurement from the map of the state, to contain an area of one hundred and fifty acres; and it was judged by your committee to be of at least that size. A depth of two feet upon one hundred and fifty acres, will contain ninety-eight million and ten thousand, which, at the rate of six hundred and thirty-one thousand gallons in twenty-four hours, would give us a full supply of the capacity of the pipe for one hundred and fifty-five days, without any assistance from the natural flow. A dam which should raise the water one foot, and a slight excavation of the outlet, which should enable us to draw one foot below the present surface, would give an ample supply during the longest drouth, and could be made at a moderate expense, without comprising much land not comprised within the sandy beach of the lake, or laying bare much of the bottom.

Samples of the water of Ashley brook, taken monthly, between January and June, were submitted, for analysis, to Dr. C. T. Jackson, the state-assayer; and the average of all the analyses for the six months, gave the following result: Total solid matter in an imperial gallon, three and eighteen hundredths grains; matter of organic origin, one and forty-four hundredths grains; of mineral nature, one and seventy-four hundredths grains. The mineral ingredients were sulphate of lime, carbonate of lime, carbonate of magnesia, sea-salt, and oxide of iron, with traces of phosphates and sulphates.

Doctor Jackson also examined ten samples of well-water, from different sections of the village. The purest of these samples, which was taken from a well on Fenn street, contained twenty-nine grains of solid matter; fourteen of a vegetable, and fifteen of a mineral character. The most impure specimen was drawn from the well at the residence of Dr. Robert Campbell, on East street; one gallon of which contained no less than fifty-six grains of solid matter; twenty-four of vegetable origin, and forty-two of a mineral character. The Springside water, brought in lead-pipes to the Young Ladies' Institute, was comparatively pure; yielding only fifteen grains of solid matter, of which eleven were mineral.

The principal mineral-salts in the well-waters were the carbonates of lime and magnesia, the sulphates of soda and potash. Some phosphates were also present in noticeable quantities. In a letter to the committee, Doctor Jackson asked: "Do not your citizens have calculi in the bladder, from the deposits of your very calcarious waters? I do not see what prevents them from forming, if your folks, as I suppose they do, really drink the well-water of the town."

Doctor Jackson's inquiry might have been answered emphatically in the affirmative. Very painful and frequent cases of the disease mentioned, and others of a like character, were directly traceable to the use of these waters; and the collection of calculi, in the cabinet of the Medical College, was startling for the number and size of its specimens.

The report of the committee was submitted to the district, in November, 1851, and the postponed resolution, to request the selectmen to petition the legislature for authority to build the water-works, was warmly pressed by Messrs. Hoadley, McKay, Tyler, and others, and as strongly opposed by Messrs. Newton, Martin, and Laflin. Finally, the opponents of the measure having raised some doubt as to the accuracy of the estimates of cost, the following committee was appointed to re-examine that matter, and also to present a plan for defraying the cost of construction: Gordon McKay, T. F. Plunkett, George W. Campbell, George S. Willis, E. A. Wells, J. C. West, and W. H. Tyler.

This committee reported, January 1, 1852, that the estimates were correct, and recommended a loan to defray the cost of the work. These recommendations were adopted, with an amendment requiring that the charter should only be accepted by a two-thirds vote in both a town and a district meeting.

The desired powers were conferred by the legislature of 1852; those of the district to be exercised during the construction of the works through three commissioners, to be chosen by ballot. To defray the cost of the undertaking, the town was authorized to issue water-scrip, to an amount not exceeding fifty thousand dollars, and payable in not less than thirty years; and to indemnify itself by taxing the polls and estates of the district. This scrip was to be delivered to the district, to be disposed of at its discretion, for the purpose for which it was issued.

No vote upon the question of accepting the provisions of this act was reached for nearly three years. But everything connected with the subject was discussed with spirit in the newspapers and in public meetings; so that, when a vote was taken in 1855, the result was a foregone conclusion. In the district, the vote was seventy-five to four in favor of acceptance, and in the town, one hundred and eighty-five to eleven.

On the 26th of February, Ensign H. Kellogg, Thomas F. Plunkett, and John E. Dodge, were elected commissioners; and on the 29th of March, they reported that they had made surveys, ascertained the amount of work and material required, and received proposals from various contractors. The meeting requested them to go on with the work at their own discretion, and they proceeded with vigor. A dam was built at Lake Ashley, sufficiently high to raise the surface four or five feet above its summer-level. A point for a filter and reservoir was selected on Ashley brook, three miles from the Elm-street bridge, at an elevation of one hundred and thirty-six feet above the level of the park.

The question of the best material for pipes was considered by the commissioners a very grave one. Recent experience in this country and Europe, they said, had developed great defects in that generally used, viz., iron; which becomes so encrusted with rust and tubercles, as in many instances to seriously diminish the capacity of the pipes, and in some to destroy it altogether. They determined, therefore, to examine into the merits of Ball's Patent Indestructible Cement Pipe. This pipe, which was made at Jersey City, consists of a thin core of iron coated within and without by a peculiar cement. It had been used in several cities and towns, which were visited by the commissioners, who, after ascertaining proximately the terms which the patentees would offer, reported to the district in favor of its use.

Their recommendation was adopted, and a contract was made with the Jersey City company, who agreed that the works should be completed October, 1855. They were finished before that date; but the person employed in supervising their construction was unfaithful, and in some respects incompetent; and, moreover, in his angry impatience, let the water into the pipes with reckless haste. A great number of breaks was the result, and the time required to repair them extended so far into the winter, that very little service-pipe was laid till the spring of 1856. The leaks were, however, supposed to be thoroughly repaired, and the contractors readily consented to an allowance of seven hundred and seven dollars for the delay, which the commissioners accepted as just.

The price paid for work and material according to the terms of the contract, with the above deduction, amounted to forty-four thousand four hundred and fifty-two dollars and ninety-two cents. The amount of pipe laid was twenty thousand one hundred and eleven feet of ten-inch diameter; seven hundred and fifty-five feet of eight-inch; one thousand one hundred ninety-six feet of seven-inch; three thousand six hundred and forty-eight feet of six-inch; four thousand seven hundred and eighty-five feet of four-inch; seventeen thousand nine hundred and thirty-seven feet of three-inch. Thirty-one fire-hydrants were provided under the contract, and also the necessary air-vents, gates, and other appurtenances.

The commissioners expressed the utmost confidence in the cement-pipe as the best material for conducting water, then known, and the same opinion is still held by many; but, unfortunately, circumstances prevented a conclusive test of its merits in Pittsfield. Few, if any, persons in 1857 were aware of the extreme depth to which the frost sometimes penetrates the earth in Berkshire; and no one took into consideration that the water, entering the pipes at a temperature approaching the freezing point, helps to chill its bed, and yet further deepen the frost. The contract, therefore, only provided that the pipes should be laid at a depth of four and a half feet, reckoning from their top; while later experience has given some instances of the earth's freezing to the depth of six feet. The first winter after the pipes were laid was severely cold, and the water in many of the distribution-pipes, being unused and motionless, was frozen; but few of them were burst. A still more severe winter followed; a number of the distribution-pipes were again frozen, and a considerable number burst.

These repeated disappointments were extremely vexatious to all parties. Still it was hoped that with the increasing use of the water, and by a liberal provision of waste-pipes, for the severest weather, freezing would be prevented. No remedy, however, proved sufficient until the pipes were re-laid.

Experience has shown that had iron-pipe been laid at the same depth, it would not have sufficed; and it is equally evident that the cement-pipe, at whatever depth laid, would have been, with the imperfections caused by the faithlessness of the overseer, subject to constant leaks. The commissioners did indeed suppose that the injuries had been thoroughly repaired. But it is a peculiarity of the cement-pipe, that, although when broken by freezing, it is not so completely shattered as iron is, yet it cannot be mended with its own material so as to be at once ready for use, but must be left to harden. When hasty repairs are required, the fracture is first wound with some other substance, over which the cement is laid; and it often happens that when the winding decays, the break re-appears; and this happened frequently in this case. The breaks continued to occur year after year; the patience of successive water-boards was exhausted; and whenever the new pipe was to be laid, iron was employed; and, after a few years' experience, at a greater depth. In 1876, very little cement-pipe remains, except in one of the mains between the village and the reservoir, which, being rarely used, can be effectually repaired when broken.

The act of the legislature empowering the district to build the water-works, provided that after their completion they should be managed by such officers and agents as it might determine upon. On the 13th of April, 1857, therefore, it was voted to commit the works to the charge of three commissioners; the first board to be chosen with members holding office for one, two and three years respectively; their successors for terms of three years. Under this arrangement, the commissioners have been: E. H. Kellogg, 1857–1859; T. F. Plunkett, 1857–1859; Seth W. Morton, 1857–1859; Thomas Colt, 1859; Jabez L. Peck, 1859–1863; George Brown, 1859–1862; Edwin Clapp, 1860–1864; N. G. Brown, 1866–1872; William R. Plunkett, 1864–1876; John Feeley, 1864–1876; Henry Colt, 1864–1865; S. T. Chapel, 1872–1875.

The duties of these later commissioners have by no means been confined to the mere management of the water-works. The large increase of the population of the village has rendered great and costly enlargement necessary; and, lacking the aid of that indispensable teacher, experience, the early committees made errors, the correction of which has not been without cost. They over-estimated the size of Lake Ashley, and neglected to take into account the evaporation from its surface, which in summer is much larger than would be believed without actual experiment. They underrated, also, the ordinary wastefulness of water-takers, and the great drain necessary in winter to keep the water in such motion as will prevent its freezing in the pipes. A "cold term" does more to exhaust the lake than a "dry spell." They did not anticipate the constant decrease of water in Lake Ashley—which has a very limited water-shed—on account of the destruction of forests around it, nor the diminished flow of Ashley brook, arising from a similar cause. And, yet again, the projectors of the water-works, although they believed the lake capable of supplying a city of fifty thousand inhabitants, did not in their plans for its use count upon the rapid growth of the village, requiring the extension of the pipes until they are several times their original length, and into streets whose existence was not dreamed of in 1855. The cost of the water-works, as they were reported completed in 1857, forms a comparatively small portion of the construction-account as it stood in 1875.

Although the water has never failed, or fallen short of the ordinary wants of the people, there have been several times when economy in its use has been deemed prudent; and liberal measures have been taken to augment the sources of supply, and hold it more largely in reserve. In 1867, the dam at Lake Ashley was raised twenty-eight inches at a cost of two thousand one hundred and eighty-seven dollars. In 1868–9, a reservoir with a capacity of over one million gallons was built near the old reservoir, three miles from the village; and the old dam, which was carried away by a freshet in October of that year, was rebuilt with improvements; the entire expenditure being eleven thousand one hundred and seventy-three dollars.

Sackett brook, which unites with the Ashley below the reservoir, has an ordinary daily flow of nearly one million gallons of water, characterized by that purity which distinguishes all the streams of this silicious slope; and it was long looked upon as likely at sometime to afford a valuable re-enforcement to the water-supply of Pittsfield. No near necessity for its use was anticipated; but in 1873, an opportunity occurring to purchase the Merry mill-privilege, which covered the right to the water of the brook, it was purchased at a cost of four hundred and fifteen dollars.

Authority to use the brook for the water-supply of Pittsfield, was obtained from the legislature of 1874; and, in reporting the fact to the district, the commissioners said: "The Ashley lake and brook are fully equal to the present wants of the town, unless a very dry summer should be followed by an unusually long and cold winter." And this contingency happened in the years 1874 and 1875, although there were heavy rains in the early summer of the former year. The commissioners did not wait for the succession of unfavorable seasons to be completed; but, in December, 1874, when the price of iron-pipe had fallen from sixty or seventy dollars per ton, to forty, they advised the district to take advantage of the market, and at once connect Sackett brook with the Ashley. This combination, they represented, would furnish a sufficient supply for ordinary seasons; leaving the lake wholly in reserve for exceptionally dry terms. And, even in these, they thought, only a small part of its water need be used.

They proposed to effect this junction by laying a ten-inch iron-pipe from the Merry mill-dam, to a point in the twelve-inch iron-main, five thousand feet below the reservoir; the whole extension being ten thousand eight hundred and fourteen feet; making the distance from the Elm-street bridge to the Merry mill-dam, four miles. At the latter point, they proposed to build a substantial dam of uncemented mountain-stone, the level of which should be forty feet higher than that of the reservoir.

The district adopted the recommendations, and they were carried into execution during the summer of 1875, at a cost of eighteen thousand dollars, being seven thousand dollars less than the estimates.

The winter of 1874–5 was excessively cold; and the frost penetrated the earth deeper than at any other time since the building of the water-works. More pipes than ever before, were burst by freezing; but the commissioners did not attribute this altogether, or chiefly, to the intensity of the cold. The authority to fix the grade of the streets belongs to the town and not to the district; and had been exercised in some instances without regard to the safety of the water-pipes. And to this the commissioners attributed a majority of the cases of freezing; the pipes having been laid sufficiently deep before the reduction of grade. They add, however, that "the main pipes are generally much deeper than the service-pipes (which are laid by the water-takers); andt he mains have not frozen, until the larger share of the service-pipes have frozen and stopped the current of water." It was found necessary to re-lay many of the street-mains, and it was done at an expense of about seven thousand dollars.

The total length of the main and distributing pipe laid in 1875 was nine miles and a quarter. Between that date and 1868, there was an increase of fourteen miles and a half. And every succeeding year has brought a new extension, generally of thousands of feet.

A ten-inch cement-pipe was originally laid from the reservoir to the village; and a new twelve-inch iron-main has since been laid, parallel with it, at a cost of about $46,000.

These several items of improvement and addition have increased the cost of the water-works, from fifty thousand dollars to one hundred and ninety-three thousand four hundred and seventy dollars and thirty-one cents. The following is an abstract of

THE CONSTRUCTION-ACCOUNT.

Original construction,	$50,000 00
Expended for re-laying and extending pipe prior to 1866,[1]	14,000 00
Extension of pipes after 1866,	22,917 53
Re-laying street-mains after 1866,	28,772 63
New twelve-inch mains, including land-damages,	45,423 32
Raising dam at Lake Ashley,	2,186 88
Lower reservoir and dam in 1873,	13,172 60
Addition of Sackett brook to water-works,	18,329 94
Total,	$194,802 90

The following is the

AMOUNT OF WATER-RATES RECEIVED IN DIFFERENT YEARS.

To January	1, 1857,	$787 81
"	1, 1858,	1,546 98
April	1, 1859,	2,098 56
"	1, 1860, 15 months,	3,242 04
"	1, 1861,	3,098 92
"	1, 1862,	3,150 00

[1] Prior to 1866 no separate account of extension and re-laying was kept.

HISTORY OF PITTSFIELD.

To April	1, 1863,	$3,450 00
"	1, 1864,	3,970 00
"	1, 1865,	4,212 10
"	1, 1866,	4,788 43
"	1, 1867,	4,901 21
"	1, 1868,	5,514 02
"	1, 1869,	6,165 04
"	1, 1870,	8,202 32
"	1, 1871,	8,371 21
"	1, 1872,	9,354 00
"	1, 1873,	10,303 14
"	1, 1874,	10,630 48
"	1, 1875,	10,801 36
"	1, 1876,	13,054 98

The legislature of 1867 authorized the district to choose three commissioners of main-drains, common sewers, and sidewalks, in the same manner and for the same terms as are prescribed in the case of the water-commissioners. Under their direction, in accordance with the votes of the district, an excellent system of drainage has been in part established; and the sidewalks, which were defective in grade and construction, have become uniform and well built, as a rule. The commissioners have been George S. Willis and Charles T. Rathbun, from 1867 to 1875. George W. Foote, from 1867 to 1869. D. C. Munyan, from 1869 to 1875.

Since 1863, the district has appropriated money for lighting the streets, increasing from three hundred dollars in that year to two thousand five hundred in 1867; the whole amount being paid for gas; the posts being provided by individuals, at points approved by a committee of the district.

CHAPTER XXIV.

BERKSHIRE JUBILEE.

[1844.]

Origin of the jubilee—Preparatory measures—Reception and public exercises—Farewell-addresses—Biographical sketches of George N. Briggs, Julius Rockwell, and James D. Colt.

OF the events in Berkshire county which have obtained a national celebrity, and whose memory is most cherished at home, with the exception of the first cattle-show, perhaps the most noted, and certainly the most unique, was the gathering of the sons of the county, held in the year 1844, and known as the Berkshire Jubilee. There probably was never a nobler family-reunion. The following account of its inception was given by Rev. R. S. Cook, in his response to the address of welcome:

A gentleman whose official relations led him to travel extensively in this country, and who was brought into contact with a great number of intelligent men, found those in influential and useful stations, in nearly every principal city and state, who hailed from Berkshire. Returning to the county, as he always did once or twice a year, he found the people of a particular town ignorant of the fact that distinguished men had emigrated from adjacent towns; the emigrants themselves were unaware of the Berkshire origin of men with whom they were familiar in commercial, political, or ecclesiastical circles. The idea was conceived, five or six years' ago, of bringing together the emigrants from this county, with the view of forming a band of brotherhood between them; awakening on the part of the citizens of the county an interest in the fame and usefulness of its sons, and furnishing an illustration of the influence which New England is exerting on the country and the world.

Wherever the idea has been suggested, it has been cordially approved. The time for its realization has been delayed for various reasons, but chiefly with the hope of such relieving prosperity as the country now enjoys. A year ago last April, he had the pleasure of meeting our respected orator (Hon. Joshua A. Spencer) in the rail-cars west of Albany, and the thought occurred that he had been named as one of Berkshire's honored sons. The inquiry was made whether he retained any affection for his native county. "Yes," said he, " it is a part of my religion to go back there once a year." The plan for this gathering was suggested, and he entered into it with all his heart. The programme for the occasion was made, on a card, essentially as it is now arranged. On the return of the individual of whom I speak, to the city of New York, he met the late lamented Colonel Stone, who promised, and gave, the aid of the *Commercial Advertiser* in forwarding the plan. When preparing an article for the *Journal of Commerce*, suggesting a meeting of the emigrants residing in New York, it became necessary to have a title, and " THE BERKSHIRE JUBILEE " was first written.[1]

At the meeting in New York, called through the *Journal of Commerce*, the plan prepared by card in the cars, by Messrs. Cook and Spencer—viz., a sermon, a poem, an oration, and a dinner or a great tea-party, " where talk might be *ad libitum* "—was suggested and approved. And Rev. Dr. J. C. Brigham, in behalf of a committee appointed by this meeting, addressed a letter to a gentleman in Pittsfield, asking him, after a consultation, to give information on the following points :—1st. Is such a social gathering desirable and practicable ? 2d. Would the citizens of the county take an interest in it ? 3d. If yea, when and where should the meeting be held ? 4th. What, in your opinion, should be the exercises ?—" That such a meeting, at some time," said Mr. Brigham, " would be attended with pleasing and useful results, I can hardly question. It would make that old American Piedmont (Berkshire county) still more honorable than she now is."

This letter was communicated to a respectable meeting, which unanimously resolved that the proposed gathering was highly desirable and practicable, and that it should be held at Pittsfield at as early a day as possible.

The following gentlemen were chosen to communicate with the committee in New York: Rev. John Todd, Thomas B. Strong, Julius Rockwell, Lemuel Pomeroy, Jason Clapp, James D. Colt, E. R. Colt, Edward A. Newton, Rev. Edward Ballard, George N. Briggs, Henry H. Childs, Phinehas Allen, Oliver P. Dickinson,

---

[1] Mr. Cook was himself the gentleman indefinitely mentioned in his speech as first suggesting the jubilee.

and Thomas A. Gold. The letter to the committee in New York was written by Rev. Mr. Todd, who, although he had very recently become a resident of the town, was made chairman of the Pittsfield committee. We reprint the concluding paragraphs.

The pride of Massachusetts is her sons and her daughters. They constitute her glory, whether they remain here to beautify and enrich the old homestead, or whether they go out to expend their indomitable energies under sunnier skies and on richer plains. Among these, Berkshire has furnished her full share—sons who would honor any parent. These we should rejoice to see gathered in the bosom of their mother, to hold a day of congratulations and sweet reflections. We love these sons and daughters none the less because they have gone from us, and we wish to have the home of their childhood live green in their memories. We would bind them, through their affections, to the place of their birth, and have their memories linger among these scenes, and their hearts warm at the thought of their early homes. The chain that binds them to us is more than golden, and we would have its links grow brighter and stronger. We would cordially respond to your proposal then, and, at the unanimous request of our fellow-citizens, respectfully invite your committee to call such a meeting, to be held at Pittsfield, at as early a day as possible.

Of the convenience and suitableness of holding the meeting here, we need not speak. In making this invitation we are certain that we express the mind and feelings of the inhabitants of this town, while we most cordially invite the meeting to share our hospitality, to command our aid, and to feel that they come among none but warm friends.

While we thus extend this invitation, and express it as our opinion that this is the most convenient and suitable place, we trust that we should not be the less ready to co-operate, should your committee judge otherwise.

We would have it an occasion of deep cherished joy, such as will move old Berkshire—the memory of which will thrill in after days. We hope it will be every way worthy of her glorious soil, and of her sons and daughters. Let it be the lighting of a beacon on these hills that will show that the watch-tower of affection is still tenanted, and that the flame of love has not yet begun to grow pale.

The New York committee was composed of the following gentlemen:

Samuel R. Betts,	Mason Noble,
Marshall S. Bidwell,	Thomas Egleston,
J. C. Brigham,	Robert Center,
D. D. Field,	H. P. Peet,

R. S. Cook,
Theodore Sedgwick,
William C. Bryant,
Orville Dewey,
Russell C. Wheeler,

Joseph Hyde,
Ruel Smith,
Drake Mills,
Edward Williams,
William Sherwood.

A meeting of the citizens of the different towns in the county was held, which elected a county-committee as follows:

Rev. John Todd,
Thomas B. Strong,
Julius Rockwell,
Lemuel Pomeroy,
Jason Clapp,
James D. Colt,
O. P. Dickinson,
Thomas A. Gold,
Ezekiel Bacon,
Nathan Willis,
Hosea Merrill, Jr.,
Thomas F. Plunkett,
James Root,
Elijah Robbins,
John Weller,
Abel West,
Henry Root,
Jared Ingersoll,
Theodore Hinsdale,
Jabez Peck,
Richard C. Coggswell,
Parker L. Hall,
Titus Goodman,
James Francis,
Charles Churchill,
Otis Peck,
Henry Hubbard,
Walter Laflin,
Ensign H. Kellogg,
Calvin Martin,

E. R. Colt,
Edward A. Newton,
Rev. Edward Ballard,
George N. Briggs,
H. H. Childs,
Phinehas Allen,
James D. Colt, 2d,
Theodore Pomeroy,
Henry Colt,
Thaddeus Clapp,
George S. Willis,
Phinehas Allen, Jr.,
Robert Colt,
William M. Walker,
David Campbell,
E. P. Little,
George P. Briggs,
Gordon McKay,
Timothy Childs,
Charles Bush,
Robert Pomeroy,
Alanson P. Dean,
Edwin Clapp,
Samuel A. Churchill,
Ethan Janes,
Oliver S. Root,
George W. Campbell,
Robert Campbell,
Franklin Root,
Robert Francis, Jr.

Subsequently auxiliary town-committees were appointed. It was determined that the jubilee should be held at Pittsfield, on the 22d and 23d of August, 1844. Julius Rockwell, Ensign H. Kellogg, and Phinehas Allen, Jr., were selected as a financial committee in Berkshire; and Thomas A. Gold, Dr. O. S. Root,

HISTORY OF PITTSFIELD. 577

Ezekiel R. Colt, George P. Briggs, and Robert Colt, as a committee of reception.

The citizens of Pittsfield, and adjoining towns, agreed to offer their hospitality without stint of labor, time, or money. The programme of public exercises was an oration by Hon. Joshua A. Spencer of Utica, a poem by Rev. William Allen, D. D., of Northampton, and a sermon by Rev. Mark Hopkins, D. D., of Williams College. Odes and poems by several authors.

The following officers for the jubilee were selected:

President, Gov. GEORGE N. BRIGGS.

Vice Presidents,

Henry H. Childs,
George Hull,
Ezekiel Bacon,
Samuel R. Betts,
Doddridge Crocker,
Marshall S. Bidwell,
William P. Walker,
Charles A. Dewey,
Nathan Willis,
John Whiting,
Lemuel Pomeroy,
Cyrus Stowell,
Edward A. Newton,
Josiah Q. Robinson,
Phinehas Allen,
Russell Brown,
William Porter, Jr.,
Horatio Byington,
Lester Filley,
Parker L. Hall,
Edward Stevens,
Eleazer Williams,
Thomas F. Plunkett,

Henry Hubbard,
Samuel Rossiter,
Wilbur Curtiss,
Henry W. Bishop,
James D. Colt,
Keyes Danforth,
John Mills,
Oliver P. Colt,
Calvin Martin,
Rodman Hazard,
Jason Clapp,
Isaac Hills,
Charles Sedgwick,
John Chamberlin,
Harvey P. Peet,
James Larned,
Daniel N. Dewey,
Thomas Robinson,
Increase Sumner,
Homer Bartlett,
Samuel Gates,
Josiah Quincy,
Jonathan Allen,

Deodotus Noble.

Secretary, James D. Colt, 2d.

Chaplains,

Rev. Samuel Shepard, D. D.,
Rev. John Alden,

Rev. James Bradford,
Rev. D. D. Wheedon,

Rev. Samuel B. Shaw.

The emigrant sons of Berkshire were formally received at the town-hall at eleven o'clock, on the morning of Thursday, August 22d; Thomas A. Gold, Esq., making the address of welcome, and Rev. R. S. Cook responding. Mr. Cook said:

The occasion which assembles us is altogether unique. The elements of interest differ widely from those of ordinary gatherings. No sectarian or partisan zeal; no selfish or ambitious purpose has called us from our business and our homes. We have left all political prejudices and animosities, and all business-cares and troubles, behind us; and have devoted these few days to social and patriotic feeling. We have come from the mountains of the north, and the plains of the south; the cities of the east and the prairies of the west; from the four quarters of the land, we have come to our Berkshire home, to revive the friendships and associations of boyish years, and live over again in memory and imagination the days of our youth.

After other remarks in a similar strain, Mr. Cook said in conclusion:

In behalf of the New York committee and the emigrant sons of Berkshire, I accept and thank you for the generous welcome with which we are received. The preparations are on a scale of characteristic hospitality. The greeting we have received is more than a compensation for the sacrifices made in coming, as many of us have, a thousand miles or more to attend this festival.

At two o'clock in the afternoon a procession was organized at that grand local center, the park, and moved to the eminence west of the village, since known as Jubilee hill. This elevation which commands a superb view of the Berkshire valley, although now thickly populated, then had but a single house, the homestead built by the patriotic Dr. Timothy Childs, and then occupied by his widow. On this hill a stand for speakers, and seats for an audience of several thousand had been erected, and between five and six thousand persons, a large portion of them ladies, were speedily collected.

An anthem, "Wake the Song of Jubilee," was sung, and a prayer was offered by Rev. Dr. Shepard of Lenox. But at this point the clouds, which for several hours had threatened rain, poured down showers which dispersed the assembly "in most admired disorder," to reassemble, however, very soon, in the old First church. The services were re-commenced by the singing of a psalm, after which Rev. Dr. Hopkins preached the sermon, occupying about an hour and a quarter in the delivery. It was such as was to be expected from its author.

"And this," he began, "is the Berkshire Jubilee! We have come—the sons and daughters of Berkshire—from our villages, and hill-sides, and mountain-tops; from the distant city; from the far West; from every place where the spirit of enterprise and of adventure bears men, we have come. The farmer has left his field, the mechanic his workshop, the merchant his counting-room, the lawyer his brief, and the minister his people, and we have come to revive old and cherished associations and to renew former friendships; to lengthen the cords and strengthen the stakes of every kind and time-hallowed affection. Coming together as natives and citizens of a state, on the eastern border of which is Plymouth Rock, what so suitable as that our first public act should be to assemble ourselves for the worship of the God of our fathers, and our God. This is a local thanksgiving in one sense, but extended in another sense. This day our family affection is thrown around a whole country. It is fit then that we should adopt the language of the psalmist in the words which I have chosen for my text: 'Return unto thy rest, oh, my soul, for the Lord hath dealt bountifully with thee.' Psalm cxvi : 7."

The reverend doctor then proceeded to notice the agency of God in the affairs of men, and what was meant by dealing bountifully with man, and applied the language of the text as peculiarly applicable to those present on the occasion. God had dealt bountifully with them in granting them those aspects of nature and influences of society by which they were surrounded. He gave a graphic description of our loved Berkshire; bestowed high compliment upon the industry and benevolence of its citizens, and upon those who had achieved a distinguished and enviable fame in the walks of literature. "It is remarkable," he said, "secluded as this county has been, that the three American writers most widely and justly celebrated in their several departments, have lived and written here. It was in the deep quiet of these scenes that the profoundest treatise of our great metaphysical writer was produced. It was here that the powers of our 'truest poet,' —one who, in his own line of poetry, has not been excelled since the world stood—became known and came to their maturity; and here are still entwined, greener by time, the home-affections of one whose peculiar social qualities have given her a place as eminent in the hearts of her friends, as her power and grace of style, and her universal sympathy with all that is human, have given her as an author, in the public estimation."[1]

The speaker concluded by a word of welcome to those who had vis-

[1] Jonathan Edwards, William Cullen Bryant, and Catharine M. Sedgwick.

ited their old homes: "Natives and former citizens of Berkshire, I welcome you—not to Bacchanalian revelry, not to costly entertainments, not to the celebration of any party, or national triumph, but, to the old homestead; to these scenes of your early days, to these mountains and valleys, and streams, and skies, to the hallowed resting-places of the dear departed. I welcome you to the warm grasp of kindred and friends, to rational festivity—to the BERKSHIRE JUBILEE."

Rev. Dr. Allen then read a poem of a hundred and eight stanzas, alluding to many historical events and personages of Berkshire.

Hon. Julius Rockwell read two graceful poems by William Pitt Palmer, entitled "The Mother Land's Home Call," and "The Response of the Home Comers," after which the public exercises of the day closed with the doxology and a benediction.

The evening being very stormy, visitors from abroad were prevented from calling, as generally as had been contemplated, at the residences of citizens, where generous preparation had been made for their reception.

Interesting informal meetings were held on the morning of Friday. The weather became pleasant at eleven o'clock, and a still larger assemblage than upon the previous day collected upon Jubilee hill. The exercises commenced with the singing of an ode written by Hon. Ezekiel Bacon.

Prayer was offered by Rev. David Dudley Field, D. D., of Stockbridge, the historian of Berkshire and of Pittsfield. A song, "Come to the Old Roof Tree," written for the occasion by a lady, was sung.

Then followed the oration by Hon. Joshua A. Spencer. Mr. Spencer began by touching allusions to the scenes of the day, and the memories of former times, which were vividly recalled by them to the minds of every son and daughter who had returned to their old Berkshire home. The beautiful scenery, the woody hill-side, the pleasant valleys, the silvery lakes, and gurgling rills, all were treated as familiar friends and brothers. "The hearts of thousands," says the writer who thus reports the address, "responded to the thrilling description by the speaker of his own feelings upon his return to these scenes of his childhood. All felt that the home of their youth was worthy to be the home of their more mature days, and was more endeared to them from the years which had elapsed since they left the old homestead to seek their fortune in other climes." The orator then passed to a historical sketch of Berkshire county, to which justice could only be done by reprinting it in full.

Of Pittsfield, he said: "May not Berkshire, too, well rejoice in the prosperity of her metropolitan village? Not the first to begin, but the first in the course of all the lovely places of business-activity and quiet retirement within her borders. Pittsfield's long, well-shaded streets, her deeply embowered dwellings, with their spacious pleasure-grounds, wear the distinctive and charming livery of New England village-scenery. Here is the home of comfort, refinement, and, as we know, of hospitality. In the midst of the enchantment, her far-famed elm lifts its lofty branches to meet the sun in his coming.

> 'Wise with the lore of centuries,
> What tales, if there were tongues in trees,
> That giant elm could tell.'"

In concluding, Mr. Spencer said, "When will the sons and daughters of Berkshire hold another 'jubilee?' Never certainly another *first* jubilee; that pleasure is vouchsafed unto us: but another jubilee? Whether it shall be in our day, or be reserved for our children, or for our children's children, we know not; but come when it will, we do know that they will find a hearty welcome. These beautiful hills, by which we are surrounded, shall not be more enduring than the love their people bear for their absent kindred."

Charles Sedgwick, Esq., then read a long and beautiful ode to Berkshire, by Miss Frances Ann Kemble. Hon. Ezekiel Bacon read "The Stockbridge Bowl," furnished for the occasion by Mrs. Lydia H. Sigourney, and an ode written by the same lady was sung.

An ode "To Hills that Cradled Childhood's Home," by Mrs. Laura Hyde, was read; and Mrs. Heman's "Hymn of the Mountain Christians—" "For the strength of the Hills we bless Thee—" was sung.

At two o'clock the assembly proceeded to the grounds of the Young Ladies' Institute, where, under a large pavilion, tables were arranged, calculated to accommodate over three thousand persons. Nearly that number, in about equal proportions of ladies and gentlemen, took seats for the dinner.

A blessing was invoked by Rev. Dr. Shepard. After the cloth

was removed, Governor Briggs, president of the day, addressed the audience in one of the happiest of those efforts in which he was always peculiarly happy. After some humorous remarks in regard to the exercises of the day, and an epitome of the history of the county, admirable for its correctness, conciseness and piquancy, he concluded as follows :

"In the freshness of this gushing joy, a sad reflection comes over the mind, that this glad jubilee will be the last that many of us will ever witness. Of the present we are secure, and for its blessings we thank Heaven, around this family-table. You have come, my friends, to walk in the green meadows over which your boyish feet once ran with the lightness of the roe ; to ramble over the pasture where once you lingered after the returning cows ; to look into the old well, and see its dripping bucket; to gaze upon that old apple-tree where you gathered the early fruit ; to walk on the banks of the winding stream, and stand by the silver pool over which the willow bent, and in which you bathed your young limbs ; to visit the spot where with your brothers and sisters you gathered the ripe berries ; to look upon that old school-house, where you learned to read and to spell, to write and to cypher, where sometimes you felt the stinging birch ; to re-ascend that well-remembered rock upon which in mirth and play you spent so many happy hours, to see if it looks and appears as it used to ; to walk once more up the alley of that old church where you first heard the revered and loved parson preach and pray ; and you have come to visit the peaceful grave-yard, to walk among its green mounds and drop the tear of affection and friendship upon the silent resting-place of loved ones who sleep there. You have come here to re-kindle at this domestic fireside the holy feelings of youth. To all these we bid you welcome ! Welcome to these green valleys and lofty mountains. Welcome to this feast, to our homes, to our hearts. Welcome to everything. Once more I say welcome ! I give you a sentiment: The County of Berkshire—she loves her institutions and her beautiful scenery ; but feeling the sentiment and borrowing the language of the Roman mother, she points to her children and exclaims, " These are my jewels."

The remainder of the day was occupied by speeches, and toasts all pertinent to the occasion, and many of them eloquent. We select extracts from those the most representative in their character.

Dr. O. W. Holmes asked to be allowed, before he opened the paper in his hand, to assure his friends of the reason why he found himself there. He said :

Inasmuch as the company express willingness to hear historical incidents, any little incident which shall connect me with those to whom I cannot claim to be a brother, seems to be fairly brought forward. One of my earliest recollections is of an annual pilgrimage made by my parents to the west. The young horse was brought up, fatted by a week's rest and high feeding, prancing and caracoling to the door. It came to the corner and was soon over the western hills. He was gone a fortnight; and one afternoon—it always seemed to me it was a Sunday afternoon—we saw an equipage crawling from the west towards the old homestead; the young horse, who set out fat and prancing, worn thin and reduced by a long journey—the chaise covered with dust, and all speaking of a terrible crusade, a formidable pilgrimage. Winter-evening stories told me where—to Berkshire, to the borders of New York, to the old domain, owned so long that there seemed a kind of hereditary love for it. Many years passed away, and I traveled down the beautiful Rhine. I wished to see the equally beautiful Hudson. I found myself at Albany; a few hours' ride brought me to Pittsfield, and I went to the little spot, the scene of this pilgrimage—a mansion—and found it surrounded by a beautiful meadow, through which the winding river made its course in a thousand fantastic curves; the mountains reared their heads around it, the blue air which makes our city-pale cheeks again to deepen with the hue of health, coursing about it pure and free. I recognized it as the scene of the annual pilgrimage. Since then I have made an annual visit to it.

In 1735, Hon. Jacob Wendell, my grandfather in the maternal line, bought a township not then laid out—the township of Pontoosuc—and that little spot which we still hold is the relic of twenty-four thousand acres of baronial territory. When I say this, no feeling which can be the subject of ridicule animates my bosom. I know too well that the hills and rocks outlast our families. I know we fall upon the places we claim, as the leaves of the forest fall, and as passed the soil from the hands of the original occupants into the hands of my immediate ancestors, I know it must pass from me and mine; and yet with pleasure and pride I feel I can take every inhabitant by the hand and say, If I am not a son or a grandson, or even a nephew of this fair county, I am at least allied to it by hereditary relation.

Doctor Holmes then read the verses commencing, "Come back to your mother, ye children," which are published in his poems.

Hon. John Mills of Springfield, who spoke in behalf of his native town, Sandisfield, said:

It is not, I believe, until life is considerably advanced, that we feel any particular solicitude as to the place where it may terminate; and I doubt whether those who have the good fortune to spend their days where they were born, are conscious of the true cause that gives the

charm to that locality. If there be in this village one who was here
born and has here passed his days, one who has survived the friends and
companions of his youth, he will tell you that the remnant of life can
be more happily spent here than elsewhere, and would probably assign
as a reason, that here are the graves of his fathers, and here too, he
desires to make his own. But remove him permanently to some other
section of the country, and he would soon be sensible of another cause
for this local preference. The place to which we may suppose him
removed, might have charms, if possible, superior to those of your village. From his window, or in his walks, the most delightful scenery
should be presented to his view, and he should be able fully to appreciate its beauties ; still there would be something wanting ; the eye
would nowhere rest on certain well-known objects of inanimate nature,
intimately entwined with his earliest impressions. "Where," he would
exclaim, "where is the great elm around whose trunk, and in the shade
of whose branches, I gamboled with my youthful companions, sixty
years ago ? Where the beautiful curve-crested mountain-range in the
west ? The higher elevation at the north, and those in the east ?
Elevations on which I gazed with admiring wonder, before my tongue
was able to articulate their names. Elevations, the view and contemplation of which, gave the first impress of grandeur and sublimity to
my imagination." Such would be the language of his heart ; and,
could you place the Alps or the Pyrenees in a position most favorable
for effect upon his vision, they would be inadequate substitutes for
those I have named ; the form and size of which, with their garniture
of light and shade, would be blended with, and in fact constitute a part
of, his moral existence.

Theodore Sedgwick of New York, gave the following senti-
ment: "The stock of New England — It is the stock of old
England—their virtue, their intelligence, with equality added."
And in response to this toast, and to an allusion to the great
English tragedian, Macready, Governor Briggs called upon that
gentleman, who came forward, and recited Leigh Hunt's poem,
"Abou Ben Adhem."

David Dudley Field, Esq., of New York, said :

It has happened that most of us who emigrated from this county,
went away in early manhood. This I conceive to have been a great
advantage. I conceive it gives us not only familiarity with this most
excellent scenery, but it gives us the impression, which we could not
have got in many other parts of the country, of the sort of society which
is peculiarly the product of American institutions. If I were to point
out to a foreigner anywhere in this country, an example of a commu-

nity whose social law and beauty were what I should say should be the production of American institutions, I should point out the county of Berkshire. It is around us—it is at our feet. It is the spectacle of that social equality without rudeness, accompanied by refinement such as I apprehend few parts of this country can show. Young men living in such a community, with such influences of scenery and of social law, can it be otherwise than that all of us should have gone away deeply impressed with the scenes which we have left, and that we should carry them with us as long as our hearts continue to beat?

Rev. Joshua N. Danforth of Alexandria, D. C., and a son of Colonel Danforth of Pittsfield, said:

We stand here to-day, numbering forty in relationship—twenty-five of us the direct descendants of David Noble of Williamstown, the upright judge, the exemplary Christian. * * * * The scenes we witness to-day, are, indeed, impressive. Genius is pouring out his treasures with a generosity suited to the great occasion. Poetry is weaving her most beautiful garland. Friendship brings her costly offerings to this altar. Even history has a portion in the reminiscences of this auspicious day. The muses and graces have conspired to honor the occasion. And if the joys of the living must be mingled with those sorrows which affection pays to the dead, the depth of the emotion attests the value of the tribute.

The president read a tribute by Miss C. M. Sedgwick to Dr. William Ellery Channing, whose last public address had been delivered at Lenox, on the first of August, 1842, the anniversary of emancipation in the West Indies, and who died in that town shortly afterwards. The tribute closed with the following passage from that address:

Men of Berkshire, whose nerves and souls the mountain-air has braced, you surely will respond to him who speaks of the blessings of freedom, and the misery of bondage. I feel as if the feeble voice which now addresses you, must find an echo in these forest-crowned heights. Do they not impart something of their own power and loftiness to men's souls? Should our commonwealth ever be invaded by victorious armies, Freedom's last asylum will be here. Here may a free spirit, may reverence for all human rights, may sympathy for all the oppressed, may a stern, solemn purpose to give no sanction to oppression, take stronger and stronger possession of men's minds, and from these mountains may generous impulses spread far and wide!"

"God grant," added Miss Sedgwick, "that this appeal, made by a voice now hushed in death, may meet a perpetual response in the hearts of our people, from generation to generation, while time shall endure. May they not be satisfied with the distinction of being natives of Berkshire, but strive in whatever clime, under whatever circumstances they may be placed, to wear always the Berkshire badge—Industry, Uprightness, Humanity."

Hon. Julius Rockwell being called upon by the president, as a Connecticut boy, but a Berkshire man, responded:

Sir, you have rightly said, I am not one of Berkshire's sons. But I have done all I could to make my position better; and I say to every young man who hears me, go and do likewise; for with the most persevering exertions, he can obtain, if he be not too late, a Berkshire wife.

One of the gentlemen who has spoken here, has told you how fortunate it is in young life, to go from Berkshire; I can tell him how fortunate it is in young life to *come to* the county of Berkshire. Another gentleman, with great beauty and power, spoke of the feeling that pervades every heart on this occasion, as the feeling of the young eagle returning to the eagle's nest. What think you is the feeling of the eagle mother, as she sees her young strong in pinions, strong in all that becomes and ennobles their kind, returning to their mother's nest?

Dr. Orville Dewey of New York, in the course of remarks distinguished by his peculiar eloquence, said:

We may have found wealth, splendor, fame, elsewhere; but there is no spot of earth like this. If I express my own feelings, all other aspects wear an air of strangeness and foreignness, in comparison with these. And yet, after all, I feel how utterly vain are my efforts to express this sentiment. There is something coiled up in this sentiment which I cannot unfold. It reminds me of an anecdote of one of the venerable fathers of the church in this county—Doctor West, one of the most learned, pure, gentle spirits that ever lived. I recollect one day of hearing a little child read the scriptures. Its voice had nothing remarkably impressive; it was a child's voice. I found myself moved in the most extraordinary manner, and yet unable to tell why, for I understood not what she uttered. On a few moments' reflection I discovered that the tone of that little child's voice was like the voice of Doctor West in prayer. So I think it is with home-affections; we are moved, we can scarcely tell why, at the sound of the word home. It is good for us to cherish these affections. Antaeus, the child of Terra and and Neptune, of earth and sea, only on the earth could be strong, could draw his replenished energies, enabling him to hold contest with the foe; and thus it is we turn hither on the waves of life; we spread our sails for the haven of honor; but after all, the re-afforded strength and courage to fight with perils is drawn from the home-affections.

Mr. Rockwell read the following sentiment, sent by Mrs. Sigourney:

THE OLD BAY STATE.

> You scarce can go, where streamlets flow,
> In prairie, or western glen,
> Or among the great, in halls of state,
> But you'll find the Berkshire men :
> May the blessing of health and well-spent wealth,
> And stainless names await,
> (With the treasured glee of this jubilee.)
> The sons of the old Bay State.

In addition to those already mentioned, speeches were made by Marshall S. Bidwell of New York, Judge Charles A. Dewey of Northampton, Josiah Quincy of New Hampshire, Prof. Chester Dewey of Rochester, N. Y., Rev. J. C. Brigham, D. D., of New York, and Timothy Childs of Rochester. Sentiments were offered by Drake Mills of New York, Thomas Allen of St. Louis, Charles R. Gold of Buffalo, Reuel Smith of New York, Dr. Charles Goodrich of Brooklyn, Rev. Heman Humphrey, D. D., of Amherst College, Dr. L. A. Smith of Newark, N. J., Silas Metcalf of Kinderhook, D. C. Whitewood of Michigan, and William P. Palmer of New York. Mr. Palmer's sentiment was in honor of Dr. Alvan Hyde, of Lee:

> Saint! in thy loss we learn this blessed lore,
> That not to breathe is not to be no more!
> Oh, no; to those whose days like thine have passed,
> In self-denying kindness to the last,
> Remains, unfading with the final breath,
> A green and sweet vitality in death!

The hour of parting having come, Judge Samuel R. Betts, chairman of the New York committee, made the farewell-address in their behalf; at the close of which he said:

The opportunity has been afforded me during the past few days, in visiting a series of your beautiful towns, to compare, to some extent, the present, with the state of the county in 1806, when my residence in it ceased. Since that period, the doubled population, the improved culture of the land, the thrifty appearance of villages, and farm-residences, and manufactories, the increase of churches, schools and academies; all denote an eminent and solid advance in wealth, refinement, and the substantial comforts of life. In view of this great and interesting progress and improvement in well-being here, the thought seems appropriate to us, that we emigrants should realize that there is much before us to do, to render our conditions abroad of equal fellowship with those in old Berkshire at home.

Rev. Dr. Todd, chairman of the Berkshire committee, responded in a touching speech, in which was the following paragraph:

We have often thought, Sir,—thought with pride, of our gorgeous hills and valleys, which have been so beautifully celebrated at this time; we have often taken pride in this, our home, and in all that is included in the term "Berkshire," and thought that we had scenery unsurpassed in nature. We thought that this occasion would bring bright and loved beings around us — brighter and more loved than whom, could not be found on the face of the earth. But, I doubt not, this pride in the present occupants of Berkshire, has been justly rebuked and deeply humbled. We had no conception of the beauty, the interlect, the character, and the real nobility of nature, which this meeting would call home; and hereafter we shall look back upon this gathering as one of the brightest and most beautiful occasions in our earthly pilgrimage. We have been thinking how we could erect some monument of this jubilee. In our wisdom, we have spoken of several, but after all, God has been before us, and His mighty hand hath reared the monument. That hill, from which we came to this pavilion, will hereafter bear the name of "Jubilee Hill," and when our heads are laid in the grave, and we have passed away and are forgotten, we hope our children, and our children's children, will walk over that beautiful spot and say, "here our fathers and mothers celebrated the *Berkshire Jubilee!*" This monument shall stand as long as the foot-stool of God shall remain.

At the close of Doctor Todd's speech, hearty cheers were given for the old homestead; and, in response, for the emigrants. The band played a farewell-strain. The multitude separated, most of them in tears; and the Berkshire Jubilee was over. It had certainly accomplished all its originators anticipated, as explained in Doctor Cook's opening speech.

In the course of the jubilee, Rev. Messrs. John Todd and Edward Ballard, Charles Sedgwick, Esq., William Cullen Bryant, and Dr. Henry L. Sabin, were appointed a committee to edit a volume containing the speeches, odes, hymns, sentiments and other proceedings. The volume, containing two hundred and forty-two large octavo pages, was published; and contained, in addition to the proceedings of the day, an historical sketch of the Stockbridge Indians, by Thomas Allen, an article on the Literature of Berkshire, a list of missionaries from Berkshire, and chaplains in the French and Indian, and revolutionary wars, by Rev. William Allen, D. D.; and the Last chapter of the Chronicles of the Berkshire Jubilee, by Miss Catharine M. Sedgwick. The reason that no contribution from William Cullen Bryant appears in the programme of the exercises is explained by the following letter from Mr. Bryant to Judge Betts, which illustrates the well-known fact that even the truest poet cannot always write occasional verses to order:

NEW YORK, August 14, 1844.

MY DEAR SIR:—I wrote you that I would supply a few verses to be set to music for the Berkshire celebration; but I find, after attempting again and again, I produce nothing that would not disgrace me by its flat and commonplace character. I have torn up the verses, and acknowledge that I cannot fulfill the engagement. It is mortifying, but I find no alternative. The committee, I am sure, will see that it may be difficult for some minds to summon up a poetic rapture upon a given occasion, and will indulgently take the attempt for the deed.

In many respects the year selected for the jubilee was one of the happiest—probably the most happy—which could have been selected in the annals of Berkshire or of Pittsfield, for such a festival. Both the town and the county were in the first flush of many prides. Four years before, the completion of the Western railroad had opened for the county communication with the great world without, and had given to Pittsfield new prominence and prosperity. The year 1844, was, moreover, one of unusual success in all industrial enterprises. In less material glories, the county, through the pens of Bryant and Miss Sedgwick, had long been growing up to a fame which then seemed fully ripe. The great colleges and schools of Berkshire flourished more than ever. For the first time in the history of the commonwealth, its chief magistrate had the year before been elected from the old county, and Pittsfield was proud that he was one of her own citizens. One of the most popular of her sons had also been elected at the same time to succeed the governor in the national house of representatives. Rev. Mr. Todd, already famous as an author, and then in the full vigor of his intellect, had recently become pastor of the First Church, and contributed much by his wonderful tact and aptitude in management, to the smooth working of the programme. A more happy combination of circumstances could hardly have been desired.

Perhaps we shall find no more fitting place than this to introduce sketches of Messrs. Briggs, Rockwell and Colt.

George Nixon Briggs was born at South Adams, April 12, 1796. His father, Allen Briggs, was a native of Cranston, R. I., and his mother, whose maiden name was Nancy Brown, was born in Cumberland, in the same state. When George was seven years old, the family removed from South Adams to Manchester, Vt., and two years afterwards to the village of White Creek, in Washington county, New York. Here he was subjected to influences which had a decisive effect upon his after life. "His training," says his biographer, Prof. W. C. Richards, "had always been of a decided religious character, * * * and, while he was in his fourteenth year he became the subject of personal religious experience, and was soon after baptized and received into the Baptist church at White Creek."

He entered with characteristic eagerness into the new and almost fascinating interests of the religious services, and soon began to exhort in the meetings. His youth gave a charm to his appeals. "His eloquent, and what were deemed almost miraculous, addresses in religious meetings," says his friend, Hon. Hiland Hall of Vermont, "drew together great crowds of people, and elicited very general and extensive appreciation and admiration."

To the faith which he then embraced and the church into which he was then baptized, he continued devotedly and affectionately faithful to his life's end. Forty-five years afterwards, in reply to a remark, which he overheard, that it "seemed strange that the governor of Massachusetts, should be president of a Baptist missionary society," he replied, "Sir, I think it more honor to be president of a Baptist missionary society than to be governor of Massachusetts."

Shortly after his conversion, George spent three years in learning the hatter's trade; but, although he had become sufficiently master of the art to set up in business for himself, he abandoned it, and in 1813, with five dollars which he had earned at haying, in his pocket, he left home, and commenced the study of the law with —— Kasson of South Adams. In 1814, he removed to Lanesboro and continued his studies in the office of Luther Washburn, Esq. He was admitted to the bar in 1818. A few months before, he had been married to Harriet, only daughter of Ezra Hall of Lanesboro. The first office which he held was that of town-clerk of Lanesboro, to which he was chosen in 1824. In 1826, he was appointed by Governor Lincoln, chairman of the board of commissioners of highways for Berkshire county, which place he held until the board was superseded by county-commissioners elected by the people. He was also division-inspector of militia, which he resigned in 1830, and was succeeded by E. R. Colt. The estimation in which he was held at this period of his life may be inferred from the following extract from an article in the *Sun* of 1827, giving an account of wool growers and manufacturers: " George N. Briggs, Esq., displayed an accuracy of knowledge, and depth of thought and reasoning upon the great topics of the meeting, and the future prospects of the country in regard to them, answering to the high appreciation which the county entertains of his abilities." He was elected to congress in the fall of 1830, and was successively re-elected, until July, 1841; his career there being distinguished for devotion to the cause of American manufactures, and the consistency of his life with his religious and temperance principles. In 1842, he removed from Lanesboro to Pittsfield. In the fall of 1843, he was chosen governor of the commonwealth, which office he held by annual re-election until 1850. Of his public life up to this time, he says:

I was six times elected to congress from the Berkshire District, and seven times chosen Governor of Massachusetts. I never asked a man to vote for me for either of these offices, or asked a man to attend a political convention when I was nominated, or to use any influence in any way to promote my election to either of those offices. * * * No man ever said to me that the interest of the whig party required, or would be promoted or injured by my doing or omitting to do anything. * * *

This last statement is remarkable, and as honorable to the whig leaders as to the governor; for, it is to be remembered that during the later years of his administration occurred the Mexican war, involving the question, what Massachusetts should do in regard to raising volunteers for what the governor and a large portion of his party regarded as an injust invasion of a sister-republic; the anti-slavery and free-soil agitations, and the coalition between the free-soil and democratic parties, which resulted in his own defeat and that of his party. And in the very last year of his gubernatorial life there came before him the question of the pardon of Professor Webster, convicted of the murder of Doctor Parkman; a question which agitated the people of the commonwealth almost as much as any of the great political contests of the day. In 1851, Governor Briggs resumed the practice of the law, and continued in private life until August, 1853, when he was appointed, by Governor Clifford, a judge of the court of Common Pleas; which office he held until that court was abolished in 1858, and the Superior Court established in its stead. This closed his official career.

During its whole course, he had been distinguished for his efforts in behalf of religion and morality. Of his love for the church with which he was identified, something has already been said. His regard for morals was not confined to any one branch —public or private; but he was the special advocate of temperance. His labors in this cause began in the very first dawn of the temperance-reformation in 1828, and from that time they were unintermitted. His speeches in that behalf were innumerable; his attendance upon conventions and public meetings was as constant and frequent as his public duties permitted. And his private and personal effort was not less assiduous.

Public education, from that of the college and the normal academy, down to the primary-school, was an object of his constant solicitude; and some of his characteristic speeches were made at their anniversaries. At the inauguration of the state normal school in Westfield, speaking of common schools, he said:

> I can recall the case of a poor boy who once sat upon the hard plank seat in one of these schools, in one of the poorest districts in this state, while his father was toiling at the anvil for his daily bread; who, under the smiles of a kind Providence, has been honored by his fellow-citizens infinitely beyond his deserts, and who, as chief magistrate of this commonwealth, deems it his highest honor to plead for the cause of common-school education.

Governor Briggs's closing days were saddened by the gathering clouds and bursting storm of the great rebellion, and the departure of his youngest son for the seat of war. But danger and death are not met upon the battle-field alone. They came to him one still afternoon, in the very sanctuary of his own peaceful home, unannounced by any warning voice of disease.

In the afternoon of the fourth of September, 1861, while preparing to carry to their home some ladies, whose carriage had broken down in front of his house, while taking down his overcoat, he overthrew a loaded gun which had been misplaced under it. It was discharged, and the contents were lodged in the side of his face, inflicting a terrible wound. His friend, Dr. H. H. Childs, was called, and other surgeons were soon in attendance. From the first, it was Governor Briggs's impression that the injury would prove fatal; but Dr. Childs felt some little confidence that if he could inspire the sufferer with hope, his life might be saved; and for a brief time the result seemed to answer his expectations.

The wound, however, soon again obtained the mastery, and the patient continued to sink until the evening of the eleventh, when he fell into a gentle slumber, from which he never awoke.

The news of his death was everywhere received with the warmest expressions of sorrow, both from the press and from public bodies. With many of the latter, indeed, he was officially connected : Among them the American Tract Society, The Baptist Foreign Missionary Union, The National Temperance Alliance, The State Sabbath School Union, and the Berkshire Life Insurance Company, of all of which he was president, and several colleges of which he was trustee. [1]

In Pittsfield, every possible demonstration of respect was paid to his memory. All the leading citizens of the town, with many distinguished men from abroad—among them ex-Governors Washburn and Clifford, Chief-Justice Bigelow, Hon. John Z. Goodrich, and the delegates of several of the societies beforementioned, were among the congregation which thronged the Baptist Church at his funeral. The sermon was preached by his pastor, Rev. Dr. Porter, and all the other Protestant clergymen of the town took part in the exercises, which were exceedingly impressive. The sun had already set when the procession

---

[1] He had also declined several similar positions ; among them, that of secretary of the American Sunday School Union, secretary of the American and Foreign Bible Society, and chancellor of the Madison University, New York. In Pittsfield, every possible demonstration of respect was paid to his memory.

reached the spot in the beautiful cemetery where he now rests beneath a handsome and appropriate monument.

A meeting of the citizens of the town was held at the First Congregational Church, and the Sunday evening next after his death, in order to express their sense of the loss they had sustained. Rev. Dr. Todd presided, and addresses were made by him, by Hon. Messrs. Henry H. Childs, James D. Colt and Thomas F. Plunkett of Pittsfield, Hon. Oliver Warner, secretary of the commonwealth, Rev. Dr. Marsh, secretary of the American Temperance Union, Rev. Dr. Warren of Boston, Hon. Thomas Colt, and James Francis, Esq., senior deacon of the Baptist Church in Pittsfield. A similar meeting was held in his old home at Lanesboro. At a meeting of the Berkshire bar, Hon. Increase Sumner, chairman, and Henry W. Taft, Esq., secretary, resolutions reported by Messrs. H. W. Bishop, Increase Sumner and George J. Tucker, eloquently portraying the character of Governor Briggs, and their grief in his death, were passed. Mr. Sumner, in reporting them to the court, paid a most classical tribute to his deceased friend. Chief-Justice Bigelow responded in similar terms, and in the course of his remarks, said :

The death of Governor Briggs will be widely and deeply felt throughout the commonwealth. During the many years which it was his fortune to pass in public life, he became more generally known to the people of the state than most persons who are called to fill high official stations. His great affability of manner, and the republican simplicity which characterized his intercourse with others, allowed every one to approach him with perfect freedom, and he won the hearts of all by the genial traits which distinguished him.

In all the eulogiums which the death of Governor Briggs called forth, there were no more truthful words than these. If there was any one art in which he excelled more than in others, it was that of making friends. In many points, he was a man of eminent talents; in this, of genius. He never missed an opportunity of creating a new friendship, or of deepening an old one ; and the day rarely passed when one or the other, or both, were not accomplished, in personal intercourse ; while, by his public acts and addresses, he reached the hearts of thousands whom he never knew. In closing this imperfect sketch of the man, we cannot do better than to employ the words which a true poet wrote concerning a great soldier:

> Since he had the genius to be loved,
> Let him have the justice to be honored in his grave.

Hon. Julius Rockwell was born at Colebrook, Conn., April 26, 1805. He attended the common-schools, and worked on his father's farm, until he left home to commence his preparatory studies for college. These he pursued with Rev. Dr. Ralph Emerson of Norfolk, Conn., and Rev. Dr. Cooley of Granville, Mass., and entered Yale College in 1822; graduating in 1826. He studied law at Sharon, Conn., at the law-school in New Haven, and with Hon. Henry Hubbard, at Pittsfield. He was admitted to the Berkshire bar in 1830, and commenced the practice of his profession as partner with Mr. Hubbard.

He married, in 1836, Miss Lucy Forbes, daughter of Hon. William P. Walker of Lenox. For four years, from 1834 to 1837, he was a representative in the legislature from Pittsfield, and, for the last three speaker of the house. From 1838 to 1840, he was one of the bank-commissioners. In 1843, he was elected representative in congress, which office he continued to hold until 1854, when he declined re-election; being appointed in that year, by Governor Washburn, to fill the vacancy in the senate, caused by the resignation of Edward Everett. He held the seat during part of the sessions of 1854 and 1855, but was defeated in the legislature of the latter year, by the sudden accession to power of the American party, to which he declined to give his adhesion.

In 1853, he was, with Governor Briggs, a member of the constitutional convention. In 1858, he was again chosen to the legislature from Pittsfield, and was again made speaker of the house of representatives. At the organization of the superior court in 1859, he was appointed one of its judges. In 1865, he removed to Lenox.

James D. Colt was born October 8, 1819, being the eldest son of Ezekiel R. Colt. He graduated at Williams College in 1838; after which he passed two years as tutor in a private family in Natchez, Miss., where he also commenced the study of the law. In the fall of 1830, he returned to Pittsfield, and continued his legal studies with Hon. Julius Rockwell, and at the Cambridge law-school. In 1842, he was admitted to the bar, and entered into a partnership with Mr. Rockwell, which continued until Mr. Rockwell's appointment as judge in 1849. It was a somewhat remarkable compliment to the firm, that both its members were tendered this appointment at the same time. Mr. Colt, however, declined the offer, and, associating with himself his brother-in-law, Thomas Perkins Pingree, he continued in the practice of the law until 1865, when he was appointed one of the justices of the supreme judicial court. His health failing, he resigned in 1866, and visited Europe. His search for health proving successful, and a new vacancy occurring in 1868, he was re-appointed to the supreme bench upon which he still remains.

Besides his judicial office, he was one of the selectmen of Pittsfield in 1848, and represented the town in the legislatures of 1853 and 1854, holding in them the position of chairman of the judiciary committee. On the death of his uncle, Dr. Robert Campbell, in 1866, he was chosen director of the Western railroad.

CHAPTER XXV.

BURIAL-PLACES AND CEMETERIES.

[1754–1875.]

Earliest burial-places—Condition of the first central ground—Movements for a new—Purchase of the First-street ground—The town-lot—Grants and sales of portions of the first burial-ground—Friends object to the removal of the dead—A rural cemetery proposed—Town grants a site to a cemetery-corporation—Preparation of the grounds—Their dedication—Subsequent history—St. Joseph's cemetery.

THE burial-ground near the first meeting-house, established probably about the year 1754,[1] continued in use until the year 1834, and was for that time the exclusive resting-place of the dead of the town, with the exception of a yard in the East Part, and two, used at different times, in the West Part, all of limited size. That at the East Part, in which lie buried the remains of the first white woman who made her home in the town, still remains, and is cared for respectfully; the same is true of the second burial-ground at the West Part; but the first is overgrown by woods, and is only recognized by a few sunken and moss-covered head-stones, which may be seen by the traveler, on his left hand, as he begins to ascend the mountain, on the road to Lebanon Springs.

The first movement for a new burial-ground was in the year 1826,—in that most spirited decade in the town's history, during which so many improvements were made—when an article was inserted in the warrant for town-meeting, "to see if the town would appoint a committee to inquire into the expediency of closing the central burial-ground, and opening another where the ground is less valuable, and better adapted for that purpose."

The town declined to make the inquiry then; and in 1830,

[1] See vol. I., page 159.

Nathan Willis, Calvin Martin, John Churchill, Lemuel Pomeroy, Samuel M. McKay, E. R. Colt, and Butler Goodrich, were appointed to report upon a proposed enlargement of the old ground. Nothing came of it that year; but in 1831, Edward A. Newton, Simeon Brown, and S. L. Russell, who were appointed committee on the same subject, reported before the adjournment of the meeting, recommending the purchase of a new ground, and the planting of shade-trees upon it. Other recommendations contained in the same report were adopted by the meeting; but upon this they were requested to report further. They probably reiterated their recommendation, although no record of it remains; for in 1833, the town directed a committee, consisting of selectmen Nathan Willis, Thomas B. Strong, and Oren Benedict, with Edward A. Newton and John B. Root, to take the matter of procuring land for a new burial-ground into consideration. This committee reported, that for various reasons it must be obvious to every one who would give the slightest consideration to the subject, that, with slight reservations, burials in the old ground must soon cease. It was already so entirely occupied, that it was a common occurence in opening new graves to find them already tenanted by the dead of the past. Indeed, with the exception of a few spots which had been reserved, by common consent, for the use of certain families, this experience was the rule, rather than the exception.

We can well credit the committee's statement. The burial-ground contained only about four acres, some portion of which was a ledge; and it had been in use, at the least, seventy-two years. With its dust was mingled, not only that of the fathers of the town, but that of some of the invaders, and some of the defenders, of the country, in two wars.

The committee recommended the purchase of a lot containing about eight acres, in the south-east corner of the estate of Thomas Melville; being the same which was afterwards known as the new, or First-street, burial-ground. This land was offered for one hundred and twenty-five dollars an acre, with the understanding that a street three rods wide, to be taken, one-half from the purchase, and one-half from the remaining portion of the Melville estate, should be laid along its west side, and be continued, by another small purchase, to connect with the street already opened from East street, through the grounds of Hon. Jonathan Allen.

It seemed to the committee, that the price of the lot offered them was reasonable, and that it was very suitable for the desired purpose; being as near the center of the village as was desirable, generally free from rock, and in particular, as not being subject to the continual objection of a thickly-settled population, becoming daily more thickly settled.

They deemed the amount of land to be purchased full small for its purpose, and would have bargained for more, had they not thought it probable that an addition on the north could, at any time, be purchased on satisfactory terms.

But the progress of events soon proved the fallacy of this latter opinion. The eight acres recommended were purchased, and established as a burial-ground; but a very few years later, the Western railroad was laid through their northern border, and Messrs. Edward A. Newton and Thomas B. Strong, a majority of a committee appointed to purchase of the Melville estate five acres on the north, as had been suggested by them in 1833, reported that they had purchased them for eleven hundred and forty-four dollars. "They were obliged," they said, "to pay for this lot, a higher price, in consequence of the competition of the railroad-company, who wanted it for a gravel-bed; a use which would have greatly injured the neighboring property." This, and the fact that there was no other vacant lot near the center so valuable for the proposed purpose, determined them to make the purchase. The committee concluded their report with the following opinion, which proved as fallacious as their earlier one: "a provision is now made for the remains of the dead, for many years to come, in all respects suited to the wants and character of the town; but as it will not all be actually required for this use, for several years, the committee recommend the leasing of it, as it may be needed."

This plot was never used for burial-purposes; but became known as the Town Lot, and was the scene of cattle-shows, menageries, and circuses, until it was sold in 1863 to Samuel W. Bowerman and Robert W. Adam.

Encroachments upon the limits of the old First burial-ground began with the taking from it a portion of the park, in 1790. They were continued by the lease to Dr. Timothy Childs, and the sale to Jonathan Allen & Brother, mentioned elsewhere. Other sales and grants followed, until the whole western border of the ground, to the depth of seventy-six feet, was disposed of. The last sales in this quarter took place in 1848, when the line between the portion sold and that retained, south of School street, was straightened, by the sale of certain pieces of land for the sum of six thousand and fifty dollars, which, by vote of the town, was divided among the Protestant parishes in it, in the following proportion: eleven hundred and forty dollars each to the First and South Congregational, the Baptist, Methodist, and St. Stephen's parishes; and two hundred to the Second Congregational; reserving one hundred and fifty dollars to defray the expenses of the sale, and of the removal of the dead to the new cemetery. Lots of land from the burial-ground had previously been granted to the Baptist, Episcopal, and Methodist churches, which the two last had sold, and the other parishes had built upon, as stated in the account of their respective churches. In 1849, another portion, in the north-east corner, was set apart as the site for a high-school house.

All, or nearly all, these appropriations of the burial-ground to the purposes of the living, required the removal of the dead, at first to other portions of the old ground, and to the new ground after that was opened.

This disturbance of their deceased friends was generally acquiesced in by the living, although very reluctantly. A few, however, refused their consent; and one gentleman even preferred to leave the remains of his mother, buried before the door of the lock-up, which the town had built in its vicinity, rather than to have her grave disturbed.

But, in the spring of 1849, Mr. Joel Stevens, a member of one of the oldest families in the town, received a note, to the following effect, from the selectmen:

In disinterring and removing the remains of the dead from the old burial-ground to the new yard, according to a vote of the town, we have arrived at the graves of your grandfather's and father's family, and request you to be present to-morrow morning, as their remains will be removed.

In response to this summons, Mr. Stevens appeared promptly on the spot, and seeking out the chairman of the selectmen, Col. George S. Willis, notified him that he forbade the disturbing a particle of the earth that surrounded the graves of his friends, warning him that he would sue both the town and every person engaged in the act, if it were done; adding, "if you wish to see the title to that ground, read it on the moss-covered head-stones. Remove these remains as you propose, and in ten years you must remove them again. Then what will you find to remove?"

Colonel Willis expressed his sympathy with Mr. Stevens' feelings; and, meeting him the next day, informed him that the board had determined not to subject themselves or the town to legal troubles, and would let the matter rest until the next town-meeting.

Mr. Stevens replied, that, since their interview, he had been thinking over the feasiblity of a cemetery, that should be large enough to suffice the town for some hundreds of years, and where the dead might rest undisturbed for all time. If such were provided, he would consent to the removal of his friends; and he thought that others, like situated, would also be satisfied. Colonel Willis, after brief consideration, warmly approved the idea, although he doubted whether the town would be ready to adopt it. He, however, drafted a petition, requesting the selectmen to call a town-meeting for the purpose of considering the subject, and Mr. Stevens undertook to procure the requisite number of signatures.

In doing so, his first effort was to procure the signature of some prominent citizen to head the petition; but after applying to several—some of whom refused on account of the hopelessness of the plan, although they approved it, and others because they deemed it unnecessary—Mr. Stevens headed the list with his own name, and was able easily to obtain the signatures of other respectable citizens, although not distinguished for wealth or position; and that in the space of twenty minutes.

The meeting thus called was attended by an unusually large proportion of the voters of the town, nearly all of whom agreed that something must be done in the proposed direction. Hon. E. A. Newton, one of those who, although approving the object, had declined to head the petition, opened the discussion by saying:

I am overwhelmed with surprise, Mr. Chairman, to see before me such a gathering of the citizens of this town, to consider the establishment of a cemetery, for the lasting repose of our dead. * * *

When my friend Stevens requested me to sign a petition for the calling of this meeting, I thought that anything of the kind would be premature. But this assemblage, and the feeling expressed here, satisfies me that now is the time to act. I thank my friend Stevens for originating this project, and his perseverance in it. I hope he will go on with the assurance, as far as it lies in my power, of my most hearty co-operation.

Mr. Newton's remarks were received with applause, and everything, thenceforward, went smoothly for the project. The only practical action of the meeting, however, was the appointment of Thomas B. Strong, Thomas A. Gold, Samuel A. Churchill, Ensign H. Kellogg, and Joel Stevens, as a committee to take into consideration the whole subject of the present and future accommodation of the town, for the burial of its dead, and report a plan for that purpose, looking to the permanent security of their remains. Of course the removal of the dead from the old ground was suspended. At the meeting of this committee, Mr. Stevens proposed the purchase of grounds containing from one hundred to one hundred and fifty acres, and the proposition was finally agreed to. They also visited a number of spots suggested as suitable for a cemetery, and became fully satisfied that the farm of George W. Campbell, on the west side of Wahconah street, and three-quarters of a mile north of the park, was the best adapted to that purpose, and very nearly all that could be desired. They reported this opinion to the town, in September, 1849, and, at their own request, were discharged; Solomon L. Russell, Thomas F. Plunkett, and Oliver S. Root, being appointed to continue the inquiry as to a proper location.

In April, 1850, the last-named committee reported, sustaining the recommendations of its predecessor, as to the necessity of a cemetery, and the advantages of Mr. Campbell's farm as a location. This farm, they said, contained one hundred and thirty-one acres of land, of which one hundred would make good burial-ground. It was at a convenient distance from the village, and its general features were favorable for making it meet the requirements of taste ; the land being rolling, having two or three small groves, and facilities for two or three fountains.

The town accepted the report, and passed the following resolutions:

Resolved, That the town purchase the farm of George W. Campbell at the price reported by the committee, viz.: five thousand five hundred and fifty dollars, payable, with its annual interest, in five or ten years, as the committee may determine.

Resolved, That a committee of ten be chosen, to make a contract with a cemetery-corporation, provided such a corporation should be duly organized under the laws of the state; by which said corporation shall be under obligations to furnish for the use of the town, out of the land so purchased, ample provision for free burial for all who may not be disposed to become owners of lots in said cemetery; and that the treasurer of the town is hereby authorized and directed to execute a deed, and convey said farm to said corporation, when organized, under such conditions and restrictions, giving them such privileges and powers as said committee may direct, to be inserted in the deed, and which shall secure the town ample and free sites.

The committee appointed under these resolutions consisted of Calvin Martin, Solomon L. Russell, James D. Colt, 2d, Thomas G. Atwood, Moses H. Baldwin, James Francis, Edward A. Newton, Abel West, Olcott Osborne, and George W. Campbell.

A cemetery-corporation was organized, under the general law for that purpose, on the 8th of April, 1850; and, at meetings held on the twenty-second and twenty-third, by-laws were adopted, and the following officers elected: president, Calvin Martin; directors, Solomon L. Russell, M. H. Baldwin, O. S. Root, Thomas F. Plunkett, George W. Campbell, N. S. Dodge, Henry Clark, Robert Colt, David Campbell; treasurer, James H. Dunham; secretary, Elias Merwin.

The grounds conveyed to this corporation by the town are happily described in the pamphlet-account of the dedication of the cemetery, as of rare fitness for the purposes for which they were set apart. "Alternate woods and lawns vary the scene. The irregularity of its surface, now breaking away into gentle inclinations and rounded knolls, adds greatly to its attractions. * * * Fine trees dot the landscape. Rural sights meet the eye wherever it is turned. Hidden within the deep shade of the woods, the wanderer is shut out from the world; but as he emerges upon the uplands, the spires of the village, the quiet homesteads of the valley, and the distant mountains, break upon him with a beauty almost enrapturing."

The corporation accepted these grounds upon the prescribed terms, and in its turn, intrusted the whole matter of transforming them into such a rural cemetery as was desired, to the hands of its directors.

Most of this board were men of liberal and cultivated tastes, well aware of the difficult and delicate nature of the task imposed upon them; but they entered upon it with hopefulness and zeal; having, moreover, the hearty sympathy and co-operation of the many of the same class in the town. "Feeling," they say in their final report, "the responsibility attached to their doings; aware that the alternative for Pittsfield, between a cemetery of rural beauty, and the repulsive hillocked grave-yard, rested upon their deliberations; fully informed of the conflicting opinions that agitated the public mind in relation to the spot selected; they yet resolutely and earnestly, with entire confidence in the ultimate taste, judgment, and public spirit of the people, set about their task."

The corporation had no funds, and the directors had only the sale of lots in the future to look to for the reimbursement of any outlays which they might make. Relying upon this, however, one gentleman of the board advanced five hundred dollars, and pledged three hundred more when it should be wanted. Other members, as the work went on, furnished funds for its completion upon the same guarantee.

Dr. Horatio Stone, of New York, an artist who had already achieved a reputation by his skill and taste in laying out and embellishing other cemeteries, was engaged, first to prepare the designs for that contemplated on the Campbell farm, and then to carry them into execution. To his fine taste and peculiar genius, it is primarily due that the great capabilities of the location for park-like effects were as fully developed as the means at the command of the corporation would permit.

In the meantime, the board was busily and faithfully devoted to its work. Meetings were held weekly. Committees of design, of farming, of finance, and of inspection were active in their duties. Visits were made to the cemeteries of Albany, Springfield, New York, Providence and New Haven; and correspondence seeking advice was carried on with the trustees of other similar institutions. In short, all the multitudinous work which was required of such a board was performed with enthusiastic faithfulness.

At the close of the summer of 1850, although Doctor Stone's plans had been but incompletely carried out, it was determined to consecrate the cemetery, and to open it for use, in accordance with an earnest desire of the people who reluctantly continued to inter the dead in the old burial-grounds. But, although much remained to be done, much also had been accomplished. Without trenching upon their wild-wood character, the groves had been rounded into grace, and freed from the unsightliness of decay and of careless destruction. Man had restored to nature something of the symmetry of which his rude and hasty greed had robbed her. The waters of Onota brook had been trained in a winding stream to a beautiful lawn, where they spread into a small lake, reflecting its fringe of trees in mirror-like perfection. Miles of roads and paths wound in gentle curves through every part of the grounds; while along its western border, one broad straight avenue was prepared to receive its long vista of trees. Everywhere the beautiful present prophesied a more beautiful future.

Monday, the 9th of September, was assigned for the dedication of this lovely spot to its solemn uses, by appropriate ceremonies, and by the best consecration which eloquence and poetry could give it. All classes of citizens had, from the first inception of the work in town-meeting, given it their cordial aid and sympathy, and it was determined that all should take part in hallowing the ground, where each might expect to find his last resting-place.

The appointed day dawned, bright and beautiful; and, at an early hour, the people began to gather in the cemetery. At half-past ten o'clock in the forenoon, the procession, escorted by the Housatonic and Pontoosuc engine-companies, and consisting of the officers of the corporation, the clergy and other invited guests, citizens and strangers, in carriages and on foot, formed at the park, under the direction of Col. George S. Willis, as chief marshal, and moved to the grounds. Here, after marching through the avenue around the lake, named in honor of St. John, the beloved apostle, the assembly grouped itself about the speaker's stand on the northern slope of Chapel hill.

Calvin Martin, Esq., president of the association, opened the exercises by a brief sketch of the burial-places of the town. There were religious exercises, in which Rev. Mr. Miner of the Baptist Church, Rev. Dr. Chapman of the Episcopal Church, Rev. Dr. Todd of the First Church, and Rev. Dr. Humphrey took part. Original odes by John C. Hoadley, Mrs. Emily P. Dodge and Mrs. J. R. Morewood, were sung by a choir under the direction of Col. Asa Barr.

The dedicatory address was delivered by Rev. Henry Neill of

Lenox, and consisted chiefly of reasons why living men should institute memorials for the dead; the argument being illustrated by exquisitely-told instances from history. We quote the opening passage:

"Have we been persuaded—an assembly of the living—to look upon the very ground where we may sleep? Impelled by a desire to do honor to the dead, have we come within the precincts of a spot where every shadow seems now to deepen, and where the mountains point so significantly to the skies?

The sense of an unpaid tribute has summoned us from our homes. Affection, in its reverence, and depths of tenderness has longed to give itself expression in some outward, significant and permanent form, until it can no longer be denied. Out of the hearts of a large community the declaration at length has come; that the remains of departed worth shall hereafter find a safe retreat, and pledges of remembrance foretokening their recompense of a higher reward."

The dedicatory poem, one of the choicest productions of its class, was delivered by Dr. O. W. Holmes, and is published in his works.

A quarter of a century has elapsed since that day of consecration, during which the cemetery has constantly increased in beauty. The earth that was then untenanted has become the resting-place of the dead of all the town's past. It is hallowed by the commingling dust of the patriots who fought in all the nation's wars; of the divines who have preached the word of God to all the generations since the town first had a settled pastor; of the statesmen whose fame has been that of Pittsfield, and the men of business, who have built up her fortunes. To those who have read these volumes, the names which are inscribed on the monuments which dot these grounds, will indeed be eloquent.

A few incidents in the history of the corporation since the dedication of the cemetery, remain to be noted. Calvin Martin continued to be president until his death, in 1868, when he was succeeded by George W. Campbell, who still holds the office. John Lane became clerk and treasurer in 1852, and was succeeded in 1854, by Dr. Oliver S. Root, who continued in office until his death in 1870. George P. Briggs, Esq., has held the office from that date.

The bounds of the cemetery have been slightly altered and

enlarged, by an exchange of lands with John Weller, and by a bequest of ten acres from Elisha Tracy, which helped to rectify its south boundary.

Among the earlier projects in connection with the cemetery, was a building on the summit of Chapel hill, in which funeral-services might be held, and in which busts, statues, and other sepulchral monuments, too delicate for exposure to the weather, might be preserved. And in connection with it was to be a receiving-tomb. The plan for a chapel fell gradually into neglect; but a receiving-tomb grew more and more a matter of necessity, as that in the First-street burial-ground became more and more unfit for the temporary deposit of the dead in winter. In 1858, a committee was appointed by the directors, to report plans before they took any definite action, and the subject was a matter of continued deliberation, committees being annually appointed to consider it, until 1866. There was much difference of opinion as to the class of stone and the general character of the tomb, as well as its location; but the delay in building it was mainly due to the lack of funds. And in the year named, the directors, finding the condition of the treasury such as to warrant the expenditure of two thousand dollars for the purpose, the proposal of C. A. Werden, to build the tomb for that sum, was accepted; and Rev. Henry Clark, Mr. William G. Backus, and Dr. O. S. Root, were appointed to superintend the work. The location selected was on the south side of Chapel hill, and the tomb is a Gothic structure of gray marble finished with oak.

In 1871, a plan by which proprietors of lots might provide for their perpetual care, was submitted by a committee consisting of Messrs. James D. Colt, and George P. Briggs, and adopted by the corporation.

Under this plan, the corporation receive on trust from the proprietors of any lot, a sum of money, not less than one hundred dollars, which they deposit in some savings-bank of the state, and apply the income, whenever it may be necessary, to keep in suitable repair and preservation, the lot designated. The directors, twice every year, cause an inspection of these lots, in order that the trust may be duly executed. Should any surplus of the income from this fund remain, it is applied to the ornamenting and preserving of the cemetery-grounds, or to some other purpose for which the funds of the corporation may lawfully be used

The fund for the perpetual care of lots now amounts to one thousand dollars, and is deposited in the Berkshire County Savings Bank.

The original projectors of the cemetery anticipated that it would be the burial-place of all the dead of the town, whatever their religious belief. The Catholic population, however, desired a ground consecrated by their peculiar rites, and set apart for their exclusive use, and it was found impossible to appropriate such a portion of the cemetery as would be satisfactory to them, for that purpose.

In May, 1853, therefore, Rev. Patrick Cuddihy, pastor of St. Joseph's Church, purchased ten acres of land upon a beautiful elevation, some hundred rods north of the Pittsfield cemetery, and on the opposite side of Onota brook. This was properly graded, planted, and intersected with walks, making it a very beautiful and tasteful spot; after which it was duly consecrated under the name of St. Joseph's Cemetery.

Being largely used for the interment of persons dying in neighboring towns, as well as in Pittsfield, it soon became apparent, however, that its extent was altogether too limited, and in 1873, Rev. Edward H. Purcell purchased twenty acres adjoining, so that additional space might be added, as it was required. And in the summer of 1875, ten acres of this tract were added to St. Joseph's Cemetery, and properly laid out and planted.

CHAPTER XXVI.

THE CIVIL WAR—THE SOLDIERS' MONUMENT AND IMPROVEMENT
OF THE PARK.

[1861-1872.]

Pittsfield soldiers of 1775, and 1861, compared — Pittsfield Guard — Allen Guard—First soldiers for the war—Henry S. Briggs—Pollock Guard and Tenth regiment—William Pollock—Twentieth and Twenty-first regiments —Lieutenant-Colonel Richardson—Western Bay State or Thirty-first regiment—Thirty-fourth regiment—Camp Briggs—Thirty-seventh regiment— Forty-ninth regiment—General W. F. Bartlett—Eighth regiment—Other regiments—Bounties—Recruiting and patriotic speeches—S. W. Bowerman—Labors of the selectmen—Ladies aid-societies—Death of a patriotic young lady—Mrs. C. T. Fenn—Mrs. J. R. Morewood—Soldiers' monument —Improvement of the park—Dedication of the monument—Speeches of General Bartlett and Hon. Thomas Colt—Oration of George William Curtis.

IN the history of Pittsfield, the years 1860 and 1861 presented a remarkable parallel to the revolutionary epoch of 1774 and 1775. That the people of the town in the later crisis of the nation's fate, manifested the same spirit which their forefathers exhibited in the earlier, and that the measures which they adopted had a general similarity, was by no means peculiar. The same was almost universally true of old New England towns. That which we think remarkable in the Pittsfield story, was the almost exact repetition of military measures in their details. Happily, there was no occasion for the reorganizing and regulating action which distracted the town at the opening of the revolution. The government and the people were in full accord ; and, instead of the rich and powerful tory-faction, which the fathers found it necessary to repress with a strong hand, those who opposed patriotic action in the war against the rebellion of 1861 were altogether of insignificant influence. The problem was simply to organize and make effective an almost unanimous public sentiment.

Many years previous to 1860, the spirit of reform had, in Massachusetts, swept away the old militia-system, with its annual musters, its gorgeous generals and colonels, its spirited and trim volunteer companies, its Falstaffian "flood-wood," and its many vexations and abuses. In the new law, provision was made for a few well-trained volunteer corps in the cities and large towns; and these proved what the theory of the law contemplated, the nurseries of military spirit and skill. But, from the disbanding of the Berkshire Grays, about the year 1836, there was no military company in Pittsfield until 1853, when the Pittsfield Guards were organized. This corps, for several years, maintained an excellent reputation, under the command successively of Captains George R. Groot, Henry S. Briggs, John Van Vechten, Robert W. Adam, Lemuel Wild, and Charles M. Whelden. But, in the summer of 1860, when Governor Banks, with wise forethought, was striving to revive the military spirit of the commonwealth, the company was in a hopelessly languishing condition; and, in the excitement of the pending presidential election, every attempt to re-organize it on a better footing failed.

In this dilemma, Mr. D. J. Dodge appealed for aid to Hon. Thomas Allen, who promptly responded by a gift of fifteen hundred dollars. This fund was increased from other sources to two thousand dollars. The company was reorganized under the name of the Allen Guard, and Henry S. Briggs, resigning the position of major, was chosen captain. The company was already supplied with a full complement of the most approved arms and equipage; and in November it was in an effective condition.

On the 16th of January, 1861, Governor Andrew issued his order directing commanding officers of volunteer companies to discharge all men who, from any cause, would be unable or unwilling to respond at once to any call of the president of the United States, and to fill their places with others ready for any exigency which might arise. This order was considered by the company on the 31st, and the following resolutions, prepared by Captain Briggs, adopted; all the members except one assenting:

> Whereas, the commander-in-chief has, by general order declared that recent and passing events require that Massachusetts should be ready to furnish her quota of troops upon any requisition of the president of the United States, to aid in the maintenance of the laws and peace of the Union; and has, by the same order, notified the volunteer-militia to be in readiness to respond at once to the call of the president of the

HISTORY OF PITTSFIELD.   611

United States; at the same time advising the immediate discharge of such as may be indisposed or unable so to respond,

Resolved, That the members of Company A, 1st Battalion of Infantry, having recently enlisted and been enrolled under the laws of the commonwealth, take this occasion to re-affirm the declaration deliberately made in the adoption of the company by-laws, wherein we avow that one, and a prominent, object of our association is to prepare ourselves to preserve those rights and privileges that have been transmitted to us from our patriotic forefathers, in the happy and admirable government we now enjoy.

Resolved, That, while none more than we regret the "recent events" that have called forth the order of the commander-in-chief, and none would more than we deplore the realization of the apprehensions which have made it the wise precaution of the executive authorities of the state and nation to prepare for the protection of the government against the assaults of its enemies; yet, with a full recognition and just appreciation of the responsibilities which we have assumed or incurred by our enlistment, we have no disposition to repudiate those obligations, nor will we seek to avoid any sacrifices which may be demanded of us as citizen-soldiers in the sacred cause of the Union, the constitution and the laws.

The Allen Guard, by this act, became what would in 1774 and 1775, have been called minute-men.

The winter of 1860-61 passed very much as that of 1774-5 passed. The minds of the people were gradually familiarized with the idea of a conflict which, although all knew it to be imminent, few realized as an almost present fact. The clergy, the press, and patriotic leaders gave voice and pen to rouse and sustain the spirit of devotion to the Union; but passing events, now as in the opening of the revolution, proved more eloquent than words. The bombardment of Fort Sumter, like the "Regulating Acts" of 1774, made broad the line between those who would defend and those who would surrender what Massachusetts believed to be legitimate government. But, not as in the revolution, now, no traitorous voice, sufficient to be heeded, was raised in opposition to the most strenuous measures in defense of freedom.

In the meantime the Allen Guard maintained a system of semi-weekly drills, and were cheered by the encouragement of citizens; and, what the young soldiers most prized, of the ladies, who once a month witnessed the evolutions at their armory. It was well understood that the call to arms might be received at any moment; but when it came, like most long-expected events, it startled the community.

Early in April, Governor Andrew received from President Lincoln a request for fifteen hundred men, and the number was almost immediately increased to a force of four regiments. The circumstances did not admit of delay, and at first he did not intend to draw any troops from the western counties, but to take those nearest Boston. The Eighth regiment, however, lacked two companies, and Captain Briggs[1] who chanced to be in Boston, representing that his company was prepared for immediate service, it was attached to that corps; and Pittsfield thus obtained the distinction of being the only town in western Massachusetts which contributed a company to the first contingent of troops which the commonwealth sent to the defense of the Union.

On the evening of April 17th, Captain Briggs transmitted, by telegraph to Lieutenant H. H. Richardson, the order for the company to report the next evening at Springfield, where it would join the regiment on its way to Washington. The night of the 17th, and the following day, was an interval of excitement, animation and preparation, such as had not been known in Pittsfield since the revolution. The members of the guard and their families were of course busy in making their personal arrangements. And as soon as the order calling for the company became public, a large number of the wealthier citizens met and guaranteed the sum of five thousand dollars, to provide for the comfort of its members and the aid of such of their families as might need assistance during their absence. At noon on the 18th, the ringing of the bells, for the first time during the war, summoned the citizens to the town-hall, where the venerable H. H. Childs presiding, addresses were made by the chairman, Messrs. James D. Colt, Ensign H. Kellogg, Walter Laflin and others. A vote was passed, thanking the guard

---

[1] Henry Shaw Briggs was born at Lanesboro, August 1, 1824, being the second son of Governor George N. Briggs. He graduated at Williams College in 1844. Studied law at the Cambridge law-school, and was admitted to practice in 1848. He represented Pittsfield in the legislature of 1856, was police-justice of the town in 1857, and justice of the district-court of central Berkshire from 1869 to 1873, and was auditor of the commonwealth from 1865 to 1869. In 1873 he was appointed one of the five general appraisers of the United States custom-houses. He married, August 6, 1849, Mary E., daughter of Nathaniel P. Talcott of Lanesboro.

for their alacrity in responding to the call of the government, and declaring that the town ought to make abundant provision for the members of the company and their families. And to carry this vote into effect, a committee was appointed, consisting of Thomas F. Plunkett, William Pollock, Theodore Pomeroy, E. H. Kellogg, Thomas Allen, and Thomas Colt.

At about half-past six o'clock in the evening, the guard— seventy-eight men strong—in their rich uniform of gray and gold: soon to be laid aside for the loose blouse and trousers of active service—marched through the crowded streets to the depot, and took the cars for Springfield; just twenty-three hours after the receipt of Captain Briggs's order; thus a little bettering the time of the minute-men who left Pittsfield, in the Lexington alarm on the 22d of April, 1774. The latter had, however, to collect their men from a wider extent of territory, and to await the gathering of the regiment from all central Berkshire.

The scenes and emotions which marked this first departure of Pittsfield soldiers in the war for the Union, cannot be described; and the meager outlines which we are able to give, will but feebly suggest the true picture to those who have not participated in similar events. Railroad square was thronged with men, women, and children, surging with excitement and enthusiasm; and evidently brought by the scene before them to a clearer realization of the grandeur and sadness of the conflict, which the thick coming telegrams of the day foreshadowed; while, on the platform, closer around the position of the guard, were witnessed the varied partings of kindred, lovers, and friends, with those never so well loved as then; partings in which pride and joy struggled strangely with grief and sad forebodings.

Within the next four years, the spot became but too familiar with similar scenes; but there never could come again the same emotions as when, for the first time, in the presence of a great, unaccustomed and unmeasured peril, men recognized in their intimate friends and acquaintances, the compeers of the heroes of Lexington and Bunker hill. As, amid cheers half choked with feeling, the cars bore away their precious burden, they left a people inspired by the events of the previous twenty-four hours, not only with a greater, but with an essentially new, sense of faith in and devotion to their country.

The march of the Eighth regiment to Philadelphia, was distinguished only by the enthusiasm which marked the passage of all the earlier Union troops through the northern states. Arriving at Philadelphia on the evening of the 19th, it was quartered at the Girard House; but at two o'clock on the following morning, the Allen Guard and the Salem Zouaves were aroused from their repose on the bare floor. On the day before, the slaughter of the Massachusetts soldiers, of the Sixth regiment, had taken place at Baltimore; and now General Butler, who accompanied the Eighth regiment, learned that it was the intention of the rebels to seize the ferry at Havre de Gras, thus closing the only remaining line of railroad-communication between the north and Washington. It was General Butler's intention to send the two companies forward by steamer, to thwart this design of the enemy. But not being able to obtain the steamer, the whole regiment was sent forward by rail; and when within two miles of the ferry, the two companies were again detached for their original purpose.

Perryville, which is the north terminus, was reported to be occupied by a rebel force; and, for the first time, the order was given to load with ball. All believed that they would shortly be in action, and there was doubtless even more trepidation than is generally experienced by young recruits in similar circumstances, as officers as well as men were entirely without experience, and they expected to fight superior numbers in an enemy's country. They, however, displayed perfect coolness, and in some instances even chivalric ardor; although it was not put to the final test of actual conflict.

The ferry-boat—the large steamer Maryland—was occupied without opposition. Adjutant-General Schouler, in his history of Massachusetts in the war, states that the Maryland was sent to Perryville by order of President Felton of the Baltimore and Philadelphia railroad, for the express purpose of conveying the Eighth regiment to Annapolis. If this was the case, neither the officers or men of the Allen Guard ever heard of it until the publication of Mr. Schouler's book, although the whole regiment at once proceeded in the steamer to Annapolis, and the fact would seem likely to have been made known by her officers and crew.

After a brief service at Annapolis, on board the frigate Constitution, the Allen Guard were sent to Fort McHenry, Baltimore harbor, and did not rejoin the regiment for three weeks. During the remainder of its service, the guard was employed at Washing-

GREYTOWER. RESIDENCE OF MRS. WILLIAM POLLOCK.

ton, Baltimore, and neighboring points. It returned home without having met the enemy in battle; but it proved an excellent military school, and its members showed good soldierly qualities. The greater part of them afterwards served in other corps, either as officers or privates; there being among them one brigadier-general, two lieutenant-colonels, one major, four captains, and seven lieutenants.

Shortly after the departure of the Allen Guard, came the president's call for seventy-five thousand men to serve for three years, six regiments being assigned to Massachusetts, of which one—the Tenth—was recruited in the western counties. The system of recruiting, by calling upon towns to furnish their proper quota, not having been yet established, Governor Andrew commissioned Messrs. Thomas Colt and George H. Laflin, to raise a company in Pittsfield and its vicinity.

These gentlemen entered upon their work with zeal, and received the heartiest co-operation of the town and its citizens. William Pollock, Esq.,[1] gave one thousand dollars towards the outfit of the company, and it took the name of the Pollock Guard. In the Tenth regiment, it was designated as Company D. It went into barracks at the hall on the agricultural grounds, May 2, 1861, and on the 4th, Thomas W. Clapp, who had been a cadet at West Point, was chosen captain.[2]

[1] William Pollock was born at Neilston, Renfrew county, Scotland, February 9, 1809. In 1836, he went to Canada, where he purchased a farm of one hundred acres, a large portion of which he cleared up with his own hands. But not liking farming, he sold his land and went to Brainard's Bridge, Columbia county, N. Y., where he was employed as a mule-spinner, by a Mr. Rider, who soon appointed him superintendent of his entire cotton-warp mills. He afterwards removed to South Adams, as superintendent of a similar mill, owned by the same gentleman. This mill he soon purchased, and after running it a few years, built a large, stone factory upon its site. Having become one of the most prosperous manufacturers in Berkshire, he removed to Pittsfield in 1856, where he purchased the handsome stone cottage erected by Mr. Gaius Burnap, on Elm street. This place was surrounded by very ample and beautiful grounds, and Mr. Pollock, in 1864-5, enlarged the house to a spacious and elegant mansion, to which he gave the name of Gray Tower, it being built of gray lime-stone. During his residence in Pittsfield, he was one of the most successful business-men of the town. He married October 17, 1855, Miss Susan M. Learned, of Watervliet, N. Y. He died December 9, 1866.

[2] After the war, Captain Clapp, who was a son of Col. Thaddeus Clapp, took the name of Warren T. C. Colt, by permission of the probate court.

While they remained in barracks, the committee, appointed April 18th, provided rations at the expense of the town, the average cost per week being one hundred and eighty dollars; and also expended for clothing about four hundred dollars, in addition to the gift of Mr. Pollock. On the 15th of June, the guard took the cars for Springfield, and joined the regiment. A short time before their departure, they had done excellent firemen's service at the burning of the Pittsfield Woolen Mills, and they left the town under the half-burned national flag of the factory, which had been given them by the proprietors.

Captain Briggs of the Allen Guard was appointed colonel of the Tenth regiment On the 16th of July, it left Springfield. It first went into battle May 31, 1862, at Fair Oaks, Va., where Colonel Briggs was severely wounded; and before his recovery, he was appointed brigadier-general.

The regiment afterwards took part in the following engagements: Battles on the Peninsula, Fredericksburg, Chancellorsville, Gettysburg, Rappahannock Station, Wilderness, Spottsylvania, North Anna River, Cold Harbor.

The Allen Guard returned to Pittsfield, August 8, 1861, and were received with enthusiasm; Ex-Governor Briggs presiding over an assemblage in the park, where Hon. Thomas Allen made a speech of welcome, and presented a banner in behalf of his sisters.

Lieut. Henry H. Richardson, who came home in command, immediately announced his intention to take the field again, and was commissioned captain in the Twenty-first regiment, for which he raised a number of recruits, whom pressing exigencies of the service rendered it necessary to send to the Twentieth. Still he took with him a good number of Pittsfield men for the Twenty-first; in which he distinguished himself as a gallant officer, and rose to the rank of lieutenant-colonel.

On the 1st of October, 1861, the adjutant-general of the army issued an order forming the six New England states into a military department, and providing that Maj.-General Benj. F. Butler should command it while recruiting his division. A controversy arose from this measure, between the war-department and Governor Andrew, which we have not space to enter into. A statement of but one side of the story occupies thirty pages of Schouler's History of Massachusetts in the Civil War. But in spite of the governor's remonstances, General Butler proceeded to raise two regiments in Massachusetts, known respectively as the Eastern and Western Bay State regiments. The latter was recruited in the fall and winter of 1861, and had its barracks at the agricultural hall, in Pittsfield, which took the name of Camp Seward. The regiment, while in barracks, was under the command of Charles M. Whelden of Pittsfield, who received a warrant from General Butler, to act as lieutenant-colonel, with the promise of that rank when the regiment should be finally organized. The men were raised rapidly and economically, and were well drilled.

The regiment was mustered into the United States service in the latter part of 1861, and left the state February 21, 1862. The special service for which the six regiments were required, turned out to be the expedition which resulted in the capture of New Orleans; and the Western Bay State was, according to General Butler's promise, the first to enter that city after its surrender. In the winter of 1862, the controversy between the war-department and the governor was settled, by the transfer of the regiments in question to the state, and the Western Bay State became the Thirty-first Massachusetts. The governor, however, confirmed most of the appointments, but refused commissions to Lieutenant-Colonel Whelden and a few others.

The regiment was mustered out of service in December, 1864; but left a battalion of five companies, which remained until September, 1865. It took part in the engagements at Bisland, Port Hudson, Brashear City, Sabine Cross Roads, Cane River Crossing, Alexandria, Governor Moor's Plantation, Yellow Bayou, and in the several actions during the siege of Mobile.[1]

In the Thirty-fourth regiment, mustered into service at Worcester, August 13, 1862, were two companies raised at Pittsfield, by Captains Andrew Potter and William H. Cooley. No regiment suffered more severely, or sustained itself more gallantly. It was with General Hunter in his starvation-march up the Shenandoah; and in the first battle one-half the men in the Pittsfield companies were either killed or wounded. It fought in the battles of New Market, Piedmont, Lynchburg, Snicker's Gap, Martinsburg, Halltown, Berryville, Winchester, Fisher's Hill, Cedar Creek, Hatcher's Run, Petersburg.

[1] Lieutenant-Colonel Whelden, after the change in the officers of the regiment, served on General Butler's general staff, and in other positions.

In August, 1862, a camp of instruction for the reception of recruits from Berkshire, Hampden, and Hampshire counties, was established at Pittsfield, under the name of Camp Briggs; the grounds selected being those afterwards occupied by the Berkshire Pleasure Park, on Elm street, and about a mile and a half east of Park square. Col. William R. Lee, of the Twentieth regiment, was assigned to the command; but was relieved on the 12th of August, by Adj. Oliver Edwards of the Tenth, who was commissioned major, and instructed to organize the Thirty-seventh regiment. Two weeks afterwards, the regiment was organized with the following officers: Colonel, Oliver Edwards of Springfield; lieutenant-colonel, Alonzo E. Goodrich of Pittsfield; major, George L. Montague of Hadley; adjutant, Thomas G. Colt of Pittsfield; quartermaster, Daniel J. Dodge of Pittsfield.

On the 5th of September, in reply to an inquiry how soon the Thirty-seventh would be ready to proceed to Washington, Colonel Edwards wrote, " we are ready and ask no delay; but await orders." The regiment was not quite full; General Lee was in Maryland, and Washington was also threatened on the south side. The Thirty-seventh, therefore, left Pittsfield on Sunday, September 7th, and soon afterwards was attached to Couch's division of the Sixth Corps, then at Downsville, Maryland. From that time to the close of the war, it performed the most gallant service, and was engaged in the following battles: First Fredericksburg, Va., Mayres Heights, Salem Heights, Second Fredericksburg, Gettysburg, Rappahannock Station, Mine Run, Va., the three days Wilderness, four engagements at Spottsylvania, two engagements and five days fighting at Cold Harbor, battles at Petersburg in 1864, Fort Stevens, Snicker's Ferry, and Charlestown, Va.

Immediately after the evacuation of Camp Briggs by the Thirty-seventh regiment, it was occupied by the Forty-ninth, which was the only regiment raised exclusively in Berkshire county; and was enlisted for nine months, although it served for twelve. The first company to go into camp was that of Capt. I. C. Weller, which had been four days in barracks at Burbank's hall. Company B, Capt. Charles R. Garlick, followed on the same day; and, before the 14th, each of these companies numbered a hundred men. Both were commanded by Pittsfield captains, and shortly following them, came Company C, Capt. Charles T. Plunkett;

early in October, Capt. Zenas C. Renne, also of Pittsfield, joined the regiment with eighty-eight men.

On the 20th of September, Capt. William F. Bartlett of the Twentieth regiment, who was invalided on account of the loss of a leg at the siege of Yorktown, took command of the post. Captain Bartlett, although a severe disciplinarian, soon became extremely popular with the regiment, as well as the citizens, and, the officers being instructed by him daily, their companies showed great efficiency.[1]

The regiment left Pittsfield for Camp Wool, Worcester; and there the subalterns, who had been previously elected by the respective companies, chose the following field-officers: Colonel, William F. Bartlett of Boston; lieutenant-colonel, Samuel B. Sumner of Great Barrington; major, Charles T. Plunkett of Pittsfield. Colonel Bartlett appointed his college-friend, Benjamin C. Miflin of Boston, adjutant, and Henry B. Brewster of Pittsfield, quartermaster, which gave them respectively the rank of first-lieutenant. The non-commissioned staff were sergeant-major, Henry J. Wylie, Pittsfield; quartermaster-sergeant, George E. Howard, Pittsfield; commissary-sergeant, H. H. Northrop, Cheshire; hospital-steward, Albert J. Morey, Lee.

The regiment reached Carrolton, seven miles above New Orleans, February 7, 1863, and first went into battle May 21st, at Plains Store, where it exhibited great gallantry. In this battle, Lieut. Joseph Tucker of Lenox, lost a leg while acting as aid to Colonel Chapin.[2]

During its whole term of service, the Forty-ninth fully maintained the fame which the Berkshire soldiers won in former wars.

---

[1] William Francis Bartlett was born at Haverhill, June 6, 1840, being the son of Charles Leonard Bartlett. His grandfather, Bailey Bartlett, was a member of the congress of 1800. When the civil war broke out, W. F. Bartlett was a student in Harvard University; but in April, 1861, he enlisted as a private, and in July, was commissioned captain in the Twentieth regiment. After the return of the Forty-ninth, he was made colonel of the Fifty-seventh regiment, and in June, 1864, was promoted brigadier-general for conspicuous gallantry at Port Hudson, and commanded a division of the Ninth corps. In 1865, he was breveted major-general. In October, 1865, he married Agnes, daughter of Robert Pomeroy of Pittsfield, and became a citizen of the town.

[2] Lieutenant Tucker, who was lieutenant-governor of the commonwealth in 1870-73, was appointed judge of the district-court for central Berkshire, in 1873, when he became a citizen of Pittsfield.

At the siege of Port Hudson, no corps excelled it in gallantry and efficiency. We are precluded by a rule, necessarily adopted, from relating special instances of heroic conduct; but the stories of the Forty-ninth and the Tenth regiments have been published in well-written volumes, and that of the others, doubtless, will be. It would be impossible to do any of them justice in the space at our command.

The Forty-ninth left Baton Rouge for home, August 9, 1863, passing by steamer up the Mississippi to Cairo, and thence by railroad to Pittsfield, which was reached on the twenty-third.

The regiment left Pittsfield with nine hundred and sixty-two men. It returned with six hundred and seventy-six, including officers. During its absence, eighty-two men died of disease, and thirty-two of wounds; fifty one were sent home sick, and twenty were left behind sick; thirty-two deserted, two were missing, and fifty-six were discharged. After the return of the regiment, several died of disease contracted or wounds received in service.

For several weeks before the regiment reached Pittsfield, preparations had been making for such a welcome as would express the feeling of the county towards those who had done so much for its honor; and the vexatious delays, which from time to time postponed its arrival, were borne with impatience. When at last intelligence was received that it was surely near at hand, the news was at once dispatched to all parts of the county, and on the morning of the twenty-third, the streets were thronged as they rarely have been. The town was beautifully decorated with flags, evergreens, triumphal arches, and appropriate mottoes. The regiment was received at the depot by a procession consisting of a cavalcade of citizens, Stewart's band of North Adams, the Pittsfield and Lee fire-companies, the St. Joseph's Mutual Aid Society, the Pittsfield Liederkranz, and Schreiber's band of Albany. After marching through the principal streets, the procession halted at the park, where Hon. James D. Colt made an address of welcome: after which the soldiers partook of a collation in the park. From beginning to end, the reception was marked by genuine feeling. Never did returning soldiers receive a prouder ovation.

After the Forty-ninth regiment was mustered out of service, Colonel Bartlett was assigned to the Fifty-seventh, of which Edward P. Hollistèr, also of Pittsfield, was lieutenant-colonel, and which contained several Pittsfield men. It was engaged in the following battles: Wilderness, Spottsylvania, North Anna, Cold Harbor, Petersburg, Weldon Railroad, Poplar Spring Church, Hatcher's Run. The regiment left the state April 16, 1864, and Colonel Bartlett was promoted brigadier-general in June.

In November, 1864, the Eighth regiment of militia was again called into service, and a Pittsfield company, under the command of Captain Lafayette Butler, was attached to it. The service was for one hundred days, and it did not go into battle; but two of the Pittsfield soldiers died of disease.

The Sixty-first regiment was recruited in the fall of 1864, for one year's service. One company was raised at Pittsfield. The regiment took part in the battle before Petersburg.

The Twenty-seventh regiment, Colonel Horace C. Lee, which has a most honorable record in the war, had a considerable number of Pittsfield men. It fought at Roanoke, Newbern, Washington, Gum Swamp, Walthal, Arrowfield Church, Drury's Bluff, Cold Harbor, and other battles before Richmond, and South-west Creek.

The town was also represented largely in the First, and to some extent in the Second, Third and Fifth regiments of cavalry. And it furnished soldiers to a number of other regiments in all branches of the service, whose names will appear in the roll printed in the appendix.

During the first year of the civil war, the soldiers of Pittsfield hurried to the field, as we have seen, with no thought save the imminent danger of their country; and the contributions of their fellow-citizens in their aid were spontaneous, and not the result of previous contract. Afterwards, as the prolonged contest demanded more and more of pecuniary sacrifice on the part of those who represented the town in the field, a part of this sacrifice was assumed, in the form of bounties, by those who remained at home. Those who received this aid were, however, assured that it was only in compensation for their pecuniary losses. For the dangers which they were to encounter, for the lives which they might lose, the reward which was proffered them, next after the satisfaction of having fulfilled their duty, was, that they should be forever held in grateful memory as brave, true, and patriotic men.

The first bounty offered was when, early in July, 1862, it was made known to the people of Pittsfield, that, under the president's call for three hundred thousand men, the quota of the town would be one hundred and two men. The exigency did not admit of the delay necessary for calling a legal town-meeting, but the citizens assembled and passed a resolution to offer a bounty of one hundred dollars on each enlistment prior to August 15th. They also passed unanimously a series of resolutions, among which were the following :

Resolved, That the forces of the United States should be adequate to suppress domestic insurrection and to repel foreign invasion, and that in order to maintain the authority of this government, and the integrity of the Union, the militia of the United States ought immediately to be placed upon a war-footing, so that a million of soldiers, if necessary, in addition to the federal armies now in the field, may be ready to respond to any draft which may be made by the President of the United States.

Resolved, That in the opinion of this meeting, the exigencies of the country demand that the government should at once call for a draft of at least half a million of men in addition to the three hundred thousand already called for, and that they should at once be placed in the field for service.

Resolved, That the governor of this state should at as early a day as possible put the militia of the state in readiness for such a call.

The action of this meeting, which was held on the 7th, was immediately communicated by the chairman, Hon. Thomas Allen, to Governor Andrew, who replied on the 9th, in a letter of which the following extract shows the spirit: "Nothing can exceed the patriotic spirit of the people of Pittsfield. The town has already most nobly connected its name with the brightest pages of this war, and now it is the first to take hold in the right way to raise its quota for the new demand. I find that the cities and towns are taking hold with a will; and I feel very much encouraged that we shall get our quota, not only without drafting, but before any other state has got half its share." On the 2d of August, Mr. Allen also reported the action of the informal assemblage of citizens to a regular town-meeting, by which both the resolutions and the offer of bounties were ratified. Bounties in the meanwhile had been paid in the faith that this would be the case. On the 25th of August, 1862, the town voted to offer fifty dollars bounty to each recruit for the nine-months service. On the 27th of June, 1864, it offered a hundred and twenty-five dol-

ELMWOOD. RESIDENCE OF HON. EDWARD LEARNED.

lars for each enlistment for three years; and on the 7th of December, increased the amount to one hundred and fifty. Large sums, in addition, were contributed by individuals, and the whole expenditure for raising the volunteers from the town, in bounties and other aids to enlistment, was over one hundred and twenty-two thousand dollars.

On every call for troops, public meetings were held in the park, when the weather was suitable, and at other times in the town-hall, where patriotic speeches were made by the best speakers of the town and vicinity. Hon. Samuel W. Bowerman [1] and Major Charles N. Emerson were untiring in this class of effort, and few meetings passed without an address from one or both of them, distinguished both for eloquence and good judgment. Among the other prominent speakers were E. H. Kellogg, H. L. Dawes, Edward Learned, Joseph Tucker and P. L. Page. The most remarkable of these meetings was that held July 7, 1862, to which allusion has already been made. Addresses were made by Hon. Thomas Allen, who presided, Dr. H. H. Childs, Rev. Dr. Todd, Colonel H. S. Briggs, who was at home on account of wounds received at Fair Oaks, and Major Emerson. But the unique feature of the occasion was the appearance upon the platform of Doctor Childs, then seventy-nine years old, Captain Jared Ingersoll, an officer of the war of 1812, who was seventy-five years old, and others of like age and character, who volunteered to "enlist or send a substitute."

Throughout the war similar occasions constantly recurred, presenting scenes which can never be forgotten by those who witnessed them. Sometimes ordinary business was suspended, and the people were called together at mid-day by martial music and the ringing of bells. Sometimes they assembled in the park by moonlight or torch-light. In urgent crises the solemn hours of the holy Sabbath were devoted to the same patriotic purpose. In most cases the assembly felt the presence of a great and immediate danger to the country. The orators spoke, and the people listened in profound consciousness of that presence; and in the

[1] Samuel W. Bowerman was born at North Adams, May 8, 1820; graduated at Williams College in 1844; was admitted to the bar and commenced practice at South Adams in 1847. He removed to Pittsfield in 1857. He was a member of the state-senate in 1859, 1867 and 1868, and a member of the house in 1866.

same consciousness the young men to whom they appealed, enrolled themselves in the army of the republic. But we must leave the adequate description of those great days of danger, anxiety and excitement to other pens. Enough that they gave a new consecration to a spot before made sacred by the memories of the revolution.

John C. West, Henry Colt, and Chauncey Goodrich were selectmen from the beginning to the end of the war. During the first year much labor and anxiety devolved upon them; but after the system of assigning quotas to towns was adopted, their work was perpetually laborious; often perplexing and involving the gravest responsibilities. These duties they assumed cheerfully and performed with untiring assiduity. The chairman, Mr. West, on whom a large share of the active labor naturally devolved, had made up his mind in the beginning, that, if it was possible to avoid it, the town should do its whole duty without the aid of a draft; and, except in one case where a mistake occurred at Boston, too late to be rectified, he succeeded. Distinguished for firmness of purpose, of great personal influence, and furnished by the town with abundant pecuniary resources, he was everywhere present with persuasive tongue and purse, both when public meetings were in session and when private effort was demanded. In addition to this, he was in constant correspondence with the agents of the government, and of the town, keeping himself watchfully informed of the coming needs, in order to be prepared for them. He was with good reason proud of the result.

The Allen Guard had hardly left Pittsfield, in April, 1861, before the ladies began the labors for the purpose of furnishing the soldiers of the town with articles of health and comfort, which continued and increased until the end of the war. Among the earliest and busiest were the young ladies of Maplewood, in connection with which a sad incident occurred. One of the pupils was Miss Lilla Reeves, a daughter of Lieutenant-Colonel Reeves of the Eighth United States infantry; one of the officers stationed in Texas, who were captured through the treachery of General Twiggs. Miss Reeves was a young lady of scarcely seventeen years, of marked personal beauty, and a favorite of her school-mates. As a soldier's daughter, she was naturally foremost in their labors for the volunteers. And, indeed, was so assiduous that her teachers feared its effect upon her health, and induced her to join in an excursion to Wahconah Falls, a romantic resort, some ten miles from Pittsfield. On reaching the falls, some of the party, in the exuberance of their spirits, ventured too far on the slippery rocks, which extend into the whirlpool below the falls; among them Miss Reeves, who, turning hastily, fell into the water, and being stunned, was carried beyond the reach of aid.

At first, the efforts of the ladies in procuring comfort for the soldiers, like those of the gentlemen in enlisting them, were somewhat more earnest than well-directed, and did not perfectly accomplish their purpose; but as the needs of the soldiers began to be better understood, and the fact that the war must be protracted was realized, a ladies' soldiers' aid-society was formed, and a spacious hall in Martin's block, devoted to its use. The organization was peculiar. There were no officers, or records, or votes. By spontaneous consent, Mrs. Curtis T. Fenn became sole director and manager, taking advice and asking aid of whom she would, but under no control or supervision save that of public opinion; and, so well was she sustained by that, that to the close of the war, almost all donations for the army and contributions to the sanitary commission—not only from Pittsfield, but from several neighboring towns—passed through her hands. Boxes were constantly forwarded to the regiments containing Pittsfield men, to the sanitary commission, and to the hospitals. A New York society, for the aid of the hospitals and garrisons around that city, received very large contributions through Mrs. Fenn, who personally visited the stations at David's Island, and aided at the soldiers' thanksgiving-dinner. The regiments returning from the south-west, and passing through Pittsfield, were all handsomely entertained—the well with solid refreshments, and the sick with wines and delicacies. Long before the war closed, the name of Mrs. Fenn was one of those most familiar by the camp-fire and hospital. The amount of Pittsfield contributions expended under her direction may be fairly estimated at over ten thousand dollars. For the whole period of the war she gave herself up almost entirely to her duties as directress of the soldiers' aid-society.[1]

[1] Mrs. Curtis T. [Parthenia] Fenn was born in 1798, being the daughter of Captain John Dickinson. She had worked for the soldiers of 1812, and for the Greek patriots in 1824, and for her whole life has been noted for kindly services to the sick and suffering.

Nearly every lady of the town took some part in the labors of the ladies soldiers aid-society, and many of them with a zeal and self-devotion almost, if not quite equal to that of Mrs. Fenn. Among those who were most distinguished for their efficiency and assiduity, were Mrs. Dr. N. Wilson (afterwards Mrs. Albert Tolman), Mrs. L. F. Sperry, Mrs. Daniel J. Dodge, Mrs. Willard Carpenter, Mrs. Joseph Gregory, Mrs. J. P. Rockwell, Mrs. Phinehas Allen, Jr.

These ladies were always ready on every emergency, even if necessary to the sacrifice of their personal comfort and pressing personal engagements. The soldiers returning through Pittsfield from the war, had special occasion to remember them with gratitude.

A lady whose services and encouragement were most enthusiastically recognized by the soldiers, was Mrs. J. R. Morewood, who extended them a liberal hospitality, and presented them with flags to be carried to the field as tokens of her interest in their exploits. In return, they gave her name to their camps, while she was living, and since she died, bestow upon her grave, annually, the same floral testimonials with which they decorate those of their fallen comrades.

The calls upon the town for soldiers had hardly ceased, before its attention was directed to the pledges which had been made in its name, that it would hold in perpetual memory and honor, the names of its sons who had died in the field. Committees were appointed to consider the best means of redeeming these pledges, by the erection of some monument; and from time to time made partial reports. But final action was delayed, at first on account of the town's desire to avoid all expenses not immediately necessary in order to speedily extinguish the debt incurred in the war; and, when that was accomplished, from some difference of opinion whether the monument should take the form of a pillar, statue, or a memorial hall.

While the town was thus considering its plans, independent action had not been neglected. Immediately after the close of the war, Mrs. Fenn devoted herself as energetically to obtaining the means for a monument to the memory of the fallen soldiers, as she had before to the service of the living. By soliciting contributions, and by a fair in co-operation with other ladies, she obtained a considerable fund. But, while it was felt that it would give additional interest to the monument, that the ladies should have a conspicuous share in providing it, it was also generally deemed proper and fitting, that the town, in its corporate capacity, should take the greater part in thus honoring the memory of its representatives in the armies of the republic. Mrs. Fenn, therefore, suspended her labors and deposited the fund raised by her, in the savings bank, to await the action of the town.

In the spring of 1871, it had there accumulated to the sum of three thousand dollars, and it appeared to gentlemen who had from the first been interested in the matter, that there should be no longer delay. At the April town-meeting, Hon. S. W. Bowerman moved an appropriation of seven thousand dollars for the erection of a "suitable and appropriate soldiers' monument." The motion was advocated by Mr. Bowerman and by Hon. Thomas Colt, who left the moderator's chair for the purpose; and was unanimously adopted. The following gentlemen were then appointed a committee, with full powers to carry the vote into effect: Samuel W. Bowerman, Thomas Colt, William F. Bartlett, Henry S. Briggs, William R. Plunkett, Ensign H. Kellogg. John C. West, Henry H. Richardson, Alonzo E. Goodrich, Edward S. Francis, and Henry Stearns.

Mr. Colt was chosen chairman of the committee, and Messrs. Bartlett, Colt, and Plunkett, were appointed a sub-committee for procuring the monument. Several designs were submitted, but that offered by Mr. Launt. Thompson of New York, an artist of distinguished reputation and acknowledged genius, was so original in thought, so striking and appropriate in character, that the committee had little difficulty in making their selection.

The monument, as finally erected, consists of a bronze-statue of a color-sergeant standing upon a square granite-pillar composed of pedestal, base, shaft, and capital. The height of the pillar is fifteen feet and four inches, and the figure of the standard-bearer is six feet and three inches; above which the spear-pointed staff of the colors rises four feet, making the extreme height of the monument, to this minute apex, twenty-five feet and six inches. The sergeant is represented standing in line of battle, looking eagerly into the distance. The figure is erect, but slightly supported by the staff of the colors, which is clasped by both hands; the right gathering the flag—the stars and stripes—into graceful folds. The statue is correct in detail, as well as truthful in its grand effect; the uniform and accoutrements being faithfully copied from those of a color-sergeant at Fort Hamilton. Both face and figure are of a peculiar military type—as unique and easily recognized as that of the French zouave or Cossack trooper—which the war for the Union developed from material which it found rough-moulded in every New England village. One sees, at a glance, that the sculptor's ideal was a bold, frank man; resolute rather than defiant; self-reliant but modest; capable of either commanding or obeying; looking into the future as well as into the distance.

The base of the pillar is truncated at the top, leaving a projection upon each face, which bears in bronze-relief: on the west, the arms of the United States; on the east, the arms of the commonwealth; on the north and south, shields inscribed with the names of the Pittsfield soldiers who fell in the war.[1]

The dedicatory inscriptions are carved upon the shaft, and read as follows:

On the west face:

FOR THE DEAD

A TRIBUTE.

FOR THE LIVING

A MEMORY.

FOR POSTERITY

AN EMBLEM

OF LOYALTY TO THE FLAG

OF THEIR COUNTRY.

On the east face:

WITH GRATEFUL RECOGNITION

OF THE SERVICES OF ALL HER

SONS

WHO UPHELD THE HONOR AND

[1] Mr. Thompson gave much attention to the modeling of the Massachusetts coat-of-arms, procuring a complete Indian hunting-suit, as a study for the principal figure, and copying the head from that of Spotted Tail, the famous western chief.

HISTORY OF PITTSFIELD.

INTEGRITY OF OUR BELOVED

COUNTRY

IN HER HOUR OF PERIL,

THE TOWN OF

PITTSFIELD

ERECTS THIS MONUMENT IN

LOVING MEMORY OF THOSE

WHO DIED THAT THE

NATION

MIGHT LIVE.

The names inscribed on the monument are those of citizens of Pittsfield who died in the war, either from wounds, or, before their discharge, from disease contracted in the war; not including citizens of other places, who served on her quota. They are as follows:

SECOND REGIMENT.

Charles W. Robbins, died in hospital at Louisville, Ky.
Michael Mullany, died in 1862.

EIGHTH REGIMENT.

Charles C. Broad, died at Pittsfield, November 4, 1864.
Daniel S. Morgan, died at Baltimore, August 9, 1864.

TENTH REGIMENT.

Sergt. Haskel Hemenway, killed July 1, 1862, at Malvern Hill.
Sergt. Thomas Duffee, killed at Spottsylvania, Va., May 12, 1864.
Samuel D. Burbank, killed May 10, 1864, at Spottsylvania, Va.
James Cassidy, killed May 5, 1864, at Wilderness, Va.
Richard S. Corliss, killed July 1, 1862, at Malvern Hill, Va.
Nelson N. Grippen, killed July 1, 1862, at Malvern Hill, Va.
Charles F. Harris, Jr., died Sept. 17, 1862, at Newport News, Va.
Alfred C. Hemenway, killed May 30, 1862, at Fair Oaks, Va.
Gardner B. Hibbard, died November 13, 1861, at Washington, D. C.
Michael Hogan.
Henry Noble, killed May 12, 1864, at Spottsylvania, Va.
Richard Ryan, killed May 12, 1864, at Spottsylvania, Va.

TWENTIETH REGIMENT.

Lieut. Lansing E. Hibbard, killed May 10, 1864.[1]
Sergt. John Merchant, killed October 21, 1861, at Balls Bluff, Va.
Oliver S. Bates, died August 19, 1864, at Alexandria, Va.
James Carough, died of wounds December 15, 1862.
Jonathan Francis, died of wounds December 13, 1862, at Fredericksburg, Va.
Charles Goodwin, killed in the Wilderness, May 5, 1864.
George F. Kelly, killed October 21, 1861, at Balls Bluff, Va.
James K. Morey, died December 28th, at Salisbury, N. C.
Wilbur Noble, died in June, 1862, in New York, while on his way home.
John A. Sloan, died October 8, 1862, at Bolivar Heights, Md.

TWENTY-FIRST REGIMENT.

Capt. William H. Clark, died of wounds, August 16, 1864.
Sergt. Justin S. Cressy, killed September 1, 1862, at Chantilly, Va.
Sergt. Evelyn A. Garlick, killed September 1, 1862, at Chantilly, Va.
Corp. Charles L. Woodworth, killed March 14, 1862, at Newbern, N. C.
Henry F. Chamberlain, died April 6, 1862, at Newbern, N. C.
George W. Jarvis, killed June 2, 1864, at Cold Harbor, Va.
Hobart R. McIntosh, killed September 1, 1862, at Chantilly, Va.
George E. Menton, killed March 14, 1862, at Newbern, N. C.
Samuel Wright, died March 30, 1863, of wounds.

TWENTY-SEVENTH REGIMENT.

Sergt. Willard L. Merry, died April 19, 1862, at Newbern, N. C.
Sergt. William H. Monnier, died December 4, 1864, at Annapolis, Md.
James S. Bentley, died September 4, 1862, at Newbern, N. C.
David Bolio, killed June 3, 1864, at Cold Harbor, Va.
Charles H. Davis, killed June 18, 1864, at Petersburg, Va.
James Donlon, died July 20, 1864, at Andersonville, Ga.
Joseph Goddit, died June 27, 1864, of wounds, at Point of Rocks, Md.
Eleazur Wilbur, died August 24, 1864, at Andersonville prison, Ga.
James Williams, died in Libby prison, Va., June 8, 1864.
John Wilson, died May 21, 1864, at Norfolk, Va.

THIRTY-FIRST REGIMENT.

Capt. William W. Rockwell, died December 3, 1863, at Baton Rouge, La.
Louis H. Daily, died June 29, 1865, at Donaldsonville, La.

---

[1] Lieutenant Hibbard's commission as captain was issued, but he had not been mustered into his new rank, when he was killed.

Henry Holder, died October 13, 1863, at Cairo, Ill.
Edward E. Quigley, died December 24, 1861, at Chester, Mass.
George L. Martin, died October 12, 1864, at New Orleans, La.
John B. Ross, died April 11, 1864, at New Orleans, La.
James Tute, died June 17, 1864, at New Orleans, La.
Jonathan F. H. Harrington, Jr.

THIRTY-FOURTH REGIMENT.

Lieut. James L. Dempsey, died October 17, 1864, at Winchester, Va., of wounds received at Cedar Creek, October 13th.
Corp. Noah A. Clark, killed October 18, 1863, at Ripon, Va.
John Casey, killed June 6, 1864, at Piedmont, Va.
Charles H. Dill, died August 20, 1864, at Staunton, Va.
William E. Donnelly, killed at Newmarket, Va.
Edgar P. Fairbanks, died November 6, 1862, at Fort Lyon, Va.
John Grady, died November 12, 1865, at Salisbury, N. C.
Nelson Harned, died January 7, 1864, at Harper's Ferry, Va.
Thomas Leeson, died April 3, 1864, at Martinsburg, Va.
John Shaw, died August 27, 1864, at Staunton, Va.

THIRTY-SEVENTH REGIMENT.

Miles H. Blood, killed September 19, 1864, at Winchester, Va.
Oliver C. Hooker, killed May 6, 1864, at Wilderness, Va.
Patrick Hussey, killed July 3, 1863, at Gettysburg, Pa.
Robert Reinhart, killed August 21, 1864, at Fort Stevens, D. C.

THIRTY-NINTH REGIMENT.

Elbert O. Hemenway, died at Salisbury prison, N. C., January 1, 1865.

FORTY-NINTH REGIMENT.

Corp. Allen M. Dewey, died March 23, 1863, at New Orleans, La.
James B. Bull, killed July 13, 1863, at Donaldsonville, La.
Luther M. Davis, killed May 27, 1863, at Port Hudson, La.
Seth R. Jones, died May 16, 1863, at Baton Rouge, La.
Daniel M. Joyner, died July 2, 1863, at Baton Rouge, La.
Samuel G. Noble, died July 14, 1863.
Charles E. Platt, died June 6, 1863, of wounds, at Port Hudson, La.
William Taylor, died March 20, 1863, at New Orleans, La.
Charles F. Videtto, died April 14, 1863, at Baton Rouge, La.

FIFTY-FOURTH REGIMENT.

Eli Franklin, died July 20, 1863, at Beaufort, S. C.
Levi Bird, died July 10, 1865, at Charleston, S. C.
John Van Blake, died December 21, 1863, at Morris Island, S. C.
Henry Wilson, died July 31, 1865, at Charleston, S. C.

FIFTY-SEVENTH REGIMENT.

Corp. George H. Hodge, died June 5, 1864, at Arlington, Va.
William G. Bourne, killed May 6, 1864, at Wilderness, Va.
Chester H. Daniels, died July 29, 1864.
Lowell Daniels, killed May 18, 1864, at Spottsylvania, Va.
Horace Danyon, died July 18, 1864, at Washington, D. C.
Peter Monney, killed May 12, 1864, at Spottsylvania, Va.
Patrick Thornton, died May 18, 1864, of wounds.
Lester Tyler, killed May 6, 1864, at Wilderness, Va.

SIXTY-FIRST REGIMENT.

Thomas D. Beebe, died February 12, 1865, at City Point, Va.
Martin F. Mallison, died September 12, 1864, at Galloup's Island.

FIRST REGIMENT OF CAVALRY.

Charles-T. Chapman, died August 28, 1863, at Annapolis, Md.
Hiram S. Gray, died August 17, 1864.
Michael Hanly, died August 22, 1864, at Andersonville, Ga.
John F. Hills, died February 18, 1865, at Richmond, Va.
John P. Ober, killed June 17, 1863, at Aldie, Va.
Edward O. Roberts, died September 21, 1864, at Andersonville, Va.
Giles Taylor, died at City Point, Va.

THIRD REGIMENT OF CAVALRY.

Abram Malcom, died October 13, 1864.
Charles Ollinger, killed at Kelley's Ford.
Allen Prichard, died August 11, 1865, at Fort Leavenworth, Kan.

OTHER REGIMENTS.

Timothy Reardon, second battery light artillery, killed April 8, 1864, at Sabine Cross Roads.

Sergt. Byron W. Kellogg, One Hundred and Seventy-third New York Volunteers, died of wounds June 30, 1863, at Baton Rouge, La.

Charles M. Shepardson, Twelfth New York Cavalry, died October 30, 1864, at Newbern, N. C.

Isaac Johnson, Fifth Massachusetts Cavalry, killed July 28, 1864, at Point Lookout, Va.

Capt. Henry H. Sears, Forty-eighth New York.

Sergt. John W. Smith, United States Army, died January, 1863, at Harper's Ferry, Va.

James Donahue, One Hundred and Twenty-first New York Infantry, died at Alexandria, Va., April, 1865.

THE PARK. 1876.

One name, which the committee reluctantly, under the strict interpretation of their rules, omitted from the inscription, was that of Lieut. George Read, of the Forty-ninth regiment, who died at Cleveland, O., before reaching home, but after his discharge from the service on account of ill health.

The cost of the entire monument was ten thousand dollars, besides which, Mr. Thompson received a number of condemned cannon, granted for the work by congress, through the efforts of Hon. H. L. Dawes.

It was determined to place it at the west end of the park, in or near which, a large portion of the Pittsfield soldiers volunteered, and which possessed many other associations of patriotic interest; and the park, however beautiful, being not considered in a proper condition for the reception of the contemplated work, the town placed in the hands of the committee before-named, a further sum of seven thousand dollars, for the purpose of making some long-desired improvements. The nature of these improvements was left to the discretion of the committee, by whom the following changes were made: The oval plot which constitutes the park, was surrounded by a handsome and substantial coping of granite, outside of which a broad gravel walk, with granite curbing, was built. The surface of the plot was graded, and a considerable number of trees, which had become so thick as to impede each other's growth, were felled. The Old Elm had fallen in 1861. In addition to this, the grade of Park place was reduced so as to make it more uniform with that of Bank row.

While these alterations were in progress, the town voted an appropriation of twenty-five hundred dollars, to enable the committee to dedicate the monument to its great purposes, with such impressive words and ceremonies, as should fix them, for at least one generation, in the minds of the community; and at the same time add to the honors which the town bestowed upon the memory of its heroic dead.

To carry these intentions into effect, the committee had the good fortune to secure the services of so eminent an orator as George William Curtis. It was afterwards determined to have other exercises than those of the platform; and such as would require very great industry, zeal, experience, and good judgment. The committee, therefore, called to their aid fifteen gentlemen, distinguished for those qualities, viz.: Messrs. James M. Barker,

Graham A. Root, Israel C. Weller, William H. Teeling, Thomas G. Colt, Samuel E. Nichols, William W. Whiting, Frederick A. Francis, William H. Coogan, Michael Casey, Seth W. Morton, George S. Willis, Jr., D. J. Dodge, Henry B. Brewster, and Erdman Leidhold. By this committee, the exercises of the day, with the exception of those on the platform, were arranged and carried out, consultation being had with the town-committee whenever occasion arose.

The pillar having been previously erected, the statue was raised to its place at noon, on the 23d of September, 1872, and immediately draped with the national flags belonging to the two political parties in the town, which had, for the day, been removed from the street, in order that no reminder of political differences might, by any chance, mar the harmony of the occasion.

The day fixed for the unvailing of the statue was the 24th of September, in that week of the year which is most unfailingly characterized by the most delicious of autumn days; and never were September skies more cloudless, or September days more genial in Berkshire, than those which favored the ceremonies with which Pittsfield honored her soldiers.

The streets were brilliant with red, white, blue, green and yellow bunting; the flags of many nations, arranged with greater regard to the effects of color, than to significant grouping. And, in this view of it, the result was excellent; the gay colors of the banners, and of the few trees which had begun to put on their autumnal hues—mellow and rich, but not yet gaudy—contrasting finely with the verdure which the foliage had this year retained in unusual freshness. Nature and art combined to make a gala-day, and the people of western Massachusetts did not incline to resist its attractions. On the morning of the 24th, long trains of cars, from all directions, came in, crowded to their utmost capacity, and the town was soon thronged as it never had been on any similar occasion; not even at the reception of the Forty-ninth regiment.

The Second regiment of the Massachusetts Volunteer Militia— belonging to Berkshire, Hampden, Hampshire, and Franklin counties, was holding its annual encampment, and acted as escort for the procession, and the following gentlemen were selected as marshals:

Chief marshal, High-Sheriff Graham A. Root; aids, Michael

Casey, Lieutenant-Colonel Thomas G. Colt, Col. Henry H. Richardson, Capt. F. A. Francis, William W. Whiting, William H. Coogan, Lieutenant-Colonel I. C. Weller, Lieut. William H. Harrington, J. L. Peck, and George S. Willis, Jr.

The procession moved in the following order—cheering, as it went, the appropriate mottoes at different points along its route, and receiving the plaudits of the crowds which lined the streets—

Gilmore's Band of Boston.
Second Regiment, M. V. M., Colonel Parsons.
Governor, Orator, Chaplain and President of the Day in Carriage.
Governor's Staff and other distinguished guests in Carriages.
Second Regiment Band.
Berkshire Commandery, Knights Templar.
Brown's Boston Brigade Band.
Springfield Commandery, Knights Templar.
Florence Band.
Northampton Commandery, Knights Templar.
Viall's Band of North Adams.
Veterans of the Tenth, Twenty-first, Twenty-seventh, and Thirty-fourth Massachusetts Regiments.
Colt's Armory Band of Hartford.
Veterans of Thirty-seventh, Forty-Ninth, Fifty-seventh, and Sixty-first Regiments.
Grand Army Posts of Berkshire County.
Doring's Band of Troy.
Pittsfield Fire Department.
Erdman's Band of Pittsfield.
St. Joseph's Mutual Aid Society.

The procession reached the park—where an appropriately decorated platform had been erected—at half-past twelve o'clock; and, the assembly having been called to order by Hon. Thomas Colt, president of the day, the exercises commenced with a prayer by Rev. Dr. Todd.

Major-General W. F. Bartlett, chairman of the sub-committee, under whose immediate supervision the monument was erected, then rose, and addressing Mr. Colt, delivered it to him, in a brief speech, in which, after eulogizing the services of Mrs. Fenn, and complimenting the genius of the sculptor, he concluded as follows :

He has taken for his subject, not the private soldier nor the commissioned officer, but a greater hero than either—the man on whom so often hung the fate of battle; the man on whose self-forgetting bravery and unflinching firmness the steadiness of the whole line depended; the man who bore the colors; and, comrades, was there ever any flag half so well worth fighting for, half so well worth dying for, as that which we followed? As I look upon your faces that I have seen amid the smoke of battle, and remember how you closed up the gaps made by the fall of those whom we honor to-day, I am conscious that to you also belongs a share of the honor, but with this difference: their fame was achieved and secured by dying heroic deaths; yours must yet be maintained and preserved by living blameless lives. How well the hand of genius has succeeded in carving in lasting bronze a living memorial of duty done in the past, which shall be to us and to those who shall come after us, an incentive to faithfulness, you shall now judge.

As General Bartlett closed, the veil of flags which had hitherto covered the statue fell, and it was greeted by the band with appropriate music, and by the people with approving shouts.

Mr. Colt then accepted the monument in behalf of the town, concluding thus:

I receive this monument,—and let us all here receive it,—in trust for succeeding generations, not alone as a monument to perpetuate the memory of those brave heroes who died fighting for their country, and who sleep in honored graves, but as an eminent and lasting evidence of the value of that country for which they laid down their lives. To the present generation this monument will be a constant reminder of sacrifices, of doubts, of dangers, and of glorious victory. To the surviving soldiers who took part in the great conflict it will be a memento of their own hardships, of deadly battles, of lost comrades and of splendid achievements. To those who in future years shall read these inscriptions, it will teach the duties they owe to a government handed down to them through the blood of martyrs shed for its preservation.

On this very spot, where the sacred stillness of the Christian Sabbath has been broken by the clamor of martial music and the tramp of departing soldiers, and where the voice of the patriot preacher has been raised in prayer for their safety and victory, let it stand as an enduring pledge that the devotion and the deaths commemorated on this stone have not been in vain. Let this color-bearer stand with his face to the setting sun, holding up this emblem of liberty to its last lingering rays until the last hopes of liberty shall have expired forever.

Then came the oration of George William Curtis, characterized by all its author's classic and glowing eloquence, overflowing with historic allusions and illustrations, and full of the lessons taught by the war, and the civil struggle for human rights which preceded it. He opened with a rapid sketch of the history of the the Pittsfield soldiers in the revolution, and in the civil war, and closed with the following lesson :

The educated Germans made better soldiers. The triumph of Germany was a moral victory. It was not cannon and powder and shells— it was character, human quality, that won. Eloquence, says Emerson, is that speech in which there is a man behind every word. Victorious war, says history, is that contest in which intelligence and morality serve the guns.

And how rich was our war in these personal qualities ! How profound the influence of this statue in showing us that the heroic excellence of human character which we associate with the past, and suppose to be the exclusive property of tradition and poetry, are of our own age and country as much as of any other ! We read Plutarch until our imaginations flame with the Grecian story. The trophies of Miltiades will not let us sleep. History and poetry and heroic legend make the names of Marathon and of Salamis, of Thermopylæ and Platea, names of unrivaled glory. Pericles, Themistocles, Alcibiades, Demosthenes, Timoleon, stand in our fancies proudly aloof and superior, removing the meanness of later men and the bitterness of modern times. But our own history is not less heroic. The mighty torrent of Asiatic barbarism that threatened for a time to sweep away Grecian civilization was not more formidable than that which threatened American liberty. If the statesmen and the heroes who stayed that earlier desolation, and the fields on which their battles were fought, are renowned and precious to Americans to-day, how much more our own fields and our own brothers ! Xerxes sent a herald to Leonidas, ordering him to give up his armies. "Let him come and take them," said Leonidas, and for a whole summer day he held all Asia at bay at Thermopylæ. "Surrender! Surrender !" cried a rebel leader to the commander of a Union company in Missouri, cut off from the main body. "Not much," replied the Union captain, and he won the victory.

The war has taught us that the poetry of heroism is in the deed, not in the distance. The brave youth seems a poetic hero when we see him, three hundred years ago, called Philip Sydney, riding into the fight against the Spaniards, on a misty morning, upon the Isel. Suddenly he sees his friend Lord Willoughby surrounded and sorely pressed, and Sir Philip dashing to the rescue is shot and mortally wounded. Borne fainting upon his horse from the field, he asks for water. But as it is brought to him and he is raising it to his lips, he sees the eyes of a dying soldier fixed upon it with passionate longing. Then leaning from the saddle, the gentleman of gentlemen, the flower of English manhood, hands the cup to the soldier, and the dying hero whispers to his dying comrade, "Friend, thy necessity is yet greater than mine." History will never tire of the beautiful story. But more than three hundred years later a gunner at Gettysburg falls mortally wounded by his gun, which is sorely pressed by the enemy. The battle rages on, and tortured by thirst, the dying man says to his comrade, serving the gun alone, " Johnny, Johnny, for the love of God give me a drop of water." " Ah, Jamie," says his comrade, " there's not a drop in my canteen, and if I go to fetch it the rebs will have the gun." " No matter, then, Johnny, stick to your gun," is the answer, and when, after a desperate struggle, with a ringing shout of victory, the line moves forward, it is over Jamie's dead body. Does it need three hundred years to make that self-sacrifice as beautiful as Sidney's? Jamie is not less a hero than the Englishman, and the brave Sidney clasps his hand in paradise. The past was a good time,. but the present is a better. Themistocles standing upon his galley and driving the enemy at Salamis, the image of Greek valor in the war with Persia, is not a nobler figure than Farragut lashed into the maintop of the old Hartford at Mobile, the image of American liberty in the war with slavery. When Timoleon, the patriot general of Corinth, freed Sicily, the citizens of Syracuse put even the wives and daughters of the opposing general to death. When General Grant by his final victory secured the emancipation of a race and the perpetuity of the Union, he spared the enemy every humiliation, and would not even enter their capital, while in the same great spirit his fellow-citizens forbore to shed one drop of blood. The shadow of a political scaffold has never stained the land; and to-day, with the exception of the ineligibility to office of some two hundred persons,—a disability which the same wise and humane policy will soon sweep away—the laws of the United States rest with perfect equality upon every part of the land.

Let us be grateful for Greece two thousand years ago, and thank God that we live in America to-day! The war scattered the glamour of the past and showed us that we, too, live among great virtues, great characters, and great men. Through these streets the culture of Greece, the heroism of Rome, the patriotism of our own revolution, have marched before your eyes. These elms, like the trees of Ardennes, have shed their tears in dew-drops over the unreturning brave. The ground upon which we stand is consecrated by the tread of feet gladly going to the noblest sacrifice. And from these throbbing drums and wailing horns, still peals the music to which they marched away. They were your sons, Pittsfield and green Berkshire! They were your comrades, Massachusetts soldiers! They were the darlings of your homes, tender hearts that hear me! And here in this fair figure of heroic youth, they stand as you will always recall them—the bloom of immortal youth upon their cheeks; the divine hope of youth in their hearts; the perpetual inspiration of youth to every beholder. For this is the American soldier of the Union; the messenger of liberty to the captive and of peace to the nation. This is the perpetual but silent preacher of the gospel of liberty and justice as the only sure foundation of states. "Beautiful on the mountains are the feet of him that bringeth glad tidings, that publisheth peace, that saith unto Zion, thy God reigneth!"

After the exercises in the park, the procession was formed again, and marched to the corner of Wendell avenue and East Housatonic street, where dinner had been provided in a mammoth pavilion. Here the public celebration of the day closed; Hon. Thomas Colt presiding, and addresses being made by Gov. Washburn and Lieutenant-Governor Tucker.[1]

A full list of the soldiers furnished by Pittsfield in the civil war will be found in the appendix.

[1] An account of the exercises of the day, including Mr. Curtis's address in full, has been publishêd.

CHAPTER XXVII.

LIBRARIES AND ATHENÆUM.

Early private libraries—Pittsfield social libraries—Pittsfield Young Men's Associations — Berkshire Athenæum — Thomas Allen—Calvin Martin—Phinehas Allen—Thomas F. Plunkett—Rev. Dr. Todd—Henry L. Dawes.

THE number of the earliest citizens of Pittsfield who were familiar with the best literature of their day, was unusual in frontier settlements; and allusion, in their letters, as well as bequests in their wills, show that several of them owned choice libraries, which they knew how to prize. Woodbridge Little, Colonel William Williams, Israel Dickinson, Israel Stoddard, Captain John Strong, Rev. Mr. Allen, and probably others, possessed collections as large, in proportion to their means, as gentlemen in corresponding circumstances now own; and there is sufficient evidence that they used them to as good advantage as their successors.

The old tory-families seem in particular to have indulged in a love for the more elegant class of literature; and an incident of a little later date, shows how, in adversity, this sometimes became a passion with them. The family of Graves, which was nearly allied to those of Stoddard and Williams, was one of those which served the king's cause most boldly and actively; and they suffered for it both in purse and person. Still one of them, Moses, retained some portion of his estate, and his son of the same name was in business in the early part of the nineteenth century. But afterwards his fortunes declined rapidly; he became a pauper, and was taken to the alms-house, doubtless keenly feeling his position. The authorities, however, had not the heart to deprive him of his books; and, as he rode to the sad refuge of poverty, seated upon the box containing his little library, he exclaimed, cheerfully, that he could bear his fate with resignation as long as they were left to him.

HISTORY OF PITTSFIELD.   641

Social libraries were established as early as 1796, and the town was afterwards rarely without one or more of them. The catalogue of the Pittsfield library of 1800, is preserved in the Berkshire Athenæum, and shows eighty very well selected volumes. The Young Men's Association, a society, which, between the years 1836 and 1849, was of great service, collected an excellent library. Before 1850, this society had become practically extinct, and its collection had dwindled to a set of Ree's encyclopedia and a few other books. In that year the Pittsfield Library Association was founded, with the intention of establishing a permanent and general library for the town. By its constitution, any person might become a member by purchasing a share at the cost of five dollars, subject to a yearly tax of one dollar. One person could hold an unlimited number of shares, and, unless they were used, be exempt from taxation upon all except one. Non-shareholders were admitted to the use of the library on payment of two dollars a year.

Several very earnest workers devoted themselves with ardor to laying the foundations of this institution; and, among the most indefatigable were Rev. Dr. Humphrey, Rev. W. H. Tyler, Rev. S. C. Brace, Dr. Stephen Reed, Hon. Julius Rockwell and John C. Hoadley. By the efforts of these gentlemen, in the first year, ninety-six shares were taken, and eight hundred volumes purchased at a cost of five hundred dollars. The books, among which were the relics of the young men's library, were most judiciously selected and bought by Mr. Brace. The rules of the association excluded forever all prose-works of fiction; and theological writings could only be admitted by a unanimous vote of the directors.

For some years the association flourished; successful courses of lectures were given under its auspices, and its library increased. But, probably on account of its rigid exclusion of the more popular class of literature, the public interest in it after a while languished; the books were consigned to a small room, rudely finished, which was opened only one evening in the week, by the dim light of a lantern. There was danger that the library would soon cease to be.

In this crisis, Rev. Dr. Humphrey published an appeal in its behalf, in response to which James M. Beebe, a wealthy gentleman of Boston, who was, in his boyhood, a resident of Pittsfield, sent his check for five hundred dollars, to be used at Doctor Humphrey's discretion for the benefit of the library.

This timely donation inspired the institution with new life. A considerable number of members were added to the association, some of whom gave themselves to its interests with the same spirit which its founders exhibited. A handsome hall in Francis' block was hired; new books were purchased; more successful courses of lectures were instituted, and a lively public interest created. The rule regarding works of fiction was construed more liberally than it had been; and, although with great caution, standard novels were admitted. Both classes of book-takers increased so rapidly that it required the utmost efforts of the directors to even proximately meet their demands. Between 1860 and 1866, the Library Association had an interval of hard-earned prosperity.

In the fall of 1865, it was determined to institute a new young men's association; and it was organized November 20th; its object being the intellectual, moral and physical improvement of its members by means of a library, a reading-room, a collection of curiosities, and provision for amusement and exercise. The officers elected were : President, Thomas Colt; vice-president, Samuel W. Bowerman; corresponding secretary, Rev. E. L. Wells; recording secretary, Buel Lamberson; treasurer, M. H. Wood; directors, E. S. Francis, Jabez L. Peck, Rev. Edward Strong and William G. Harding.

Spacious and handsome rooms in James H. Dunham's building on North street, were fitted up, a liberal supply of newspapers was subscribed for, and an attractive recreation-room opened. The institution at once obtained public favor, and entered upon a brilliant career. For six years its rooms afforded a pleasant resort to its members, and added much to the credit of the town with visitors who received its hospitality. It provided many eloquent and instructive lectures, as well as social reunions and musical entertainments of a high order, all of which were enjoyed and prized by the intellectual public of Berkshire. A scientific section of the association was organized, by whose members many valuable papers were read, an interesting cabinet collected, a popular interest in science created, and several successful field-meetings held at various points in the town and vicinity. The association formed a pleasant bond of union among the young men of the town, and they probably never knew a more agreeable period, nor one more favorable to the formation of character than during its existence.

In their eagerness, however, to make the institution all that it should be, they unfortunately allowed their expenditures to exceed their receipts, with the hope of increasing prosperity. Mr. Colt paid the yearly deficiency while he remained president, and great exertions were made by the other officers by personal contributions of money, and by arduous labor in the management of lectures and otherwise; the most conspicuous service being performed by Messrs. James W. Hull, Samuel E. Nichols, James M. Barker, Albert B. Root, Irving D. Ferry and Thomas G. Colt. With the approaching depression of business in March, 1873, it nevertheless became apparent that all exertions to maintain the organization would be in vain, and measures were taken to discontinue it.

When the Young Men's Association was organized, an attempt was made by some of its friends, to induce the Pittsfield Library Association to endow it with its books. But they, deeming the new corporation even less permanently founded than their own, declined the proposition, although one of its rooms, being peculiarly adapted to the purpose, was hired, and the library removed to it.

In 1861, Hon. Thomas Allen expressed his intention of doing something which would put the library of his native town upon a creditable and permanent footing; but this purpose was postponed by the disorders in Missouri, caused by the civil war. Mr. Allen meanwhile continued his interest in the institution, of which he was made president. Hon. Thomas F. Plunkett was a liberal friend of the library, and while it occupied the hall in Dunham's building, his donations were of indispensable service. Calvin Martin, Esq., for many years a friend of popular education, shortly before his death, made known his wish to contribute towards a public library. Neither of these gentlemen were satisfied with the character of the old organization, in regard to permanence, it being in law merely a private corporation, liable to be dissolved at the will of its stockholders.

While they were deliberating, they learned that the Agricultural Bank building, on Bank row, could be purchased for eight thousand and eight hundred dollars, if appropriated for the purposes of a library-room. This building was handsome, substantial, convenient, and well located; and the price being very low, they determined to buy it; Mr. Martin contributing five thousand dollars, Messrs. Allen and Plunkett each nineteen hundred. There being some delay in the sale, the donors made a gift of the price to themselves as trustees for a library, when one should be established in accordance with their plans. When the building was finally purchased, in October, 1868, Mr. Martin having died in the interval, the deed was made to Messrs. Allen and Plunkett, in trust.

In April, 1869, the legislature authorized the trustees of the Medical College to sell its real and personal estate, and pay the interest of the proceeds, in equal proportions, to the Library and Young Men's Associations, until the organization of the proposed athenæum, when it should receive the principal; providing, nevertheless, that so much of the personal property as it was deemed desirable to preserve, should be deposited with the Young Men's Association until the athenæum should be prepared to receive it. In 1870, the legislature changed the name of the Library Association to the Pittsfield Athenæum, but without altering its constitution. In 1870, Mr. Allen fitted the Agricultural banking-room with handsome book-cases, at a cost of nine hundred dollars; and, together with Mr. Plunkett, invited the Pittsfield Athenæum to occupy it without rent. The offer was accepted. In 1870, the Medical College having been sold, the library, cabinets, and scientific apparatus of that institution, were also removed to the athenæum.

The trustees of the Berkshire Athenæum were incorporated March 24, 1871, "for the purpose of establishing and maintaining, in the town of Pittsfield, an institution to aid in promoting education, culture, and refinement, and diffusing knowledge by means of a library, reading-rooms, lectures, museums, and cabinets of art, and of historical and natural curiosities." This board fills vacancies in its own number, and is authorized to hold real and personal property to the amount of two hundred and fifty thousand dollars. Power was also granted to the town to appropriate money towards the support of the institution, so long as it maintained a free library for the use of its inhabitants. The trustees named in the charter were Thomas Allen, Ensign H. Kellogg, Thomas Colt, George Y. Learned, Edward S. Francis,

John Todd, Henry L. Dawes, Edwin Clapp, William R. Plunkett, William F. Bartlett, and James M. Barker. The corporation was formally organized May 13, 1872, the principal officers being Thomas Allen, president; William F. Bartlett, vice-president; James M. Barker, clerk and treasurer.

On the same day, the trustees received from Messrs. Allen and Plunkett, a deed of the Agricultural Bank building. The trustees of the Medical College also paid them four thousand four hundred dollars, being the residue, after the payment of debts, of the price received by them for the college-building.

Soon after their organization, the trustees of the athenæum began to take measures for the extension of their grounds; partly in order to control the use of the neighboring property, and partly in anticipation of a larger edifice; and in June, 1872, a committee was appointed to carry out the latter purpose. In December, 1873, Mr. Allen addressed a letter to his associates, offering to erect a suitable building, at his own personal cost, not exceeding fifty thousand dollars; and make a free gift of it to the institution, if satisfactory assurance was given within a reasonable time, that a sufficient fund would be raised to free the site from incumbrance, and maintain the athenæum in perpetuity.

In 1872, Phinehas Allen died, leaving an estate valued at over seventy-one thousand dollars; and making the athenæum his residuary legatee, after the payment of certain legacies, and the termination of three annuities, which were secured to relatives of the testator for their lives. After the payment of the legacies, about fifty thousand dollars of the estate remained, which is managed by Elias Merwin of Boston, and Edwin Clapp of Pittsfield, as trustees, until the bequest to the athenæum shall take effect.

Under these circumstances, the trustees of the athenæum instructed William R. Plunkett, Esq., to submit to the town a plan for making Thomas Allen's offer immediately available; and, on Mr. Plunkett's motion, the following votes were passed at the annual town-meeting of 1874 :

Voted, That Theodore Pomeroy, Owen Coogan, William H. Murray, Robert W. Adam, and Jarvis N. Dunham, be a committee with power to direct the treasurer of the town, who is hereby duly authorized to issue its obligations in such form as said committee may direct, as follows :

First, To the amount of sixteen thousand dollars for the discharge of the mortgage now upon the land of the trustees of the Berkshire Athenæum.

Second, For a reasonable sum to be paid for the conveyance to said trustees of the land now owned by the Berkshire Mutual Fire Insurance Company.

Third, For a reasonable sum to be paid for the conveyance to said trustees, of a strip of land in the rear of land now owned by said trustees, to be used for the purposes of a new athenæum:

Provided, that the obligations, so to be issued by the treasurer aforesaid, shall not exceed twenty-four thousand dollars in amount; and provided, also, that said committee shall be satisfied that a suitable building for the athenæum and free library of said trustees, will be erected within a reasonable time, without expense to the town of Pittsfield;

And that, upon the erection of a new athenæum-building without expense to the town of Pittsfield, for a free library for all its citizens, and for other purposes, the town hereby agrees to pay annually to the trustees of the Berkshire Athenæum, for the maintenance of said free library, and the care of said building, the sum of two thousand dollars annually, until such time as said trustees shall receive the bequest of the late Phinehas Allen, Esq., or such portion thereof as shall enable them to realize from the increase thereof, the said sum of two thousand dollars yearly; and the erection of said building shall bind the town to the agreement in this vote contained.

Under this vote, the trustees enlarged their estate, free of mortgage, to a frontage of one hundred and forty-four feet, with a uniform depth of ninety-nine feet and six inches, as follows: They had purchased, in 1871, the lots west of their library-building, on which stood two old wooden stores, for twenty thousand dollars, of which they paid four thousand dollars, obtained from the sale of the Medical College; securing the remainder by a mortgage, from which the town now freed them. Between these lots and the athenæum was the office of the Berkshire Mutual Fire Insurance Company, which was bought for four thousand dollars; and twenty-four hundred dollars were paid the heirs of Calvin Martin for a strip of land in the rear; making the amount paid by the town twenty-two thousand and four hundred dollars.

In the spring of 1874, the library was removed to the wooden store which occupied a space which is finally to be left vacant; and all the other buildings were demolished or removed.

After considering many designs for the proposed structure, Mr. Allen finally accepted one submitted by William A. Potter of

THE BERKSHIRE ATHENÆUM.

New York, a gentleman specially distinguished in library-architecture. The contract for the erection of the athenæum was was awarded to A. B. & D. C. Munyan, who associated with themselves, Patrick Treanor of Boston, by whom it was completed.[1]

A very solid foundation was built in the fall of 1874, and the superstructure was nearly completed in the following year. The general appearance of this noble monument to the gentlemen to whom it owes its erection, and in which centers so much evidence of the love of the citizens of Pittsfield for the town, will be best shown by the accompanying beautiful and accurate engraving. It is a much admired specimen of the richer Gothic style, and has few equals among the public libraries of Massachusetts. The chief material is the dark blue lime-stone of Great Barrington, left with a rock face, and laid in courses, while the same stone hammered, and thus becoming a lighter blue, forms a portion of the dressing. The remainder of the ornamental stone-work is of the red Longmeadow free-stone, and the red granite of Missouri; the latter of which is almost identical, in character, with the Aberdeen granite of Scotland. The frontage of the building is ninety feet, and the general depth sixty feet. A projection in the rear gives a depth of eighty feet to the main library-room, which is thirty feet wide.

The other principal divisions of the first story are a reading-room, trustees' room, librarian's room, consulting room, janitor's room, and a spacious entrance-hall. In the second story are two halls, which are to be devoted to natural and general history. Between them is a large apartment designed for a fine art gallery. It is lighted entirely from the roof, which, above the gallery, is constructed of Lenox plate-glass. The library-room furnishes space for about thirty thousand volumes, and the other rooms are amply spacious for the purposes for which they are designed.

The nucleus of the library was that of the Pittsfield Athenæum, which was transferred to the new organization in November, 1872, on condition that it should be kept free to the citizens of the town. It contained four thousand and two hundred volumes, of which the greater part were of a choice character, and

---

[1] Mr. Treanor obtained his first reputation as a builder, by the construction of St. Joseph's Church, Pittsfield. He was afterwards the builder of the cathedral at Boston, and other noted public edifices.

scarcely any worthless. To these was afterwards added the Medical College library, of about a thousand volumes, of which a portion were medical works, many of them obsolete. But beside these, it contained a very valuable collection of pamphlets upon general subjects, dating back to the beginning of the century, and some rare books. Hon. H. L. Dawes subsequently presented to the institution about fifteen hundred volumes of public documents, among which were some very valuable series. Mr. Phinehas Allen presented the complete files of the *Pittsfield Sun*, from 1800 to 1872, and a few other rare newspapers. Rev. E. Livingston Wells, presented several files of leading newspapers of dates previous to 1820. Hon. Thomas Allen, among other books, presented an interesting collection of French pamphlets of the era of the Consulate and Empire. Hon. Thomas Colt presented a rich collection of historical manuscripts, pertaining chiefly to western Massachusetts, and the French and Indian wars in New York. Franklin E. Taylor, of New York, gave the splendid work of Luigi Canina, on the edifices of ancient Rome.

Dr. W. E. Vermilye gave the natural and documentary histories of the State of New York. The trustees received the loan from the state-department at Boston, of the duplicate files of the *Boston Advertiser* from 1844 to 1871. There has been a very liberal contribution of smaller but exceedingly interesting donations, including the earlier newspapers of Pittsfield and Stockbridge; and the library contains much to interest the general, as well as the local, historian ; a very unusual amount, indeed, for an institution of so recent a date. The cabinets are also of great value, although the classification of that of mineralogy has been postponed until the completion of the new building. It includes the collection made for the medical college, principally under the direction of Professor Dewey; the small but rich collection made by the scientific section of the Young Men's Association ; several hundred specimens gathered by the national survey of the fortieth parallel ; and many fine single specimens contributed by individuals. Among the most notable of these is a very large and beautiful polished fortification agate, given by Mr. B. C. Blodgett, who bought it in the rough at Mount Blanc. A thorough examination of the collection of agates in the British museum failed to discover its equal.

The athenæum is still in a somewhat inchoate state; but it has

RESIDENCE OF HON. THOMAS ALLEN.

been placed upon a foundation which renders its permanence secure. We proceed to give sketches of its principal benefactors.

Hon. Jonathan Allen first married Elizabeth, daughter of Dr. Perez Marsh of Dalton, and a granddaughter of Col. Israel Williams of Hatfield. His second wife, Eunice Williams, daughter of Darius Larned of Pittsfield, was also a granddaughter of Colonel Williams. There were two children of the first marriage, and eight of the second; of which the third, Thomas, was born August 29, 1813. After preparation at the Berkshire gymnasium, then just established by Professor Dewey, he entered Union College in 1829, and graduated in 1832. He commenced the study of the law at Albany; but its prosecution was interrupted by the approach of cholera to that city in its first fearful visitation to America. Family misfortunes, involving much loss of property, rendered it impossible for Mr. Allen to resume his studies as before; and with twenty-five dollars only for capital, he repaired to the city of New York, where he was able to earn a salary of three hundred dollars per annum as copying-clerk in a lawyer's office. He was also for eighteen months editor of *The Family Magazine*, a very popular illustrated monthly journal; and, by this and other literary work, contrived to live. For editing a digest of the decisions of the New York courts, he received a small but select law-library.

In 1835, he was admitted to the bar; and in 1836, his uncle by marriage, General Ripley, then a representative in congress from Louisiana, offered to resign to him his law-practice in New Orleans. Intending to accept this office, Mr. Allen spent the winter of 1836-7 in Washington, observing the short but excited session of congress. But General Ripley's health failing in the spring of 1837, and his death soon following, Mr. Allen gave over his project of removing to Louisiana, and undertook the publication and editorship of the *Madisonian* newspaper; the first number being issued August 16, 1837. In the ensuing election for congressional printer, Mr. Allen was chosen, after three days' contest; the other candidates being the veteran publishers, Blair & Rives of the *Globe*, and Gale & Seaton of the *National Intelligencer*.

The *Madisonian* obtained a remarkably large circulation for that era, and contributed greatly to the election of President Harrison. But Mr. Allen left it in 1842, and removed to St.

Louis, where, on the 12th of July, he married Miss Ann C., daughter of William Russell, Esq.

At St. Louis, he soon gave up the practice of the law and devoted himself to public interests, prominently in connection with railroad-projects. After several years of study and preliminary measures, he commenced in 1848, those public labors in that direction, which have accomplished results then hardly hoped for by the most sanguine. The United States had then only about seven thousand miles of railroad, of which not a mile was beyond the Mississippi. Various projects had been broached for a line to the Pacific coast; but they were almost universally scouted as impracticable, and it was very largely through his influence that the first road of that character was begun in 1850, by a company of which he was president, and which obtained aid from congress, and the state-legislature, mainly by his efforts. When he resigned its presidency in 1854, thirty-eight miles of the road were in operation, and over one hundred more under construction.

In 1850, he was chosen state-senator from St. Louis, for four years, during which he served as chairman of the committee of internal improvements. In 1854, he declined a re-nomination, and for several years gave his attention to his private affairs, which had suffered from his absorption in the business of the Pacific railroad; his property consisting in great part of city-lots then unoccupied. In 1858, he founded the well-known banking-house of Allen, Copp & Nisbet, of which he is still the head.

Meanwhile, in 1855, he commenced at Pittsfield, a spacious and elegant mansion, on the lands received by his grandfather as the first settled minister of the town. A considerable portion of these grounds had always remained attached to the homestead; and, by re-purchasing the portion sold for a democratic hotel in 1809, Mr. Allen rendered them ample, and opened the view to Park square. The house, which is an excellent specimen of the Elizabethan style, is constructed of the peculiar dark-blue limestone of Great Barrington, one of the most admired building-stones of Berkshire. It was completed in 1858, and Mr. Allen has since occupied it in summer; retaining his winter-residence in St. Louis.

Mr. Allen continued this double residence during the civil war, and manifested in St. Louis the same zeal for the Union which he exhibited in Pittsfield; and in the same practical manner.

On the completion of his house at Pittsfield, Mr. Allen intended to pause in his business-career, and give himself up to literary and rural pursuits. But he was soon tempted from that life by an opportunity to purchase the Iron Mountain and St. Louis railroad. We will not attempt to relate the story of his management of that great work or its extension, by means of the Cairo and Fulton road, across the state of Arkansas to the northern border of Texas. His labors in completing these roads have been enormous, and form a conspicuous feature in the history of the Mississippi valley.

Besides the places of trust and power of which we have spoken, Mr. Allen has held numerous others of great importance to the state of Missouri and the country. The railroads of which he is president have an aggregate length of over seven hundred miles; and, including these, he is president of nine different corporations, which employ a very large number of men. The amount of other property, besides his own personal estate, which is administered by him, is also great. But in these numerous and arduous labors for the development of the material resources of his adopted state, he has not forgotten the interests of science. By persistent effort, he carried through the legislature in 1852, a bill for the geological survey of Missouri. In 1871, he endowed a chair of mining and metallurgy in Washington University at St. Louis. In 1872, he was chosen president of the newly-formed university-club of St. Louis, and at the opening of their club-house, delivered a philosophical address which was published and made a deep impression. Indeed, wherever he has had opportunity he has manifested a warm interest in all institutions intended to promote classical learning or practical science; and his addresses at their public meetings have been numerous and valuable.

Calvin Martin was born in Hancock, August 7, 1787, and was admitted to the Berkshire bar in 1814. From that time to his death, September 6, 1867, he was a lawyer and a prosperous citizen of Pittsfield. He was a director of the Agricultural Bank, and the first president of the cemetery-corporation. Throughout his life he was a friend of popular education, and his gift to the athenæum was a proof that his interest in that subject continued to the end.

Phinehas Allen, the younger, was born in 1807, in the gambrel-roof cottage, which had served as a printing-office for four newspapers. At the age of six years, he began to be initiated into the mysteries of the printer's craft; a pedestal of boxes being built to enable him to reach the type in their cases. He soon became an enthusiast in the art; and, long after his pecuniary means freed him from the necessity of mechanical labor, he was accustomed, on many days, for mere pleasure, to set more type than is the ordinary task of a journeyman. In 1829, his father, the founder of the *Sun*, admitted him as a partner in its publication and editorship.

Filial love and reverence were among the most prominent traits in his character, and he adopted without reserve the political opinions and business-habits of his father. Even after his father's death, the bookstore and newspaper were conducted under the old firm name of P. Allen & Son, and as nearly as the junior partner could judge, as his father would have done in the same circumstances. The younger Mr. Allen was of course an unfailing supporter of the democratic party, and for many years a prominent member of its managing committees in the state, as well as the county.

On the death of Hon. Jonathan Allen, in 1845, he was appointed postmaster, and held the office, except for a brief interval, till 1861, performing its duties in all respects so as to command the popular appreciation. In the estimation of the department he ranked as second among the postmasters of the Union in point of faithfulness and accuracy. Neither partisan jealousy or private pique could find anything in his administration to impeach. His views of editorial duty were not always in accord with popular opinions; but none doubted his sincerity. His conduct towards all institutions for the public good, from those for the support of religion, morality and education, down to those of a minor, but still important, character was uniformly generous. His views of life were genial and charitable, and his personal character was beyond reproach. He was a firm and faithful friend, and his affection for those whom he especially esteemed, was most ardent and trusting.

He married, in 1833, Miss Maria, daughter of Jason Clapp, who died in 1866. He died July 4, 1873.

His last act in the endowment of the public library, after a just provision for those who had claims upon him, was consistent with his whole life.

In one of the later years of the eighteenth century, Hon. William Walker of Lenox, needing a farmer upon his place, obtained the services of Patrick Plunkett, a young Irishman, of whom we have the following spirited story :

He had come out to America " to see the world," in company with a fellow-countryman named Gracie—a "scribe," who had lived in Lenox, and knowing that Judge Walker wanted a capable helper, recommended Plunkett. He was thoroughly honest, and, although uneducated, had the naturally sagacious judgment which places a just estimate on the best things in life.

A kind Providence, and his own wise instinct, helped him in choosing for his wife one who was in all respects a remarkable woman. Patrick had worked for Judge Walker two or three years, when an irrepressible longing to see somebody from the old country seized him. He was then the only Irishman in all this region, and he resolved on a trip to New York. Just then—1795-6-7—many were fleeing from Ireland, driven forth by the disorders of the rebellion; and among those who sought refuge in New York, were a well-to-do gentleman and his wife, who had brought with them their fatherless niece, Mary Robinson, whose brothers were active participants in that struggle. They were all boarding in New York, with no thought but to return to green Erin as soon as the country should be pacified ; when the homesick young man from Lenox arrived in town he saw the blooming Miss Mary ; was conquered, and asked for her hand. He was bidden by her prudent guardians to wait awhile; but he returned to Lenox, with a new hope in his heart, and a new light in his eye, literally to labor and to wait ; and to add to the tidy sum which he had already saved.

On the day after Christmas, 1799, he married Mary Robinson, and, from that hour, wisely gave himself up to the guidance and inspiration of a superior spirit. She was an industrious, frugal, resolute, God-fearing woman ; and seldom did heat or cold, or storm detain her or her household from the ministrations of Doctor Shepard—a sample Puritain—in the meeting-house on the hill. The stern doctrines of the assembly's catechism were learned in the district-school by every pupil; and they must have helped to mould the minds which so received them.

Both Mrs. Plunkett and her husband had an almost superstitious reverence for that wisdom which is condensed between the covers of books. They lived isolated, on a farm, and were the only Irish family in the region ; so that they had little temptation to spend their evenings abroad. And, as soon as the children could read well, these evenings were consecrated to the acquisition of that wonderful book, knowledge, which to their unlettered parents, seemed a talisman, sure to put its possessors ahead in the race of life. At that day the Lenox library could all have been carried in a bushel-basket ; but it contained some of the old matchless masterpieces : the *Spectator*, Doctor Johnson's works, and the like. One by one, these were carried to the cottage of the Plunketts, and read aloud to the household-circle. The father and mother listening as eagerly as the children, until every book-no matter how obstruse, had been mastered; so that when the sons went forth to seek their fortunes on the broad arena of the world, they had no mean portion of the culture which comes from acquaintance with the best literary models. And the useful and honorable careers of these sons, and the steps which each took, in his own town, to promote the diffusion of knowledge is a priceless comment on their influence and value.

These sons were William C. of South Adams, Charles H. of Hinsdale, and Thomas F. of Pittsfield, all of whom worked their way to wealth and honorable position. The youngest, Thomas F., was born at Lenox in 1804. His education, so far as schools went, was simply what could be obtained from that excellent institution, the Lenox Academy. For the rest we quote from the account of which we have already made use.

At the age of eighteen, after two years of vain endeavor to like a mechanical handicraft, he entered the broad field of the world ; traveling from town to town through eastern New York; conducting a trade with householders and country-dealers, which, in those days of infrequent communication, rose to considerable proportions ; meeting at the country-inns the more social spirits of each village, and listening with the hungry eagerness of youth to discussions of questions of the day, often viewed from stand-points novel to him.

It was during these five years of sharp apprenticeship to life that Mr. Plunkett gained a shrewd knowledge of men, a keen tact in influencing them, and a small moneyed capital. He always declared that this was the great labor of his life. With it he went to Chester, Mass., and commenced the manufacture of slat window-shades. When these passed out of fashion, he purchased a small cotton-factory ; and, in it, in eight years, accumulated a moderate fortune, with which he felt that he was free to choose a home from the wide world. And he came to Pittsfield in 1836. A landed domain had always been one of his dreams, and he purchased the farm on Unkamet street, next east of the railroad.

But he soon wearied of the slow processes of agriculture, and, in 1839, commenced the cotton-manufacture, as we have related

in the proper connection. In 1866, he closed his business in Pittsfield as a manufacturer. But he had previously become senior-partner in the firm of Plunkett, Wyllys & Co., cotton-manufacturers at South Glastonbury, Conn., of which his son, Major Charles T. Plunkett, is business-manager. Without removing from Pittsfield, he continued this business until his death; and also invested largely in the Union Manufacturing Company of North Manchester, Conn., of which his son Thomas F., is treasurer and agent, and of which Mr. Plunkett was president at the time of his death.

As a financier, Mr. Plunkett held many honorable positions. For twenty-seven years he was a director of the Agricultural Bank, and for five its president. From the first organization of the Berkshire Life Insurance Company, he was among its most influential officers; and, upon the death of Governor Briggs, in 1861, he succeeded him as president. His business-talent contributed essentially to the remarkable success of the company. His services to the town in connection with the gas and water works, Housatonic, and Boston and Albany railroads, the removal of the county-seat, and in other particulars, have been of great value.

In political life, Mr. Plunkett would doubtless have been more fortunate had his convictions permitted him to choose a side more popular in Massachusetts. But, as it was, his success was honorable. He represented Chester in the legislatures of 1834, and 1835, and Pittsfield in those of 1868, 1869, and 1875. He was senator from Berkshire in 1842, 1843 and 1862. He was twice nominated by the democratic party for lieutenant-governor, and once for representative in congress. These positions were, however, but faint indications of the esteem in which he was held. Official place sometimes offered him opportunity to effect cherished objects; but, as a rule, his influence did not depend upon it.

In April, 1830, Mr. Plunkett married Miss Hannah S. Taylor of Chester, who died in 1844. In October, 1847, he married Miss Harriet Merrick Hodge of Hadley. He died October 31, 1875.

Mr. Plunkett was a man of original and energetic thought, uniquely fitted for the places which he filled. He was a close observer of men and things, with a happy faculty of adapting all he learned to whatever purpose he had in hand. His sympathies were quick, and nothing which pertained to the welfare of the community, or of the country, was foreign to them. For forty years he was fully identified with the public affairs of Pittsfield, and during all that time there was hardly a project for public improvements in whose discussion he did not take part, and few which he was not concerned in carrying out.[1]

The peculiar love which the inhabitants of mountainous regions bear to their homes, is a matter of trite remark; and is perhaps due to the distinctness of outline and feature, which individualizes each locality, and renders it easy for the imagination to endow it with life and character. This individuality, Pittsfield, by the completeness and picturesqueness of its encircling bounds, possesses in an unusual degree; and it seems to have inspired in many of its best citizens, a corresponding affection. We have already noted this attribute in several of the subjects of our biographical sketches; and, to some good extent, it characterized most of them. In the character of Mr. Plunkett it was a prominent feature. He never wavered in his love for and loyalty to the county of Berkshire and the town of Pittsfield. On his return from a tour in Europe, he declared, with enthusiastic emphasis, that, in his estimation there was no place in the entire world that could equal Pittsfield as a place of residence, and this feeling he constantly manifested in his life.

Rev. Dr. Todd shared largely in this sentiment. Indeed, it began to be inspired long before he became a resident of the town, when in the summer of 1834, passing through it on a trip to Saratoga, he was struck with its beauty, and celebrated it eloquently in the Northampton newspapers. His biographer says, with striking truth:

* * * No one knew him thoroughly who did not know him in Berkshire county, in Pittsfield, in the First Church, and in his own family.

The county of Berkshire was to him the most beautiful region in the world. He would often point out its natural charms to strangers, and speak of them in his family letters, with the enthusiasm of a mind highly sensitive to the beautiful and poetic. In all this region he was recognized as a kind of bishop, partly, in later years, on account of his age and experience; partly because of his being pastor of the leading church in the county; but most of all, on account of his strong common sense and practical wisdom, and his unconscious tendency

---

[1] The statements and opinions regarding Mr. Plunkett, given in the text, were in part communicated to the Pittsfield newspapers, by the writer, at the time of his death. In repeating them here, the same language is sometimes used.

Yours truly,
Jno. Todd.

to push to the front and take the lead, from sheer weight and energy of character. There was scarcely a convention or anniversary, a dedication or an installation, or a meeting or gathering of any kind, secular or religious, which did not demand his presence.

The story of Doctor Todd's pastorate in Pittsfield is included in our account of the First Church, and a general sketch of his life is rendered unnecessary in this place by the publication of an excellent and universally read biography.[1]

Still some general account of one who loved the town so well and conferred so much honor upon it will naturally be expected.

John Todd was born at Rutland, Vt., on the ninth of October, 1800. A few months before, his father, Dr. Timothy Todd, a noted physician of that town, and a member of the governor's council, met with an accident, which crippled him until his death which occurred when his son was six years old. Mrs. Todd being abruptly informed of the accident, and being pre-disposed to insanity, became at once a hopeless lunatic. Before his death, Dr. Timothy Todd, after several changes of residence and business, finally settled at Killingworth, Conn. In these changes his property had been nearly dissipated, and his family was left so destitute, that it was necessary to borrow shoes for his youngest son to wear at the funeral. The family was scattered, and John was received into the family of his father's youngest sister Matilda, who had married John Hamilton, of North Killingworth.

In the year 1810, Mr. Hamilton being a prisoner among the Spaniards, and his wife breaking up housekeeping, John lived for several months with his cousin Jeremiah Evarts, of New Haven, who had married a daughter of Roger Sherman; but, Mr. Hamilton returning in the spring, he again became a member of his family. In the fall of 1812, he went to live with his uncle, Dr. Jonathan Todd, at East Guilford, in order to obtain better schooling. In 1815, his cousin, Mr. Evarts, who had removed to Charlestown, to become editor of the *Panoplist*, again offered him a home in his family, which was accepted. Mr. Evarts was treas-

---

[1] JOHN TODD, the story of his life, told mainly by himself, compiled and edited by his son, John E. Todd: New York, Harper & Brothers, 1876. John Edwards Todd, eldest son of Rev. Dr. Todd, was born at Northampton, December 6, 1834, graduated at Yale College in 1855. He was for several years pastor of the Central Church, Boston, and has since held the same position in the Church of the Redeemer, at New Haven.

urer of the American Board of Commissioners for Foreign Missions, and was connected with several other societies; but he seemed not to have recognized the talents of his cousin, and suffered him to work his way in his family by petty and tedious labor. Young Todd, however, steadily pursued his classical studies, with some dim view of sometime entering college. In 1817, a revival of religion commenced in Charlestown, and he was one of its subjects. This circumstance revived and intensified his desire to obtain a college-education, with the ultimate view of becoming a missionary; and, although utterly without means, and but illy fitted in his studies, he determined to make the attempt, and was admitted to Yale College in the fall of 1818. Poverty and ill health haunted him through his whole college-course, but he sustained himself by school-teaching, and by writing for several publications; receiving also some aid from Christian ladies and gentlemen who had become interested in the promising young divinity-student.

Immediately upon graduation he entered the Theological Seminary at Andover, where he maintained himself in the same way as at college, although with improved health and rather better pay for his literary labors. Here he was in danger of giving himself up to a literary and editorial life, having at one time determined to accept the editorship of the *Boston Recorder and Telegraph*. His love of preaching saved him. In June, 1825, he was licensed to preach by the Suffolk Association of Congregational Ministers, and in May, 1826, he left Andover to take charge of the Orthodox Congregational Church at Groton. Here he had a stormy pastorate of six years, the Unitarian denomination being in a majority in the town, and sectarian feeling running high

In 1832, he removed to Northampton and became pastor of the newly organized Edwards Church. Here he had a pleasant pastorate and remained until 1834, when he accepted a call to the Clinton street Congregational Church at Philadelphia. This church, which originated in a Sabbath-school, was the first of its denomination in the city, where Presbyterianism was predominant; the undertaking at once excited the bitter opposition of that sect, and Mr. Todd led a laborious, vexatious, and disagreeable life while engaged in it. He was, however, well-nigh successful in establishing the church on a firm basis. In December, 1839, he resigned

its charge, and in January commenced preaching for the First
Congregational Church at Pittsfield, over which he was installed
pastor on the sixteenth of February. He thus gives his first
impressions of his new home: "Everything seems strange to me
here. It seems strange to see the mountains all around me covered
with snow. It seems strange not to be able to leave the stove for
half an hour without having all the fire burned out and the room
cold. It seems strange to find the water frozen in your room,
though you make up a hot fire at ten o'clock, and get up at four.
It seems strange to go to meeting when the thermometer is six
below zero, and stranger still to see the Baptists go down to the
river and baptize seven, when the thermometer is six below zero,
and a man has to stand with a rake and keep the pool from freezing over. Last Sabbath you might have seen the richest man in
town going to church with a large buffalo-robe under his arm,
which he used in his pew; and I actually had my toes touched
with frost in the pulpit." His biographer thus completes the picture.

Fronting the little oval park by the side of the old town-hall, which
thirty years more have not yet improved, stood the long, cupola-
crowned white frame meeting-house of the First Church—an object of
great admiration to its original builders, but somewhat the worse for
wear, and presenting a strange contrast with the new and elegant edifice
which the pastor had just left. In the interior, low galleries ran around
three sides, one of them being appropriated by men, the opposite one
by women, and the middle one by the choir, who were not crowded by
an organ. In the back corners, under the galleries, lingered two or three
box-pews claimed by some of the older families; along the fronts of
the galleries ran interminable stove-pipes, which dripped pyroligneous
acid abundantly on the well-stained carpets, but diffused little heat;
behind the lofty pulpit, a supposed window was concealed by faded and
dingy crimson tapestry. But the cheery disposition of the new pastor,
determined to look on the brightest side of everything, found something even here to approve. "The church has a good bell, a *very* good
town-clock on it, and a good clock inside, on the gallery fronting the pulpit." In his new *people* he found much greater cause for satisfaction.
"It is a great, rich, proud, enlightened, powerful people. They move
slowly, but they tread like the elephant. They are cool, but kind, sincere, great at hearing, but very critical. I have never had an audience
who heard so critically. There is ten times more intellect that is cultivated than we have ever had before. You would be surprised to see
how much they read. The ladies are most abundant, intelligent,

refined, and kind. A wider, better, harder, or more interesting field no man need desire. It is large enough to make him tremble, and desirable enough to satisfy his most fastidious wishes."

How well Doctor Todd filled this field in his pastoral relations has been shown already; but he was also deeply interested in all the efforts for public improvement, and in the literary institutions of the town. No one of its citizens was more jealous of its honor, or more anxious to enhance its reputation. He was an earnest advocate of the introduction of pure water, of the beautifying of the public streets and squares of the rural cemetery, and of all similar works, and of all measures of public instruction.

The Medical College, the Young Ladies' Institute and other seminaries; the Young Men's Association, and the public library were all deeply indebted to him. For many years he, as well as Rev. Dr. Humphrey, plead eloquently for some such gifts as afterwards laid the foundation for the athenæum; and his selection as one of the trustees was a just recognition of his previous efforts. Doctor Todd's reputation as an author reflected honor upon the town, and a brief record of his works will not be out of place here. He appears to have had an early predilection for literary work. Indeed, at one time he seems to have been in doubt, although not very long, whether he should abandon the pulpit for the editorial chair. This was in 1825, when, being a student at Andover, he was invited to become editor of the *Boston Recorder and Telegraph;* and did edit the *Christian Almanac.* He first began the writing of books at Northampton, in 1833, his object being to aid himself in the support of his insane and widowed mother. His first book and one of his most popular was Lectures to Children. This was followed by Simple Sketches and the Student's Manual; which last, his biographer rightly considers as on the whole, perhaps, the most important of all his published works. "For nearly forty years," says Mr. Todd, "it has found a place in students' libraries, and to this day enjoys the singular distinction of being the only standard authority in the field which it occupies. During his whole life, the author was constantly receiving letters of thanks from men in this and other lands, for the influence exerted upon them by this book. It has passed through a great many editions in England, as well as in this country; over one hundred and fifty thousand copies having been sold to young men in London alone."

HISTORY OF PITTSFIELD. 661

In 1847, Doctor Todd published Stories on The Shorter Catechism, and in 1867, "two little books * * * Serpents in the Dove's Nest; a plain and forcible treatise upon certain prevalent vices; * * * and Woman's Rights, a presentation of his views upon that much discussed subject."

In 1869, he visited California, and took part in the ceremonies at the uniting of the eastern and western sections of the Pacific railroad. On his return, he delivered a course of lectures, the profits from which he gave to the Young Men's Association. They were published in a handsome volume, and formed one of the most popular and interesting accounts of the golden state.

Besides his larger works, he wrote many smaller tracts and newspaper-essays which were quite as widely read, and had as powerful an influence. Among these, one of the most valued in Pittsfield is that styled Polished Diamonds; being an account of the Christian life of his eldest daughter during a painful illness of many years.

Henry Laurens Dawes was born at Cummington, Hampshire county, Massachusetts, October 30, 1816. His family is a branch of that of the same name which is distinguished in politics and literature in eastern Massachusetts. He graduated at Yale College in the class of 1839. While a student at law he taught school and edited the *Greenfield Gazette*. He was admitted to the bar in 1842, and commenced practice at North Adams, where, for a time, he edited the *Transcript*. He also represented that town in the legislatures of 1848, 1849, and 1852; and in the constitutional convention of 1853. In 1850, he was elected to the state-senate. From 1853 until 1857, he was district-attorney for the western district of Massachusetts. In 1857, there being a very decisive contest pending, regarding the future status of political parties, Mr. Dawes, being the exponent of republican principles in the westernmost district of Massachusetts, was chosen by a large majority over the democratic and American candidates. And he represented this district until 1874, when he declined a re-nomination. In the following session of the legislature, he was chosen a senator of the United States.

CHAPTER XXVIII.

MISCELLANEOUS.

[1800-1876.]

Agricultural society—Schools—Newspapers—Removal of county-buildings—Banks and insurance company—Academy of Music—Abraham Burbank—Edward Learned—New manufactures—Valuation and census.

THE Berkshire Agricultural Society, whose story we left in the year 1825, has continued to flourish, and its transactions have often been interesting and important; but none specially connect it with the town of Pittsfield, until the purchase of exhibition-grounds, in the year 1855.

This was not at that time an entirely new project. As early as 1822, on motion of Thomas Gold, the society voted " to provide a permanent location of land, in Pittsfield, for a show-ground—either by purchase or leasing, as might be most for the benefit of the society—and that the executive committee look for some suitable place, ascertain the terms, and report at a special meeting." There is no mention of any such report; but at the annual meeting of 1823, on motion of Hon. Phinehas Allen, Samuel D. Colt, John Dickinson, and Thomas B. Strong were appointed a committee to correspond with Henry W. Dwight, then at Washington,[1] to ascertain if the society could lease the Cantonment grounds, and if so, to obtain the terms from the government. The committee were directed to report at the next quarterly meeting of the executive committee, who were authorized, if they should deem the terms advantageous, to lease the premises for one or more years. No mention is made in the record of any farther action, and the project seems to have slumbered until 1855.

On the 9th of January in that year, the society voted that the time had come to purchase land for its annual cattle-show and

[1] Mr. Dwight was at this time president of the society as well as member of Congress.

fair; and the following committee were appointed to consider the feasibility and expediency of the plan : E. H. Kellogg and Henry Colt of Pittsfield, Socrates Squier, Justus Tower and Eli Bradley of Lanesboro, William E. Johnson and Asahel Foote, of Williamstown, and Joshua R. Lawton of Great Barrington.

At a special meeting, May 1st, the committee reported favorably, and, after much discussion, the society gave them full powers to make arrangements for the purchase.

On the 7th of July the committee—to which Hon. Julius Rockwell was added—were authorized to purchase the land for which they had taken a bond of William W. Goodman; and, on the 31st, these grounds—which embrace twenty-nine and two-thirds acres on the west side of Wahconah street a mile and a half north of the park—were deeded to the society by Mr. Goodman, the price paid being twenty-two hundred dollars.

On the 23d of July, Socrates Squier, Henry Colt and Robert Pomeroy were appointed a sub-committee to erect such fences and buildings as they might deem necessary, and prepare suitable grounds for the exhibition of horses.

The eastern portion of the land purchased of Mr. Goodman is rather an abrupt hill-side, which leads to a broad and nearly level surface, in much the larger portion of the estate. On this elevation, which commands superb views of the neighboring scenery, the committee erected, near the brow of the hill, a plain wooden building of one story in the form of the letter T, having a length of one hundred feet, and a breadth of forty. The traverse is one hundred and twenty long by forty wide. The interior was left rough without paint or plaster. The roof was surrounded by a railing and seats, and furnishes a delightful promenade. A few rods west of this building, which is styled Agricultural Hall, an excellent half-mile track, on a perfectly level surface, was built for the exhibition of horses and the trial of their speed. On the north-east of the hall a block of booths, containing some fifteen stalls, was provided for the sale of refreshments and other articles. In 1860, a dining-hall, forty feet square, was added to the north end of the exhibition-building, giving it the shape of a cross. Sheds and barns for the protection of stock brought to the cattle-shows have since been added at different times.

The expenditures, in 1855, were as follows : for the hall, built by Abraham Burbank, twenty-two hundred dollars; for the fence, built by Thomas G. Atwood, eight hundred dollars; for track and roads, built by O. H. Beach, eight hundred and fifty dollars. Total, three thousand eight hundred and fifty dollars.

There has been since expended: for additional booths, seven hundred and fifty dollars; for dining-room and secretary's office added to the hall, six hundred dollars; for barn, eight hundred dollars; for sheds, four hundred dollars; for new gate and treasurer's office, five hundred and fifty dollars. Total, thirty-one hundred dollars—making the grand total of expenditures on the grounds, except for ordinary repairs and some small items, six thousand nine hundred and fifty dollars.

Up to the year 1855, the cost of premiums and the small incidental expenses of the society were defrayed by the annual interest of the notes of members and the state-appropriation, with occasional private donations.[1]

The exhibitions of cattle and other stock, were made at first on the park, and afterwards upon the town-lot on First street, north of the Boston and Albany railroad. Household-manufactures, agricultural implements, vegetables, fruit and the like small articles were displayed after 1832 until 1848, in the town-hall, and after the latter date in Burbank's hall, on North street. Both of these rooms were usually crowded to suffocation on the exhibition-days—as even the larger exhibition-hall on the society's grounds still is.

Prior to 1855, there was no charge for admission to any of the departments of the society's exhibitions, and it derived no income from the rent of booths; but from that date the receipts from rents and entrance-fees for four years were as follows: 1855, thirteen hundred dollars; 1856, fifteen hundred and fifty dollars; 1857, seventeen hundred dollars; 1858, fifteen hundred and seventy-five dollars. In 1875, the receipts from these sources were seventeen hundred and twenty-four dollars.

The premiums awarded in the four years after the exhibition

[1] These private donations were very rare after the state began to grant its aid to the society. Before that, they were an essential part of its income. In 1813, Allan Melville, brother of Major Melville, and father of Herman and Allan Melville, obtained a hundred and thirty-eight dollars for it from friends in Boston, and T. Storm, of New York, made it a donation of fifty dollars. It awarded, that year, three hundred and sixty-six dollars in premiums. In 1814, Major Melville obtained one hundred and twenty-five dollars from citizens of Boston, and the premiums amounted to five hundred and twenty-three dollars.

was removed to the society's grounds, varied from nine hundred to eleven hundred and seventy-five dollars. In the four years ending with 1875, they were as follows: 1872, three thousand five hundred and twenty-two dollars; 1873, three thousand four hundred and forty-six dollars; 1874, three thousand two hundred and forty-five dollars; in 1875, two thousand eight hundred and seventy-five dollars.

In 1855, also, a change was made in the basis of membership in the society. The practice of accepting the notes of members as an endowment of the institution, and the payment of the interest as an annual fee was done away with, and provision was made for two classes only: honorary and ordinary. The honorary members consist only of distinguished agriculturists, or eminent advocates of the agricultural interest, residing out of the county. They are elected by the executive committee, and may speak but not vote in the meetings of the society. Ordinary members become such either by the payment of one dollar annually, or the payment of ten dollars in advance, which constitutes them life-members. Ladies become life-members on the payment of five dollars. In 1875, the society numbered one thousand and fifty-one members, of whom four hundred and twenty-one resided in Pittsfield, and one hundred and six in Lanesboro. About half were members for life. The receipts from annual members in 1875, were four hundred and eighty-seven dollars; from new life-members they were one hundred and twelve dollars. These figures will serve to show something of the growth of the society. Still other changes incidental to the purchase of the cattle-show grounds were the extension of the festival from two days to three, and increased encouragement for the exhibition of horses. At the cattle-show of 1853, there was only one division of this class of animals, and the premiums amounted to only sixty-six dollars. In 1854, there were two divisions—horses, mares and colts—and the premiums were seventy-one dollars. In 1855, the number of divisions became five, besides one for female equestrianism; and one hundred and forty-one dollars awarded in premiums. In 1857, there were six divisions, and the premiums were one hundred and eighty-four dollars. Since then the policy of the society has varied in regard to the amount appropriated for the encouragement of trotting-horses.

The society celebrated its semi-centennial anniversary on the second day of the cattle-show of 1860, by a dinner in its new dining-hall. The exercises were under the charge of a committee consisting of E. H. Kellogg, Thomas Colt and Phinehas Allen. Speeches were made by Messrs. Kellogg, president of the society, Thomas B. Strong, its first secretary, Ex-Governor George N. Briggs, who was elected president of the society in 1830, but being a young lawyer was too modest to take the head of a society of farmers; Henry Hubbard; Henry Chamberlain of Dalton, the only survivor of those who took premiums at the first cattle-show; and John C. Grey of Boston. Hon. William J. Bacon, of Utica, N. Y., spoke as the representative of his father, a letter from whom was read by him. A letter was also read from Francis Brewer, of Springfield, who was a witness of the first cattle-show of which he gave pleasant reminiscences.

At the cattle-show of 1849, an incident occurred which conferred so much honor upon the society that it must be recounted, associating its name with the noblest Georgic ever written by an American or English poet: THE PLOUGHMAN, written by Oliver Wendell Holmes. This poem is so familiar to most readers that it is useless to reprint it here. We will, however, relate the circumstances under which it was produced. At the cattle-show of 1849, Doctor Holmes being then a summer-resident of Pittsfield, was appointed chairman of the committee on the plowing-match, and prefaced his report as follows :

The committee on the plowing-match are fully sensible of the dignity and importance of the office entrusted to their judgment. To decide upon the comparative merits of so many excellent specimens of agricultural art is a most delicate, responsible and honorable duty.

The plow is a very ancient implement. It is written in the English language p-l-o-u-g-h, and, by the association of free and independent spellers, p-l-o-w. It may be remarked that the same gentlemen can, by a similar process, turn their coughs into cows; which would be the cheapest mode of raising live stock, although it is to be feared that they (referring to the cows,) would prove but low-bred animals. Some have derived the English word plough from the Greek *ploutos*, the wealth which comes from the former suggesting its resemblance to the latter. But such resemblances between different languages may be carried too far: as for example, if a man should trace the name of the Altamaha to the circumstance that the first settlers were all tomahawked on the margin of that river.

Time and experience have sanctioned the custom of putting only plain, practical men upon this committee. Were it not so, the most awkward blunders would be constantly occurring. The inhabitants of our cities, who visit the country during the fine season, would find themselves quite at a loss if an overstrained politeness should place them in this position. Imagine a trader, or a professional man, from the capital of the state, unexpectedly called upon to act in rural matters. Plowshares are to him shares that pay no dividends. A coulter, he supposes, has something to do with a horse. His notions of stock were obtained in Faneuil Hall market, where the cattle looked funnily enough, to be sure, compared with the living originals. He knows, it is true, that there is a difference in cattle, and would tell you that he prefers the sirloin breed. His children are equally unenlightened; they know no more of the poultry-yard than what they have learned by having the chicken-pox, and playing on a Turkey carpet. Their small knowledge of wool-growing is lam(b)entable.

The history of one of these summer-visitors shows how imperfect is his rural education. He no sooner establishes himself in the country than he begins a series of experiments. He tries to drain a marsh, but only succeeds in draining his own pockets. He offers to pay for carting off a compost heap; but is informed that it consists of corn and potatoes in an unfinished state. He sows abundantly, but reaps little or nothing, except with the implement which he uses in shaving, a process which is frequently performed for him by other people, though he pays no barber's bill. He builds a wire-fence and paints it green, so that nobody can see it. But he forgets to order a pair of spectacles apiece for his cows, who, taken offense at something else take his fence in addition, and make an invisible one of it, sure enough. And, finally, having bought a machine to chop fodder, which chops off a good slice of his dividends, and two or three children's fingers, he concludes that, instead of cutting feed, he will cut farming; and so sells out to one of those plain, practical farmers, such as you have honored by placing them on your committee, whose pockets are not so full when he starts, but have fewer holes and not so many fingers in them.

It must have been one of these practical men whose love of his pursuits led him to send in to the committee the following lines, which it is hoped will be accepted as a grateful tribute to the noble art whose successful champions are now to be named and rewarded.

Doctor Holmes then read the poem now known to fame as The Ploughman.

Since the organization of the society the following citizens of Pittsfield have held its most laborious offices.

PRESIDENTS.

Elkanah Watson, 1811 to October 6, 1814; Thomas Melville, October 6, 1814 to 1816; Thomas Gold, 1816, 1817; Thomas Melville, 1818;

Jonathan Allen, 1820, 1821, 1822; Samuel M. McKay, 1824 ; Thomas B. Strong, 1827, 1828 ; Lemuel Pomeroy, 1831, 1832; Edward A. Newton, 1840; George S. Willis, 1848, 1849; Julius Rockwell, 1854, 1855; Ensign H. Kellogg, 1860, 1861; Thomas Colt, 1862, 1863, 1864 ; John E. Merrill, 1870, 1871.

SECRETARIES.

Thomas B. Strong, 1811; Samuel D. Colt, 1812 to 1814; William C. Jarvis, 1815; Jonathan Allen, 1816, 1817; Thomas A. Gold, 1818 to 1822; Ezekiel R. Colt, 1823, 1824; Josiah Hooker, 1825 to 1827; Henry K. Strong, 1828, 1829; Daniel B. Bush, 1830; Julius Rockwell, 1831 to 1843; Ensign H. Kellogg, 1844 to 1848; Thomas Colt, 1859 to 1861 ; John E. Merrill, 1862 to 1869 ; William H. Murray, 1870, 1876.

TREASURERS.

John B. Root, 1811 to 1814; Ebenezer Center, 1815, 1816; Samuel D. Colt, 1817 to 1844; James Buel, 1845, 1846; Walter Laflin 1847 to 1849; Stephen Reed, 1850 to 1857 ; Henry M. Pierson 1858 to 1876.

Hon. E. H. Kellogg was born at Sheffield in 1812, his father being Elisha Kellogg. He graduated at Amherst College in 1836. He moved to Pittsfield in 1838, and commenced the practice of the law, but after a few years abandoned it for manufacturing. In 1841, he married Miss Caroline L., daughter of David Campbell. Since his residence in Pittsfield he has been prominent in public affairs, and many times represented the town in the legislature, commencing in 1843, and being twice speaker.

Hon. Thomas Colt was born at Pittsfield, June 28, 1823, being the youngest son of Ezekiel R. Colt. He graduated at Williams College, in 1842. In 1856, he was chosen member of the executive council and presidential elector at large. In 1855, he married Catherine M., daughter of William B. Cooley, of Pittsfield, and granddaughter of Rev. Timothy M. Cooley, D. D., of Granville.

The common schools of the town appear to have been generally as good as the average of those in western Massachusetts. Probably there were few of its teachers so incompetent, as Doctor Humphrey describes himself to have been when he first taught a Connecticut district-school. The schools, except in the center-districts, were taught by men in winter, and by women in the summer, until recent years when women have been employed in many of the districts, and indeed as a rule throughout the year. The change has been found advantageous. In 1830, the Center district was divided into the Center, East Center and West Center.

In 1844, there were fifteen districts, and the number had not increased in 1849. The plan of abolishing the district-system in accordance with the views of the State Board of Education was constantly pressed upon the town, but was resisted stoutly by most of the outer districts; and in 1849, Hon. Edward A. Newton offered, as a compromise, a resolution that the school-houses of the several districts, many of which were unfit for their purpose, should be rebuilt by the town. The resolution, with amendments to it proposed in town-meeting, was referred to Calvin Martin, Abel West and James H. Dunham. The committee reported that the town ought to procure a plan or model for all the school-houses so that all should be alike except as to size; and that they should be built by the town, the districts giving the old buildings —the houses to be built two each year, and the first in the districts where they were most needed. The districts were to furnish sites and keep the buildings in repair.

The report was adopted and all the school-houses in the town were rebuilt in the course of a few years. In 1869, the district-system was entirely abolished.

In 1874, a system of graded schools was established for all except a few outer districts. The system as at present established consists of a High school, a First Grammar school, two Secondary Grammar schools, Intermediate and Primary schools. Mr. George H. Cary, principal of the First Grammar school, gave very valuable assistance in fixing this system of organization.

In 1868, Mr. Lebbeus Scott was elected superintendent of schools, but the office was continued only one year. In 1873, it was re-established, and Dr. John M. Brewster was chosen superintendent. At the annual meeting, in 1876, it was again abolished.

From the beginning to the end of the administration of the schools in town, its management has been so much a matter of conflict and the record is so imperfect, that we are able to give only a bare outline of its story. Very great credit is, nevertheless, due to a large number of gentlemen who have labored in the cause of education. About 1824, much feeling was manifested throughout the county on account of the imperfection of the common schools, and an educational society was established for the purpose of reforming their character, of which Henry Hubbard, of Pittsfield, was president, and Henry Marsh, of Dalton, secretary. Thomas B. Strong and Samuel M. McKay were prominent members, and the latter gentleman was appointed by Governor Lincoln, commissioner of education. Their labors doubtless were valuable; and with those of other gentlemen in other parts of the commonwealth, prepared the way for the great improvement in public education, which was accomplished under the lead of Horace Mann. But it was many years before the common schools of Pittsfield became such as they should be.

Dr. Stephen Reed, Dr. O. S. Root, Dr. O. E. Brewster and Rev. Dr. Heman Humphrey, as well as several younger gentlemen, have contributed much towards the later improvements of the schools. Mr. William Renne advocated the rebuilding of the school-houses, in a series of influential articles in the *Culturist and Gazette* newspaper.

In 1827, Thomas Melville, Jr., M. R. Lanckton and Thomas B. Strong were appointed a committee to consider whether the town would establish a separate school for black children; and under their advice the town refused to take any measures in that direction.

Previous to the year 1844, the appropriations for schools in addition to the school-fund, did not exceed sixteen hundred dollars annually. From that time it increased rapidly; the amount being in 1845, seventeen hundred and fifty dollars; in 1849, three thousand and two hundred dollars, including the state-fund; for the year 1853, five thousand dollars, including the High school; in 1860, six thousand and three hundred dollars; in 1865, eight thousand six hundred and fifty dollars; in 1866, thirteen thousand four hundred and fifty dollars; in 1869, nineteen thousand and two hundred dollars; in 1871, twenty-one thousand dollars; in 1872, twenty-two thousand three hundred dollars, with the addition of twenty-five hundred dollars for evening-schools; in 1873, twenty-six thousand and three hundred dollars; in 1874, twenty-eight thousand and five hundred dollars; in 1876, twenty thousand dollars, there being no appropriations for evening-schools.

The ordinary district-school system of Massachusetts prevailed in Pittsfield until the year 1869. To this was added for a portion of the time the Grammar school, required by the laws of the state. There was, almost from the first, a conflict between those who desired an improved system, or a more liberal administration of the old one, and those who were content with a bare compliance with the law, or even less. As early as 1781, under an article in the warrant for a town-meeting, "to see if the town will raise money to set up a grammar school to save the town from a fine," it was voted "that the selectmen be instructed to inform the grand jurymen that the town is not deficient in maintaining schools both summer and winter; although at present a grammar school is not maintained." And the town did not comply with the law until 1792, when a committee was chosen "for the purpose of hiring a master to teach a grammar school, and to attend, with the Rev. Mr. Allen, to visit and inspect the several schools in this town; and that the committee consist of Dr. Timothy Childs, Woodbridge Little and David Bush." In that year a grammar school was established in the new town-house,[1] which was maintained until the year 1824; but with exceedingly varying appropriations, which were rarely sufficient to support the school independently of tuition. In 1824, it was voted, "that instead of appropriating moneys for the support of Latin Grammar schools, the money voted by the town shall be appropriated in the several school-districts for the support of teachers well qualified to instruct youth, in the mode prescribed by an act of our legislature passed February 18, 1822."

From this time the Pittsfield Grammar School, or Academy, appears to have ceased to be a public institution. At this time, however, the system of paying back to parents the taxes paid by them for schooling, to be expended at their discretion for tuition, prevailed, and much of the money returned was received by the Grammar school.

This practice was abolished in 1830, and for many years no grammar school was maintained by the town. The school was, however, continued as a private institution.

In 1849, the town voted that a suitable house should be built on the old burial-ground for a grammar or high school, for the benefit of all the inhabitants of the town; and Thomas F. Plunkett, Walter Laflin, James Francis, John C. West and James D. Colt, 2d, were made a committee to select the site, build the

---

[1] See Volume 1, page 446.

house, and sell so much of the town-land east of the Baptist church and north of the street laid out in part in 1848, between said church and land sold to L. E. Davis, as might be necessary to meet the expense.

No sufficient offer was made for the land during the summer; and a motion at a special meeting in September, that the committee forthwith build, at an expense not exceeding three thousand dollars, was defeated. But the agitation in favor of the school continued, and at the April meeting of 1850, Nathaniel S. Dodge, George S. Willis and James Francis were appointed a committee to build a suitable house for a grammar or high school, at a cost not exceeding three thousand dollars, to be completed in season for the school to commence November 1st. And Dr. O. S. Root, Rev. Henry Clark, and Dr. Oliver E. Brewster were appointed to employ suitable teachers, to determine the qualifications for admission to the school, and to have the oversight and supervision of it.

The school-house, a neat and commodious building for the time, was built, upon plans furnished by J. C. Hoadley, in the north-east corner of the burial-ground, and streets leading to it were opened from it to North and East streets. The school was organized by Mr. Jonathan Tenney, a teacher of very high ability. The succeeding principals have been A. B. Whipple, S. J. Sawyer, W. H. Swift, J. E. Bradley and Albert Tolman.

In 1867, the High-school house was rebuilt, two stories high. In 1870, the Medical College building being for sale, was purchased for eight thousand five hundred dollars, and remodeled at an expense of seven thousand five hundred dollars, for the use of the High and First Grammar schools. In April, 1876, it was burned by an incendiary fire, and in the succeeding summer was rebuilt at a cost of sixteen thousand dollars.

The first public institution in Pittsfield for the higher education of young women, was suggested by the successful efforts of Miss Nancy Hinsdale, in instituting a select female school about the year 1800. Appreciating the efforts of Miss Hinsdale, several gentlemen determined to give their aid in still farther elevating the school; and in 1806, Joshua Danforth, Joseph Merrick, and Ezekiel Bacon, with such as they might associate with themselves, were incorporated as the trustees of the Pittsfield Female Academy, with authority to hold property, in addition to the value of the building, the annual income of which should not exceed twelve hundred dollars.

The first board of trustees erected on the east portion of the present site of the athenæum a commodious building of two stories.[1] Miss Hinsdale was principal until about 1813, commencing with about forty pupils, and closing with about ninety. Miss Eliza Doane, of Boston, instructed the school from 1814 to 1818, and other ladies for shorter periods.

After the dissolution of the Union Parish, the Academy was transferred to the lower story of its meeting-house, on South street, which was fitted up for that purpose. In 1826, the trustees, for the accommodation of a principal and for pupils from abroad, erected a large three-story brick-building, on South street, nearly opposite the school-room.

In April, 1827, the seminary was opened as a boarding-school, under the charge of Eliakim Phelps, assisted by accomplished ladies; and the standard of education was raised. In the fall of 1828, Mr. Phelps was succeeded by Mr. and Mrs. Jonathan L. Hyde, who conducted the school with great ability until 1834. Nathaniel S. Dodge, afterwards an author of some reputation, was principal from 1834 to 1838, when he was succeeded for one year by Rev. Ward Stafford.

About this time the seminary appears to have been abandoned as a corporate institution; but Miss Fanny Hinsdale, niece of its first instructress, opened a select school in the south lecture-room. She was assisted by two female-teachers, and gave instruction in French and Latin, and the higher as well as the lower English branches.

In 1845, Miss Clara Wells hired the boarding-house of the seminary, to which a school-room was afterwards added. Miss Wells had previously acquired a reputation as a teacher of a young ladies' select school, and she soon began to raise the character of the seminary, which she conducted until 1870. During this time, she was generally assisted by a full board of skillful male and female teachers; and the graduates of the institution were excelled by none in accomplishments, or in their acquirements in the more solid branches of learning.

During the few latter years of Miss Wells's connection with the

[1] See view of the park in 1807.

school it was conducted for a time in the Childs Mansion on Jubilee Hill, and the Dr. Robert Campbell House on East street; but, being in ill health, she was unable to fully maintain the standard of the school; and in September, 1870, she went to California, where she died.

Before leaving, however, she associated with herself, Miss Mary E. Salisbury, a lady every way competent to sustain and elevate the institution. In 1872, Miss Salisbury removed the school to the building on South street, erected by Mr. Dillingham, which had been purchased by Prof. Charles E. West, of Brooklyn, who, in 1875, much enlarged and completely remodeled it, making it, with its ample grounds, one of the most pleasant and commodious buildings of its class. Here Miss Salisbury has succeeded in restoring the Pittsfield Young Ladies' Seminary to the prosperity of its best days.

After closing his connection with the Pittsfield Seminary, Mr. N. S. Dodge, for a while, kept a boarding-school for young ladies, in the buildings on the Cantonment grounds, left vacant by the suspension of Professor Dewey's gymnasium. While occupied by him the middle building was burned, and the school was given up.

The Pittsfield Young Ladies' Institute, the most noted and successful institution of learning which has ever existed in Pittsfield, was established by Rev. Wellington Hart Tyler, in the fall of 1841, in the building previously occupied by the gymnasium.

Mr. Tyler was born at Harford, Susquehanna county, Pa., October 14, 1812, being the son of Deacon Joab and Mrs. Nabby (Seymour) Tyler. He graduated at Amherst College, in the class of 1831, taking high rank as a scholar. In 1831 and 1832, he was a student in Andover Theological Seminary. From 1832 to 1834, he taught an academy in Kentucky; from 1834 to 1836, he was tutor in Amherst College; and from 1836 to 1838, principal of the academy at Manlius, N. Y. In 1839, he was licensed to preach, by the Hampshire association, but after preaching a few months at Hadley, his voice failing, he went to Columbia, S. C., where he was principal of a young ladies' seminary until 1841.

In the summer of that year, Mr. Tyler removed to Pittsfield, and hired, of Mr. Pomeroy, the gymnasium-grounds and buildings, in which he immediately established the Pittsfield Young

Ladies' Institute. So little was the public confidence in the undertaking, that the principal was refused credit for a barrel of flour at the opening of the school. But he was not a man to be discouraged or to fail; and in 1845, he was able to purchase the gymnasium-property, with the seven and a quarter acres of the Cantonment grounds which lie west of First street, paying for them nine thousand dollars. In the following year he built, in place of the burned dormitory, a brick-chapel upon an elegant classic model.

Mr. Tyler was pronounced by Rev. Dr. Todd a "model teacher," and he possessed an energy and ambition which rendered success certain. More, perhaps, than all, he had a wife characterized by the same qualities, who gave all her abilities and energies to the same end. It was Mr. Tyler's ambition to make the school at least the equal of the best of its kind in the country; and, in order to do so, he employed a large number of the best teachers. In music and the fine arts, as was fitting for a seminary for young ladies he endeavored especially to excel. But he desired to make the whole course of study harmonious, and such as would not only cultivate all the moral and intellectual faculties of the pupils, but develop healthfully their physical constitution. It was, at one time, his intention to give the institution a collegiate character; and in March, 1853, to aid him in doing this, he called a convention of gentlemen distinguished for their interest in education. Rev. Nathaniel Hewitt, D. D., of Bridgeport, presided, and Rev. S. C. Brace was secretary. Among the members were Gov. George N. Briggs, President Hopkins of Williams College, Rev. Drs. Henry Neill, Samuel Harris, John Todd, A. McEwen and Absalom Peters. The discussions were very thorough; and a very exhaustive report, prepared by the Rev. Dr. Harris, was adopted and printed under the title of The Complete Academic Education of Females.

By these and other means, the Pittsfield Young Ladies' Institute won a most honorable national reputation, and came to be warmly appreciated at home. For years no entertainments were more keenly enjoyed by the people of the town than the concerts and other exhibitions given by the young ladies in the beautiful chapel and in the spacious hall of the gymnasium.[1]

[1] The gymnasium, remodeled from the Congregational meeting-house of 1794, was divided into two stories; of which the first contained recitation-

Of course the Institute flourished, and at times the large dormitories were not sufficient to accommodate all who applied for admission.

Mr. Tyler was one of the most public-spirited citizens of the town, and always displayed a liberal, enlightened and active interest in its improvement. No man exerted himself more energetically than he in behalf of the water-works, the library, and the removal of the county-seat to Pittsfield.

After twelve years of successful effort, Mr. Tyler found the constant labor and intense activity required in the management of the school too exhausting to be safely continued, and in 1852, he admitted Rev. J. Holmes Agnew, D. D., a distinguished scholar and writer, as a partner. And in 1874, he sold to Doctor Agnew, for forty-seven thousand dollars, the grounds, buildings, furniture, and good-will of the institution.

In 1855, he removed to the city of New York, and engaged in mercantile business, which was unsuccessful, and in which he lost all the fortune which he had accumulated in Pittsfield. In 1861 and 1862, he made an attempt to resume teaching in the Cincinnati Female Seminary; but finding the task too great for his strength, he made a health-voyage to Hudson's Bay, where he died at North West River, Labrador, August 19, 1863. His remains were brought to Pittsfield in 1864, and buried in the rural cemetery, where a fine granite-monument was erected over them by the voluntary contributions of his pupils.

In the fall of 1857, Rev. C. V. Spear[1] purchased the personal property of the institution, and together with Rev. Prof. James R. Boyd, conducted the school for three years. In 1864, Professor Boyd retired, and Mr. Spear purchased, for twenty-seven thousand dollars, the grounds and buildings, which had before

rooms, and apartments for the male teachers, while the second formed a spacious and handsome hall, which was liberally furnished with gymnastic apparatus.

[1] Charles V. Spear, son of Nathaniel and Esther (Dyer) Spear, was born November 13, 1825, at Randolph, now Holbrook. He graduated at Amherst College, in 1846, and was soon after engaged by Mr. Tyler as teacher at the Institute. While in this position he studied theology with Rev. Dr. Todd, and was licensed to preach in June, 1851. He was pastor at Sudbury, Mass., for three years. He was, for many years, one of the most devoted officers of the Library Association, and was its last president. He married, in 1851, Miss R. L. Holbrook, daughter of E. N. Holbrook, of Holbrook.

passed into the hands of James Mabbitt, of Mabbittsville, N. Y. Mr. Spear has since conducted the institution successfully, under the name of The Maplewood Young Ladies' Institute, which was given to it by Professor Agnew, in 1854.

In the year 1826, the Cantonment grounds were sold at auction, under the act of 1819, authorizing the sale of military posts which had become useless; and the whole twenty acres, with the buildings upon them, were purchased by Lemuel Pomeroy for seven hundred and sixty dollars. The next year, Mr. Pomeroy removed the barracks to the lot on North street, since occupied by St. Joseph's Church, and erected in their place three large three-story brick-buildings, which were immediately occupied by his son-in-law, Prof. Chester Dewey, who established a seminary for young men, under the name of the Berkshire Gymnasium. This school which was incorporated in 1829, was taught by a corps of competent teachers, among whom was Mark Hopkins. Professor Dewey was himself unsurpassed as a teacher and as the governing head of collegiate institutions. The school was conducted on the general plan of the European gymnasia; the pupils were taught all the branches of education usual in the higher classes of seminaries below the rank of colleges; and some which were not then usual in such schools. Professor Dewey was specially distinguished for his attainments in natural science, and his school was noted for excellence in that department. He was also possessed of a fine taste, and, under his direction, was begun that system of adorning the grounds with trees and shrubbery, which, carried out and enlarged by his successors, have made Maplewood famed throughout the country for its beauty.[1]

Professor Dewey continued the school until 1836, when he accepted an invitation to become principal of the collegiate institute of the city of Rochester, which position he held until the institute-buildings were destroyed by fire, about 1850. He then accepted the position of professor of chemistry and the natural sciences in the University of Rochester, which he held until he resigned, in 1861.

Several gentlemen, afterwards of note, laid the foundations of their education in the Gymnasium: among them Hon. Thomas Allen and Prof. Charles E. West.

In June, 1826, Mr. Charles Dillingham established an excellent

[1] See Volume 1, page 36.

boarding-school for lads between the ages of six and fourteen years, for which he erected, on South street at the corner of what is now Reed street, a large two-story brick-building, with wings of one story. It had a capacity for forty pupils, and soon there were nearly that number, mostly from Philadelphia, New York and Albany. Mr. Dillingham died December 15, 1834, at the age of thirty-five; deeply mourned by the community which had learned to prize him highly as a citizen, as well as in his profession.

He was succeeded in the school by Mr. Robert M. Chapman, who had been his assistant, and who continued the institution until October, 1838. Mr. Chapman afterwards became an Episcopal clergyman.

In the fall of 1838, Rev. J. Adams Nash, a native of Conway, and a graduate of Amherst College, became principal of the institution, which took the name of the Pittsfield Commercial and Classical Boarding-school. Mr. Nash had previously taught a select school in New York city, for five years, and had also been pastor of a Presbyterian church in Binghamton, N. Y. His associate-principal was Lester M. Clark, A. M.; there was also a teacher of French, and another of penmanship. The course of instruction embraced, besides the ordinary English branches, Greek, Latin, French, Mathematics, vocal music and drawing. Mr. Nash remained principal of the school until 1848, when he was succeeded by Edward G. Tyler, A. M., a graduate of Amherst, who had previously been associate-principal with his brother in the Young Ladies' Institute. In 1849, Mr. Tyler sold the institution to Rev. S. C. Brace, who continued it for three years.

In 1856, Rev. Charles E. Abbott purchased the residence of Abraham Burbank, on a commanding elevation half a mile north of Maplewood, and remodeled it for a boarding-school, of the higher class, for lads. He made an excellent and successful school; but in 1866, sold it to Rev. Prof. William C. Richards, the well-known author and naturalist, who had been previously pastor of the Baptist Church. Both Mr. Abbott and Professor Richards made great improvement in the building, and added a gymnasium and school-rooms.

The story of the later newspapers of Pittsfield may be briefly told. The *Sun* continued to be published by Phinehas Allen, alone, until 1829, whenhe admitted his son of the same name, as

HISTORY OF PITTSFIELD. 679

partner in the publication and editorship. The senior partner died May 8, 1868, but his son continued the paper until May, 1872, when he sold it to his kinsman, Theodore L. Allen. The new proprietor, after conducting it creditably from May to August of that year, sold it to William H. Phillips, of North Adams, who removed to Pittsfield, and has since made many improvements in the office. The *Sun* still continues to support the democratic party, but gives up a large portion of its space to local interests.[1]

From the suspension of the *Berkshire Reporter*—probably soon after the year 1815—until 1827, the *Sun* had no rival in Pittsfield. But in May of that year, the *Argus*, a handsome sheet twenty-one inches by sixteen in size, was commenced by Henry K. Strong, who had been for some years principal of the grammar school, or Pittsfield Academy. Mr. Strong, having become financially embarrassed, left the state, and was succeeded May 1, 1828, by Samuel W. Bush, who conducted the paper until September 1, 1831, when he removed it to Lenox and united it with the *Berkshire Journal*, then published by John Z. Goodrich. Both Mr. Strong and Mr. Bush were good writers, and judicious and spirited editors; the lack of pecuniary success in the *Argus* was due in part to a fault in its business-management, and in part to the number of journals of the same political character in neighboring towns. While the *Sun* was the sole organ of the democratic party in a large section of western Massachusetts and adjoining states, there were no less than four representatives of the opposing political school among the newspapers of Berkshire alone.

In removing to Lenox, the *Argus* dropped from its heading a neat view of the Pittsfield park, which had adorned it; and the paper took the name of the *Journal and Argus*. Mr. Bush continued to edit it until September, 1838, when Mr. Goodrich became editor as well as proprietor. In the issue of August 27th, the name was changed, without any announcement or explanation, to that of the *Massachusetts Eagle*. In March, 1838, Messrs.

[1] Hon. William H. Phillips was born at Lanesboro, March 16, 1830, being a son of Dr. H. P. Phillips. He studied at Williams College, but did not graduate. In 1857, he established the *Hoosac Valley News*, and soon after combined with it the *Transcript*, which he had purchased. In 1866, he sold the *News* and *Transcript*, and was afterwards engaged in newspaper-enterprises at Bridgeport and Worcester. He was a member of the state-senate from northern Berkshire in 1875.

Eastman and Montague became publishers, with Henry W. Taft as editor. Charles Montague became sole proprietor in July, 1838; and on the retirement of Mr. Taft, in 1840, he assumed the editorial chair. In 1842, Mr. Montague removed the paper to its old home at Pittsfield, where he continued its publication until November 20, 1852. Being then in a not very prosperous condition it was purchased by Samuel Bowles & Co., of Springfield, who replenished the material of the office and leased it to Otis F. R. Wait. Mr. Wait much improved the editorial management and changed the name to the *Berkshire County Eagle*. But, at the end of one year, the establishment was sold to Henry Chickering of North Adams,[1] and Henry A. Marsh of Pittsfield, who conducted it until July 20, 1855, under the firm-name of Chickering & Marsh. At that date Mr. Marsh was succeeded by James B. Davis, and the firm continued to be Chickering & Davis until January 1, 1859, when Mr. Davis withdrew, Mr. Chickering conducting the paper in his own name until July 1, 1865, when William D. Axtell, previously a successful printer in Pittsfield and Northampton, became associated with him in its ownership and management. In 1876, the firm is still Chickering & Axtell.

The *Berkshire County Whig* was established in 1840. It was edited by Hon. Henry Hubbard and his son, Douglas S. Hubbard; the latter also being publisher. Independent in its political course, it supported the whig party, but not uniformly or without reserve. When the first native American party nominated Henry Shaw, of Lanesboro, for governor, it gave him its support. And in 1848, it entered earnestly into the free-soil movement. In 1849, its publisher joining in the new migration to California, the paper was discontinued.

In 1844, T. D. Bonner, a violent temperance-reformer, established the *Cataract*, as an organ of his peculiar views regarding

[1] Hon. Henry Chickering was born at Woburn, Mass., September 3, 1819, being the son of Rev. Joseph Chickering, who removed with him in 1822, to Phillipston. He was educated in the common schools, and for short terms in the academies at Westminster, Greenfield and Andover. At the age of fourteen he began to learn the printer's trade at Andover; and in 1844, engaged with John R. Briggs in the publication of the *North Adams Transcript*. After a few months, Mr. Briggs retired, and Mr. Chickering continued publisher and editor of the *Transcript* for twelve years. In 1855, he removed to Pittsfield. From 1852 to 1854, he was a member of the executive council. Since 1861, he has been postmaster of Pittsfield.

that interest. It was grossly personal and scurrilous, and its office was at one time mobbed; the only instance of that kind in the history of Berkshire. After two years it passed into the hands of Quigly, Kingsley and Axtell, who continued it eighteen months, and then sold the subscription-list to an Albany publisher.

In 1847, William D. Axtell, afterwards of the *Eagle*, published for six months, an extremely sprightly and pleasant paper, entitled the *Star*.

In 1840, Thaddeus Clapp, 3d, published a small campaign sheet, entitled, "*Old Tip*." "It supported General Harrison for president," says Holland's History of Western Massachusetts, "and General Harrison was elected."

During the existence of the Berkshire Gymnasium, the students of that institution published a small sheet of the same name, which numbered among its editors, Thomas Allen, Charles E. West and other men afterwards of note. It was entitled to a fair rank among papers of its class.

The *Institute Omnibus* was a small but sparkling sheet, published by the pupils of the Young Ladies' Institute for several years.

The *Berkshire Agriculturist* was commenced in 1847, by Charles Montague, the publisher of the *Eagle*, and E. P. Little, a bookseller. Rev. Dr. Todd was editor for the first eleven numbers, although his connection with it was not made public. Mr. Little left town at the end of that term and the paper was continued by Mr. Montague until 1848, when he sold it to Dr. Stephen Reed, who changed its name to the *Culturist and Gazette*. Doctor Reed was a graduate of Yale College in the class of 1824, and was for some years a practicing physician in Richmond, Mass. He was a devoted student of natural science; and, in geology, particularly, was an original investigator and thinker. He obtained a wide reputation by the discovery of the ice-strewn trains of boulders from the mountains of Columbia County, N. Y., across the Taconic range and the valley of the Housatonic.[1] He was also ardently interested in all efforts for the promotion of social, moral and intellectual culture, especially by means of common schools, and libraries. Every local undertaking in this direction had his hearty aid; and, although agri-

[1] See Lyell's Antiquity of Man.

culture continued to be a leading feature of the paper, these characteristics of the editor were constantly displayed in it, and justified its change of title. Doctor Reed continued to edit it until 1858, when its publication was suspended.[1]

In 1861, Professors William H. Thayer and R. Cresson Stiles published the *Berkshire Medical Journal*, a monthly magazine which contained many able original articles and much valuable medical information.

The business of the town having increased so as to need much more ample accommodation than could be afforded by the Agricultural Bank, the Pittsfield Bank was chartered in April, 1853, with a capital stock of one hundred and fifty thousand dollars. The first meeting of the stockholders was held in May, 1853, and the following directors were chosen: David Carson, John V. Barker, Gaius C. Burnap, Robert Pomeroy, Henry Stearns, Thomas Colt, George W. Platner. David Carson was chosen president, and Junius D. Adams, cashier. The succeeding presidents were: Hon. Julius Rockwell, elected April 6, 1858; Hon. Thomas Colt, elected January 18, 1870; John V. Barker, Esq., elected July 29, 1873; Hon. Julius Rockwell, re-elected January 20, 1874.

On the death of Mr. Adams, Edward S. Francis was chosen cashier April 1, 1864.[2]

The capital of the bank was increased to three hundred thousand dollars in March, 1854; and to five hundred thousand dollars in May, 1857. It was reorganized as the Pittsfield National Bank, in June, 1865.

The Berkshire County Savings Bank was incorporated in 1846, the original corporators being Henry Shaw, Thomas A. Gold, Thomas F. Plunkett and Charles Sedgwick. These corporators met March 28, 1846, Henry Shaw being chairman, and Thomas A. Gold secretary, when forty gentlemen, from all parts of the county, were elected associate members of the corporation. The

---

[1] During the existence of the *Culturist and Gazette* under Doctor Reed's editorship, the publishers were Reed, Hull & Pierson, and Reed & Pierson. Mr. Varnum Hull, a printer, and H. M. Pierson, Doctor Reed's partner in an agricultural warehouse, being associated with him.

[2] Edward S. Francis was born in Pittsfield, December 20, 1835, being the son of James Francis. He was clerk in the Pittsfield Bank from 1852 to 1856, and cashier of the Shelburne Falls Bank from 1856 to 1864.

following officers were elected April 29, 1846: president, Henry Shaw; secretary, Thomas A. Gold; vice-presidents, Charles M. Owen, Phinehas Allen, Samuel Rossiter, Sanford Blackinton; trustees, Jason Clapp, Jabez Peck, Thomas F. Plunkett, Thaddeus Clapp, George W. Campbell, Solomon L. Russell, Comfort B. Platt, Stephen B. Brown, Zenas M. Crane, Henry W. Bishop, George W. Platner, Samuel Gates, John C. Russell, Socrates Squier.

At the first meeting of the trustees, June 3, 1846, James Warriner was elected treasurer, and held the office until his death in 1865, when he was succeeded by Robert W. Adam, who still holds the office. Mr. Gold was succeeded as secretary in 1855, by John R. Warriner. On the resignation of Mr. Shaw in 1847, Hon. George N. Briggs became president, and was succeeded, in 1852, by Hon. Thomas F. Plunkett, and in 1863, Hon. Julius Rockwell succeeded Mr. Plunkett, and in 1876 is still president.

The first deposit was made July 11, 1846, by David Stockbridge, the amount being twenty-five dollars. The sixteenth depositor was Robert A. Merriam, who, on the 16th of November, 1846, made a deposit of a hundred and fifty dollars, and has ever since kept a deposit in the bank, and, of course, has now the oldest account.

The growth of the institution is shown by the following statement of the amount of deposits at different intervals:

January, 1850, twenty-one thousand five hundred and ninety-six dollars; January, 1855, ninety-four thousand nine hundred and sixty-four dollars; January, 1860, one hundred and eighty-seven thousand seven hundred and thirty-six dollars; January, 1865, four hundred and eighty-eight thousand two hundred and seventy-two dollars; January, 1870, one million nine hundred and fifty-three dollars; January, 1875, one million nine hundred and twenty thousand and eighty-three dollars.

The Agricultural Bank, incorporated in 1818, has had, from the first, a successful history. The successive presidents have been elected as follows: Thomas Gold, April 27, 1818; Edward A. Newton, October 2, 1826; Henry Shaw, April 28, 1830; E. A. Newton, October 5, 1840; Henry Shaw, April 24, 1845; Nathan Willis, October 11, 1845; E. A. Newton, October 2, 1848; George W. Campbell, October 17, 1853; Thomas F. Plunkett, October 8, 1861; Ensign H. Kellogg, January 9, 1866.

Ezekiel R. Colt was elected cashier, June 20, 1818, and held the office until his resignation, August 1, 1853, when John R. Warriner, who has since held the place, was elected.[1] What Mr. Colt's services to the bank were, has been elsewhere stated. The capital stock of the bank was increased, in 1851, to two hundred thousand dollars. Its present combined capital and surplus fund is four hundred thousand and four hundred dollars. It became a national bank in 1865.

The Berkshire Life Insurance Company, which has been one of the most successful business-institutions in the town, and contributed much to its beauty and prosperity,[2] was chartered in May, 1851, and organized in September, 1851, when Hon. George N. Briggs was chosen president. On the death of Governor Briggs, in September, 1861, he was succeeded by Hon. Thomas F. Plunkett; and upon the death of Mr. Plunkett, Edward Boltwood became president in January, 1876.

In May, 1874, all the water-power of the town being occupied, and there being a strong public desire to extend manufacturing, after a series of public meetings, a company was organized, with a capital of forty-two thousand dollars, for the purpose of erecting a building with steam-power, to be leased, in such portions as might be needed, to other parties. The first officers were, president, Nathan G. Brown; secretary and treasurer, A. J. Waterman; directors, William R. Plunkett, D. J. Dodge, J. H. Butler, E. D. Jones, Daniel Sprague, and George N. Dutton.

A site for the building was presented by Hon. E. H. Kellogg, and it was erected at an expense, including engines and other machinery, of fifty-two thousand dollars. It is two hundred feet long by fifty wide, besides some out-buildings. The third story was leased from October, 1874, to Edward Saunders, who established in it the Saunders factory, for the manufacture of silk-thread.

The lower story was leased to the Pittsfield Tack Company, which was organized August 7, 1875, with the following officers: President, Jabez L. Peck; clerk and treasurer, George N. Dut-

---

[1] John R. Warriner, son of James Warriner, was born at Pittsfield, March 22, 1827. He was clerk in a dry-goods jobbing-house from 1845 to 1850, clerk in the Springfield Bank until the fall of 1851, and cashier of the Hadley Falls Bank until August, 1853.

[2] See Volume 1, page 38.

ton; directors, J. L. Peck, George N. Dutton, J. R. Warriner, Edwin Clapp, E. S. Francis. Its capital is thirty thousand dollars, and it has thirty machines, making every description of tacks, brads, nails, etc.

The most extensive builder in Pittsfield has been Abraham Burbank, who was born at West Springfield, June 10, 1813, and was the son of Arthur Burbank. At the age of twelve years, he was compelled to begin earning his own living; and at the age of fifteen began to learn the trade of carpenter and joiner with William Blinn, at East Springfield, with whom he afterwards moved to Utica, N. Y. After leaving him, he moved to Schenectady, and built three and a half miles of the railroad between that city and Saratoga Springs, in 1832. In the same year, he removed to Pittsfield. In 1834, he was married, and in 1836, he removed to the State of Michigan, but not liking the west, returned to Pittsfield in July, 1837, and the location of the Western railroad having been determined, he commenced building, which he has continued to the present time; having also been engaged at various periods in the market and hardware and hotel business.

Mr. Burbank commenced life without pecuniary means and with no one to lend him a helping hand; but he has been one of the first in aiding the growth of the town, with personal hard work, and by the expenditure of hard-earned money. In 1842-44, he purchased a number of lots on North street, and erected two blocks of wooden dwellings, which have since been changed to stores. In 1847, he purchased of E. H. Kellogg a lot of land adjoining his other lots, on which he erected a brick-block, one hundred and forty-two feet long by sixty-two feet deep, the lower story being occupied by six stores, and the third by a large public hall. In 1860, he purchased of Parker L. Hall, the large property now occupied by the American and Berkshire houses, and by the large wooden block which he erected on it. He has also opened several streets, and built a large number of houses in various portions of the town, including the Burbank Hotel, and the buildings occupied by the Springside school.

Hon. Edward Learned was born February 26, 1820, at Watervliet, Albany county, N. Y. His father, Edward, was born at Salem, Mass.; his mother, whose maiden name was Crawford, was born in the north of Ireland. Mr. Learned attended school until he was fifteen years old, at which time he engaged in civil engineering, as rodman on the Hudson and Berkshire railroad. His advancement in his profession was so rapid, that the construction of the most difficult portion of the road—that from Mellenville, then Hardscrabble, to the river at Hudson—was placed almost exclusively in his charge. From this beginning, Mr. Learned soon became engaged in the construction of other public works, and has continued his relations to such undertakings till the present time; although his business-capacity has not been confined to such operations, but has found abundant employment in other channels, including manufacture of woolens in Berkshire county, manufacturing iron near Marquette, and mining copper and silver on Lake Superior.

In public affairs, whether local, state, or national, he has always taken a lively interest and occupied decided and active positions. He was elected to the state-legislature from Pittsfield, in 1857, and served in the years 1873–1874, for two terms as senator from the Berkshire district.

He was married in September, 1840, to Caroline, daughter of Lewis Stoddard of Pittsfield. He became a resident of Pittsfield in 1853, having purchased the place on which he now resides, and which he has beautified and extended, until "Elmwood" is recognized as one of the most elegant country-seats in Massachusetts.

The removal of the seat of the county-courts to Lenox, in 1787, soon became a source of conflict between the northern and southern portions of the county, which continued until the year 1868—a period of eighty-one years—with serious evils to the county.

The jail having been burned, Dr. Timothy Childs and others, in the year 1812, memorialized the legislature, stating that the public good required that the public buildings of the county of Berkshire should be located in Pittsfield. They said, "we state it to be an incontrovertible fact that this town is more conveniently situated for the transaction of all concerns in the courts of law and in the public offices than the town of Lenox. This is apparent from the peculiar local situation of this town, it being a spacious common center for the people of the county of Berkshire to assemble for the transaction of all public business."

These brief sentences were the basis of all the arguments of the people of Pittsfield, and of northern Berkshire, in favor of the change in the county-seat, which were repeated and amplified and sustained by redoubled proof, until they were finally successful.

The petitioners further stated that the citizens of Pittsfield would erect pleasant and suitable buildings at their own expense, and in turn, only asked that the county-property at Lenox should be transferred to them; "together with the money lately granted for erecting fire-proof offices for the public records, together with such sums as an impartial committee might judge necessary for rendering the jail secure; and for altering, repairing and rendering convenient the present court-house." They therefore asked the appointment of a legislative committee to view the situation, and examine all the circumstances touching and relating to the subject.

The desired committee was appointed, and at the April town-meeting of 1813, the following committee was chosen to present the case of the town before them: Timothy Childs, Thomas Gold, Ezekiel Bacon, John W. Hulbert, John B. Root, Ebenezer Center, Joshua Danforth, William C. Jarvis and Jonathan Allen.

The viewing-committee reported to the legislature that under certain conditions, provision should be made at the ensuing session of the legislature for the removal of the courts from Lenox to Pittsfield. Among these provisions were the following:

First, that Pittsfield should build on a suitable lot, of not less than one acre, and adjoining The Green so-called, a court-house of solid materials, with two jury-rooms, and all such fire-proof offices as are required by law, besides a jail and jail-house of such dimensions as the legislature might direct; and further to pay the town of Lenox two thousand six hundred and sixty-six dollars.

At a town-meeting held November 15, 1813, the following gentlemen were appointed to take the report into consideration: John C. Williams, John W. Hulbert, Oliver Root, Capt. John Churchill, Hosea Merrill, Butler Goodrich, Ezekiel Bacon, Thomas Gold, Oren Goodrich, Joseph Shearer, Simeon Griswold and Joseph Merrick. This committee thought that it would cost fourteen thousand dollars to comply with these conditions. A private subscription of nine thousand dollars had been raised towards this fund. The committee believed that if the town were authorized to use the money voted by the county for fire-proof offices, and to sell and use the old county-buildings, the whole expense of removal would be provided for. The location on the green was objected to, as it did not seem practicable to procure a site there of the required size. The committee also thought it might be shown that the required payment of two thousand six hundred and sixty-six dollars to the town of Lenox was unjust. These views were presented at the spring session of the legislature of 1814; and together with petitions in aid of the proposed removal, from the towns of Lanesboro, Dalton, Hinsdale, Washington, Peru, Savoy and Adams, were referred to the succeeding session, with due order of notice. But in the meanwhile the towns were directed to hold meetings to ascertain the opinion of the voters upon the propriety and expediency of the measure.

At this time, twenty citizens of Lenox banded themselves together with the resolution that while they lived, Lenox should remain the county-seat. But indeed, the whole town seems to have been actuated by the same spirit. And it had citizens who acted as leaders, and who were unsurpassed in ability and influence in the county. And as the preponderance of population had not passed absolutely to northern Berkshire, they labored for and obtained this practical reference of the matter to the people. By their efforts, also, it became prestige, and long continued the essential obstacle to the removal; and the legislature clung to it long after it became apparent, to the whole commonwealth, that the public interests demanded a change. In its first operation, its effect was decided by the vote of the town of Richmond; several citizens of Lenox having given a bond to that town agreeing to idemnify it for its share of expense in erecting new buildings, at Lenox. The vote was, therefore, against the removal, and the new county-buildings were erected, and occupied in 1816.

The question was revived in 1826, when Pittsfield voted to petition the legislature for the removal of the county-seat, and appointed Jonathan Allen, John Churchill, Lemuel Pomeroy, Joseph Merrick and Henry Hubbard to manage the matter. There was an earnest but brief attempt to carry out the desires of the town; but at the February session of the legislature, the petitioners had leave to withdraw.

In December, 1842, the completion of the Western railroad, having given Pittsfield great additional advantages, and the county-commissioners having contracted for remodeling the jail

HISTORY OF PITTSFIELD. 689

as a house of correction, at a cost of five thousand two hundred and fifty dollars, and the citizens of Pittsfield and other towns having subscribed more than the same sum for the purpose of removing the county-seat to Pittsfield, on motion of M. R. Lanckton, the town agreed to guarantee its payment; and also voted to give a durable lease of land between the store of Tracy & West and the First Church, for a court-house, and to furnish a suitable site for the jail. The following committee was appointed to forward the removal by all honorable means: Hosea Merrill, Jr., E. H. Kellogg, J. D. Colt 2d, Lemuel Pomeroy, Lyman Warriner and George Campbell.

The following extract from the town-records tells the remainder of the story:

Whereas, by a resolve passed by the legislature, the removal of the county-buildings is submitted to a vote of the people on the 3d of April, and the almost impassable state of the roads has prevented the friends of removal from giving that information to the voters necessary for a fair understanding of the question; therefore, resolved, that we, the citizens of Pittsfield, in legal town-meeting assembled, decline voting on the subject.

Resolved, That, in the opinion of this meeting, the necessities of the county do not require the immediate erection of a house of correction, at a cost of five thousand dollars, and the county-commissioners are requested to postpone action until such time as a full, fair and deliberate decision upon the location of all the county-buildings can be had by the citizens of this county.

And then the matter rested again, although not very quietly, until the year 1854, when—the Housatonic railroad having been extended through southern Berkshire to Pittsfield—the agitation was revived; several towns, Great Barrington taking the lead, petitioning the legislature for a change in the county-seat. In February, a Pittsfield town-meeting, on motion of Hon. Julius Rockwell, passed a long series of resolutions favoring the movement, and declaring that the town ought to take action without delay. These resolutions declared, that while the citizens of the town sincerely regretted that a movement of this kind must be attended with a collision of local interests, and some excitement of personal and local feeling, all must be aware that questions of this kind must be determined by the general interests of the people of the whole county and state, and that the interest of par-

690   HISTORY OF PITTSFIELD.

ticular towns must yield to the general public accommodation. Upon this predicate, the resolutions argued that the question of the location of county-seats belonged to the legislature exclusively; and that it ought to keep in view the "interests of the commonwealth, at whose expense, and by whose judges and other officers the laws are administered; and for this end it should provide the location where the business could be most conveniently transacted, with the most economy of the valuable time of the judges." They fully recognized, however, the interest of the people of the county in the question; but considered that the proper mode for the people to represent their wishes, was by petition to the legislature, and not by a final reference of the question to their decision.

It was further resolved, that there ought to be no farther delay in the removal of the county-seat; and a committee of thirty was appointed, with full powers and an ample appropriation of money, to procure that result. This committee consisted of Wellington H. Tyler, George S. Willis, John V. Barker, Theodore Pomeroy, Hosea Merrill, James Francis, David Campbell, N. G. Brown, R. W. Adam, S. A. Churchill, Henry Stearns, Edwin Clapp, Henry Colt, Elisha S. Tracy, M. R. Lanckton, Calvin Martin, Thomas G. Atwood, Henry Noble, William M. Walker, O. W. Robbins, John Weller, P. L. Page, F. W. Gibbs, William R. Plunkett, H. S. Briggs, John C. West, Joel Stevens, Jerome Hulburt, Josiah Carter, Elisha Peck.

At the March meeting of 1855, the following gentlemen were appointed to meet a committee of the legislature at Lenox, and were authorized to expend five hundred dollars to further the objects of the petitioners for removal: S. L. Russell, James Francis, Thomas Colt, George S. Willis, John E. Dodge, Robert Pomeroy, Julius Rockwell, and S. A. Churchill.

The whole subject was fully discussed in the newspapers of the county, and produced much angry discussion; but the legislature finally submitted the following questions to town-meetings of the people of the county, November 8, 1854.

"Do you desire a removal of the courts from Lenox; and, if so, name the town or towns to which they shall be removed."

In Pittsfield the vote stood for removal six hundred and fifty-eight; against it, three. There were three hundred and eighty-one votes in favor of the removal to Pittsfield, and two hundred

BERKSHIRE COUNTY COURT HOUSE.

and fifty-five for double county-seats, at Pittsfield and Great Barrington. The county decided, by a majority of about fifteen hundred, in favor of Lenox. No further decided movement was made in favor of a change, until the year 1868; but public opinion constantly tended in that direction, and in that year, when Hon. T. F. Plunkett made a movement in the legislature to effect it, the opposition was comparatively feeble. Mr. Plunkett managed the matter with great discretion, and was aided in the same spirit by other gentlemen of the county. The propriety of the measure was generally recognized; and, by a direct vote of the legislature, the county-seat was established at Pittsfield, on condition that the town should furnish suitable sites for the court-house and jail, and provide rooms for the courts, until a court-house could be built.

We forbear comment upon the means by which this result was so long delayed, and also upon the cost which the delay imposed upon the county and its citizens.

The town accepted, without hesitation, the conditions upon which the change was to be made, and appointed the following committee to select and purchase the sites for the court-house and jail: S. W. Bowerman, Theodore Pomeroy, Thomas Colt, John C. West, J. V. Barker, E. H. Kellogg, Edwin Clapp, John E. Merrill, W. B. Cooley, Owen Coogan, and Abraham Burbank. The committee manifested a most liberal spirit, and the town sustained them in selecting the best and most costly sites, which were demanded for those purposes. Thirty-five thousand dollars were paid for the John Chandler Williams place, with its noble surrounding of elms, on the corner of Park square and East street, as a location for a court-house. Six thousand five hundred dollars were paid Abraham Burbank for a site for a jail and house of correction.

The legislature granted three hundred and fifty thousand dollars, to be assessed on the county, for the erection of the county-buildings. One hundred and ninety thousand dollars were expended for the jail, and the remainder for the court-house. Subsequently twenty-eight thousand dollars were appropriated for furnishing the buildings, of which the greater portion was expended for the court-house.

Architectural plans were furnished for the buildings by Louis Weisbein of Boston, and the contract for constructing them was awarded to A. B. & D. C. Munyan. They were completed in the fall of 1871. The court-house, which is one of the finest in the commonwealth, is constructed of white marble, from Sheffield, resting on a basement of light-blue marble from the same town. It was first occupied at the September term of the supreme court, in 1871, all the judges being present, and Henry W. Taft, Esq., delivering an historical address.

The jail, which stands on North Second street, is built of marble and pressed brick; the latter material being chiefly used.

The business brought to the town by the establishment of the county-seat, is not more valued than the accession of citizens of high character, which it involved in the residence of such officers as High-Sheriff Graham A. Root; Henry W. Taft, the clerk of the courts; Andrew J. Waterman, register of probate; George S. Tucker, register of deeds.

Some idea of the growth of the town, in its later decades, may be obtained from the following statistics: In 1865, the population was 9,679; the valuation was $6,402,666. The taxes were $84,197. The valuation per capita $661. In 1875, the population was 12,267, and the valuation $8,412,236. The total tax was $111,309, and the valuation per capita was $685.

We have thus traced the progress of the town from its early hopes and early disappointments, to a success and position which the best might envy. We should have been glad to have given, more in detail, the account of the manufacturing enterprises which, in later years, have aided in building up its prosperity. But space, and the plan to which we are limited, forbid. We may, however, mention that among them are the tannery, which Mr. Owen Coogan has carried on as the successor of James and Simeon Brown; the shoe-factory established by Robbins & Kellogg; the manufactory of magic oil, and other medical and essential preparations carried on for twenty-five years by William Renne; the carriage-factories of Ebenezer Dunham and George Van Valkenberg; the boiler-manufactory by Hezekiah Russell; the machine-works by E. D. Jones and W. H. Clark; and the foundry of E. D. Bonney. Other gentlemen, engaged in professional and mercantile business, may have contributed as much or more to the prosperity of the town, but there is a certain permanence and distinction in manufacturing-enterprise, which permits it to be more positively recognized.

THE ACADEMY OF MUSIC.

The elder citizens of Pittsfield, in 1875, remember with delight literary and artistic entertainments in the old South-street lecture-room, in the two town-halls, in the more commodious halls provided by Messrs. Burbank and West, and in some smaller rooms of the same class. There are many who even remember joyous hours in the old assembly rooms over the Female Academy, and the Berkshire Hotel. Nor are the chapel and gymnasium of Maplewood forgotten. But, until 1872, the town was entirely without any building approaching the character of a theater or any hall well fitted for a dramatic or musical entertainment of a high character. In that year, by private enterprise, it obtained an opera-house as spacious as the requirements of the location demanded, and worthy to rank in other respects with the best edifices of its class.

It was styled the Academy of Music, and was built in the summer of 1872, by Cebra Quackenbush and Messrs. A. B. and D. C. Munyan. The Messrs. Munyan were the practical builders and the capital was furnished by Mr. Quackenbush, who subsequently became the sole owner. The builders took great pride in their work, and by a very liberal expenditure the town was furnished with one of the most beautiful and commodious buildings of its class in the country. It is one hundred and thirty-two feet long, eighty feet deep, and seventy high. The materials are brick and iron with dressings of blue stone and tile, and richly ornamented. The lower story contains six large stores. The theater, with its parlors and offices, occupies the whole of the upper portion of the building, except that in the mansard roof. The auditorium, which is very elegantly finished and furnished, affords eleven hundred and fourteen seats. The stage is eighty feet wide, by thirty-six deep. The parlors are handsome and commodious, and the manager's and other offices are large and convenient. The stairways are of liberal proportion and of easy ascent. In beauty, comfort, and convenience, the Pittsfield Academy of Music is unexcelled by any edifice of its class in the country. Its acoustic properties and the capabilities of its stage are particularly admired.

The story of the academy in the mansard roof is occupied by a smaller hall, so far as it is not required by stage-machinery.

There is one other gentleman whose services to the town, during a not very extended residence, were so marked that they ought to be recognized, and will create a desire to know more of him. John C. Hoadley was the son of Lester Hoadley and the grandson of Philemon Hoadley, the fourth in descent from William Hoadley, who was a resident of Saybrook, Conn., in 1663, and in 1664 became one of the founders of the town of Bradford. John C. Hoadley was born in Martinsburg, Lewis county, N. Y., in December, 1818. He learned to read at his mother's knee, and had read the New Testament through before his fourth birthday. His subsequent education was eclectic; being partly gathered at the academies at Potsdam and Utica, but chiefly wherever he could find a teacher in men, books, or nature. In 1835, he was employed as chainman and rodman in the preliminary survey of the railway from Utica to Binghamton. In May, 1836, he entered the service of the State of New York, on the surveys for the enlargement of the Erie canal. This work being completed in 1842, he was retained in the employ of the canal board. But in December, 1844, he took charge of the mills at Leominster, Mass., then erecting by H. N. & E. B. Bigelow, where he remained until 1848, when he removed to Pittsfield, and became a partner of Gordon McKay, in his machine-works. Here he was enthusiastically devoted to all the interests of the town. A part, and only a part of these services appear in these pages. In 1852, together with Mr. McKay, he removed to the city of Lawrence, where he became interested in a series of manufactures. He was elected a member of the legislature in 1858, and presidential elector in 1872. He married in 1847, a daughter of Rev. Daniel Kimball, of Needham, who died June 12, 1848. On the 15th of September, 1853, he married Catherine Gansevoort, daughter of Allan Melville and Catherine Gansevoort.

APPENDIX.

LIST OF PITTSFIELD SOLDIERS WHO SERVED IN THE WAR FOR THE
PRESERVATION OF THE UNION.

[1861–1865.]

EIGHTH REGIMENT INFANTRY, M. V. M.

ALLEN GUARD.

Henry S. Briggs, Captain: Colonel 10th Mass. Vols., June 12, 1861.
Henry H. Richardson, 1st Lieutenant: Captain, June 15, 1861.
Robert Bache, 2d Lieutenant: 1st Lieutenant, June 15, 1861.
Alonzo E. Goodrich, 1st Sergeant: 2d Lieutenant, June 15, 1861.

Non-Commissioned Officers.

Daniel J. Dodge, Sergeant.	Frederick Smith, Corporal.
Samuel M. Wardwell, "	Cornelius Burley, "
Israel C. Weller, "	Albert Howe, "
Charles R. Strong, "	

Musician.
Edwin Merry.

Privates.

Alden, Henry	Butler, Lafayette
Atwood, Andrew J.	Chamberlain, Robert
Barnard, William E.	Clark, W. H.
Bassett, Almon F.	Castello, William
Bentley, Perry C.	Davis, Charles H.
Blinn, George	Dodge, Emerson J.
Bonney, Harvey	Fuller, Andrew J.
Bonney, Nicholas	Garrett, William H. H.
Booth, Dexter F.	Goggins, James
Brown, Charles	Greelis, Robert
Burbank, George W.	Harrington, William F.

Hemenway, Elbert O.
Hemenway, F. A.
Hemenway, Harrison
Hopkins, Chester H.
Hughes, Daniel
Joyce, Thomas
Jordan, Dwight
Lee, John M.
Lloyd, Frank
Marks, Constant R.
Mullany, Anthony
McIntosh, Hobart H.
McKenna, James
McKenna, William
Mitchell, Wells B.
Montville, Mitchell
Morse, J. A.
Nichols, Abram J.
Powers, Richard

Randall, Jason B.
Reed, George
Read, William D.
Reynolds, George
Rockwell, William W.
Rouse, John T.
Sedgwick, Irving M.
Skinner, Frederick A.
Taylor, Charles H.
Van Loon, Lyman W.
Vedder, Jacob
Volk, Abraham
Wark, John
Wells, John
Whipple, Albert H.
Whittlesey, Elihu B.
Wood, Thaddeus
Wright, Theodore S.

EIGHTH REGIMENT INFANTRY, M. V. M. (100 Days.)

Lafayette Butler, Captain.
William D. Reed, 1st Lieutenant.
James Kittle, 2d Lieutenant.

Non-Commissioned Officers.

Edward B. Mead, 1st Sergeant.
George A. Holland, "
Edwin F. Russell, "
George S. Willis, Jr., "
John T. Power, "
Dwight Holland, Corporal.

Timothy Drew, Corporal.
John K. Packard, "
Orson B. Kendall, "
William D. Bliss, "
John S. Smith, "
John L. Dalrymple, "

Privates.

Adams, John H.
Aldrich, Cornelius S.
Barber, Joseph
Bardeau, Peter
Broad, Charles C.
Brian, Isadore
Burbank, Charles H.
Burt, Charles A.
Casey, Patrick
Chickering, John A.

Collins, John
Curron, Marcus
Fabricius, William
Fagan, Alonzo D. E.
Forward, William
Gallipaux, Lewis
Goodrich, Frank H.
Green, William H.
Gunn, Charles H.
Hemenway, Willard F.

APPENDIX. 697

Houlohan, James
Jeffers, Edgar
Kendall, Eben W.
Labare, John J.
Lawrence, Joseph E.
Mallison, Lugene
Marshall, Alfred
Massey, Milo T.
McDonald, Frank
Meeks, Thomas
Moore, Albert
Moore, Charles
Moore, John 1st
Moore, John 2d

Morgan, Daniel S.
Murphy, Joseph P.
Prentiss, Charles
Pritchard, Allen
Rensehausen, Henry
Rockwell, Charles A.
Rolland, Ausanda E.
Ryan, Edward J.
Ryan, John
Sears, James H.
Smith, Henry H.
Smith, William H.
Walker, Eleazer

FORTY-NINTH REGIMENT INFANTRY, M. V. M.

[This being a nine-months regiment, raised exclusively in Berkshire county, we give the roll of staff and field officers and the Pittsfield members by companies.]

Field and Staff.

Colonel, William F. Bartlett, Boston.
Lieutenant-Colonel, Samuel B. Sumner, Great Barrington.
Major, Charles T. Plunkett, Pittsfield.
Surgeon, Frederic Winsor, Boston.
Adjutant, Benjamin C. Miflin, Boston.
Quartermaster, Henry B. Brewster, Pittsfield.
Sergeant-Major, Henry J. Wylie, Pittsfield.
Quartermaster-Sergeant, George E. Howard, Pittsfield.
Hospital-Steward, Albert J. Morey, Lee.

Pittsfield Roll.

COMPANY A.

Israel C. Weller, Captain.
George W. Clark, 1st Lieutenant.
Frederick A. Francis, 2d Lieut. Sept. 18, 1862; 1st Lieut. Dec. 31, 1862.
George Reed, 1st Sergeant, Sept. 18, 1862 ; 2d Lieut. May 23, 1863.

Non-Commissioned Officers.

Albert Howe, 1st Sergeant.
Charles P. Adams,   "
David Greber,   "
Thomas Biety,   "
Henry J. Wylie,   "
George E. Howard,   "
John Priestly,   Corporal.
Erastus D. Barnes,   "

George H. Kearn, Corporal.
Lyman J. Read,   "
Michael F. Dailey,   "
John B. Scace,   "
William E. Tillotson,   "
James Kittle,   "
Joseph H. Allen,   "

88

HISTORY OF PITTSFIELD.

Musicians.

John C. Merry, Michael H. Hanley,
Emile Neuber.

Privates.

Abbe, Merrick L.
Aldrich, Cornelius S.
Bailey, Julius F.
Bassett, James W.
Blake, Frank V.
Bogard, Robert
Bryce, John, Jr.
Burt, Orville D.
Clamann, William
Clark, John B.
Clark, William E.
Coleman, Charles A.
Colt, Merrick R.
Daniels, Peter
Davis, Luther M.
Drew, Timothy
Dunlap, Thomas
Endie, Emile
Fuller, George
Green, Robert A.
Grewe, Henry
Hall, Thomas E.
Holland, George A.
Hubbard, Lewis F.
Hufneagle, Frederick
Jones, Seth R.
Jones, William
Joyner, Daniel M.
Kendall, Chauncey E.
Kimball, John
LeBarnes, George E.

Macoy, Martin
Malcomb, Joseph
Marion, Andrew
Marion, Lewis
Maxwell, John
Nicholas, William
Noble, Samuel G.
O'Brien, William
Packard, John K.
Platt, Charles E.
Rairden, Hugh
Rairden, Timothy
Reed, William
Rheel, Henry
Root, Henry L.
Robbins, Henry M.
Rechsteshell, Henry
Rogers, Judson B.
Rogers, John
Shaw, William
Swart, John
Swart, John W.
Stupka, William
Taylor, William
Tuggey, William
Vanderburg, Charles B.
Videtto, Charles F.
Warner, Henry C.
Watkins, Charles B.
Watkins, Willard L.
Weidman, John

COMPANY B.

Charles R. Garlick, Captain.

COMPANY C.

Charles T. Plunkett, Captain : promoted Major, May 11, 1862.
Charles R. Lingenfeldter, Captain, January 3, 1863.
William M. Wells, 2d Lieutenant.
James N. Strong, 2d Lieutenant.

APPENDIX. 699

Non-Commissioned Officers.

William H. Cranston, Corporal.   Frank H. Haskins, Corporal.
Allen M. Dewey,   "

Privates.

Baker, Robert H.   Lee, John H.
Bastianella, James E.   Merry, Edward F.
Braunwalder, Daniel   Merry, Henry N.,
Campbell, Henry J.   Moore, Henry
Camp, John R.   Ollenger, Charles
Daniels, Michael   Smith, Henry
Dudley, Charles   Stelfax, William
Knox, Francis M.

COMPANY D.

Henry R. Fowler, Corporal.

COMPANY H.

Privates.

Hills, John F.   Knickerbocker, George
Doten, John

COMPANY I.

Zenas C. Rennie, Captain.

Non-Commissioned Officer.

George L. Geer, Sergeant.

Privates.

Avery, Peter   Mallison, Martin
Dresser, Gilbert W.   McKenna, James
Gallipaux, Joseph   Merrills, John W.
Groat, Rufus   Rockwell, Charles A.
Harris, Addison I.   Van Line, Peter
Howard, Alberjus W.   Vandenburgh, Richard
Jeffers, Lewis R.

SIXTY-FIRST REGIMENT INFANTRY, M. V. M. (ONE YEAR SERVICE.)

William H. Brown, 1st Lieutenant, September 22, 1864.
Henry T. Johns, 2d Lieutenant, Sept. 6, 1864.   1st Lieut. Jan. 15, 1865.
George H. Kearn, 2d Lieutenant, March 15, 1865.

Non-Commissioned Officers.

Thomas Bietty, 1st Sergeant.   John B. Scace, Sergeant.
George H. Kearn, 1st   "   Charles L. R. Strong,"
Lewis Merriam,   "   Warren W. Wade,   "
Judson B. Rogers,   "   James W. Bassett, Corporal.

Pindar F. Cooley, Corporal.
George H. French, "
John H. Holland, "

James McKenna, Corporal.
Herman H. Shaw, "
Chas. W. Thompson, "

Principal Musician.
Edwin S. Joy.

Privates.

Austin, William H.
Bagg, Edwin
Barnes, James
Bedford, James, Jr.
Beebe, James H.
Beebe, Thomas D.
Bonney Nicholas D.
Boughton, John W.
Brown, William H.
Bundy, Alexander D.
Caden, James H.
Chapman, Nathaniel C., Jr.
Cowan, Harrison J.
Curley, Michael
Dailey, Joseph T.
Davis, Daniel
Davis, Michael L.
Dick, William J.
Dunn, James
Ferron, Edward
Flansburg, Peter
Follen, Michael
Forward, Daniel
Francis, George
Gandley, James
Gilbert, Henry, Jr.
Goodell, David
Gottschald, Herman

Grey, William
Hallenbeck, Augustus P.
Hancock, John
Harrison, Henry A.
Hemenway, Francis A.
Holdridge, Israel D.
Horton, Emery S.
Howard, George E.
Hubbard, Josiah N.
Kellard, John
Kerr, Peter
Larkin, Michael
LeBarnes, George E.
Loudon, Thomas L.
Loring, William G.
Lovejoy, Alfred H.
Mallison, Martin F.
McKenna, Thomas
Morrow, John
Porter, Andrew J.
Ransehausen, William, Jr.
Roberts, Peter J.
Robinson, George E.
Shepton, George
Spaulding, Silas D.
Ward, James
Webley, Edward
Widmaier, Christian

THREE YEARS' REGIMENTS.

THE Regiments whose rolls are already given were called in special emergencies, for brief periods. Those which follow were enlisted for three years' service.

TENTH REGIMENT INFANTRY, M. V.

Henry S. Briggs, Colonel, June 21, 1861. Promoted Brigadier-General July 27, 1862.

APPENDIX. 701

Thomas W. Clapp, Captain.
John W. Howland, 1st Lieutenant.
George Hagar, 2d Lieutenant.
Elihu B. Whittlesey, 2d Lieutenant.

Non-Commissioned Officers.

George E. Bailey, Sergeant.
Henry R. Davis, "
Haskell Hemenway, "
Dwight Hubbard, "
Almond Bassett, Corporal.
Thomas Duffee, "

James Finnican, Corporal.
Gardner B. Hibbard, "
John S. Smith, "
Walter B. Smith, "
Timothy Murphy, "

Privates.

Bolter, Peter C.
Breyer, Frank L.
Brown, Thomas
Burbank, Samuel
Carey, John
Cassidy, James
Colt, Thomas G.
Dailey, John E.
Dudley, Charles
Ginn, John N.
Green, Jerry
Harris, Charles F., Jr.
Bosworth, Henry C.
Baird, Andrew
Eagan, John
Hemenway, Alfred C.
Hemenway, Harrison
Hogan, William
Irving, William
Jones, John
Joy, Edward S.
Kellogg, George S.
Lane, William T.
Larkin, Thomas G.
Loomis, Daniel
Mann, Benjamin
Magee, Nelson

Martin, John
Menton, George
Mullett, Daniel A.
Mullett, John S.
Newton, Henry D.
Noble, Henry
Prentiss, George L.
Packard, Charles
Phipps, Charles W.
Reinhardt, Robert
Reardon, Daniel
Ryan, Richard
Ross, John H.
Shannon, Thomas
Simons, Wolfe
Slate, Marshall F.
Stockbridge, Lyman
Tahan, Albert A.
Vetter, Jacob
Viddeto, William H.
Wetherbee, James W.
Wallace, William
Williams, James
Wilbur, Eleazer
Wilson, Ephraim
Wilcox, Darvil M.

ELEVENTH REGIMENT INFANTRY, M. V.

William R. Bassett, 1st Lieutenant, July 11, 1863.

TWELFTH REGIMENT INFANTRY, M. V.
Privates.

Claffee, John	Hemenway, Elbert O.
Evans, John	Phelps, Dexter M.

SEVENTEENTH REGIMENT INFANTRY, M. V.
Privates.

Cozzens, Michael	Murphy, Thomas
Guinar, Andrew	Nugent, Hugh
Lawler, James	O'Mara, John

EIGHTEENTH REGIMENT INFANTRY, M. V.
Privates.

Cannon, Patrick	Dwyer, James

NINETEENTH REGIMENT INFANTRY, M. V.
Privates.

McCabe, Joseph	Smith, James
	Thornton, James

TWENTIETH REGIMENT INFANTRY, M. V.

Walter B. Smith, Captain: transferred from 37th Reg., March 4, 1865. Lansing E. Hibbard, 1st Sergeant, Aug. 31, 1861; 2d Lieut., Nov. 12, 1862; 1st Lieut., June 16, 1863. (Lieut. Hibbard's commission as Captain had been made out, but he had not been mustered into his new rank when he was killed, May 10, 1864.)

Non-Commissioned Officer.
John Merchant, 1st Sergeant.

Privates.

Chapman, David G.	Lew, Thomas
Chase, Hollis S.	Packard, Charles
Corbett, John	Polie, Frederick
Devine, James	Reed, John
Feathergill, George W.	Shannon, Thomas
French, William, Jr.	Sloan, John A.
Kelley, George F.	Smith, Thomas
Kennedy, John	Strong, King
Lewis, Arthur S.	Tenna, John A.

APPENDIX. 703

TWENTY-FIRST REGIMENT INFANTRY, M. V.

Henry H. Richardson, Captain, Aug. 21, 1861; Major, Dec. 18, 1863;
  Lieutenant-Colonel, July 16, 1864.
William H. Clark, 1st Sergeant, Aug. 10, 1861; 1st. Lieut., March 3,
  1862; Captain, Oct. 30, 1862.

Non-Commissioned Officers.

Justin S. Cressey, Sergeant.
Samuel G. Dunovan, "

Charles E. Johnson, Sergeant.
Richard Stevens, Corporal.

Privates.

Atwood, Andrew J.
Atwood, Charles L.
Bedford, Samuel
Costello, William
Davidson, John H.
Davis, Charles P.
Dudley, Sidney
Farelly, John
Garlick, Evalyn A.
Hazard, Alfred M.
Jacquot, Jules
Jarvis, George W.
Jordan, Xavier
Kelley, Jeremiah
Lombard, Robert R.

McIntosh, H. R.
Messenger, John
Mountain, Edward
Murphy, Hugh
Potter, George E.
Reed, Thomas E.
Russell, Henry
Russell, Samuel P.
Scolly, Augustus
Sharp, George W.
Sperry, Henry H.
Volk, Abraham
Whipple, Samuel P.
Wright, Samuel

TWENTY-FOURTH REGIMENT INFANTRY, M. V.

Non-Commissioned Officers.

James R. Cranston, Sergeant. | Timothy Riardon, Corporal.

Privates.

Gifford, Stephen E.
Grisworld, Theodore D.
King, Henry
Lynch, James
McCarthy, John
McKenna, John

Malcomb, George
Pennock, Charles L.
Powers, Peter
Pratt, Edward L.
Quinn, Michael
Scriver, David

TWENTY-SEVENTH REGIMENT INFANTRY, M. V.

Robert M. Roberts, 1st Sergeant, Dec. 4, 1863; 1st Lieut., May 15, 1865.
Wm. F. Harrington, 1st Sergeant, Sept. 29, 1861; 2d Lieut., June 4, 1863.

Non-Commissioned Officers.

Charles H. Blood, 1st Sergeant.
Willard L. Merry, 1st "
Franklin Hunt, "

W. H. Monnier, Sergeant.
Laville F. Hall, Corporal.

Privates.

Bentley, James L.
Bentley, William G.
Bolio, David
Gorman, John
Groat, Rufus
Donlan, James
Eagan, John
Fisher, David
Fisher, Francis
Goddett, Joseph
Groat, Rufus
Jackson, Stillman
Jones, Thomas
Lander, Robert
McCombs, Henry
Marian, Andrew

Harrington, Walter S.
O'Brien, William
O'Conner, Dennis
Patterson, Nathan W.
Davis, Charles H.
O'Brien, William
O'Conner, Dennis
Patterson, Nathan W.
Root, James W.
Teelhan, Albert A.
Tucker, John
Weed, Charles
Welsor, John
Wilson, John
Wilson, William
Wilbur, Eleazer

TWENTY-EIGHTH REGIMENT INFANTRY.

Non-Commissioned Officer.
Henry Ruckeshell, Corporal.

TWENTY-NINTH REGIMENT INFANTRY.
Michael Mullany, Corporal.

Privates.

Cassidy, Francis
Clamann, William
Jackman, Henry L.

Mercer, William
Owen, Richard
Raftes, John

THIRTY-FIRST REGIMENT INFANTRY.

Robert Bache, Major.
Elbert H. Fordham, 1st Lieutenant, Feb. 20, 1862; Capt. Sept. 6, 1862;
    Major, April 15, 1864.
Francis E. R. Chubbuck, Chaplain.
Edward F. Hollister, Captain.
William W. Rockwell, Captain.

APPENDIX. 705

Geo. W. Sears, Sergeant, Feb. 17, 1862; Hospital Steward, Feb. 14, 1862; 2d Lieutenant, April 1, 1864.
Charles S. Burt, Quartermaster-Sergeant.

Wagoner.

John L. Weller.

Non-Commissioned Officers.

Abraham I. Nichols, 1st Sergeant.
William H. Rich, 1st   "
Emerson J. Dodge,   "
William McKenna,   "
Benjamin Taylor,   "

Charles H. Adriance, Corporal
Frederick Blauss,   "
Thomas Harrington,   "
George E. Millen,   "

Privates.

Agar, John
Anthony, George
Atwater, William E.
Ball, Henry
Ball, Horace C.
Barber, John L.
Barker, Daniel E.
Barnard, William E.
Bentley, Commodore P.
Berry, Albert L.
Bidwell, George A.
Bickmyer, William
Bohonet, John
Booth, Dexter F.
Byrne, Edward
Carney, Patrick
Carr, Homer E.
Carver, John W.
Clark, John
Clary, Franklin
Corbett, Robert
Crandal, Rollin E.
Dailey, Lewis D.
Daley, Lafayette
Daniels, Peter
DeCorgin, F. Lewis
Forrest, Joseph B.
French, William
Galapaux, Peter
Garlick, Latham
Gear, Myron L.

Glynn, John
Goodrich, Ami B.
Goor, John L.
Gould, Samuel E.
Hanselman, Andrew
Holder, Henry
Hopper, Martin
Hubbard, James E.
Hubbard, William P.
Hughes, Daniel
Jarvis, James
Jaundrea, Joseph
Jaundrea, William
Jones, John
Kelley, George
Kelley, Thomas
Kendall, Thomas
Knight, Joseph G.
Knight, George E.
Koehlert, Louis
Lambert, John
Lassure, John
Leppers, Joseph
Liston, John
Lynes, Henry J.
McCann, Peter
McDonald, Patrick
Main, Ichabod D.
Main, James A.
Malcolm, Samuel
Malcolm, William

Martin, George L.
Matthews, Charles
Mehan, William
Merrill, John W.
Merry, John C.
Mexcur, George N.
Montville, Michell
Moore, William
Morse, James
Mullen, George E.
Mullany, Michael
Mure, Andrew
Myers, Peter
Naragan, Edgar
O'Neil, Michael
Palmer, Rosa
Quigly, Edward E.
Roberts, Daniel J.
Roony, William H.
Ross, John

Ross, Joseph M.
Ross, Peter
Russell, Joseph
Schlader, Diedrich
Shannon, Daniel
Spelman, Dominick
Stone, Charles
Sullivan, William
Tate, James
Taylor, Benjamin
Thornton, William H.
Tobin, Thomas
Volk, Abram
Walker, David T.
Wentworth, Hiram
Whipple, Stephen
Willard, John
Wood, William
Young, Hiram O.

THIRTY-SECOND REGIMENT INFANTRY.

Privates.

Hemenway, Elbert O.
Anderson, James

Phillips, Dexter M.
Scolly, Augustus

THIRTY-FOURTH REGIMENT INFANTRY.

Andrew Potter, Captain, Aug. 6, 1862; Major, Sept. 24, 1864; Lieutenant-Colonel, Oct. 14, 1864.
Lafayette Butler, 1st Lieut., July 15, 1862; Captain, June 24, 1863.
William H. Cooley, Captain, August 6, 1862.
Lyman Van Loan, 1st Lieut., Aug. 6, 1862; Captain, Sept. 24, 1864.
Samuel H. Platt, 2d Lieut., Aug. 6, 1862; 1st Lieut., March 18, 1864.
Melville F. Walker, 2d Lieut., June 18, 1863; 1st Lieut., June 6, 1864.
Lemuel Pomeroy, Sergeant-Major, Aug. 1, 1862; 2d Lieut., Nov. 29, 1864.
James R. Fairbanks, Hospital-Steward.
Michael F. Mullen, Quartermaster-Sergeant.

Non-Commissioned Officers.

Cornelius Burley, 1st Sergeant.
Henry H. Clark, 1st "
James Dempsey, 1st "
Edward B. Emerson, "

James D. French, Sergeant.
Arthur Marks, "
William Mink, "
Elisha Chapin, Corporal.

APPENDIX. 707

Noah A. Clark, Corporal.
James Cowan, "
Michael Hayden, "

Charles H. Moulton, Corporal.
William H. Porter, "
Nathan L. Robinson, "

Musicians.

George H. Carpenter, | Edgar P. Fairbanks.

Wagoner.

Julius F. Rockwell.

Privates.

Anthony, Edward P.
Anthony, John M.
Baptist, John
Bell, James A.
Bridgeman, Charles J.
Burns, Edward
Burns, William
Burt, Napoleon
Byrnes, Edward
Cady, Henry C.
Chase, William H.
Casey, John
Chapman, Nathaniel C.
Dailey, Hiram
Dill, Charles H.
Eastman, William H. H.
Garry, Patrick
Grady, John
Haggerty, Michael
Harned, Nelson
Harrison, Edson J.
Hogan, William
Hubbard, Samuel H.
Kelley, William

Kiffe, John H.
King, Henry
Jarvis, William
Leason, Thomas
Logan, Jerry
Lynch, James
McGilp, Henry
Malcolm, George
Mandego, William
Manx, Stephen
Morse, Jeremiah
Mullen, Michael
O'Connor, Thomas
Otis, Philip
Powell, Thomas
Quin, Michael
Shaw, John
Smith, James
Snell, George H.
Sprague, Tyler
Stevens, Louis
Trabold, Sebastian
Wilmot, John
Werden, Willis P.

THIRTY-SIXTH REGIMENT INFANTRY.

Privates.

Jaquot, Jules
Kelley, Jerry

Murphy, Hugh
Whipple, Samuel P.

THIRTY-SEVENTH REGIMENT INFANTRY.

Alonzo E. Goodrich, Lieutenant-Colonel, August 27, 1862.
Frank C. Morse, Chaplain, August 27, 1862.

Thomas G. Colt, 1st Lieutenant, August 5, 1862; Captain, September
    23, 1864; Brevet Lieutenant-Colonel.
Daniel J. Dodge, Quartermaster.
Walter B. Smith, 2d Lieutenant, August 27, 1862; 1st Lieutenant,
    April 5, 1864; Captain, March 4, 1865.
Michael Casey, 1st Sergeant, September 2, 1862; 2d Lieutenant, March
    2, 1865; 1st Lieutenant, June 26, 1865.
James C. Chalmers, 2d Lieut., Nov. 20, 1862; 1st Lieut., Dec. 5, 1863.
Thomas F. Plunkett, Jr., 2d Lieut., Nov. 2, 1862; 1st Lieut., Dec. 5, 1863.
Richard E. Morgan, Hospital Steward.

Non-Commissioned Officers.

Thomas Fallon, Corporal.   Robert Howe, Corporal.

Privates.

Blood, Miles H.
Chalmers, John
Clough, Francis W.
Donlan, Andrew
Fallon, John
Farrell, Christopher
Fuller, William
Ginn, John N.
Hemmenway, Harrison
Hooker, Oliver C.
Hussey, Patrick
McGheehin, John

Packard, Charles
Peters, William L.
Rice, William
Rodgers, James
Royce, Charles H.
Reinhart, Robert
Shanley, William F.
Shannon, Thomas
Sutcliff, William
Wademan, Peter
Welch, John
Young, Michael

THIRTY-NINTH REGIMENT INFANTRY.

Privates.

Caffrey, John   Phillips, Dexter M.
Hemenway, Elbert O.   Wright, Theodore S.

FORTIETH REGIMENT INFANTRY.

Oliver E. Brewster, Surgeon, Aug. 20, 1862; Resigned Oct. 3, 1862.

FIFTY-FOURTH REGIMENT INFANTRY.

Samuel Harrison, Chaplain, Sept. 8, 1863.
Edward B. Emerson, 2d Lieut., June 3, 1863; 1st Lieut., June 19, 1863;
    Captain, March 30, 1865.

Non-Commissioned Officer.

George W. Ringgold, Corporal.

APPENDIX.

Privates.

Bird, Levi
Foster, Moses
Franklin, Eli
Gaines, Alexander
Green, George W.
Hamilton, Paul
Hoose, Edward
Jackson, Samuel D.

Jones, Henry E.
Jones, Samuel
Peters, William
Potter, Charles
Thompson, Abraham
Van Blake, John
Wilson, Abraham
Wilson, Henry

FIFTY-SIXTH REGIMENT INFANTRY.

Privates.

Bedford, Samuel
Jaquot, Jules

Kelly, Jerry
Whipple, Samuel P.

FIFTY-SEVENTH REGIMENT INFANTRY.

Edward P. Hollister, Lieutenant-Colonel, Dec. 21, 1863.
James H. Marshall, 1st Lieut. Oct. 7, 1864.
Charles H. Royce, 2d Lieut. Jan. 7, 1864; 1st Lieut. Oct. 7, 1864.

Non-Commissioned Officers.

Joseph Gallipaux, Corporal.
George H. Hodge,   "

Lester Tyler, Corporal.
Charles E. Stone,   "

Privates.

Avery, Peter
Bassett, Joseph
Beckwith, Joseph H.
Bourne, William S.
Clark, John
Daniels, Charles S.
Daniels, Lowell
Danyon, Horace
Dudley, Charles F.
Dudley, Lyman

Gouch, Edwin J.
Hunt, Alvah A.
Morrissey, Peter
O'Clair, Peter
Peeardet, George
Putnam, Rufus E.
Thompson, Andrew C.
Thornton, Patrick
Vince, Benjamin A.

FIFTY-EIGHTH REGIMENT INFANTRY.

Private.

Daniel Higgins.

LIGHT ARTILLERY.

SECOND BATTERY.

John W. Swart, Corporal. | Henry Welch, Corporal.

Privates.

O'Donnell, Peter | Riardon, Thomas
Riardon, William |

THIRD BATTERY.

Malony, David N.

SEVENTH BATTERY.

Belcher, Edward | Brady, Hugh

TWELFTH BATTERY.

Boynton, Nathaniel B. | Powers, Philip
Keefe, Thomas C. |

HEAVY ARTILLERY.

FIRST REGIMENT.

Emanuel B. Bleeo, Corporal. | John O'Rouke, Private.

SECOND REGIMENT.

Bates, Henry | Murphy, Thomas
Cuzzens, Michael | O'Mara, John
Lawler, James |

THIRD REGIMENT.

James Halpin, Corporal. | Nelson, John
Greenwood, James | Schermerhorn, Daniel
Nelson, James |

FIRST BATTALION.

Thomas Duffee, Private.

THIRTIETH UNATTACHED COMPANY. (One year.)

William Johnson, Private.

FIRST REGIMENT CAVALRY.

Non-Commissioned Officers.

John B. Fields, Sergeant. | Clark B. Blood, Corporal.
James F. Lloyd,   " |

Privates.

Allen, Stanton | Avery, Franklin M.
Andrews, Charles E. | Bellon, Patrick
Atwood, Benoni W. | Bennett, Richard

APPENDIX. 711

Bowen, Nelson O.
Bramer, Josiah
Casey, Maurice
Carter, Nelson
Chapman, Charles T.
Clark, William
Cole, James
Conway, Anthony
Coste, Henry
Dennis, Edward
Dolan, James
Estes, William H.
Fairbanks, Charles F.
Feeney, Martin
Fernet, Henry
Garley, Thomas
Gallipaux, Charles
Guinan, James

Hatch, Moses
Hoin, Theodore C.
Howe, John
Hull, William H.
Jansen, Eilart
McArdie, James
Madden, George G.
Miner, Smith
Morse, William
Palmer, William D.
Putnam, John
Rouse, John D.
Shannon, Daniel
Shannon, Edward
Taylor, Giles
Waterman, Irving
Williams, Henry

SECOND REGIMENT CAVALRY.
Privates.

Abbott, Sturges
Benjamin, James N.
Bran, John
Donahue, Thomas

Heckory, Charles
Huych, Nicholas H.
McCreith, John
Odell, John

THIRD REGIMENT CAVALRY.
Privates.

Barber, Joseph P.
Brown, Nelson S.
Conlin, James
Corron, Marcus
Fagan, Dennis A.
Green, Jerry
McKenna, Daniel

McKenna, William E.
Malcolm, Abraham
Pritchard, Allen
Quinn, Thomas
Ray, Charles
Solon, James

FOURTH REGIMENT CAVALRY.
William Cook, Private.

FIFTH REGIMENT CAVALRY.
John F. Porter, Sergeant.
John A. Williams, "

John E. Gillard, Corporal.
Augustus Fields, Private.

U. S. REGULAR ARMY.
Privates.

Connolly, Timothy J.
Dane, Joseph E.
Gould, David H.
Moran, Hugh
Noonan, Morris
Powers, Richard

U. S. VETERAN VOLUNTEERS.
Privates.

James Malcomb. | John W. McGinnis.

U. S. COLORED TROOPS.
Privates.

Richard Birdsound. | Abraham Reynolds.

FIRST COMPANY SHARP-SHOOTERS.
William F. Bunnells, Private.

VETERAN RESERVE CORPS.
Privates.

Albert, Charles.
Barrett, James A.
Brady, James
Brady, Michael
Broderick, Patrick
Brown, James
Craven, Anthony
Dalton, William
Dugan, Joseph
Ersenberger, Rudolph
Finicane, James
Fitzgerald, Peter
Gaddis, James
Guinan, William J.
Hart, Daniel
Hunt, John
Hedgeman, George
Hea, Jacob
Hoffman, Germany
Hooker, George
Jackson, Charles L.
Kennedy, Thomas
Leary, John
Leary, Patrick
Lyman, Charles
Lynch, John
McCabe, George
McIntyre, Michael
McRichards, Joseph
O'Callahan, Eugene
O'Hanen, Hugh
O'Neil, Hugh
Parker, Joseph
Quinlian, William
Rapp, William
Reed, Samuel W.
Read, John S.
Schneck, Charles
Spear, Charles H.
Taylor, Abraham
Thompson, William
Underwood, Edward E.

APPENDIX. 713

ENLISTMENTS IN ORGANIZATIONS OF STATES OTHER THAN MASSACHUSETTS.

Henry H. Sears, Captain, 48th New York Volunteer Infantry.
Byron W. Kellogg, Sergeant, 173d New York Volunteer Infantry.
John Camp, 1st Regiment New Orleans Infantry.
Charles M. Shepardson, 12th New York Cavalry.

INDEX.

A.

Abbe, Lyman, 505.
Abbott, Rev. Charles E., 678.
Academy of Music, 693.
Adams, Rev. Nehemiah, D. D., 433.
Adam, Robert W., 429, 599, 610, 683.
Adams, Junius D., 682.
Adams, town of, 20, 329, 546.
Adams, George W., 506.
Agnew, Rev. Dr. J. H., 676.
Agriculture, 30; early, et seq.; price of land and stock, 35.
Agricultural society, Berkshire, 316, et seq. (See heading, Chapter 15.)
Agricultural societies, early in Europe and America, 316; claims to priority, 319; Elkanah Watson's part in founding, 324; call for first meeting, 328; first cattle-show, 328; first fair after incorporation, 333; sheep-raising a prominent object, 329; early struggles, 333; manufactures a prominent object, 335; efforts to interest the ladies, 340; plowing-matches, 344; society developed by degrees, 345; effects on the county, 345; attempts to make the fairs migratory, 345; poem by William Cullen Bryant, 350; later history of the society, 662; poem and report by Oliver Wendell Holmes, 666; list of Pittsfield officers, 667; permanent show-grounds established, 662; early donations to, 664.
Albany, 46.
Allen, Capt. Elisha L., 255, 388.
Allen, Dr. Elisha Lee, 220, 221.
Allen Guard, 610, 614, 616.
Allen, Horace, 48, 186, 188.
Allen, Hon. Jonathan, 5, 48, 75, 195, 211, 267, 299, 321, 332, 353, 356, 364, 379, 387, 388, 398, 465, 480, 509, 511, 528, 649, 652.
Allen, Capt. Jonathan 2d, 133, 175, 195, 299, 310, 381.
Allen, Hon. Phinehas, 66, 79, 82, 186, 267, 271, 299, 303, 379, 381, 387, 550, 662, 678.
Allen, Phinehas 2d, 561, 576, 651, 652, 679.
Allen, Rufus, 5, 38, 44.
Allen, Rev. Samuel A., 418.
Allen, Solomon L., 221.
Allen, Samuel L., 222.
Allen, Rev. Thomas, 5, 53, 54, 66, 72, 74, 102, 104, et seq.; 133, 186, 195, 200, 203, 222, 419, 640.
Allen, Thomas 2d, 5, 74, 107, 181.
Allen, Thomas 3d, 187, 368, 589, 610, 613, 622, 623, 643, 648, 649, 677, 681.
Allen, Theodore L., 679.
Allen, Rev. William, D. D., 76, 107, 191, 200, 263, 265, 266, 274, 277, 280, 418, 419, 580, 589.
Amherst College, 299, 304.
Andrew, Gov. John A., 622.
Anecdotes. Of Ashbel Strong, 15; trustees of Williams College, 71; Henry Van Schaack, 72; H. H. Childs, 77; Joseph Shearer, 79; Solomon L. Allen, 82; Hon. Phinehas Allen, 83; Hon. Ezekiel Bacon, 85; certain federal young ladies, 91; Mrs. C. T. Fenn, 12; Rev. Billy Hibbard, 153; Capt. Hosea Merrill, wife and daughters, 166; James Strandring and Phillips Merrill, 168; Lemuel Pomeroy, 190; General Weinbold and certain disorderly prisoners of war, 216; Twenty-first regiment, 220; Washington Benevolent Society, 234; Rev. Billy Hibbard and a Boston federalist, 256; Rev. Dr. Humphrey, 286, 289; Timothy Hall, 360; resurrectionists and body-snatching, 361, 362, 364; Abel West, 385; Shakers, 389; Henry C. Brown, 401, 402; Berkshire Hotel, 9; Phillips Merrill, 22.
Appleton, Nathan, 6.
Ashley, David, 140, 141.
Ashley, Lake, 560, 563, 566. (See Waterworks.)

716 INDEX.

Aspinwall, Lieut.-Col. Thomas, 205, 206, 210.
Athenæum, Berkshire, 644, et seq.
Atwood, Thomas G., 505, 551, 553, 603, 664.
Axtell, William D., 680, 681.

B.

Bacon, Hon. Ezekiel, 85, 124, 186, 195, 545, 580, 581, 687.
Bacon, John, 85.
Bacon, W. Frank, 500.
Backus, William G., 553, 637.
Bailey, Dr. Charles, 373.
Bailey, Rev. Rufus W., 416, 418, 419.
Baker, Aaron, 37.
Baldwin, Moses H., 367, 426, 432, 463.
Ballard, Rev. Dr. Edward, 456, 457, 458, 459.
Baptist church. (See headings, Chapters 7, 16, 20.) Early zeal of, 135; re-established in Pittsfield, 136; early place of baptism, 137; Rev. John Francis the first pastor, 138; readmitted to Shaftsbury Association, 139; prominent members of, in 1819, 435; pastorate of Rev. Mr. Beach, 436; Berkshire Association established, 437; builds its first church, 438; rebuilds, 440; remodels, 442, 435, 590, 593.
Barber, Matthew, 37.
Barber, Nathan, 504.
Barker, Charles T., 496, 555.
Barker, Dr. Daniel, 219.
Barker, Gardner T., 495.
Barker, James M., 633, 643, 645.
Barker, John V., 493, 496.
Barker, Otis R., 496.
Barkersville, 37.
Barnes, Amos, 424, 434.
Barnes, Henry P., 551.
Bartlett, Rev. E. O., 420.
Bartlett, General William F., 619, 620, 621, 627, 635, 645.
Batchelder, Dr. J. P., 355, 356, 360.
Bates, Ezekiel, 214.
Beach, Rev. Augustus, 393, 436.
Beach, O. H., 664.
Beebe, James M., 641.
Bedell, B. C., 442.
Benedict, Oren, 381, 445, 598.
Bently, Arnold, 298.
Berkshire Agricultural Society. (See Agricultural Society.)
Berkshire Jubilee, 573, et. seq.
Betts, Judge Samuel R., 587.
Bible class, list of in 1823, 287.
Bissell, E. M., 388.

Bissell, Josiah, 188, 195, 236, 260, 282, 303, 332, 361, 362, 379, 381, 394, 418.
Bishop, Nathaniel, 325.
Bliss, George, of Springfield, 536, 541.
Blodget, B. C., 648.
Boltwood, Edward, 684.
Bonney, E. D., 692.
Boston, 229, 244, 245.
Bowden, Rev. James A., 459.
Bowerman, Samuel W., 623, 627, 642.
Boyington, Rev. Charles B., 433, 533.
Brace, Rev. S. C., 641, 675, 678.
Bradley, J. E., 672.
Brewster, Henry B., 619, 634.
Brewster, Dr. John M., 6, 412.
Brewster, Dr. John M. 2d, 669.
Brewster, Dr. Oliver E., 670.
Briggs, George N., 83, 299, 393, 441, 487, 577, 582, 590, 595, 675, 683, 684.
Briggs, George P., 577, 606, 607.
Briggs, Henry S., 551, 601, 612, 616, 623, 627.
Brinsmade, Rev. H. N., 418, 419, 422.
Broadcloth, early manufacture of, 161, 162, et. seq.
Brown, George, 563, 568.
Brown, Henry C., 356, 359, 361, 379, 381, 382, 398, 409.
Brown, James, 41, 186, 332, 692.
Brown, Colonel John, 400.
Brown, Captain John, 283.
Brown, John, 563.
Brown, N. G., 563, 568, 684.
Brown, Simeon, 41, 186, 381, 459, 598, 692.
Brown, Rev. William R., 445, 449.
Browning, William, 199, 222, 224.
Bryant, William Cullen, 350, 588, 589.
Bryant, John, 142.
Buel, James, 184, 195, 197, 382, 38, 409, 472, 473, 474, 477.
Bucklin, Capt. A. J., 199.
Buckley, Gershom, 236.
Bulkley, Charles T., 505.
Burbank, Abraham, 422, 553, 554, 685.
Burbank, Dr. Asa, 356, 360.
Burbank, George W., 553.
Burdick, Rev. C. F., 449.
Burial-grounds, 597.
Burt, Z., 5.
Bush, David, 7, 94, 187.
Bush, Eli, 4, 5.
Butler, George, 361.
Butler, James H., 362, 445, 446.

C.

Cadwell, Capt., 54.
Cadwell, Timothy, 123, 267.
Cadwell, William, 35.

INDEX. 717

Callender, Henry, 397, 550, 553.
Campbell, David 1st, 70, 184, 330, 379, 410, 413.
Campbell, David 2d, 181, 195, 197, 329, 382, 472, 483.
Campbell, David 3d, 603.
Campbell, George, 490, 689.
Campbell, George W., 367, 425, 483, 490, 565, 602, 603, 606.
Campbell, Dr. Robert, 240, 381, 411, 544, 549, 550, 553, 563, 564.
Canal proposed, 515.
Cantonment, 192. (See War 1812.)
Carding machines. (See Manufactures.)
Carhart, Rev. Dr. J. Wesley, 140, 448, 449.
Carey, Avery, 431, 432.
Carpets, rag and other, 50.
Carruthers, Rev. William, 433.
Carter, Josiah, 430.
Cary, George H., 669.
Catholic churches, 460, 461; Catholic cemetery, 608.
Cattle-shows, early, 324, 325, 328.
Cemeteries, 596, 597, 600.
Center, Ebenezer, 181, 184, 472, 477, 487.
Chadbourne, Paul A., 370.
Chapman, Daniel, 88, 123, 124, 267.
Chapman, Rev. Dr. George T., 451, 456, 459, 605.
Chapel, Richard S., 254, 329, 332, 468, 470.
Cheshire, 20, 177, 204, 211, 213, 242, 328, 329, 546.
Chickering, Henry, 680.
Childs, Dr. Henry H., 77, 122, 134, 195, 267, 288, 297, 299, 307, 314, 332, 350, 374, 375, 379, 381, 385, 398, 417, 430, 443, 550, 574, 612, 623.
Childs, Dr. Timothy, 5, 10, 11, 14, 48, 50, 73, 122, 181, 184, 217, 223, 297, 332, 379, 508, 599, 686, 687.
Childs, Dr. Timothy 2d, 369.
Childs, Thomas, 221.
Churches, Baptist. (See headings, Chapters 7, 20.) Catholic, 460; Congregational. (See headings, Chapters 6, 12, 13, 19.) Episcopal, 450; Lutheran, (German,) 463; Methodist Episcopal. (See headings, Chapters 7, 20.)
Churchill, Charles, 384.
Churchill, John, 438, 598, 687, 688.
Churchill, Samuel A., 602.
Churchill, Spencer, 504.
Churchill family, 195.
Clapp, Edwin, 548, 551, 556, 568, 645.
Clapp, Jason, 84, 195, 381, 382, 388, 393, 424, 429, 473, 510, 552, 574, 652.
Clapp, Lyman, 502.

Clapp, Col. Thaddeus, 475, 483, 484, 490,
Clapp, Thaddeus 3d, 165, 490.
Clapp, Thomas W., 615.
Clark, George H., 505.
Clark, Rev. Henry, 441, 603, 607.
Clark, Jonathan Yale, 186, 297, 298, 299, 307, 309, 384, 528.
Clark, William H., 196, 205.
Clay, Henry, 452, 482, 492.
Clothiers, 36. (See Fulling Mills, Cloth, Home-made Woolen, product of Berkshire County in 1808, 177, 179.)
Clough, Aaron, 430.
Clymer, Rev. J. F., 449.
Coggswell, Richard C., 550.
Coogan, Owen, 645, 692.
Coogan, William H., 635.
Cooley, William B., 414.
Cooley, William H., 617.
Coleman, Dr. William, 528.
Cole, Otis, Jr., 505.
Collins, Dwight M., 501.
Colt, Ezekiel R., 81, 92, 184, 314, 379, 381, 382, 384, 388, 394, 401, 409, 493, 550, 574, 598, 684.
Colt, Henry, 428, 500, 545, 568, 624.
Colt, J. D. & S. D., 5, 14, 43, 77, 197.
Colt, Capt. James D., 408.
Colt, James D. 2d, 5, 10, 173, 176, 181, 195, 248, 373, 375, 408, 473, 574.
Colt, Judge James D., 545, 552, 577, 594, 595, 603, 612, 620, 671, 689.
Colt, John and Jabez, 444.
Colt, Robert, 288.
Colt, Samuel D., 78, 288, 328, 329, 330, 332, 379, 384, 422, 465, 472, 474, 477, 482, 528.
Colt, Thomas, 429, 503, 504, 551, 560, 568, 613, 615, 627, 635, 636, 644, 648, 666, 668, 682, 690, 691.
Colt, Thomas G., 618, 634, 635, 643.
Comb-plates for carding-machines, 167.
Congregational churches. (See headings, Chapters 6, 12, 13, 19.) Ministerial fund of, 272; zeal of clergymen in 1800, 156; discipline in, 111, 126, 128.
Connecticut Valley, new emigration from, 79.
Constitutional convention of 1820, 305. (See heading, Chapter 14.)
County-buildings, removal of to Pittsfield, 686, et. seq.; committees upon, 687, 688, 689, 690, 691.
Councils, ecclesiastical, 105, 119, 120, 122, 128.
Crofoot, Dea. Daniel, 275, 422.
Crocker, John R., 421.
Crowther, Rev. Thomas, 433.

INDEX.

Cuddihy, Rev. P., 461.
Curtis, George William, 633, 636.

D.

Dalton, 205, 211, 255.
Dancing-parties and balls, 53, 205.
Danforth, Col. Joshua, 14, 43, 46, 73, 88, 99, 123, 173, 180, 188, 242, 265, 299, 420, 508, 558, 687.
Danforth, Rev. Joshua N., 585.
Danforth, S. A., 417.
Daniels, S. V. R., 441.
Davis, Henry G., 430.
Dawes, Henry L., 623, 633, 645, 648, 661.
Dean, H. N. & A. P., Stowell & Benjamin, 503.
Dearborn, Gen. Henry S., 200, 399.
Deism, 145.
Democrats, list of, in 1810, 186.
DeLamater, Dr. John, 360.
Dewey, Prof. Chester, 356, 359, 360, 366, 418, 648.
Dexter, Andrew, 181.
Dexter, Samuel, 229, 404.
Dickinson, Israel, 17, 640.
Dickinson, Joel, 558.
Dickinson, John, 9, 88, 195, 201, 265, 299, 332, 385, 428, 473, 559, 625.
Dickinson, Oliver P., 332, 381, 438, 574.
Dillingham, Charles, 677.
Dimock, Rev. Samuel R., 433.
Dodge, D. J., 610, 618, 634, 684.
Dodge, Mrs. D. J., 626.
Dodge, Mrs. Emily Pomeroy, 605.
Dodge, John E., 566.
Dodge, N. S., 563, 603, 674.
Dorn, Alexander, 503.
Dress, fashions of, 1800, 51.
Dunbar, George S., 555.
Dunbar, Henry, 480.
Dunham, Ebenezer, 430, 432, 692.
Dunham, Helen, 421.
Dunham, James H., 397, 421, 430, 431, 433, 434, 603, 669.
Dunham, Jarvis N., 555, 556, 645.
Dutton, George N., 428.
Dwight, Henry W., of Stockbridge, 382, 393, 662.

E.

Easton, Col. James, 6, 44, 77.
Earle, Dr. Pliny, 370.
Eli, Alexander and Elisha, 174, 325.
Elm, The old, 188, 383, 633.
Emerson, Charles N., 623.
Emigration to the West, and to Vermont, 21; to the West grows excessive, 22; causes of, 23; counterbalancing influences, 22.

Ensign, Eli, 236.
Ensign's pond, 4.
Episcopal church, 450, 453, 458, 460.
Explosion of powder-magazine, 395.

F.

Factories. (See Manufactures.)
Fairfield, Joseph, 110, 123, 267.
Fairfield, Nathaniel, 123, 267.
Fairfield family, 33, 88.
Fanning, Oramel, 196, 208.
Farmers' diaries and farm-work, 82.
Farm products, prices of, in 1795, 35.
Farming, early, 30. (See heading, Chapter 15.)
Feeley, John, 554, 555, 568.
Fenn, Curtis T., 404, 424, 430, 431, 433, 502.
Fenn, Mrs. Curtis T., 9, 12, 201, 205, 625, 626, 627.
Field, Rev. David Dudley, D. D., 580.
Ferry, Irving D., 643.
Fire-department. (See heading, Chapter 23.) Before 1844, 549; re-organized, 550; fire-district, 549; fire-companies: Housatonic, 551; Pontoosuc, 552; S. W. Morton, 552; Greylock hook and ladder company, 553; Edwin Clapp steamer, 556; George Y. Learned steamer, 556; list of engineers, 553.
Flowers, flower-gardens, and wild flowers, 12, 13, 14.
Foote, Daniel, 267, 275.
Foote, George W., 572.
Foot, James, 449.
Ford, Dr. Corydon L., 370.
Foster, Rev. Roswell, 433.
Francis, Almiron D., 442.
Francis, Charles B., 388, 393, 439.
Francis, Daniel H., 137, 435, 439.
Francis, Edward S., 627, 682.
Francis, Eldad, 356, 439.
Francis, James, 441, 442, 603, 671.
Francis, J. Dwight, 490.
Francis, John, 137; pastor of the Baptist church, 139, 140, 291, 435, 440.
Francis, Josiah, 137, 138, 139, 195, 291, 435, 439.
Francis, Luke, 435.
Francis, Robert, 8, 420, 441.
Francis, William, 8, 195.
French, Edmund, 8.
French revolution, 96.
Fulling-Mills, 36. (See Manufactures.)

G.

Gambling, 65.
Garlick, Charles R., 618.
Gates, Rev. David W., 449.

INDEX. 719

German population, 463.
Gerry, Gov. Elbridge, 228.
Gibbs, F. W., 503.
Goodhue, Dr. Josiah, 365, 366.
Goodman. Joseph, 181, 329.
Goodman, Titus, 328, 330.
Goodrich, Alonzo E., 618, 627.
Goodrich, Butler, 9, 195, 236, 363, 384, 428, 528, 598, 687.
Goodrich, Caleb, 504, 505.
Goodrich, Capt. Charles, 17, 33, 37, 68, 123, 195, 269, 271, 276, 558.
Goodrich, Charles, Jr., 123, 124, 129, 195, 267.
Goodrich, Chauncy, 624.
Goodrich, Ebenezer, 505.
Goodrich, Jesse, 8, 195.
Goodrich, Levi, 298, 426, 427, 550.
Goodrich, Noah W., 581.
Goodrich, Oren., 134, 299, 428, 438, 559, 689.
Gold, Thomas, 5, 6, 195, 247, 248, 265, 332, 379, 420, 477, 480, 508, 509, 687.
Gold, Thomas A., 388, 473, 528, 576, 559, 602.
Graves, Perez, 5, 48.
Graves & Root, 14, 43.
Great Barrington, 20, 306, 689.
Green, Rev. Robert, 48, 123, 141, 188, 291.
Green, Dr. William Warren, 370.
Gregory, Mrs. Joseph, 626.
Groot, George R., 556, 610.
Groot, Henry, 553.
Grotrian, Rev. Augustus, 453.

H.

Hall, Parker L., 382, 544, 545.
Hall, Timothy, 360.
Halls, public, 693.
Hampshire county, 249.
Haegar, John David, 464.
Hancock, 20, 141.
Harding, William G., 642.
Harris, Rev. Samuel, 418, 433, 450.
Harrison, Rev. Samuel, 434, 450.
Hartford, 11, 19, 96, 162, 194.
Hartford convention, 249.
Haskell, Timothy, 123, 129, 267.
Hawley, Rev. Bostwick, 449.
Hawthorn, Nathaniel, 7.
Herrick, William Z., 140.
Hibbard, Rev. Billy, 142, 213, 255, 291.
Hicock, Aaron, 38.
Hinsdale, Miss Nancy, 672.
Hinsdale, town of, 177.
Hinsdale, Theodore, 172, 181, 195, 247, 248, 379, 430, 431.

Hinsdale, Rev. Theodore, 121, 123.
Hitchcock, Rev. Edward, D. D., 366.
Hoadley, John C., 367, 127, 560, 563, 605, 641, 660, 672.
Holland, Dr. Joshua G., 372, 373.
Hollister, Edward P., 620.
Hollister, William, 208, 381, 385.
Holly, Nathaniel, 28.
Holmes, Dr. O. W., 582, 606.
Honasada street, 517.
Hopkins, Rev. Dr. Mark, 372, 578.
Hosmer, James B., of Hartford, 162.
Horse-breeding, 34.
Hotels, Merrick's inn, 9, 185, 413; Pittsfield [democratic] hotel, 9, 185, 186, 356. Campbell's coffee-house, 185, 213, 413; William Clark's tavern, 205; Jesse Goodrich tavern, 8; Berkshire hotel, 413, 414; Ingersoll tavern 5, 10.
Housatonic railroad, 546.
Household-furniture in 1800, 50.
Houses in 1800, 5, et seq.
Howard, Welcome S., 431.
Hubbard, D. S., 680.
Hubbard, Henry, 76, 297, 298, 314, 355, 358, 387, 392, 393, 405, 438, 443, 450, 528, 529, 595, 670. 680, 688.
Hubbard, Rev. Jonathan, 405.
Hubbard, James, 186, 267, 275.
Hubbard, James, Jr., 267.
Hubbard, Thomas, 141, 265.
Hudson, city of, 18, 43.
Hulbert, Chauncey, 236.
Hulbert, John W., 10, 85, 181, 182, 195, 238, 240, 241, 325, 687.
Hull, James W., 643.
Humphrey, E. F., 434.
Humphrey, Col. Gad, 387.
Humphrey, Rev. Dr. Heman. (See heading Chapter 13.) 282, 302, 303, 312, 355, 357, 367, 391, 416, 417, 418, 430, 641.
Humphries, Col. D., of Poughkeepsie, 329.
Hulburt, Charles, 552, 563.
Hyde, Alexander, of Lee, 400.
Hyde, Rev. Dr. Alvan, of Lee, 587.
Hyde, Jonathan L., 673.

I.

Imprisonment for debt, 63.
Independence day, celebration of, 293
Ingersoll, Capt. Jared 1st, 173, 186, 199.
Ingersoll, Capt. Jared 2d, 225, 550.
Ingersoll tavern, 5, 10.
Insurance-companies, 381, 382; Berkshire Mutual Fire-Insurance Company, 382; Berkshire Life-Insurance Company, 684.
Iron-forges and manufactures, 37.

J.

James, Dr. Daniel, 195.
James, Henry & Company, 188, 236.
Janes, Ethan, 187, 214.
Janes, William, 187, 214, 216.
Jarvis, William C , 299, 355, 356, 361, 381, 403, 472, 482, 687.
Jennings, Rev. Ebenezer, of Dalton, 237, 279, 286.
Jewish synagogue, 464.
Jinks, Ahab, 188.
Jones, Jonathan M. & Sons, 505.
Jubilee. Berkshire. (See heading,Chapter 24, 573.) Committees and officers, 574; history of, published, 185; jubilee hill named, 588.

K.

Keeler, Joseph, 37, 485.
Keeler's mills, 37.
Kellogg, Ensign H., 367, 426, 490, 549, 566, 568, 602, 612, 623, 627, 644, 663, 668, 689.
Kernochan, Frank E., 500.
Kinderhook, 7, 18, 46.
Kingsley, Jonathan, 142.
Kingsbury, Rev. A., 440.
Kirby, Reynolds M., 221, 222, 225.
Kitteredge, William, 558.

L.

Ladies' societies, and social meetings, 53, 54, 625.
Laflin, George H., 615.
Laflin, Walter, 382, 563, 612, 671.
Lafayette, General, his visit to Pittsfield, 387.
Lanckton, M. R., 381, 443, 453, 512, 528, 670.
Lanesboro, 20, 177, 211, 329, 688.
Larned, Darius, 9, 649.
Larned, Simon, 6, 33, 43, 46, 47, 48, 173, 181, 182, 183, 195, 508, 558.
Learned, Albert, 503.
Learned, Edward, 499, 500, 623, 685.
Learned, E. McAlpine, 500.
Learned, George Y., 556, 644.
Lee, S. H. P., 550.
Leland, Elder John, 103, 138, 204, 436, 440.
Lemarque, Rev. Mr., 463.
Leidhold, Erdman, 634.
Lenox, 29, 177, 255.
Libraries, 640.
Life, social and domestic. (See heading, Chapter 4.)
Linseed oil, manufacture of, 43.
Little, James S., 505.
Little, Woodbridge, 8, 68, 107, 108, 113, 117, 123, 271, 420.

Looms, Scholfield's manufacture of, 163, 174.
Looms, Hand and Power, 474.
Longfellow, Henry W., 6, 7.
Lotteries, 63.
Luce, Benjamin, 329, 450, 473.
Luce's Mills, 43.
Lutheran [German] church, 463.

M.

McGlathery, Rev. William, 460.
McKay, Gordon, 367, 426, 552, 553, 560, 563, 565.
McKay, Samuel M., 297, 298, 299, 303, 313, 314, 355, 384, 403, 404, 421, 443, 482, 492, 502, 523, 528, 530, 598, 670.
Manners and morals. (See headings, Chapters 4, 17. pp. 53, 392, 393, 395, 402.)
Manufactures. (See headings, Chapters 3, 8, 15, 21, 28.) Early difficulties of, 485, 489 ; early woolen, 36, 158, et. seq.; fulling-mills, 37, 164; iron-forges, 37; tanneries, 41; potasheries, 42 ; nails, 44 ; economy of manufacturing, 159; difficulties in the introduction of cotton and woolen manufactures, 159; early mills, 164; claim of Pittsfield to priority in woolen manufacture, 162; carding-machines, looms, and spinning-jennies. (See Arthur Scholfield.) Profits on home-made broadcloths, 177; Pomeroy's musket-factory, 189; action of agricultural society for protection by tariff, 335, 342; condition of manufactures in 1840, 377; household-manufactures predominant in 1812, 465; first broadcloths, 467; sail duck, 467, 468; rope-walk, 467.
Manufacturers of Pittsfield; act in favor of protection by tariff, 480, 487; early struggles of, 476.
Manufactories ; Housatonic mill, 468; Pittsfield woolen and cotton factory, 472; Pomeroy woolen mills, 478; Pontoosuc woolen manufacturing company, 483; Barkersville and Stearnsville, 493 ; Russell woolen factory, 496 ; Peck's factory, 498 ; Taconic woolen mill, 499; Pittsfield and Bel Air woolen companies, 499 ; Osceola woolen mill, 401 ; Pittsfield cotton factory, 502 ; Coltsville paper mill, 503 ; Wahconah flouring mill, 504; Shaker flouring mill, 506 ; Osceola flouring mill, 506 ; Kellogg steam-power works, 684; Saunders silk-factory, 684; Pittsfield tack-factory, 684; Various manufactories, 692.

INDEX.

Maplewood, Young Ladies Institute, 7, 201, 419, 625, 674.
Markham, Zalmon, 502.
Markets, 46.
Martin, Calvin, 381, 393, 421, 432, 598, 605, 643, 644, 651, 669.
Marsh, Henry A., 680.
Masonry, Free, 9, 293, 297.
Maynard, Eli, 108, 110, 189, 468.
Medical College. (See heading, Chapter 16.)
Medical societies, 373.
Medical fee-table of 1812, 375.
Meeting-houses. (See Churches.) Seating and dignifying of, 312, 315.
Melville, Allan, 7, 8, 664.
Melville, Herman, 7, 8, 664.
Melville, Robert, 7.
Melville, Maj. Thomas, 7, 176, 195, 206, 211, 212, 213, 247, 324, 380, 398, 598, 664, 670.
Mercantile affairs and merchants, 44, 45, 188; trade by barter, 47.
Merriam, Daniel P., 424.
Merriam, Robert A., 683.
Merrick, Joseph, 9, 172, 173, 181, 185, 195, 303, 328, 329, 332, 384, 392, 472, 509, 511, 528, 687, 688.
Merrill, Dr. A. P., 497.
Merrill, Caleb, 38.
Merrill, Capt. Hosea, 22, 33, 166, 213, 332, 421.
Merrill, Hosea, Jr., 382, 456, 689, 690.
Merrill, Orsemus C., 28.
Merrill, Phillips, 22, 39, 168, 332.
Merwin, Elias, 368, 603, 645.
Methodist church. (See headings, Chapters 7, 20.) Early seal of, 146, 147, 148; formation of the Pittsfield Circuit, 140; religious society incorporated, 141; schism of Reformed Methodists, 142; first church built, 139; second church built, 443; third church built, 445; fourth church built, 445; Wesleyan Methodists, 449; list of clergymen, 448; lists of early members, 140, 141.
Militia, 188, 189, 246, 250, 609, 610.
Millard, Royal, 187, 470.
Miller, William, the Second Adventist, 144.
Mills, Jason, 189.
Ministerial fund, Congregational, 421, 422, 431.
Miner, Rev. Bradley, 440.
Missions, A. B. C. F., meetings of, 419.
Monument, soldiers', 626; names inscribed on, 629.
Monroe, Dan, 165.
Montague, Charles, 430, 680, 681.
Morals and moral societies, 35; 392.

Morewood, J. R., 7.
Morewood, Mrs. J. R., 605, 626.
Morgan, Charles, 506.
Morgan, Richard P., of Stockbridge, 52
Morton, S. W., 552, 554, 555, 556, 568, 68
Moseley, T. E., 417.
Munyan, A. B. & D. C., 572, 647, 692, (
Murray, William H., 544, 645.
Music church, 421.

N.

Nail-factory, 44.
Names, catalogues of:
[We should have been glad to have given in this index every name mentioned in the body of the work, but it would have swelled it to an unreasonable length, and in cases where large bodies of persons are mentioned in the same connection, we are able only to refer to the lists. We have done so under the proper heads, and here repeat them in a condensed form.]
Residents of Pittsfield in 1800, 5; members of Union church, 123; early members of Baptist church, 136, 142, 435; early members of Methodist church, 140, 141; corporators of Berkshire bank, 181; democrats of 1808, 186; politicians of 1812, 195; miscellaneous, 265; Bible class of 1821, 288; signers to the call for the first cattle-show, 328; exhibitors, 329; early members and officers of the society, 332; corporators of Agricultural bank, 379; first members of South congregational parish, 430, 431; clergymen of Methodist church, 448; committees on Western railroad, 528. Petitioners for Pittsfield and West Stockbridge railroad, 532; first Pittsfield shareholders in Western railroad, 539; members of fire-companies and committees of fire-district, 550, 551, 525, 553; engineers of the fire-department, 553; committees and officers of Berkshire jubilee, 575, 576, 577, 587; Pittsfield soldiers killed in the war of the Rebellion, 629; list of soldiers who served in the war for the preservation of the Union, 695; Pittsfield officers of the Berkshire agricultural society, 687; first directors of Pittsfield bank, 682; officers of Agricultural bank, 683; officers and depositors of Berkshire savings bank, 682, 683.
Natural History, Lyceum of, 365.
Neill, Rev. Dr. Henry, 605, 675.
Nettleton, Rev. Asahel, 56, 92, 296.
New Marlboro', 19, 20.

INDEX.

ṿ measure men, 417.
ѵspapers, early influence of, 24; Cen-
.inel, 24; Berkshire Chronicle, 25; rules
?or conduct of, 26; post riders, 26, 29;
erkshire Gazette, 28.
ѵspapers, recent; Sun, 82, 678; Argus,
.9; Eagle, 679; Cataract, 680; Whig,
˜0; Star, 681; Culturist and Gazette,
ȝi; Medical Journal, 682; minor pa-
ers, 681.
.wton, Edward A., 6, 379, 382, 383, 384,
385, 392, 397, 407, 434, 453, 456, 550, 563,
574, 601, 669.
ˆ˜˜ton, Miss Lucretia E., 458.
˜ˡ˒ˡ ɔls, Samuel E., 634, 643.
ˀˣˢˡ˒, Daniel, of Williamston, 356.
˜ˀˢˡ˒, Capt. David, 44.
˜ˀˢˡ˒, Flavius P., 445.
Not˒˒, Henry, 446.
ˢˀˢ˒ hampton, 41, 56, 182.
orth woods, 17, 137, 139.

O.

ɹ'Callahan, Rev. Jeremiah, 460.
Ɔil-mills, linseed, 43.
Ɔsborne, Olcott, 451, 503, 603.
Osborn, Vivus, 278.
Otaneaque street, 17, 18.

P.

Page, P. L., 430, 623.
Palmer, Dr. A. B., 370.
Palmer, Dr. David, death of, 367.
Parker, Frederick S., 442.
Parker, Linus, 8, 187.
Parker, Titus, 37.
Park, the, and Park square, 108, 383, 384, 633.
Parks, Rev. Stephen, 444, 449.
Partridge family, 17.
Partridge, Dr. Oliver, 373.
Parvin, Robert J., 459.
Peck, Elijah, 422, 424, 498.
Peck, Rev. E. M., 459.
Peck, Jabez, 382, 498.
Peck, Jabez L., 428, 498, 554, 555, 568, 635, 642, 684.
Pepoon, Daniel, 181, 325.
Perry, Rev. David, of Richmond, 111, 128, 130.
Perry, Lieut. David, 199.
Phillips, William H., 679.
Pierson, Henry M., 668.
Pierson, Capt. Nathan, 641.
Pingree, Thomas P., 596.
Plunkett, Charles T., 618, 619.
Plunkett, Charles H., 654.
Plunkett, Patrick, 653.

Plunkett, Thomas F., 426, 502, 504, 547, 549, 563, 565, 566, 568, 576, 594, 602, 603, 613, 643, 653, 671, 684.
Plunkett, William C., 654.
Plunkett, William R., 568, 627, 645.
Political feuds between federalists and democrats, from 1798 to 1815. (See headings, Chapters 6, 10, 11, 12.)
Politics in 1820. (See heading, Chapter 16.)
Pollock, William, 613, 615.
Pomeroy, Edward, 478.
Pomeroy, John, 443, 456.
Pomeroy, Josiah, 477, 478, 501.
Pomeroy, Lemuel, 6, 37, 79, 84, 176, 189, 195, 197, 271, 332, 370, 396, 417, 422, 423, 431, 454, 477, 482, 501, 509, 511, 544, 574, 598, 677, 688, 689.
Pomeroy, Robert, 6, 478, 500.
Pomeroy, Theodore, 429, 478, 500, 615, 645.
Pontoosuc, 37. (See Manufactures and Fire-companies.)
Population, 20, 89, 378, 692.
Porter, Rev. Lemuel, D. D., 135, 136, 440, 441, 442, 450, 593.
Post-office, post-riders, and postmasters, 29, 652, 680.
Potash-making, 42.
Powder-magazine explosion, 395.
Prindle, Rev. Cyrus, 444, 449, 450.
Punderson, Rev. Thomas, 129, 418.
Purcell, Rev. Edward H., 461, 608.

Q.

Quackenbush, Cebra, 693.
Quevillon, Rev. Joseph, 463.
Quigly, 681.

R.

Railroads. (See heading, Chapter 22.)
Western, 572, et. seq.; Housatonic, 546; Stockbridge and Pittsfield, 545; Pittsfield and North Adams, 545; Boston and Albany, 544; Pittsfield directors of Western, 544.
Rathbun, Charles T., 445, 446, 572.
Rathbun, Daniel, 142.
Rathbun, Sylvester, 311, 443.
Rathbun, Valentine, 37, 94, 136, 138, 142, 165.
Reed, Dr. Stephen, 641, 681, 690.
Reeves, Miss Lilla, 624.
Religionists, philosophical, 144.
Religious denominations, equality of in law. (See headings, Chapters 7, 11, 13, 14, pp. 307, 309, 311.)
Remington, John, 342.
Renne, William, 445, 447, 679, 692.

INDEX.

Resurrectionists, 209, 360.
Riall, General, 213, 240.
Rice, Amasa, 551.
Rice, William B., 434.
Rice, William K., 434.
Richards, Rev. Prof. William C., 442, 595, 678.
Richardson, Col. Henry H., 434, 612, 616, 627.
Richmond, town of, 20, 38, 177, 329.
Ripley, Gen. E. W., 210, 220.
Roads, 15, 17.
Robbins, Elijah, 186, 430.
Robbins, Oliver, 137, 435, 468.
Robbins, Oliver W., 441, 692.
Robbins, Sylvester, 443.
Robinson, Rev. R. H., 449.
Rockwell, Julius, 426, 512, 574, 586, 595, 623.
Rockwell, Mrs. J. P., 626.
Root, Albert B., 382, 643.
Root, Azariah, 5, 237.
Root, Ezekiel, 5, 11, 48, 408.
Root, Graham A., 634, 692.
Root, John B., 14, 48, 134, 186, 195, 265, 328, 329, 465, 468, 687.
Root, Col. Oliver, 11, 33, 60, 61, 186, 247, 687.
Root, Dr. Oliver S., 315, 352, 430, 431, 432, 606, 607, 670.
Root, Roswell, 328, 332.
Root, Samuel, 133, 265, 435, 443.
Ross, Merrick, 430, 431, 432, 550.
Russell, Charles L., 497.
Russell, E., 24, 26.
Russell, Frank W., 497.
Russell, Hezkiah S., 497, 555, 692.
Russell, Joseph, 497.
Russell, Solomon L., 314, 382, 412, 422, 598, 603.
Russell, Solomon N., 497.
Russell, Zeno, 413, 497.

S.

Sabbath, observance of, 555.
Sackett, Erastus and Solomon, 328.
Saint Joseph's church, 460.
Saint Joseph's cemetery, 608.
Saint Stephen's parish, 428, 432, 460.
Salisbury, Miss Mary E., 674.
Sandys, Rev. Edwin, 440.
Sandys, Edwin F., 382.
Sawyer, S. J., 672.
Scholfield, Arthur, 162, 329, 332, 466, 471, 472, 504.
Scholfield, Isaac, 473, 505.
Scholfield, John, 163, 164.
Schools, 668, et seq.

Scott, Lebbeus, 554, 555, 669.
Scythe factory, 485.
Sedgwick, Theodore, 29, 96, 100.
Sedgwick, Theodore, Jr., 382, 517.
Sewers, 572.
Seymour, John U., 385.
Shade-trees and shubbery in 1800, 17.,
Shaker society, 383, 464,
Shaw, Hon. Henry, 356, 382, 482, 483, 487, 517, 680.
Shearer, Joseph, 18, 78, 79, 187, 195, 328, 332, 356, 379, 426, 509, 687.
Sheep and sheep-culture, 35, 171, 483. (See Agriculture, Agricultural society and Manufactures.)
Shepard, Rev. Samuel, of Lenox, 110, 121, 122, 123, 127.
Sigourney, Mrs. Lydia H., 587.
Skinner, Thompson J., 134.
Slaves, fugitive, 52.
Smith, Chester, 28.
Smith, Dr. J. V. C., 359.
Smith, Rev. Lemuel, 140.
Smith, Rev. Thomas, 395.
Snow, John, 503, 538.
Social life of 1800, 53.
Spalding, Rev. C. H., 139, 432.
Spear, Rev. Charles V., 676.
Spencer, Hon. Joshua A., 580.
Sperry, Mrs. L. F., 626.
Spinning-jennies, 163, 174, 178.
Spooner, Mr., 28.
Sprague, George W., 506.
Springfield, 26; excursion to, 512.
Sprong, Daniel, 551.
Squier, Socrates, 490.
Stanton, Ludowick, 187, 328.
Stanton, Robert, 187, 265.
Starks, Rev. D., 449.
Stearns, Daniel, 177, 493, 494, 496, 506.
Stearns, Daniel 2d, 494.
Stearns, Henry, 441, 494, 549, 627.
Stearns, Henry, of Springfield, 509, 511.
Stearns, Jirah, 310, 494.
Stearns, Rev. John, 460.
Stevens, Abner, 188.
Stevens, Joel, 140.
Stevens, Dr. Joel, 600.
Stevens, William, 444.
Stewart, Rev. William H., 459.
Stiles, Zebediah, 5, 123, 132.
Stockbridge, town of, 20, 29, 157, 177, 306.
Stone, Horatio, 604.
Stoddard, Israel, 14, 70.
Stoddard, John, 14, 48, 99.
Stoddard, Lewis, 430, 432, 686.
Storrs, Rev. Leonard K., 460.

Storrs, Roger, 25, 27, 28, 29.
Story, Judge Joseph, 436.
Strandring, James, 164, 167, 485.
Strong, Ashbel, 5, 14, 15, 58, 70, 100.
Strong, Rev. Edward, D. D., 433, 642.
Strong, Henry K., 224, 392, 393.
Strong, Capt. John, 5, 6, 94.
Strong, Nelson, 298, 396.
Strong, Noble, 435.
Strong, Thomas B., 13, 310, 313, 328, 332, 381, 405, 421, 443, 472, 487, 574, 662, 670.
Sunday-schools, 287.
Swift, William H., 672.

T.

Taconic factory. (See Manufactures.)
Tack-factory, 684.
Taft, Henry W., 594, 680, 692.
Tanneries, 41, 692.
Tappan, Rev. Dr. Henry P., 393, 416, 418, 419.
Taxation, 692.
Teeling, William H., 551, 634.
Temperance-organizations, 392, 393, 395, 402.
Temperance and intemperance, 60, 414.
Tenney, Jonathan, 672.
Thayer, Dr. William H., 670.
Theaters, 393.
Thompson, Launt, 627.
Tillotson, Otis R., 501.
Todd, Rev. Dr. John, 12, 84, 85, 191, 367, 419, 422, 423, 424, 434, 858, 613, 656, 681.
Todd, Rev. John E., 657.
Tolman, Albert, 672.
Tolman, Mrs. Albert, 626.
Town-hall, 653.
Town-lot, 599.
Tracy, Appleton, 187.
Tracy, E., 265.
Travel, facilities for, 18, 514. (See heading, Chapter 22.)
Tremain, Isaac and Nathaniel, 123, 132, 276.
Treanor, Patrick, 647.
Tucker, George S., 692.
Tucker, Joseph, 623, 639.
Turnpikes and Railroads. (See heading, Chapter 22.)
Tyler, Rev. W. H., 425, 430, 463, 641, 674.
Tyng, Dudley Atkins and Susan C., 408.
Tyringham, town of, 20, 197.

U.

Union church and parish, 118, 119.

V.

Valuation, 692.
Van Schaack, Henry, 7, 11, 71, 108, 290, 450, 508.
Van Sickler, Martin, 502.
Vermilye, Dr. W. E., 648.
Village of 1800, mapped and described, 3.
Virginia, politics and politicians of, 103.

W.

Wadsworth, Joseph, 470.
Wait, Otis F. R., 680.
Walker, John A., 382.
Walker, William M., 430, 454.
Walker, Hon. William, 325, 332.
Ward, William M., 430.
Warriner, James, 397, 683.
Warriner, John R., 683.
Warriner, Lyman, 414.
Warriner, Solomon, 381.
Warner, Moses, 381.
Washburn, Luther, 439, 443.
Washburn, Rev. Sanford, 449.
Waterman, Andrew J., 684, 692.
War of 1812. (See headings, Chapters 10, 11.) Influence of on Pittsfield, 199; Cantonment established, 200; difficulties and expenditures of the quartermaster and commissary, 206, 211; Cantonment made a depot for prisoners of war, 210; patriotic resolutions, 230, 247; town and county militia called out, 244; proposition of the Berkshire regiment to march for the relief of Maine, 257; celebration of peace, 260; first troops arrive, 202; hospitality to the soldiers, 204; prisoners of war, 214, et seq.; Cantonment, 205; Thomas Melville appointed commissary, marshal and agent for prisoners of war, 206; influence on the business of Pittsfield, 206; Ninth regiment, 206; troubles from political slanders, 206; Jonathan Allen appointed deputy quartermaster-general, 211; numbers and disposition of the prisoners, 212, 213; kind treatment of, 215; reluctance to return to Europe, 216, 217; surgical services of Dr. Timothy Childs, 217; bravery of Pittsfield soldiers, 219, et seq.; celebration of Washington's birthday by the Washington Benevolent Society, 235.
War of the Rebellion. (See heading, Chapter 26.) Thirty-seventh regiment, 618; Forty-ninth regiment, 619; Camp Briggs, 618; Thirty-first regiment, 616; Ladies' Soldiers Aid Society, 625; sol-

INDEX.

diers' monument, 628; list of Pittsfield soldiers killed in the war, 629; list of soldiers who served in the war, 695.
Water-works, early, 558; Ashley water-works, 560; Sackett Brook added to, 569; commissioners of, 568. (See heading, Chapter 23.)
Waters, Rev. W. G., 449.
Watson, Elkanah, 170, 173, 176, 195, 316, 328, 332, 465, 467.
Watson, Rev. D. S., 442.
Weller, Capt. Daniel, 5, 41.
Weller, Maj. Daniel, 5.
Weller, Enoch, 5, 41.
Weller, Col. Israel C., 334, 335.
Weller, John, 607.
Weller, Royal, 503.
Weller, William, 471.
Wells, Miss Clara, 673.
Wells, Rev. E. L., 460, 642.
Wendell, Judge Oliver, 119.
Wentworth, Rev. Erastus, 445, 446, 449.
West, Abel, 384, 385, 603, 669.
West, Prof. Charles E., 386, 674, 677, 681.
West, Gilbert, 386.
West, John C., 425, 551, 563, 565, 624, 627, 671.
Westfield, emigrants from, 53.
Weston, Jonathan, 123, 129.
West Stockbridge, 20.
Whelden, Lieut. Col. Charles M., 617.
Wheeler, Samuel H., 328, 329, 332.

Whipple, A. B., 672.
Whipple, S. T., 442.
White, Ebenezer, 5, 502.
White, Enoch, 428, 502.
White's Mills, 37.
Whitney, Asa, George, Joshua, and Porter, 37, 40.
Whiting, William W., 685.
Willard, Josiah, 329.
Williams College, 71, 77, 300, 355,
Williams, John Chandler, 5, 6, 56 118, 123, 124, 125, 132, 182, 185, 1 333, 421, 456, 458, 508, 687.
Williams, Col. William, 10, 11, 12, 649.
Williamstown, 20.
Willis, George S., 411, 549, 550, 5 572, 600, 605.
Willis, George S., Jr., 554, 634 635.
Willis, General Nathan, 188, 307, 30 357, 361, 379, 382, 384, 410, 421, 47 515, 598.
Wilson, James, 503.
Wood, M. H., 642.
Woolen manufactures. (See Manufac tures.)
Wrigley, James, 472, 473.

Y.

Yates, Rev. J., 449.
Yeomans, Rev. John W., 416, 418, 419.
Young Men's Associations, 641, 642.

ERRATA.

The figures 1872, in the second line of the note on page 15, should e 1772, and on page 17, fourteen lines from the bottom, "west" ould read "east."

Later investigations than those in our possession when the text was written, show that the first Hubbard, George, came first to Watertown, Mass., about 1634, and soon went to Wethersfield, Conn., thence to Milford, and about 1650 to Guilford, where he died. His son John removed to Hadley. There is no evidence that either ever lived in Saybrook. See page 405.

www.ingramcontent.com/pod-product-compliance
Lightning Source LLC
Chambersburg PA
CBHW052107010526
44111CB00036B/1490